Dedicated to My Children,
Beth, Ted, and Sam

Contents

Acknowledgments

All 50 schools were extremely cooperative in recommending prospective contributors to this book and/or supplying information and statistics.

Nevertheless, the opinions and viewpoints expressed in the profiles remain those of recent graduates of each school. The opinions and viewpoints expressed in the book as a whole are those of the editor.

I would like to thank the following individuals and schools for their cooperation.

AMHERST COLLEGE—*Terry Allen*

BATES COLLEGE—*Betsy Kimball*

BOSTON COLLEGE—*Patricia Delaney*

BOWDOIN COLLEGE—*Norma McLoughlin*

BROWN UNIVERSITY—*Mark Nickel*

BRYN MAWR COLLEGE—*Debra Thomas*

CALIFORNIA INSTITUTE OF TECHNOLOGY—*Carole Snow*

CARLETON COLLEGE—*Jim Shoop*

CARNEGIE MELLON UNIVERSITY—*Kyle Fisher*

CLAREMONT McKENNA COLLEGE—*Robert Daseler*

COLLEGE OF WILLIAM AND MARY—*Peggy Shaw*

COLUMBIA UNIVERSITY—*Frederick Knubel, Larry Momo*

CORNELL UNIVERSITY—*Nancy Meislahn, John Spenser*

DARTMOUTH COLLEGE—*Barbara Whipple, Rick Adams*

DAVIDSON COLLEGE—*Jerry Stockdale, John Kelton*

DUKE UNIVERISTY—*David Roberson*

EMORY UNIVERSITY—*Jan Gleason*

GEORGETOWN UNIVERSITY—*Gary Krull*

GEORGIA INSTITUTE OF TECHNOLOGY—*David Arnold*

HARVARD UNIVERSITY—*Peter Costa, J. Sharad Apte*

HARVEY MUDD COLLEGE—*Julie Quinn*

HAVERFORD COLLEGE—*Pam Sheridan*

JOHNS HOPKINS UNIVERSITY—*Rod Sauder, Dennis O'Shea*

MASSACHUSETTS INSTITUTE OF TECHNOLOGY—*Michael Behnke, Bette Johnson, Travis Merritt, Clara Diebold*

MIDDLEBURY COLLEGE—*Ron Nief*

NORTHWESTERN UNIVERSITY—*Kenneth Wildes*

POMONA COLLEGE—*Nina Ellerman*

PRINCETON UNIVERSITY—*Justin Harmon*

REED COLLEGE—*Harriet Watson*

RICE UNIVERSITY—*Grethe Pollis, Kirsten Omnen*

STANFORD UNIVERSITY—*Sandi Risser, Jim Montoya, Rich Kurovsky*

SWARTHMORE COLLEGE—*Lorna Shurkin*

TUFTS UNIVERSITY—*Rosemarie Van Camp*

UNIVERSITY OF CALIFORNIA/BERKELEY—*Jesus Mena, Pat McBroom, Ernie Hudson*

UNIVERSITY OF CALIFORNIA/LOS ANGELES—*Karen Mack*

UNIVERSITY OF CHICAGO—*Ted O'Neill, Stephanie Kalfayan*

UNIVERSITY OF ILLINOIS/URBANA-CHAMPAIGN—*Judith Rowan*

UNIVERSITY OF MICHIGAN/ANN ARBOR—*Janet Mendler*

UNIVERSITY OF NORTH CAROLINA/CHAPEL HILL—*Mike McFarland*

UNIVERSITY OF NOTRE DAME—*Dennis Brown*

UNIVERSITY OF PENNSYLVANIA—*Carol Farnsworth*

UNIVERSITY OF TEXAS/AUSTIN—*John Durham*

UNIVERSITY OF VIRGINIA—*Louise Dudley*

VASSAR COLLEGE—*Dixie Sheridan*

WAKE FOREST UNIVERSITY—*Paul Orser*

WASHINGTON AND LEE UNIVERSITY—*Evan Atkins*

WELLESLEY COLLEGE—*Laurel Stavis*

WESLEYAN UNIVERSITY—*Bobby Wayne Clark*

WILLIAMS COLLEGE—*Jim Kolesar, Ellen Berek*

YALE UNIVERSITY—*Martha Matzke*

Preface to the
Third Edition

Getting into a Top 50 college remains as difficult as ever, if not more so. Applications to the top schools have increased faster than enrollments. Costs have also grown. Tuition, room, and board for a year broke the $25,000 barrier at a number of schools, while all reported healthy increases. Nevertheless, the good news is a Top 50 degree has also become more valuable. College-degree holders continue to earn more money than high school graduates, and more important, the college-educated acquire critical skills and contacts necessary for success later in life.

Anything worth having requires determination and effort. A degree from a Top 50 college is no exception. I hope this book is helpful in getting a Top 50 degree. Good luck.

Tom Fischgrund
BA Tufts University
MBA Harvard University
PhD Massachusetts Institute of Technology

Introduction

The college decision becomes increasingly important in the 1990s. As costs for a four-year education break the $100,000 barrier and with career, friendship, earnings, and outlook on life largely determined in college, the choice is critical.

Given the significance of this decision, it is no wonder that getting into a good school is so paramount. Top colleges are generally recognized to have stronger academic programs, more well-known professors, and better students. Degrees from top colleges are more broadly recognized and accepted. They also provide contacts with many successful alumni. Going to a top college can provide a superior educational experience.

High school students and their parents seem to agree because thousands of hours are spent studying, taking the PSAT and SAT I, and preparing to get into top schools. Deciding where to go and then getting in, however, are not easy tasks. Choosing which schools to apply to is particularly difficult for a number of reasons. First, good unbiased information about schools is limited. College catalogs, which are written by the schools, provide good basic information about requirements, course offerings, and so on, but present only the positive side. Information in guide books is more objective, but very limited. These guides do only a brief one- or two-page review of each school.

Second, it is difficult, expensive, and time-consuming to visit more than a half dozen colleges. Because the top schools are spread from coast to coast, the schools a student can visit are often determined more by geography than by other important factors such as academic program and social atmosphere. Third, inside information about the top schools is almost nonexistent. The primary way to get an insider viewpoint is to visit the college and talk with students. However, this random collection of views can be very accurate or inaccurate depending on whom you talked to and their mood that day. Finally, many graduating high school seniors don't know exactly what they want. This is understandable given that this is the first major decision many students have had to make, good information is limited, and personal desires and needs change frequently.

Even once the decision about where to apply is made, getting into a top college is a challenge. The top schools accept only a fraction of those who apply, anywhere from a low of 14% to a high of 75%. For the most part, the median

SAT I scores of accepted students at top schools are from about 1200 to 1400. Moreover, successful applicants are usually well-rounded students who often excel in a particular area or field. Even if you think you are among the best, filling out the application is still a killer. Applications range from three to ten pages, take hours and sometimes days to complete, and must be accompanied by application fees ranging from $25 to $50. Given that college is the culmination of your high school career and a major factor in your future success, the amount of anxiety and stress can be overwhelming.

CHOOSING COLLEGES

This book is designed to provide help in deciding where to apply and getting into the best school possible. Deciding which colleges to apply to often is done in an unorganized, haphazard way. Most students decide based on a half hour talk with a guidance counselor, brief discussions with friends, some input or pressure from parents, and information gathered from college catalogs and guide books. It appears that very few students actually follow a systematic approach. Often more time, thought, and organization are given to selecting a new car than the right college. Yet to maximize your chances of getting into the best school possible and the one that is right for you, the following five-step process should be used:

Step 1—Establish Selection Criteria

What is the most important factor to you in picking a college? the second most important?

What are you looking for in a school? academics, social life, athletics, and so on?

What is the proper balance?

Do you have geographic preferences?

Do you have financial constraints?

Step 2—Develop a Broad List of Possible College Choices

Which schools meet the criteria you have just established?

Have you included both the obvious and not-so-obvious choices?

Step 3—Collect Information on the Different Colleges

What is the school's philosophy of education?

What are the academic requirements?

How difficult is it to get in?

What is it really like to go to that school?

Step 4—Evaluate the Choices

Which schools best meet my selection criteria?

Which do I think I can get into?

Which are dream schools?

How many do my financial circumstances and my time constraints allow me to apply to?

Step 5—Make the Decision
Where should I apply?

The time of decision has arrived. Choose wisely, choose carefully, choose well, and enjoy. College should be four of the most enjoyable years of your life.

GETTING INTO TOP COLLEGES

Now that you have decided where to apply, getting in will not be easy. However, someone has to be accepted. Why shouldn't it be you? How can you maximize your chances of being accepted by the top schools you have chosen? Here again, a simple three-step process will help.

Step 1—Understand the Admissions Process
How are applications processed?
Who reads them?
When is the best time to apply?

Step 2—Decide Why a College Should Choose You
Why should the college choose you over the thousands of other applicants competing for the same place?
What makes you unique?
What are your strengths and weaknesses?

Step 3—Take Your Time and Give Plenty of Thought to Filling Out the Application
How important is this decision to you?

These simple steps and tips to help you choose schools and get in are covered more fully in Part II of this book.

FORMAT OF THE BOOK

Going to college is more than just academics and attending classes. It is a total experience. Formal classes are only one small part of a total learning environment. It is talking with other students. It is meeting with friends. It is learning independently. It is both a place and a process. Therefore, in picking a college you should consider the entire program, including the school's philosophy of education, its academic environment, social activities, student interaction, and so on. In short, you must consider what it is *really* like to go to school A or school B.

Part I of this book addresses these questions. Recent graduates of each of the top 50 colleges have written an in-depth profile of their schools. These profiles have focused on providing an insider view, i.e., what it is actually like to go there. In addition to descriptions of the school, the students relate personal experiences *that give added insight*. Each of the chapters covers seven major areas and addresses questions related to those areas. The format for each chapter is as follows:

THE PROGRAM

- What is the school's philosophy of education?
- What are its defining characteristics?
- What do most students major in?
- What is it actually like to go there?

GETTING IN/FINANCIAL AID

- How difficult is it to get in?
- What is the composition of the student body?
- What financial aid is available and what percentage of students receive it?

ACADEMIC ENVIRONMENT

- What is the academic program?
- What are the requirements?
- What is the academic atmosphere?
- What majors are available?
- What are the predominant teaching method, class size, and so on?

SOCIAL LIFE

- What is the social life on and off campus—for upper and lower classmen and women?
- What is the school's reputation and is it accurate?

EXTRACURRICULAR ACTIVITIES

- What activities are available?
- Which activities are most popular?
- Are there fraternities, sororities, eating clubs?
- What is the housing like?

GRADUATES

- What do most students do after graduation?
- What are most students doing five years after graduation?
- How strong is the alumni network?

SUMMARY OVERVIEW
- Summary of Program
- Strengths and Weaknesses

Part II provides tips on choosing and getting into a top college. Five major topics are addressed: selecting colleges, filling out applications, getting in, obtaining financing, and succeeding at the top schools. These tips are based on advice provided by students, graduates, and school administrators from the top 50 colleges.

In conclusion, Part III offers comments from the directors of admission offices at three of the top universities—Caltech, Michigan, and Yale. All three discuss what they (and their institutions) look for in applicants, and they provide counsel and suggestions on approaching the application process as it relates to their schools.

PICKING THE TOP 50 COLLEGES

There are more than 3000 colleges and universities in the United States. At least 100 colleges proudly state they are in the top 50. Therefore, selecting the top 50 undergraduate institutions is understandably difficult.

Various evaluators use such criteria as SAT I scores, president's ratings, faculty resources, and so on. Despite these measurement differences, there is a remarkable consensus on which schools are at the top. For example, Harvard, Stanford, and Yale are on everyone's list of top colleges. This is because many of the criteria used to determine quality are highly related, that is, colleges that are highly selective and whose applicants have high scholastic scores also have excellent reputations and significant academic resources. Therefore, a few important measures can be used to select top colleges.

The most powerful and most objective measures relate to school selectivity (acceptance and enrollment rates) and academic achievement (SAT scores). Other measures are more difficult to determine, such as school resources, or are more subjective such as academic reputation.

To determine the top colleges for this guide, a system was developed based on three simple, set effective measures:
- Percent Accepted   (number of applicants accepted vs. number who applied)
- Percent Enrolled   (number of students who enroll vs. number accepted)
- SAT I scores   (combined verbal and quantitative scores)

Statistics for each school are listed on pages xvi–xvii.

Although these estimates are not perfect, there is general agreement that each of the colleges profiled in this guide has excellent programs and certainly belongs in any list of top schools.

MEASUREMENT CRITERIA FOR SELECTING TOP SCHOOLS

School	Applications	Acceptances	Enrolled	% Accepted	% Enrolled	SAT I
Amherst College	4,823	976	418	20	43	1303
Bates College	3,754	1,250	458	33	37	1250
Boston College	15,522	6,378	2,250	41	35	1210*
Bowdoin College	3,662	1,097	431	30	39	1275*
Brown University	13,222	2,901	1,423	22	49	1300
Bryn Mawr College	1,583	846	329	56	39	1280*
California Institute of Technology	2,012	500	231	25	46	1396
Carleton College	2,782	1,596	528	57	33	1285*
Carnegie Mellon University	8,647	5,100	1,150	59	23	1230
Claremont McKenna College	2,066	864	232	42	27	1280
College of William and Mary	8,169	3,076	1,256	38	41	1230
Columbia University	7,856	1,921	870	24	46	1290
Cornell University	20,076	6,668	3,103	33	47	1280*
Dartmouth College	9,521	2,188	1,057	23	49	1360
Davidson College	2,724	1,001	451	37	45	1260
Duke University	14,324	4,258	1,730	30	41	1365*
Emory University	9,653	4,718	1,190	49	25	1225
Georgetown University	12,652	3,072	1,449	24	47	1250*
Georgia Institute of Technology	7,875	4,679	1,798	59	38	1233
Harvard University	15,261	2,149	1,619	14	75	1340*
Harvey Mudd College	1,388	562	170	40	30	1400
Haverford College	2,466	952	314	39	33	1290
Johns Hopkins University	7,794	3,350	952	43	28	1300
Massachusetts Institute of Technology	7,136	2,166	1,097	30	51	1388*
Middlebury College	3,871	1,238	493	32	40	1250*
Northwestern University	13,515	5,230	1,867	39	36	1260
Pomona College	3,293	1,179	379	36	32	1320**
Princeton University	14,363	2,043	1,161	14	57	1350

*estimate   **mean

School	Applications	Acceptances	Enrolled	% Accepted	% Enrolled	SAT I
Reed College	1,966	1,396	327	73	23	1235
Rice University	7,779	1,686	620	22	37	1370*
Stanford University	14,609	2,942	1,589	21	54	1342
Swarthmore College	3,349	1,006	328	30	33	1350**
Tufts University	7,880	3,547	1,170	45	33	1240
University of California/ Berkeley	19,873	8,252	3,206	42	39	1250*
University of California/ Los Angeles	23,406	11,790	4,130	50	35	1128
University of Chicago	6,262	3,146	924	50	29	1290*
University of Illinois/Urbana-Champaign	15,616	11,843	5,734	75	50	1139
University of Michigan/ Ann Arbor	19,393	13,276	5,068	68	38	1190
University of North Carolina/ Chapel Hill	15,041	5,977	3,331	40	58	1121
University of Notre Dame	9,300*	3,900*	1,878	42	48	1250
University of Pennsylvania	13,739	4,984	2,346	36	47	1276
University of Texas/Austin	14,320	9,468	5,545	66	59	1135
University of Virginia	14,921	5,713	2,764	38	48	1217
Vassar College	3,760	1,886	612	50	33	1235
Wake Forest University	5,923	2,607	948	44	36	1200*
Washington and Lee University	3,620	1,055	443	29	42	1280*
Wellesley College	3,385	1,297	570	39	44	1280
Wesleyan University	5,482	1,955	727	36	37	1260
Williams College	4,673	1,224	500	26	41	1350
Yale University	12,991	2,372	1,308	22	54	1390

*estimate   **mean

Part I

The Top
50 Colleges

Amherst College

THE PROGRAM

Most guidance counselors, tour guides, and college handbooks describe Amherst College as "a small, liberal arts college located in western Massachusetts." They are right. It *is* small: about 1575 students, all undergraduates. It *is* dedicated to the liberal arts, awarding only a B.A. degree. And it *is* in western Massachusetts, in Amherst, a town of 35,000 people.

For someone shopping for colleges, the most important of these general facts is Amherst's liberal arts inclination. "Inclination" may be too understated. Founded in 1821, Amherst has long established itself as a bastion of the liberal arts philosophy: to prepare for life by preparing a well-rounded mind. The most popular majors are in the humanities, with English, American studies, and history usually topping the list, although social sciences like political science and psychology also have strong followings. The economics department has a tough reputation but attracts its share of majors, as do some of the "hard" sciences—biology is especially popular. No matter what your major, though, you will find the emphasis in classes to be the development of independent, critical thinking. Most classes are small enough for frequent discussions, but even in the "lecture courses," students do their share of speaking—and writing.

"Amherst professors love to have students write. Most class assignments are papers: short papers, long papers, lab write-ups, critical essays. I had gone to a large public high school with frequent standardized testing, and when I first came to Amherst, I missed multiple-choice exams greatly. After a few years, when I was going to take the GRE, I had to go out and buy a #2 pencil. Even the final exams in college, down to the math and science problems, are written in blue exam booklets. But the professors themselves grade each exam and paper, somehow—no TAs at

3

Amherst—and write extended comments. Then you go on and write more papers…"

Amherst is an old school, but it wears its traditions modestly. Many of these traditions have changed. Remembered by some as an all-male school heavily dominated by fraternities (Amherst students always catch the reference to the school, by name, in *Animal House*), the college actually went coeducational in 1976, and fraternities were abolished in 1984.

Some things do not change. It is a beautiful campus in the Pioneer Valley, ringed by the Holyoke Mountains, with hundreds of adjacent acres preserved undeveloped by the college. Freshmen are required to live on campus, but housing is guaranteed to all students each of their four years. Most choose to live in college housing, taking their meals in the central dining hall. These factors make Amherst an intimate campus. It is hard not to know people, or to be known by them, after only a very short time there. This has its disadvantages, especially if campus gossip centers on you. But it also means that when you leave Amherst, you will have connections to the college and friends from there for the rest of your life.

GETTING IN/FINANCIAL AID

Before you leave, however, you have to get into Amherst. This is no easy job, and it may be getting harder. Already one of the most selective schools in the country, Amherst has, in the past few years, experienced an increase in its average class membership. Greater numbers of accepted students than the admissions office has calculated have decided to attend—an honor, to be sure, but also a headache at a school that guarantees room and board. The completion of the New Dorm and the college's lease of a half-dozen or so off-campus apartments recently helped alleviate the problem.

The admissions office is doing its job to keep the class size around the ideal of 390 by tightening up its already selective policies, making Amherst one of the most difficult schools to get into. Only 20% of the applicants for the class of 1996 were accepted. Almost every student came from at least the top fifth of his or her high school class, and the overwhelming majority — some 84% — from the top tenth.

"There is a point during freshman year when you begin to wonder what in the world you're doing at Amherst. Everyone seems smarter, quicker, more articulate. It's a big shock to some people, who were the kings and queens of the heap back in high school. I mean, everyone is bright. Some people have difficulty getting

through this, especially if academic success came easily to them in high school. The time comes, though, when you find your place, and you can enjoy being surrounded by some of the finest students anywhere."

The administration and admissions staff have pledged themselves to encourage "diversity" in the student body with some success. Amherst is coeducationally balanced — about half of the students are women — but many feel that the representation of minorities still needs work. Students and administrators alike were overjoyed, then, that a quarter of the class of 1996 were minorities. Up from an earlier figure of around 15%, this is an improvement that the college hopes will continue.

Fortunately, financial need is not considered as a criterion of admission. About 45% of the students receive aid, the average amount offered being $15,200. Even students not receiving aid or on work-study programs can supplement their income with a campus job, and two thirds of the students hold one. Valentine Hall (the dining center) and the libraries are the biggest employers although other jobs are available, especially within certain departments.

Despite all these figures, the question remains: How do you get in? Admissions staffers recommend the following high school program:
- four years of English
- mathematics up to precalculus
- three to four years of a foreign language, if possible
- one year of history and social science
- three years of science, with at least one of laboratory science.

Applicants are also advised to take the SAT I and three SAT II exams, writing being one, or the ACT. Of course, the personal application will be the most important consideration.

"Since Amherst is so selective (and may become more so), it's important to make sure that your application represents the best of yourself. I write, so I enclosed some short stories I'd done. A musician friend of mine said that he'd sent a tape of some of his songs. Perhaps it didn't help, perhaps they did not read the stuff or listen to the music—but we did get in."

Interviews are not required, but if you live within a couple of hundred miles, they are recommended, and if you think that you interview well, they can't hurt.

Should you be accepted, you have the choice of deferring attendance for a year, your placement guaranteed in the class the year after. Fewer and fewer students seem to be using this option, but it is still there.

ACADEMIC ENVIRONMENT

Amherst has a two-semester academic year. Students take four courses per semester, a total of 32 to graduate. The college gives no advanced placement credit, but good AP scores help in course placement. Aside from specific courses needed to complete your major, the only required class at Amherst is Introduction to Liberal Studies (ILS), which is taken the first semester of freshman year. The eight different ILS topics, taught interdepartmentally, attempt to examine a subject or problem with different perspectives. Recent ILS offerings have included "War," "Romanticism and the Enlightenment," and "The Mind."

Students are free to choose their schedules. Everyone has a faculty member as an academic adviser, and every faculty member is an adviser. Freshman year, the adviser is assigned. At the end of the sophomore year, when students must declare their majors, they are reassigned to someone in the department they choose.

Majors at Amherst are: American studies, anthropology, Asian languages and civilizations, astronomy, biology, black studies, chemistry, classics, dance, economics, English, European studies, fine arts, French, geology, German, history, mathematics, music, neuroscience, philosophy, physics, political science, psychology, religion, Russian, sociology, Spanish, theater and dance, and, the most recent additions, women's and gender studies.

A quarter of the students double-major; in addition, Amherst allows the design of independent, interdisciplinary majors with a faculty member. You do not have to create an independent major to work closely with a professor, however. Seniors wishing to do honors work undertake a year-long project with a member of the faculty as a guide and critic. Research usually culminates in a long essay and a defense of your findings. Almost half the students graduate with honors.

Amherst has plenty of course offerings and takes part in exchange programs as well. The Five-College Exchange allows undergraduates to get credit for classes taken at Smith, Mt. Holyoke, and Hampshire colleges, and at the University of Massachusetts. These are all within a ten-mile radius and are served by a bus system, free during the academic year. Additionally, Amherst accepts and sponsors many study-away programs. About a quarter of each class chooses to spend a semester or a year at another college or university—more often than not, abroad.

Courses at Amherst are either seminars or lectures. Although the actual student-to-faculty ratio is under ten to one, enrollment in individual courses varies depending on the level, department, and popularity of the professor. For every course there is a heavy amount of reading, sometimes a ridiculous amount.

"Once I was interviewing a professor and I asked him about the reading load, why it was so extensive. He said that he remembered a professor who had cut down on the number of readings, hoping instead to concentrate more intently on what he'd left.

*His course became a "gut," students whizzing through their
work so that they could spend time doing the heavy reading for
their other courses. To keep the class challenging, he had to
increase the reading list again.*

*"Students and professors justify this by saying that it's good
training for the future, when we will have to skim quickly large
amounts of material, picking out the important points."*

There is, as I've said, a lot of writing as well. Amherst has its own writing counselor, with whom students can meet to get help in improving their writing skills. When students have to write, they can use the resources of the Computer Center, which is open 24 hours on weekdays and long hours on weekends. There are 65 terminals and microcomputers, with many printers. During midterm week and finals, and in the spring when the seniors' honors theses are due, the Computer Center is packed, the sound of printers never ceasing. Most rooms on campus are now wired to connect personal computers with the VAX8550 computer; between this, the resources of the Computer Center itself, and the options to purchase a computer through the college at a reduced rate, most students now seem to do their writing in front of a terminal.

SOCIAL LIFE

Amherst is a rigorous school, but it is not just a work camp. Students work hard, but they play hard too. Some students call the college "Camp Amherst," especially during Interterm. Campus life is varied to say the least.

You may have heard stories, dating from the all-male, fraternity days, about the principal social activities being beer guzzling, road tripping to Smith and Mt. Holyoke, and thinking up new ways to humiliate Williams College. Beer is still the drink of choice at all campus parties, a few males still road trip (usually freshman year and usually no more than twice), and Williams still takes its share of abuse. But a lot has changed.

Social life for underclassmen is about the same as for upperclassmen. Amherst is too small a school, the students too intimate, to have it any other way. This intimacy is part of the social life. Most social happenings occur on campus. The town of Amherst is small, and what nightlife it has is dominated by students from the University of Massachusetts 1½ miles away. Students slip off to cultural events at the other four colleges, to see movies, or to shop in Northampton or at the nearby malls, and they sometimes make weekend trips to Boston (90 miles) or to New York City (150 miles). But the real social life happens only a short walk from your dorm.

Fraternities were abolished by the trustees in 1984, in part because of declining popularity. Some of the frats went underground and still attract a few students each year, but they have ceased to contribute significantly to campus life. Frat-style all-campus parties remain, as do certain traditions such as Wednesday Night Tap, but in other ways the temper of campus activities is changing also. Amherst opened its new Campus Center in 1987, and its facilities have helped smaller group activities to flourish—finally fulfilling what many saw to be a social vacuum left in the wake of the fraternities' closing.

> *"My freshman year was the first without the fraternities. They had gone out of style, it was clear, but it was also clear that no one knew what exactly would take their place. The big beer bashes and weekly taps still went on—still go on—but I think it's been only in recent years that the social offerings have expanded. There are more Open Mikes and Talent Nights now, more small group meetings and theme parties. It's easier to get funding for single-group or single-dorm activities as well."*

The Campus Center houses a game room, snack bar and coffee shop, a campus store, the post office, a movie theater, and a large open room for concerts or lectures, called the Frontroom, as well as offices for student groups and open lounges.

Homecoming Weekend in the fall is always popular, as is the late winter evening of Casino. During Casino, Amherst gets a night's gambling license from the state, and students run an actual casino in the rooms of the dining hall. There are limits on the amount of money that you can win, and all house proceeds go to charity. Casino is a night to dress formally and live a fantasy of wild sophistication. But even Casino pales in comparison to Interterm.

Interterm is the three-week period in January immediately after winter break, when the campus is open but when attendance is not required and there are no formal classes. Classes are offered, but they are noncredit, with many taught by students—everything from ballroom dancing to beer making—and the list changes every year. Seniors most likely will use the time to work on their honors theses, and even nonseniors are encouraged to explore academic interests that might not be covered in a traditional course, but in general Interterm is a three-week-long weekend of skiing, sledding, and partying.

> *"During my freshman year, a friend of mine actually went home for a few days to rest from Interterm. Amherst students are as intense about their play as they are about their work."*

EXTRACURRICULAR ACTIVITIES

> *"You may hear it time and time again: some of the best moments of college exist outside of the classroom. I know that when I think*

*back on my college years, I remember not only a fantastic politi-
cal science lecture, but also the fine spring day when I arrived
late to philosophy, put my hand on the doorknob to turn it and
walk in and sit down, then changed my mind, walked out of the
building, and watched the trees bud for an hour instead. I
remember squirt-gun battles with my roommates, the snowball
fights with U Mass students every first snowfall, and the aches
after intramural soccer games. There are so many groups to join
and people to meet, so much that we learn and do that isn't listed
in the course catalog."*

There is a multitude of groups and activities in which to participate—more
activities than there is time to do them, or even to list here. I'll cover only some of
the most popular.

Sports are popular although there is no physical education requirement.
Amherst participates in 19 intercollegiate sports: baseball, basketball, crew, cross
country, football, golf, field and ice hockey, lacrosse, skiing, soccer, squash, swimming, tennis, indoor and outdoor track, volleyball, and wrestling. Some sports, like
water polo and men's and women's rugby, are club sports, meaning that those teams
compete with clubs from other colleges. Then there are intramural sports, which
frequently change in offering and in participation, although more than three quarters of the students play at least one intramural sport. The new gym and swimming
pool, both redone after a devastating fire in 1985, are frequently used by students,
as are the indoor dirt track, the Nautilus and weight rooms, the ten squash courts,
the 36 outdoor tennis courts, and the ice rink. A small golf course is also within
walking distance of campus.

Music is popular. One of Amherst's nicknames is "The Singing College." Up to
one fifth of the students participate in the Choral Society, which includes the male
Glee Club, the female Chorus, and the coed Choir. The Gospel Choir also holds
performances, as do the *a cappella* groups the Zumbyes and the DQ, for men, and
the Sabrinas, for women. There are the Jazz Band, a Five-College Symphony, and
the Amherst Collegium Musicum, if instrumental music better suits you, as well as
active theater and dance groups. The Frontroom holds frequent folk and blues evenings and talent shows. And, even if all you can do in the way of performance is put
a needle on a record and turn up the volume on the stereo, there is always WAMH,
the student radio station, to join.

Writing is popular. The *Amherst Student* is the weekly campus paper, *In Other
Words* and the *Spectator* offer political articles, and the *Sabrina* is the college's
lampoon. The yearbook, the *Olio,* accepts writings and photography, and the
Amherst Review is the school's literary magazine.

Participation in awareness groups is heavy. Activities offered by groups such as
the Asian Students Association, the Black Students Union, the Lesbian, Bisexual, Gay
Alliance, and the Women's Center all bring higher social consciousness to the
Amherst campus.

When you go back to your room at the end of the day, your walk is not far. Most students live in campus housing, in one of the 30 dorms or houses owned by the college. Freshmen live in doubles and triples in all-freshmen dorms or in "mixed" dorms, meaning mixed with upperclassmen. All dorms are coed, though some dorms have single-sex floors. The "social dorms," on the east side of campus, contain suites of four to ten single rooms around a common living room and bathroom. The most popular rooms, however, are those in the old fraternity houses, renamed and refurbished (and, I understand, *extensively* cleaned) after the frats were shut down. The houses have kitchens, large social areas, and fantastic rooms.

GRADUATES

"One Graduation Day, our college president called the diplomas 'eviction notices written in Latin.'"

No matter how good or bad the college years are, they come to an end sometime. As a liberal arts college, Amherst cannot claim to train its students for a career in any specific field. There are not even special premed or prelaw programs offered, although members of the faculty are available to advise students who hope to pursue these fields. And while it's true that there are as many opportunities available for Amherst graduates as there are Amherst graduates, some trends in what an Amherst grad does after receiving the diploma are evident.

Twenty-five percent of a graduating class immediately enters graduate school or some other higher-education program. Within five years, 80% of the class will have earned or will be enrolled in programs to earn an advanced degree. Business schools, law schools, and medical schools are the three most popular places for graduates to attend, and the average acceptance rate of Amherst graduates to these schools is 90%. Many also continue their education in their undergraduate fields.

A growing number of students choose to delay entering graduate school for a couple of years after finishing Amherst. Some of them teach at various public or private schools. Some of them enter the business or law professions: investment banking and paralegal work in particular are very popular pursuits in these in-between years. Over 65 companies recruit and interview on campus. They seem to like the school and its reputation well enough—the trick is to get them, in one or two interviews, to like *you.*

"There is the time each spring when the company representatives arrive on campus, conducting interviews and having breakfast meetings with seniors. It's a funny, strangely moving thing to see one of your friends sharing a table in the dining hall with a couple of older people dressed in business suits. Then you notice that your friend is in a suit as well. Suddenly, you realize that Something Important is going on. Within a few weeks, your

friend will be receiving a letter that either asks for a second inter-
view or begins with the phrase 'We regret to inform you....' You
realize that this marks the beginning of the end and the start of
something completely new."

Organizing information about upcoming interviews and job fairs is the Office of
Career Counseling (OCC). The OCC serves Amherst students during the undergraduate years, especially during the final year, and even after graduation. For undergraduates, it is a clearing-house of information on summer job programs and
national testing dates for graduate exams. It provides the names of alumni already
established in certain fields as contacts for students wishing to explore those fields.
Through its sponsored workshops on career planning, résumé writing, and interviewing, it helps to train students in all the skills necessary to open the doors not
already ajar from the reputation that precedes them as alumni of Amherst College.

For Amherst does have a reputation. It is a school recognized for the excellence
of its graduates. Amherst grads recognize this as well, and consequently the alumni
network is impressively strong, as is the college's endowment. It is the privilege
and reward of having attended Amherst to have ties to it for the rest of your life.

SUMMARY OVERVIEW

In summary, I'll end as I began: Amherst College is a small liberal arts college in
Massachusetts. It is solely an undergraduate institution, and the members of the
faculty are there primarily to teach. Students and faculty become acquainted with
each other; they cannot help doing so because the classes are small enough to make
frequent intellectual exchange the norm. The advantages of this system are that you
become familiar—often, even good friends—with some of the top scholars in their
fields. The disadvantages were once concisely explained to me by my thesis
adviser: "Amherst spoils you," he said.

The college is small. With only 1575 students, there is room for great individual
expression and development. You will come to know most of your fellow students
and will have with them the shared experience of an Amherst education for the rest
of your lives. On the debit side: the other students will also come to know *you*,
perhaps in ways that you might find uncomfortable, for the intimacy of the campus
can sometimes be stifling.

Amherst encourages individual thinking and decision making. Its course selection policy reflects this. Beyond the completion of one ILS course the first semester
of your first year and the requirements needed to fulfill a major, there are no course
requirements at Amherst. Although this policy will not change in the immediate
future, it does have its critics among some of the faculty and administration and
even among some of the students. These critics would like to see a core curriculum

of some sort established—even though studies of undergraduate transcripts show that over 80% of the students would already fulfill most of the hypothetical core's requirements. Amherst students, for the most part, have a good sense of the value of a balanced, liberal education.

Amherst works its students hard but fairly. The close student-faculty interaction and the impressive system of tutors and counselors, both academic and psychological, challenge and support each student.

The intellectual atmosphere and the composition of the students and faculty include great diversity, but despite its improvements, Amherst is still sometimes haunted by the ghost of its wealthy, all-male tradition. Student awareness groups campaign sometimes against open hostility, but more often against a kind of disinterest more frightful than mere ignorance. It is sometimes easy for students to become involved exclusively with their own intellectual and social interests, at the expense of confronting the challenges that cause one to grow as a person.

I graduated from Amherst satisfied that I had received—better: had given myself—one of the best educations around. Amherst lights intellectual fires that promise to keep burning throughout life. Perhaps that is why its motto on the college seal reads "*Terras Irradient.*" Perhaps its students and graduates really will light up the world.

Kevin Williams, B.A.

Bates College

THE PROGRAM

"First year orientation. Outing Club trips. Convocation. Eight o'clock classes. Fall foliage on the quad. Soccer and football games on crisp Saturday afternoons. Den Terrace parties. Great friends. Trips to Freeport and the coast. Midterms. Triad. Harvest Dinner in Commons. Science trips to Morse Mountain. Basketball games in Alumni. Winter Carnival. Newman Day. Tacky Party. Den cookies. Flo and the Hi Guy. Skiing at Sunday River. Skating on the Puddle. Critical Theory, Statistics, a City on a Hill, Organic Chemistry, Psych 101, Political Theory, and Senior Theses. The President's Gala Ball. St. Patrick's Day Dip. The Goose, the Cage, and Luiggi's. The Sedgley Place. Late nights in the library. Pizza parties at President and Mrs. Harward's house. Final exams. Short term. Cell Hell and Philosophy of Star Trek. Barbecues on the quad. Intramural softball. Range Pond. The Old Port. The Pub Crawl. Sunsets on Mount David. Midnight Madness. Graduation. Curious?"

Ever been to Maine? If not, you are in for a treat. After all, according to signs along U.S. Route 95, as you cross the border from New Hampshire, Maine is "The Way Life Should Be."

Students arrive on the Bates campus each September ready and eager to learn, having chosen to pursue a liberal arts education rather than some more specific training offered at other institutions. The college philosophy on education is that exposure to and knowledge of a variety of different fields is preferable to intensive training in only one field. To this end, Bates does not attempt to train students for any particular career. Instead, Bates aims to prepare students for any and *every* career.

Students do not graduate with a specific blueprint for success, but rather take from Bates a general knowledge and understanding of the world around them. Students learn how to question, how to think, and how to solve problems. While the most popular majors are English, biology, and psychology, students are exposed to a variety of different fields, even those for which they may have never before felt a need or an interest. This is all part of the Bates package, and is the main ingredient that makes a liberal arts education so valuable.

Bates is a particularly appealing place to get a liberal arts education because of the environment in which students learn. Bates was the first college in New England, and the second in the nation, to accept both men and women. "Coed before coed was fashionable," as I once heard it put. Bates didn't decide to accept women because of some national trend—rather, Bates helped start the trend. In addition, Bates has never in its history allowed fraternities or sororities on campus. In theory and in practice, all college-sponsored organizations and activities are open to all members of the student body. This history of openness, which continues to pervade campus life today, is perhaps Bates' most defining characteristic.

These historical trademarks are complemented by a student body of overwhelmingly friendly and outgoing people. It may sound corny, and I certainly won't win any literary awards for using the word friendly as my most descriptive adjective, but a trip to Bates anytime students are around will confirm this. Step onto campus, talk with students and professors, and you will immediately feel welcome.

> *"The first few days of college are often among the most challenging of students' academic careers. I spent the summer before my first year at Bates living away from home with friends, where college was about the last thing on my mind. When September rolled around I made my inaugural drive up to Bates, pulled into my new dorm's parking lot, unloaded my stuff, waved goodbye to my parents, and was immediately struck with a Herculean case of anxiety. 'What if this?' 'What about that?' 'Where do I . . . ?' 'What should I . . . ?' It was not my finest hour.*
>
> *"Within hours, however, I realized I had nothing to worry about. At a barbecue on the quad that evening, I found myself engaged in a touch football game with people whom I today call old friends. I met my academic advisor, talked to some professors and, along with my new roommates, tried to meet as many people as possible. That was not difficult, as everyone else seemed to have the same agenda.*
>
> *"That is something I found throughout my Bates years—the people at Bates just seem to want to know you. Students are outgoing and friendly and are, by and large, not satisfied with just knowing a certain number of people. Whether they are hosting prospective students, tutoring undergraduates, or just striking up conversations with unfamiliar faces at parties, Bates students are always looking to expand their circle of friends."*

People at Bates have a good perspective in that regard—obviously, all students come to Bates to get one of the best educations around, but they also understand that there is more to life than the classroom and the library. That students take the time to talk to prospective students, to encourage them, to answer questions and ask some of their own, is just one example of this. A great social life, widespread participation in campus clubs, music groups, and athletics, and a love of recreational and social activities in general, help to round out students' academic lives.

But don't take my word on what kind of place Bates is—visit for yourself. Follow the Maine Turnpike north through thick forest, up and down rolling hills, past metropolitan Portland, and on up to Exit 12. Follow signs to the campus through the neighborhoods of Auburn and Lewiston, and park along Campus Avenue in front of Lindholm House—a beautiful white Victorian that houses the college's admissions and financial aid departments.

Start exploring.

Enter the quad, passing under an ivy-laden brick archway, from which hangs a lantern symbolizing the light of knowledge. Up the path directly in front of you stands Hathorn Hall. One look, and you will know that you are standing on the grounds of the quintessential New England college campus.

Hathorn, constructed in 1856, is the perfect college building. It too has an ivy-covered façade, with granite steps climbing to an entryway that beckons you inside, and pure, white columns that grab your gaze and direct it skyward to the clock and bell tower, which has kept students and professors alike on time for nearly a century and a half.

Hathorn and the quad are the focal points of the entire 109-acre campus. Towering elms flank pathways that branch out in every direction, providing a canopy of leaves to lead members of the college community from building to building—a select few of which sit nobly along the quad's borders.

Dana Chemistry Hall is to the right of Hathorn, followed clockwise by the old Coram Library, which could never be mistaken for anything other than a home of academia. Behind Coram rises the new Ladd Library, which has earned multiple architectural awards for its design, and which was based on the lines of old New England saltbox-style houses.

While this description may make the quad seem quite staid and stoic, in reality it is anything but. Between classes, the area is especially alive, becoming both a bustling pedestrian highway and the campus social center for about ten minutes before and after classes change. Students can generally be found engaging in activities on the quad at all times of the day, though during January and February, students' strides become more purposeful and driven, and socializing becomes a predominantly indoor activity. Of course, students aren't afraid to make good use of all the snow Maine enjoys, so the threat of getting clobbered by a snowball thrown by a friend makes the walk to class a little more interesting. (This, naturally, is only applicable to first-year students—not because of their maturity, but merely because they have not yet experienced the discomfort of sitting through a class with snow clinging to their Levis and melting slowly down the back of a turtleneck. Hey, it's a rookie mistake.)

The quad is also home to many campus-wide events, including Convocation, Baccalaureate, Commencement, and, on the nonacademic side, barbecues and parties in the fall and spring. Also, the ever-popular naked run, performed by members of the cross-country running teams (and others who feel the urge) is the unofficial kickoff to the last party of every year, Midnight Madness, starting at midnight and lasting (for some) until graduation the next morning.

Other student favorites are the ancient Alumni Gymnasium, where Bates and Colby basketball teams clash annually in one of Division III's great rivalries, and the recently opened Olin Arts Center, a fantastic facility for studio and fine arts classes, exhibitions, and performances, which has been molded into a gentle hillside on the far end of tiny Lake Andrews (the Puddle to Bates students). The Puddle is itself the scene of the annual St. Patrick's Day Dip, when an ever-increasing number of students (all are welcome, not just the Irish) chop a hole through the thick ice and take the plunge into the freezing water, celebrating the holiday and thumbing their noses at the worst of Maine's winter weather.

Because more than 90% of the student body lives on campus, the annual housing lottery held each spring is a major campus-wide event. The college guarantees housing for all four years, and continually seeks to provide students with as many variations of campus living as possible. The newly opened student Village, comprised of three suite-style dorms and a student center, is the most recent manifestation of this goal. The Village, along with any of the nearly 30 college-owned Victorian houses lining College and Frye Streets, are the most sought-after student-housing options.

The entire Bates campus seems to just flow together. Everything fits. While it is clear than each building is home to some serious teaching and learning, the campus still seems to exude a friendly, casual atmosphere. None of the buildings are *too* big—none are at all domineering; you don't feel intimidated or humbled in their presence. Instead, like other communities throughout Maine, Bates has an open, small-town feel to it. This particular community invites students in to grow and learn, and it is an invitation Bates students relish.

Any of the schools in this book will give you a solid college education. It is the people at Bates, however (from students to faculty to administrators), the college's history of openness—the lack of a Greek system and early switch to coeducation— openness that continues to set the tone for campus life and its liberal arts tradition, that set it apart from the rest. At Bates you will get a big time education in a small town atmosphere, where friendly, supportive, energetic people create a community you'll wish you could take with you when you leave.

GETTING IN/FINANCIAL AID

Becoming a Bates student is no easy task. Bates' reputation for academic excellence has grown steadily over recent years, and it seems that every year the admissions department announces that the applicant pool was "the strongest ever." As talented students across the country and around the world continue to make Bates their school of choice, admissions standards continue to rise correspondingly. It is not surprising to hear older alumni comment that, if they were applying to Bates today, they might not be able to gain admission. Bates is currently listed as one of the nation's most competitive colleges by *Barron's Profiles of American Colleges*, and gets the equivalent ranking from other major college review publications.

There are no clear-cut rules defining what makes a perfect admissions candidate. According to the college admissions literature, Bates "seeks promising individuals from a variety of educational, ethnic, socioeconomic, cultural, and geographical backgrounds. Academic, extracurricular, and personal achievements are considered in the evaluation of a candidate's preparation, aptitude, and character."

As for the application process itself, the Bates procedure is refreshing in that it *does not* require the submission of standardized test scores. The admissions team will look at your scores if you wish, but they realize there may be flaws in the makeup of the major standardized tests. Instead of placing students' admissions fate in the hands of tests, the people who read your application will be concentrating on your high school record, academic pursuits and honors, extracurricular activities, community involvement/personal interests, and other ways you have spent your free time, and will look carefully at your teachers' and school's recommendations. So, while most students who apply to Bates have scored well on SAT I and the ACT, the Bates admissions team does not automatically discount those who have not.

> *"While a campus visit and interview are not required, they are strongly encouraged. My first visit to Bates came during the fall of my sophomore year in high school, when I tagged along on many of my older sister's college trips. During those trips, I was generally only interested in collecting as many college sweatshirts as possible, but something besides nice sweats must have struck me about Bates, because it was on my very short list of schools I was interested in when it was time for me to face the whole college admissions process.*
>
> *"I returned to Bates for an interview and a closer look around during the fall of my own senior year in high school. Like most others who travel to Maine to look at schools, I have to confess that I also made stops at Colby and Bowdoin. It was Bates, though, that really stood out on this trip.*
>
> *"I had a great interview with a recent Bates graduate who asked me a variety of thought-provoking questions, and who was*

eager to share with me all of her experiences as they related to the questions I had about the college.

"After my interview, I took a campus tour, and then sat in on a history class. Feeling totally overwhelmed, I tried to make myself as inconspicuous as possible. The professor noticed me, however, and made sure he pulled me aside after class to introduce himself and see if I had any questions about Bates that he might be able to answer. While I thought it a bit odd for a professor to take such an interest in a high school student who hadn't even made up his mind to apply to Bates, it is a scene I saw repeated a hundred times during my subsequent four years as a Bates student. Prospective students are always welcome on campus and in classrooms. Class sizes are small, so professors always know when visitors are sitting in, and always do their best to make sure those visitors know they are welcome."

If and when you decide Bates is for you, you have a couple of options in terms of actually applying. The regular admissions process is complemented by two different early decision deadlines, deferred admission, January admission, transfer admission, and the possibility of attending Bates as a visiting student.

Financial aid is available to help defray the expense of attending Bates. More than 40% of the student body receives college-endowed scholarship funds, and around 55% receive some sort of financial aid, whether in the form of scholarships, loans from Bates and outside sources, and/or payment for a wide variety of on-campus jobs.

Probably the only thing you need to know about financing a Bates education is the name Lee Campbell. Give Lee a call in the financial aid office, and he'll take it from there, skillfully and devotedly guiding you through the whole process and explaining all the different financial aid avenues available for you and your family to explore.

"One of my Bates friends recently called Lee with some questions about financing her graduate school studies. She reported to me, skeptically, that Lee, upon hearing her name, said 'Oh sure! I remember you!' She really doubted that Lee had any idea who she was, as she couldn't remember ever having been anywhere near the financial aid office. The fact that she had not been on financial aid doesn't really matter—Lee just makes it a point to get to know people around campus.

"I asked Lee about this particular friend last time I spoke with him, and, as I expected, he had been right on when he told her he remembered her. 'History major, rugby player, blond hair. Right?' Lee said to me. 'I try to see a couple of their games every year.' Indeed, outside of the financial aid office, athletic events are probably the best places to look for Lee. The sport doesn't really matter—although he is partial to basketball—Lee just enjoys watching students showcase their talents.

"Oh, and not only did Lee remember my friend, he also gave her great advice. Financial problems were the last thing she needed to worry about while in grad school, and, with Lee's guidance, she now hits her textbooks without worrying about her checkbook."

More financial aid questions? Honestly, just give Lee a call.

ACADEMIC ENVIRONMENT

"I was scared at my convocation dinner. Dean Celeste Branham addressed all of us new Bates students, a captive-but-restless audience in our coats and ties, skirts and heels, with this heady welcome. 'All of you graduated in the top of half of your high school classes. Half of you will graduate in the bottom half of your college class.' That was enough to get our attention. Now everyone sat up a little straighter, focused earnestly on our speaker. 'Oh, man,' I thought, 'this is it. This is college. Time to hit the books.'

"That particular moment was probably the most nervous time of my college career. I felt threatened, like I had to prove my adequacy. That really was the only time I had that feeling, however, and within a few weeks all students realize that the focus at Bates is on getting a great education, and not just on getting great grades."

The Bates academic year is set up on a 4-4-1 calendar. This means, simply, that there are two consecutive semesters during which the normal course load is four classes, followed by one five-week session (called Short Term) during which students take only one class, thus, 4-4-1. To graduate, students must complete 32 courses and two Short Term units. Bates does offer the option of completing one's studies in only three years; requirements differ slightly for the few students who attempt this.

While students have a lot of leeway in choosing their courses, there are a number of General Education requirements that must be completed. Because it is the college's aim to expose students to as many different areas as possible, the General Education requirements ensure that all students must branch out beyond their major field of study. These requirements include:

• at least three courses from the curriculum in biology, chemistry, geology, or physics and astronomy;

• at least three courses from the curriculum in anthropology, economics, political science, psychology, or sociology;

• a cluster of five courses (three of which fit a general theme) in art, English, foreign languages and literatures, history, music, philosophy, religion, rhetoric, or theater; and

- at least one course in which the understanding and use of quantitative techniques are emphasized.

While this may seem like quite a list to complete, my experience and that of most of my friends was that the majority of the requirements get fulfilled just by taking classes in which you are interested. Some students complain about the "cluster" requirement, but this can be fulfilled in so many different ways that you'll never have to take à class you don't find worthwhile.

"For me, the requirements were a blessing. Coming out of high school I had a phobia of sciences, and would have been plenty happy to have never set foot in another science lab. The requirement, however, forced me to open myself up to science again, and I was happily surprised at how much I enjoyed the geology and astronomy classes with which I fulfilled the requirement. I actually enjoyed geology so much that I became a teaching assistant for an introductory class when I was a sophomore. If you had asked me in high school if I thought I would ever be interested in or able to explain the difference between a moraine and a serac, I would have just laughed in your face. 'No way. You will never see me in another science lab,' I vowed. Well, this political science major found his geology classes to be some of the most rewarding units he took at Bates. Mapping a section of coastline at Bates' own Morse Mountain Preserve, exploring the alpine environment on top of Mount Washington, and standing waist deep in the Saco River collecting sediment samples, were far cries from the humanities and social science classes I had planned on, and were events that helped make my Bates experience more complete—and that is exactly what liberal arts is about—getting a complete education. Without the requirement, I would never have ventured into any Bates science class, and would consequently have missed out on a couple of really interesting fields and some wonderful professors."

Bates professors are, in a word, excellent. More than 95% of full-time teaching faculty members hold doctoral degrees or other terminal degrees appropriate to their disciplines. They have a diverse background, and vary from fresh faces who are eager to share their experiences to the wise, older sages who have the benefit of years of teaching already behind them. What they all have in common is a love of learning, a love of teaching, and a desire to help students learn to think and grow and find success themselves.

Because Bates is a small college, devoted entirely to undergraduate education, professors teach all their own classes. There are no graduate students on campus, so having students teach is not even an option. Upperclass students do have the opportunity to work as teaching assistants and, in that regard, have the chance to oversee language lab work or to help out in science laboratories.

Class structure varies from introductory lectures to specialized seminars, and all combinations in between. Overall class size averages 15 students, while half the classes offered have fewer than ten.

With a student-faculty ratio of 10.5:1, Bates professors are overwhelmingly accessible. All professors hold regularly scheduled office hours when students can drop by with questions or problems to discuss; all professors will schedule one-on-one meetings with students, and the vast majority will linger after class for further discussion of class materials, and will schedule review sessions to help students prepare for midterms and finals.

Relationships between students and faculty members can and do flourish outside the classroom. Bates professors are, by and large, an outgoing, active group, and can often be found enjoying their hobbies, from hiking to skiing to ultimate frisbee, with students. Professors serve as advisors for campus clubs, sharing their experience, knowledge, and enthusiasm in these arenas as well as in their classrooms. The faculty consistently fields one of the strongest teams in the winter intramural basketball league, so it is not impossible that the same professor could stump you with a question in class during the day and then block a jump shot in your face during a game that night. Pretty humbling, but it helps to remind you that your professors are as well-rounded as the students they teach.

> *"One of my best nonclassroom experiences with professors was hiking with professors Mike Retelle and Dyk Eusden in the Presidential Range in New Hampshire. Mike and Dyk are two of the nicest people you'll ever meet anywhere. They can play the classroom heavy when necessary, but it doesn't come naturally.*
>
> *"This particular hiking trip, with a handful of other students, came early in my Bates career, in the fall of my first year. Getting to know both of these professors as people, not just as teachers, really helped me associate with the rest of my professors throughout my four years at Bates. Mike was actually the first person I saw when I finished the oral defense of my thesis in the spring of my senior year. I had to leave the room as my examiners deliberated whether I should be granted honors and, as I waited in the hallway, Mike walked by and stopped to chat. He hung out with me the whole time the panel deliberated, obviously realizing that I was pretty nervous. That just sort of struck me—I mean, he definitely had been on his way somewhere when he walked by, but he put it off to hang out and give me some support. While you wouldn't expect that at many schools, at Bates it is all part of the package."*

Despite the fact that the faculty are extremely supportive of their students, academic tensions can still run very high at Bates. There is not really a sense of competitiveness among students, but everyone has their own personal drive to do their absolute best on all their work. While few would consider Bates a four-year grind, at times it may seem like your whole life is spent in the library. Stress levels run highest, not surprisingly, during midterms and final exams, but students tend to keep a pretty positive perspective even during these weeks. While students may complain about their workloads—comparing workloads with friends is a popular pastime, with everyone believing that their particular load is heaviest—Bates students are not afraid to push themselves and spend long hours in the library hunched over books.

The Bates curriculum is divided into three parts: the humanities, the social sciences, and the natural sciences, which are in turn broken down into 19 departments and 28 major fields in which students can earn either a Bachelor of Arts or Bachelor of Sciences degree.

Most of these majors have a senior thesis as one of their departmental requirements. (Those that don't offer a thesis option require students to pass comprehensive exams during their senior year.) The senior thesis—one semester for most students or a two-semester honors thesis for those who have performed especially well within their department—is a daunting project that culminates all of a student's prior learning, and helps to refine reading, research, and writing skills that will be invaluable in all areas of potential graduate study. When the project is completed, students are left with a tangible piece of work consisting of their own research, tested hypotheses, and conclusions, and have the knowledge and confidence to undertake similar assignments in the future.

While thesis crunch time is perhaps the most stressful time of Bates students' academic careers, all students make it through—some with only minutes to spare before their deadline—and when the product is finally laser-printed, bound, and passed in, few would argue that it was not a worthwhile endeavor. Many other institutions have stopped requiring a senior thesis, but Bates continues to stand by the program, which gives its students a leg up on others as they head down career paths, and if and when they move on to graduate school.

The Bates experience is complemented by a variety of off-campus opportunities, widely popular among students. Many take advantage of Bates-sponsored programs in France, Spain, Germany, Japan, and Ecuador, as well as a number of other locales including Russia and the Galapagos Islands during Short Term. Students can also participate in North American programs set up with other colleges, including semesters at American University in Washington D.C., McGill University in Montreal, Morehouse and Spelman Colleges in Georgia, and the Mystic Seaport Program in American Maritime Studies in Mystic, Connecticut.

Students may choose to study abroad in hundreds of other locations throughout the world, from Austria to Australia, and Ireland to India. These programs, offered by other colleges or private institutions, merely need to be approved by the off-campus study advisor. In this way, students can complement their college experience by learning firsthand about another way of life, and by facing all the challenges and excitement involved in doing so.

SOCIAL LIFE

Despite the heavy workload, Bates boasts a healthy social life. Social activities revolve around the campus to a large degree, primarily because 94% of students live on campus. From campus-wide parties on weekends to student-run coffeehouses on Wednesdays, from Friday-night film showings to noontime musical offerings, there is always something happening on campus, with enough variety to sate all students' palates.

Student groups sponsor parties every weekend, and the college itself sponsors a number of social events throughout the year, the biggest being the annual President's Gala Ball (to which the entire college community is invited) and at which the Count Basie Orchestra recently performed. The Student Activities Committee does a good job of bringing nationally known bands to play on campus—in recent years The Samples, The Indigo Girls, and The Spin Doctors have all performed.

Lewiston-Auburn, with a combined population of around 60,000, provides other opportunities for social life. Multiscreen cinemas, a variety of restaurants (priced in both the affordable and Parents' Weekend-only ranges), and easy access to the Maine coast and mountains, both within an hour's drive, are among the best offerings.

For those who are more metropolitan-minded, Portland is only 35 miles south down the turnpike. While students don't make the trip very often, Portland (though fairly small by city standards) does offer a great nightlife in the bar and brew-pub-lined Old Port, as well as a fine art museum and symphony. For those who yearn for more big-city life, Montreal and Boston are both options for weekend road trips.

Another popular off-campus destination spot is Freeport, Maine, home of L.L. Bean (open 365 days a year, 24 hours a day), and a slew of other outlet stores, ranging from Patagonia to Banana Republic to Pepperidge Farm (yes, it's actually possible to buy cut-rate Goldfish Crackers). Freeport is only about a half hour away, and is especially popular for off-hour trips to L.L. Bean, and shopping trips during Parent's Weekend.

Social life is basically the same for the upper and lower classes, with the obvious difference that those over 21 have the added option of going to The Goose, The Cage, and any of the other area bars. Basically, Bates students know how to have fun and they aren't afraid to put down the books when there is a great social opportunity that should not be passed up.

Social life becomes even more lively during Short Term, when students have the burden of only one class. While this one class might meet every day, the work load is invariably lighter than during the normal school year, giving all students ample opportunity for more nonacademic pursuits. Virtually all students have been heard to mutter—usually while knee-deep in textbooks and notes—"College would be heaven if it weren't for all this work!" Well, Short Term is about the closest thing to this fantasy that students can experience. While there is work to be done, the main point is to afford students a chance to study something outside their major within a less-stressful academic atmosphere, but it is also a five-week socialite's dream. Seniors especially relish this time, as it is one final hurrah before good friends head their separate ways into the real world that lies beyond the quad.

Happily for many students, the long Maine winter has conveniently come to an end by the time Short Term begins, and a large part of campus social life moves back outside, where it started back in September. All-campus barbecues take place weekly on the quad, and student groups often throw parties on any number of outdoor terraces. The spring intramural softball league is extremely popular, as are trips to the coast for beachgoing and the annual Outing Club-sponsored clambakes. Range Pond State Park is another favorite student spot, consisting of a beautiful evergreen-encircled lake with ample beachfront, only ten minutes from campus.

> *"For many people, the first thing that comes to mind when they hear the word* Maine *is lobster. Bates does its best to make sure that all students get a chance to participate in this integral part of Maine living by sponsoring authentic Maine clambakes on the beach every fall and spring. These much-anticipated events are among nearly everyone's favorite social events. Students pile into buses and friends' cars for the one-hour drive to the coast, where they eat their fill of lobster, steamers, corn on the cob, and all the trimmings for less than $10. Most people make an afternoon of it, and impromptu touch football and ultimate frisbee games pop up along the beach. The bravest (most foolish?) students take quick dips into the icy Atlantic, and many just slip into a food coma and nap on the rocks. The clambake is a great way to meet new people too, as everyone's true colors shine through when they attempt to conquer a one-and-a-half pound lobster armed with nothing but their fingers and plastic forks. For the uninitiated, it is, to say the least, a messy affair."*

It is a fact of life that alcohol plays a role in the social life of nearly every student on every college campus across the country, and, at Bates, things are no different. If students want alcohol (primarily beer), it is available, but it is definitely not a compulsory aspect of campus social life. As one of my friends put it, "Of course there is drinking at Bates, but no more than at any other similar school." College students will probably always drink beer, and college administrators will probably always frown upon student consumption. The Bates administration is still relatively laissez-faire in terms of alcohol regulation, but it has taken steps in recent years to comply with national and state laws. This has manifested most noticeably into more college-sponsored nonalcoholic events, as well as campus security regulation of on-campus keg parties.

For students who are 21, popular off-campus destinations consist of two local bars, The Goose and The Cage, both within walking distance. While social centers on campus tend to wax and wane, the popularity of both The Goose and The Cage is constant. The Cage's main draw is a wonderful Wednesday night institution called

"Burgers and Beer"—consisting of an incredible burger and, yes, beer, for a ridiculously small amount of money. The Goose, a true dive, is even more popular among students. It's main draws are even cheaper prices, an atmosphere only a college student could like, and its proximity to another much-adored establishment, Luiggi's Pizzeria, which happens to be right next door. While you can't take beer from The Goose into Luiggi's, you are more than welcome to bring a pizza—2 small cheese for $5—into The Goose. All colleges seem to have one neighborhood bar that students feel is their very own—Hamilton has The Rock, Williams has The Pub, Bates has The Goose. They are institutions themselves, and students love them.

EXTRACURRICULAR ACTIVITIES

As with social life, extracurricular opportunities at Bates are both plentiful and popular. Many students are attracted to the multitude of outdoor activities available in the state of Maine, and Bates' location provides ample opportunity to take advantage of all Maine has to offer. Mountain biking and skiing are both extremely popular—students can start bike rides from campus—and superb skiing is only about an hour away at Sunday River, and only about a two-hour drive to Sugarloaf/USA, two of the best ski resorts in the East.

Another popular after-class activity is jogging on the three- and five-mile loops that branch off from campus and wind through the residential neighborhoods of Lewiston. On any given afternoon there are dozens of students and professors out running, all pounding out the stresses of the day.

In terms of college-sponsored activities, the options are seemingly endless.

"My first nonacademic Bates experience—as it is for many others—was as a member of an Outing Club-sponsored prefreshman orientation wilderness trip. Mine was a three-day canoe trip down the Kennebec River with seven other first-year students and two sophomore group leaders. Besides being both a great time and a great introduction to the wilds of the state of Maine, these trips are excellent ways for students to get to know a handful of their peers, and to get some of their college jitters out of the way before orientation even starts. The group leaders are excellent sources of information for inquisitive new students and, on my trip, we peppered our leaders with every question imaginable about Bates over the course of our three days. What are classes like? Homework? Professors? Exams? Parties? Dating? We wanted to know everything, and our more worldly sophomore superiors were only too happy to give us the lowdown on every aspect of Bates life. While we were definitely not seasoned Bates veterans by the time we emerged from the woods, all eight of us new stu-

dents had formed friendships that would last throughout our four years, and had asked enough nervous questions to help us avoid at least a few common freshman pitfalls."

The Outing Club, in operation for more than 70 years, also runs a well-used equipment room in the basement of Hathorn Hall, where any student can cheaply rent everything from bikes to skis to tents, and everything else necessary to enjoy the outdoors. The club also runs student trips throughout the year, ranging from trail maintenance on the Appalachian Trail to sea kayaking on the coast.

Other popular clubs include the foreign language clubs, the Film Board, the Ultimate Frisbee Club, the college radio station, the Volleyball Club, the Waterpolo Club, the Quimby Debate Council, a variety of political clubs, music clubs, the weekly newspaper, the yearbook, a variety of volunteer clubs, and the Crew and Rugby clubs, to name only a few. All these organizations are open to all students and, even as a first-year student, it is possible to play a significant role in any club's operations.

Many students find time for on- or off-campus jobs, or for volunteering at local schools, nursing homes, political offices, and other organizations around town. Other students fulfill internships at local hospitals, law offices, and local businesses. While not as popular, some students do make weekly trips to Portland for internships there.

Probably the most popular extracurricular activities are varsity, intramural, and club sports. This is due mostly to the active nature of Bates students, and is aided by the fact that graduation requirements do include physical education units (which can be fulfilled by participating in the above-mentioned groups).

Among the most popular club sports are crew, rugby, and hockey, all three of which field both male and female teams. Popular intramurals, all coed, are soccer in the fall, basketball during the winter and, the most popular, softball (usually played with a keg of beer on the field) during Short Term in the spring. Intramurals are open to students of all abilities, and many students participate.

"I am 6'2", and the question I was probably asked most often in high school was 'Why don't you play basketball?' Well, I'm not sure why I never played, but I never did. As a result, I am a downright miserable basketball player. But, as bad as I am, there was a place for even me in the Bates intramural basketball league. The league has four categories—A is the best, followed by B+, B, and C. You can guess which category my team was in. The year of the Persian Gulf War, we named our team the Scuds—after the Iraqi missiles that just couldn't seem to hit their targets. We similarly had a hard time getting the basketball into the hoop. As bad as we were, we always had a great time and I think we even won a few games (the talent pool in C league being pretty thin). Win or lose, intramurals at Bates are a terrific way to get your mind off academics for an hour or two, and are invariably social events where ultracompetitiveness and poor sportsmanship are viewed about as warmly as is an 8:00 o'clock exam."

Bates has all the varsity sports one would expect, with the one glaring omission (for a school in Maine) of varsity hockey. However, a new rink has just been completed, so varsity men's and women's hockey teams may not be far off.

Bates participates in NCAA Division I for men's and women's alpine and nordic skiing, and these teams consistently place well in New England and national competitions.

For all other sports, Bates participates in the NCAA Division III New England Small College Athletic Conference, which includes Bowdoin, Colby, Williams, and Middlebury, among others. Despite being Division III, the quality of play is high on all teams and many, like men's and women's soccer, women's lacrosse, women's volleyball, and men's tennis are particularly strong. All sports require huge time commitments, and athletes must learn to balance their time between academics and athletics—with academics as the top priority.

As with academics, Bates students are extremely supportive of one another's extracurricular activities. Students are avid fans of Bates sports teams and, on fall Saturday afternoons, the only place to be is out watching the Bobcats compete. The fields are all within a couple hundred yards of each other, so it's possible to keep an eye on the rugby, football, tennis, soccer, and field hockey teams, who may all be engaged in contests on the same afternoon. While the teams are hard at work on their respective fields, other students are hard at work cheering them on, or at least are around for some sideline socializing.

Bates' biggest rivals are Bowdoin, a half-hour drive to the south, and Colby, an hour drive to the north. Clashes with teams from these schools, especially Colby, draw large crowds and tend to bring out the best in athletes' performances. Because of their proximity, fans often travel to away events, and emotions always run high between opposing sidelines. In general, though, the rivalries are friendly, due primarily to the fact that many of the students at the colleges have friends at the other schools. So, while athletes and fans give their all during contests, everyone puts their rivalries aside after events, lingering awhile to catch up with old friends.

Emotions definitely run highest for the twice-yearly meetings between the Bates and Colby basketball teams. For the Bates fan, there is no greater thrill than to watch the Bobcats battle it out against the White Mules of Colby in the intimate confines of the aging Alumni Gymnasium on the Bates campus. Other teams dread coming to play in Alumni, because the size of the gym means fans literally line the sidelines, leaving opposing players feeling completely outnumbered on the floor. Dean of Students James Reese always shakes his head and laughs when he describes to students how much he and his Middlebury teammates used to hate to play in Alumni during his undergraduate basketball days.

"For the Colby games, the gym is packed to standing-room only, and school spirit is the highest of any time during the year. Books are left unattended in the library and dorm rooms, to be picked up again that evening only if Colby manages a victory. After Bates wins, however, fans leave the books alone and head down

to The Goose or to spontaneous parties that pop up around campus, everyone celebrating their good fortune of being a Batesie.

"The Bates-Colby game my junior year was by far the biggest basketball event of my four years. The Bates team was in the midst of its best season ever, and Colby was having a great season as well. The gym was, as always, packed to overflowing—so full that my friends and I had to sneak in a back door after tennis practice just to get in.

"The game itself was fantastic, with the teams trading leads throughout. Despite Bates' great record, we were still the underdog, so the fact the Bobcats had the lead late in the fourth quarter had everyone in a frenzy. Bates fans were on their feet and cheering like mad for at least the last ten minutes of the contest. Colby surged in the final minutes, but the Bates players stepped it up a notch and pulled away to secure their biggest and most satisfying win of the year. The crowd went absolutely wild, spilling out of the bleachers and onto the floor to hug and high-five all the Bates players.

"After the game, the parties started immediately, the biggest one in the house where a number of the team's seniors lived. One great thing about a small school is that you know the people you are cheering for at sporting events. At Michigan or North Carolina, or any other large university, the athletes are often larger than life, more like professionals than students. At Bates, the athletes you cheer for are your chemistry lab partners, your freshman roommates, and your best friends, making wins all the more special, and making post-game parties all the more fervent.

"That evening the parties lasted deep into the night, everyone trying hard not to think about all the work that was being left undone. The baggy eyes and smiling faces at breakfast the next day were the best indicator of the great time people had the night before.

"Don't ever let anyone tell you Division III sports aren't worth getting excited about."

GRADUATES

As with other liberal arts institutions, Bates does not train its students for any one particular career. Instead, Bates instills in its students a breadth of knowledge and gives them the luxury of knowing how to think and respond to new and ever-evolving situations—leaving career choices wide open.

To try to characterize life after Bates in any one way would be an exercise in futility. There is no particular path graduates follow after leaving the college. Pick anything, and it's a safe bet there is a Bates grad out there somewhere doing it. Teachers, doctors, politicians, business leaders, professional athletes, volunteers, writers—even a host of "The Today Show"—whatever you can think of, Bates graduates make careers and find happiness in a myriad of ways.

One thing many graduates do share in common is the motivation to continue their education. Around two thirds of graduates continue on to graduate school within five years of graduation. Again, however, it would be impossible to detail all the different programs Bates grads enroll in, or to try to list all the universities they attend.

The Bates alumni network is strong. The annual Alumni Fund Drive receives widespread support. Alumni also meet regularly in Bates Clubs across the country, conduct off-campus admissions interviews, and return to Lewiston in droves for yearly June reunions and October homecomings.

The college's small size gives graduates a sense of camraderie. You can always rely on other alums to assist in networking and job searches, and alums are always eager to reminisce about their Bates years.

> *"One of my classmates has a great story about receiving his first job offer after graduation. He was in New York for an interview and, upon leaving the building his meeting was in, managed to walk in the exact opposite direction of where his car was parked. Quickly realizing his mistake, yet still unsure of exactly which way to head, he was happy to notice a Bates decal in the window of a car parked on the street next to where he was standing. Luckier still was that the car's owner was approaching his vehicle at that moment. My friend introduced himself as a recent graduate, to which the car's owner responded with a huge smile and the acknowledgment that he too was an alum. They quickly slipped into a discussion of Bates then and now, both of them with a healthy dose of Bates pride.*
>
> *"At the end of the conversation, my friend walked off with directions back to his car, and with an honest, earnest job offer. Although they had only spoken for about ten minutes, this older Bates grad was impressed with my buddy as a person and, of course, had absolute confidence in his academic preparedness and his ability to excel in his profession. It's a great example of Bates grads wanting to see one another succeed, and of their desire to assist them whenever possible."*

SUMMARY

Pick up any college guidebook or magazine, and you will find Bates listed among the top schools in the nation. The quality of education is at the forefront of what is offered in this country and around the world. Bates was founded on egalitarian ideals, ideals that are still manifest in all aspects of both the academic program and college life in general. To this end, all campus opportunities remain open to all students, with no sense of exclusivity. The college also continually strives to offer diverse educational opportunities in tune with society's demands—not as a follower of these trends, but as a leader.

Bates' small size fosters a sense of community and support within that community, the likes of which cannot be duplicated at other, larger institutions. Bates students encourage one another in all aspects of college life, and Bates professors are always there to make sure everyone is getting the most out of their classes. While no one will hold your hand and make college easy, at Bates the support system is there to ensure that any student who is willing to work hard will receive the best education possible, and will always get personal attention when needed.

While by this point it must be completely obvious that I am a huge fan of the Bates experience and am 100% satisfied with the education I received, Bates does have a couple of faults that even I am not blind to. These are the small size of the college's endowment as compared with those of similar institutions and the colleges relative lack of name recognition outside the Northeast. In Bates' defense, the endowment has been steadily rising over recent years (the annual Alumni Fund seems to set new records every year), and the Bates name and word of the quality education it provides continues to spread around the nation and indeed around the world. Bates has offered its students a great education for years, but is a relative newcomer in the highest echelons of institutions for higher learning. As the college continues to produce great thinkers and leaders, the endowment and name recognition will both continue to grow.

A possible third drawback for some students is Bates' location. Some lament the long Maine winters and/or the college's distance from a major metropolitan area. The vast majority, however, relish the location—if not before they arrived, at least by the time they graduate. Many would argue that you should come to Bates *because* it is in Maine, not in spite of that fact. As the college's literature is fond of saying, "Graduates from other parts of the country and the world often leave subtly changed by the experience of living in this special place for four years."

So, even for the student who is more comfortable in a city than in the country, or who is more comfortable in shorts and sandals than in L.L. Bean flannel shirts and boots, I would still say, "Come to Bates." The quality of education, the intimate size, the sense of community, and overwhelming feelings of friendliness and supportiveness you experience on campus make it a truly wonderful place to spend four years.

Oh, and when you're through, you too can proudly say, "Ayuh, been to Maine."

J. Reese Madden, B.A.

Boston College

THE PROGRAM

When one mentions words such as: Jesuit, religious, Society of Jesus, Saint Ignatius Loyola, Catholic, or any phrase remotely hinting of a spiritual essence, the average young adult may well hesitate. Indeed, opting to spend perhaps the most important four years of your life in a place where such words are commonplace may not be the desired collegiate experience; especially for those who do not consider themselves overly religious. Such a preconception would be a grave mistake when contemplating attending Boston College. Yes, it is Jesuit and yes, it is considered a "religious" institution of higher learning. However, Boston College is so much more.

Boston College has long been nicknamed the Jesuit Ivy, due largely to its lofty academic aspirations. In many respects, these aspirations have been realized. The college was founded by the Society of Jesus in 1863. The university very much models itself after the tradition and religious influences of the very first Jesuit school. The institution was established in Messina, Sicily in 1548 at the time of the Reformation. Although these religious roots are never stifled, you need not fear becoming overwhelmed by them. Boston College is as religious as you want it to be.

The college originally was established for the purpose of providing education to the ever increasing population of immigrant Catholics who settled in the flourishing port city of Boston. Located in the South End, the fledgling college was committed, not to turning out model Jesuit priests, but rather to educating Boston's young men. Curriculum in the early days consisted of rigorous study in such traditional disciplines as Latin, Greek, history, science, math, literature, and rhetoric. This core curriculum, a shadow of which still exists today, was designed not only to educate, but to develop the moral, intellectual, and social awareness of each student.

The Boston College experience is a study in dualism. There is equal emphasis given to the development of the spiritual person as well as the critical thinker. The academic intention of the university is to encourage each student to think for himself or herself as opposed to merely memorizing random facts only to forget them after the exam is graded. Above all else, however, Boston College encourages a Christian outlook on life. This perspective is focused on developing morally responsible individuals who rise to spiritual challenges. This Christian outlook never overpowers, it guides.

It is this spiritual presence, I believe, that shapes and influences the Boston College student. It doesn't make us overtly religious. Rather, it heightens our awareness of the world around us and encourages us to effect change. Most importantly, it encourages us to believe in ourselves and have faith in the conviction that we are capable of making a difference in the world. Boston College also offers its students outlets for the purpose of making these differences. Currently the Wallace E. Carroll School of Management sponsors a program entitled Business Basics. Its intention: introducing business concepts to elementary school children. Consisting of sessions on marketing, budgeting, and organization, management students go to area elementary schools and teach young children philosophies of the business world.

Another offered program that serves in heightening our awareness of the world around us is entitled Pulse. This program is usually undertaken as part of the philosophy/theology core requirement. It involves hands-on experience with various social service organizations. Participants are presented with a myriad of opportunities from work in homeless shelters to soup kitchens to legal research to the Boston correctional system. The rewards are far greater than the accompanying course credit. This type of participation serves to demonstrate over and over again that we are capable of making a difference in society.

Academic achievement is equally important at Boston College. Along with commitment to the spiritual person comes a commitment to developing the critical thinker. Every class, from requirements to advanced electives, is designed to encourage participation and inquiry. This allows students to question what they are learning. This participation comes in all forms, not just question and answer sessions. Instructors at Boston College are concerned with the opinions and questions of all students. Disagreement is never stifled but is welcome. This disagreement and questioning leads to the intellectual development of every student who experiences Boston College.

> *"One of my most powerful encounters with this commitment to developing critical thinking came during a course on four of Shakespeare's major plays. The first task was to be* Hamlet, *a work that most are first introduced to in high school. My professor was a man feared among English majors. He was known as D+Duhamel, not because of unfair grading practices, but because he expected a lot out of his students, and he usually received it. Hamlet is a character renowned for his indecision. Much of the play is concerned with his dilemma over how to avenge the death of his father. Professor Duhamel wanted us to*

write "the scene that Shakespeare forgot": Develop a scene in which Hamlet discovers absolute proof of his father's murder and decides to avenge it. Needless to say I felt somewhat daunted. My classmates and I joked that the Great William Shakespeare was probably turning over in his grave because perhaps his most famous character was being tampered with by mere undergraduates. That assignment taught us more about Hamlet than endless hours of lectures by the most prestigious experts. By pondering Hamlet's indecision on our own we were able to come up with many interpretations of this great character. A rousing class discussion after the scenes were graded led to a heightened understanding of this complex literary character."

Attendance at Boston College, however, develops much more than the socially aware and committed individual. Through instruction and guest speakers, the college attempts to heighten our political awareness as well.

"My most memorable encounter with this awareness came as I was beginning my junior year. As the semester commenced, rumors surfaced, hinting that the colorful and very controversial Oliver North would be putting in an appearance at The Heights. These rumors proved true and North arrived amid considerable animosity.

"As an active member of Boston College's Fulton Debating Society, I made it a practice throughout my college career to attend the lectures of most of the speakers scheduled on campus, particularly the headliners. In the case of Oliver North I was on a mission to understand this man's extraordinary ability to appear sincere in the face of supreme adversity. I was aware of the Iran Contra scandal. However, I really hadn't given much thought to North's sincerity or lack thereof. The audience was fairly evenly divided between fans and foes. It was a rare observer who was content to just listen to what North had to say. Rather, the lecture hall was teeming with citizens who were aware of the nuances of this controversy which had rocked the nation to its very foundations.

"As I sat in that audience, I was overwhelmed with the ramifications of Iranscam and finally understood the gravity of his wrongdoing. It is one thing to read the paper and watch the trials. It is entirely another to actually witness the accusations and defenses offered by North himself as well as those expressed by the audience. Local media likened the combination of animosity and admiration displayed at the event to the best of the demonstrations in the 1960s. I took that experience and have never let its power diminish. It shaped my opinion of this political figure and made me realize for the first time just how grave his actions really were. That experience forced me to question the power of the government and the extent to which rules were bent or

downright ignored. This experience heightened my own political awareness. It also led to the realization that Boston College is a place which provides countless opportunities for its students to question beliefs and open the mind. All of this leads to the development of the critical thinker."

Like its students, Boston College has grown and undergone many changes over time. After it had been in existence for about 50 years, the college outgrew its city campus and relocated to nearby Chestnut Hill, a suburb of Boston. With emphasis on Gothic architecture and magnificent landscaping, Boston College has become an impressive and beautiful place. The first building erected on this newly purchased campus was Gasson Hall, recognized today as the physical embodiment of the ideals of the university. Its architectural beauty, inside and out, is unparalleled on campus. Bells in the Gasson Tower toll on each quarter hour, quickly becoming part of the routine of each member of the Boston College community. This lofty tower has earned the college the nickname: The Heights.

Although no longer in the city of Boston, the university still benefits from its proximity to a large metropolitan area. Three subway lines are within walking distance from the campus, and provide direct access downtown. Once you are Boston bound, a large menu of activity is readily available. You can enjoy a baseball game at the famed Fenway Park, reflect upon the variety of pieces on display at the Museum of Fine Arts, or take in a show of Broadway caliber. In addition to the cultural and social distractions available, Boston has become known as the city of colleges. Over 30, four-year academic institutions can be found within 60 miles of downtown Boston. This provides countless opportunities for the Boston College student, from theater to lectures to social activity to library use.

As Boston College physically expanded, so too did its academic aspirations. Eventually women were included in this scheme. It may well seem impossible to imagine that women were once excluded from most of this country's institutions of higher learning. However, that fact was driven home to the Chestnut Hill campus as recently as the fall of 1989. You see, it was only at this late date that women were included in the school's century-old fight song, "For Boston." One change that was made includes the phrase: "For here all are one and their hearts are true," in place of "for here men are men…" These alterations are symbolic of the changing nature of the Boston College population. When the song was introduced by Thomas Hurley of the class of 1885 the school was not yet coeducational. Today, Boston College's undergraduate population consists of roughly 10,300 undergraduates. Women make up more than half the student body (about 5650) and over 45% of the school's alumni population.

Above all, the Boston College experience can provide you with the ultimate balance between development of the spiritual person and the intellectual person. Like the Jesuits of old, contemporary faculty are committed to nurturing the critical thinker and to creating a spiritually fulfilled individual. Boston College is a place where the attainment of both is entirely possible.

GETTING IN/FINANCIAL AID

Since the early 1970s, admission to Boston College has become increasingly competitive. For a recent class, some 15,500 applications were received for 2250 available slots. Like all top universities, Boston College is searching for the candidate who not only qualifies academically, but who is a contributor in terms of talents or drive. No minimum test scores or class ranks have been established. However, the admissions committee tends to seek out that individual who has performed well in an academically challenging high school program. This could include honors as well as advanced placement courses. The best course of study is one that includes four years of English and three or more of math, science, history, and a foreign language.

Admission to the College of Arts and Sciences and the Wallace E. Carroll School of Management is highly competitive. The successful candidate should have a B+ or better and rank somewhere in the top 10% of his or her graduating high school class. Average SAT scores for recent classes have ranged from 520–620 verbal and 580–680 math. However, I cannot emphasize strongly enough that all of these are only averages. There are no minimums in determining admission to Boston College.

One attractive quality about the Boston College population is its national and international diversity. The current undergraduate population includes students from all 50 states as well as over 70 foreign countries. Most students, however, do come from the New England and Mid-Atlantic regions. Alumni play a pivotal role in interviewing potential Boston College undergraduates. Although not required, the interview is a valuable admissions tool, and can be undertaken by a Boston College graduate in your state of residence. Individuals also come from a variety of socio-economic and cultural backgrounds, making Boston College a place to experience the unfamiliar. At Boston College you will encounter a little bit of everything. Incoming freshman arrive from the most prestigious prep schools, from private Catholic schools, and from inner-city schools. Applicants range from the very wealthy to the middle and lower class echelons of society.

> *"The people who decide to attend Boston College are unique. They come from all aspects of life. One of my close friends throughout my college career was a young man named Pete whose father traveled extensively. As a result, he had lived in rather exotic places. When he started at Boston College, he was from Panama City, Panama. Everyone called him Panama Pete and the name stuck, even though his place of residence changed about seven times. He moved to Venezuela, Holland, and Nigeria, just to name a few. My friends and I referred to him as the nomad and often asked him why he chose the United States, since he had ties to so many different places. He always told us that he*

had heard about Boston College when he was small and wanted that university to be the place where he experienced yet another culture. His English was excellent but his writing skills left a bit to be desired. I was privileged to experience his progress in this area firsthand. You see, he would always ask me to proofread his papers. When we were freshmen, these so-called papers consisted of the topic, an idea, and nothing else. It was a real challenge for him to put his ideas coherently on paper. By the time we were seniors I needed a dictionary to understand some of his adjectives!"

International students like Pete are not uncommon. There are about 500 students from countries other than the United States.

A Boston College education is an increasingly expensive one. Fortunately, a generous amount of financial aid is made readily available to those who qualify. Over two thirds of each class receives some form of financial aid. This includes student loans, grants, need-based scholarships, and employment. All together, over $35 million is distributed. Requests for financial aid have absolutely no bearing on admissions decisions. If you are wondering how you will finance your education, and the neighborhood of $100,000 (the estimated cost of completing degree requirements) seems a little daunting, don't hesitate to apply for assistance. For those who qualify and express the desire, the money is there to help finance attendance.

ACADEMIC ENVIRONMENT

The academic environment of Boston College is a reflection of the Jesuit ideal. This involves emphasis on learning for learning's sake and the never-ending pursuit of knowledge. Because the college is so dedicated to learning, a core curriculum has been established. It is very much the core of old, with emphasis on developing the free thinker. This core differs very slightly depending on the school to which you apply. As an undergraduate English major, I was a member of the College of Arts and Sciences. This required me to complete a series of liberal arts courses including two semesters of the following: philosophy, theology, science, English, European history, and social sciences, and demonstration of intermediate proficiency in a foreign language. Also, the core requires coursework in mathematics, cultural diversity, writing, and the arts. Courses in the latter may include drawing, pottery, Renaissance painting, the Impressionists, or the Flemish Masters, just to name a few.

As I reflect upon my academic life, I realize that some of the most enriching experiences have come from those courses developed as requirements. Although all involved different academic departments (philosophy, theology, language) they shared a common goal: challenging us to think for ourselves.

> *"I can remember taking a theology class with emphasis on New Testament criticism. Having attended Catholic school all my life, the content of this work was not unfamiliar. In fact, I will admit now that I took the class precisely for that reason: because I expected few surprises. After all, a requirement is something you should just take and then be done with, right? Wrong! My professor introduced me to a variety of different perspectives and possibilities for interpretation. That class turned into one of my most enjoyable and definitely most illuminating of my college career. I took the class in the spring and would gaze onto the lawn thinking: 'Wow, this is what college is all about, learning about important things I normally wouldn't take the time to ponder.' We studied things that I had always taken for granted such as the Four Gospels. She pointed out the vast differences between John's Gospel and the Gospels of Matthew, Mark, and Luke and offered a series of possibilities as to why this was the case. Since the four books deal with the events of Jesus's life, I had always thought that they were roughly the same. I couldn't have been more wrong. She showed us how certain events were treated with importance in one gospel and ignored in the others. We would break down into groups and offer speculation on this strange situation. Not all of the class was Catholic and I think it turned out to be more of a challenge to those who were. We were forced to let go of many previously held beliefs about the New Testament."*

Theology classes at Boston College are not only confined to these religious topics. Courses are offered entitled "Modern Moral Problems," "Person and Social Responsibility," and "Nature, Dignity and Destiny of the Human Person."

> *"Another memorable academic challenge also appeared in the guise of a mere requirement. Students of all majors must demonstrate proficiency in a foreign language. Having spent half of my high school career learning about Latin, I decided to continue along that path. It happened to be my very first encounter with a college academic environment. I was placed in a class with a relatively equal distribution of freshmen, sophomores, juniors, and seniors. We all shared roughly the same attitude: 'Latin is a dead language so let's just get a good grade, get our credits, and then put all those declensions out of our minds!'*
>
> *"I don't think any of us were quite prepared for the man who would be determining our progress over the next several weeks. He arrived wearing flowing academic robes and informed us that this was the manner in which he would be attired for the rest of the semester. A young man who would become one of my*

closest college friends turned to me and mumbled: 'A man wear-
ing a dress is our teacher.' We could not help but surpress giggles
at this ridiculous looking man! For him, it was symbolic of the
atmosphere he intended to create: one of academic reverence
and inspiration. He quickly informed us that he would succeed
in inspiring us to really want to learn about the language and its
history. Well, he succeeded admirably.

"Very few ever missed a class and Latin became second nat-
ure. He encouraged us to treat it as a puzzle which would inevita-
bly be deciphered. I realized that even though Latin was
considered a dead language, it was an invaluable tool; and not
just for potential doctors or those about to take the SAT. It
increased my vocabulary and helped in all my classes. I learned
so much about becoming a free thinker and challenging myself
academically from that slightly eccentric gentleman. I also dis-
covered that learning just for the sake of learning may prove
more rewarding in practical terms than you might believe. I
learned how to think, among other things. It is an experience I
wouldn't trade. If not for that sometimes cursed core curricu-
lum, none of this challenge would have been experienced."

The predominant teaching method at Boston College is a combination of lecture and discussion. Unfortunately, many of the core classes, particularly in the realms of history and science, are large impersonal lecture atmospheres. This is rectified somewhat by the existence of weekly discussion groups and/or laboratory assignments. In addition, many professors require individual meetings when assignments such as term papers are distributed. This eliminates much of the impersonal feeling of the large classes. Once core requirements are completed and students are concentrating more on specialized areas of study, which usually takes about three semesters, class size decreases considerably. It then takes on more of a seminar tone. Most of the undergraduate advanced electives are seminars.

Grading is done using the 4.0 grading scale. Plus and minus grades are also given. The allocation is as follows: 4.0 = A; 3.67 = A −; 3.3 = B+; 3.0 = B.... Professors consider C grades as indicative of average work, B grades as above average, and A grades as excellent—in much the same manner as high schools allot grades. Academic pressure at Boston College is definitely not overwhelming. One of the qualities I especially like about the college is the perception that each student makes his or her own pressure in terms of grades. There is a definite balance between social and academic. This is not to say that Boston College is not difficult. Rather the general attitude of the faculty is that learning is the responsibility of the student. Thus, academic pressure varies with each student.

Students at Boston College are increasingly drawn to the areas of elementary education, finance, and English. These have become the majors of choice in the School of Education, the Wallace E. Carroll School of Management, and the College of Arts and Sciences, respectively. In an average academic year about 980 students pursue degrees in English, 568 in finance, and 216 in elementary education. The large enrollment in English reflects the respectable nature of the college's English department as well as an increased commitment to study in the humanities. Interest in finance has much to do with the nature of the economic community. Interest in education is also a sign of the times. Studies indicate that there will be a shortage of teachers over the next two decades. Increased salaries also have made the teaching profession an attractive and rewarding option. Other popular majors at Boston College include political science, communication arts, economics, psychology, secondary education, marketing, and accounting.

SOCIAL LIFE

One of my first memories of Boston College social life comes from the dark and sometimes ominous days of Freshman Orientation. Two enterprising seniors were selling T-shirts in my residence hall for a bargain price with the witty caption: "Boston College is a great party school. . .with a twenty thousand dollar cover charge." Imagine bringing that one home to parents who are struggling to meet staggering tuition payments! Admittedly, the description is wildly extreme, but I think it accurately characterizes your initial perception of the Boston College social scene, particularly during those first weeks of parental freedom.

Well, Boston College isn't *that* much of a decadent place. A great deal of study and academic inquiry does go on at Boston College. However, there is also a healthy mix of parties and nights on the town. The housing on campus is designed so as to allow for those students above the legal drinking age to exercise that right in the privacy of their residence halls. Underclass residence halls are designated as "dry," which means that absolutely no alcohol consumption is allowed. Upperclassmen are permitted to register parties with the Office of Housing. This provides for a controlled drinking environment, thus reducing risk.

In terms of social life, the most fun at Boston College comes from these on-campus parties. Very often, they develop on the spur of the moment and grow by word of mouth. In fact, most choose to remain on campus during weekends because the social scene is so diverse. Some parties are small gatherings, whereas others are focused on a particular theme. The most fun I ever had at any party was one where the theme of the night was "The Seventies." People dressed in appropriate attire and the only music allowed throughout the night was from that decade and ranged from disco to heavy metal. Everyone danced until the wee hours.

Boston College has a major intercollegiate football team so fall picnics and games are an integral part of the social scene during the first semester of each academic year. Along with that comes the annual Homecoming celebration, complete with a semiformal ball. Other social events worth mentioning are Middlemarch and the famed "SYR."

Middlemarch is an elaborate evening designed around a particular theme. Past themes have included "The Arabian Nights" and "The Great Gatsby." A limited number of tickets are made available but you must earn them. Three sets of clues are published that hint at a series of ticket-selling locations. The first 20 people in line at the right locations on the designated selling day earn a ticket. It makes for high-spirited competition and a great night for the lucky ones.

> *"Sometimes just waiting out for the tickets is great fun, even if morning comes and you discover that you are waiting in the wrong place. I was privileged to attend one Middlemarch Ball but didn't have any part in the searching since I was asked by a friend. I think I had more fun waiting to purchase a ticket of my own when I was a senior. It was a spur of the moment decision which led to rousing fun. I waited with my roommates who had been pondering the clues for weeks. We huddled in the foyer of the library from midnight until eight in the morning. Temperatures had dropped below zero that night and we were numb. To pass the time we told ghost stories, took turns leaving our hideout to gather refreshments for all, and gossiped about potential dates if we were in the right spot. Well, we weren't, but the experience of staying up in sub-zero weather for nothing proved to be a memorable one!"*

SYR stands for "Surprise Your Roommate," and the results are often hilarious! It is a semiformal dance where your escort is someone handpicked by a roommate or close friend, without your knowledge or input. It certainly makes for an evening to remember.

Overall, Boston College offers a variety of social distractions. One commendable quality about this social environment is the equal distribution between on-campus and off-campus recreation. Boston nightlife provides everything from movies to the theater to elaborate restaurants and exciting dance clubs. On-campus parties are not uncommon, as well as dances and sports events.

One of the qualities that attracted me to Boston College was its absence of fraternities and sororities, eliminating the artificial social barriers that such institutions can foster. Boston College operates under a unique housing system. The majority of incoming freshmen are only offered three years of on-campus housing. For these students, junior year is designated as "off." What this means is the opportunity to experience life as a true independent. It is not nearly as threatening as it may sound. Rather, my time off campus was rewarding and filled with adventure. By the time this experience presents itself, students have established social networks and are comfortable with the Boston College environment. This makes for a less threatening endeavor.

The housing that is available comes in all forms. Freshmen are housed on two separate campuses: upper campus and Newton campus. Upper campus is located adjacent to the college's main campus and consists of single, double, and triple rooms. Newton campus is located about a mile and a half away from the rest of the college. Shuttle bus service is provided, which runs roughly every ten minutes. At first glance, being a mile and a half away from the main action may seem far from ideal. This is far from the truth. As a "graduate" of Newton campus, I found my time there far from frustrating. Roughly half of the freshman class was also housed there so plenty of opportunity existed for developing friendships. In fact, a real sense of community developed. Most importantly, we were able to experience the benefits of a large college while enjoying the comforts of a small campus.

Sophomores, seniors, and the small percentage of juniors who receive housing are placed on the main campus. Residence halls run from the traditional doubles to apartments complete with air conditioning and dishwashers. Depending upon the building, apartments house from four to eight undergraduates comfortably. Housing assignments are determined using a lottery system.

EXTRACURRICULAR ACTIVITIES

Boston College boasts over 135 clubs and organizations—academic, social, athletic, preprofessional, political, and honor. There is a great deal of administrative support for all existing organizations as well as the encouragement to start new programs.

As an officer of the Boston College debate/public speaking society (the Fulton Debating Society), I was able to experience firsthand the commitment of the school to its extracurricular endeavors. The society recently celebrated its centennial year amid tremendous administrative support—everything from financial to spiritual. The college was generous in terms of dollars; we were able to attend certain contests for the first time ever. The society hosted two major speaking events on campus and a large percentage of the administration was on hand.

As with the Fulton Debating Society, many of the school's existing organizations have traditions and histories as rich and colorful as the school itself. The Dramatics Society is one such organization. Each year it presents musicals, dramas, comedies, and period pieces. Its various branches include the Contemporary Theater, the Children's Theater, and the People's Performing Arts Company. Since its inception over a century ago, the society has expanded to allow for every imaginable form of artistic expression. Many of the plays are written, directed, and performed entirely by students. The most popular organizations include various preprofessional organizations such as the Bellarmine Law Academy, and government organizations such as the Residence Hall Council and the Class Government Council. There is indeed something for everyone in terms of extracurricular activities.

Boston College is also rich in sports. The Boston College Athletic Association offers five types of athletic participation: intercollegiate competition, intramural sports, club sports, sports instruction, and unstructured recreation. Boston

College has 16 varsity teams for men and 15 for women in areas such as football, basketball, diving, skiing, wrestling, and water polo.

Over 40% of the Boston College population participate in intramural sports programs. These include such areas as touch football, tennis, water polo, volleyball, rugby, and judo. In addition to team sports, Boston College also provides instruction in various areas. Students may take lessons in such diverse areas as figure skating, modern dance, and water safety.

GRADUATES

Boston College is indeed committed to its nickname: "The Jesuit Ivy." Founded over 125 years ago, the school is dedicated to turning out socially responsible men and women as well as critical thinkers. Because of this commitment many individuals go on to pursue graduate degrees or contemplate law. The Boston College Law School is one of the top 20 in the country today. As such, it represents a popular postgraduate endeavor. Many Boston College Alumni go on to complete studies in law at institutions across the country. About 20% of the senior class go on to pursue graduate studies immediately, whereas roughly 80% plan to resume studies within ten years.

The existence of the Boston College Career Center presents students with the opportunity to explore various career options. Many organizations recruit on campus and enable most seniors the luxury of finding employment before graduation. The strong alumni network comes into play in this respect. Many alumni recruit on campus for their companies or organizations, offering employment as early as October.

SUMMARY OVERVIEW

The unique nature of the Boston College experience is due largely to its Jesuit heritage. The college's major strengths include its spiritual backbone, its balance of academic and moral development, and its diversity. Because it was founded by the Society of Jesus, much spiritual meaning is factored into the Boston College experience, which is what makes the college so special. It guides and serves as a source of inspiration. This spiritual presence enhances the overall collegiate challenges.

Despite this spiritual essence, Boston College is exceptional in balancing the development of the academic and the moral person. The institution recognizes the fact that a true education consists of the perpetual nurturing of both intellect and spirit. Countless programs exist that are concerned solely with turning out socially responsible and spiritually rich young adults.

Boston College is also a very diverse environment. This too, is a source of the college's power. At Boston College you will be exposed to different cultures and religions. You will be able to take classes in anything from the most traditional to the most unique. You will enjoy the benefits of a thriving metropolis as well as the peace of the suburbs. The college truly has something for everyone.

However, its weaknesses mirror its strengths. The religious nuances may not be for everyone. Some individuals may not want to attend a school with such a religious orientation.

Although the religious nature of Boston College is by no means overwhelming, it is there. Masses are held quite frequently, particularly on the weekends. Jesuits and religious faculty are a presence on campus. It is virtually impossible to ignore the spiritual nature of the college.

Boston College is a place for self starters. This atmosphere may not be for everyone. Students take primary responsibility for their own education. Professors leave it up to each individual to achieve academic success; certainly, they are always willing to help, but they will never push those who are not themselves interested in learning.

Overall, however, Boston College is a great place to be while pursuing higher education. Through its unique Jesuit history, the commitment to experiencing the ideas of Western culture is illuminated. These ideas are not merely instructional in nature. They are symbolic. These ideas represent the true objective of a Boston College education: development of the spirit, intellect, and conscience.

Alison Mills, B.A.

Bowdoin College

THE PROGRAM

As you begin to look at top colleges, you will probably run across a group of schools that are pretty much characterized the same way: small, highly selective, liberal arts colleges, each with a lovely New England campus, situated in an idyllic New England town. Bowdoin College, in Brunswick, Maine, is one of these schools. The first trick is proper pronunciation: *Boe-din*. But there is a lot more that allows Bowdoin to stand out from its counterparts in addition to pronunciation. Principal among these assets are Bowdoin's knack for experimentation and innovation, its superb faculty, which excels not only in the traditional humanities and arts but also in the hard sciences, and its location on the coast of Maine.

Bowdoin's knack for innovation covers a wide spectrum, from its pioneering microscale chemistry lab, for which the creators won wide acclaim, to the on-campus Peary-MacMillan Arctic Museum, which houses artifacts from the travels of two of the world's most famous arctic explorers and many other arctic-related exhibits. Bowdoin is also home to a Language Media Center that features live television broadcasts from around the world to assist students in understanding foreign languages and cultures. The curriculum, with its relatively loose requirements, encourages experimentation by the student, particularly in the area of independent study. Bowdoin is remarkably strong across the curriculum, without a single truly weak department. Economics, government, and history tend to be the most popular majors, while English and art are also very strong. Majors in newer disciplines like Asian studies and Latin American studies, as well as a program in women's studies, also dot the curriculum. But some may not realize that Bowdoin's hard sciences are recognized nationally as being among the best. The Hatch Science Library, opened in 1991, is emblematic of Bowdoin's commitment to the sciences. The facility houses 60,000 volumes of scientific material as well as study and conference space.

"The key to any good college is its faculty, and Bowdoin's is excellent across the board. You will find professors who want to teach, not spend every moment striving to publish another article in an obscure journal. In the classroom, relatively few courses are large, lecture-type classes. Professors prefer the seminar style, with a small class sitting around a table in animated discussion. Faculty members are available outside of class, whether for a one-on-one discussion of a paper topic or a casual lunch and debate of that day's lecture.

"But the area in which the Bowdoin faculty truly shines is independent study. I worked closely with one professor for the entire year on a senior honors project. It was the highlight of my academic career and the culmination of a great relationship with my favorite professor."

Life outside the classroom at Bowdoin is filled with possibilities. Most everyone does something athletic, from the three-sport varsity star to the most casual jogger or intramural softball player. The many clubs and organizations also enjoy great popularity. The role of the coeducational fraternities in campus social life has dwindled some in recent years, but the fraternities continue to be an important facet of campus life. The campus pub is a popular hangout, and Brunswick and its environs offer ample choices for those who wish to escape the confines of campus once in a while.

The Bowdoin campus is a mix of old and new, typical for old colleges (Bowdoin was founded in 1794). The buildings range from stately Massachusetts Hall, constructed in 1802, to the modern architecture of the Visual Arts Center and everything in between. The campus isn't perfect. Some of the facilities desperately need updating, but a recently constructed science library demonstrates Bowdoin's commitment to doing just that. Bowdoin is also somewhat characterized by its weather. The campus is gorgeous when the fall colors are at their peak, and beautiful again from mid-April on. The intervening months can be long, dark, cold, and occasionally depressing. An appreciation of snow is recommended. Also, Bowdoin is small (about 1400 students). While this can be great in terms of class size and access to professors, it can be constricting because there are few secrets in the student body.

"When I am asked to describe what Bowdoin is like, I usually find myself describing what Maine is like. I first saw Bowdoin when I was nine years old, accompanying my brother to campus for the start of his freshman year. I thought it looked like paradise then, with the tall pine trees on campus and all around, the ocean minutes away, and the mountains a short drive in the opposite direction. When I looked at Bowdoin for myself nine years later, I felt exactly the same way. Maine is a beautiful place, but it is also an attitude, an attitude of not taking life too seriously, of not worrying about everyone else too much, of finding your own path through life. That's what I loved about it."

Maine isn't just a recreation area for Bowdoin students, though drives to the beach, the rugged coast, or the mountains are popular getaways. Maine is also a part of the educational experience of Bowdoin. For many students, that experience begins with a Preorientation Trip. About one-third of incoming students take a four-to five-day trip with about a dozen other new students and upperclass leaders. Options include biking, hiking, canoeing, sailing, or rock-climbing. Not only do you get to see some of Maine on these trips, but you also return to campus with a group of friends, or at least familiar faces, to help you through the first few days of college. Bowdoin's location is later incorporated into the classroom, particularly in the natural sciences. A trip to the coast might supplement a marine ecology course, while budding ornithologists might visit nearby Coleman Farm, a stop-over point for migrating birds.

In general, Bowdoin is a college in the traditional liberal arts mode, but by no means is it stuck in the past. Bowdoin is constantly looking forward, changing and adapting when the times warrant it, and now and again helping to push the established boundaries of education.

GETTING IN/FINANCIAL AID

Admission to Bowdoin is highly competitive. Most recently, 1097 students were accepted out of 3662 applicants, or about 30%. Approximately 431 students eventually matriculated. The application process is fairly standard, with high school transcripts, the application essay, and teacher recommendations all playing significant roles. Interviews are strongly encouraged but not required, and can be done either during a campus visit or through an extensive network of alumni interviewers around the country. Bowdoin also encourages the submission of supplementary materials to the basic application, welcoming musical tapes, works of art, or anything else you think might be appropriate.

There is one extremely important distinction to the Bowdoin application process, and it is one that shouldn't be overlooked. The submission of SAT I scores has been optional since 1969. Bowdoin looks carefully at your entire portfolio in evaluating your application. Whether SAT I or ACT scores are part of this portfolio is your choice. About one-third of all applicants don't submit their scores, and about one-third of admitted students don't submit them.

Bowdoin has two Early Decision programs. The first requires application by November 15, with notification in mid-December. The second requires application by January 15, with notification by mid-February. Both Early Decision rounds are binding—you are required to sign a form upon applying that says you will enroll at Bowdoin if admitted through the Early Decision.

"I ended up applying to Bowdoin, and getting in, through the Early Decision program. I did interview at several other schools,

and I found Bowdoin to be far and away the least stressful. Bowdoin uses senior interviewers—seniors who have been selected and trained to assist the Admissions Committee by handling some of the interviews. I happened to get one of these seniors when I interviewed, and she and I had many of the same interests. We simply had a conversation for an hour. Bowdoin was the only school at which I never once felt as though I was being viewed under a microscope during the interview.

"I submitted my SAT scores. They were solid, not overly spectacular, but I felt they were a reasonable reflection of whatever ability it is the SAT tries to test. I also submitted a tape of two of my music performances, which were critiqued for the Admissions Committee by members of the Music Department. And by December, I was into college. It sure made the rest of senior year more relaxed!"

About half the student body comes from New England, with Massachusetts providing the most students every year. Maine, the target of heavy state-wide recruiting, provides a substantial portion of the student body. Most years, about 45 states and 15 countries are represented. It wouldn't hurt to be a good student from a far-away state, like South Dakota. Women were first admitted to Bowdoin in 1971, and the male-female ratio hovers around fifty-fifty, though there are usually slightly more men when the final figures are tallied. A little more than sixty percent of the student body comes from public high schools.

Diversity at Bowdoin has become a volatile issue in recent years. Both the student body and the faculty are predominantly white. Part of this undoubtedly stems from the fact that the state of Maine itself has tended to be a relatively homogeneous place. Bowdoin has worked hard to improve recruitment of students and faculty of color, and slight gains have been made, but it continues to be an uphill struggle.

Bowdoin is dedicated to meeting the financial needs of all admitted students. There are no athletic or merit scholarships, so Bowdoin provides financial aid through need-based grants, loans, and work-study. The financial aid office is aware that a year of Bowdoin education carries a hefty price tag—now in the $25,000 range—and works hard to alleviate it for all who need assistance. About 40% of the student body receives assistance, to the tune of over $7,000,000. Another 20% receives aid from non-Bowdoin sources.

ACADEMIC ENVIRONMENT

The overall academic atmosphere at Bowdoin tends to be fairly laid back, though finals time does bring out a campus-wide high-stress level. Overt competitiveness is usually frowned upon, but there is certainly a portion of the student body that seems to spend most waking moments in the library. At the same time, there is a relatively low number of slackers on campus. Bowdoin students want to do well, but without killing each other or themselves!

Bowdoin offers a B.A. degree in 35 departmental or interdisciplinary majors, and also allows students to design their own specialized majors if they wish. Many students have double majors, and the departments also offer minor programs. There are no graduate students at Bowdoin. The 130 full-time faculty members are at Bowdoin to teach undergraduates, and they enjoy doing so.

> *"The Bowdoin viewbook claims that almost two-thirds of the classes have 20 or fewer students enrolled. In my experience, that was certainly true. In four years at Bowdoin, I took only four classes that I considered 'large'—more than 50 students. All four were introductory classes I took during my first two years. Fully half of my classes were in the 15-student range. My course load was primarily humanities courses, which may have contributed to the small class size. Classes in economics, government, and most of the sciences tend to be slightly larger. But, in general, if you're looking for a place where you can be an anonymous number in a large lecture hall, Bowdoin probably isn't the school for you. But if you enjoy sitting around a table with 10 or 12 other students and a professor and engaging in intense discussion, this is the place."*

The small class size starts during the first year. A number of departments offer First-Year Seminars, which are limited to 16 students. They are designed to introduce you to college-level study. They are tough and writing-intensive, but by the time they are finished, your abilities to think critically about what you read and to argue effectively in your writing will be radically enhanced. Later, as students press deeper and deper into their majors, they will work more and more closely with individual professors.

Bowdoin is strongly supportive of independent study, and about eight of every ten students do some kind of independent work. A significant number of students complete a one-on-one collaboration with a professor on a senior honors project. Honors projects cover a remarkably wide range of subjects, and can take many forms. Art students might present exhibitions of their work; a student in chemistry might coauthor a publishable research paper with a professor; a psychology student might devise a study to run on fellow classmates. Whatever your interest, there is likely to be a professor ready and willing to guide you.

Bowdoin made a stab at abolishing distribution requirements, but reinstituted modest ones in the mid-1980s. Two courses are required in each of three areas: natural sciences and mathematics; social and behavioral sciences; and humanities and fine arts. In addition, two courses in non-Eurocentric studies, such as Asian or African studies, must be chosen from any of the three categories.

> *"The purpose of distribution requirements, of course, is to provide the well-rounded education that is the goal of a liberal arts college. The benefit is the exposure to areas you might not other-*

wise have explored. With me, it was psychology. It started my first year with Psych 101, which I took ostensibly to fulfill a requirement. I loved the class and later decided to minor in psychology. The distribution requirements are, in some ways, an annoyance. But they can also open doors that otherwise would have remained forever closed."

Bowdoin recently changed its grading system to the traditional A, B, C, D, F system. For about 20 years, the school followed a four-grade system: High Honors, Honors, Pass, and Fail. The decision to change was met with outrage by the student body, but, actually, the old system probably had more drawbacks than positive factors. Bowdoin also has a Credit/Fail option, with restrictions on how many courses can be completed in this fashion. Normal course load for a semester is four, with 32 courses required for graduation.

Every year, about 200 students, mostly juniors, choose to study away from Bowdoin. This can include such far-flung options as spending a semester in Sri Lanka or South India on programs that Bowdin cosponsors, or it can consist of spending a year at another American institution, through the Twelve-College Exchange or other domestic programs.

"I spent the first semester of my junior year studying in Wales. It was perfect: not only did I experience all the wonderful results of living in a foreign country, but I came back to Bowdoin with a renewed appreciation of the place and enthusiasm that lasted the rest of my career."

SOCIAL LIFE

Several years ago, Bowdoin acquired an unfortunate reputation as a drinking school. Most of that drinking revolved around fraternities, which sponsored frequent, campus-wide parties, usually consisting of hundreds of students standing around in a beer-soaked basement. Fortunately, crackdowns in recent years on underage drinking and out-of-control fraternity parties have radically changed the social landscape. These days, fraternities are more likely to have smaller get-togethers for house members and invited guests.

The social scene no longer revolves around fraternities. Parties continue, but they are quieter and smaller, located perhaps in a senior's apartment or in a suite in the 16-story Coles Tower. A typical weekend also features a large assortment of plays, concerts, movies, lectures, and performances whose popularity varies according to the subject. Each semester a few truly noteworthy speakers or bands come to campus.

The town of Brunswick is something less than a booming metropolis, and thus provides limited night-life options. There are a couple of good bars frequented by older students, and one loud dance club — if dancing to pulsating music amid flashing lights strikes your fancy. To expand the options, however, a car is a real asset. Of course, not everyone on campus has a car, but it isn't usually hard to find someone willing to drive.

> *"Having a car on campus opened up a wealth of options. There was the possibility of driving out to the nearby islands for a lobster dinner, or heading to Portland (about a 30-minute drive) for a movie or a visit to one of the many bars in the Old Port. In the winter, I would occasionally drive two hours to some of the best skiing in New England with a friend or two. In the spring, the two-and-a-half hour drive to Boston for a Red Sox game was an annual event."*

It is true that Bowdoin can seem, at times, rather claustrophobic, particularly in the middle of winter. The campus is finally working on long-overdue student activity space, which should alleviate some of the problems.

The dating atmosphere at Bowdoin tends to be low-key. The size of the school can be an annoyance in this area, as one's current dating habits are likely to be fairly widely known. There are more "serious" couples on campus than casual dates, but no particular protocol exists for getting from one level to another.

Bowdoin continues to improve in the area of becoming coeducational in practice as well as policy. Some tradition-minded alums and trustees still fit the "old boy" image, and the administration is lacking in high-ranking females, but, in general, the current campus has an increased awareness of women's issues and sexism.

STUDENT LIFE/EXTRACURRICULAR ACTIVITIES

There are a myriad of extracurricular options available to Bowdoin students. *The Bowdoin Orient*, the weekly student newspaper, is the oldest continuously published campus paper in the country. Masque and Gown, the drama club, puts on a variety of plays each semester. WBOR, the student-run radio station, is perfect for those who long to spin the latest tunes on the air. Miscellania, the female *a cappella* singing group, and the Meddiebempsters, their male counterparts, perform regularly on campus and on the road. There are a multitude of other publications, organizations for dancers or musicians, active African American, Latin American and Asian societies, and clubs for political, religious, and cultural purposes as well. Bowdoin also has a popular student volunteer organization, which provides opportunities for involvement with a Big Brother/Big Sister Program, a local homeless shelter and a wide variety of other programs.

> *"Like most students, I went off to college with few concrete ideas about what I wanted to do with my life. Many people find the*

answer to that question in the classroom. I found mine in an extracurricular activity—the student newspaper. I had no prior experience in any aspect of journalism, but I was welcomed enthusiastically when I joined the advertising department during my first year. I soon switched to the editorial side of the paper, and by senior year I was editor-in-chief. I knew by that time that I wanted to focus on journalism, or something closely related, as a career, and that's what I have done. I probably spent more time at Bowdoin working on the newspaper than I did working on academics. But that's what liberal arts education is all about. Bowdoin provides an atmosphere where everyone can find their own niche, whether in the classroom, on the playing fields, or somewhere else."

Bowdoin is a very active place, and athletics are extremely popular. Whether it is playing for one of the 29 varsity or four junior varsity teams, participating in the popular intramural competitions, or joining a regular aerobics class, almost everybody on campus is doing something. Varsity men's hockey is the most popular spectator sport, and Bowdoin has a long tradition of having one of the best teams in the nation. Women's soccer, men's lacrosse, and the swimming and cross-country teams have also enjoyed great success in recent years. One doesn't have to be a superstar to play on most varsity teams, and determination and enthusiasm are usually the priority. Club sports like rugby and crew are also appealing to many, while the three levels of intramural competition are wildly popular with fraternities, dorms, or just groups of friends. Bowdoin has a splendid indoor athletic facility, built in 1987, which includes a track, tennis courts, a swimming pool, weight room, and aerobics room. There is also an active Outing Club on campus, which sponsors trips of all types in the wilderness near and far, from hiking and backpacking to rock climbing and skiing. Bowdoin isn't a "jock" school, but there are relatively few idle bodies.

One of the strongest features of life at Bowdoin may come as a surprise: the food. Bowdoin has been unanimously praised for its food, and rightly so. Wentworth Hall's cuisine is almost always exceptional, and features a salad bar that rivals any restaurant. The Maine coast provides excellent seafood, which is regularly incorporated into the dining plan. The outdoor lobster bakes at the beginning of the academic year and at Commencement Weekend are traditions. The Dining Service is also remarkably receptive to student suggestions, including recipes. Crowding is a problem at the two dining halls. Wentworth is the larger and more social, and tends to have long lines at peak hours. The Moulton Union dining room also features quality food in a smaller, more intimate setting.

Dorm housing for first-year students is typically short on luxury and privacy. Most first-years will be housed in two-room triples (usually arranged as one bedroom and one living room) in one of six fairly similar brick buildings. A few lucky first-years get housed in smaller, house-like dorms. After the first year, each class has a lottery, with the lowest (best) numbers going to seniors. The quality of living increases each year.

"My housing experience after the first year was somewhat atypical. My sophomore year, my roommate and I hooked up with two juniors and shared a four-bedroom suite in the 16-story Coles Tower. Tower quads tend to go mostly to juniors, with some seniors and a few sophomores mixed in. Most sophomores live in one of the unspectacular, but sufficient, college-owned apartment complexes. I was abroad for the first semester of junior year, and when I returned I shared a two-bedroom campus apartment with two friends who had also been away. Seniors with the best lottery numbers usually snap up the luxurious Pine Street and Harpswell apartments, located at the edges of campus and open only to seniors. I lived with three friends in the Tower again during my senior year, on one of the top floors. With the great views and a bedroom for everyone, it was the best situation, in my opinion."

All apartment complexes have kitchens, and Bowdoin provides various partial board options for those who wish to cook for themselves. There are also a few theme houses on campus, including a Wellness House.

The other housing option is one of the eight coed fraternities on campus. About 40% of the student body joins one of the fraternities and about 12% actually live in the houses. Fraternities must comply with strict standard-of-living codes, but the rooms still run the gamut from opulent to squalid. All the fraternities must be completely coeducational: college policy dictates that a fraternity's national organization must admit women, or else that a Bowdoin fraternity must be only a local organization. House governance must also be coed. For the most part, women are treated equally in the houses. In a few of the more tradition-bound houses, however, the change from all-male membership has been a slower process.

Each year, a small number of students pursue their own housing arrangements around Brunswick. Some live in apartments or houses in town, while others share a house on the ocean with a few friends. Some spectacular locations on the water are available, but a car and a sense of discipline (in order to drag oneself out of bed on a winter morning and drive to class) are necessities.

GRADUATES

Bowdoin certainly prepares its students for a wide variety of careers. Graduates are businesspeople, doctors, lawyers, and just about everything else. Notable alumni include both current U.S. senators from Maine, Democratic Leader George Mitchell (1954) and Republican Senator Bill Cohen (1962), as well as 1984 Olympic Champion Joan Benoit Samuelson (1979). About two-thirds of the graduates go on to graduate or professional school within five years. Some of the more popular degree programs in recent years include medicine, law, and the MBA, but a large percentage go on to earn advanced degrees in more strictly academic fields as well.

If graduate school isn't your thing, the Office of Career Services has a wealth of resources for job searches. The staff helps students write quality résumés, and routinely presents workshops on successful interviewing. One-on-one interview training with an alum, which can include critiquing a videotaped practice interview, is also available. The office has information on over a thousand internships across the country, as well as full-time, postgraduate employment in any part of the country. Alumni offer job counseling and networking. Every year, a large number of corporations visit campus to interview candidates. Secondary schools, eager to recruit new teachers, also visit campus, as do approximately 60 graduate schools each year.

> *"A lot of people think the Bowdoin degree is a regional one, that it only gets recognition in New England. But my friends and I found that word has spread, and Bowdoin now looks impressive on a resume in all parts of the country. I have friends working on both coasts, and everywhere in between, and the Bowdoin degree was instrumental in their job searches.*
>
> *"If you're the type who chooses a particular place to settle first, and then worries about finding a job in that city, then Bowdoin alumni can be an invaluable resource. The Office of Career Services has a directory that lists alumni by field and location, and they are generally more than willing to talk to students. Whatever city you choose, whatever field interests you, chances are there is a Bowdoin alum in the area, more than willing to lend you a hand."*

The alumni of Bowdoin are generally wildly supportive of the college, often bordering on the fanatical. Bowdoin is annually among the leaders in terms of alumni support to the alumni fund, and reunions and Homecoming always draw big crowds back to campus. Active alumni clubs in cities throughout the country can make moving to a new location much easier. The average Bowdoin grads, young or old, will gladly talk endlessly about their own Bowdoin experiences.

SUMMARY OVERVIEW

Bowdoin is a great place for the students who want an excellent liberal arts education and are up to the challenge of finding their own path. The requirements are relatively loose and thus encourage the taking of risks and the broadening of one's own academic horizons. It is not a cutthroat atmosphere, but one in which most students strive to meet their own standards. The professors want to teach undergraduates, not bury themselves in some remote office, and it shows.

Outside of class, the food is great and housing options varied and appealing. A plethora of opportunities for athletics and extracurricular success exist, and students are again encouraged to explore something new. The state of Maine is spectacularly beautiful, and anyone with even a drop of outdoor enthusiasm will grow to love it. However, a certain level of tolerance for ice cold winters is recommended.

Bowdoin continues to work hard at improving its most obvious weakness: the homogeneity of the campus. "White, suburban, New Englander" still characterizes many of the students, though in recent years, increased nationwide recruitment has significantly broadened the profile of the student body. Students from the Midwest and Far West now make up 15 to 20% of a typical entering class. Cultural diversity, however, continues to be a problem area.

The small size of the college can be wonderful or maddening, depending on one's mood. On the one hand, classes are relatively small, professors readily accessible, and most everyone you pass on campus is likely to smile and give a friendly "hello." On the other hand, students tend to know a lot about each other's business, and social life can feel constricted at times.

Overall, Bowdoin is a place where students get a top-notch education and are almost universally happy while doing so. Nearly everyone loves their time on campus, regrets leaving and remains fiercely loyal after graduation. In a state that prides itself on being "the way life should be," Bowdoin College is the way liberal arts education should be.

Michael Townsend, A.B. and Mark Wanner, A.B.

Brown University

THE PROGRAM

Progressive. Untraditional. Diverse. Challenging. All these are words that spring to mind when considering Brown University. For independent, self-motivated, open-minded students who want all the intimacy of a college as well as the benefits of a research university, it is the perfect place to spend four years—even if it is in Providence, which isn't as bad as some think.

Providence often gets a bad rap. It isn't as developed as Boston or as quaint as Cambridge (both an hour north) and it can't begin to compete with New York (four hours south), but it does have its own appeal. People claim that the Providence skyline was used for the opening credits in the old *Superman* series. It isn't true, but that's the feeling that Providence has. It's almost toy-like and as such is a completely accessible and manageable city. Brown is located on a hill on the East Side, as it's called. It's an upscale, residential area with old houses and tree-lined streets, and because Brown lies in the middle of a neighborhood as opposed to in the middle of downtown, the feeling isn't overwhelmingly urban. For those interested in exploring the city, the center of downtown Providence is an easy ten-minute walk "down the hill," and students who want to escape the city can head for Rhode Island's beaches (including Newport of America's Cup fame), which are easily reached by bus or car. Of course, most people don't come to Brown because of its location. They come to get a top-of-the-line liberal arts education.

Despite its many graduate programs, the emphasis at Brown is undergraduate education. From the open stacks in the library to the computer facilities to the professors themselves, undergraduates have access to everything that Brown has to offer (except the Graduate Center Bar)—and Brown offers a lot. More than anything, Brown offers an education tailored to the individual. The school is not governed by hard-and-fast rules concerning the academic program. Because Brown has no core curriculum and no distribution requirements, each student, in conjunction with an adviser, makes his or her own rules in establishing educational priorities and values. In setting those priorities, students are encouraged to take risks, to move beyond what is known, safe, and easy. The administration also understands that not every risk yields positive results, so there is latitude to make mistakes and guidance to help students get back on track if they wander too far from their chosen paths.

The paths that Brown students choose vary widely. The majority of students concentrate on traditional subjects, including English, history, biology, engineering, and computer science. However, there are also many students who pursue degrees in organizational behavior and management, environmental studies, biomedical engineering, and Afro-American studies. If none of the standard concentrations offered by the university is of interest, a student can design an independent concentration. Each year more than 50 students choose this option, pursuing topics such as "Dance and Sculpture," "Computers and the Shape of the Human Intellect," and "Disability: Physiological Causes and Sociological Response."

But it is not only concentrations and course work that make up the Brown program. The university expects that students will complement their formal education with experiences outside the classroom. As evidenced by the libraries' hours (they close at midnight Sunday through Thursday and at ten on Friday and Saturday), students are not expected nor encouraged to study all the time.

> *"When I came to Brown, I went out for the crew team. I had never been a star athlete, nor had I ever really dedicated myself to any kind of physical endeavor. I'd played on teams in high school, but I certainly didn't consider myself a jock. Working out on the crew team—lifting weights, running up and down hills in freezing rain, rowing six days a week for nine months—was by far the most challenging thing I had ever done in my life. I learned about commitment, about trusting my teammates, about overcoming doubts in my mind to push my body harder than it had ever been pushed before. For my first two years at Brown, it was, without question, the most important thing in my life. If it was a choice between studying or getting enough sleep so I could work out hard, sleep almost always won out. I still did my work, still got As and Bs, but my main focus was not in the classroom. By my third year, I wanted to get more involved in my courses, so I changed my priorities. That's one of Brown's greatest strengths: it allows students to set their own priorities, their own goals."*

When students aren't studying or spending time on extracurricular activities, they will most likely be hanging out with other students. Brown's student body is one of its greatest assets. It is difficult to make a generalization about the type of person who attends Brown; the university attracts all types of people, from intellectuals, artists, and socialites to hippies, jocks, and political activists. Thus, it is a place for people who are more interested in exposing themselves to the differences between people than in spending four years in a homogeneous environment. It is often said that the way to conform at Brown is not to conform. That isn't to say that everyone is so individualistic that there are no cliques on campus. There are, but the variety is so great that almost everyone fits in somewhere and no one group dominates (though some would like to believe that they do!). In addition to being diverse (I know, it's a word that is overused when describing Brown, but it does apply), the student body is, on the whole, open and friendly. Brown is a school where students genuinely enjoy interacting with all different kinds of people. The atmosphere is noncompetitive and supportive, which allows students to be who they want to be and do exactly what they want to do.

GETTING IN/FINANCIAL AID

For a recent class, Brown accepted only 22%, or roughly one out of every five students who applied. Based on this statistic alone, it is clearly very difficult to get into Brown. As the admissions officers repeat over and over again, there are many more qualified applicants than there are available places for them. Students and administrators alike often joke that the Director of Admissions carries all the applications to the top floor of the admissions building and slides them down the stairs and sends acceptance letters to the 2901 students whose applications reach the bottom floor first. Indeed, to the student who has all the right credentials but still doesn't get it, the selection process can seem quite arbitrary, but, by the admissions office's own account, it isn't.

The university strives to create a class that is well-rounded. Brown is like a company looking for different kinds of individuals to do various kinds of jobs. Some of these individuals are responsible for supplying the school with its top students. Others provide the orchestra with its musicians. Still others have the job of filling out the university's athletic teams. Then there are those whose strength is not a particular talent or area of expertise but a particularly engaging personality that contributes to the spirit and friendliness of the campus. Applicants should be aware that the admissions committee will be asking what a particular student can contribute to the university community. This is something that applicants should think about and try to convey in their essay or interview.

> *"The year I applied to Brown, the college received more applications than in any other year and more applications than any other Ivy League school. That was the year that Brown became the "hot" college, and I had serious questions about whether or not I was a hot applicant. I had good grades, but they were far from straight As. I played on several varsity sports teams, but I wasn't the MVP. I talked up a storm in my admission interview but didn't feel like I hit it off with the interviewer. Then there was*

my essay. I wrote about running for office of student body president and losing. I wrote about how the fear of failing had almost kept me from entering the election at all, how I overcame that fear, and what I learned about the importance of taking risks when the chance of failure far outweighs the chance of success. I wrote about learning to put myself on the line. I can't pretend to know what got me into Brown, but I have a feeling that my essay helped a lot. Through that page and a half, I indicated that even though I wasn't a valedictorian or a concert violinist, I was someone who would fit in well with Brown's structure and philosophy of education, which encourages experimentation and risk-taking."

Brown's student body is diverse on all levels. Comprised of students from all 50 states and 42 countries, including Turkey, Belize, Algeria, Pakistan, and Australia, Brown is geographically and ethnically diverse. If students are curious and open, they can gain a wealth of knowledge about the world just by talking to their classmates. Brown is also committed to racial diversity. Blacks, Puerto Ricans, Asian-Americans, Native Americans, and Hispanics make up 20% of the student body. Unfortunately, enrolling minority students does not ensure that the university will be integrated in spirit as well as in fact. If often seems that various minority groups stick together, as do the white students. This is not to say that there is an overwhelming amount of racial hostility at Brown; it just indicates that all students must make an effort to interact with people of different backgrounds or heritage if the university is to become truly integrated.

Brown also strives to keep the university economically diverse. Given the high price of a private college education, it would be all too easy to populate the school only with those who can afford it. Happily, Brown's policy of awarding financial aid to every student who demonstrates need helps to keep the student body economically varied. Forty percent of all students at Brown receive some form of financial aid. Some of that aid is provided through outside sources such as private scholarships or grants. Brown provides aid through scholarships, loans, and student jobs, all awarded based solely on need. The school doesn't award scholarships based on athletic, academic, or artistic excellence. Brown uses the Financial Aid Form (FAF), which is processed by the College Testing Service, to determine a student's financial needs. The university also takes into account family situations such as divorce and other children in college when determining a student's financial need.

For the most part, admission to Brown is "need blind," meaning that the Board of Admissions does not take into account whether a student is applying for aid when they make their admissions decision. Only after 95% of the class has been selected does the admissions committee look at applicants' financial situations. This ensures that, as much as possible, financial aid applicants aren't discriminated against.

ACADEMIC ENVIRONMENT

Many people are shocked, appalled, then thrilled to learn that Brown University has no distribution requirement, no core curriculum. The Brown curriculum, as it's called, allows students to create their own academic programs. Students take courses based on their curiosity and interests as opposed to someone else's idea of what they should learn. The name of the game is academic freedom, "but with freedom comes responsibility." This is a phrase that Brown advisers love to use, and though they may say it with their tongues lightly pressed against their cheeks, it's true. At no other college or university are students given so much responsibility for their academic choices. That responsibility and the number of decisions students must make can be daunting at times. So daunting, in fact, that Brown's greatest strength can become its greatest weakness.

> *"My first year at Brown, I was like a kid in a candy shop. After 18 years of prescribed education, I could finally take exactly the courses I wanted. Over two semesters I enrolled in eight different courses in eight different departments, dipping into everything from creative writing, religious studies, and psychology to political science, geology, and calculus. It felt terrific to be able to experiment, to give myself a chance to expand my interests, but I sometimes found myself overwhelmed by the choices available to me.*
>
> *"Both my adviser and I were new to Brown in the fall of my freshman year, so he didn't know any more about Brown than I did. Although I had an interesting, exciting year, I might have made more informed decisions had I sought the input of another dean or adviser. Part of the problem is that the advising system at Brown is so large, so complex, that it was difficult to know where to turn. Of course, all it took was a few phone calls to put me in touch with some very helpful, reassuring people. Once I'd met them, they never forgot who I was. There was a dean I met with once during my sophomore year. I was worried about my concentration and my overall feeling of directionlessness. He helped me explore my options but also reassured me that I didn't need to rush into any decisions. For the rest of the time I was at Brown, anytime the dean saw me on campus, he addressed me by name and asked how everything had worked out."*

It definitely pays to seek out guidance from students, professors, deans, and advisers. Not only can they offer advice, but in a school where students are as independent as they are at Brown, it helps to feel that someone is looking out for your best interest. But like everything else at Brown, it's up to the student to ask for help or support if he or she wants it. It's out there, but no one is going to call and tell a student that he or she has to make an appointment for academic counseling or make sure that he or she is doing a good job of planning an academic program.

Along with the new Curriculum come several misconceptions. Academic freedom does not mean that a student can spend four years at Brown bouncing from course to course, department to department. First of all, each student must earn a minimum of 30 credits (one credit per course) in order to graduate. Most students take four courses a semester and graduate with 32 credits. Once a student has selected a concentration, as majors are called at Brown, there are very specific requirements within each department that must be fulfilled. Some departments require students to write a thesis, others do not. Some concentrations require eight courses, others as many as 20. As far as fulfilling concentration requirements, different students have different approaches. Some people come to Brown, know exactly what they want to do, and spend the first years taking courses required for their degree. Others have no idea what they want to do and so wait until the last possible moment to decide, always making jokes about how many times they've changed their concentration. It's not uncommon to see these students trying frantically to take those last required courses before graduation. Most people, though, fall somewhere between these two extremes, taking courses in the area that interests them the most and then experimenting with other courses before they make a final decision about their concentration.

> *"When I came to Brown, I was uncertain about what I wanted my concentration to be. I was interested in literature and writing but also intrigued by religious studies and political science. For my first two years of college, I took courses in these subjects and dabbled in other areas as well. By the end of sophomore year, I was all set to concentrate in political science, that is, until I took my first fiction writing course. By the end of the course, I was hooked. The professor encouraged me to enroll in the combined English/Honors in Creative Writing concentration. I did, and spent my last two years at Brown taking my required English courses and writing workshops."*

Most people, including those who didn't go to Brown but who have an opinion anyway, will say that, academically (and in most other ways too) Brown is a laid-back place. This is not to say that people don't take their studies seriously. Most students do. It's just to point out that Brown is not the place for students who thrive in a cutthroat, competitive environment. The emphasis is on students (and professors) learning together, not fighting to see who can get the highest grade. Academic or performance pressure usually comes from within the individual (or from the individual's parents) as opposed to from professors or other students. Some professors are more demanding than others, but ultimately how hard a student works, how much effort is put into courses, is up to the student. It all goes back to Brown's basic educational philosophy. Students are responsible for their own educations. Unless a student is on the verge of failing a course or flunking out of school, no one is going to tell him or her to work harder. It's an individual choice. As a result, students spend time talking about their classes, not about how hard they're working. They discuss what they're learning, not the grades they're getting. Part of this attitude stems from Brown's pass/fail option.

At Brown, students can take any and all of their courses satisfactory/no credit or S/NC. (Alternatively, this option is called C/NC for cookies/no cookies.) The philosophy behind this option is that if students aren't worried about a grade, they might be encouraged to take courses in departments outside their chosen discipline. For example, an engineering student who is interested in but also intimidated by the twentieth century novel might elect to take the Proust, Joyce, and Faulkner course S/NC. Other students take their courses S/NC simply because, philosophically, they don't believe in grades. Of course, there are those who abuse the system. They wait until the first exam or paper and then decide, based on their grade, whether or not to take the pass/fail option. Happily, this group is a minority.

Another progressive aspect of Brown's grading system is that there are no Ds or Fs. Anything below a C is no credit. Courses for which a student receives no credit do not appear on any external record. The student knows that he or she failed the course and Brown knows, but outside the university, it is as though the course was never taken. The hope is that this policy encourages students to take academic risks instead of always playing it safe and taking courses in which they know they can do well. One consequence of these policies is that an A is hard to come by, a B is considered an average grade and a C indicates that the student did just enough to get by. Fortunately, most people at Brown care enough about their education that they don't slide by with a 2.0 GPA.

One of the best things about Brown is the notion that it is a college within a university. Most courses, from the introductory to the advanced, are taught by full professors. Students at Brown can take a small seminar with an expert in religious studies who is also an ex-priest, do research with a leading biologist, hear lectures by a well-known scholar of twentieth century art. Regardless of the class size—which can range from five to 200 people—students always have access to their professors. Professors have office hours each week when students can come in to ask questions, talk, discuss a paper. It is not unusual for students to invite their professors for dinner or to meet them for coffee.

Most large lecture courses are accompanied by a discussion section once a week. Sections are supposed to provide students with an opportunity to discuss the issues of a course in a more intimate setting. Sections, though, vary a great deal in quality. If the section leader (either a teaching assistant [TA] or the professor) is well-informed, dynamic, and challenging and the students are interested, inquisitive, and have done the reading, sections can add a lot to the course. If, on the other hand, the TA isn't excited about the material and the students aren't participating in the discussion, sections can be a colossal waste of time.

Teaching methods vary from person to person. One professor uses the *Paper Chase* model of calling on students by name and asking them to answer a specific question or discuss a particular issue. Students who take this professor can be seen quaking prior to their class, hoping that, if called on, they can rise to the occasion. Other professors give more traditional lectures, and, of course, some are better at it than others. One piece of advice always given at Brown is to take professors, not courses. No matter what the subject matter, if the professor is energetic and enthusiastic, the student is bound to become engaged in the topic of discussion. Ask upperclassmen and shop around. Students can learn more about a course or professor from people who've already taken the course than they can from the course catalog.

> *"One of the best professors I ever had at Brown was Professor Cobb. He taught the American Political System and was totally committed to his teaching. Rumor had it that every morning he would get up early, run 12 miles, and then, on the way back from his run, stop off at the classroom and write the outline of his lecture on the board. He wrote the different sections of the outline in different colors of chalk, and his writing (miraculously) was completely legible. Unlike many profs, he followed his outline to the letter, and for every concept he presented, he had hysterical examples from various events in recent political history. As he lectured, he would get so excited about his subject that he would run his hands, all covered with colored chalk, through his quarter-inch hair. By the end of the lecture, I could almost always see bright pink or orange chalk dust on his scalp. He was demanding—his tests were content-specific, so it was absolutely necessary to do all the reading and to attend all the lectures. Even at nine o'clock in the morning, this was no hardship. The professor was often given an enthusiastic round of applause at the end of the period."*

Brown offers four different degree programs and over 80 regular concentrations (majors). Although it is difficult to say which departments are the strongest, it is possible to make some general statements about where Brown's academic strengths lie. The economics department is considered one of the strongest in the country and the newly completed Center for Information Technology puts Brown on the cutting edge of computer science. For students interested in language studies, Brown offers instruction in 30 languages including Biblical Hebrew, Hindi, Sanskrit, Korean, Akkadian, and of course French, Italian, German, and Latin. In addition, math, physics, theater arts, creative writing, political science, and history are all noted for their excellence. Applicants should be aware, though, that at a school like Brown, the major strength is not in a particular program or department but in the overall structure and philosophy of the academic program. The opportunity to do interdisciplinary work, the freedom to create programs suited to individual needs, and the chance for undergraduates to do independent projects and research with full professors all add to the high caliber of individual departments.

Over two thirds of Brown's students are candidates for a Bachelor of Arts (A.B.— I have no idea why it isn't a B.A.). A.B. candidates can concentrate in such varied areas as human biology, semiotics (the study of the theory of signs and symbols), engineering, media and culture, and Afro-American studies. If none of the regular concentrations addresses an issue that particularly interests a student, the student can, with the help of a faculty adviser, design his or her own independent concentration.

Another third of the students at Brown are candidates for the Bachelor of Science degree. This degree offers students an intensive education in a variety of areas, including applied mathematics, computer science, engineering, and psychology. These programs are specialized and concentrated and designed for those who have a strong ability in science and mathematics. Sc.B. candidates are also likely to embark on careers in these areas or continue with advanced study at the graduate or professional level.

It is also possible to study for a combined Sc.B./A.B. degree. This degree, obtained over five years, allows students to pursue both the sciences and the humanities. The two degrees can be related and complementary or completely unrelated.

Finally, Brown offers the unique Program in Liberal Medical Education (PLME). The PLME combines a liberal arts education with a medical degree and takes eight years to complete. It is not a way of speeding up medical school. The time involved is the same as with a traditional medical education. Rather, it is a way of integrating medical education into a liberal arts curriculum. The hope is that the PLME will produce more humane, well-rounded physicians than sometimes emerge from medical school programs that don't incorporate non-science courses.

SOCIAL LIFE

Students' social lives are as diverse as everything else at Brown, and no one group of people or set of activities dominates the social scene. Freshmen live in residential units with 35 to 50 other students, and these units are the center of social activity for most freshmen. It is not unusual for an entire unit to head off to dinner together or strike out for a party en masse, during the first few months of school. The units provide a home base for incoming students, but there is also plenty of opportunity for freshmen to make friends with upperclassmen and participate fully in the social activities of the Brown community.

Much of the social life at Brown takes place on an informal level. Indeed, many claim that more socializing goes on in the library than anywhere else, that people don't go there to do their work but to see their friends. This isn't entirely true, but one is just as likely to see students talking in a library lounge as reading in a study carrel. People also gather on the college green, which, on a sunny day, is a terrific place to people watch and visit with friends.

On a more structured level, the variety of activities in which students can partake is endless. On any given night, students might go see a movie at the Cable Car (where half the seats are sofas) or one put on by the Brown Film Society (where the seats are hard wood), cheer on the Bruins at a hockey match or basketball game, go out for a study break beer, listen to a student play acoustic guitar at the Underground (the campus pub), hear a concert at the Civic Center in downtown Providence (also the arena for the annual truck-and-tractor pull), or see a play at one of Brown's four theaters. If Brown and Providence don't provide enough activity, ambitious students can easily skip up to Boston for the night or New York for the weekend. Of course, when students ask about the social life of a college, they are often really asking about the parties, of which there are plenty at Brown.

People tend to work hard during the week and play hard on the weekends, which often begin on Thursday. One of the favorite ways Brown students have of releasing their tension is by dancing. Thursday night at the Underground is Funk Night. After a few hours in the library, people often head across the green to this small, crowded, but always hopping place to dance to "funk" music spun on turntables by a student disc jockey. No need to have a partner. It's so small that everyone tends to dance with everyone else.

On weekends, there are usually several parties to choose from. Though by no means the only place to head for fun, the fraternities at Brown provide many people (whether they are members or not) with the majority of their social structure. If students want to drink a lot of beer and dance to blaring rock and roll in a room packed with people, this is the place to go.

For mellow parties that are still fun, students head to off-campus houses. People still drink and dance, but the parties are smaller and more intimate. More of the people tend to know each other. Freshmen are just as welcome at off-campus parties as anyone else, but unless they have friends who are upperclassmen, they aren't likely to know about them.

Even though there are plenty of parties, there is little pressure to attend them or to drink oneself into oblivion once there. Many people see Brown as a "party" school, one where students neglect their work and their health in order to drink the keg dry. Yes, students at Brown like to have a good time, but the majority of students don't live to party and there isn't any pressure to do so. People tend to respect each other's decisions about how to conduct their lives, so whether students choose to spend Saturday night studying, eating dinner with friends, or dancing until dawn, they can feel comfortable doing it.

> *"My junior year, I lived with seven friends in a large off-campus house about two blocks from the main green. Each night of the week, one person in the house was responsible for dinner. Because we lived so close to campus, people were always stopping by to hang out for a while. Needless to say, more than a few would show up just in time for dinner. During that year it was rare that dinner for eight didn't turn into dinner for ten or twelve. That house and those dinners were the focus of my social life that year. Sometimes we threw huge parties (we could feel the*

*floorboards springing under our feet because there were so many
people dancing), but most of the time, our parties were informal
extensions of our dinners where a few people would dance, listen
to music, talk, and have a beer or two.''*

One other aspect of Brown's social life on which students tend to comment is
that people don't date. For the most part, this is true. Students, even if they are part
of a couple, tend to go out in groups. Some people lament this situation, but it
eliminates social pressure that might be there otherwise. Instead of "courting,"
couples get to know each other by being in classes together, playing on the same
intramural team, or eating in the dining hall with a bunch of people. When students
do get involved in relationships, they tend to be "serious" and "long term" though
the majority of students at Brown tend not to have this type of relationship.
Although students spend a fair amount of time lamenting their partnerless lives, no
one feels as though he or she is the only one. Not that many people have boyfriends
or girlfriends, so it's hard to feel bad about it. Instead, people have many friends of
both sexes. Sponsored by the Gay/Lesbian Student Alliance, social activities, such
as dances, concerts, forums, and parties organized specifically, but not exclusively,
for homosexual students are also a part of campus life.

Like any school, Brown has identifiable social cliques. Preppies, deadheads,
jocks, beautiful people (B.P.s—the chic crowd), Euro-trash (the chic crowd with
accents), intellectuals, pseudo-intellectuals, political activists, granola-heads—
they all exist at Brown. One of the best things about Brown is that anyone and
everyone can move (fairly) comfortably among the groups, all types of people.
There are no rigid lines, and thankfully, most people are accepting of differences
among themselves and their classmates.

The housing at Brown is neither its best nor its worst aspect. Every freshman at
Brown lives on campus and, except in rare circumstances, every freshman lives in a
double. The dormitory buildings are not especially warm and charming, but the
rooms themselves, as college dorm rooms go, are spacious enough to accommodate the two beds, desks, dressers, and students required to share the space for the
year. The university does a fairly good job of matching up compatible people, and it
isn't unusual for first year roommates to remain friends all the way through Brown.

After freshman year, students have several options. Several of Brown's fraternities
have housing on campus where members can live in double rooms. The houses are
essentially the same as the rest of the Brown dorms, so no one should be under the
illusion that a fraternity offers the charm that other residential buildings lack. Sophomores can also live in one of the several social dorms, which sponsor parties and in-
house activities but are not selective in any way. Whoever lives in the house
automatically becomes part of the social dorm. Most sophomores live in double
rooms.

Brown also owns several houses just off campus as well as some apartments. In
these houses and apartments, students usually have their own rooms, as well as a
living room and a kitchen. Juniors and seniors who do not live in a single room in a
campus dorm usually choose to live in these buildings.

All Brown housing is assigned through lottery numbers. Each class has its own set of lottery numbers, and the senior class has first priority. There are some residence halls reserved exclusively for juniors and sophomores, so even students with high lottery numbers can usually find an acceptable place to live. Everyone is guaranteed on-campus housing.

EXTRACURRICULAR ACTIVITIES

Brown has almost as many extracurricular activities as can be imagined. Whether students are interested in competing in varsity athletics, writing for the newspaper, doing community service, joining the croquet club, or acting in a play, they usually can find an organization that supports their interest. If not, it is always possible for students to create new clubs or add a sport to the intramural roster.

Athletics, both intercollegiate and intramural, is one of the most popular non-academic pursuits at Brown. At the varsity level, Brown fields, among others, football, soccer, hockey, basketball, volleyball, lacrosse, crew, track, gymnastics, and swimming teams. Even if students don't actually play on a particular team, they often participate as a cheering section. Tailgating at a football game is a terrific way to spend a crisp, clear fall day (though expect to spend more time socializing than actually keeping track of the downs), and cheering at an ice hockey match is a surefire way to release stress and get the adrenaline going. Diehard crew fans gather on the banks of the Seekonk (Providence's industrialized version of the pastoral Charles River, which divides Cambridge from Boston) in the early morning to catch a glimpse of the eights gliding across the finish line. So whether students come to play or watch, many take part in the athletic activities at the university. If they want to play a sport on a more informal level, there are also intramurals. In addition to the more traditional sports such as basketball, soccer, and baseball, Brown also offers innertube water polo, ultimate Frisbee, and croquet.

After sports, the various campus publications are popular. The *Brown Daily Herald*, which, despite the title, is published five days a week, is the campus newspaper. There is also a monthly magazine called *Issues*, which publishes articles on national and international politics, topics of interest to the university community, interviews with celebrities, and student fiction and poetry. For those with an interest in the arts, there are several literary magazines.

Brown also boasts the first student radio station in the country. WBRU has both an AM and an FM station (DJs usually train on the AM before moving up to the FM station), which are entirely run by students. Recently, Brown began a cable television station that airs campus news and a soap opera, among other things.

Students can also pursue interests in karate, backpacking, politics, gardening, and community service. Brown is also supportive of the performing arts as evidenced by the four theaters on campus, which always have something either "up" or in the works. Students can also sing in one of the many *a cappella* groups or play in the orchestra or the crazy marching band.

The Brown Lecture Board brings interesting and often controversial speakers to campus and the Sarah Doyle Women's Center, the Third World Center, and all academic departments offer an endless calendar of interesting activities. At Brown, it will never be a question of not having enough to do. Rather, the challenge will be in deciding what to do and how to find time for it.

> *"I remember once during my sophomore year, I had been trying to get hold of a good friend of mine. As an exhausted member of the crew team, I usually spent my evenings doing my homework in my room and then tucking into bed early to get enough sleep to get through the next day's workout. No matter when I called my friend, she wasn't home to answer the phone. Finally, after about a week, I bumped into her on the street. When I asked where she'd been, what she'd been up to, she breathlessly told me of the seven lectures she'd heard over the last six days. She'd learned about glass blowing from a visiting artist at the Rhode Island School of Design, the political situation in the Middle East, and the homeless in America. The night I saw her she was off to see a performance by the composer and musician Philip Glass. In addition to that she had been working out at the athletic center, spending time with her "little brother," and somehow finding time to study. This is definitely the way of the world at Brown."*

GRADUATES

It is the question that every senior asks as graduation approaches: "What am I going to do next year?" Underlying that seemingly simple question is the more complicated, overwhelming question: "What am I going to do with my life?" By the end of four years of college, some students have a crystal clear vision of their goals and how to achieve them. Others have no idea what they really want to do and so have a hard time making post-graduation plans. The variety of things that people choose to do following their education reflects the variety of ways that they feel about themselves and what they want to do in the world.

About a quarter of the class go on to graduate school just as soon as they have those Brown diplomas in their hands. Most of the remaining three quarters, who aren't yet sure that they want to be doctors, lawyers, businessmen or businesswomen, engineers, midwives, astrophysicists, or academics, head out, bravely, into the job market. About half of those work in business. Yes, even at laid-back, noncompetitive Brown, there are still plenty of individuals who become investment bankers, Wall Street traders, and commercial real estate brokers. The other half of the graduates who pound the pavement in search of employment seek out positions in the fields of science (often graduates become research assistants for a year or two before making a final decision about medical school), social service, education, health, and arts and communication. Of course, not everyone goes to graduate school, and not everyone looks for a career path job. Many take the proverbial year "off." Presumably this means "off" from "real" life, though I'm not exactly sure what a fake life would be.

> *"When I graduated from Brown, I didn't have a clear idea of what I wanted to do. My boyfriend had applied to medical school and was trying to decide whether to go right to school or to defer for a year. Given our mutual states of indecision, we decided to stay in Providence, at least for the summer. I worked doing landscape construction, and he was a chef in a gourmet take-out shop. By the end of the summer, he'd decided to defer medical school, and we decided to work a while longer, then travel. He kept his job, and I began working as the coordinator of the Writing Fellows Program at Brown. I also volunteered to teach a course in reading and writing fiction at a local high school. In February, we quit our jobs and headed for West Africa to visit friends in the Peace Corps. From there, we went to Israel where we read about but did not personally see the fighting. Next, we traveled in Turkey, Greece, Italy, and France. We returned in midsummer, he to begin medical school, I to begin the graduate fiction writing program at NYU. What we chose to do right after graduation was somewhat atypical, but there are plenty of graduates who choose not to take the main route."*

Five years after graduation, most people are either in graduate school or working in some sort of steady job. The university does not have specific statistics but just from speaking to people and tuning in to the post-grad grapevine, after taking some time away from school, many people go on to get advanced degrees.

The alumni network at Brown is strong. The Maddock Alumni Center has a complete listing of Brown graduates in various fields. This is a helpful reference when students are trying to find more information about specific jobs. In reading the alumni magazine, it is clear that the longer people are away from Brown, the more interested they become in keeping in touch with the life of the university. In "The Classes" section, which publishes blurbs about what graduates are doing, the class with the least information is the most recently graduated one. Somehow, it isn't quite "cool," at least not right away, for grads to write in and let everyone know what they're up to.

SUMMARY OVERVIEW

Brown University is a research university that offers the benefits of a small liberal arts college. Located in Providence, Rhode Island, it is within easy reach of Boston and New York City. The academic program is top-notch and is complemented by a broad selection of extracurricular activities.

One of Brown's greatest strengths lies in the Brown curriculum. This program allows students to plan their own course of study instead of having to take a slate of required courses. This freedom requires students to take responsibility for their own education and forces them to assess where their true interests lie. In addition to freedom and flexibility, Brown also offers an incredible variety of courses and concentrations. It is rare that students have the opportunity to study in areas such as Judaic studies, biomedical engineering, or psycholinguistics at the undergraduate level. Independent concentrations (majors designed by the students themselves) make the programs available virtually limitless. Beyond sheer variety, Brown students also benefit from the opportunity to do independent projects or research with professors. Though Brown has graduate programs, the emphasis is on the undergraduate students, so they have access not only to professors but also to all university facilities.

In addition to the academic side of life at Brown, students are encouraged to have active extracurricular lives. This creates an atmosphere that is intellectually rigorous but not intense or cutthroat. The feeling at Brown is supportive and friendly as opposed to pressured and competitive. Brown is a school where most students lead balanced lives, involved not only with their studies but also with sports, art, publications, clubs, and friends.

Of course, there is a downside to Brown. It is definitely a place where the greatest strength, academic freedom, can become the greatest weakness. Sometimes students are overwhelmed by all the choices they are called upon to make or don't know exactly what they want to do, so they end up wandering aimlessly through various courses, never really finding a focus. Part of the problem stems from the hands-off nature of the advising system at Brown. Students are assigned advisers for freshman year, but after that people must seek out the advice that they want or need on their own. Because the advising program is so extensive and so decentralized, it is often difficult for students to know to whom they can turn for help. Thankfully, there are advisers, but students must take the initiative in seeking them out.

Another complaint about Brown is that it is *too* individualistic. Brown encourages students to "do their own thing," but this sometimes means that students don't feel connected to the Brown community as a whole. The university isn't big on tradition. Most students (at least the ones that I know) don't know the school song, and there isn't any activity (except for Spring Weekend) in which the majority of students participate. Students tend to find communities within particular groups or activities—the radio station, sports teams, theater groups, publications—as opposed to considering Brown as a whole their community. For applicants looking for a school where they will immediately feel a part of things, Brown is the wrong place. It is a school where students must seek out whatever sense of belonging they have.

With the ups and downs, Brown is, in the end, a terrific place to go to school. More than anything, it is a place where students are encouraged to think and act independently. Brown challenges people to explore—both intellectually and personally—with the belief that through such exploration, students will discover their own ideas about what is important. Brown does not provide students with answers. It is not a school for people who want to be told what they should know after four years. It is a university where students are given the opportunity to get a top-notch education while also questioning and redefining exactly what a "top-notch" education is.

Pamela Bol, A.B.

Bryn Mawr College

THE PROGRAM

"I didn't choose to come to Bryn Mawr because it is a women's college. Like most applicants, I looked at its single-sex status as something of a drawback, a blemish on an otherwise perfectly clear complextion. If I really thought about it, I might say, yes, Bryn Mawr is that great, academically tough, individualistic place—which also happens to be a women's institution. I braced myself for encounters with rabid feminists who would, no doubt, try to convince me to hate men, leave my legs unshaven, and wear woolen knee socks beneath Birkenstock sandals.

"I still shave my legs, and my love for the male of the species remains unwavering. But after four years at Bryn Mawr, I now think of it as that great women's college whose toughness and individuality are not apart from the student body's gender, but rather grow out of the college's commitment to women's education."

Like most institutions, Bryn Mawr has been plagued by a number of stereotypes that persist in spite of their patent silliness. First off, there's my initial reaction to the school: Because it's an all-women's college, it's obviously a roiling mass of radical lesbian feminists. Another interesting Bryn Mawr myth is that it's a finishing school: Mawrtyrs, as Bryn Mawr students are called, are bluestockings, teapot handlers, lace hanky users. Diametrically opposed to the latter is the hunchback-of-the-library theory: Mawrtyrs are all grinds who wear clunky eyeglasses (through which they squint myopically), take far too many years of Greek, and scurry away at any mention of fun. Not surprisingly, the reality is that you cannot pin down a "typical" Bryn Mawr woman's character, and you cannot really define what it means to be educated at Bryn Mawr, because the school's philosophy encourages neither strict definition nor rigid categorization.

Throughout its hundred-odd years of existence, the college has maintained the integrity of its original belief in the soundness of a liberal arts education—"liberal" meaning "free." And this freedom includes the right to question, to denounce, to advocate ideas, and especially to undertake an understanding of—and responsibility for—the world outside one's own blinkered perspective. Bryn Mawr encourages the belief that to achieve that end, you have to be courageous enough to say radical things *and* civil enough to listen to other people's views *and* literate enough to base your arguments on reason, not prejudice. As highfalutin as this last might sound, it really is true that you come away from the place fairly bursting with a sense of your own freedom and your own potential, whether you prefer to spend Saturday night dancing at the local country club, or curled up in bed with Ovid's Greatest Hits (and, by the way, not many Mawrtyrs major in Greek—English, economics, chemistry, and political science are the majors of choice).

The campus reflects both the diversity of the student body and the philosophy of the college: the collegiate Gothic gray stone buildings (the first American examples of this architectural style) are lovely edifices that speak of seriousness of purpose and grace of form (and, no, the walls are *not* ivy covered). As one rambles about the campus, though, one continually stumbles across hidden places, each with its own style and personality. The Cloisters in the middle of Thomas Library is a particularly fine spot for whiling away a pleasant hour or two with a meaty book, and there are enough small gardens, shady groves, and the like to please the most dedicated nature lover. Near the center of campus stands the college's first building, Taylor Hall, whose construction was supervised in 1883 by Bryn Mawr's founder, Dr. Joseph Taylor, who built the school for the education of young Quaker women.

The undergraduate college, composed of about 1200 students, still admits women only (the graduate schools admit men). Although the college has divested itself of any religious affiliation, it's still strongly influenced by such Quakerly attributes as responsibility to the community, modesty (Mawrtyrs tend to avoid flashy academic display—for example, there's no Bryn Mawr chapter of Phi Beta Kappa, or dean's list), and open-mindedness. When it opened, Bryn Mawr was the first women's college to offer the A.B., the M.A., and the Ph.D. degrees, becoming the first institution in the United States to offer graduate study leading to the doctorate for women. M. Carey Thomas, president of Bryn Mawr from 1894 to 1922, was largely responsible for the school's special identity as a college determined to prove that women could successfully complete a curriculum as rigorous as that offered to men at the best universities. Her life, and her work at Bryn Mawr, was a constant effort to prove that women have equal powers of the mind, and should be accorded, therefore, equal educational opportunities.

In spite of a certain austerity stemming from this serious scholarly background, Bryn Mawr can be a delightfully campy place, in part because the first women who came to Bryn Mawr had sense enough (and sense of humor enough) to begin traditions—strange (and sometimes touching) displays of affections, solemnity, and, occasionally, outright goofiness that pop up at odd times during one's years at Bryn Mawr. All first-year students, for example, receive colored lanterns from their second-year counterparts in an eerie, academic robe swathed, Greek song infested ceremony known as Lantern Night. All seniors (in various stages of undress) run to the top of Taylor tower to ring the bell, thereby marking the end of their academic careers at Bryn Mawr. And then there's Hell Week…

Philadelphia, which is about 15 minutes or a buck fifty away from Bryn Mawr, provides a nice counterpoint to the sustained silliness of traditions and the sustained pressures of abundant course work. It's a great city, not as overwhelming as New York, but personable, easily accessible, and filled to the gills with museums, art galleries, alternative music venues and movie houses, and great places to eat. The town of Bryn Mawr—really the whole Main Line (a suburban strip of townships west of Philadelphia)—is a safe, residential community with a fairly good mix of people (leaning toward the snobby side), a number of good places to eat, drink, hear music, and go for long walks or bike rides.

GETTING IN/FINANCIAL AID

Like most schools of its caliber and reputation, Bryn Mawr's admission standards are tough. About 1600 applications are received and about 800 of those are accepted for the freshman class. Prospective students can apply for early decision, with deadlines of November 15 and January 1; the deadline for regular admissions is January 15. Of those admitted this year, all graduated in the top half of their high school class, and 95% were in the top fifth. Median SAT I scores are 650 verbal, 630 math. Bryn Mawr's office of admissions suggests the following school program as giving the best preparation for the college: four years of English grammar, composition, and literature; at least three years of math with emphasis on basic algebra, geometry, and trigonometry; three years of one modern or ancient language, or a good foundation in two languages; some work in history; and at least one course in a laboratory science, preferably biology, chemistry, or physics. But the admissions department is not looking for academic automatons (women who make the grades by studying and regurgitating dry facts through four years of high school). They're looking for creative people who have a variety of interests and who have demonstrated leadership and community involvement as well as intellectual curiosity and discipline. An interview, either at the college or with an alumna representative, is required, and gives you a good chance to explain yourself, to check out the college, and to impress the admissions officer with your innate style and wit.

"As a Southerner and a prospective transfer student, I felt that I already had two strikes against me. I had never been north of the Mason-Dixon line, never seen a city as large as Philadelphia, and I thought that whatever credentials I had acquired at my former college would sound puny and unsophisticated in the presence of

an admissions officer used to hearing: 'I'm an accomplished flutist, president of my senior class, captain of the varsity soccer team, and, oh, yes, I just got back from a summer in Brazil, where I helped design a sanitation system for a whole village.'

"But I did get in, and I think what did it wasn't my GPA, or my test scores, or the essays on my application. I think I got in because I was ready for Bryn Mawr, and the interviewer recognized that potential. Admissions isn't looking for 325 superwomen; they're looking for interesting people with potential to give their best and get the most from the college."

The student body is diverse in terms of personality, outside interests, geographical distribution, and racial and cultural origins. Only 11% of the student body comes from Pennsylvania, 27% of this year's freshman class are American minorities, and 12% come from countries other than the United States. The breakdown of minority women on campus is 5% black (compared to 12% of the national population), 3% Hispanic (4% nationally), and 19% Asian-American (3% nationally). For a school of its size, then, Bryn Mawr is really quite diverse in anyone's terms. The college makes a genuine effort to attract and enroll women of color, and to support women of color on campus. For example, all entering students are now required to take a Pluralism workshop, which encourages people to talk about the differences and the similarities of different cultures, and to be sensitive to issues of culture, class, race, and gender.

Bryn Mawr is also supportive of students who need financial aid to enroll. No admissions decisions are based on financial needs. Forty-two percent of the student body receives financial aid, and 90% of admitted students are offered full demonstrated need. Once on campus, a variety of work-study programs are available, from checking I.D.s in the gym to being a tour guide for the admissions office. All the usual college and federal loan programs exist, although Bryn Mawr offers no scholarships based on athletic prowess or academic achievement in high school. Financial aid is given freshman year; it is guaranteed for four years if one continues to need it. In addition, financial aid is available to upper-class students, should their financial circumstances change.

"I was fortunate enough not to need financial aid as an undergraduate, but most of my friends had good financial aid packages and good jobs on campus. Many people, as a matter of fact, say that Bryn Mawr offered them better financial aid packages than any of the other schools they applied to. As to my own experience, when I applied to Bryn Mawr's graduate school program as an A.B./M.A. candidate, I had very little trouble getting full tuition.

"Contrary to popular belief, your parents do not have to be in a stratospheric tax bracket in order for you to come to Bryn Mawr. The college is, frankly, more interested in its academic standards than its endowment."

ACADEMIC ENVIRONMENT

Women come to Bryn Mawr prepared to study, and to study damned hard. The curriculum is intense—four courses is considered a full load, and sometimes even that seems almost too much to handle. During the first two years, students are encouraged to take a broad spectrum of liberal arts courses on which to base their final two years of concentration in the major. Course offerings are very diverse, and close cooperation with Haverford College, which shares some departments with Bryn Mawr, widens one's options considerably. Many students choose to major at Haverford, and many Haverford students major at Bryn Mawr, so if you think that Haverford's philosophy department is particularly fine (it is), you have the option of doing your major work there. In addition, Bryn Mawr students can take courses and use the libraries at Swarthmore College, the University of Pennsylvania, and Villanova University, so there really is no limit to the diversity of the curriculum.

People tend to hear the name Bryn Mawr and imagine course offerings that center solely on the "classical" curriculum: you come to Bryn Mawr to learn about white male history, to study literature written by dead white men, to learn the philosophy of white male culture. Wrong. The curriculum is hard. You may have to read Plato. You probably will read Shakespeare and Milton and Keats. On the other hand, it is perfectly possible to go through four years of Bryn Mawr without ever studying white Western culture. The idea of a Bryn Mawr education is to teach each student to think for herself and to expand her world view. Bryn Mawr is not a technical school, so if you come here planning exclusively to cram science in preparation for medical school, be prepared to have your bubble burst.

Most women at Bryn Mawr fill the requirements without really noticing that that's what they're doing—except if, like me, you notice that math has once again wrecked your happy world. Incoming freshmen take two semesters of English literature and composition (unless they make a five on the AP exam, in which case they're exempted). Everyone must take a course to meet the quantitative skills requirement (math!), work to demonstrate proficiency in at least one foreign language, and complete seven courses to meet the divisional requirements: two social sciences, two natural sciences, and three humanities. In addition, of course, every woman must complete a major subject sequence, and enough electives to make up 32 units of work. Oh, yes, I forgot the scourge of Bryn Mawr: Everybody has to pass a swim test and take eight units (four semesters) of gym before she can graduate.

> *"Every time the course guide came out, I went through a couple of days of intense soul-searching. Wasn't it time that I started learning Chinese? If I gave up a couple of hours of sleep every night, couldn't I squeeze in that 8:00 A.M. class on Sex, Culture, and Society? How could I resist a course called 'Problems in Netherlandish Art?' Luckily for me, I had fulfilled most of my requirements before I transferred to Bryn Mawr, so I could graze freely in*

various far-flung fields of academic discipline. But even the courses I took to fulfill the divisionals were anything but oner-ous. Most of the time, my problem wasn't having not enough choice, but having too much, like trying to settle on one entrée from a menu with hundreds of options.

"The courses I took were universally difficult. Exam period became a week-long hell of sleeplessness, coffee jag, cigarette burnout, and stomach-acid mayhem. Most of my friends felt the same way. I sometimes cursed myself for even considering a notoriously rough course in the optimistic days of the semester's opening. But, as difficult as it is to make straight 4.0s, it's also almost impossible to fail a course. More importantly, I learned to have confidence in myself, because I was continually pushed, and I consistently came through."

One of the greatest things about going to Bryn Mawr is the honor code, which governs both academic and social life on campus. In the academic sphere, the exist-ence of the honor code means that exams are unproctored; professors are not present during class quizzes or midterms; and nobody asks any other student what was on an exam, how hard it was, what the format was, or what grade the other student received for a paper, an exam, or a course. Nobody cheats. The idea behind the honor code is that Mawrtyrs are not in college to make grades, but to learn and, astonishingly for one who came to Bryn Mawr from a school rife with well-policed exams on which people cheated anyway, the honor code works very well. Because pressure from competing with other people's grades doesn't exist, Bryn Mawr doesn't have any cutthroats, which means no papers snitched out of professors' boxes, no ruined chemistry experiments, no nosy questions from friends about the contents of the French final. So, whereas the academic atmosphere is extremely tough, it is not cutthroat. Women compete with themselves, not with each other, so the pressure is internal and self-generated.

And what better way to generate some internal pressure than to contemplate in what subject one will major? Bryn Mawr offers about 35 major subjects, some rather run-of-the-mill, others a bit on the unusual side. Normal sorts of majors include: anthropology, astronomy, biology, chemistry, classical languages, classical studies, economics, English, fine arts, French, geology, German, Greek, history, history of art, history of religion, independent major, Italian, Latin, mathematics, music, phi-losophy, physics, political science, psychology, religion, Russian, Russian studies, sociology, and Spanish. If one wishes to stray from the middle of the road, one can choose to major in classical and Near Eastern archaeology (one of very few depart-ments of this kind in existence), East Asian studies, growth and structure of cities, Hispanic and Hispanic American studies, or romance languages. In addition, Bryn Mawr offers a number of interdepartmental majors and minors such as peace stud-ies and women's studies, and programs like the international economic relations concentration. The programs in Greek, Latin, archaeology, art history, and Russian are particularly well-known nationally.

"Because the classes I took were so small (15–25 students—one had only five), and because most were discussion format, not straight lecture, they had a very personal feeling. I knew that the professor cared about what she (or he) was teaching, and was learning from the class while she taught. Most Bryn Mawr courses have a true give-and-take atmosphere, probably because the place isn't a large research university, but a small liberal arts college with a student/faculty ratio of nine to one. Attention was lavished on me; extensions were freely given, my ideas and comments were treated seriously by professors and students alike, and particularly stupid statements were politely passed over. I had one professor who seemed too convinced of the sanctity of his own opinion to be really effective (he got canned), and another who was just plain bad, but the college seems to attract professors who are totally focused on their students rather than upon getting grants or publishing reams of articles every year."

SOCIAL LIFE

First, let me refresh what you know about oxymorons: Jumbo shrimp. Icy heat. Military intelligence. Near miss. Bryn Mawr social life.

Oh, okay, it's not really all that bad, but that's the Bryn Mawr reputation. With the strenuousness of the academic program, people do tend to let their hair down rather extravagantly on the weekends, and, as people have remarked from time to time, you really can have any kind of social life you want at Bryn Mawr. If you like big parties, Haverford (within walking distance of Bryn Mawr's campus) has a biggie almost every weekend. If you like to see films and plays, or listen to live music and distinguished lecturers, or go to dances, Bryn Mawr has many such events just about every week. Most socializing, though, seems to go on among small bunches of friends (although the school isn't particularly cliquish) who get together to drink wine, chew the fat, and bitch about the fact that they have more work than any reasonable human being could be expected to finish. But other alternatives for on-campus socializing abound. The college-run Campus Café, for example, has become a favorite nighttime hangout, because it offers a menu of various sinful dessert concoctions and gourmet coffees, and often has live music and comedy performances in the evening.

Off campus, there's always Philly, which is an extremely hip, clean, and safe city. Favorite student destinations include a small but nifty Chinatown, and South Street, which is a sort of scaled-down East Village with art galleries, alternative music bars, good restaurants, and punk shops. Nearby in Ardmore and Bryn Mawr, students often catch a flick, browse through records at Plastic Fantastic Record Shop, eat a burger at Roach's bar and grill, or quaff a beer at Mallory's pub. The drinking age in Pennsylvania is twenty-one, so some of these places aren't available to lowerclasswomen, but in general, students from all classes mingle freely. Age or experience are never barriers to socializing at Bryn Mawr.

> *"By the time I got to Bryn Mawr, I was all finished with partying, so the social life suited me perfectly. I've never been very comfortable at huge shindigs, and the few big parties I went to at Haverford or Villanova usually ended badly. I do enjoy being with a group of close friends, playing cards or Trivial Pursuit or whatever. What my friends and I did was never so important as what we talked about.*
>
> *"When I craved excitement, I went to Philly to walk around, or cruise South Street, or catch a band at the Chestnut Cabaret. I never felt deprived of a social life, or of male companionship. Contrary to popular belief, going to a women's college doesn't mean floating in a manless limbo for four years. As a matter of fact, I met more interesting men, and learned more about friendships with men, than I ever had anywhere else."*

EXTRACURRICULAR ACTIVITIES

It is the Bryn Mawr way to overextend oneself in about a zillion different directions. If a student doesn't belong to at least one campus organization, hold a dorm or class office, and play a varsity sport, why, she feels that she's not using her time to full effect. Hence the name "Mawrtyr."

Perhaps in order to feed this insane predilection for being constantly busy, opportunities for campus involvement abound. Available activities include the Self Government Association (S.G.A.), the student-run governing body that makes all decisions about campus life, mediates social and academic disputes through the Honor Board, handles budgeting of the student activity fee, and contributes to decisions about the curriculum. Other activities are the Eighth Dimension, a very popular organization that sends students two or three times a week to tutor children in Philadelphia and the surrounding area; the International Student Association; the Bisexual, Gay, and Lesbian Association; the Sisterhood, an organization for women of color; the Minority coalition; the newly formed debating society; the Bryn Mawr chapter of N.O.W.; and the Student Investment Committee. In addition, there are numerous opportunities for those interested in dance or theater (there are two student-run theater groups, a Bi-College theater department, and an available independent major in theater), and there are two student-run newspapers, the *College News*, which covers Bryn Mawr exclusively, and the *Bi-College News*, which covers Haverford and Bryn Mawr.

Sporting people can participate in varsity athletics, including basketball, soccer, field hockey, gymnastics, tennis, lacrosse, and badminton (don't snicker, it's a tough sport). Because there is a gym requirement, many people do participate in sports, if not at the varsity level, then in intramurals. And the gym itself is terrific, with an Olympic-size pool, a weight room, two full basketball courts, and a dance and gymnastics studio.

> *"I scorned the gym requirement, and hated every lap I swam to fill that requirement. A lot of formerly sedentary seniors (myself included) end up second semester swimming madly, jumping rope at all hours of the day or night, and taking the wellness seminar to work off the odious eight units. It's quite ironic (and very funny) that the physically laziest people in school ended up being the most active their last year of college.*
> *"I suppose that the 'sound mind in a healthy body' thing is well and good, but I would have been content with a sound mind in a saggy (and well-rested) body."*

Most people have some involvement with S.G.A. over their four years, either as dorm reps, class reps, or members of various committees, and the organizations that support community involvement, like the recycling project and Eighth Dimension, are particularly popular. Bryn Mawr women are generally very involved in their school and very vocal about their place in the community, so extracurricular activities have an important place on campus.

Bryn Mawr has no sororities, which tend to be exclusionary rather than group oriented. Because Bryn Mawr is an all-women's college, and because the student body is so small, the whole campus is really one large sorority. Dorm life, too, adds to a feeling of campus-wide camaraderie. There are eight dormitories, plus Haffner, the language house, and Perry House, the black cultural center (which has a library of black history as well as huge, gorgeous rooms for women of color). For the most part, the dorms are beautiful. I'm partial to the older ones — Denbigh, Pembroke East and West, Rockefeller, Rhoads, Brecon, and Radnor. The rooms in these buildings are fantastic, many with open fireplaces, huge bay windows, interesting ceilings, and loads of dark woodwork. I think that Erdman, a huge gray thing modeled on a castle and built in the sixties, is particularly ugly, but some folks swear they love it.

First-year students all have roommates, but almost all upper-class women have singles or suites, unless they choose to live with a particular friend. Two of the dorms are coed, with Haverford men enjoying the Bryn Mawr ambiance, and Mawrtyrs also have the option of living in suites (coed or single-sex) at Haverford. The dining service (in Erdman, Haffner, Brecon, and Rhoads) is great, because the college runs it; it's not one of those generic, catered things like the dreaded food service, and the people who manage it provide a variety of options, like vegetarian foods.

> *"The worst experience of my life at Bryn Mawr was living in the French house at Haffner. I had just gotten back from a year in France, and thought that it would be great to practice the*

*language every day, live with French scholars, and so on. Wrong.
First of all, nobody there spoke French. Ever. Secondly, the building was designed in the sixties by a person who decided to make it
like a 'medieval village.' The effect was that I never saw any of
my dormmates, since the rooms don't open into a common hallway, but are situated in clusters of three at each corner of the
dorm. I'd occasionally glimpse an apparition scooting down the
hall to the bathroom, or catch sight of some hapless person's feet
under the shower curtain, but that was it. Haffner is known for
having bad parties and being peopled with the most antisocial
lot of students on campus. If only I'd known!*

*"By contrast, I spent my second year in Brecon, which is a bit
off campus, so everybody sort of bonds together in the dining hall
and the TV room. My room was great—three large windows looking out over an open field, a window seat, and a huge closet."*

GRADUATES

One thing that all alumna say is that, after Bryn Mawr, graduate school is a
breeze. About 29% of last year's Bryn Mawr graduates went on to graduate school,
although most took jobs, and 13% went straight to medical, law, or business
schools. In the latest study, Bryn Mawr ranked first in the percentage of undergraduates who received non-science doctorates; the school ranked fourth overall. Interestingly, though Bryn Mawr is a small school, and the physics department not enormous, the college awarded 1% of all graduate degrees in physics in a recent year.
The percentage of current physics majors is currently 29 times that of the national
average.

*"After studying at Bryn Mawr for two years, I needed a break. I
did work toward my M.A. in English, but my heart just wasn't in
it after busting a gut as an undergraduate. Most of my friends
have gone on to medical school, graduate school, or law school,
but I'm content to futz around for a couple of years and catch my
breath. My mother, who is a Bryn Mawr graduate as well, took
about 15 years off before she went back to school to get her law
degree. Bryn Mawr encourages women to use their education,
and it's true that I feel slightly guilty that I'm not carrying the
Bryn Mawr standard in professional or graduate school.
Someday."*

Like myself, a lot of Bryn Mawr women seem to rest up for awhile after graduation. But after five years, most are in professional fields (about 40%), and another
30% have gone into secondary or university-level education. The college puts a lot

of emphasis on training women for careers in academia, and has a few programs at the undergraduate level that encourage people to choose careers as teachers and researchers. It's interesting to note that graduates of women's colleges are more than twice as likely as their coed counterparts to receive doctorates, and they produce a higher number of graduates who go on to medical school and careers in the sciences. One third of the women board members of the Fortune 1000 companies are graduates of women's colleges, even though these graduates comprise a small fraction of the nation's female graduates.

SUMMARY OVERVIEW

Women's colleges like Bryn Mawr produce a number of high-achieving professional women, and the experience of attending Bryn Mawr for four years certainly has a great effect upon the future success of its graduates. Yet, although most of Bryn Mawr graduates offer nothing but the highest praise for their alma mater, the typical undergraduate Mawrtyr suffers through a peculiar love-hate relationship with her school. Thus, it proves difficult to separate and enumerate the assets and deficits of attending the college.

The best way to approach this issue is to say that Bryn Mawr's best points are also its worst, at least in the eyes of a sleep-deprived undergraduate who, though she dearly loves the study of fifteenth century Norwegian dynastic history, must produce a 40-page paper on the subject by 9:00 A.M. tomorrow morning. Bryn Mawr's refusal to lighten up on its academic requirements means that its students get a superior grounding in scholarship: the curriculum is designed to produce women who are curious about their world, analytical in their approach to problem solving, and dedicated to knowledge. The downside of the excellent curriculum is, of course, that Mawrtyrs live with a great deal of stress—it is not easy to transform oneself from a callow, mush-brained freshman to a sophisticated, steely-eyed Bryn Mawr alumna.

Another item on Bryn Mawr's love-hate slate is the college's size—with only about 1200 undergraduates, one learns one's fellows' names and faces quickly, which, again, has its good and bad points. At Bryn Mawr, one is never a number in an enormous lecture hall—classmates and professors get to know, not just your face, but the quirks of your thinking, what you like to do outside the classroom, whether you're likely to add much to an 8:30 A.M. class—in short, Mawrtyrs are known and appreciated for their individual personalities, not for their marks in a roll book or their presence on the Dean's list (which doesn't exist at Bryn Mawr).

Bryn Mawr's size, though, does have its drawbacks. I can remember feeling, at times, quite stifled on campus, as if I couldn't be anonymous even when my somewhat grumpy self desired anonymity. Knowing everyone and having everyone know you sometimes makes for a certain lack of privacy, a feeling which I usually remedied by escaping to Philly or New York.

Finally, we come to the fact that Bryn Mawr admits only women to the undergraduate college. Again, most graduates consider that attending an all-women's college was one of the best moves they ever made. Being in an atmosphere in which one is judged, not by one's gender, but by one's intelligence, is refreshing, to say the very least. After spending a couple of years in the corporate world, being called "baby" and condescended to, Bryn Mawr grads look back gratefully to a place where such atrocities do not exist.

Ah, but what about men? What red-blooded eighteen to twenty-one year-old woman wants to go to a place where for four years she and ten other women will do battle each Saturday evening for the privilege of being escorted to Al-E-Gator's by a Haverford freshman who looks like a bespectacled glass of milk. Who needs it? Regardless of what the admissions office may say, men are in short supply, and if one yearns for continual romance, one is not as likely to find it at Bryn Mawr as elsewhere.

The women who graduate from Bryn Mawr are a fiercely loyal lot who are very involved in the future direction of the school. I was strongly influenced to come to Bryn Mawr by my mother's adoration of the school, and by the delight that her alumna friends took in being involved in prospective student interviews and recruitment at local high schools. Bryn Mawr sends people out into the world feeling grateful for their education and hopeful about their opportunities as women. As Bryn Mawr's most famous alumna, Katharine Hepburn, puts it: "I came to Bryn Mawr by the skin of my teeth, and by the skin of my teeth I stayed. It was the best thing I ever did."

Sarah E. Davis, A.B.

California Institute of Technology

THE PROGRAM

Beyond the textbooks, beyond the classrooms, beyond today's knowledge, is Caltech. A place where you will learn to *write* the textbooks that others will read, *teach* the students of the future, and *create* the knowledge that will shape tomorrow's technology. Throughout Caltech's more than 100 years, this philosophy, of going beyond the known, has led to scientific advances such as the discovery of quasars, anti-matter, quarks, and the nature of the chemical bond. These have been breakthroughs that affect more than just scientists and science fiction writers — the establishment of the Richter Scale, the development of the principles that govern modern aviation and jet flight, and how birds know which way to fly every winter. The Caltech experience provides undergraduates with the opportunity to learn in the same environment that has fostered such ground-breaking discoveries, in research-focused academic surroundings where a small student population creates an extremely low student-to-faculty ratio of three to one, and as members of a community that live and work under an honor system that encourages responsible adults to govern themselves.

All of Caltech's undergraduate options center around math, science, and engineering, combining a rigorous core curriculum with a specialized research-based education in a four-year program leading to the Bachelor of Science degree. Core classes include two years of math, two years of physics, and one year of chemistry. Through these courses, which occupy much of the freshman and sophomore years, students learn a little bit about a lot of things. This belief, that the mathematician, scientist, and engineer of the future must have a little bit of each within themselves, is as old as Caltech. And you will discover that the "little bit" you have learned, turns out to be a lot. Homework assignments and exams are designed to test understanding rather than recollection. Students are taken beyond the "how to," and thrust into the exciting world of "why."

"ME 171 is called 'Computer-Aided Engineering Design.' At first glance, this might seem like a course that would teach you to draw things using a Computer-Aided Design (CAD) package, but that would be too easy. ME 171 taught us how CAD programs work as opposed to what they do. We answered questions such as how do you explain to the computer to rotate the image on the screen just by turning a dial, how do you define a complex surface, and how would you make the propeller you drew spin? The objective was not to determine how to design something using a computer, but rather to discover the strengths and weaknesses of geometric modeling, and how they can help or hinder the design process. And you did start using a CAD program toward the end of the term. It was very primitive, and it didn't have a fancy name, but you used it anyway. After all, you wrote it."

Providing the foundation are the educators, along with the abundant amount of resources they control. Among the past and present faculty and alumni, 21 Nobel Laureates share 22 Nobel Prizes, four of which belong to professors currently in residence. The three-to-one student-to-faculty ratio mentioned earlier is based only on tenure-track faculty, 100% of whom have Ph.D.'s. The faculty are at Caltech not only to pursue their own projects, but also to train undergraduates, both by helping them to make important contributions to faculty research, and encouraging them to develop and cultivate their own original endeavors. Each year, the Summer Undergraduate Research Fellowship (SURF) Program sponsors nearly 200 undergraduates to participate in summer research, based on their own proposals that are written and submitted in collaboration with a sponsoring faculty member. SURF students work either in small groups, or in many cases one-on-one with faculty members, on their summer projects and they receive a stipend for this work. They are required to write a technical paper summarizing the results, and present this paper during SURF Seminar Day in the fall.

Though the SURF program is mainly geared toward those with plans to continue in research, there are also ample opportunities for students who choose not to participate in this program. These other students can take advantage of Caltech's abundant resources through upper division classes that are designed around individual or small group projects, lab work, and "hands on" training.

"One of the highlights of the Caltech mechanical engineering program is ME 72, 'Mechanical Engineering Design.' Everyone is given an identical bag of 'junk,' and is expected to build a vehicle out of the raw materials to compete against classmates' vehicles at the conclusion of the course. My year, the contest was a tug-of-war between two vehicles, each moving in the same direction but joined by a long piece of surgical tubing that ran around a pulley, through 'sand' composed of tiny plastic pellets. Because style counts as much as performance, there were many different types of vehicles: tanks, catapults, tractors, and walkers, all presenting unique design challenges. We were encouraged to

learn about our own devices — what made them fast, what made them strong, what made them tip upside down and spray plastic pellets all over the place. And, somehow, we crossed that bridge between theory and reality, with only a few minor cuts and abrasions, all together.

Both upper and lower division courses are designed to foster group, as well as individual study, leading to a strong feeling of camaraderie. Whether it is in the mechanical engineering shop, in someone's room at a ridiculously early hour of the morning, or in the dorm lounge, students can always be found working on homework sets, studying for tests, or arguing over which soft drink has the most caffeine. Everyone seems to share the feeling that because they are so individually talented, as a team, they are untouchable.

"Though ME 72 culminates in the final competition, the real fun and drama occurs throughout the course, when everyone would be down in the machine shop refining their vehicles, challenging each other in mock contests, and helping each other solve problems. Striving to win was important, of course, but there was always a strong 'esprit de corps' that encouraged us to share our ideas freely. If someone came up with a new process, or found out how to make something useful that might improve another's design, for example, they shared the information rather than keeping it to themselves. Because of this, the overall quality of the devices was much higher than it would have been under a more competitive or 'cut-throat' environment."

Team spirit and fellowship extend into all aspects of campus life, from academics, to athletics, to social events, and is helped along by an honor system that really works. Many schools have an honor system. Some are just empty words so that there's something to put on the title page of the school catalog; some, like Caltech's, become so much a part of campus life that they become not merely the most important rule, but the *only* rule. The Caltech Honor System requires that, "No one shall take unfair advantage of another member of the Caltech community." Under this system, exams are never proctored and most of them are "take-home," 24-hour lab and classroom access is made possible by the issuing of keys, students are often encouraged to work in groups on homework assignments and in lab, and there are no fines for overdue library books. A Board of Control (BOC), composed entirely of undergraduates, enforces the honor code, through a process that is truth-seeking, rather than punitive.

"Panic is a great catalyst for human nature to conflict with ethics, especially when you find yourself looking at a page full of midterm exam questions — some that just look hard, some that you don't even, recognize — and your textbook is invitingly perched on a shelf just inches away. I think there comes a point in almost everyone's Caltech career when they are tempted to dip

> *their hand into the cookie jar and see if there are math answers inside. For me it was during the Math 2a midterm. (The average turned out to be something like thirty out of a possible 175.) I remember thinking, during the exam, about why I came to Caltech, and reminding myself that learning meant not concentrating on getting a better grade than anyone else in the class, but rather doing the best you can do, and seeing how far that takes you. I figure it was time well spent, since I had no idea how to do the third problem anyway."*

Dorm life is similarly structured around social interaction. There are seven on-campus houses, each with a distinctive personality, and almost everyone, by choice, is affiliated with one or more of them. They are all self-governing, and derive their own policies and procedures regarding room pick, how house dues are spent, and keeping morale high. In addition, there is a separate group of upperclass committeepersons who serve as peer counselors, working with the Resident Associates in each house to solve personal and individual problems, as a supplement to the formal counseling program available through the Caltech Health Center. There are single house and multiple house parties from time to time, along with events, such as picnics and ski trips, organized by the houses themselves. The student organization, Associated Students of CIT (ASCIT), sponsors periodic social events also. Federal alcohol control guidelines are observed, of course, but this has not seemed to diminish either the spirit, or even the frequency of social events.

There are about 70 clubs and organizations on campus, and even if you don't find something you're specifically interested in, if you can get a couple of people together with the same idea, then you've got club 71. In addition, there is an athletics program that boasts a no-cut policy, which can provide an outlet for your competitive side as well as the opportunity to get out and exercise a little.

> *"Even though we don't have to leave campus to have fun, we often did anyway. It sometimes seemed like getting out of Pasadena on the weekends to go see a movie in Westwood, visit Mickey and his friends in Anaheim, or spending money we didn't have down at the South Coast Plaza was essential in order to maintain our sanity. Now, years after graduation, I don't know what I was complaining about. In retrospect, Pasadena is a great city. Everything we needed, from movie theaters, to grocery stores, to Tower Records, is there. And if we felt the urge to hike, or ski, or swim in the ocean, an hour in a car got us there. Pasadena is a pretty central place, just minutes from Los Angeles. Want Chinese food at 2:00 A.M.? No problem. Want to see a movie premiere on Hollywood Boulevard? No problem. Six dollars for an ice tea on Rodeo Drive? Well, after all, it is L.A."*

Of course, students don't come to Caltech because of the clubs, athletic teams, or to get really good seats for the Rose Parade. Students come to learn to be mathematicians, scientists, and engineers. They come because of Caltech's reputation for providing an unequaled education specifically in those fields. And sometimes it goes beyond being a good math school, or a good science school, or a good engineering school. For example, why would the high school varsity football star think the Caltech chemistry program was more exciting than the world of college sports, or why would the woman who performed at Carnegie Hall last year think that coming to Caltech and becoming a scientist would be more rewarding than a career as a professional musician?

> *"There's a passion that accompanies the pursuit of science that goes beyond science. I think the attraction of a place like Caltech, is that it not only allows, but inspires, multi-talented individuals to express themselves to their full, possibly as yet undiscovered potential. We left with pieces of paper that proclaimed us Bachelors of Science, but, more important, we left with the responsibility to make sure the world kept moving, to never be satisfied with the way things worked, and to always remember that the only real four letter word is 'can't.'"*

GETTING IN/FINANCIAL AID

Caltech admissions policies can best be described as tough, but fair. Yes, like most or all of the other schools you will probably be applying to, it is difficult to get into Caltech. The specific reasons for this are as varied as the individual personalities on the Freshman Admissions Committee itself. Composed of faculty, staff, and current undergraduates, each with their own diverse opinions, the committee often cannot even agree on the thermostat setting of the room, let alone who and what defines the ideal "Caltech student."

In general, the strongest applicants are those who manage to couple exceptionally strong academic backgrounds, especially in the areas of math and science, with a well-rounded high school experience. Typically, admitted students will have come from the top 10% of their high school class, and have challenged themselves with the most rigorous course work their high school offers, sometimes pursuing courses through other schools or area colleges and universities when local opportunities are exhausted. Extracurricular activities are often an important consideration.

The average SAT I composite score for the most recent freshman class is 1396. Since this is an average, this obviously means there were scores below, as well as above, this number. The SAT I and SAT II exams provide important standardized indicators of performance, but by themselves, they cannot demonstrate the ability to succeed in a college environment. As is the case with grade point averages (GPAs), there are no minimum scores at which your application will not be considered. Your GPA will be recalculated by the application processing group, so it is not necessary to worry about factors like weighing or not weighing for honors courses because everyone's GPA is recalculated the same way. The actual courses taken are carefully considered, since everyone on the committee was once a college appli-cant and they are not easily fooled by students who take easy courses just to get a good GPA.

The personal essays are influential because Caltech does not interview. In order to be fair, either all prospective applicants should be interviewed, or none of them should be. The applicant from Alaska, for example, should have the same opportuni-ties as those who apply from Los Angeles. To replace the value of an interview, the essay questions were all revised, and are now designed to allow self-expression with the maximum amount of freedom. An important point to keep in mind, is that about one-half of the applicants are academically qualified to attend Caltech, but only about one-quarter are accepted. Because of this, the committee is continually searching for those factors that might distinguish each applicant from other appli-cants who may look identical on paper. Along these lines, applicants are encouraged to enclose any additional material with the application that they think will better describe them.

Caltech receives about 2000 applications every year, and the Freshman Ad-missions Committee reviews every single scrap of paper in every single one of them. Twice. During the actual decision process following the readings, there are no rules, no restrictions, no guidelines passed out—only the instructions to admit everyone the committee thinks belongs at Caltech.

California applicants do not have any advantage during the admissions process, and there is no in-state vs. out-of-state tuition difference. (The reason a large per-centage of students come from California is that more students from California apply.) In addition, Caltech obviously does not discriminate, either for or against applicants, and admissions are "need blind," which means that the admissions com-mittee does not know if you're applying for financial aid when considering you for admission.

Financial aid is often the most misunderstood part of the application process. About 65% of the Caltech student population receives some sort of financial aid. Schools with high tuition can sometimes be even less expensive to attend than schools with low tuition, depending on their individual financial aid policies. Caltech calculates your demonstrated need by subtracting the amount you and/or your family are able to pay for your college education (as determined by Caltech and the government) from a "total estimated expenses" estimate, which includes tuition, fees, books and supplies, room and board, and personal expenses (like flying home for the holidays and seeing a movie once in a while). Not every school in-cludes the same items in the total estimated expenses. Caltech promises to meet 100% of your demonstrated need through three methods: grant money (gift aid), loan money, and work study, wherein you work during the school year and receive paychecks.

The items to compare against other schools are the average per student indebt-edness after four years (Caltech's is around $7,000), the average number of hours worked per week under work study (Caltech students average between six and ten hours per week), and what will happen to your aid package if you have outside scholarships (Caltech will not touch gift aid until loan and work study are depleted).

ACADEMIC ENVIRONMENT

Caltech concentrates on a specialized education centered around math, science, and engineering. About 35% of all students end up majoring in engineering and applied science; 24% pursue physics or applied physics; 15% explore electrical engineering; 24% choose chemistry, chemical engineering, biology, or math; the remaining 2% explore fields such as astronomy, economics, geology, literature, and social science (even the options such as literature and social science strongly encourage the aggressive and parallel pursuit of math, science, or engineering). Engineering and Applied Science (E&AS), the most popular option, is a great way to expose yourself to more than one engineering discipline, while at the same time, emphasizing a specific area. Because E&AS encompasses many different fields, such as aeronautics, applied mechanics, civil engineering, computer science, environmental engineering science, materials science, and mechanical engineering, and you can generally choose courses from any of the above fields to satisfy many of the E&AS elective requirements for graduation, you can actually create your own custom-tailored major.

Common to all options is the teaching philosophy: teach the students not *what* to learn, but *how* to learn. And push them. Hard.

> *"I asked my friend Roy Hashimoto what he thought was the best and the worst part of his Caltech experience. The best part was 'winning Interhouse volleyball.' The worst? 'EE 114.' The academic curriculum at Caltech sort of resembles the old cliché, 'drinking water from a fire hose,' except that a fire hose will eventually be shut off or the water will run out. Caltech's will not. And they won't let you out until you drink a lot! For example, most majors, including engineering, require math courses that go beyond those required of math majors at some other universities."*

Caltech will provide you with an environment where you are forever challenged, where you cannot ever hit the upper limit that you might have run up against in high school. This entails a certain amount of academic rigor that has been described as "relentless." Is it too much so? That depends on the level of commitment and the sometimes elusive ability to prioritize time. The assistant vice president for Student Affairs comments that often when academic problems arise, it is not so much that students can't do the work, it's that they need a bit of help managing their lives.

Fortunately, life is made a little easier during freshman year through a mandatory pass/fail grading system regardless of what classes you are taking, not allowing part-

or full-time jobs during the first term of freshman year and only by special permission during the second and third, and guaranteed on-campus housing for freshmen. (Some sort of Caltech housing is guaranteed for all four years as long as you turn in your housing contract on time.)

> *"You are kind of spoiled at Caltech, especially as a freshman. Many of the mechanics of living are taken care of. There is a custodial department that cleans all on- and off-campus rooms once every two weeks, empties the trash, and cleans the bathrooms and house kitchens. You can exchange sheets and bath towels twice a week if you want, and there is a sink provided in all on-campus rooms so that no one except your roommate really has to see what you look like first thing in the morning."*

Take-home exams are just like any other, with a time limit and often a policy that you cannot consult any references. The distinction is that it allows you to take tests in your dorm room, at the library, outside on the grass under a tree — wherever you want and whenever you want (before they're due of course). The faculty generally supports this system because it allows them flexibility and it also removes most of the excuses for bad performance, such as having to study for two exams that are scheduled for the same day.

The only place there seems to be "real" academic competition, when students are reluctant to share notes or homework problem hints, for example, is with the graduate students in upper division classes containing both undergraduate and graduate students. Competition among undergraduates is rare, and mostly friendly anyway. The graduate students, however, sometimes seem to be much more concerned with relative performance than their undergraduate classmates. This is probably due to the fact that they have come from other institutions that do not have an honor system with the scope and depth of Caltech's. (Caltech undergraduates are typically discouraged from Caltech graduate programs because the faculty believes that a diverse education requires study at different institutions.)

In large part due to these policies, more than 95% of the freshmen return, and a little more than 80% end up graduating in four years. So what happens to those who don't make it? As you can probably tell from the section on "getting in," admitted students are generally more than capable of at least surviving academically. As a result, very few leave or flunk out ("flame") because they cannot pass enough courses or have to study too much. It's more or less up to individuals how much they will push themselves and how quickly they will learn how to budget their time.

> *"I personally probably pulled fewer than ten 'all nighters' during the four years I was at Caltech. Some of my classmates never stayed up all night studying, while for others, 24-hour study periods seemed to be a part of their lives. Prioritization of time seems to be one of the most important skills college can teach you. We found that we had to learn that one quick, so we could find time for the luxuries in life such as eating and sleeping."*

For the most part, students who leave do so because they discover that Caltech is not right for them. They find that their goals could better be met by a more liberal arts oriented education, or maybe they feel that math, science, and engineering were not really what they expected them to be. In addition, most students were at the top of their high school class; many were valedictorians. By definition, half of them will now be in the bottom half of their class—and they don't like it. So they go to a school where they can be the best again.

Caltech isn't for everyone. Larger institutions can offer a broader education: the opportunity to choose from a greater number of humanities and social science classes, the ability to order take-out from a pizza franchise right on the campus, and the luxury of shopping at a bookstore that rivals some shopping malls. Caltech balances this with a low student-to-faculty ratio and an extensive availability of resources.

> *"Though most of the faculty are blessed with low teaching loads and small classes, they are sometimes busy with their own individual projects, and often complain that they wish they had more time to allocate to the students. Some members of the faculty go way out of their way to interact with students, while others cannot seem to find the time. The good news is that the Deans' Office would always make sure we got what we needed somehow. In addition since upper division classes are really designed around research and lab work, I actually found that my option advisor was extremely accessible because we were often in lab together."*

The students will tell you that they believe the Caltech undergraduate curriculum is the toughest in the nation. Whether it is true or false, academics really provide the main course for everything that goes on at Caltech. The rest are only appetizers, side orders, and dessert.

> *"For me, the biggest challenge was to accept that it might be better to be mediocre among the very best than to be the very best of the mediocre. It doesn't seem to be such a bad thing anymore to say that I came to Caltech and was an 'average student.' Caltech sort of redefined what that meant."*

SOCIAL LIFE

Social life actually centers around student interaction, whether that means a few individuals piling into a car and driving to Westwood on Saturday night, checking out the dance party going on in one of the house courtyards, or fighting over which movie to rent at the local video store. Caltech is sort of like a small town. Since everyone tends to know everyone else, finding something to do on the weekends is usually as simple as walking out of your room into the hall and looking bored. There's a lot to do in Los Angeles if you feel like venturing off campus — everything from attending a symphony concert, to riding rollercoasters, to eating at places that serve caviar pizza. Everything is only a car-hop away, providing of course, there's nothing worthwhile going on at Tech. Caltech parties range from the amazing to the bizarre, depending on the mood of the students at the time. Many parties are hosted by either individual or multiple houses. Because they control their own budgets, the scope of the event depends on how much they can spend. In general though, if it's a choice between a new couch for the lounge and a Friday night bash, you can probably count on people sleeping on old couches early Saturday morning.

To a large degree, social satisfaction revolves around being happy with the people with whom you will interact everyday. Caltech has traditionally had to combat the stereotypical image of students wearing thick-rimmed glasses with heavy lenses and tape on the frame, carrying laptop computers and wearing plaid. There are people like that at Caltech, just as there are at any school in the country. The best way to try and determine what the students are like at Caltech is to look around your AP math, physics, and chemistry classes. Look at your fellow students who are also applying to the same schools you are. Look at yourself.

> *"When I first set foot on the Caltech campus seven years ago, I didn't know what to expect. The inside covers of my senior high school yearbook are decorated with numerous 'thank you for everythings,' 'keep in touches,' and 'remember that time in AP Physics when Robert threw the ball of paper' stories, but there is also that ominous note: 'P.S.: Say hello to all the nerds at Caltech for me.'*
>
> *"I had an extremely positive high school experience; the friends I made there will be my friends for life. It is difficult to leave an environment like that, and there was a great deal of fear associated with the prospect of meeting new people and making new friends. During the first few days at Caltech, I remember quickly finding the first-year students and upperclassmen from my home town. I remember freshman orientation at Catalina Island and how our small circle of friends expanded to include many others who had never been to a beach, never had a Christmas that wasn't white, and didn't eat Spam by choice. I remember looking at my new classmates and feeling very relieved that they did not have pocket calculators nestled in quick-draw holsters, or plastic pocket protectors to hold their pens. I remember thinking that they were just like some of my old friends. I remember thinking that they were just like me."*

Caltech is not immune from other, more standard issues that plague all college campuses, like substance abuse and crime. Caltech is taking steps toward increasing awareness in these areas and actively addressing the difficult issues. Frankly, there simply isn't enough time to abuse drugs or alcohol and still survive academically; it's sort of self-correcting. The director of Residence Life is there to provide support and direction for any student needing counseling, or just to listen. She is there to be both a friend and confidant, and to see that everyone's basic needs are met so they can busy themselves with becoming brilliant. In addition, there is a professional counseling center which provides discreet, confidential, and specific professional advice on painful and troublesome topics such as alcoholism, date rape, and sexual harassment.

> *"Now, I am almost sure if my mom read this section before I went to college, she would have chained me to my bedroom door and never let me out of the house again. It's a scary world, and Los Angeles is a big city. On the other hand, Caltech students are extremely supportive and protective of each other. Please, please remember that no matter what college you select, there is no substitute for good judgment and common sense!"*

Caltech is predominately a male institution. A little more than 25% of the students are female. While this ratio still needs to be improved, there are now about twice as many women on campus as there were back in the mid-eighties. This has resulted in a dramatic improvement in campus dynamics, and, though the situation improved, there are still problems associated with the fact that this is a campus with more men than women. The good news is that there are more women now, and they have found a stronger voice. Will it keep getting better over the next few years? Well, Caltech is trying to make that happen. Trying *hard*. The admissions office is actively pursuing an increase in applications from women and minority students. On campus there are continuing signs of improvement, such as the recent approval of a new Caltech Women's Center. Another thing to keep in mind is that the science and engineering industries today are predominantly male. Many female Caltech alumni have commented that they have seen coworkers from other more "integrated' institutions have real problems with this type of working environment.

> *"Fortunately, life is not without miracles. Love is a funny thing; no matter how difficult you make it, two people will somehow find each other through the confusion perpetuated by misinterpreted actions, political correctness, and physics problem sets. I have a real appreciation for the women who come here because I think they have to put up with a lot of garbage; yet somehow they manage to make friends, secure solid relationships, and still turn in the calculus homework on time!"*

EXTRACURRICULAR ACTIVITIES

To maintain your sanity and mental health, there are a large variety of clubs and organizations available, including men's and women's glee clubs, a jazz band, chamber ensembles, Christian fellowship, martial arts, skiing, hiking, windsurfing, sailing, ballroom dancing, and almost anything else you can think of. There's even a frisbee club. The athletics program includes baseball, basketball, cross country, fencing, golf, soccer, swimming, diving, tennis, track and field, water polo, and ice hockey. Most of these sports field both men's and women's teams. In addition to intramural athletics, there are traditional and nontraditional "challenges" being made all the time between the different student houses. ASCIT hosts a movie every Friday night, as well as a formal dinner and dance in the spring. The student newspaper, called *The California Tech*, comes out every Friday; the yearbook is called *The Big T*. There are opportunities to participate in a number of different faculty/student committees, such as Freshman Admissions, where students participate in the actual decision-making process, and Undergraduate Academic Standards and Honors (UASH) which allows student participation in determinations concerning probation, suspension, or expulsion for academic reasons.

> *"I was afraid that because Caltech was so small, there wouldn't be anything to do outside of studying. Surprise! It's a real school! There are so many opportunities to get involved. Where else can you participate in house government, be an editor on the yearbook, play tennis, and perform with the chamber music group in the same term? I did it, and so did many others. Among the great things about Caltech are the opportunities given to undergraduates, academically and socially, along with extracurricular activities."*

Much of the routine extracurricular activity centers around the student houses. During the first week of classes, freshmen participate in a "rotation" process where they visit each house, meet the current residents, and then rank where they want to live in order of preference. The new students are "picked" into houses at the end of "rotation" through a method that attempts to insure that the needs and wishes of everyone in the freshman class are maximized. The advantages of Caltech's house system are that it gives everyone a chance to belong to a group, and there are always seniors, juniors, sophomores, and freshmen living in the houses, allowing for ample opportunity to receive advice on what classes to take, how to do the last problem on the physics assignment, and where to find the nearest McDonald's. On the down side, similarities tend to get reinforced when living among the same group of people for four years. Fortunately, house personalities change quickly because each freshman class brings with it a different group of individuals, and though the house may be very different during your senior year than it was three years earlier, often it's for the better.

GRADUATES

If you have been following the Southern California job market in recent years, you are probably aware it's not the best time to be seeking technical employment.

Caltech graduates, however, seem to be holding their own. Perhaps it is that they are stubborn; perhaps it is because they don't like to take "no" for an answer; perhaps it's that there will always be a market for good people. In any event, the Career Development Center (CDC) reports that 58% of the most recent graduating class are pursuing graduate school immediately, 24% have found jobs, 4% have other plans, which leaves 14% who are listed as "No Information Available" or "Uncommitted." The average starting salary was $37,632, up 2.9% from last year. This is due in part to the active role the CDC assumes, which includes counseling, the promotion of on-campus career days, and organizing on-campus company interviews. The rest is due to the fact that the students themselves are extremely marketable.

> *"There is a power associated with graduating from Caltech. You may not notice it when you are in school, because you are probably more concerned with how much sleep you'll be able to get that night rather than what your career plans are years from now. The Caltech graduates with whom I worked following graduation were all very well respected, quickly earned a reputation for being authorities in their various job areas, and were soon training others with years of experience many times theirs."*

Because theory and understanding are stressed over specific training, Caltech's graduates are not only well prepared for jobs related to their majors, but are also able to adapt to positions that bridge the gap between math, science, and engineering, and other fields, such as law and business. Caltech encourages you to do your best at whatever you do, whether it is getting a Ph.D. in physics, working for NASA, or maybe even developing a stomach condition as an investment banker on Wall Street. You are taught to use the talents you have developed, to be a leader through example. If it is true that an institution is reflected through its graduates, then Caltech has been, and will continue to be, a proud and important contributor to society and the associated technological community.

SUMMARY OVERVIEW

There is only one Caltech. There is only one place that can offer you the opportunity to be not at, but defining, the leading edge of technology, to learn in a small school research-centered environment with a three-to-one student-to-faculty ratio complemented by extensive resources, and to eat, sleep, study, and play under a single rule that basically says to be nice to each other.

The future is being created and shaped with new discoveries. Each new discovery has a home, and the birthplace for many of today's inventions that become the resources of tomorrow is at Caltech. This process is fostered by the opportunities that are created where there are no waiting lines for chemistry lab space, where un-that are created where there are no waiting lines for chemistry lab space, where undergraduates are not only allowed, but encouraged to pursue independent research projects, and where everyone works together as a team. The Honor System provides the foundation for all of these advantages, by allowing the pursuit of knowledge that is unencumbered by excess academic pressure, competition, and fear.

As always, nothing is perfect. If your interests lie outside of mathematics, science, or engineering, or if you can't really decide between chemical engineering or motion picture directing, then Caltech isn't right for you. Likewise, if you lack the passion that drives Caltech students to seek and question and learn; if you don't feel comfortable in an environment with very few rules, or if you want a more diverse education, then perhaps you would be better off selecting a school where you could take it easy and have more fun.

However, if you're looking for a place that will challenge you, a place that will excite you, a place where you will learn to laugh at the word "impossible," then consider Caltech. Consider that it's not just a piece of paper that makes you a Bachelor of Science, but rather the knowledge and skill that backs it up. Consider that just as Caltech may not be the right school for you, it might be the *perfect* school for you. Consider touching the future, today.

> *"Caltech is a very different place now than it was when I left. I think it has become stronger; the students who are there now are, in some ways, better than we were. They understand life a little better. They enjoy life a little more. Caltech as an institution has traditionally resisted change, but it's coming, through new ideas, fresh faces, and imagination that builds upon what we defined as imagination many years ago. I left Caltech with many new friends, a revised opinion of what my limitations were, and a better understanding of how the world worked. I left Caltech with a smile, a tear, and yes, the warm welcome feeling that I would finally be able to get some serious sleep!"*

> *Garrett W. Choi, B.S.*

Carleton College

THE PROGRAM

"Whenever I tell people that I went to Carleton College, I can tell by the look in their eyes that they've never heard of it and are probably assuming it's some backwoods community college. Or maybe they have a vague notion that it's a liberal arts school somewhere in the Midwest. But the ones who know it, immediately register a glint of respect, recognizing that Carleton is one of the nation's best colleges. No, it may not be a household name that jumps to people's lips. However, nestled in the quaint town of Northfield, Minnesota, an hour away from Minneapolis/St. Paul, Carleton College is a dynamic and stimulating intellectual environment."

Carleton, in its essence, is a small, academic institution that offers a broad liberal arts program. This program seeks to expose students to the traditional arts and sciences, and requires them to take courses in a variety of disciplines. Yet it also leaves room for students' own unique academic interests and self-designed majors. What makes it different from other schools of this description is a combination of intelligent, involved, and multitalented people, with an atmosphere of open, friendly respect for people and ideas, derived from its location in the Midwest.

Every member of the community tries to be aware of the social, political, and academic issues at the college—and in the world—and each strives to create an arena where these issues can be heard and discussed. This holds true academically; students and faculty are both heavily involved in the educational process, and classrooms really are open forums for the discussion and exchange of ideas. And in the college community, representatives from the student body, the faculty, the staff, and administration are all present on committees that determine everything from the college's academic policies to its budget to its future investment plans.

The people who make up this arena are a varied group, whose backgrounds and talents also help create Carleton's unique atmosphere. Despite its size, Carleton manages to draw a very diverse student body and faculty. Its 1707 students hail from all 50 states and 17 foreign countries. Most of them graduated at or near the top of their high school class, but they really are distinguished by their outside accomplishments.

> *"I lived down the hall from a friend for two years before I learned that she not only played left wing on the women's first string varsity soccer team, she also played first clarinet in the orchestra. When I went to one of her concerts, I spotted my Greek professor on the bassoon. It seems everyone here participates in many diverse activities."*

Carleton attracts and cultivates the Renaissance student, and in true liberal arts fashion, it seeks to broaden a student's horizons both inside and outside the classroom. Academically, students must digest a well-balanced diet of courses selected from a wide variety of departments. In the extracurricular realm, students also have full schedules with all of the artistic, athletic, political, and social activities that Carleton has to offer—plus a few of their own. Carleton's size allows for participation in plenty of activities, and students take advantage of it.

On the surface, one hardly would guess that Carleton is a primarily academic school. If students are so involved *extra*curricularly, when do students find time for curriculars? They do their share of studying...and then some. However, Carleton's academic program calls for more than a variety of learning, it calls for depth of learning as well. Classes are rigorous, and the demands made on students are many—both from the faculty and the students themselves. This makes for a very intense academic environment.

Fortunately, this intensity is balanced by a supportive community and a respect for the seriousness with which students apply themselves to their endeavors. In fact, there are several places to find stress relief, such as the dean of students' office, your resident assistant—an upperclass student dormitory supervisor, a peer counselor—an upperclass student minority adviser, or even the professor who gave you all the stress in the first place. He or she probably will be glad to talk over any assignment with you. And of course, there's always a student at the next study carrel in the library who will be more than happy to swap stress stories with you over a cup of coffee at Sayles Hill Campus Center.

Another intensity beater is the campus itself. Carleton's physical plant ranks among the finest in beauty. There are more than 55 buildings spread over 900 acres, and each edifice possesses it own unique architectural style. The main campus overflows into a 400-acre arboretum, which is part of the college and is filled with ski and jog trails, open fields, and endless flora and fauna. Did I say ski? Sorry, it just slipped out. Yes, Minnesota does get its share of snow and sub-zero temperatures. But the sun shines almost every day, and besides, where else can you go skating 24 hours a day on the outdoor rink in the middle of campus? Or grab a cafeteria tray and go sledding (or traying) down Evans Hill? The weather really can be a source of fun, and believe it or not, the snow melts by March or early April, and we have a genuine spring season, fully equipped with ultimate Frisbee games, outdoor classes, and lots of mosquitoes.

For those who brave the cold and the relative obscurity of the school's name, Carleton can be a gold mine of opportunity to explore, challenge oneself, and meet an extraordinary community of people. Carleton draws from the nation's best students, throws them together in a scenic and invigorating environment, and then lets them run free. In this way, students are pushed by their classmates and professors to extend the boundaries of their limitations and abilities, and thus to discover the rewards of a first-rate liberal arts program.

GETTING IN/FINANCIAL AID

Being accepted into Carleton is by no means an easy feat. In a recent class, only 57% of 2782 applicants were admitted. About 88% were in the top fifth of their high school classes, and to add to that, there are more National Merit scholars at Carleton (94 in the most recent freshman class) than at any other undergraduate institution of its kind. Statistics, however, do not make up the student body. The Carleton admissions staff takes great pains to create a diverse and unique freshman class. They look past the alphabet soup of GPAs, SATs, and ACTs. A student's academic record is considered carefully, but so are those other achievements, activities, and experiences that shape his/her life.

> *"I remember talking with my roommate about our admissions experiences. I had done everything by the book—sent in exactly what the application required and no more. She told me she sent in writing samples that had appeared in her school's literary magazine and a local newspaper. Another floormate said that he had made a tape of his solos in community choir. I realized later, after working in the Carleton admissions office as a tour guide/ office assistant, that the admissions officers really appreciate the extra materials; it helps them to get to know the people behind the applications."*

Through the grueling admissions process, which includes three separate readings of each file plus a personal interview, the admissions staff has created a current undergraduate student body of 872 men and 844 women, of whom 14% are minorities and 3% are international students. The geographic distribution is as follows: 20% from the East, 16% from the West, 8% from the South, and 54% from the Midwest. Their interests and intellectual pursuits are as diverse as their geographic distribution—from the Montana-born biology major who organized the intramural badminton tournament, to the English major from Chicago who composed and staged his own musical in the experimental theater, to the political science major from New York City who co-coordinated Northfield's "Take Back the Night" march and rally.

Carleton operates on a need-blind admissions policy, so there are no financial barriers to admission. And with the help of a fair financial aid system, there aren't too many barriers to matriculation. It is not inexpensive to attend Carleton College, but the financial aid office does try to match a family's need. Approximately 64% of Carleton students receive some form of financial assistance, and through Carleton grants, scholarships, loans, and work-study programs, it is usually possible for any student who so desires to afford a Carleton education.

The work-study option is quite popular on campus. About 88% of the students hold some type of campus job. As a freshman, your employment is assigned, and it's just luck whether you end up as a cafeteria worker or a library assistant. But after a few weeks on campus, you find out how to secure a cushier position, such as a gallery monitor or a lifeguard at one of the pools. Because the majority of students work eight to ten hours per week, there is no stigma attached to campus employment. Plus, it's a great place to gain some practical experience; many students work as lab assistants, tutors, and computer monitors, which can beef up a résumé nicely. (You'll have something concrete to show for your four-year liberal arts degree.)

Financially needy students should not be scared off by that five-figured number ($19,620) called tuition, printed in the admissions literature. If you're good enough to be accepted into the school, Carleton will do all it can to help you enroll.

ACADEMIC ENVIRONMENT

"Carleton College as a whole is committed to the integration of knowledge and to the pursuit of order, balance, and breadth in its academic programs," states the immortal Carleton Viewbook. In other words, the college fosters a broad liberal arts education, where students learn not what to think, but *how* to think.

The college operates on a trimester system, which provides for an interesting schedule. Students take an average of three courses per term, each term being ten weeks long. There is an unusually long break between fall and winter trimesters (from Thanksgiving through New Year's), allowing students to enjoy a long vacation to use for travel, a career internship, or just to relax at home for the holidays. But while *on* campus, the academic schedule and environment are intense. Students may have fewer classes here than at a semester school, but a semester's worth of work is packed into ten weeks. With a student-to-faculty ratio of 12 to one, students have the opportunity (and the responsibility) of working in an informal manner, where classroom participation is the norm. Students lead discussions, design and present elaborate research projects, and read and write more pages than probably is healthy. Students also must take certain courses to round out the educational experience. Distribution requirements are as follows: two courses in humanities, two courses in arts and literature, three courses in social sciences, and three courses in natural sciences, plus four terms of physical education. There are also foreign language and writing requirements. Most students are able to complete this list within two years without sacrificing any of their first choices—because most of the courses lie in disciplines that they would have chosen anyway. Many of the requirements can be fulfilled with credits from AP exams or through placement testing during Freshman Week. Once students choose a major, they must take a minimum of seven six-credit courses in their field, plus they must complete a comprehensive exercise (affectionately called comps), which entails a year-long written and/or oral integrative project.

> *"Comps was one of the most difficult—and rewarding—things I've ever done. During the countless hours of research on the intertwinings of myth and character in the plays of Euripides, I finally came to the conclusion that I had no conclusions. I wanted to kick and scream and give up entirely. But my adviser pushed me to dig deeper. After many more hours in the library and several rewrites, I handed in a piece and gave an oral presentation that I was proud of. Dreaded though it is by nearly every Carleton senior, comps really does hone your academic skills to their most effective core, and challenges you to reach beyond your previous standards of achievement."*

Because comps can be so time-consuming, it is difficult to double-major at Carleton. Those who accomplish it usually finish one set of comps during their junior year. Most students opt for a single major with a concentration in another area. With more than 30 majors and 12 concentrations, plus an option for designing your own major, it's not hard to find a course of study that's right for you. Some of the more popular majors are English, history, political science, economics, and the sciences.

Even with all the academic requirements, more than 65% of students spend at least one term on an off-campus program. Carleton itself offers some 15 overseas programs, taught and supervised by Carleton professors. These programs range from seminars on economics in Cambridge, to international relations in Geneva, to sociology and anthropology in Nepal. Carleton also allows students to participate in study-abroad programs from other schools, so there's no limit to where students can study. Carleton encourages students to take part in off-campus study, and I strongly recommend that students grab the opportunity.

> *"During my senior year I spent a term in London. After the program ended, I had the chance to backpack for a month through Europe. I remember once standing in front of a painting in the Vatican and realizing that I had written a paper on it a year ago*

in an art history class. Seeing the original work in its original setting was an overwhelming experience, but the fact that I was applying my knowledge from Carleton to the real world—to this painting—was an even greater one. I came home with a truer appreciation of my education and a better perspective on Carleton."

One of Carleton's greatest academic assets is its faculty. About 96% of the 157 members hold the highest degree in their fields. But they are more than well trained, they are devoted to teaching. They know they are dealing with serious students, so they try to design their courses to be not only challenging, but stimulating as well. They often allow their students to shape the academic pattern of their classes, and many of them act as supervisors for students' self-assigned independent studies. The faculty generally are very accessible, and they have a vested interest in their student's progress. They stay after class to answer questions or continue an important discussion, or they extend their office hours to work around a student's schedule. They even invite students to their homes for class or just for coffee and doughnuts.

"At the end of spring term my freshman year, my Roman Satire professor held our last class at his house, from five to seven in the evening. As the party went on I found myself sitting with my professor and four classics majors on the porch, throwing awful Latin puns across the room at breakneck speed. It was nine o'clock before any of us realized what time it was. To this day that professor stops and chats with me whenever I see him on campus—and he always has a bad classics joke to share."

The faculty are not the only teachers on campus. Although it does not have teaching assistants, Carleton does have a terrific tutoring system, made up of student tutors in every department, plus two major centers for math and writing: the Math Skills Center and the Write Place. In addition, there are two computer centers on campus, one of which is open 24 hours, that house four large VAXs, three micro VAXs, and over 450 personal computers. The library contains 460,000 volumes, and through a system called minitex, students have access to materials at the University of Minnesota library. The science facilities house two electron microscopes, a superconducting FT NMR spectrometer, plus a 16-inch visual refractor telescope—all of which are unusual for a school of Carleton's size and help to make Carleton's science program one of the strongest in the country among undergraduate institutions.

The top-notch facilities, faculty, and students themselves all help to make the academic experience at Carleton rich, challenging, and unforgettable. I may have been pushed to limits I never thought I could or would have to reach, but the depths of learning to which it exposed me are invaluable. Carleton claims to train its students to think independently, openly, and analytically. Talk to any Carleton student and you'll find that it fulfills this mission admirably.

SOCIAL LIFE

Because there are no fraternities, sororities, eating clubs, and no all-freshman dorms—in fact very little distinction between classes at all—there are few social barriers to break through at Carleton. Students can mix and mingle in various different crowds and social situations with ease. Carls shudder at the mention of those traditional college pastimes: the frat parties, the football cheering squads, the hazing, and the homecoming courts. They are proud of their antiestablishment attitudes, not only towards the traditional social institutions of college life, but towards many traditional political and economic institutions as well. Some would accuse us of having no school spirit. But students would rather sacrifice spirit in order to maintain Carleton's open social atmosphere.

So where can you go in this open social atmosphere for a good time? The main student events organization on campus, the Carleton COOP, provides many weekend activities, such as dances in the campus center, with entertainment by professional bands imported from Minneapolis/St. Paul. They also sponsor Wednesday night coffee hours and campus movies—two popular films each weekend, plus a midweek foreign or special interest film. In addition to COOP events, there are countless student activities happening on campus every day, from theater productions, to concerts, to art shows. Carleton also brings in culture from the outside world through a weekly lecture series called Convocation. Every Friday, the entire school schedule is rearranged around an hour period in the morning so that everyone who wants to can attend. Past convo speakers include radio personality and writer Garrison Keillor, Colorado congresswoman Patricia Schroeder, playwright Wendy Wasserstein, and anthropologist Richard Leakey, to name just a few. And because Carleton's tuition includes activity fees, all of these events are free to the entire Carleton community.

For those who enjoy the hanging out type of social life, there are plenty of places to satisfy those desires. Sayles Hill Campus Center is open until one in the morning for students to stop by and pick up their mail, lounge at the tables on the main level or on the comfy couches upstairs, to enjoy a bite to eat at the snack bar, or to play a little Ping-Pong in the game room. It's the busiest place on campus; if you're looking for a place to waste some time or shoot the breeze, you can't help but find a friend at Sayles.

Students who prefer to hang out off campus will find comfort in the intimate Northfield establishments, such as the Reub or Grundy's Bar and Grill for the rowdier crowd, and Hattie's or Treats for students who enjoy a quiet cup of gourmet coffee or a great deli sandwich. If you're short on cash, take a walk over to Dacie Moses's house for some homemade cookies. The house was left to the college by Dacie herself, who asked that it always be kept well-stocked with cookies and ingredients for students to drop in to bake or eat.

For those who like an even bigger environment in which to enjoy themselves, Carleton provides three daily buses that make the 50-minute trip to the Twin Cities. The buses make several stops around the two towns, where students can take in the delights of the big city, such as the Guthrie Theater, the Walker Arts Center, or the Metrodome—home of the Twins and the Vikings. Most students would agree that you don't have to leave town in order to have fun. Usually it's just the opposite—you don't want to leave because there's too much to do *on* campus. Still, it's nice to know the option is there. You can always escape for a day or a weekend for a change of pace.

At the risk of sounding clichéd, Carleton really does offer the best of both worlds—plenty of small town charm with easy access to a huge metropolitan area. Add to that the many activities happening right on campus and you'll find you have very few dull evenings at Carleton.

EXTRACURRICULAR ACTIVITIES

"My parents used to call me up worrying that I was trying to do too much, that one of these days I was going to burn myself out. 'Don't worry,' I'd tell them, 'I never let my academics interfere with my extracurricular activities.' I was only half joking."

The extracurricular offerings at Carleton are as many and diverse as the students who attend the college. About 35% of students participate in one or more intercollegiate sports. Men's varsity sports include football, soccer, cross country, basketball, swimming, wrestling, indoor and outdoor track, tennis, golf, and downhill and cross-country skiing. Women's sports include tennis, volleyball, basketball, cross country, indoor and outdoor track, swimming, soccer, softball, and downhill and cross-country skiing. Although Carleton is not known specifically for its athletics, its athletes excel both at the conference and national Division III levels.

If you want to participate in a sport without the serious competition, there are many alternatives to varsity teams. There are club teams that compete intercollegiately, but are run by students. Some such clubs are the men's and women's ultimate Frisbee teams, women's field hockey and lacrosse, and men's volleyball and water polo. By far the most popular sports activity is intramurals. In addition to the more traditional games like intramural basketball or volleyball, Carleton also has a few of its own unique sports: Rottblatt—essentially a student/faculty softball league named after a forgotten White Sox pitcher, and broomball—a form of ice hockey played in tennis shoes, using brooms for sticks and a rubber ball for a puck. Finally, if you don't want any type of organized physical activity, you can exercise on your own time at either the West Gym, at Cowling Recreation Center, or at Laird Stadium. Between them there are two pools, two weight rooms, several exercycles, racquetball/squash courts, 12 tennis courts, and a dance studio.

Carleton students also are very involved in the arts. There are two theaters on campus—the 460-seat Arena Theater, and the smaller 100-seat experimental theater in Nourse Hall. The Players, the mainstream campus drama group, produces about five faculty-directed plays each year, whereas the Experimental Theater Board (ETB), run entirely by students, puts on 15–20 productions a year, including a full-scale student musical and productions by the Black Dramatic Arts Group. ETB accepts proposals from students for their own dramatic ventures, and because there is no formal theater major, anyone who wants to can produce, direct, design, or act in a show.

Music groups are also popular. Singers can get involved with the 100-member chapel choir or the 32-member Chamber Singers who perform everything from sacred choral works to Gilbert and Sullivan operettas. In addition there are two popular *a capella* octets—the Knights and Knightingales. Both perform all over campus, around town, and on tour. Instrumentalists can join the Carleton orchestra, the jazz band, or any of the other small student ensembles. Dancers have a home in either Kalochoros or Ebony II. Both specialize in modern dance and both hold concerts that almost exclusively are choreographed by students. There are also various campus rock bands that spring up all the time. They usually get a chance to show their stuff at Mai Fete, a spring festival where student bands play nonstop all day out on an island on one of the lakes in the arboretum.

Music is provided in other ways besides live performances; a large amount of students are disc jockeys on the student-run AM/FM radio station KRLX. Other communicative extracurriculars include the *Carletonian,* the weekly student newspaper; the *Algol,* the college yearbook; plus various literary magazines, such as *Manuscript* for prose, poetry, and art, and *The Observer* and *The Bull Moose Journal*, two magazines discussing student views on controversial and political issues.

For those with an itch for political or public service, there's the Carleton Student Association Senate, which governs and allocates the budget for most student activities, the Minnesota Public Interest Research Group (MPIRG), plus several community service organizations, such as Acting in the Community Together (ACT), and Volunteers for Youth. There are too many more special interest groups to name here, from religious organizations to multi-ethnic support groups, but I can guarantee there's something for everyone. And if you can't find the specific group you're looking for—create it yourself. There is plenty of room for new and different clubs on campus.

> *"During my sophomore year a friend approached me about starting up an improvisational comedy troupe. I thought it was a terrific idea, but we weren't sure if we could make it successful We advertised in the Noon News Bulletin (a one-page flier announcing all campus activities for the week) and got a good response. We began rehearsing and, with the support of the students and staff, 'Cujokra' has become one of the major campus attractions."*

RESIDENCE LIFE

Some people don't need to join an outside activity to fill their time; there's always something to do right at home in the dorm. Floor life is practically an extra-curricular activity in itself. Every floor of every dorm has its own character, its own spirit. Some of them are extremely close-knit—they even print up their own T-shirts. Floors plan parties, organize intramural teams, and hold weekly study breaks where they discuss campus issues or just relax in the floor lounge. Ninety-three percent of students live in campus housing, which includes nine large residence halls (approximately 200 students in each) and several off-campus and special interest houses. All are located within a few blocks from campus. With the exception of one all-male and one all-female floor, all campus dorms are coed, and almost all of them house a sampling of students from each class. Most students live in doubles or triples, but a fair amount of singles are available for upperclassmen, as well as a few quads, quints, and sextets scattered about the campus. Freshmen are assigned their rooms and roommates, but after the first year, students can choose their living companions, and by an infamous lottery system, choose their living spaces.

There are some apartments available in Northfield, that many seniors (and a few juniors) can rent with permission from the housing office. However, Carleton guarantees housing all four years to every student, so there's no pressure to find a place off campus. There are four dining halls on campus, and students may eat at any one of them, regardless of where they live. Although few college food services are ideal, Carleton's does try to provide a good variety of dishes, including a vegetarian entree, plus a fully stocked salad bar at every meal.

No matter where you choose to spend your time, life outside the classroom is hectic, to say the least. The difficulty will not come from *how* to get involved, but with *what* activities to become involved. It isn't often in a person's life that he or she is confronted with so many stimulating activities, in such a convenient location. Believe me, Carleton students are the first ones to take the fullest advantage of it.

GRADUATES

At first, the thought of leaving a place like Carleton is a bit scary. Liberal arts schools are notorious for preparing you for everything and nothing at the same time. And although there are no doors closed to you upon graduating, it usually takes some time to figure out what kind of job or profession you want to pursue and to get used to the new parameters of the outside world. But no matter where its graduates want to go, Carleton will not leave them to sink or swim alone in the world. There is a very active alumni network that strives to tighten the bonds between graduates and the college. There are 40 alumni clubs throughout the country, and they hold all sorts of events to bring past Carls together, from holiday gatherings, to dinners with visiting Carleton staff, to career guidance sessions. All of them are great places to meet graduates from different classes, employed in a variety of fields. Past Carls usually are very willing to help out a recent graduate in the world of job hunting. Another good source for career guidance is the Career Center. This campus office helps students prepare for the real world by providing everything from research materials on postgraduate programs to seminars on job interviews and résumé preparation.

Approximately 75% of students attend some form of graduate or professional program within five years of graduating, and they tend to be in the areas of law, business, medicine, social services, and education. Many alumni have worked their way into some pretty high-powered positions, such as a United States foreign ambassador, or a news anchor and correspondent for a major television network.

One strange phenomenon of Carleton graduates is their ability to find one another—even years after they graduate. Large groups of Carleton grads can be found living in close quarters in several metropolitan areas. In Minneapolis/St. Paul this group is referred to jokingly as the Carleton Ghetto because so many grads have found it a comfortable place to settle. More and more of these Carleton clusters are popping up in other major cities throughout the country. In addition, there is a very high marriage rate among Carleton graduates, and quite a large number of children of graduates who have attended or are currently attending the college. These facts are just proof that the Carleton experience runs deep and lasts far beyond the walls of the campus.

SUMMARY OVERVIEW

Carleton offers students an exacting yet stimulating education in an open-minded and supportive environment. This environment is provided directly by the people on campus and indirectly by the wholesome and warm qualities of the Midwest. Carleton also offers a faculty that is committed to teaching and is accessible outside the classroom for student inquiries, discussions, or just plain friendly conversation. There is also a wealth of extracurricular activities at Carleton that allows students to discover and/or develop their multitude of talents. Because of Carleton's small size, students can participate heavily in both their education and their outside activities. They also can get involved with groups that help shape the present and future policies of the school.

At the best of times, students can take advantage of all this while maintaining a healthy balance between work and play. At the worst of times, students pile on too much and tip their emotional and physical scales. Although Carleton encourages and promotes the well-roundedness of its undergraduates, some students often overextend themselves in both their academic and extracurricular pursuits, thus turning the campus into a pressure cooker. But as individuals go through Carleton, they learn how to monitor their intensity and find that all the brilliant accomplishments in the world won't make up for a neglected body and soul.

If there's any other reason to complain about the school, it's that it creates an idealistic environment that rarely exists in everyday society. The time spent at Carleton, though unique and intense, doesn't last forever, and sometimes Carls have difficulty facing the reality of a less than perfect world. However, most Carls do very well at adapting themselves to the life beyond the Ivory Tower and go on to become extremely successful in their chosen fields.

No matter how far those graduates go, the spirit of Carleton never dies in them. It continues to be called home by its students long after they've left the place, because their years on campus instilled in them a celebration of diversity and individual thinking, plus a belief that the education they received there will take them wherever they want to go. Any Carl will tell you that it's not just a belief, it's a reality.

Becky Biegelsen, B.A.

Carnegie Mellon University

THE PROGRAM

Arriving at Carnegie Mellon's campus is an experience analogous to the school itself. Because it is nestled in its own corner on the periphery of Pittsburgh, there is no warning that you are approaching the campus. Suddenly, you are there—surrounded by old and new academic buildings, residence halls, grassy areas, and students.

Similarly, Carnegie Mellon's aura of academic excellence sneaks up on its students and visitors alike. But it doesn't take long to realize that this is an intensely dedicated and fiercely competitive university. Renowned in certain circles for its computer science and engineering curriculums, recognized in the art world for its fine arts and drama programs, Carnegie Mellon as an entity is not yet a household word in most parts of the country. Graduates are just as likely to receive "Carnegie what?" as an impressed and knowing nod in response to their alma mater's name.

But with each graduating class spreading the work in the academic and corporate worlds, and increasing recognition being given to the work of faculty members and researchers, this private and diverse school of approximately 4300 undergraduate and 2500 graduate students is becoming the university of choice for students looking for a challenging and dynamic education.

> *"It wasn't until the middle of freshman orientation that I realized that Carnegie Mellon was truly a high-caliber school. My entire class—all 1200 of us—were assembled, and those who were valedictorians of their high school class were asked to stand. I was expecting a handful, maybe a hundred, but was not prepared for the hundreds of freshmen who responded. That's when I knew—the students here would be as eager to learn and as accepting of the challenges presented to them as I was. What a stimulating feeling!"*

Carnegie Mellon has undergone several transformations—as well as name changes—since steel magnate Andrew Carnegie founded the Carnegie Technical Schools at the turn of the century. An established national university has grown from the small Pittsburgh-focused trade school, but one thing has undoubtedly remained unchanged: Carnegie Mellon University remains true to its founder's belief that innovation is the basis of excellence; education essential for knowledge.

The university is divided into the Carnegie Institute of Technology (CIT), the College of Fine Arts (CFA), the College of Humanities and Social Sciences (H&SS), the Mellon College of Science (MCS) undergraduate colleges, the Graduate School of Industrial Administration (GSIA), the H. John Heinz III School of Public Policy and Management, and the School of Computer Science. Each class is divided almost equally among the four undergraduate colleges—a few more in CIT, fewer in CFA. Within each college, students choose specific majors, such as civil engineering, biology, or graphic design. All are four-year programs with the exception of architecture, which requires five years.

One of the most frequent questions people have asked when they hear I'm a Carnegie Mellon graduate is, "Did you have to buy a computer?" Part of the university's renown is thanks to its early involvement in the computer revolution. On some level—whether it be simply using the machine or learning how to program or mastering computer drafting—computers are a part of all course curricula at Carnegie Mellon: fine arts as much as electrical engineering, English as much as architecture.

Although the idea often is bandied about, there is no mandate that students must purchase a computer. Healthy discounts at the campus computer store do encourage students to do so on their own and every dormitory room is equipped with the wiring that allows students with computers in their rooms to hook into the mainframe computer system. Twelve computer clusters are available all over campus and many are open 24 hours a day.

Carnegie Mellon's involvement in the computer revolution is indicative of the university. This is a school with its eye on the future—progressive, academically charged, encouraging of individual innovation. Founder Andrew Carnegie was always looking for a better, more efficient, more economical way of doing things; he would be proud of the progress his school is making in the computer revolution.

There is no typical Carnegie Mellon student: 4300 undergraduates hail from 50 states and 77 foreign countries. Drama students, electrical engineers, literary and cultural studies majors...their course work is as varied as their outlooks on life, and they make an exciting and interesting group. One shared trait brings them together—a commitment to personal excellence and to accomplishing goals. They are innovators.

Carnegie Mellon offers great opportunities and challenges, but it is only realistic to accept that it is not the ideal school for everyone. Some colleges encourage students to dabble in a variety of courses, to experiment before deciding upon a major, or even to create a self-defined major. Although some of these options are available, Carnegie Mellon's programs are more focused with specific choices within course work. Transferring between colleges can be difficult—although possible—and changing majors may delay a student's graduation date.

Carnegie Mellon once marketed itself as the professional choice—a slogan that perfectly describes its students, who are eager to apply their knowledge to the outside world. For the most part, the student body is very driven. Students know what they want out of life and how they are going to get it. Because Carnegie Mellon offers a wealth of educational opportunities, there is a perfect blend between hard-working students and a great university.

GETTING IN/FINANCIAL AID

"Brochures and speeches by admissions counselors are informative, but they can't show what a school is really like. The final factor in my decision to attend Carnegie Mellon was sleeping bag weekend. The admissions office invited me to visit the school overnight—it was a chance to talk to real students and to determine if Carnegie Mellon was the school for me. We 'baggers' roomed with current students on campus, attended classes, ate meals in the cafeteria. The weekend allowed me to truly experience Carnegie Mellon, and convinced me that I'd fit in there. That trip made a lasting impression on me. In my high school, being serious about your schoolwork meant being labeled a grind. But on that weekend visit to Carnegie Mellon, I saw students who excelled at their classes and were still lots of fun. I mean, we stayed up until all hours that Sunday night joking and discussing Plato's Republic. *And maybe that sounds hopelessly boring, but I had a blast! That weekend, I knew I had found a place where I could discuss my ideas and form my own opinions. I made my decision to attend Carnegie Mellon the day I returned home."*

Like its student body, Carnegie Mellon is eclectic. Its engineering and science programs often are compared to those of Cornell, Stanford, and Emory. The arts programs are outstanding, boasting famous alumni such as Ted Danson of "Cheers," Stephen Bochco, the creator of "L.A. Law," and artist Andy Warhol. Astronaut Judith Resnik also held a degree from Carnegie Mellon, and graduates serve as chairmen, presidents, and executives at many Fortune 500 companies. The liberal arts program's professional emphasis and strong base in analytical skills makes it a unique and practical choice.

The school is competitive in admissions. About 60% of the approximately 8600 applicants are accepted; those who enter comprise a class of about 1150. The male/female ratio for the entire university is 67/33; there are considerably fewer females in the engineering and science colleges. Nearly 7% of the student body is international; the percentage of minority students is a bit higher, with support groups and special services existing to assist these students.

Admissions officials look for different traits according to the applicant's potential major: engineering and science applicants should have strong math and science aptitude; liberal arts applicants are encouraged to have a well-rounded course load with an emphasis on written skills; fine arts students should have some experience in their chosen curriculum.

The school places a heavy emphasis on getting to know its applicants personally. Campus visits and interviews are encouraged, as is attending a sleeping bag weekend. Area programs offered in various parts of the country and visits with alumni are also good ways for you to become familiar with the school.

Approximately half of the admissions decision is based on high school performance—grades, challenging course load, and involvement in extracurricular activities. Another 20% comes from standardized testing (i.e., SAT I or ACT and SAT II scores), whereas the remainder of the decision is determined by personal essays on the application, recommendations, and the applicant's personal involvement with Carnegie Mellon (campus visit, interview). The latter is often the deciding factor in the big decision.

Carnegie Mellon is evolving to find its niche in academia. Its start as a technical school, relatively short history (having been founded in this century), and its location (some people think of Pittsburgh as a steel town, rather than as a high technology capital), mean that Carnegie Mellon doesn't immediately top most lists of prestigious universities, although it consistently ranks in the top 25. The school's emphasis on innovation is its greatest tradition.

There may not be ivy on the walls of Baker Hall, but the level of intellectualism and seriousness of Carnegie Mellon's students give MIT and Cornell a run for their money. And as the years go on, the university seems to be striving for more of an association with the schools farther north—in recent years, Carnegie Mellon University's nickname changed from CMU to Carnegie Mellon, and its logo was revamped.

Carnegie Mellon's tuition is comparable to the Ivy League's price tags. The cost of tuition for the current academic year is $16,000. Room, board, and other incidentals bring the total estimate to $22,760. With a price tag like that, some financial aid is a necessity for many applicants. About 65% of all undergraduates receive financial aid (scholarship and grant assistance). The average grant award is about $12,000.

Traditionally, freshmen receive financial aid packages—combinations of different types of financial support. These can include scholarships, grants, loans, and work-study employment. The school subscribes to the self-help concept that education is an investment that students and parents ought to have a financial stake in. Therefore, part of a student's aid package undoubtedly will include work-study and loans. The work-study amount specified in a student's aid package usually includes expected summer earnings. In most cases, students are not encouraged to work more than 10 to 15 hours per week.

There is a great variety of on-campus student jobs. Positions in the libraries, departmental offices, and child-care facilities, and as faculty assistants are most popular. Late night and early morning assignments are available to residence hall desk attendants and food service workers, among others. Job openings are posted biweekly by the financial aid office. More skilled positions are available to upper-classmen, who are more qualified having completed a significant portion of their course work. Positions as teaching assistants, research associates, and resident assistants are excellent résumé builders and can lead to summer or postgraduate employment.

ACADEMIC ENVIRONMENT

"I breezed through my freshman year, but with sophomore year came statistics class—and trouble. It seemed that the harder I tried, the worse things got. Finally, I asked my professor for help. We met one-on-one three times each week for the rest of the semester. The work still wasn't easy, but I struggled through. I was more proud of the C I earned in that class than my other—higher— grades! But I learned more than just analysis of variance from that professor. I found that if I put my mind to it, I could accomplish anything. And that confidence made the next two years a lot easier. Carnegie Mellon taught me more than just facts. And that after all is what a good university should do."

The academic program is as much about innovative thinking and exploration as it is specific subject matter or facts and formulas. By integrating technical courses with liberal arts courses (a Carnegie Mellon combination dating back to the 1930s), the university encourages students to develop a good mix between the cultural and intellectual enrichment of liberal education and the career preparation of professional education. This translates into a rigorous and demanding program. But the result—a student body of independent thinkers—is well worth the extra work.

"I didn't truly appreciate what Carnegie Mellon teaches until I'd graduated and started working. That's when I realized—the courses I took focused on developing problem-solving skills, rather than memorizing details with limited applications. I'm confident that I can tackle whatever may come up; with creative thinking and innovative solutions I can adapt to numerous work situations. My education has liberated me to look for the back door entrance, and to believe that I'm equipped to find it."

The curriculum for each department, and each major, varies. However, the average academic load across departments is similar, between 45 and 54 units per semester. (Units are approximately equivalent to the hours per week required for that course.) This is fairly accurate, give or take 10 hours of class preparation time.

Because of the diverse focuses and requirements of the four undergraduate colleges within the university, the following discussion includes a profile of each of the colleges.

Carnegie Institute of Technology (CIT) houses a variety of engineering options, biomedical, chemical, civil, electrical and computer, engineering and public policy, and materials sciences and engineering. CIT is very similar to the Mellon College of Science (MCS), which is comprised of biological sciences, chemistry, math/computer science, and physics.

During a student's freshman year, both CIT and MCS require a core curriculum of math, science, and computer programming, and liberal arts courses. Students declare their majors at the end of freshman year, and begin their specific major course work in the fall of sophomore year. A concentration in liberal or fine arts is also required, and specific course sequences are offered.

The normal course load — five classes per semester — means that most students spend their evenings doing homework — reading assignments, problem sets, assigned papers, and projects. Most students split their weekends — half the time in social and extracurricular activities, the other half spent preparing for the week. Don't be surprised to see the libraries crowded on weekend afternoons, but they empty out considerably later in the day. Time management is an important lesson, and most students strike a balance early in their years between working and playing at Carnegie Mellon.

Another lesson to be learned at Carnegie Mellon is that grades count. Students joke that when they enter as freshmen, the questions are, "Where are you from? What's your major?" These soon are replaced by, "What grade did you get? What was your GPA last semester?"

As graduating seniors, the pressure moves to, "Who offered you a job? What is the starting salary?" In such an intellectually charged environment, competition runs rampant. However, this is friendly competition, because working as a group — especially in the science, engineering, and arts-related majors — is absolutely necessary for survival.

Introductory and general classes are taught in a lecture format (no larger than 250 students) with smaller recitations (20 to 30 students). The male-to-female ratio in CIT and MCS is more imbalanced than in the other colleges, but this is improving as more females are encouraged to pursue careers in the sciences.

"After hearing so many horror stories from older friends at other universities about lecture halls so large that they were equipped with TV monitors just so the students could see the professor, I was a bit fearful of my first college class. Coming from a high school that graduates only 100 students each year, a graduating class of 1200 seemed huge to me. All of my worrying was for nothing—the largest lecture hall at Carnegie Mellon holds only 250

students. And even in classes of this size (which are broken down into small classroom-size recitation sections once each week), the professors make an effort to get to know as many students as possible. My physics professor actually required that each student in his classes stop by during his office hours, and when I ran into him in the nearby shopping district of Squirrel Hill, he not only recognized me but remembered my name! The same cannot be said about all Carnegie Mellon professors—but it's true more often than not."

Students in the College of Humanities and Social Sciences (H&SS) do not officially declare their majors until the middle of sophomore year. Prior to this time, they take courses in a core curriculum that includes each of the humanities departments, as well as science and computer programming classes.

Of the eight departments within H&SS, many have focuses that are nontraditional for a liberal arts program. Again, this reflects the professional, application bias of Carnegie Mellon—this is not a find-yourself school. Economics offers two majors: economics and managerial economics, which is appropriate for students planning to pursue advanced professional education. The English department offers five majors: professional writing, technical writing, creative writing, rhetoric, and literary and cultural studies. The history department offers social and applied history degrees, and the philosophy department combines tradition with an emphasis on logic, computational linguistics, and the philosophy of social science.

Psychology is cognitive-focused, examining biological, social sciences, and behavioral analysis. The social and decision science department is empirically based and methodological and offers four majors: social and decision sciences, political science information and decision sciences, and policy and management. The other H&SS departments are modern languages and statistics.

The department of industrial management, through the Graduate School of Industrial Administration, offers a junior and senior program for students who are interested in preparing for management through a broad educational base. Students are admitted to this program in their sophomore year, thus spending their first two years gaining a broad core base. Industrial management (IM) majors may choose concentrations in marketing, production or finance, or a major in graphic communications management.

Students are provided with a solid background in each department, which is excellent preparation for graduate school. But, as the professional liberal choice, all departments keep practical application foremost in the curriculum. Theory and practice are melded together in an ideal way.

The College of Fine Arts is the first school of total art, administered and guided by a single philosophy, in the Western world. Under one roof, the school combines architecture, art, design, drama, and music. The department of architecture's program requires five years and is multidisciplinary, encompassing art, engineering, management, history, and design. The art program offers concentrations in drawing, painting, and printmaking; sculpture; installation and site work; and electronic and time-based work. Through the design department, students can specialize in either graphic or industrial design. Drama (students in this major are affectionately called dramats) includes options in acting, music theater, production, directing, and design. The music department considers itself the best of two worlds—a conservatory in a university setting. The performance-based program combines diverse musical experience with academic opportunity. A music teacher certification program requires an additional year.

Each of the four colleges is very different, attracting students with individual interests and talents. Through the core curriculum, course concentrations outside a student's major, double majors, and extracurricular activities, the colleges are able to capitalize on their diversity.

> *"Senior year, three graphic design students, one electrical engineer, and a physics major took the same literature course I did. Like most of the English courses, this one revolved around discussion of the novels we read. But I think that the composite of the class made a big difference. My stereotypes took a nosedive the day the engineer vividly described how moved he was by John Updike's* Rabbit, Run. *And I never paid particular attention to color in a book until one of the designers pointed out how it correlated with the protagonist's mood. Exposure to such a variety of opinions changed the way I now read—and think of others."*

SOCIAL LIFE

"We work hard and we play hard" is the typical description of the social life at this school where students are serious about their work and, in many cases, just as serious about their fun. Myth often depicts students here as geeks or grunts—noses forever in a book or, worst yet, Saturday nights spent in one of the campus's dozen computer clusters. And although you'd be hard pressed to find a student who hasn't—at some point in his/her college career—spent at least part of a weekend in front of a computer screen, the stereotype is not typical of Carnegie Mellon's majority.

> *"I think the difference between Carnegie Mellon and other universities—and even high school—is that the social life here doesn't just happen. You have to make an effort to meet people and to get involved. Opportunities don't just fall into your lap, but once you start looking you'll find as many ways to relax and have a good time at Carnegie Mellon as at any other school. It's easy to say, 'I don't have time to join a club; I can't go to the movies—I have a test on Monday.' Time becomes a precious*

commodity, and I often found myself weighing the benefits: join-
ing Student Dormitory Council versus participating in Greek
Sing. Too many choices; too little time."

Because of the dedicated nature of the student body, socializing per se is restricted to weekend nights. But schoolwork itself can be an opportunity for socializing—without working together, many problem sets are next to impossible; in the wee hours of the morning, it is not unusual to hear jokes being told in the computer room or to see study groups enjoying a pizza break. The secret that Carnegie Mellon students have discovered is that having fun isn't reserved for out-side of class—it's an all-the-time thing related to course work and to enjoying what you're doing.

Weekend socializing revolves for the most part around the Greek organizations. Approximately 30% of the student body are members of fraternities or sororities, but parties during fall rush are open to all of the campus, and attended by many. During the rest of the year, parties are restricted to guest lists. At all times, alcohol consumption is limited to those over the age of twenty-one—a rule that increas-ingly is enforced by the students themselves.

Scotland Yard, Carnegie Mellon's student-operated pub, is another great place for socializing. Its finger foods menu (nachos, veggies, and great desserts) and non-alcoholic blender drinks are a refreshing change from cafeteria food. Entertain-ment ranges from a wide-screen TV during the week to student bands and entertainers on the weekends. A masquerade party and the Sexy Body Parts Contest are perennial favorites. On-campus movies are shown four nights per week, and a variety of speakers, comedians, and musicians perform throughout each semester.

The residence halls also offer a change of pace for students. The housing office strives to provide activities that are cultural, educational, and just plain social. From half-price tickets to the Pittsburgh Symphony to make-your-own-ice-cream-sundaes in the dorm lounge, or even an AIDS awareness discussion, residence life offers more than just a bed to sleep in and a place to study.

Situated on 103 acres and next to Schenley Park, Carnegie Mellon certainly has the space for socializing. But a study a few years ago on the quality of student life at the school indicated that better facilities—namely a university center that incorpo-rated club offices and athletic facilities, socializing space, and cafeterias—were needed. Already, the campuses now include a new residence hall and a dining and stadium complex. The fund-raising process is still underway for a new University Center.

But what if students want to get away from campus? Within walking distance of Carnegie Mellon is Oakland, home to the University of Pittsburgh. Although sepa-rated by good-natured animosity (Carnegie Mellon students refer to Pitt's massive Cathedral of Learning as the Tower of Ignorance), they often visit the fast-food restaurants and shops surrounding Pitt. In opposite directions but still within walk-ing distance, Squirrel Hill and Shadyside also offer repose from campus life. All three of these areas are rich with apartments and houses to rent—an option many upperclassmen pursue.

Downtown Pittsburgh, with its breathtaking entrance and beautiful skyline, is easily accessible—the 15-minute bus ride costs only $1—and offers department stores and shops, restaurants, and a variety of cultural activities. No longer the smoky city of the steel era, Pittsburgh—with thanks to Carnegie Mellon and Pitt—rapidly is becoming a high technology capital. Recently touted as one of Rand McNally's "Most Livable Cities," Pittsburgh combines big city conveniences with small town friendliness and affordability.

Like most things at Carnegie Mellon, social life ultimately depends on the individual student's desires and initiative. Often, students who spend little time going out do so by choice. Such a diverse student body, reflecting so many different interests and opinions, certainly has a lot to offer.

EXTRACURRICULAR ACTIVITIES

"It didn't take long for my husband (also a Carnegie Mellon graduate) to arrive at this conclusion: 'If all I do in college is go to class and do homework, I'll miss out on an awful lot.' He joined a fraternity and became a photographer for The Tartan. *And when it came time to put together a résumé, his grades weren't the dean's list quality that many companies look for, but his list of activities showed future employers that this was a student who had enjoyed college immensely, made a lot of friends, and most importantly, learned how to interact with people.* Tartan *staff meetings showed him how to be a leader, which is essential for project leaders in his field. Being a resident assistant taught him to organize his time and balance responsibilities simultaneously—that's crucial in the professional world. And the time spent at the fraternity? He will have those friends and memories forever."*

To one student, being involved extracurricularly may mean joining an honor society that meets twice a semester. To another, involvement could translate into countless hours spent tracking down a story for the school paper, or comparing experiences with fellow minority students. Involvement might take the form of a religious discussion group, intramural football, or varsity soccer.

In any group of almost 7000 people, interests are bound to vary. Carnegie Mellon is no exception, and this diversity is reflected in more than 100 organizations, athletic teams, and discussion groups. From the Student Dormitory Council, with representatives from each residence hall, to the gay and lesbian club, vocalizing an alternative viewpoint; from Student Senate to the Ultimate Frisbee Club; and including the Kiltie Band, Society of Women Engineers, and 19 Greek organizations, there is a group for practically everyone to call his or her own. Some are larger than others or require a greater time commitment — this variety allows a better fit with individual student's desires.

For students who have an interest in drama, but are not theater majors, there is Scotch n' Soda, an amateur group that puts on two shows a year. It was a Scotch n' Soda member who wrote *Godspell*; the group also claims *Pippin*'s playwright among its former members. For those whose tastes run to the literary, the school newspaper has a monthly insert for fiction, poetry, and design; there is also an annual literary magazine. Intramural sports—from football, basketball, and softball to darts and chess—are very popular at Carnegie Mellon, because they offer athletic involvement and enjoyment without a great time commitment. Teams range from fraternity brothers to students on the same dormitory floor in the same classes. Carnegie Mellon is a member of the University Athletic Association (competing against schools such as Emory and University of Chicago) for varsity athletics.

Students also spend their time helping the Pittsburgh community. Members of the Carnegie Mellon chapter of Big Brothers/Big Sisters spend their free time with disadvantaged children; Alpha Phi Omega, a coed service fraternity, is involved in numerous projects from raising money for the needy to producing and distributing a campus phone directory. And many Greek organizations, clubs, and honor societies pitch in—from organizing a campus recycling program to tutoring children to raising funds for community programs.

In the event that a student finds the extracurricular scene lacking, the chartering of new organizations is encouraged. That's how an alternate student newspaper, the student pub, the cycling club, and the rowing team—and countless other great ideas—got started.

Carnegie Mellon's extracurricular activities and social life reach their peak during one spring weekend: Spring Carnival. The three-day festival features game booths constructed by student organizations, musicians, and carnival rides. But the highlight of Carnival is the unique to Carnegie Mellon sweepstakes buggy races. The racecourse is on the peripheries of campus and Schenley Park, its ups and downs provided by the naturally hilly Pittsburgh terrain. Buggies—powered by five-person push teams who shove the buggies uphill—are only five feet long and inches from the ground. Inside them, small females (the smaller the better) steer around curves at speeds of 35–40 mph. The competition is stiff, pitting independent groups, fraternities, and sororities against one another for the honor of being racecourse champion. Spring Carnival is *the* event at Carnegie Mellon, attracting alumni like no homecoming celebration ever will.

GRADUATES

" 'You don't really appreciate Carnegie Mellon until you're away from it' my friends and I have concluded. It wasn't until six

months after graduation—in the throes of my first job—that I really appreciated the problem-solving skills I had gained in my computer programming course. Although I'm still convinced that no boss will ever ask me to write a Pascal program, I realize that it taught me to approach problems more logically and to look for innovative solutions.

"The other thing that I took for granted while at Carnegie Mellon was the camaraderie of the student body. While on campus, we had our cliques and our groups, but in the real world I look forward to meeting other Carnegie Mellon graduates. I felt proud when the person next to me at a restaurant noticed my Carnegie Mellon wristwatch and struck up a conversation, and although she was a fine arts major and I was a writer, we shared a common thread, a laugh about Spring Carnival. Episodes like that make up for the man who stopped me in Disney World when I was wearing an (outdated) CMU T-shirt and asked me if I also went to Central Michigan University. Perhaps he too was looking to share his CMU experience, just as I am always looking for fellow Carnegie Mellon alumni."

Carnegie Mellon's nearly 46,000 alumni are sprinkled across the globe. Those in the United States are linked together by clans—alumni organizations located in key cities. The 38 area clans organize alumni dinners and happy hours, lectures and seminars, as well as social outings and bowling leagues. They also can provide assistance to an alumnus or alumna relocating to a new city.

Presently, the alumni office is putting into place an alumni network that will link graduates to established alumni in a specific field or geographic area. This will be an enormous asset in alumni job searches.

However, the Carnegie Mellon job placement rate already is quite high. The Career Services and Placement Office (CSP), which provided career assistance to students, estimates that more than 75% of each graduating class accepts a position within six months of commencement, and nearly 22% proceed to full-time graduate school.

A large portion of these students began their job searches at the CSP office, attending sessions on career decision making, résumé writing, and interview skills. In a recent year, they participated in 7500 on-campus interviews with the 460 potential employers who visited Carnegie Mellon. Only 10–15% of the companies represented were Pittsburgh based—a fact that demonstrates Carnegie Mellon's growing national prominence.

The majority of employers who visit Carnegie Mellon are looking for technical, scientific, or business-focused students. They represent a mixture of business and industry—manufacturing, retail, finance, insurance, scientific, and government—which excludes many H&SS and CFA students. Unfortunately, positions of the type these students are looking for usually are not filled through recruiting efforts. However, the CSP makes an effort to train students in the art of auditioning and portfolio presentation, and offers assistance with independent job searches. A direct referral service in the CSP matches registered students with employers who have job openings but are not recruiting. This service led to 500 interviews.

Believing that practical job experience leads graduates to a more successful job search, the CSP employs a full-time career counselor to assist undergraduate students with internship, part-time, and summer job searches.

SUMMARY OVERVIEW

Carnegie Mellon's greatest strengths include its cutting edge academic programs, the intensity of the student body, and the diversity of students and faculty.

Nothing is more exciting than attending a class where the professor describes the latest discovery in that field—from firsthand experience. Because faculty members are required to spend a portion of their time doing research or publishing, Carnegie Mellon students often are privy to the latest advances in science or the most modern theories in liberal arts. Students sometimes have the opportunity to work as faculty research assistants, which provides valuable work experience.

The intensity of Carnegie Mellon's student body is one of its most stimulating attributes. Here is a university where the students truly want to learn and experience new things. Although their majors and interests may differ, the students all share that desire for knowledge. Sure, they like to go to parties and football games, but they also have a great time learning new things.

The diversity of interests and backgrounds of the student body is another great thing about Carnegie Mellon. Here is a school with engineers, graphic designers, mathematicians, and historians at the same university. They hail from all corners of the world, and have varying backgrounds and talents. As much learning takes place outside the classroom as does inside.

The diversity of the student body and faculty also tops the list of Carnegie Mellon's weaknesses. The school does not do enough to encourage the different colleges within the university to work together. As students get more involved in their majors, there is less time to spend with the students outside their majors. Exceptions to this rule—such as the Physics of Music class, which brings science and art together, or the human relations workshops, noncredit classes, which encourage students to look beyond stereotypes—serve as hopeful signs of the university's future.

Similarly, there is not enough faculty/student interaction on campus. To truly learn, students need to see their professors as people, not just lecturers. With research requirements on top of their teaching responsibilities, many faculty members find themselves backed into a corner without enough hours in the day.

And finally, Carnegie Mellon remains a school that helps those who help themselves. This is not a liberal arts, find yourself university. Instead, it provides a strong education and a firm background for those looking toward the future. Although it is not easy to switch majors or transfer between colleges, Carnegie Mellon does build confidence in its students, showing them that they are capable of achieving great innovations.

Would I do it differently if I could? Without question, I would attend Carnegie Mellon in a heartbeat. I believe that it provided me with an outstanding education that has no comparison. This is a university whose time is just approaching. Rather than being steeped in tradition, it is making headway into the future — a future I am proud to be a part of.

Natalie Capone Gillespie, B.A.

Claremont McKenna College

THE PROGRAM

Tradition. It seems to go part and parcel with a description of the country's most selective colleges. Tradition means a storied past, a glorious future, and instant credibility. It also means a huge endowment, a buzzing network of high-level alumni eager to hire new graduates, and the comforting thought that you will never be asked where you went to college more than once. Collegiate tradition is an established heritage to join, a proud history waiting for your chapter...normally. Claremont McKenna College's tradition, however, is something being created right now. Although the school's history is already distinguished, it is perhaps the youngest top school in the nation. Because of this actively developing tradition, CMC students participate daily in something their contemporaries at other top-ranked colleges and universities can only read about in dusty old yearbooks.

The Claremont McKenna experience is an intensely personal one. As at other schools, your formal education begins at Freshman Orientation and ends at graduation with a handshake from the school president; what separates CMC from those other schools are all the handshakes you make in between.

> "'Read Wouk's The Caine Mutiny for next week's class.' Our literature professor called it an assignment, but to my freshman ears it rang more like a pronouncement of doom. For a single upcoming two-hour seminar, I had been sentenced to digest a novel of over 1000 pages in only seven days. That night, as I resignedly pushed back the book's cover, I grumbled that God had it easier the week He created the universe.
>
> "Because my other professors had maliciously assigned their normal work loads, I lugged Wouk's substantial paperback everywhere I went—so I could sneak in page chunks during bathroom breaks and boring conversation.

"During the week, my initial anxiety over being able to intelligently discuss such a compendium of pages receded, building confidence that actually I knew what I was doing. Marathon sessions under a tree on Parents Field left me with a new appreciation for Wouk's dramatic irony, his subtle turn of phrase, his bitter symbolism—this was literature! Weary yet triumphant, I strode into the seminar and was promptly slammed into a brick wall by the prof's very first question, 'Who can tell me why this book is sloppy writing; what is its fatal flaw?'

"A week spent chained to this book, about 950 pages too long to be anything but a classic, and he wanted to know why it was lousy! My mind whirled with disbelieving frustration and homicidal fantasies. Worse still, I felt I had failed; after tasting of the Pierian Spring, I had really understood nothing. However, upon much reflection, I came to understand my professor's real lesson plan: that intellectual analysis begins by drawing a line between artifice and the artificer. Doing the reading, regardless of length, was only half the job because piercing analysis requires a stepping away from the text, extricating yourself from the author's plot, and seeing what's then laid out before you. Grand themes and symbolism, as well as Wouk's broken plot scheme, become apparent only to the eye looking for that line.

"Kindergartners know what many college freshmen have long forgotten—that learning begins with listening. It could be that being humbled is necessary to unclog the ears of a high school hotshot. Whatever the case, I look back on that class as the day my Claremont McKenna College education really began. It hasn't stopped since."

Although the college years are often a time of personal self-definition, CMC's size, faculty, resources, and educational philosophy are all geared to ensure that students' quest for personhood is accomplished as a cohesive group. Since Claremont McKenna College was established in 1946 as the third of five Claremont colleges, the group concept has been fundamental to CMC's very existence. Modeled after England's Oxford University and her famed tradition of multiple small colleges, The Claremont Colleges pool their individual resources to provide every student with the kind of facilities and course selection beyond the reach of any isolated single college.

Simultaneously, each Claremont College maintains its own faculty, students, and identity. CMC's academic identity is revealed in its Latin motto, *Crescit Cum Commercio Civitas* or "the City is built upon Commerce." Thus, the primary emphasis at CMC is on economics, political science, international relations, and public affairs. Critical to this academic environment is a unique relationship between teacher and student, rivaling the intellectual interaction of the Oxford tutorial system.

"When people ask me why I chose to attend Claremont McKenna College, my mind drifts back to my senior year at Pearl City High

School in Hawaii. A registered letter and a plane ticket arrived at my house, inviting me to compete with other top applicants for the inaugural McKenna Achievement Awards. The thought of being flown to California to convince a quorum of professors that I was more promising and/or brilliant than other top applicants from across the nation was more daunting than exciting. However, economic necessity is the wellspring of courage so I kissed my parents good-bye and headed up to sell myself to CMC.

"In terms of physical beauty, I was so taken aback by CMC's grandeur that I snapped a few pictures of what I later discovered was Scripps College. CMC's campus and buildings were nice but not spectacular. Even my lunch at Faculty House was nice but not spectacular. (Ever try to impress someone while trying to eat chicken? It requires a measure of social grace and physical dexterity which I do not possess.) However, I did discover something nice AND spectacular about CMC. It was a most obvious thing but perhaps not back then. 'It' was CMC's professors: The men and women I had fully expected to be grilling me, popping impossible questions, and frowning or scribbling at wrong answers instead proved to be the highlight of my experience. They made it clear that their interviews would be conducted as friendly, open discussions about life, dreams, and ambitions. I suppose we top applicants were theoretically competing but I was actually able to forget about that and enjoy my participation in the discussions.

"I was chosen to be one of the first McKenna Scholars so my initial impression of CMC could be positive because of that. But I don't think that's the reason. Beyond the boundaries of that single competition, what impressed me then about CMC is what impresses me still, the special attention, humanity, and intellectual respect shown to me by the professors of Claremont McKenna College."

CMC's educational philosophy of individuals working in concert toward a common end carries over to the social environment. Primarily because of the school's location and small size, CMC'ers form a close-knit, on-campus community. Thought-provoking classmates double as interesting dinner dates; the dormmate who caught your touchdown pass in intramural is also your "Bank Sim" (Theory and Practice of Commercial Banking) partner—all because the CMC environment ensures that socializing and academic work need not be mutually exclusive.

This sense of community is CMC's most valuable attribute. It is also necessary for enticing the college bound youth of the world to come out to Claremont, a sleepy little college town, which the *Los Angeles Times* once described as "Norman Rockwell, U.S.A." Claremont lies about 35 miles as the eastbound crow flies out of downtown Los Angeles, near the foothills of the San Gabriel Valley, an area where the Los Angeles smog tends to collect in its rough bowl shape. Far from Hollywood, Beverly Hills, Malibu beaches, and Disneyland, Claremont is not exactly a hotbed of California bright lights nightlife. For those students without a car, the word marooned pretty much says it all.

Thus, the numerous social and academic benefits of going to CMC stem almost entirely from the strength of the college's own internal community. The overall program is a microcosmic manifestation of The Claremont Colleges' colloquium, utilizing CMC's select group of students and faculty by pooling the particular talents of these individuals to generate a multifaceted resource of academic and social interaction for all.

GETTING IN/FINANCIAL AID

As at other selective schools, the admissions process at Claremont McKenna College attempts to attract and create a diverse student body while maintaining the college's high academic standards. The most fundamental criterion sought in CMC's student body, however, is best described by a gift made to CMC by its first four-year graduates, the Class of 1950. In the middle of campus lies Pacesetters Patio, barely adorned yet prominent in spirit. It represents one of the ways CMC forges an evolving tradition, recruiting students who can and want to meet the demands of a participatory education—the independent thinkers who also understand how to listen. The admissions office's primary charge is to identify these potential trailblazers.

> *"In hindsight, I must have looked pretty moronic, sitting there at the dinner table, mouth agape and eyes staring at nothing in particular. But I couldn't help it—the thrall of abrupt enlightenment held me motionless. The scene—eating dinner with my friends— was familiar, yet imminent graduation from CMC somehow altered my perspective. Looking around our table of chewing faces, inside jokes, and culinary commentary, I saw not only friends eating together for the umpteenth time, but young men and women of impressive character and achievement.*
>
> *"We came from homes in Repulse Bay, Hong Kong to Kansas City, Missouri, yet during our shared time at CMC we had extended these vistas by studying abroad in Moscow, Helsinki, Japan, and London. One friend planned to use his biology degree to help run a shipping firm in Taiwan, while another had decided to use hers to study Los Angeles water quality. Sitting next to them was a self-designed communications major heading for a teaching position in Israel. Immediate futures in marketing, investment banking, accounting, and law school beckoned the rest of us. How the admissions office could've used a photo of us, for that one table ran the gamut of diversity—*

wealthy to barely middle class, private school and public school, male and female, widely different majors with ethnicities from three continents and religions ranging from Christianity to agnosticism. But, diversity for its own sake is worthless—my sudden insight was that most CMC students are consciously aware of that fact. As different as CMC'ers are, the collegiate community we come to belong to encourages us to learn and grow from the inevitable collisions of perspective which occur in and out of class. Voicing personal beliefs takes guts but listening to, rather than just tolerating, other opinions takes even more intestinal fortitude. More than anything else, this is the common thread running throughout CMC's student body.

"And, we all know how to enjoy a fresh burrito, even when someone at the table chews with his mouth open."

Although CMC has no minimum SAT I score or high school GPA requirement, the admissions numbers game still rolls up some impressive figures: median SAT I scores of 610 verbal, 670 math with the middle 50% of the freshman class having combined SAT scores of 1170 to 1360; just under 90% of the most recent class ranked in the top 20% of their graduating classes (22 valedictorians); and only 38.4% (864 of 2066) of all applicants were accepted. In addition, although personal interviews are only recommended, a well-written personal essay is perhaps the essential component of a strong CMC application.

Beyond statistics, CMC distinguishes between applicants on an overall demonstration of leadership in high school and extracurricular activities, the personal initiative and energy involved in taking advanced placement or honors courses, and the interpersonal evaluation of the student painted by written recommendations. Although roughly half of CMC's student body hails from California, a more aggressive recruiting policy ensures that geographic diversity is a factor, as evidenced by recent freshmen from 38 states from Alaska to Hawaii and Washington to Washington, D.C.; and from foreign countries including Malaysia, Brazil, and Switzerland. Ethnic minorities like blacks (5%), Hispanics and Chicanos (11%) and Asian-Americans (13%) make up almost one-third of the student population. Women constitute about 47% of the total student body.

For those students CMC does admit, however, a concerted effort is made to bring the cost of a CMC education, hovering around $21,000 a year, within reason. Almost 75% of all CMC'ers receive some form of financial aid. A multitude of need-based scholarships is available, averaging about $12,000, from alumni or community sources, whereas the median student loan is around $2500. One-third of the CMC student body works on campus, most as part of a work-study package. Many find work in the Ath (Athenaeum campus center), whereas others sort mail, do computer consulting, fry burgers at the Hub student union, or keep the peace at either Frazee or Bauer reading rooms.

In addition, the top 75 freshman applicants (roughly) are flown out to Claremont from across the nation to compete for the 30 McKenna Achievement Awards.

Unlike most financial aid, these $10,000 scholarships are not need-based. Because the competition is held over a weekend in early March, applicants must have their forms completed by mid-January. After selection and enrollment, McKenna Scholars must then maintain a GPA in the upper half of their class and carry a minimum of three courses in a semester. McKenna Scholars suffer from none of the publicized overexposure such a program might have because the scholarship rewards high school achievement and college potential; there is no need to treat McKenna Scholars any differently from their equally talented classmates at CMC. But that money does come in handy at tuition time.

ACADEMIC ENVIRONMENT

CMC's total enrollment is roughly 850 students or about the size of a large state university dorm. For the individual CMC'er, this situation means that although CMC's Poppa Computer Lab offers use of 60 access terminals to the VAX 8200 mainframe, 30 IBM PS(2)'s, 30 Apple Macintoshes, and both dot-matrix and laser printing, the underlying research for papers typed out at Poppa lab must be done at the five-college Honnold Library because CMC does not support a full library on its campus.

Nonetheless, small size is CMC's choice and its strength. CMC maintains a sparkling ten-to-one student-to-faculty ratio with the average class numbering 18 to 25 students. Yet as part of The Claremont Colleges consortium, CMC can offer its students the full range of courses, laboratories, libraries, Huntley Bookstore, and even the dining halls of the other four colleges (all literally across the street from each other). Because of the cluster's unique setup, the array of classes CMC students have to choose from rivals a university curriculum, yet each course is taught by a professor whose private college resources enabled him or her to develop a personalized course of study like The Russian Novel, Men and Masculinity, Holocaust Studies, Politics of Interest Groups, Fords, Flappers and Fanatics, or Theories of the Good Life.

Holding up these innovative electives is CMC's framework of general course requirements. This comprehensive program, encompassing the spectrum of academic disciplines from psychology to calculus, is designed to help students decide which wrinkle of the liberal arts universe to explore as a major course of study. Consequently, although about half of all CMC'ers include either economics or government in their majors, combining that with a totally unrelated field, like literature or philosophy, for a dual or double degree is more the norm than the exception. Adding to this melange of customized majors, CMC has also launched a number of nontraditional programs of study like a 3–2 management engineering degree with Stanford and other universities, a 3–3 program with

Columbia Law School, and the Oxford-born politics, philosophy, and economics (PPE) tutorial degree.

Academic involvement, however, also extends well outside the traditional classroom environment. About 50% of all CMC'ers spend at least half of their junior year studying off campus, in one of the 50 overseas programs available, in an exchange program at Haverford or Colby Colleges, or on Washington, D.C.'s internship on Capitol Hill, all for full CMC credit. In addition, all CMC majors are required to write a substantive senior thesis. The dreaded t-word (thesis) is a one-to-one research collaboration between you and the faculty adviser-reader of your choice. Whether it's a one or two semester thesis, this paradigm of scholarly pain and suffering is easily the most challenging of CMC's general requirements. If you can do this, you can do anything; CMC just forces you to prove it to yourself.

To further supplement student research experience, CMC supports no less than seven research institutes. From the Rose Institute of State and Local Government to the Lowe Institute of Political Economy to the Gould Center for Humanistic Studies, each institute generates original research and data under the direction of faculty members but entirely fueled by student fellows. Also, through CMC's participation in The Claremont Colleges Joint Science Center, professors recruit interested students for clinical work with a variety of subjects, from autistic children to military radar systems.

The flip side of having every avenue of involvement opened to you, however, is trying to find time to do it all. All Claremont professors grade on a 12.0 point scale, amplifying the impact of every single point earned or squandered through the semester. Making CMC's Dean's List for any given semester means maintaining a 10.0 average, whereas only the heights of an 11.0 GPA can qualify you as a Distinguished Scholar. A decided lack of grade inflation make these goals both worthwhile and stressful. Further, although cutthroat competitiveness among students is another collegiate tradition that CMC does not share in, the foreboding pit of academic probation awaiting those who fall below a cumulative 6.0 GPA can cause some very real stress. To make matters worse, there are times when the choking, hot weather smog, Claremont's strangely fizzy tap water, and the latest triple whammy meal from Collins dining hall amplify ordinary worries about impending paper deadlines and multiple midterms to a point of seeming hopelessness.

Recognizing this reality, CMC goes beyond the usual personal buffers of friends and phone calls to provide easy student access to academic, career, and professional counseling services. The Monsour Counseling Center, a five-college facility, provides a quiet haven for confidential advice on coping with life in general. Monsour also sponsors several self-help groups to help combat problems like eating disorders, shyness, and chronic depression. These groups hold both regular meetings and special presentations on campus for easy student access to their services.

In addition, every CMC freshman is paired up with a faculty adviser, usually not from your proposed or eventual major, who is basically your friend on the staff. Students are encouraged to talk about anything from course options to bad news about Grandma with these advisers. Most CMC'ers remain with the same faculty adviser throughout their four years, a little-recognized tribute to the personality and commitment CMC professors bring to their positions.

For more focused academic counseling CMC's English Resources Center (ERC) provides a staff of honor student and faculty tutors to help break through writer's block, listen to lines of fledgling poetry, or just proofread paper drafts. Another concrete example of CMC's evolving tradition, the ERC was created to serve both the student consumer's need for consistent constructive criticism in writing and to fill a previous dearth of practical student experience in literary critique. Because most CMC courses stress writing by resting most of your grade on it, the ERC can become a very valuable friend to have in your corner.

All this underscores the personal involvement that is the hallmark of a CMC education. Professors do not take attendance, but most classes are small enough for them to keep running brownie point totals for student tardiness or absence. Besides, because lectures are often built around class discussion, it's in the professor's best interest to have his or her students physically in the chairs fronting the lectern.

However, mere bodily attendance is never enough because CMC professors rely on student reactions—student perspectives—to complement their base lesson plan. Regardless of your major, doing the homework reading is often a matter of basic student survival. Whatever your present sleeping patterns are, during your CMC tour of duty, staying up late becomes an art form, be it to study or to grumble about studying. One quickly learns to appreciate the orchestrated beauty of a class schedule that begins at 11:00 A.M.

What turns this sweat, drudgery, and stress from work into a participatory education are the close relationships CMC's faculty members build with their students. Graduate students do not teach any classes or review sessions at CMC; in every case without exception, it is between you and the doctorate. Because of this, most CMC profs go far beyond the usual stale jokes and strained rapport of college lecturing and actually get to know their students as human beings.

This deceptively simple-looking process begins by professors talking to students in and out of class on a first-name basis. Most CMC professors readily accept spontaneous invitations to eat lunch with one or more students in Collins dining hall. Making an appointment to see a professor is a formality that most faculty members typically dispense with; the usual practice amounts to just stopping by with questions, comments, or news of the latest Dodgers' trade during their liberal office hours. It is not unusual for a professor to take advantage of the temperate Southern California climate and invigorate a sluggish after-lunch class by holding it in the shade of a tree overlooking Parents Field. Some professors will even reschedule classes at their homes, usually combining them with a backyard cookout or informal dinner. And, CMC's very own, very unique facility, the Athenaeum, provides an intimate forum for special events, distinguished guest lecturers, film viewings, and student presentations. During any given week, four or five class-related, professor-sponsored events will be going on at the Ath.

The Athenaeum is another bit of English/London tradition that CMC has borrowed to make a little history of its own. In comparison to CMC's Collins dining hall, the Ath and its food means finer dining, but it is infinitely more than that. Whereas any physical description of its four combination dining room/lounges and lobby would fail to do justice to their elegant charm, the Athenaeum's real beauty lies in its multifaceted purpose and personality. It is a comfortable haven for daily afternoon tea and conversation. A student-faculty advisory committee on academic policy can meet in a room next door to a literature class session speaking with a visiting author like John Irving, Ray Bradbury, or Joyce Carol Oates. Students and faculty exchange perspectives during regular meetings of the Women's Forum and the lighter-hearted Wordsworth Club. And in between bites of Black Forest cake, students engage in dinner conversation with as diverse a group of guest speakers as Vietnam veteran Ron Kovic, Cambodian survivor Dith Pran, Congresswoman Patricia Schroeder, business leaders Henry Kravis (CMC '67), and George Roberts (CMC '66), former Olympic volleyball star Karch Kiraly, or feminist psychologist-journalist Dr. Jean Kilbourne. CMC's Athenaeum is a single forum where one can listen to Dr. Allan Bloom discourse on the *Closing of the American Mind* a week after boxing promoter Don King proclaims that he "don't want no pie in the sky when I die, [but] something sound on the ground while I'm around." And of course, the Ath is the perfect setting for social events, hosting everything from ballroom dancing, medieval-style feasts (complete with choir, knaves, and wenches) and even the Hawaii Club's annual luau. In taking full advantage of the possibilities created by the vigorous interaction of talented students, faculty, and guest lectures, the Athenaeum provides a paradigm for CMC's merged model of intellectual energy in a cordial, social environment.

SOCIAL LIFE

Studying is the baseline behavior of the typical CMC'er during the week *and* on weekends, so, social involvement becomes a high priority item. From Friday night to Sunday afternoon parties are anything but scarce, be it a formally organized five-college bash like Monte Carlo Night, the dorm-sponsored revelry of the Boxer (shorts) Rebellion or the Night of Extremes, or one of countless impromptu get-togethers thrown in individual dormrooms. Despite the recent emergence of a stricter alcohol control policy, CMC's unofficial motto remains, "Bibo Ergo Sum" or "I drink, therefore I am." However, the party service, With A Twist, is rapidly building a following on campus by putting a dash of imagination into fruity "mocktails" like "Whiz-bangers" or "Pineapple smoothies." Additionally, the entirely student-run, all-volunteer Claremont Coffee House, held every Saturday evening at CMC's student union, the Hub, provides a tranquil haven to talk with friends and listen to fledgling jazz and folk entertainers. Coffee House is a nice, on-campus alternative for those who would rather socialize than party.

"During my sophomore year at CMC, a friend from high school stopped to see me. Giving him my usual 25-cent tour of the campus, we strolled from my dorm in south campus to the border of Pitzer College in the north, a grand total of about four blocks. While pointing out the names and anecdotes of various sites, we would stop to wave back to or chat with friends I had made over the past year. Upon returning to my dormroom, he said, much to my surprise, 'Wow, you're really popular.' Quizzically, I asked him to explain. He remarked that someone had called out to me at almost every building we passed. I chuckled, shrugged, and told him that that was probably more of a reflection of CMC than of my scintillating personality.

" 'I wish my school was like that,' he said.
Don't we all?"

Sororities, fraternities, and a wild Greek Row are neither existent nor necessary as social generators at CMC. In addition to the party scene, CMC is a residential college, so 98% of its student body lives on campus for all four years. Living, eating, and going to class together for that long almost destines students to get involved with each other. An old myth, perpetrated by other college guide books, is that CMC men still primarily date Scripps students from the north rather than go out with their female class/dormmates. This may have been true in the days right after CMC's decision to admit women in 1976, but reality paints a different picture in recent times. However, if you're going out with someone, expect everyone to know about it almost before you do. A small-town coziness pervades the campus, right down to the gossip.

Because of recent renovations and construction, the housing situation has improved, especially for women. The addition of spacious student apartments in south campus opened up a larger number of single rooms. Also, the rising number of women students is slowly resulting in a greater number of these singles being made available to female CMC'ers. Now, both men and women can generally obtain a single by junior year. Whether it's a double or a single, though, CMC's dorm rooms are large enough to personalize and seem designed to foster those philosophical three-o'clock-in-the-morning, sitting-on-the-floor-with-friends-and-a-pizza revelations.

EXTRACURRICULAR ACTIVITIES

A stranger is a hard thing to find at CMC because bountiful opportunities to get involved complement the school's comfortable size. In addition to *The CMC Forum*, a weekly campus newspaper, the *Collage*, a Five-College weekly, and the *Ayer* yearbook, CMC students write and produce various academic journals, compilations of original stories and poems (*Undercurrents*), and sundry other newsletters or handouts for campus social, service, or political organizations. Recent projects completed by Sova-East to gather and distribute canned foods to a nearby shelter for the homeless are but one example of how Claremont Colleges students involve themselves in the solution of pressing social problems.

Student political coalitions run the gamut from the Pink Triangles, a faction of the Gay and Lesbian Student Union, to the ruffled pretentiousness of the James Madison Society. Yes, to the surprise of no one, CMC'ers take their politics seriously. But, although CMC is often stereotyped as an academic fortress of conservativism, differing political ideologies often spark spirited debates among the Claremont community, between faculty members as well as students.

> *"The raucous cheering I heard coming from inside the dorm lounge piqued my curiosity. Through a picture window, I saw a crowd of students huddled around a big-screen TV. Going inside, I saw that the room had been divided into two relatively equal and certainly vocal factions, waving their arms and shouting support for their respective sides. Since it was the middle of football season, I naturally assumed it was some sort of televised game, albeit on a Wednesday night. Then I looked at the screen. To my amazement, the television broadcast that had this group of CMC'ers worked up into a rabid frenzy was one of the presidential debates. Politics never meant quite the same thing to me again."*

So, if political frenzy mimics sports fan mania, imagine what CMC athletics are like! As an NCAA Division III school, CMC offers no athletic scholarships yet has been a consistent, top-20 powerhouse in water polo, swimming, tennis, and soccer, with recent success in football and basketball. Regardless of relative rankings or records, the Battle for Sixth Street (any head-to-head competition between the Claremont-Mudd-Scripps Stags and the Pomona-Pitzer Sagehens) always generates high emotion and all-out effort for athletes and spectators alike. Club sports like lacrosse and floor hockey enjoy strong student participation, as does the ever-popular slate of intramural sports for us weekend warriors. Ducey Gym and adjoining Stag Field offer open use of Nautilus equipment, aerobics sessions, a jogging track, and even a boxing ring. Getting enough playing time in whatever sport you choose is never a problem at CMC. In fact, athletic participation is unavoidable because of CMC's general requirement of three physical education credits.

For students seeking less sweaty involvement, dean of students' advisory committees offer a personal inroad towards affecting school policy. Just as professors recruit students for work on academic research, CMC's deans and other staff are equally keen in seeking student viewpoints or utilizing student body energy on various administrative projects.

> *"As a freshman member of the Housing Committee, I helped germinate a set of plans for new student apartments. By the time I*

*was a senior, several of my friends were living in them—that's
progress. CMC's admissions office depends on us students to
recruit back home, lead campus tours, and host visiting students.
And, as a member of the food service committee, I collaborated
with our food service director to plan menus for the monthly special dinners which help break the monotony of Collins' everyday
bill of fare."*

And, besides making themselves generally accessible to students in their respective offices, CMC's deans also get involved in student life by pushing a coffee and
cookie cart around the dorms during finals week or working alongside the campus
maintenance crew for a day, complete with name tag and uniform.

Another avenue of student input is through CMC's influential student government. Intramural sports programs (like inner tube water polo), a student-run store,
and the Playbill weekly film series are all run through the Associated Students of
CMC. In addition, each of CMC's 12 dorms/student apartments, all coed, elects
dorm officers who become responsible for inventing reasons for dorm residents to
get to know each other. Such activities range from broomball, a particularly barbaric version of ice hockey; screw-your-roommate parties, where roomies set each
other up with either a dream or a nightmare; sloshball, a unique marriage of softball
and beer guzzling; and the charbroiled hamburgers and warm pickles of Friday
afternoon barbecues. Dormmates also frequently bond while dunking their classmates (and some faculty) into Flamson fountain on their birthdays—yet another
example of a daily developing tradition.

GRADUATES

Career development, both for summer jobs and permanent positions, is an
annoying demon that lurks at the back of every student's mind. CMC's Heggblade
Center is the on-campus repository for such worries and their solutions. Informa-
tional packets, résumé services, videotaped practice interviews, and plain ol' counseling and advice are all available to the confused job seeker. By virtue of CMC's
stated purpose to prepare students for careers in ethical leadership, most CMC graduates either head directly to graduate school or take a management job of some
kind with the intention of going to graduate school within five years. For example,
of the 223 graduates in a recent class, 10% went to law school, 8% to Ph.D. programs, 8% to medical school, 15% to MBA programs, and 4% to international relations programs. For that portion of the class that went job hunting, 98% were hired
within six months of graduation, at employers ranging from Big-6 accounting firms,
management consulting firms, banks, investment brokerages, federal and state government offices, and volunteer organizations like the Peace Corps.

CMC's reservoir of talent makes it a prime stop for both graduate school and employment recruiters. Further, CMC alumni generally are willing or even eager to employ current students as interns or new recruits; the networking system being as close-knit as any other aspect of CMC. Individual students, however, still need personal guidance to make the right connection: that is the Career Development Office's mission. The process is never easy but it's comforting that the counselors and staff of Heggblade Center, the people going to bat for you, actually know you as a person independent of your résumé.

SUMMARY OVERVIEW

The long and distinguished histories at most top schools in the country make finding a niche in the existing scheme of things, academic or social, a priority for their students. By comparison, the relative lack of revered tradition at Claremont McKenna College puts a premium on actively carving out a niche for yourself. The pioneer spirit of manifest destiny is a viable force because the emphasis is on building, rather than maintaining, CMC's reputation.

Literally a community in itself, CMC is best defined by the close interaction between its faculty members and their students. Professors and administrators associate students with names, faces, and personalities, instead of mere serial numbers. Cordial discussions over lunch or during a friendly volleyball game often replace the stuffy formality of an office appointment. Students work one-to-one with their professors on a variety of projects, ranging from independent studies, research institute assignments, joint publications in academic journals, and the universally required senior thesis. Largely because of the dedication and personality CMC professors pour into their positions, opportunities of student access are ready for the asking.

This kind of focused, personal attention is a necessary component of the CMC experience. As a member of The Claremont Colleges consortium, CMC can offer its students the availability of five college curriculums' worth of course choices as well as the signature compact class sizes of a small, private school. Professors generally demand a lot from their students, so studying is a constant and grade inflation virtually is nonexistent. However, busywork is equally scarce because most CMC profs also respect the intellectual prowess of their students. Course grades are based primarily on analytical and/or research papers so, like it or not, every CMC'er learns the art of effective written communication. Although this fact may not seem appealing on its face, the primacy of written reports, proposals, and memos in today's working world makes this aspect of a CMC education invaluable.

But a well-rounded college experience extends far beyond the boundaries of academics alone. CMC's comfortable size combines with a vigorous assemblage of faculty, students, and staff to form a community of open and creative involvement. CMC's numerous social, service, religious, and political organizations daily defy the contention that sororities and/or fraternities are integral to collegiate social life. Student viewpoints find ready outlets in campus news weeklies, bulletins, or periodic newsletters. An active student government controls a sizable treasury, sponsors a weekly film series, helps subsidize weekend parties, submits policy resolutions to the college administration, and runs the intramural sports program. At CMC, finding something to do is not an issue, it's finding time to do all you want to. Through this dilemma of abundance, all CMC'ers become schooled in the magic of time management.

Yet, the student who chooses to attend CMC becomes heir to a host of shortcomings as well. Most prominent is the annoying flip side to CMC's youth and lack of aged tradition. Although this opens a door of tremendous opportunity for any ambitious student, it also means that relatively few people have crossed over that threshold before you. CMC is rapidly building a name for itself, primarily through the achievements of its graduates, but even the most prominent alumni are themselves trying to establish that CMC'ers are just as capable as any Ivy Leaguer. Choosing CMC over its more established collegiate counterparts is tantamount to accepting a lifelong challenge—paving the way for a future generation of CMC'ers to enjoy instant credibility. For the present, CMC students and alumni must still endure some blank stares when asked where they go/went to college.

Although the Claremont cluster is quippingly described as the American Oxford, CMC's architecture does not inspire the slightest vision of a city of dreaming spires. CMC's tallest structures are the eight-story Auen and Fawcett residence halls. Although the squat cylinder of Bauer Center is indeed reminiscent of the Oxford Camera library, it was the practical need to house a firing range in its basement that influenced CMC's planners more than any aesthetic desire to provide an Oxfordian parallel. Recently, CMC has grown more attractive through a number of cosmetic renovations There's a four-tiered fountain where only a boring walkway lay before. The administration responded to calls for increased campus safety by installing new and brighter night lamps around the dorms and footpaths. Every dorm room is now carpeted, and just about every building got a fresh paint job. Even in light of these improvements, however, CMC's basic California contemporary layout will never rival the hammering first impression made by the campuses of other larger, older, and bigger institutions. The World War II origins of CMC dictated functional attractiveness over aesthetic beauty and that's the way it will remain.

Finally, the physical closeness of CMC's small-town community can make individual privacy a rarely enjoyed luxury. Dorm rooms generally become places for socializing rather than sanctuaries of solitude. Close neighbors and thin walls mandate that the best dormmates will be the ones who happen to share a particular taste in music. And, although the myth of "everyone knows everyone else" is definitely untrue for most CMC'ers, students almost have to sneak off to Honnold Library or a neighboring college campus to gain a measure of private thinking time. Whether you wish it or not, one's unexplained absence is always readily noticeable at CMC.

But, as CMC's famed economics department would say, the direct and subsidiary benefits of the CMC experience far outweigh any opportunity costs it may impose. For many students, the college years represent a quest to define one's personal identity. The overall program at CMC is designed to facilitate this process, with the idea that the best way to find yourself is to interact with as many people as you can. CMC purposely draws its professors and students into a close community with each other to encourage an exchange of their perspectives. Naturally, this participatory brand of education invites discussion and vocal disagreement, but although resolution may never be achieved, the individual awareness of both sides grows and the seeds of deeper general understanding will have been sown. CMC's educative group concept, the communal meshing of teacher and student, helps individuals realize, not who they are, but who they can be. The students of Claremont McKenna College discover that the search for personal identity should never end because the question "Who are you?" cannot and should not require the same answer every time.

Kenneth G. Lau, B.A.

College of William and Mary

THE PROGRAM

The College of William and Mary in Williamsburg, Virginia, is a school of firsts. It is the oldest public college in the United States. Its history dates back to 1693. Over the years, William and Mary has been responsible for the nation's first law school, the first system of elective studies, the first college honor code, and even the first national honor fraternity (Phi Beta Kappa). In fact, each of these firsts is still as important at William and Mary now as it was when its most illustrious graduate, Thomas Jefferson, studied in the same building that many students today still use. From its seventeenth- and eighteenth-century landmarks at one side of campus to the modern academic buildings and labs that spread across 1200 acres on the new campus, William and Mary has grown to offer its 5376 undergraduates a broad variety of opportunities in academics and extracurriculars.

William and Mary's educational foundation has always been a strong background in the liberal arts, social sciences, and natural sciences. Today, students are advised to sample some introductory courses from a wide variety of departments before deciding on a concentration (major) at the end of their sophomore year. Students are not discouraged from changing their concentration, and many students do, even during the second semester of their senior year!

"August, 1984. I'm confronted with the imposing sight of my first college registration. Needing to sign up for only one more course to balance out my schedule, which already has courses in math, biology, sociology, and economics, I step up to the English department's table. 'What's this ENG 211—The Study of Language all about?' I naively ask the professor. 'It's fantastic, I teach it!' he exclaims with a smile. Facing the first major decision of my college career, I ponder whether I should risk insulting him and take my registration card elsewhere or have him sign it and

go to lunch. Well, my stomach made the decision for me, and, I must say, the class turned out to be so interesting that I took another linguistics course and another. Then I decided to do a minor in linguistics, and finally, in my senior year, I took a few more courses to make linguistics my second concentration. I would never have discovered such a discipline had I not been encouraged by William and Mary's liberal arts requirements to explore new fields of study."

There are similar success stories told by those who discovered a subject they never dreamed of majoring in. William and Mary's very"liberal" liberal arts curriculum affords students a valuable opportunity to search out their true interests that might not have been uncovered in high school.

Needless to say, William and Mary students concentrate in every discipline offered. None of the college's 24 departments is window dressing to thicken the college catalog. Interdisciplinary majors are also possible, and a number of students do choose to construct their own concentration from existing courses in a number of different departments. The most popular majors (in order) are: English, government, biology, psychology, history, accounting, economics, international studies, and finance.

One reason every department at William and Mary can be considered the school's strongest department lies in the commitment of the faculty to the undergraduates. Although William and Mary is a university with half the departments offering advanced degrees, most of the faculty's time is devoted to the undergraduates who make up 80% of all students enrolled there. Not only do the professors teach all the classes, administer their own exams, conduct extra help sessions, and make themselves available to the students, but they also volunteer to serve as personal academic advisers to the incoming freshmen during their first two years as undecided majors.

The enthusiastic and personal academic atmosphere often gives the impression that William and Mary is a private institution; however, it is part of the Virginia state system with 30–40% of the students hailing from outside of the state and overseas. Therefore, William and Mary is definitely unique—a public university with all the charm and benefits of a medium-sized private college.

GETTING IN/FINANCIAL AID

"I must admit, I didn't put a great deal of time into my application to William and Mary. In fact, I copied an essay that I wrote for another school's application and mailed the whole mess in one day before the deadline. Somehow they accepted me, and I waited until April 29 to visit the campus for the first time (two

days before students are asked to send in their matriculating deposits). By that evening, I was convinced that William and Mary was the place for me. I left my deposit at the admissions office just as they were leaving for the day, and we canceled our last-minute trip to Duke. For the sanity of your parents as well as yourself, don't do this the way I did, unless colleges start offering advanced placement credits for Procrastination 101."

Statistics don't lie. William and Mary has become an extremely selective school recently. Applications for the freshman class have doubled over the past five years. Most recently, a total of 8169 students applied for an entering class of 1256 (766 of these were Virginia residents), and roughly two applicants were accepted for every available place in the freshman class. William and Mary's application process has changed recently in order to better evaluate the applicants. The application consists of two parts. Part 1 is just a data sheet, and Part 2 requires a list of extracurricular activities, employment experiences, and a response to two of four creative essay topics. The student is advised to submit Part 1 as soon as possible so that there is ample time for the admissions office to send out Part 2. The deadlines for Part 2 are November 15 for early decision and January 15 for regular decision.

"So how are admission decisions made?" you might ask. The admissions office equally weighs the following three categories in its decision-making process: standardized test scores, the strength of the high school curriculum and grades, and other personal information such as special talents and the essay responses. Interviews are not required and should be requested only if the student feels he or she needs to present information that is not expressed in the application. All applicants must take the dreaded SAT I; SAT II exams are optional but strongly recommended because they can strengthen an application. English composition with essay and foreign language achievements are advised because a good score on these will exempt the student from the college's writing and/or foreign language requirements (more on these academic requirements later).

Both Virginia and out-of-state areas are divided into regions, and the number of students accepted is proportional to the number of applicants from that region. William and Mary takes pride in the geographic diversity of the student body it has assembled from all over Virginia, every corner of the United States, and 31 foreign countries. Diversity is also seen in the various backgrounds of the students who enter William and Mary. For example, in a recent class, 10% were class valedictorian or salutatorian, 54% participated in band, orchestra, or chorus, and 23% were varsity athletic team captains. Essentially every student comes to William and Mary with some special talent.

Most of the William and Mary student body receive some sort of financial aid in terms of loans, scholarships, or employment. Because most of William and Mary's athletic programs are in the NCAA Division I, there are a number of athletic scholarships available also. Need-based funds from the college, the state, and the federal government are allocated based on the student's CSS-FAF form. This must be submitted by February 1. Additional employment opportunities are plentiful in Colonial Williamsburg, and the hours are flexible. There are not too many other places where you can earn money for dressing up like a Revolutionary soldier and loading cannons! Finally, the most obvious source of financial aid is that William and Mary's tuition is relatively inexpensive to begin with, compared to most schools similar in size, facilities, and reputation.

ACADEMIC ENVIRONMENT

One of William and Mary's greatest strengths is in its stimulating academic environment due to the breadth and depth of the academic opportunities, an accessible and dynamic faculty, and the liberal arts requirement, which can be fulfilled through a wide range of options. Basically, four requirements must be fulfilled in order to graduate. First, each student must take Writing 101 or pass a writing placement test given during orientation week. The writing requirement may also be fulfilled with a score of four or five on either AP English exam or by achieving a combined score of 1300 on the SAT verbal section and the English achievement test. By the way, credits and/or placement is available at William and Mary for every AP exam offered, so sign up for them. The second requirement is a minimum proficiency in a foreign language. This may be fulfilled by taking a four-semester sequence of courses in any classical or modern language at William and Mary. Taking four years of the same language in high school will exempt the student from the language requirement, and scores on both AP and achievement tests are considered for placement.

Third, and most enjoyable, every student must complete four semesters of physical education activity courses. These classes vary in exertion level from the relatively sedate (golf, bowling) to the active (competitive lacrosse, aerobics) to the exotic (white water canoeing, skiing in Canada, and windsurfing). The only hard part about completing the PE requirement is finding an open class for which to sign up.

Finally, the college's core requirement, better known as the area-sequence requirement, forces the student to explore a wide range of introductory courses. There are a few restrictions, but in a nutshell a minimum of 33 of the 120 credits required for graduation must be distributed among certain eligible courses in Area I (classical studies, comparative literature, dance, English, fine arts, modern languages, music, philosophy, religion, theater, and speech), Area II (anthropology, economics, government, history, psychology, and sociology), and Area III (biology, chemistry, computer science, geology, mathematics, and physics). No single course is required; therefore, the student is not *required* to take calculus if he or she would rather fulfill the Area III part of the requirement by taking courses in biology or geology. In addition, a sequence of four courses must be taken in one of the aforementioned departments outside the student's concentration. Although the student can fulfill these requirements anytime, these courses are usually taken during the first two years when students are shopping around for a concentration.

All of these requirements may seem awfully stringent, but there is plenty of time to complete them in addition to a concentration and still take lots of fun courses. No incoming freshman is asked to register for any courses until he or she arrives on campus and has had an opportunity to meet with a faculty adviser during orientation week. Then students are encouraged to keep in touch with their adviser during the first two years to make sure that the requirements are being fulfilled properly.

The participation of the faculty in the advising process is only one indication of their unfailing commitment to the William and Mary undergraduates. Every class is taught by a professor, and even in the science laboratory courses, which do utilize graduate students, the professor is ultimately in charge of the course and the grading. Every professor keeps office hours, and most even give out their home phone numbers.

> *"I couldn't believe it either. Sure, I had heard how forthcoming the faculty is, but I never thought I'd ever experience it. Well, after in-class Halloween and Christmas parties, after attending lectures and having dinner at three different professors' homes, and after receiving a call from a professor who just wanted to know how I did on a big project in a different class, I was convinced that the faculty really does care about the students. So, the moral of the story is 'get to know your professors' because at William and Mary, they want to get to know you."*

The academic atmosphere at William and Mary is really shaped by the constructive attitude of the faculty and the respect of the faculty for the students. The faculty is not out to trick the students and fail as many as possible although the grading is tough when compared to other colleges. But even with a low GPA, William and Mary students have enjoyed excellent placement in graduate and professional schools. These schools are aware that a B at William and Mary is worth more than a B at another institution where grade inflation has run rampant. Despite the grading scale, there is very little academic competition. The students very often study in groups, share textbooks and notes, and generally aid each other when preparing for an exam. Whatever academic pressure exists is usually self-imposed and is not a product of an overly demanding or ineffective faculty.

Classes can vary in size from one-on-one independent studies to large introductory lecture classes of 300 students. The student-to-faculty ratio is fourteen to one. Classes of some 15 students are seen in upper-level courses, usually taken during the junior and senior years. There are also a number of small introductory courses as well. For example, for Economics 101 and 102, students have the choice of six or seven smaller classes that meet at various times and days, or the student may sign up for the one large lecture class offered. The exams can follow a variety of formats from multiple choice to short essays to full-blown essay tests. The William and Mary Student Association publishes a course guidebook to help the student find the courses and professors best suited for his or her own preferences.

> *"Speaking of exams, my first one at William and Mary consisted of ten short-answer questions. That was no surprise. However, the surprise came when the professor said we could take our exam anywhere we wanted as long as we handed it in on time. He said he would be in his office if we had any questions and then left the room. For the first time in my life, I did not have to take an exam cramped up in a classroom while someone walked up and down the aisles watching us like a hawk. I knew William and Mary had an honor code, but I really thought it was all for show. Four take-home tests and two self-scheduled tests later, I realized that the honor code was no show, and it really made a difference in relieving a lot of the academic pressure that can needlessly drain college students."*

So important is the two-century-old honor code at William and Mary that a statement of commitment to it is printed on every application for admission. The honor code is enforced completely by the students. All decisions of innocence or guilt are made by a 16-member student honor council. The faculty's respect for the honor code results in such conveniences as self-scheduled exams, take-home exams, open stacks in the library, and academic buildings that are open 24 hours a day for student use.

SOCIAL LIFE/ EXTRACURRICULAR ACTIVITIES

> *"William and Mary students work hard, play hard, and are not afraid to try new things. When I arrived on campus, I never thought I would become a patron of the theater, a yearbook section editor, and an ace intramural hockey goaltender. There are plenty of fun things to do on campus and in the Williamsburg area when it's time to give the books a rest."*

To be perfectly honest, Williamsburg is definitely a tourist town first and a college town second, but that doesn't keep students from having fun both on campus and off. Whatever your preference, there is always something for you to get involved in at William and Mary. You just have to find it. Just a quick read of the weekly student newspaper *The Flat Hat,* and you will never miss anything that's going on.

In any event, during a given semester, there are a number of varied activities that take place across the campus. The Student Association regularly sponsors major concerts, band nights, comedians, guest speakers, and a popular weekend series of current and classic movies. If a little more culture is what you're after, William and Mary Theater, the chorus, choir, Orchesis (modern dance), band, orchestra, Premiere Theater (which features original student works), and the concert series, which brings distinguished professional artists to campus, all light up the theater in Phi Beta Kappa Hall throughout the semester.

On the lighter side, students frequently blow off some steam at the frequent fraternity parties (which can have some outrageous themes) and at the local delis. The fraternity parties are usually open to everyone except during the January rush period. With about 40% of the student body joining Greek organizations, fraternities and sororities are very active on campus but are certainly not dominant in the social scene. For those students craving a late snack and the chance to meet some friends, the delis across the street from campus are the popular choice. They can get very crowded even on weekdays, so it helps to get to know the deli owners to ensure getting in on those busy nights.

The residence halls at William and Mary are active to the extent that dorms, especially the freshman dorms, become their own fraternities and sororities. Each dormitory elects some if its residents to a dorm council, which organizes events such as parties, dances, cookouts, ice cream study breaks, and guest speakers. With 76% of the undergraduate student body living in campus housing, you usually don't have to look far to find something going on.

Besides the Colonial Williamsburg attractions, which are always free to William and Mary students, a popular local destination is the Busch Gardens theme park only five minutes away from campus. Many students purchase season passes to visit the park as often as they wish. Hampton (25 minutes away), Norfolk (60 minutes), and Virginia Beach (70 minutes) are popular destinations outside Williamsburg for their shopping, night life, and beaches. Finally, every May about one fourth of the student body makes the pilgrimage to Nags Head, North Carolina, for a week at the beach to celebrate the end of finals and say some last good-byes before the summer.

Athletics at William and Mary, either at the varsity club, or intramural level, are the most popular extracurricular activity. Over 80% of the students participate in one of the 25 intramural sports (including the ever-popular coed inner-tube water polo), 16 club sports, or 23 intercollegiate varsity teams. In fact, William and Mary has the most extensive athletic program in the state of Virginia, and one of the most successful in the nation in terms of the graduation rate of the athletes, as well as winning percentage.

There are also those unique happenings that stand out in every student's memory of their time spent at William and Mary. One of these events is the annual Yule Log Ceremony, held on a Saturday evening during final exam week in December. For this occasion, the entire college community suspends their activities of concluding another semester, and all gather together in the chilling night air at the Wren Building courtyard. The William and Mary Choir commences the ceremony with a program of Christmas carols, followed by the college president's reading of a special William and Mary version of *'Twas The Night Before Christmas*. Then everyone feeds the yule log flame with a sprig of holly before enjoying hot apple cider and gingerbread cookies. It's just another thing that shows that being a student at William and Mary is really more like being a part of a friendly, close-knit community than being just another student ID number on everyone's computer.

RESIDENCE LIFE

About half of the learning that goes on in college takes place away from the classrooms and libraries. This learning comes in the daily trials and tribulations of living on your own and living with a roommate for the first time. The residence life at William and Mary allows the best possible environment for this learning with its supply of quality dormitories on campus that house all the freshmen and 85% of all undergraduates. Most of the campus housing is coed dormitories, which are sociably arranged into large "halls." The rooms are mostly doubles, but there are some singles, apartments, and suites, occupied mostly by seniors. Freshmen are all housed in exclusively freshman dorms and are assigned roommates on the basis of an extensive roommate preference questionnaire. After freshman year, students can enter the housing lottery to remain in college housing. Because the seniors get all the best housing numbers, followed by the juniors, the sophomores have to choose from what's left over, which usually isn't all that bad.

> *"After freshman year, fearing a bad lottery number, I decided to get an apartment about a mile off campus. To be honest, that was the worst decision I made during my four years in college. Oh, the apartment was nice and comfortable, but everything else that I took for granted freshman year was gone. Gone was the opportunity to walk down the hall and bang on doors until I found someone to order a pizza with. Gone were the late-night gatherings in the lounge to watch* Letterman. *Gone were the potential lifelong friends you can make simply by living in such close proximity to so many of your peers. Gone was the ability to roll out of bed and walk (eh...stumble) to class in the morning. Needless to say, I moved back onto campus for my last two years because at William and Mary, if you don't live on campus, you miss out on half of the education and most of the fun."*

Each hall in each dorm has an upperclass resident assistant who lives on the hall and helps to plan many of the activities and administer the rules and regulations of the dormitory, which are drawn up by the residents. This policy of the residents both creating and enforcing their own rules is called "self-determination" and has long been part of the residence life at William and Mary. The residents can determine what hours the dorm will be quiet, during what hours the dorm should be placed on a card-key access lock-up system, and even how to divide up the storage space in the kitchens. Like the honor code, this system of self-government in the dorms works mainly because the students respect the system and each other's ability to carry it out.

Ok, you're still probably interested in William and Mary because you've read this far, but here comes the bad news—the food. There are only two places to eat on campus, and both are often very crowded during the prime lunch and dinner times, which, if anything, makes for quite a social hour. One cafeteria serves all-you-can-eat fare, whereas the other offers more variety but allows you only a set amount of credit toward the meal, so add up those prices carefully! A third cafeteria opened this year in the new University Center. Freshmen are required to take a full meal plan, whereas some reduced meal plans are available to those upperclassmen who desire to stay on at least a partial meal plan for ten or 15 meals per week. On the bright side, the food service is improving gradually, and it now stacks up with any average college food service. The upperclass dorms have larger kitchen facilities, so it's not unlikely to find students in the same dorm forming supper clubs. The sororities also have supper clubs open for anyone to join, and the nearby delis offer some alternatives to the college's food service.

GRADUATES

"Before I began interviewing at medical schools across the country, I made sure to be prepared to explain everything about William and Mary, assuming nobody would know about where I came from. To my surprise, I never needed to explain anything to anyone during my interviews. The interviewers were all aware that William and Mary is a top school on a national scale."

William and Mary, being a liberal arts institution with no true vocational-based majors, could be quite aloof about preparing students for the real world, but nothing could be further from the truth. Essentially there is no stereotypical path that the average William and Mary student takes after graduation. History has dictated that William and Mary graduates are prepared to take on any challenge, anywhere. Many graduates even successfully pursue fields outside their college major.

The Office of Career Services makes an aggressive effort to alert students to all the possible career opportunities available with a William and Mary education by sponsoring career days, guest speakers, and a number of informative newsletters. The office prepares students for job or professional school interviews, and many major business, scientific, government, and public service firms travel to campus annually to recruit students. Most William and Mary students move on to complete advanced degrees, but many usually work for one to five years first. This is a direct indication of the high quality jobs that a William and Mary graduate is able to attract right out of college. Although William and Mary has no preprofessional majors, it has a tremendous record of placing students into the most competitive business, law, and medical schools. In fact, one dean of a major medical school in Virginia sums up the opinion most people have of a William and Mary education: "I'm disappointed when we get only a few applications from William and Mary students. They are, by far, the best prepared students we have, year after year."

SUMMARY OVERVIEW

William and Mary is certainly a unique college even when compared with other prestigious institutions. The college's three major features are its relatively small size, its place in the Virginia state system, and its broad liberal arts curriculum. From these three characteristics stem the strengths and the weaknesses.

William and Mary's strongest points lie in its personal atmosphere, which builds strong relationships between the faculty and the students and among the students themselves. The relative scarcity of graduate programs at William and Mary allows the faculty to devote most of their time to the undergraduates. With such a devoted faculty in every department, a student can concentrate in any field and be assured of receiving a challenging education that is good preparation for any starting job or graduate school. Most students live on campus, and the housing is comfortable and convenient to all academic buildings. This creates a spirited campus life that never sleeps and a social life that is active with a good mixture of Greek-and non-Greek-supported events. The student body, which is remarkably diverse for a state-supported school, is large enough that you are always meeting new people. The campus is especially active in athletics at both the intercollegiate and intramural levels, and a brand-new physical education facility has recently opened. Finally, the tuition is low even for out-of-state residents. Over four years William and Mary can be nearly $40,000 cheaper than comparable small private universities.

However, because of William and Mary's small size and its location in a small town, it is definitely not the place for a dyed-in-the-wool urbanite. Big city-style clubs and nightlife are at least 30 minutes away. Williamsburg itself is not exactly your average small town either. On a busy day there are usually more tourists than college students creating havoc in town. On campus, although the faculty is excellent, you will not bump into any Nobel Prize-winning professors or many other world-renowned experts in their fields, for that matter. William and Mary also has a limited number of majors to choose from, which may disappoint some people who have their career plans set and wish to major in more specialized fields, such as molecular biology, advertising, or journalism. Also, William and Mary's stringent grading system can be somewhat discouraging to students accustomed to getting mostly *A*s in high school. Finally, as a state-sponsored school, William and Mary's facilities are not quite the exotic surroundings found at many private institutions.

But the strengths far outweigh the weaknesses. William and Mary is a small university that places undergraduates first on its priority list. Every student has the opportunity, and is expected, to get involved in all things academic, artistic, and athletic that William and Mary has to offer. It is the kind of place where a football player performs in a musical, a chemistry major gives a piano recital, and everyone takes courses in a wide variety of disciplines. If you've definitely decided on your college major already and do not want to be bogged down by seemingly unrelated courses or if you like the security of being just another number in the crowd, then William and Mary is not the place for you. If you want the opportunity to explore new disciplines, take advantage of an extremely forthcoming faculty, and live in a fun-loving close-knit community with 5000 of your peers, the College of William and Mary is the perfect choice.

Greg Zengo, B.S.

Columbia University

THE PROGRAM

The Columbia experience begins with the first steps through the large black iron gates that separate it from the rest of Manhattan. A tree-lined path with eight-story neo-Renaissance red brick buildings on either side leads to an open plaza. A sweeping stone stairway leads to Columbia University's monumental Low Library, the center of the six-block 32-acre campus. With its Roman columns and domed roof, the building, which is actually the main administration building and not a library, resembles the Jefferson Memorial in Washington, D.C. The focus of the plaza is the Alma Mater statue, a seated woman, who resembles the Greek goddess Athena. The open book on her lap, her outstretched arms, and flowing robes embody the intellectual atmosphere that envelopes the campus. Alma Mater, who has been part of the campus since 1903, looks out onto the Main Quad, home of the university's undergraduate college and the nation's smallest Ivy League school, Columbia College. On a first visit to the campus, the sight of the Main Quad is nothing short of breathtaking. It says academia.

Founded in 1754 as King's College, as in King George II of England, the college is the fifth oldest in the United States. The first campus was around Trinity Church and Wall Street and taught the likes of Alexander Hamilton, Robert Livingston, Gouverneur Morris, and John Jay. The school was renamed Columbia—for a mythical patriotic figure—in 1787 after the Revolutionary War. In 1857, the campus moved to 49th Street and Madison Avenue, near what is now Rockefeller Center. As it continued to evolve into a major university, Columbia administrators looked northward to Manhattan's Upper West Side. In 1897, on the site of the old Bloomingdale Insane Asylum, construction began on the current campus, a classic in urban architecture nestled between Amsterdam Avenue and Broadway, from 114th to 120th streets. Columbia retained possession of the Rockefeller Center land until 1985, when it sold it for $400 million.

The grassy quads and unified red brick dorms and academic buildings reflect the balance the college strives for in its educational mission. In academic circles, the college is perhaps best known for its hailed general education program, known as the core curriculum. A series of courses focusing on Western civilization's great literary and philosophical texts, as well as its art and music, the four mandatory core classes are regarded as the foundation of a Columbia College liberal arts education, one designed to make its students balanced, well-rounded individuals. Although a Columbia College education doesn't prepare its students for any specific career, its intention is to produce graduates who know how to deal with, respond to, and shape the constantly changing world. Even as undergraduates, students seem to take this change-the-world attitude to heart, branching out through different organizations to effect change, whether it's a campus matter or an international issue.

> *"My political awakening happened at Columbia. While I was a freshman, a student group calling itself the Coalition for a Free South Africa chained shut the doors of the main administration building—Hamilton Hall, named for Alexander Hamilton— and vowed not to remove them until the university sold off the stock it held in companies that operated in South Africa. Columbia's reputation for political action—students closed down the entire university for several days in 1968—certainly was a factor in my deciding to come here, but nothing prepared me for the three weeks the students kept Hamilton, renamed by the protesters Mandela Hall for the jailed African National Congress leader, chained shut. I helped cover the protest for the campus newspaper, the* Columbia Daily Spectator, *alongside the major networks and dailies. While the trustees didn't divest that spring, in the fall they announced that they would indeed sell off the more than $40 million in South African-connected stock. I saw firsthand how political action could indeed effect change."*

There is no one profile of a Columbia student. They come from poor inner-city public high schools and the best, most expensive private prep schools. They come from as close as five blocks and as far away as Saudi Arabia. Some spent their secondary school years learning the intricacies of complex calculus formulas and others focused on writing. Together, they make up the smallest and most ethnically diverse Ivy League college. And while the differences are great, the diversity creates a community unto itself.

Columbia students can't help but face the real world of New York City that surrounds them—a world filled with both human triumph and tragedy. The homelessness crisis in the city has not spared Morningside Heights. A walk down Amsterdam Avenue and Broadway almost always brings students face-to-face with panhandlers looking for some change or a sympathetic ear. It's a sad fact of life that students either learn to ignore or try to change, sometimes volunteering time at a local church soup kitchen. Problems aside, Morningside Heights is a college town like no other in the country. In the university, there are 15 other divisions, including the first-class School of Law, the graduate school of journalism, and social work, engineering, and medical schools. There are also six additional private colleges in the neighborhood: the Bank Street College of Education, Jewish Theological Seminary, Union Theological Seminary, Manhattan School of Music, Barnard College, and Teachers College. Morningside Heights is often referred to as an "academic Acropolis."

But it's a whole lot more. With 15 ethnic restaurants, six bookstores, a record store, nine newsstands, two jazz clubs, seven bars, a 24-hour bagel shop, three all-night diners, and three around-the-clock stores, all within a few short blocks of campus, a student can spend his or her four years at the college without ever leaving the neighborhood—something that is definitely not recommended. Although its academic reputation and Ivy League status are important selling points for the college, its location in New York City is a main draw, students say. With five bus and subway routes serving Morningside Heights and the fare still only $1.25, transportation to and from the great New York City attractions and an unparalleled night life is cheap, easy, and even relatively safe. The number of people living in Morningside Heights and the heavily traveled transportation lines in the area make getting around Manhattan a lot safer than most out-of-towners would think. And from architectural restoration projects to hospital volunteer programs to summer positions on Wall Street to newspaper and magazine internships, the city is unmatched in opportunity.

GETTING IN/FINANCIAL AID

As with any Ivy League school, academic standards are among the most stringent in the nation. Nearly 8000 applications are received for 870 spots. Ninety-five percent of the student body ranked in the top fifth of their high school classes and combined SAT scores average almost 1300. Columbia recommends, although does not require, that entering students have the following secondary-school preparation: four years of English with extensive writing practice; three, but preferably four, years of mathematics; three years or more of one foreign language; three, but preferably four, years of history; and two years or more of a laboratory science. But it is more than academic prowess that the Committee on Admissions looks for: achievement in extracurricular activities, special talents, personality, and background are also important factors. Because it strives for geographic diversity, it is a safe bet that the committee would more likely admit a candidate from the Midwest than one from New York if the only difference between the two is geography.

"I entered the cavernous Low Library for the first formal gathering of freshmen with the required beanie—the only time this

indignity has to be suffered—and looked around the room at my 750 or so classmates. The Dean of Admissions, as he does every year, tells the incoming class how great it is. More than 60 were their high school newspaper editor, as I was, and a similar number were their class president—another title I held while at Freeport High. Many were top athletes and others National Merit Scholars. It suddenly dawned on me that I was no longer a 'star.' None of us really was anymore. A new chapter had started."

The college starts accepting applications September 1, and the deadline for admission the following fall is January 1. Notification is in April. Besides transcripts and written teacher and counselor/dean recommendations, applications also include essay questions to be answered by all candidates for admission. The process may also include an on-campus interview or an interview with Columbia representatives in your region. Because Columbia draws its students from the same pool that the other top Ivy League schools do, the college is particularly interested in students who consider Columbia their first choice. Although Columbia accepts nearly double the number of students that it has room for in its entering class of 860, many of these highly sought-after candidates choose another Ivy, such as Harvard, Princeton, or Yale, when admitted to more than one. Students who are sure they want to attend Columbia should apply under the early decision program. Admission insiders say the early decision candidates, because of their enthusiasm for Columbia, have a better chance for admission than general pool applicants. Applications for early decision are due November 1 and notification of admission, rejection, or deferral to the general pool is given by late December. Transfer applications are due April 15 for the autumn semester and October 15 for the spring term.

One of the most important considerations when applying to America's top private colleges is cost. Tuition and fees, including campus housing and board, books, and estimated personal expenses recently hit over $25,000. Columbia admits students under a need-blind policy: admission without regard to ability to pay. If you are admitted, the college will make sure you can afford to attend and keep enrolling in the subsequent years. Approximately 60% of all students at Columbia College—the highest percentage in the Ivy League—receive financial aid of some kind, whether in the form of a grant directly from the university, student loans from the college or private banks, or part-time jobs on or off campus. Most financial aid packages are a mix of these programs. The financial aid office requires the submission of the Financial Aid Form (FAF) and additional family income data. If you legitimately cannot afford the costs of a Columbia education, the college guarantees it will make up the difference. Students who must work while at Columbia sometimes cannot fully participate in the student life offerings of the campus because their spare time is taken up by the job.

Extra loan burden (such as PLUS—Parent Loans for Undergraduate Students) can help offset the expected contribution from family and student and give a student more time for school work and campus life.

"When I first started to look at Columbia, my parents both nearly had coronaries when I told them that the $16,000 cost (that's how much it was when I applied) was a per year cost and did not cover the entire four years. My mother was still a housewife because of my younger brother, and my father barely made double what the tuition and other costs would be per year. Their mortgage costs were high, as well as the taxes on Long Island, so the whole idea of sending their son to an Ivy League school seemed out of the question. 'Look at state schools,' they told me at first. But then I started exploring my options. It turned out that with the Columbia grant I would receive, Guaranteed Student Loans, campus and summer jobs, and New York State aid, my parents' contribution would be no more than $2000 each year. While the four years weren't easy financially and my student loan payments now take a big bite out of my paycheck each month, Columbia was, in fact, an affordable college."

ACADEMIC ENVIRONMENT

Columbia's buildings not only look academic, but also literally explain an important part of the academic program. Around the top of the imposing Butler Library, just opposite Low Library, are inscribed some names that are very telling about the college's educational philosophy: Cervantes, Shakespeare, Milton, Voltaire, Goethe, Homer, Herodotus, Sophocles, Plato, Aristotle, Demosthenes, Cicero, Vergil, Horace, Tacitus, St. Augustine, St. Thomas Aquinas, and Dante. These famous thinkers, whose names were chiseled in when the main library was constructed in the 1930s, are still mandatory reading fare for all college students in a set of courses called core curriculum. Developed after World War I, the general education requirements have remained the foundation of the college academic experience and a model for such curriculums around the nation. The two major courses are Contemporary Civilization and Literature Humanities—students called them C.C. and Lit Hum for short—and they are among the best-loved and most-hated courses on campus. From Plato to Marx, C.C.'s curriculum covers the great philosophers and political theorists, whereas Lit Hum focuses on classical and some modern literary and theatrical works. Sixteen original texts are read each semester in seminar-style classes that never exceed 25 students. Class discussion is required, and it's not too difficult for the instructors to figure out which students read the books and which did not. Several papers and exams are also required. Although a common criticism of these courses is their length—each are a year long—another complaint, as frequently stated, is not having enough time to evaluate each work properly in the classroom.

"I found myself writing in my journal about the theories I learned in C.C. with the same enthusiasm I wrote about the new friend I was making...and thinking about how the ideas put forth in Plato's Republic *and Machiavelli's* The Prince *can be found in today's politics. And something happened in the classroom that never happened in the public high school I attended. The professor encouraged us to analyze and criticize the ideas we were reading about and argue about these criticisms at the table where we sat. And something else happened. The arguments kept going outside of the classroom, in the lounges of my dormitory, in the cafeteria, in the library, and around the quads."*

The other two core classes are semester-long courses examining music and art— Masterpieces of the Fine Arts and Masterpieces of Music. Called Art Hum and Music Hum for short, these classes require students to visit New York's finest museums and galleries and attend music performances and ballets. In the classroom, students are taught to recognize some of the classic and influential art and music pieces of Western civilization. In all four core classes, writing ability and clear thinking are of the utmost importance. Upon entering Columbia, most students must take at least a semester's worth of English composition. An examination at the start of the term determines placement. Other required courses at Columbia include three semesters of science for nonscience majors, two years of a foreign language (high school training may shorten this requirement), and a recent addition to requirements— two semesters of classes examining non-Western cultures. Following years of criticism that a Columbia education was too Euro-centric, the facility voted to require two classes that would expose students to ideas and cultures that are not derived from white European men. A less academically oriented requirement, but one the college takes seriously, is two semesters of physical education and a swim test. Unless they are physically unable, all students must pass a swim test of 75 yards before they can graduate.

Some students complain that the college's requirements take up too much time from their specific academic interests, but the faculty defend these standards as important means to a well-rounded liberal arts education. With 2,928 courses available to undergraduates, it's important to pick and choose carefully. The college offers the following areas of study: Afro-American studies, ancient studies, anthropology, architecture, art history, astronomy, biochemistry, biology, biophysics, chemical physics, chemistry, classics, comparative literature, computer science, dance, East Asian studies, economics, engineering (five years), English, environmental science, film, French, geography, geology, German, history, history-sociology, Italian, mathematics, Middle East studies, music, philosophy, physics, political science, psychology, regional studies, religion, Russian studies, sociology, Spanish, statistics, theater, urban studies, visual arts, and women's studies. The stronger departments also tend to be the more popular ones — English, history, and political science. In fact, more than one of every eight college students in a recent class were history majors. Those not opting for the professions either join the work force or head to graduate school in the arts or sciences. And while not all students continue their education upon graduation, 90% of college students attend graduate school sometime in their lives—the highest percentage in the nation. Students heading for the professional schools find exceptional success in getting accepted.

Students at the college are often taught by leaders in their fields. They include professors such as Eric Foner, a Civil War and Reconstruction scholar specializing in radical history and author of several leading tests about the period; Carol Gluck, a world-renowned professor of East Asian Studies and winner of the university's prize for Excellence in Teaching; Henry Graff, history professor and former adviser to Lyndon B. Johnson; Roger Hilsman, political science professor and former adviser to John F. Kennedy; and Edward W. Said, professor of English and comparative literature, whose specialties include theories of colonialism, literary theory, and the role of the intellectual in society. The university also sponsors a top Russian studies program based in the graduate School of International Affairs and Public Policy. College students studying Russian can watch Soviet television captured by the school's massive satellite dish.

More than fifty Columbia faculty and alumni are Nobel Prize winners, and 89 current faculty members have been elected to the prestigious American Academy of Arts and Sciences. Seven have won the National Medal of Science.

> *"The quality of teaching varies from dead boring to dynamic at the university. In the core classes, for instance, some graduate students teach. Sometimes these students are too busy with their own work and are teaching the class because they must and not because they want to. On the other hand, it's not always the case that the better teacher will be a full professor. Indeed, sometimes graduate preceptors turn out to be fine instructors. Upperclassmen and the student-published course guide can help in selecting the better sections. When it comes to the major courses, the faculty are very often on the cutting edge of research in their fields. I had several urban studies teachers, including author and historian Kenneth Jackson, who were out there writing the texts that were shaping the way the subject matter was being taught around the country. And the surprising thing about these 'big' professors was that they were very accessible. I often made the mistake of not getting to know them unless I was in trouble, but even then they were usually friendly, open, and understanding."*

Technically, the student-to-faculty ratio is nine to one, but most classes average around 15–20 students. Some large, popular classes include as many as 300 students, whereas other specialized seminar classes can be as small as three students.

SOCIAL LIFE

"I had just waved good-bye to my family as they drove off and headed back up to my freshman double. My roommate had not arrived yet, and the reality of living away from home for the first time in my life started to hit me. So did the feeling of inadequacy. If there is one thing about Columbia College that first-year students should prepare for, it's the feeling of no longer being a big fish in the small pond of high school. My roommate was a graduate of Andover Academy, the same prep school George Bush attended, and I came from a middle-class Long Island public high school. When he walked into the room dressed in his preppie poplin pants, all-cotton button-down shirt, and tie, carrying a violin case, I, in my denim shorts and T-shirt, was ready to pack up and head for the local community college. But I figured I'd give it a shot. Turns out Peter and I became the best of friends, roomed together again sophomore year, and in senior year lived in our own single rooms in a campus suite with common kitchen and lounge."

As clichéd as it may sound, never judge a book by its cover—or a person by the way he or she dresses—at Columbia. One of the greatest in- and out-of-class lessons Columbia College teaches is the removal of stereotypes of all kinds and the importance of the individual. It makes for a living atmosphere that, for the most part, is quite pleasant. When individual rights at the campus seem as if they are being violated, students don't hesitate to protest. Following a campus fight a few years back that included the hurling of racial epithets by a few individuals, student activists—white and black—mobilized to make it clear that such attitudes would not be tolerated at the college.

In 1983, Columbia College became the last Ivy League school to admit women. The move, which also came about following student protests, was seen as a long-overdue action. To address women's needs, the college set up a women's center in the student activities building and maintained a standing committee on coeducation. It also recently set up a women's studies major that draws on the resources of a women's college across Broadway, Barnard College. Barnard, which was founded by Columbia officials a century ago when the idea of men and women in the same college classroom was generally unheard of, has strong ties to the university but is independently run.

For many years, students were more or less left to their own devices, and in a city like New York that independence can sometimes be too overwhelming. But since the early 1980s, Morningside Heights—like the city itself—has experienced a renaissance. And so has Columbia socially. Despite some protest, fraternities and sororities are more popular than ever. More students stay in the neighborhood for their entertainment than in years past with the opening of nearby movie houses, jazz clubs, and bars. And while the drinking age in New York is twenty-one, enforcement varies enough in the area and in the city that many students don't have to wait until their junior and senior years before they can enter clubs and other establishments serving alcohol.

Students not familiar with Columbia sometimes think of the school as a cold and lonely place because of its location in Manhattan. In some respects, because there is so much to do in the city, the college can never develop the unified, spirited atmosphere that other campuses enjoy. This is not a place for homecoming kings and queens or bonfires. Although its students know how to have a good time—check out frat row on 114th Street on a weekend—Columbia College is for the most part an intensely serious place.

EXTRACURRICULAR ACTIVITIES

From drama clubs to ethnic organizations and from politicians to political groups, Columbia is rife with activities for its students when their noses aren't stuck in the books.

For the budding politician, there's the University Senate, which makes recommendations to the president and trustees of Columbia on policy matters. The real power at the university lies in the Board of Trustees, who have final say on all matters. While they are rarely involved in day-to-day decisions or student life issues, rest assured that Columbia is no democracy despite its elected bodies. Columbia College has its own Student Council, whose main power lies in its ability to apportion the student activity fee that all college students are required to pay. Future journalists and broadcasters can join the *Columbia Daily Spectator*, an independent student-run daily and the second-oldest college paper in the country; the campus humor magazine, *Jester*; the conservative alternate paper, the *Federalist Paper*; the metropolitan-wide student-run radio station, WKCR; or Columbia's student cable channel, CTV.

> *"In my case, my extracurricular activity became my life pursuit. I joined the* Columbia Daily Spectator *my first week in college and worked my way up to managing editor by the middle of my junior year. While I sometimes regret not having devoted more time to my studies, working for the nation's second-oldest college daily opened doors for me that undergraduate journalism schools simply can't. As an undergraduate, I served as stringer to the* New York Times *and* New York Newsday *and was selected for an internship at the* Los Angeles Times. *But more important, the* Spectator

*became a community for me within the larger community of
Columbia College. Some of my closest friendships were forged
there, and most of my lessons about human behavior and responsibility were learned there as well."*

Columbia offers a host of intercollegiate and intramural athletic programs for
men and women. Its football team recently broke a 44-game losing streak that had
made the school the laughing stock of NCAA football circles. But the school does
boast an Ivy champion soccer team and a top national fencing squad. Many of the
teams—crew, baseball, tennis, football, and soccer—practice at the school's Baker
Field athletic complex, 100 blocks north of the campus on the tip of Manhattan
island. Fully equipped gyms at Barnard and the university in Morningside Heights
offer students a wide range of activities from weight training to bowling.

Students can also join the community volunteer groups housed in Earl Hall.
Under the umbrella group Community Impact, students participate in Big Brother/
Big Sister programs, tutor local children, and work in homeless shelters and soup
kitchens. Earl Hall also is home to the campus religious, political, and special interest organizations, such as Amnesty International, Committee for UNICEF, Jewish
Students Organization, Democratic Socialists of America youth division, and the
Gay and Lesbian Alliance. Particularly popular among Columbia students are the
social-activities groups, such as the Board of Managers, which is a student-run
group that organizes theme parties, shows popular and off-beat films, lures comedy
acts, invites guest speakers, and books bands. A few years ago, the university
opened its own dance club in the basement of the student activities building. Further evidence of an improved social life is the growing number of students joining
fraternities and sororities. There are 23 such groups, many with their own brown-
stones as frat houses.

For the less raucous types, Columbia has its own coffee house, called Postcrypt,
where folk singers, poets, and actors do their thing on a dark stage in the cozy,
usually crowded cafe. Additionally, the 12 campus dormitories have their own student social organizations that put together programs designed to create dorm unity.
Almost fully residential, Columbia offers its students a variety of living arrangements, including single rooms on floors with common bathrooms, suite-style living arrangements in which groups of students live in an apartment-like setting, and
special interest housing for students trying to learn a foreign tongue or those who
are arts oriented. Newly constructed Schapiro Hall, with views of the Hudson
River, includes a student theater and practice rooms. Freshmen are required to sign
up for a board plan, but after that membership declines. Upperclassmen's housing
arrangements often include access to kitchens, and the availability of fast food restaurants, diners, pizza parlors, and Chinese food in the area offers more than
enough dining opportunities.

GRADUATES

There is no one direction for Columbia College students, and that's the way the school would have it. Students go on to careers as diverse as the student body itself. In recent years, many have headed for cushy jobs on Wall Street as management trainees, brokers, analysts, and consultants. Still others take jobs as teachers, journalists, public relations staffers, museum coordinators, and film production assistants. Although the majority of students enter the work force upon graduation, 90% eventually attend graduate school.

Columbia College's graduates go on to become influential leaders in the professions, politics, the sciences, and the arts. The list is long and diverse: American industrialist Armand Hammer; media tycoon John Kluge, one of the nation's richest men; *New York Times* Executive Editor Max Frankel and Publisher Arthur Ochs Sulzberger; singer Art Garfunkel; former NBC News head Lawrence Grossman; ABC News head Richard Wald; baseball Hall of Famers Lou Gehrig and Eddie Collins; New York State Attorney General Robert Abrams; beat poet Allen Ginsberg; actor James Cagney; former Federal Reserve Board Chairman Arthur Burns, who also served as ambassador to West Germany; and songmen Richard Rogers and Oscar Hammerstein, to name a few.

Columbia's alumni sometimes return to campus to meet with students or accept awards for their accomplishments. Although the sixties uprisings left a sour taste in some alumni's mouths, in recent years the stabilized college has enjoyed a resurgence in alumni activity. Giving is now at its highest. John Kluge donated $25 million in 1987 for a minority-aid program. Morris Schapiro gave $5 million for a new dormitory, and Lawrence Wein, owner of the Empire State Building, donated enough money through the 1980s to build football and soccer stadiums and renovate completely a campus dormitory. As the old guard comes back to its alma mater, new-guard graduates have organized an unprecedented group for recent alumni called the Young Alumni Club, designed to meet the interests of alums from the preceding ten years. Although there has been a resurgence in the alumni network, Columbia College has a long way to go to match the strong "old boy" networks of some of the other Ivy League schools.

> *"I see the product of the Columbia College education already, even as a recent alumnus. A recent graduate I know has been working for the President's Council of Economic Advisers since graduation. Others I know work 60 or 80 hours a week down at Wall Street, something I consider a nightmare. Spectator alum from the past five years have jobs at ABC News,* Newsweek, *the* New York Daily News, *the* Washington Monthly, *and a host of other prestigious news organizations. I know many who are teachers—some at prestigious prep schools like Andover, others in the public schools of the South Bronx. A few of my friends*

joined the staff of the Columbia College admissions and alumni offices, hoping to maintain and improve a college that has gotten into their blood. I even have a friend who decided to spend some time building new low-income housing in Harlem. I think the story of the success and dedication of its graduates is the most important story about Columbia College."

SUMMARY OVERVIEW

The common foundation of the core curriculum creates an important unity among Columbians, one based in ideas and texts, not in football victories or pep rallies. The diverse community allows students to meet individuals of differing political stances, different backgrounds, and different ambitions. Its topnotch academic reputation opens countless doors to graduate schools and career opportunities. Although graduates are not trained for any particular future, one of Columbia College's main strengths is that its students are prepared to deal with a host of challenges. They are taught to analyze, to criticize, and, most of all, to think.

Academics aside, students have numerous campus and off-campus activities to pursue. New organizations pop up all the time to fit the current needs of the college. The neighborhood offers restaurants, bars, shopping, and services found in few college towns. And Columbia's New York City location gives it a quality unknown at other residential colleges.

But one of the school's greatest advantages can also be one of its biggest drawbacks. To say Columbia is short on space is an understatement. In fact, the university president has suggested that the school may someday have to move certain divisions out of Manhattan if Columbia is to grow. Although Columbia owns much of the real estate in its neighborhood, new student organizations and fraternities often have to wait years before they are given their own space. When people think of the Ivy League, they think of colleges spread out on rolling acres with large shade trees and acres of grass. Although the Columbia campus does indeed have trees and some grass, the eight- to 15-story buildings create an entirely different image. Then there are the other problems of big cities: crime, homelessness, high living expenses, and pollution. Students choosing Columbia are choosing a whole lot more than top academics. They are choosing, for four years, a way of life that they had best be prepared to deal with.

"Obviously, I'm pretty happy with my Columbia College experience. I miss it dearly, and whenever I see friends who are still there, I tell them, 'Enjoy it while it lasts.' While graduation was recent, it seems already far away. But my experiences are vividly etched in my mind. I remember my first few nights at

Columbia. It seemed like everybody was having a great time during the Orientation Week activities except me. One evening, unable to sleep, I climbed to the top of Low Library's stairs and sat, knees to my chest, and inspected the campus that I had fallen in love with a year ago when I first visited. Feeling alone and homesick, I cried. I think the next time I cried while at Columbia was my final night as managing editor of the Spectator *three-and-a-half years later while taping up the box of flats that we sent every day to our printer. I had gone from 'nothing' to 'something' again, and I think my fellow editors—my friends—and I all felt the same thing we did when we were freshmen: that an important chapter in our lives had been completed and a new one was about to begin. Included in that new chapter was the separation from a community like no other I will live in again. While Columbia's diversity and the myriad of opportunities in New York City make campus unity and school spirit difficult things to foster, Columbia's fractious nature is a community-building quality unto itself."*

John A. Oswald, B.A.

Cornell University

THE PROGRAM

Cornell's philosophy of education, words uttered by founder Ezra Cornell, can be found emblazoned all over campus: "I would found an institution where any person can find instruction in any study." More than a century after its founding, with almost 100 departments and more than 4000 courses in seven different undergraduate colleges, Cornell certainly offers study in a range of fields wide enough to satisfy its founder.

The university is a unique combination of four private schools and three state schools. Its private schools are the College of Arts and Sciences, the College of Engineering, the School of Hotel Administration, and the College of Architecture, Art, and Planning. The New York state-assisted schools are the College of Agriculture and Life Sciences, the College of Human Ecology, and the School of Industrial and Labor Relations.

Although there are differences in how some observers rate each of them, academic excellence is a uniform characteristic throughout Cornell's colleges. From astronomer/TV personality Carl Sagan to Alfred E. Kahn (a chief economic adviser to President Carter) to Nobel Laureate chemist Roald Hoffman to Urie Bronfenbrenner (noted specialist in human development and family studies) to Pulitzer Prize-winning author Alison Lurie, Cornell is home to a wide range of well-known experts.

Cornell's colleges function as independent fiefdoms within the university, each with its own buildings, requirements, and personalities.

> *"In my first few weeks at Cornell, I learned the stereotypes very quickly, among them: 'Artsies' sit around and talk about Kafka but can't change a light bulb; 'Enginerds' are more interested in computing than communicating; and 'Aggies' milk cows all*

day. Soon, my own growing group of friends, including a wild, fun-loving engineer and a Wall Street-bound 'Aggie,' made me forget those generalizations."

Most of the stereotypes, of course, are dead wrong. Still, learning how wrong they are over a four-year period provides an enlightenment in itself. And the persistence of the stereotypes highlights a good-natured competition among the various schools. A traditional rivalry, for instance, pits the engineers against the architects. The engineering buildings, each constructed in a different color, are said to have been designed that way by the architects so the less-than-literary engineers could tell them apart. Engineers get their revenge each year on Dragon Day, when architects parade through campus with a huge green cardboard dragon while engineers pelt it and its carriers with eggs.

Although all students apply to and most major in only one of the seven schools at Cornell, their Cornell experience is far from limited to one seventh of what the university offers. Most of the schools have at least one course that attracts undergraduates from throughout the university. A popular senior-year semester might include these courses: Recent American History in the College of Arts and Sciences, Wines and Beverages in the School of Hotel Administration, and Human Sexuality in the College of Human Ecology.

All undergraduates, regardless of course of study, live and eat together. There are specialized libraries geared to specific colleges, but most students end up finding their own study niche in whichever library's degree of noise, nightly population, and geographic location suits them best. For thousands of students, hotelies and artsies and aggies alike, *the* place for nightly studying and mingling is the main undergraduate library, Uris.

Cornell's physical surroundings are, in a word, breathtaking. "Ithaca is Gorges," reads a popular bumper sticker, referring to the deep cliffs and fast-water streams that some gracious glacier left centuries ago. The school peers down on the city of Ithaca from East Hill, and the view on a clear day encompasses the beauty of Cayuga Lake, the charm of the town, and the tranquility of rural New York State. Several state parks, many featuring awesome waterfalls, are a short drive from campus. Most students who stay in Ithaca over a summer fall in love with the place if they have not done so before.

As for the winter: yes, it's cold, and yes, it snows a lot, but the southern tier of New York State is *not* the Arctic. In fact, Ithaca is not even in the so-called snow belt, and it occasionally gets less snowfall during a major storm than does New York City or Washington, D.C. The battle against Ithaca's winter is more of a war of attrition; wintery weather begins early, ends late, and usually involves at least a dash of snowfall several times a week. For the optimist, winter's wrath brings out another element of Ithaca's beauty and draws together the large student body in a mutual empathy. And when spring does eventually arrive, nobody appreciates it more than Cornell students. On that first sunny day when the temperature hits 50°, the arts quad comes alive with Frisbees and sunbathers.

Like Ithaca's weather, Cornell is diverse, from its academic program to its professors to its on-campus facilities. The university's resources are astounding; if you get a sudden urge to learn about livestock production or textile management or nonlinear elasticity, an expert is just a short walk away. That person walking on the arts quad might be a former White House official, a prize-winning author, or a scientist on the cutting edge of new research. Those who arrive in Ithaca worried that they left excitement behind will find a unique kind of exhilaration in the ordinary day-to-day life of a Cornell student.

GETTING IN/FINANCIAL AID

Judging strictly by geography, Cornell's is not the diverse student body that its brochures herald. About 39% of its 12,700 undergraduates are natives of New York State, more than 54% are from other states, and about 7% are foreign students.

According to a popular joke, Cornell's supposed diversity boils down to "students from all over Long Island." Indeed, the search for a ride home for winter break is quite easy for those hailing from the suburbs around New York City. Still, although playing on a certain light-hearted sensitivity to the number of Long Islanders at Cornell, the joke does not do justice to the university. There are more than 6000 non-New Yorkers at Cornell, bringing perspectives from all parts of the country and many parts of the world.

> *"My five suitemates freshman year included one from Egypt, one from Hawaii, and two from Hong Kong. After several months of living together, the two from Hong Kong came to the startling realization that back home, one of their fathers was the other father's dentist. A year later, when I lived off campus, I had as housemates people from all around New York State, Virginia, Alabama, Florida, Texas, Washington State, and Korea."*

Cornell's admissions office receives over 20,000 applications for about 3000 freshman places. These numbers are indicative of the university's high selectivity, but they should not discourage prospective applicants. Cornell's admissions process does not go simply by the numbers—SAT I scores, grade point averages, and so on. In order to maintain its wealth of activities and breadth of courses, Cornell has to look beyond statistics for leadership qualities, unique talents, and diversity of experience. Like other schools, it is interested in the class president and the yearbook editor. But it also wants to attract the farmer, the apparel designer, the Russian linguist, the sculptor—a diverse enough student body to keep up and contribute to the university's varied activities and course offerings.

The first step on the road to Ithaca is choosing which Cornell college to apply to. For those with a clear idea of what to study, this can be an easy decision. Others may find that knowing what they want to study does not complete their decision-making process. Six Cornell colleges, for instance, offer study in business, each with an emphasis in different areas. Business is taught in Industrial and Labor Relations with a focus on labor relations; in Human Ecology, with focuses on consumerism and the apparel and textile industries; in Agriculture and Life Sciences, with courses in business management, financial accounting, marketing, and business law, among others; in Arts and Sciences, with a host of economics courses; in Hotel Administration, with a focus on management in the hotel industry; and in Engineering, with courses in operations research and industrial engineering. Regardless of the programs students choose, they may take business courses that interest them in any of the other schools.

Another crucial factor in choosing which college to apply to is cost. Like most comparable institutions, Cornell for several years raised its tuition faster than the rate of inflation. But unlike most universities, Cornell's tuition varies between the private and state colleges, and within the state schools between residents and non-residents. Tuition and fees for the most recent year in the endowed colleges (Architecture, Art, and Planning; Arts and Sciences; Engineering; Hotel Administration) was $17,276; tuition for the statutory colleges (Agriculture and Life Sciences, Human Ecology, Industrial and Labor Relations) was $7056 for New York State residents, $13,306 for nonresidents.

Cornell's stated financial aid policy is one of "need-blind admissions" — meaning that applicants are considered for admission without regard to their financial need. In addition, administrators have said every year that Cornell is "meeting the full financial need" of all its students. However, since the financial aid crunch that began several years ago, more and more students are finding that they have to spend many hours working in the college work-study program while at Cornell and many years paying back loans after Cornell in order to afford an education. In short, the opportunity for a Cornell education is there, but students must be willing to work for it.

ACADEMIC ENVIRONMENT

Cornell's great academic strength is a uniformity of excellence in a wide variety of subjects. Regardless of their course of study, students are free to take courses in all seven undergraduate colleges and, in some instances, in Cornell's graduate schools. It is also possible for students who are not happy with their choice of school to transfer within the university.

With few exceptions, Cornell's high student-to-faculty ratio has ramifications throughout all its colleges. Many introductory level courses, and some higher level ones, are taught as large lectures with little or no built-in opportunity for individual instruction with a professor. On the other hand, if a student makes an effort, most professors are more than willing to spend time and meet with students. Cornell is a renowned research institution, and many professors do not make teaching undergraduates a priority, preferring instead to leave most student contact to their graduate teaching assistants. Seminars, discussion sections, and laboratory classes with small enrollment do provide one-on-one instruction, usually with teaching assistants.

UNIVERSITY-WIDE REQUIREMENTS

Under the only university-wide academic requirement, freshman must take a writing seminar in each of their first two semesters (students in the College of Architecture, Art, and Planning need take only one semester; hotel school students take one semester of a specialized hotel writing course). With a choice of up to 125 writing seminars, all students can find two that interest them. Work in the seminars includes at least 30 pages of writing spread over eight to 14 assignments and opportunities for independent conferences and revisions. Although some of Cornell's well-known professors teach freshman seminars, many are led by lecturers or TAs. Still, this requirement ensures that each incoming student will have the opportunity to work one-on-one with someone exceptionally knowledgeable in a field.

In addition, there is a university-wide physical education requirement: two semesters of classes with a variety of activities to choose from: archery, bowling, diving, ballroom dancing, fencing, rock-climbing, riflery, skiing, wind-surfing, kung fu, and yoga, to name a few. Every freshman must either pass a swim test or take swimming for a semester.

> *"Ah, the swim test. One of the first things I did as an incoming freshman was report to the pool to take the 75-yard test. It really was an education; I learned how far I could swim. Exactly 74 yards. Fortunately, a deft dead man's stroke took me the final yard. A swim instructor was waiting by the pool to sign a card affirming that I had passed, and I struggled to look like I wasn't about to die. He bought it. All that was left was the long walk home, with my roommate carrying my bag and me resting on the grass three times along the way. I was sore for days."*

What follows are descriptions of three of Cornell's schools that are most likely to invite comparisons to the other colleges and universities in this book.

ARTS AND SCIENCES

Cornell describes its College of Arts and Sciences as "a traditional liberal arts college." Indeed, students may study and major in the traditional gamut of liberal arts fields: the humanities, expressive arts, social sciences, mathematics, and basic sciences. What is less traditional about Cornell's school is the relative independence of its students, the predominance of large lecture-style classes as opposed to small give-and-take sessions, and the opportunity available at such a diverse university to dabble in so many other fields.

Arts students are required to achieve either proficiency in one foreign language or qualification in two, which may mean up to four semesters of language courses. Students who come to Cornell with a background in a foreign language can take a test during their first few days to place out of the lower-level language courses. For this reason, plus the fact that language courses are extremely time-consuming (one or more classes a day, plus daily homework and time in a language laboratory), students are well advised to tackle this requirement early in their four years at Cornell.

The distribution requirement, meant to ensure a well-rounded liberal arts education, takes a little longer to fulfill, but certainly is not burdensome or intrusive. In fact, most students will find themselves pleased that they are forced to experience the many strong departments Cornell offers. In order to fulfill the science requirement, for example, many arts-oriented students choose to enroll in two semesters of introductory astronomy and find themselves being taught by two renowned professors in one of the best departments at the university.

There are four areas to the distribution requirement. The first requires two semesters in either the physical sciences (astronomy, chemistry, geology, or physics) or biology. The science distribution requirement is the only one that honors advanced placement credit; students with sufficient scores can place out of one semester of science.

"Like many nonscientists in the arts college, I chose astronomy to fulfill my science requirement. One reason, I suppose, was because it was the one science discipline that I did not try in high school. But looking back, I remember another factor: on the campus tour I took when I was applying to Cornell, the guide made sure not only to mention the fact that Carl Sagan was a professor at Cornell, but also to point out the astronomy building 'where Carl Sagan has an office.' During my two semesters taking astronomy, however, I learned that Sagan was more of a campus whipping boy than a professor. His colleagues—usually, but not always, in good fun—hail their proximity to Sagan's office and publicly wonder exactly what he does to earn his salary at Cornell.

"In truth, Sagan—whose office number is not listed on the astronomy building directory—teaches one 600-level course for graduate students. He is most famous for his house, which is built into a cliff near campus and gives him a view of the highest vertical drop in Ithaca."

Under the three other distribution requirements, students take two courses in the areas of social science/history (economics, government, history, sociology, psychology, African studies, and women's studies, to name a few choices); humanities/expressive arts (archaeology, Asian studies, English, philosophy, and literature, for instance); and quantitative reasoning.

ENGINEERING

Cornell's 2500 engineering students choose to specialize in one of the following engineering fields: agricultural and biological, chemical, civil, electrical, mechanical, computer science, engineering physics, geological sciences, materials science and engineering, and operations research and industrial engineering. In addition, the college offers an interdisciplinary program, in which students can combine study in two engineering departments or in engineering and a field in another Cornell college.

During their four years, engineering students must also meet the requirements of the Engineering College's common curriculum, which is comprised of eight categories: mathematics, physics, chemistry, freshman writing seminar, computer programming, engineering distribution, humanities/social sciences, and electives. The Engineering Cooperative Program allows qualified students to spend eight months working for companies like Eastman Kodak, General Motors, and Hewlett-Packard.

HOTEL ADMINISTRATION

Cornell's hotel school is widely recognized as the best school of its kind in the country. It is a small school (about 700 students) and is quite centralized, with students spending much of their day in one building, Statler Hall. The curriculum is regimented, with no majors and minimal subject concentration, but students are free to take up to one-third of their courses in the liberal arts. Among the disciplines stressed in the hotel school are accounting, finance, marketing, operations, communication, properties management, computers, law, and human-resource management. Students are required to spend two summers working in the hotel business.

All seven Cornell colleges are widely known and highly regarded, and their varied academic offerings are too vast to be fairly summarized. Add to that a faculty that garners major academic awards each year, and you have a top-notch learning atmosphere with limitless opportunities for the inquisitive mind.

That's not all. Contained within Cornell's 740 acres are 19 libraries, six national research centers, sprawling farmland, a marine laboratory, an art museum, a brand new hotel (where Hotel Administration students get hands-on experience), and countless other resources. The university's well-known astronomy department operates its own telescope laboratory in Arecibo, Puerto Rico.

For the rare students who can't find one major that satisfies their academic tastes, there are dual majors and independent majors. You can study art in Rome, design in New York City, or government in Washington, D.C. For the Cornell student who wants to experience all the college has to offer, the possibilities are endless.

SOCIAL LIFE

Cornell has a well-deserved reputation for an active social life. Much of it revolves around a strong community of fraternities and sororities or takes place within a few city blocks in nearby Collegetown. Noticeably absent from the social scene is the university, which seems to disappear between Friday afternoon and Monday morning. Even before the drinking age rose to twenty-one, the university sponsored (or even acknowledged officially) only a handful of events. Of them, only one survived unscathed the switch to the higher drinking age: Fun in the Sun, an arts-quad celebration of the brief warm weather early in the fall term. But even Fun in the Sun is run more by individual fraternities and sororities than by university officials, who watch the merriment from the periphery of the arts quad.

Because of the university's laissez-faire attitude toward campus social life, students must develop and pursue their own social agendas. With the rare exception like Fun in the Sun, few organized social events are the obvious choice for the student out for a good time. Much more often, you find that your three best friends are going to three different parties on three different areas of the campus. Ah, decisions, decisions!

Cornell's fraternities and sororities fill a large part of the void in organized social life at the university. The higher drinking age has forced fraternities to downgrade what used to be enormous drinkfests open to everyone, but the fraternity party has lived on as a key component in many Cornellians' social lives. In an era when Greek organizations at many colleges have declined, Cornell's have remained active and attractive to many students. More than one third of its male students belong to one of 43 nationally recognized fraternities; about one third of its females join one of 14 national sororities. In addition, there are a handful of local fraternities and sororities.

Cornell and Ithaca offer a variety of activities as respites from studying. Regardless of the season, sports fans can choose among a variety of games and matches to watch (hockey is traditionally Cornell's best sport, and fans camp out overnight in line to buy season tickets). Cornell offers an extensive intramural program, the largest in the Ivy League, with about 65% of the student body participating in 23 sports. Each weekend, Cornell Cinema presents first-run movies on campus, and with the large number of arts-oriented campus groups, there's always a recital, play, or concert to attend. Ithaca, an arts-oriented town, offers several movie theaters, shows, and restaurants.

All new Cornellians quickly learn the art of "Facetime," a uniquely Cornell phrase translating roughly to "seeing and being seen." The mere existence of such a phrase speaks volumes about the social life at a university of 18,000 students, seven different undergraduate colleges, and a 740-acre campus. Perhaps only at Cornell could the normally simple and natural act of being seen be considered an activity in itself, one that makes the university community seem smaller.

Newcomers at Cornell quickly learn the best daily opportunities for Facetime. Lunchtime Facetime generally means eating at one of the two central campus cafeterias that honor the various meal plans Cornell offers: Okenshield's in Willard Straight Hall (the Straight) and Sage Hall Dining, located across from the Straight. Many upperclass men and women no longer on a meal plan frequent the Ivy Room in the Straight, where a variety of food is available for cash or, even better, on Cornellcard—an on-campus credit-card system that charges your account to your bursar's bill.

The basic elements of your social life at Cornell will depend in large part on your choice of where to live. Residence halls are grouped in three areas: West Campus, North Campus, and Collegetown. West Campus is traditionally popular among freshmen, with its assortment of mainly traditional dormitories— long hallways with shared common areas and bathrooms. The six University Halls (U-Halls), each named for a different class that helped fund it, house many of each year's freshmen. A recent renovation project has helped revise the U-Halls' reputation as crowded and plain, and they continue to offer students a lively environment and the opportunity to meet a large number of classmates.

North Campus offers more variety in living conditions, including more single rooms, various suite arrangements, and, in general, a quieter atmosphere more conducive to in-room study. Most of the university's theme houses are located on or near North Campus, including residences geared toward the arts, the environment, internationalism, and Third World concerns.

Collegetown (C-Town) houses two dormitories, Sheldon Court and Cascadilla Hall, which are popular because of their location. Collegetown features almost a dozen watering holes in a three-block area, plus a number of popular restaurants and other close-by conveniences.

In addition to the two dormitories, thousands of students live in apartment buildings and houses in and around Collegetown. Eventually, most students end up off campus, and Collegetown offers just about everything for a variety of prices. Living conditions vary widely: a studio apartment right on College Avenue, complete with kitchen, can run nearly $400 a month; a double room in a fairly run-down old house a couple blocks up Dryden Road might cost each roommate less than $200. One word of advice: Start your search for next year's house or apartment early in the preceding spring semester.

> *"To the shock and dismay of my parents, I spent a memorable sophomore year in a beat-up Collegetown house, living with three other men, seven women, two dogs, and a tank full of fish that were there when we moved in and, despite not being fed for one month during winter break, despite being left in the house while we 'bombed' it to kill fleas, were alive and well when we moved out. I had grown up in a house where dust was cleaned before it had time to settle, and I had always been a little wary of dogs. Somewhat to my own surprise, I not only survived that year, but thoroughly enjoyed every moment of it. Sometimes you learn and grow a lot more out of the classroom than in it."*

Like everything else at Cornell, your social life is what you make of it; rarely will there be an obvious choice about where to spend your Saturday night. At first, the choices seem daunting, but don't worry: once you settle in with a group of friends and once you appreciate the variety of activities to choose from, your own likes and dislikes will make your decisions for you.

EXTRACURRICULAR ACTIVITIES

At a university with more than 12,700 undergraduates in seven widely differing schools, there is bound to be a vast array of activities and causes. At last count, there were more than 500 student clubs and organizations active on campus. In addition to the traditional activities found at most colleges, Cornell students participate in the Agronomy Club, the Cornell Bangladesh Association, the Cornell Civil Liberties Union, Cornell International Folkdancers, the Cornell Sri Lanka Students' Association, the Cornell Prison Project, the Cornell Skydiving Club, the Cornell Cricket Club, and campus branches of the Society of Women Engineers and the American Association of Textile Technology.

Perhaps because of the wide range of choices, many groups suffer from poor attendance. But that can be a blessing, because students willing to devote their precious time to activities often can be rewarded with some sort of leadership role.

> *"Little did I know when, early in my freshman year, I attended an organizational meeting for the school newspaper that I would end up spending 50 hours a week as associate editor my senior year. Looking back, I see that what hooked me was not only the thrill of working on a daily newspaper but the opportunity to gain as friends people who shared my interests. Even though it sometimes—make that often—cut into my schoolwork, my work at the* Sun *provided me with an unofficial second major. Combined with my history degree, it gave me what I now appreciate as perfect training for a career in journalism."*

Once a center of student radicalism, Cornell now is no more active than other campuses, with literally only a few dozen students responsible for organizing protests against CIA recruitment on campus, U.S. military aggression, or other political issues. For several years, by far the loudest and largest protests have come in favor of divesting the university's money from companies that maintain ties with South Africa. Despite the uproar, the Board of Trustees has kept its course of maintaining selective divestment—investment only in companies that abide by certain guidelines in that country.

Students participate in more than 28 varsity sports, including hockey and lacrosse, teams that are perennial NCAA powerhouses. Cornell also offers an extensive intramural program, the largest in the Ivy League.

Many student-run publications circulate around campus and town. The *Cornell Daily Sun*, a completely independent, five-day-a-week newspaper, proudly serves as "Ithaca's Only Morning Newspaper." The *Cornell Review* provides periodic coverage as seen from the political right. Other publications focus on Jewish issues, student literature, and national and world politics.

Those interested in the expressive arts will no doubt find a group to their liking at Cornell. Music groups include the Cornell Symphony Orchestra, the Sage Chapel Choir, the Cornell Chorus, the Cornell Glee Club, the Collegium Musicum, and the Indonesian Gamelan, as well as various university bands, chamber music ensembles, and very popular *a cappella* singing groups. Bailey Hall plays host to a number of major artists each year, the likes of B.B. King, Itzhak Perlman, and Suzanne Vega. And if your interest is the visual arts, Cornell has its own art museum on campus—the Herbert F. Johnson Museum of Art.

This summary touches only the surface of the wealth of activities available at Cornell. There is at least one organization to attract any student's interest, and most students will have to choose between various activities that catch their eye. To quote a Cornell brochure: "You'll never find any reason to be alone with your particular passion—unless you want to."

GRADUATES

A recent annual report on Cornell graduates showed the continuation of a trend away from graduate and professional schools but also a decrease in the number of students employed soon after graduation. For the first time, a measurable number of graduates (more than 3%) reported that they were voluntarily out of the job market.

Cornell students clearly are exploring a number of postgraduate options outside of the traditional two choices of continuing education or seeking employment. An increasing number of students reported that they planned to attend graduate or professional school within two years after graduation, presumably taking time to pursue personal interests before delving into more academics. According to the report, the most popular and fastest growing employment field for Cornellians is business. About 40% of a recent graduating class entered the business field, an increase of 12% from three years earlier.

For graduates pursuing further education, Cornell was the most popular institution. Nearly one quarter remained at the university for further study in many areas, including law, business, and engineering, or traveled to New York City to attend the Cornell Medical Center. New York University and Columbia University placed a distant second and third for graduate studies.

By all measures, Cornell's alumni network is a strong and active one. In fundraising, Cornell ranks at or near the top among universities, and alumni play a critical and generous role. Many alumni are active in recruiting and interviewing applicants, and many others work through a program called the Cornell Connection to help match graduating students with potential employers in their fields. Through a program called the Cornell Tradition, alumni help students find summer employment. but perhaps the most important role of the alumni network involves keeping Cornell's graduates in touch with their alma mater and, to some degree, in touch with each other.

> *"A popular Cornell professor tells the story of traveling with his family in Mexico City, Mexico—nearly 4000 miles from Ithaca. Expecting to be strangers in this foreign place, they were quite surprised to be contacted by the Cornell Club of Mexico City. That night, local Cornell graduates—eager to hear what was new at their alma mater—treated them to dinner at the nicest restaurant in the city."*

Cornell graduates are likely to find groups of former Cornellians in whatever region of the country (or the world!) to which they move. All colleges, with the exception of Arts and Sciences, operate their own alumni association, and individual schools hold their own events. One of the most popular is the School of Hotel Administration's annual Hotel Ezra Cornell, a weekend gathering of alumni and others in the hospitality industry that allows students to show their skills. In addition, all students, regardless of their college, belong to the alumni group of their graduating class, which holds a campus reunion every five years.

SUMMARY OVERVIEW

Four years at Cornell offers not only a top-notch education in a variety of subjects but also an education about other people and about oneself. Despite the ivy on the buildings and the somewhat isolated location of the campus, Cornell is the real world, with real pressures, real challenges, and real rewards for those who work for them.

The campus and its surroundings provide a wonderful atmosphere for four years of education and introspection. Around you are cream-of-the-crop students (undergraduates and graduates) and professors with interests and expertise in a mind-boggling array of subjects. Many students will find themselves able to touch only the surface of this wealth and breadth of knowledge, leaving Cornell more aware than ever of all they do *not* know. But perhaps that is the greatest gift a university can bestow on its graduates.

Cornell has a reputation for intense academic pressure, and to some degree the reputation is accurate. The work is difficult, but the university's low attrition rate proves that most students can handle it. In addition, because of the size and somewhat impersonal nature of the university, it is all too easy to pass through Cornell practically unnoticed. Too many professors—including faculty advisers assigned to each student—depend on the student to initiate contact although students who do will find most professors to be friendly and helpful. First-year students, especially those who had high profiles in high school, may find it difficult to adjust to life out of the academic spotlight. Cornell students are many things; one thing they are not is pampered.

At Cornell, *any* student can find an interesting area of study, an exciting extracurricular activity, and a close circle of friends with similar interests. The key word is "find"; those unwilling to put in the effort to shape their own college experience will not find Cornell to their liking. But those who do choose to accept the Cornell challenge will find after four years that they have gained a lot more than a diploma.

Laurence Arnold, B.A.

Dartmouth College

THE PROGRAM

There are a few obvious differences between Dartmouth and the seven other schools in the Ivy League. The first thing you should know if you want to apply to Dartmouth is that it's the northern most of the Ancient Eight, and it has the coldest climate. (On the other hand, it does own its own skiway.) It's won more Ivy League football championships than any other school. Arguably, it has the best food. And it's the only school to call itself a college, not a university.

This distinction is a very important one at Dartmouth, and not just for semantic reasons. The difference between Dartmouth College and Dartmouth University stems from the famous "Dartmouth College Case" of 1819 in which Daniel Webster, class of 1801, argued successfully before the Supreme Court that Dartmouth should remain a private institution without interference from the government of the State of New Hampshire. Webster's eloquent peroration, which he summed up with the line "It is, sir, as I have said, a small College, but there are those who love it," may partially explain why referring to the school as Dartmouth University—an innocent slip-up for the uninformed—is regarded as a cardinal sin among students. (And just think of what would have happened to Dartmouth's marching band, the DCMB, had Webster lost!)

But the name Dartmouth College has more than merely historical significance. Dartmouth distinguishes itself from a research university by its excellent teaching, which the school is justifiably proud of, and the close mentor relationships that often develop between undergraduates and professors. Virtually all classes are taught by members of the faculty, not by graduate assistants. And professors regularly open their office doors to students, with shared scholarship becoming increasingly more common. Dartmouth considers itself a liberal arts university—lower case—in the sense that its faculty members are recognized nationally as both teachers and scholars, and its associated professional schools—the Dartmouth Medical

School (which boasts a brand-new medical center three miles from Hanover), the Amos Tuck School of Business Administration, and the Thayer School of Engineering—are highly regarded. Enhancing the intellectual climate are approximately 400 students enrolled in 12 arts and sciences doctoral programs and four master's degree programs. But the primary emphasis of Dartmouth is undergraduate education, which entitles the school to its status as a college.

It's hard to imagine a more perfect setting for an institution of higher education than Hanover. With the coming of each season, Dartmouth's magnificent architecture gains new brilliance. The classically rendered regality of Baker Library, which holds many of the college's two million volumes, and Dartmouth Row, which includes Dartmouth Hall, the main academic building, look like they were constructed with falling leaves or drifting snow in mind. The central campus Green (the grassy area, not the school color) is surrounded by ivy-covered administrative buildings, the library, Dartmouth Row, and the Hopkins Center for the Arts. "This is what a college ought to look like," said President Eisenhower at Dartmouth's commencement in 1953.

Ike would undoubtedly have been befuddled by the vagaries of Dartmouth's innovative year-round calendar system, which was instituted in 1972 when the college became coeducational. Called the D-Plan, the Dartmouth calendar divides the academic year into four ten-week terms named after the seasons (however, there's no term called "mud," which dominates the New England landscape during most of March and April). Students are required to be on campus during fall, winter, and spring of their first and fourth years, and the summer after their second year. (Summer term operates like any other academic term, except with fewer people on campus, offering a chance for students to float in the Connecticut River or relax on the sunny Green between classes.)

Since twelve terms are ordinarily required for graduation—students usually take three classes per term—the remaining five terms are scheduled according to individual preference: on or off-campus, on exchange with another institution, or on one of Dartmouth's 44 foreign study programs in 17 nations (nearly two-thirds of the students participate in these programs).

"The flexibility of the D-Plan allowed me to study music for a term in London. I had never been out of the country before, so I was amazed at the opportunities there. Coming from Hanover, London was cultural nirvana. Every night, the question in our flat wasn't 'Should we go out tonight?' but 'Should we go to the theatre, to a concert, or to a jazz club?'

"The academic part of the program was structured to give us maximum exposure to the resources of the city. We studied the music of England, I took voice lessons with a professional teacher, and we went to dozens of concerts. Although our professor said that London was our textbook, she didn't say that we'd never want to put it down again. My time abroad sparked a long-term love affair with the city of London and all things British."

Though Hanover is certainly no London, Dartmouth is remarkably well-endowed for a small New England town. The Hopkins Center for the Performing Arts (known as the Hop) sponsors dozens of concerts each semester, and the Rockefeller Center for the Social Sciences (known as Rocky) hosts an equal number of speakers and panel discussions. The Hood Museum of Art, boasting a collection of rare Assyrian reliefs, is the largest American museum north of Boston (which, by the way, is only a two-hour drive and a popular road-trip destination).

Every four years, Dartmouth gains national prominence during the New Hampshire primary season, when nearly every presidential candidate makes an appearance in Hanover. During the latest presidential campaign, the College played host to Paul Tsongas (class of 1962), Bill Clinton, Jerry Brown, Tom Harkin, Bob Kerrey, and Pat Buchanan.

Hanover also boasts a world-class bookstore on Main Street, where, on any given day, you might run into nationally known authors Louise Erdrich, Michael Dorris, Richard Eberhardt, Annie Proulx, or Sydney Lea (or, for that matter, college president and bibliophile James O. Freedman) browsing through the shelves. (And if you think you see reclusive author J.D. Salinger, who lives in nearby Vermont, you wouldn't be the first to claim such a sighting.)

But hard economic times have taken their toll on several Main Street institutions, including Campion's, a clothier that opened in 1906 but recently shut its doors. Several restaurants have come and gone in recent years. And while there's *still* no deli in Hanover, the town does boast a fantastic Chinese restaurant, a fancy Italian place for when your parents come to town, and a decent Indian establishment, as well as four or five other eating places, all of high quality. Town-and-gown relations tend to vary as much as individual personalities. Most merchants welcome the business of Dartmouth students, though most — unlike the owners of the Dartmouth Co-op — don't invite the college marching band to play inside the store after football victories.

One thing you'll have to get used to at Dartmouth is cold weather from October to April. (It's no wonder that the U.S. Army's Cold Research Lab is located in Hanover.) Winter temperatures regularly fall below zero, and while I never saw the sort of snow that friends in older classes warned me about (during Winter Carnival one year, snow had to be *trucked* in so students could build the annual sculpture on the Green), there's going to be a blizzard one of these years.

Winter Carnival is the most famous, but in my mind the least memorable, of Dartmouth's many traditions. Thousands of visitors are attracted to Hanover each year to view the snow sculptures and the skiing events that highlight the weekend. It's not surprising that Dartmouth's winter weekend is so well known; by nature of the school's location in the hills of New England — which are, fittingly enough, called the Green and White Mountains — Dartmouth students have always had something of a penchant for the outdoors. Most students get their introduction to the hills before they even pick up a textbook, from the DOC (Dartmouth Outing Club) trips for first-year students. About 85% take to the woods for three days of hiking, biking, canoeing, or fishing — led by upperclass students or faculty and administrators — an outing that kicks off their orientation to Dartmouth. Students spend the last night of the trip in the Moosilauke Ravine Lodge on Dartmouth-owned Mount Moosilauke, where they are introduced to Dartmouth legend and lore, including a special tradition involving Dr. Seuss, class of 1925. (And when Seuss [Theodore Geisel] died in 1991, members of the entire Dartmouth community staged an all-night reading of his books in freezing-cold temperatures.)

Another memorable first-year activity is the building of the homecoming bonfire on the Green. This is another occasion at which members of the class get to know each other; they stack environmentally treated wood in a fifty-foot pile, and light it on Friday evening in a conflagration that usually heralds a homecoming football victory. The accompanying pep rally, called Dartmouth Night, is another symbol of the college community rallying 'round dear old Dartmouth.

It's also an unofficial tradition at Dartmouth to fabricate myths about the school. It's not true, for instance, that Dartmouth students stage a naked snowball fight at the first sign of winter. And there are probably a fair number of tales that the average high school senior has heard about Dartmouth that are equally nonsensical. One such myth is the existence of a highly visible, right-wing conservative element on campus. Such a presence simply doesn't exist, and most students pay little attention to the highly publicized antics of a few students who run an off-campus newspaper that shares little more with Dartmouth than its name.

> *"It took me until sophomore year to realize that all of the political battles I had read about in the newspapers didn't reflect reality on campus. Though Dartmouth has received its share of negative national attention, most of it has been undeserved. During my senior year, Dartmouth led the country in addressing national issues of race, sexual assault, and diversity. And many of these positive — and constructive — efforts never made it into the papers."*

Traditions such as the bonfire, first-year trips, and yes, even Winter Carnival help Dartmouth maintain a strong sense of community. A high percentage of the college's alumni maintain a close connection to the school after graduation. (Almost 60% of alumni donated money to Dartmouth in a single year.) So it's no wonder that many of my classmates were as reluctant to graduate as I was.

> *"Just before commencement, my graduating class had a discussion over a long-standing college tradition involving Native American clay pipes, which some thought was offensive to Native Americans. (The school was founded in 1769 by the Reverend Eleazar Wheelock, according to the school's charter, "for the education of Youth of the Indian Tribes. . .English Youth, and others.") After a vigorous debate, the class voted to replace the pipe ritual with a new tradition, a midnight candlelight ceremony, which we felt would be inclusive rather than exclusive.*
>
> *"The night before graduation, our class gathered in a secluded clearing near a wooded area of campus. As we stood in a giant circle with our closest friends, we each lit a green candle that we*

had been given earlier in the evening. One by one, we blew out our candles as we remembered departed classmates and our favorite personal memories, and looked ahead to life after graduation. It was a poignant ceremony; most of my classmates agree that it was a memorable way to end four years at college. We've promised to return and relight our candles at the first class reunion, and I still keep the green candle on my desk at home as a reminder of what I left behind.

"The debate over the pregraduation ceremony is an example of the sort of discussion that characterizes politics on campus. Although Dartmouth has seen its share of contention, it has a fair share of consensus too. When I realized that what makes Dartmouth tick is a firm commitment to undergraduate education and a deep sense of history and tradition, I finally began to understand the place. And I began to love it that much more for its foibles."

GETTING IN/FINANCIAL AID

Like any Ivy League school, Dartmouth's application form is challenging and its admissions process selective. Although the school has no specific subject requirements for admissions, a strong secondary-school program that includes English, a foreign language, mathematics, laboratory science, and history is strongly recommended. Besides academic process, the admissions committee looks for evidence of personal integrity, motivation, and talent and accomplishment in nonacademic areas. Slightly more than 9500 applications were received for 1057 places in the most recent class.

"What sort of person goes to Dartmouth? There used to be an image of a Dartmouth student as an outdoorsy, well-rounded person from an elite private school. There are still lots of people who could fit that billing, but the campus is much more diverse than it was in the '60s, before coeducation. During my four years, I was randomly assigned four different — very different — roommates: a public school graduate from Connecticut who majored in government and enjoyed sailing and his fraternity; a hockey player from Minnesota who had attended a private high school; a public school graduate from Maryland who was active in the Afro-American Society and did academic research in Venezuela; and an avid bicyclist who had attended private school in Maryland and was active in community service. So it's safe to say that Dartmouth students aren't of a single ilk."

The Dartmouth alumni network helps make the interview process a casual one; most applicants are interviewed by alumni, although a personal interview with an admissions counselor may also be requested. Senior undergraduates also interview some prospective students in Hanover. The admissions office highly recommends that applicants take a campus tour — led by undergraduates — and attend information sessions while classes are in session.

> *"My college interview took place in the living room of a very friendly Dartmouth alumnus, who immediately put me at ease with his casual manner. 'Don't even think of this as an interview,' he said. 'We want you to get into Dartmouth as much as you do.' I spent the next hour conversing with two alumni who were as eager to tell stories about their own college days as they were to hear about my high school preparation. And after I was offered admission, my interviewer called me to offer his personal congratulations. That's just another example of the spirit of the Dartmouth family."*

Though it still lags behind its Ivy League neighbors, Dartmouth continues to make enormous strides in admitting applicants from diverse backgrounds. Minorities comprise nearly one-quarter of the most recent class (24%). Students hail from all 50 states, the District of Columbia, and 26 foreign countries. Remarkably for a school that became coeducational only in 1972, women constitute 47% of the student body.

Despite a nationwide budget crunch in higher education, the college is firmly committed to maintaining need-blind admissions (that is, admissions without regard to one's ability to pay). Though tuition and fees alone cost a hefty $19,000 in a recent year (with total expenses approaching $28,000), Dartmouth makes every effort to ensure that financial reasons do not prohibit admitted students from attending. More than 42% of undergraduates received aid totaling more than $25 million, in the form of grants, loans, or college work-study jobs. Dartmouth administrators are fond of saying, though, that *every* Dartmouth student receives a subsidy of about 50% from gifts to the college and from Dartmouth's endowment. This is unlikely to be comforting to the student who doesn't happen to have a spare $100,000 sitting around in a personal savings account.

> *"It's not easy to pay for a Dartmouth education, but it can be done. With a combination of grants, loans, parental support, and a 10-hour-per-week job in the art library, I was able to make ends meet. Two pieces of advice, though: (1) be sure to leave room in your budget for textbooks and travel expenses, two easily forgotten items that can quickly put you in the red, and (2) make the most of your off-campus terms. Because of the D-Plan, it's possible to go 18 months without a normal "summer vacation" earning opportunity.*
>
> *"One other word about paying for Dartmouth: Don't think that because you're on financial aid, you can't afford a foreign*

study program. Financial aid packages are usually increased—
with a combination of scholarship and loan—to meet the addi-
tional cost of these programs. I would never have been able to go
to London without the extra help."

ACADEMIC ENVIRONMENT

When President James O. Freedman addressed the college at his inauguration in
1987, he delivered a message that contrasted sharply with Dartmouth's long-standing "work hard, play hard" image. Freedman called for a firm commitment to encouraging "the life of the mind," and proposed increased collaboration between students and faculty on scholarly research.

After six years, Freedman has largely succeeded in his mission to make Dartmouth a more intellectual environment, though the school is hardly full of geeks
with pocket protectors any more than it's full of drunken fraternity boys. Rather, the
changes in academic atmosphere encouraged by Freedman are more subtle. It's no
longer anathema, for instance, to spend a Friday evening reading Joyce or Chaucer
in Baker Library's wood-paneled Tower Room. And more than 100 students participate each year in a program begun under Freedman's tenure, the Presidential Scholars Research Assistantships, which allow students to work directly with professors.

"My senior-year thesis on the English composer William
Sterndale Bennett turned out to be one of my most rewarding ac-
complishments. I worked closely with my advisor to develop a
methodology for the project, and received a grant from the Rocke-
feller Center allowing me to spend three weeks in London over
my winter break conducting original research.

"Although I wasn't technically a Presidential Scholar, I was
fortunate to have an advisor who took such great interest in my
project. He was able to steer me towards the appropriate re-
sources in England, and guided me through the often tortuous
process of writing my thesis. You won't get that kind of opportu-
nity at a large research university—they'd rather spend their
time and money on graduate students."

Even outside of one's major area, classes are generally small enough that consultation with professors is possible—and welcomed—on a regular basis. Introductory classes, particularly in government, history, and psychology, tend to draw the
most students, with upper-level seminars at the opposite end of the scale. More than
half of the 1210 courses offered during a recent academic year had enrollments of
fewer than twenty students, and more than four-fifths had enrollments of fewer than
thirty. The three most popular majors at Dartmouth are government, history, and

English, which (along with chemistry and languages) also tend to be the school's strongest departments.

French professor John Rassias has been known to rip off his shirt during class and crack eggs on a student's head. It's all part of an intensive language program called the Rassias Method, which was developed at Dartmouth and is now widely used at other schools. In addition to a professor's regular classroom instruction, language students participate in daily drill sessions where they practice grammar and vocabulary in a fast-paced 7:45 A.M. workout with an upper-level teaching assistant who is guaranteed to wake up even the sleepiest student. After completing two terms of language — German, French, Spanish, Chinese, Hebrew, and Russian are just some of the possibilities — students are generally fluent enough to enroll in Language Study Abroad (LSA) or move on to upper-level classes.

Dartmouth's offerings in the sciences are also worthy of special mention. A new chemistry facility, Burke Laboratory, which opened recently, complements the Fairchild Center for the Physical Sciences, the Kiewit Computation Center, and the laboratories associated with the engineering and medical schools. Students interested in scientific careers are not only given opportunities to conduct research, but Dartmouth's commitment to the liberal arts also ensures them a well-rounded education. In the first-rate environmental sciences program, Dartmouth's location and facilities augment a broad-based curriculum. And the Women in Science project, begun by President James Freedman several years ago, aims at encouraging more women to enter careers in research, through a variety of seminars, speakers, internships, and opportunities for collaboration with faculty on scholarly projects. More than 400 students and 85 faculty members are currently involved with the program.

Over the next decade, Dartmouth will implement the most wide-sweeping curriculum changes since the 1920s, with corollary revisions in degree requirements. Rather than the current mandate of a minimum of four courses in each of three academic disciplines (humanities, social sciences, natural sciences), the new curriculum will require one or more courses in each of eight intellectual fields (arts, literature, philosophical, religious, or historical analysis; international or comparative study; social analysis; quantitative or deductive science; natural science [including a laboratory component]; and technology or applied science). The curriculum will ensure a more rigorous liberal education for future generations of Dartmouth students. In addition, all students will be required to engage in a "culminating experience" within their major — which may take the form of a thesis, independent study project, or senior seminar — and may elect to minor in a second academic discipline.

Some of Dartmouth's existing requirements, however, will remain, including demonstration of proficiency in at least one foreign language, first-year English classes (unless exempted on the basis of Advanced Placement scores), and a first-year seminar, held in small-group discussion format on topics in every academic discipline. These last two classes form what amounts to a core experience for many first-year students, teaching principles of the academic community and writing skills. One's experience in these seminars tends to vary according to the subject and the professor; the effectiveness of the writing instruction, which tends to be sporadic, is currently being evaluated. (On the other hand, the English department's Creative Writing program is highly regarded and each year attracts noted poets and authors to present public readings of their works and teach classes. Other distinguished visitors to the campus, known as Montgomery Fellows, offer students the opportunity to learn from internationally celebrated writers, historians, artists, and scholars such as Gore Vidal, Philip Roth, Oscar Arias, Chinua Achebe, and Medeleine Kunin, who have all visited the college in recent years.)

Dartmouth faced a rewarding challenge in 1991 when it opened its new medical facility in Lebanon, New Hampshire, three miles from Hanover: What should the college do with the existing buildings and land on the north part of campus that was no longer needed for medical purposes? Tied into this question was a $425 million capital campaign, also begun in 1991, which was intended to raise funds for new facilities. The result of years of long-range planning was a blueprint for several new academic facilities, including Burke Laboratory, the Berry Library (funded in 1992 with gifts totaling $30 million, including a $25 million gift from John Berry '44), and new buildings for psychology, mathematics, and computer science, all of which will be completed by the end of the decade.

Dartmouth's library collection is first-rate, and includes more than two million volumes in Baker and its associated branches for the sciences, mathematics, business and engineering, art, and music (which alone holds nearly 15,000 sound recordings and 40,000 books and musical scores). In Sanborn Library (next to Baker and popular among English majors), studying pauses at four o'clock on weekdays for afternoon tea. Baker itself is an architectural and artistic marvel; besides its bell tower with its collection of rare books, manuscripts, and Dartmouth realia (including a pair of Daniel Webster's socks) and the academic ambiance of the Tower Room, it boasts the "Black Dan" portraits of Webster and murals by the Mexican artist Jose Clemente Orozco, painted from 1932 to 1934 in Baker's lower corridor while Orozco was artist-in-residence on campus. The murals depict the barbaric nature of American civilization and caused enough controversy in the '30s that President Ernest Martin Hopkins's one piece of advice to his successor in 1945 was, "Never have anything to do with murals."

In the Dartmouth library, the card catalog is now obsolete. Computer automation of the library's holdings, maintained under an open-stacks policy atypical of most schools, allows students to access from their dorm rooms not only the on-line catalog, but also the full texts of Shakespeare, the Bible, and the Koran. And the library's ever-burgeoning information technology makes database searches as easy as the click of a mouse. In fact, the computer has integrated itself into nearly every aspect of a Dartmouth student's life. Even when one is not writing papers on a word processor or playing Tetris, the computer calls — literally. An extensive communications network called BlitzMail has replaced the telephone as the *de rigueur* method of inviting a friend to lunch or scheduling a meeting with a professor. (The word "blitz" has entered the Dartmouth lexicon as a verb, as in "I'll blitz you those notes when I get back from dinner.") In a recent year, more than 60,000 messages were sent through campus in a week — about one message every four seconds — on the college's 9,000 Macintosh computers (every dorm room and classroom building is wired to the network, and all incoming students are required to purchase a computer upon matriculation).

> *"It's amazing how many things I used computer mail for at Dartmouth. In a typical day, I'd get a dozen messages: from the Glee Club director about an upcoming rehearsal, from my brother in Boston or a friend at Cornell, from my editor at the* Alumni Magazine *requesting ideas for a story, from a friend I hadn't seen in a few days asking when I was free for dinner, and from a professor commenting on a draft of my term paper (you can even 'enclose' word-processor documents in a blitz message!). And the computer network also lets you access everything from a paperless environmental magazine ('Its medium is its message,' says its founder) to up-to-the-minute weather reports to menus in the dining hall.*
>
> *"One of the biggest advantages of the network is that it allows you to stay in touch wherever you are on campus. On a weekday, I might leave my room at 9 A.M. and not get back until 11 P.M. But I'd check my blitzmail every couple of hours. (On the other hand, it's not easy to hide from, either; senders can request a return receipt that notifies them when you've read their mail.)*
>
> *"Don't get the wrong idea about all this; we're not automatons—and there aren't many students who understand* how *the system works. But it makes the busy life of a typical Dartmouth student easier to manage."*

SOCIAL LIFE

There are two things you need to know if you want to go to Dartmouth: (1) Hanover is not New York City, by any stretch of the imagination, and (2) the film *Animal House* (cowritten by Chris Miller, class of 1963, based loosely on his Dartmouth fraternity) was not a documentary. Keeping those two facts in mind, one can maintain a proper perspective on Dartmouth's social life. While there are a couple of bars and a movie theater in town, neither offers a sure-fire hangout spot. More than anywhere else, Dartmouth students tend to migrate towards parties in Greek houses.

Fraternity and sorority life, according to those who are involved, is often a rewarding experience. Slightly more than half of the student body belongs to a Greek organization. Members often form close relationships with their brothers and sisters and share common experiences that range from community service to eating goldfish (and I don't mean the Pepperidge Farm kind). Social life at Dartmouth is heavily concentrated in the fraternity/sorority/coed house system, especially on "big weekends" such as Homecoming, Winter Carnival, Green Key Weekend (a spring term holiday), and Summer Carnival, when there are usually several Greek houses having parties simultaneously, many of them featuring a live band.

On a normal weekend evening, Dartmouth students can be found at sporting events, movies, concerts, comedy clubs, and cultural nights. There's the occasional dorm party, of course, and special class-sponsored casino nights or formal dances. But most social activity doesn't get underway until 10 or 11 P.M., when a fraternity having a party (almost always with a DJ or a live band) will open its doors to the campus. Most students who find their social outlet in the Greek system will usually visit more than one house in a single weekend night.

There are also plenty of social opportunities outside of fraternity row. Friday night dance club in the Collis student center has become one of the more popular weekend activities, and other such offerings will certainly be expanded by the time a massive renovation of the center is completed in 1994.

Though social life is heavily concentrated in the Greek system, Dartmouth's reputation as a party school is only half-true. In a recent year, the president of the Student Assembly called for all fraternities to become coeducational, in a convocation speech that sparked discussions all over campus about the validity of the Greek system. There are some heavy drinkers at Dartmouth (as there are at any school) but there are also many students who lead healthy social lives. A student group called Asgard sponsors nonalcoholic programming and a substance-free dormitory. And a stringent alcohol policy instituted recently established a student monitoring system for parties and prohibits fraternities from serving beer from kegs.

> *"I don't feel as though I missed something because I wasn't in a fraternity. My social life revolved around the activities I participated in, such as Glee Club and marching band, and my nonaffiliated friends. I probably went to fraternity parties two or three times a term, usually at one particular house, and I always felt welcome there, even though I wasn't a member. Two of my best friends were in that fraternity, and they always let me know when the parties were."*

Hanover's small-town atmosphere has been blamed for a relative lack of dating on campus. While it's not far from the truth (as a friend of mine said, when visiting Dartmouth for the first time, that "running the lanes at Astro Bowl rates as urbane entertainment"), it's not difficult, with a little imagination, to find romantic things to do on a weekend evening. Try a moonlit stroll around Occom Pond at the northern end of campus, a midnight rendezvous in the college graveyard, or gazing across the Connecticut River down at the college docks.

Another unique element of the Dartmouth social scene is that dogs are welcome nearly everywhere on campus. In the early '30s (according to one campus publication), even though a student sent his dog to class, he was marked illegally absent anyway, "despite the diligent attention of his substitute." Some days there are as many dogs playing Frisbee on the Green as there are students in the library (or was that the other way around?). And some fraternity dogs have stayed at Dartmouth long enough to get a degree—if they had gone to classes regularly.

EXTRACURRICULAR ACTIVITIES

If you wanted to skip classes regularly, or had a dog who could take notes for you, the extracurricular activities at Dartmouth could keep you busy for weeks. Dartmouth students have developed a reputation for being well-rounded, with their participation in everything from sports to radio to music to environmental activism. More than three-quarters of the students participate in either intercollegiate, intramural, or club sports. And 25% volunteer in Students Fighting Hunger, Amnesty International, and a wide variety of local community service projects under the auspices of the Tucker Foundation. The Book Buddies literacy project, through which students travel to homes in the Upper Valley to help kids learn the joys of reading, is one of the most unique of these projects.

The Tucker Foundation is also the umbrella organization for the college's 18 religious student organizations and its two chaplains (one Jewish, one Christian). Rollins Chapel is an interdenominational house of worship and there are local churches for just about every faith. Ethnic and racial groups are represented by organizations that include the Afro-American Society, the Dartmouth Asian Organization, the Korean-American Students Association, Native Americans at Dartmouth, and La Alianza Latina. The Dartmouth Gay and Lesbian Organization is also a vocal part of Dartmouth's extracurricular activities.

All sides of the political spectrum are represented by organizations that include the Young Democrats and the Republicans at Dartmouth, and publications that range from the progressive *Bug* to the conservative *Beacon*. Students speak in tongues during the weekly meetings of the French, German, and Russian Clubs. The daily newspaper, *The Dartmouth*, is reputed to be the oldest college newspaper in the country. And when classes are in session, Dartmouth operates an AM and an FM radio station, both entirely run by students.

The college's outdoorsy image is reinforced by the Dartmouth Outing Club (the oldest and largest such club in the nation), which runs the DOC trips for first-year students and operates activities in its Cabin and Trail, Environmental Studies, and Winter Sports divisions. The Dartmouth College Skiway in nearby Lyme is a popular spot to spend a winter afternoon, and modern athletic facilities include the John W. Berry Sports Center, with indoor squash and basketball courts, a basketball arena, and a dance studio. Students are ardent supporters of the major intercollegiate sports, at least when they're winning; the football squad captured its third consecutive Ivy League title in 1992.

"The Hopkins Center alone offers dozens of extracurricular opportunities for students interested in the visual, creative, or per-

forming arts. Crafts studios, galleries, scenery shops, and film studios offer just about everything one could ask for in the arts. I concentrated on music, where I sang with a highly acclaimed mixed choral group and took voice lessons that culminated in a senior recital. There's so much to do here that it's all too easy to let classwork slide. It's a good thing I don't have a dog."

Student life is also enhanced by food that ranges from satisfactory to excellent. A new food court, the old standby all-you-can-eat cafeteria, a fast-food grill, and two areas that emphasize healthy eating make the dining options attractive to almost any hungry student. Living accommodations are also quite satisfactory; one or two dormitories could be described (without too much exaggeration) as plush. Most students live on campus in residence halls, though some live in fraternity or sorority houses or in off-campus apartments.

GRADUATES

Alumni tend to feel a strong attachment to Dartmouth and many (including myself) have a difficult time leaving the place. But once they do, they tend to come back. They come back for Homecoming, for Winter Carnival — actually, for almost any reason at all — pulled north by the intangible bonds they have to the people and to the place itself. It is said that though the Dartmouth family extends "'round the girdled earth," as the school's "Alma Mater" puts it, "her spell on them remains."

Another school song, "Dartmouth Undying," also has its effect on the alumni population. One authority says that when it's sung correctly, all alumni in the audience inwardly pledge to donate all their assets to the college. That must have been what possessed one alumnus to donate his prize herd of zebras to Dartmouth, and another to give 22 tons of corn (which, luckily, was sold by the college before it ever reached Hanover). Nearly 60% of all alumni contributed to the Alumni Fund in a recent year, though most gifts were not of the living kind. And the turnout of students who volunteer to telephone alumni during the annual fundraising effort is always high; students are just as eager to talk to alumni about their school as the alumni are to hear about it.

Many Dartmouth students use the telethon to develop their job-networking skills. A close friend has probably contacted every judge and lawyer on the east coast, and has received job offers from a handful of them. Dartmouth's Career Services department maintains extensive files on alumni who are willing to be contacted about their professions, and most will hire a Dartmouth student over an equally qualified student from another school.

With the job market bleak for recent graduates in the early '90s, many students have opted for graduate school; a large majority of students, in fact, pursue further education within five years after graduation. Many of these graduates seek higher degrees in the arts and sciences, but the numbers applying to law school and medical school are also substantial. Students who do get a job work in fields ranging from advertising to investment banking, from teaching to foreign service, and from arts administration to environmental science.

The range of fields for Dartmouth graduates is also well-represented by the prominent alumni who seem to be around every corner. Dartmouth graduates can be found in President Clinton's cabinet (Labor Secretary Robert Reich, class of 1968), in sports (former Cincinnati Bengals star Reggie Williams, class of 1976, among others), and even, not surprisingly, back at Dartmouth (former Surgeon General C. Everett Koop, class of 1937, who recently founded the C. Everett Koop Institute at the Dartmouth Medical School). Even Mister Rogers went to Dartmouth for a term before he transferred to Rollins College in Florida. How can you go wrong at a school that taught Mister Rogers, Captain Kangaroo (Bob Keeshan, class of 1943) *and* Dr. Seuss?

> *"I became so attached to Dartmouth that I didn't want my time there to end. Even after graduation, I spent the summer in Hanover, working and participating in the theater program, which I had never had a chance to do before. At the beginning of September, a friend and I left Dartmouth for a cross-country baseball trip that we had been planning since April. Though I fulfilled a childhood dream by visiting places like Wrigley Field and the Baseball Hall of Fame, my mind was often drawn to what I had left behind in Hanover. But my transition away from college was somewhat easier than I had expected. Baseball is probably the only thing that I love as much as I do Dartmouth (and I haven't even mentioned what it's like to attend a baseball game at Dartmouth), so I was able to leave without harboring any regrets.*
>
> *"As soon as the trip was over and I started a new job in North Carolina, I couldn't wait to get back to Dartmouth for a visit. My time there shaped my life in more ways than I can enumerate, and I don't think I would have been as happy anywhere else. I'm sure I'll be back there someday soon — and maybe next time for good."*

SUMMARY OVERVIEW

Dartmouth's niche is unique: a medium-sized liberal arts college in a rural environment with a devoted faculty of mentors who are firmly committed to undergraduate education. Its sense of tradition and history helps forge a bond between the school and its students, who are committed to excellence in both scholarly and extracurricular activities.

All of these positives will only be accentuated over the next decade as Dartmouth strengthens its facilities and its curriculum. A new library will place Dartmouth on the cutting edge of academia, and a new student center will help expand the opportunities for social activity outside of the Greek system. Changes to the curriculum will invigorate the faculty and will encourage students to leave Dartmouth with both a broader understanding of their world and a more sharply focused mind.

Meanwhile, Dartmouth will continue to do what it does best — offer opportunities for interaction with faculty, programs for study abroad, and outdoor activity, for intellectual, moral, and spiritual growth. Its language instruction and its computer network are unparalleled among liberal arts colleges, and a strong alumni body buttresses both the institution and individual students, through financial support and career counseling.

But Dartmouth still has many challenges to face over the next decade, several of which are similar to ones that higher education in general will tackle. Dartmouth must continue efforts to recruit both women and minority students and ensure them that Dartmouth is a place where educational opportunities are available to all. In a recent newsletter to alumni, Dartmouth's president wrote, "As the face of America changes, the only way for Dartmouth to fulfill its mission of educating leaders and to maintain its eminent stature in American higher education is for it to evolve as well. Standing still — in this area or any other — is simply not an option."

Budgetary considerations will also dominate the minds of campus administrators over the next few years. Compared to many other schools, Dartmouth is in good shape financially, although reductions in the budget of approximately $6 million over the last three years have pared away some student services. The college, however, pledges not to cut core academic functions or programs or tenure-track faculty positions, promises to keep admissions need moot, and will no longer postpone improvement of academic facilities that are inadequate for current needs. Such long-range planning, especially when new facilities are under construction, will ensure that Dartmouth remains fiscally responsible in the future.

Finally, Dartmouth must continue to reshape its national image as a place where intellectual discovery and scholarly excitement are central to the vision of the institution. The worst thing about Dartmouth is its reputation; both the college's history before coeducation and the bad press it received during the 1980s have convinced some that the Dartmouth community is not one in which they would feel comfortable. But through challenge comes opportunity, and there is great cause for the entire Dartmouth community to feel optimistic about the next decade and look forward to the rewards that come from such a vibrant and thriving institution.

Jonathan Douglas, A.B.

Davidson College

THE PROGRAM

Davidson College is not a threatening place. Red brick buildings and large old trees dot the campus located in the town of Davidson, which is 20 miles north of the city of Charlotte, North Carolina. The small-town atmosphere and friendly people make freshmen feel welcome. Despite the peaceful, quiet atmosphere, Davidson College provides one of the most demanding liberal arts curriculums in the nation for its student body of 1551 men and women. Students quickly learn the value of hard work. The combination of a challenging program and a nurturing atmosphere produces graduates who are broad based and hard thinking.

> *"From the moment I arrived at Davidson for freshman orientation I felt like I was being welcomed to a family, albeit one with an established way of doing things. From the traditional first kiss at the Student Union to the mild torture of getting my belongings into my room to my first hall meeting, every step of my first day seemed to have been planned for me. After being welcomed to the family, a process that took four days of orientation, I got a rapid welcome to the responsibility side of Davidson. I had three classes my first day. On that day my classes covered an entire chapter of German, an introductory lecture to the two-year humanities program, and a short chapter of calculus. My assignments for day two were to review the chapter of German for a quiz on day three, read the entire 'Epic of Gilgamesh,' and work a problem-set for calculus in preparation for another day-three quiz. Day one and the vacation was over."*

As a liberal arts college, Davidson has a core curriculum of 20 majors plus the option of an interdisciplinary major through the Center for Special Studies. Davidson has neither double majors nor minors, but students may supplement majors with concentrations such as applied mathematics and neuroscience. By liberal arts, Davidson means the basics. Majors have titles such as economics or history, not advertising or medieval Italian history. Liberal arts also means students receive a broad-based education that requires them to take courses in all areas of study in addition to completing the requirement for a major. By requiring students to fulfill core requirements, Davidson makes sure that science majors get out of the laboratory once in a while, and that would-be political scientists know something about chemistry, biology, or physics. Students must also pass the requirements for a foreign language, which means demonstrating proficiency at a level equal to three semesters of a language, or taking three semesters of language courses.

Although Davidson has no preprofessional majors, most Davidson graduates pursue professional careers. The more popular majors at Davidson — biology, English, and economics — reflect some of the more common career paths graduates choose. More than 80% of Davidson graduates attend graduate school. The college's reputation for producing hard-working thinkers assists determined graduates' efforts to enter any career field.

Davidson's small size gives it an advantage over other competitive schools in that students have an opportunity to become leaders in a wide range of extracurricular activities, ranging from student publications to direct involvement in college policy decisions. The opportunity to lead, to make decisions that matter, propels Davidson graduates toward leadership roles after graduation. The small student body and family atmosphere of the college provide proper nurturing to accompany the intellectual growth provided by the rigorous academic grind.

GETTING IN/FINANCIAL AID

Getting into Davidson it not easy. Only 37% of all applicants are accepted. This does not mean someone with low SAT I scores or a less-than-stellar class rank should be deterred from applying. Davidson highly values accomplishments in extracurricular activities. Due to the relatively small size of the applicant pool, the admissions staff is able to examine applicants on a more personal level. A winning interview, therefore, can nudge a borderline student into the college.

Obviously the best way to get in is to have great grades in high school and a high SAT I score and show extracurricular achievement. Such students are rare, however, even at Davidson. The breadth of the admissions application allows excellence to come through whether it is in music, a civic organization, sports, or church activities. Take your time and don't be afraid to strut your stuff.

"My parents wanted to make sure I did my best to get into Davidson. For each of the four essay questions I had to answer, I

*submitted several rough drafts for my parents' approval. I got
my application in October but sent it back only days before the
deadline. I got in and have never regretted all the time spent on
the application."*

For the borderline applicant, an interview with the admissions department is
essential. Davidson wants exceptional people as well as exceptional students. The
main thing is to convince the admissions staff that you could make a contribution
to Davidson. If you are the type of student who belongs at Davidson, that will come
through in the interview. The questions asked are not from a checklist, and no one
is looking for a right answer. Just be yourself.

Davidson has a homogeneous student body, plain and simple. The vast majority
are white. Most are from the South, and many are wealthy. Davidson has a reputation of having a WASPish student body, and the stereotype is not far from the truth.
The student body is only 7.3% minority. The college continues to make a serious
effort to increase the applications and enrollment of minority students. Several
dozen foreign students study at Davidson, and their presence brings a much needed
cultural diversity.

For the most part, however, diversity at Davidson comes in the form of personality rather than sociological differences. A student's political views, the region of
the country he or she comes from, or his or her taste in music are more likely to
make for diversity at Davidson than nationality or race.

Davidson students are by and large a wealthy group. Expensive cars are common on campus, and home addresses tend to be wealthy suburban places. Davidson will always have wealthy students because of the high cost of a private
education. Financial aid is available, and the school prides itself on meeting up to
100% of the need demonstrated by students. Approximately 65% of the student
body receive some type of financial aid, although some receive only honorary sti-
pends of $100.

ACADEMIC ENVIRONMENT

As freshmen quickly learn, Davidson's demanding work load defines the hectic
pace of the college. Davidson prides itself on the hard thinking graduates are used
to doing. The low student-to-faculty ratio in most classes allows student participation and discussion to be a major part of a Davidson education. Students must form
their own opinions about issues ranging from the causes of the American Revolution to how nuclear war can be avoided. By examining major problems and difficult
questions, Davidson graduates learn to evaluate information, form opinions, and
make decisions, skills needed in any future line of work.

"Near the end of my sophomore year I participated in a student-led discussion on the topic of fascism. At the outset of the class the discussion leader asked if he could have $4. Students quickly contributed pocket change to cover the tab. A few minutes later we were divided in half, most of the class and our professor with cans of cheap beer purchased by the collected money, the rest without. We learned those with beer were the vanguard of our fascist state, the have-nots defenders of freedom and the American way. With the class stacked in favor of the fascists, the anti-fascist group quickly learned the difficulty of arguing against the emotional appeal of fascism. Leaving the hour-long discussion, the class had a better understanding for how the people of Germany and Italy could have been seduced by Hitler and Mussolini."

Although Davidson has several especially outstanding departments, most students do not choose to attend Davidson because of a particular course of study. Most Davidson freshman either have no idea what they want to major in or change their mind one or more times between the first day of classes and the end of their sophomore year, the deadline for deciding upon a major. All of Davidson's 20 majors provide a demanding course of study in line with Davidson's philosophy of a liberal arts education. The liberal arts at Davidson means a broad range of study with a demanding work load designed to make students learn to think hard. Whether that hard thinking focuses on the works of Plato, Darwin, Einstein, or Emily Dickinson does not distract from the primary goal of the school.

Tests, papers, and quizzes come all too frequently at Davidson, where the academic pace is frantic. The unyielding work load ranges from the difficulty of regular days to the exhaustion of tests and papers to the impossibility of exams. Although regular assignments keep students comfortably occupied, every few weeks students walk the campus with serious scowls on their faces as a rash of "reviews," a Davidson word for tests, and papers hits campus. Friends disappear and the 24-hour study room in the library reaches capacity early around midterms.

The work load quickly teaches students to know what work needs immediate attention and what can be "blown off." Reading assignments are the most common casualty during tough weeks. The novel assigned in English does not seem very important when the week has a biology test and a history paper scheduled. If possible, the novel will be read in the post-crunch catch-up phase.

The masters of the college's vaunted work load, the professors, are also a key to what makes Davidson a great school. Because the school is for undergraduates only, Davidson students are taught by professors, as opposed to graduate students, in all classes except for a rare introductory class. The small class size, typically 25 students, means each student gets plenty of one-on-one instruction. Students needing help can get it rather easily as most professors keep generous office hours. Lectures are the primary form of classroom instruction, although group discussion is also very common.

The Honor Code defines the climate in which work at Davidson will be done and is the core of the Davidson experience. A simple paragraph, the Honor Code is a pledge taken by every Davidson student that simply provides that students won't cheat on their schoolwork, won't steal or lie, and will report any violations of the Honor Code. The benefits of the Honor Code are widespread. The atmosphere of trust provided by the code allows students to leave doors unlocked, permits an open-stack library, and means students can write checks virtually anywhere because people know Davidson students can be trusted. More importantly, the Honor Code permits students to have take-home tests and self-scheduled exams. Because professors know the students are honor bound not to cheat, the same test given on Tuesday can be given on Wednesday to a student who was sick. The professor simply instructs the class not to discuss the test until the remaining student has taken it. With the Honor Code, the class will not discuss even how they thought they did on the test, much less what the essay questions were.

> *"By the time classes started my freshman year, I was sick and tired of hearing about the Honor Code. I'd written an essay about the code for my admission application, heard two or three speeches about it by administrators, and had a discussion session with my freshman hall about it. Despite all the preparation, however, my first quiz under the Honor Code was spooky. It was my third day of calculus, and my professor gave us a quiz. He passed out the questions and said, 'I'll be back in ten minutes' and left the classroom. All 30 of us looked at a few other faces and then stared straight down at our paper until the professor returned. The darn thing worked after all!"*

"Intensity with honor" would be an accurate slogan for Davidson's academic environment. Students are expected to work hard and do their own work. Although this combination makes for a challenging, often grueling, college experience, these same difficulties give Davidson and its graduates their good reputation.

SOCIAL LIFE

Davidson College is not a party school. No one "road trips" to Davidson unless he or she has friends at the school. Yet this does not mean Davidson students don't like to have a good time. The school's demanding work load creates a "work hard, play hard" attitude among students. Weekends belong to celebration, at least until Sunday afternoon when the magnitude of work for the week ahead settles in across campus. By then most of the students have had some fun and are already working their way through to the next Friday afternoon.

The social life at Davidson revolves around three elements: the fraternities and eating houses of Patterson Court, the Student Union, and the nearby city of Charlotte. Patterson Court is a collection of 12 small brick buildings spread in a circle near the west end of campus. These buildings are home to national fraternities, women's eating houses, and the Black Student Coalition house. The major functions of Patterson Court houses are to provide meals and a social calendar for members. For the traditional college pastimes of drinking beer, listening to rock music, and mingling with the opposite sex, the Court is the primary scene.

Early in the fall term, freshmen are invited to visit Patterson Court and to consider membership in one of the houses. Houses may encourage students to join but are prohibited from discouraging them. Formal affiliation comes in the spring term. Every freshman has the right to select to eat and to participate in the social activities of any house through the normal Patterson Court selection process. This "normal" Patterson Court process involves choice by the freshman subject to limitations of house capacity. Approximately two-thirds of Davidson students join a Patterson Court house.

The other organization that plans major social activities on campus is the Student Union. Movies, concerts, arts festivals, speakers, and campus forums are only some of the many activities planned and organized by different committees of the student-led Union Board. The Union also organizes three annual big weekends designed to shake up the social calendar: Homecoming, Midwinters (usually in January), and Spring Frolics (April). The Union Board's dependence on student leadership makes it one of Davidson's leading extracurricular organizations as well.

When students feel the need for some city excitement, they drive 20 miles south to Charlotte, one of the nation's fastest-growing cities. It's an easy drive down Interstate 77, and many Davidson students take full advantage of Charlotte's restaurants, bars, art museums, and shopping centers. Charlotte recently opened a new 23,000-seat sports complex to house its new professional basketball team. In addition to the NBA Hornets, the Coliseum hosts rock concerts and major sporting events, including the ACC and NCAA basketball tournaments. As Charlotte continues to grow, the social options promise to improve.

"It seems like I spent a lot of time in Charlotte while I was at Davidson. I think the small size of Davidson made me a bit claustrophobic at times, and usually a trip to Charlotte was just what the doctor ordered. One of the best things about Charlotte was that the NCAA basketball tournament came to town three of the four years I was at Davidson. Each year, no matter what teams played in Charlotte, the NCAA tourney was sure to please. The best game occurred my junior year when Davidson played Kentucky in the first round. Kentucky was favored to make the national Final Four and Davidson was, well, it was like David and Goliath. For the first minutes Kentucky looked slow and Davidson hung tough. Ten minutes into the game Kentucky called time-out because Davidson was winning by five. The

crowd was going crazy. Then reality set in, and Kentucky won by 20. Still, it was fun while it lasted."

For the truly social person, however, the best times at Davidson are the impromptu parties with friends. Although Patterson Court parties are usually open to the campus and provide the major social outlet for many students, most never needed any help in having a good time. To have fun with friends, ingenuity was all that was needed.

"My freshman year, two friends introduced me to their favorite spring pastime: midnight softball. In Davidson, about a mile from campus, is a nice softball field, complete with bleachers, home-run wall, scoreboard, and, most important, lights. We would gather on campus, walk or drive out to the field and, near midnight, flip the switch that controlled the lights. Then we'd play a game of softball. The local police usually came by during our game—the lights did attract some attention—but always said 'Have fun, just keep it down.' Every spring, my friends played several games of midnight softball. The night before I graduated we played our final official game, for two hours. That final game is the most memorable social occasion I had at Davidson."

EXTRACURRICULAR ACTIVITIES

The most popular extracurricular activity at Davidson is the school's intramural sports program. More than 80% of the student body, as well as a good number of faculty and staff members, play one or more of Davidson's six intramural sports: for men, flickerball, basketball, street hockey, softball, volleyball, and indoor soccer; for women, who are welcome to play in all intramural sports, separate leagues in flickerball and basketball. The competition ranges from fierce fraternity rivalries to students just trying to have a good time.

Basketball and street hockey are played in the winter, whereas softball, volleyball, and indoor soccer are spring games. Although these sports are all universally known, the fall pastime of flickerball, a game similar to touch football, is known in only a few spots outside Davidson. In flickerball the ball may be thrown in any direction at any time. The game is tantalizingly similar to football but takes practice to master. New players must control the urge to chase the person with the ball because as soon as you do, another player gets open. The need for organization and experience makes flickerball the domain of teams from fraternities and women's eating houses. The game tends to be a humbling experience for freshman halls because their teams lack both organization and experience.

Student service both on and off campus provides an outlet for many students. For those interested in the working of the college, the Student Government Association gives students the opportunity to have their opinions heard. Known as SGA, the student government has members serving on committees concerned with issues such as the future of the athletic department, admissions, and fund-raising. The SGA also performs many campus service projects, including a Phonathon to raise money for the colleges, a career symposium, and SGA weekend for high school seniors.

Davidson Reachout is an umbrella group that organizes students interested in performing volunteer work in the local community. Volunteers do everything from visiting senior citizens at their homes to coaching youth soccer teams. National service organizations such as Habitat for Humanity also attract volunteers through Davidson Reachout.

For the would-be poet or reporter, Davidson has several student publications for student writers. The *Davidsonian* is the weekly student newspaper that provides students, faculty, and administrators with news concerning the campus and a forum for expressing their opinions. Other publications include *Quips and Cranks*, the student yearbook, and *Hobart Park*, a biannual collection of poems, paintings, photographs, and short stories.

The Student Union combines service and extracurricular activities with social activities. Union committees schedule movies and organize student discussions on important issues. Along with the Union, various campus offices and endowed programs, such as the Dean Rusk Program in International Studies, bring well-known speakers to campus. In the past few years such luminaries as authors Patsy Daniels Cornwell and Reynolds Price, theologians Walter Brueggemann and Nico Smith, psychiatrists Robert Coles and Alvin Poussaint, historian/cultural critic Garry Wills, and political scientist and government consultant Graham Allison have spoken at Davidson. Students also organize weekly open luncheons to hear speakers, and the Union presents Open Forums, in which a panel of experts discusses current issues.

The extracurricular activities at Davidson are as varied as the issues that face the campus and the world. The main ingredient in getting any activity moving forward is student involvement and effort. If for some reason the activity a student wants does not exist, he or she is welcome to start a new organization. Many currently thriving campus groups were founded by a determined student who felt the college needed a new outlet and started a club or committee from scratch.

GRADUATES

As graduation day approaches for seniors, the insidious question Mom and Dad want answered comes up more and more often: What are you going to do next year? The answer is seldom easy and is always varied, producing almost as many different responses as graduates. Davidson's liberal arts program encourages general as opposed to preprofessional majors, a philosophy that makes career choices less than obvious for many graduates. Some seniors have a clear idea of what they want to do and, anxious to pursue their professional careers, head straight to graduate school or those first steps on the corporate ladder. Others need some time to experiment with life in the real world before deciding on a career. Regardless of what first steps they take, Davidsonians have the reputation of becoming leaders in whatever fields they choose.

For the most successful of Davidson's graduates, the nation's most prestigious awards often await. During its 150 years of excellence, Davidson has produced 21 Rhodes Scholars, the fifth highest total among the nation's liberal arts colleges. Davidson leads all Southeastern colleges in the number of graduates awarded Woodrow Wilson Fellowships and Marshall Scholarships.

One of the most valuable assets Davidson graduates have in finding a job is the school's fiercely loyal network of alumni. Although the school's alumni are not large in number compared to alumni of major state universities, Davidson graduates are by and large a highly successful group that make for an excellent network of career fields, advice, and influence for the recent graduates to take advantage of. Although Davidson has changed during the last half-century, graduates from any class, no matter how long ago, feel a tie to recent graduates and often go out of their way to lend a hand.

> *"I had been a reporter in town for only about six months when I went to see a lawyer I had never met to discuss a case he was involved in that I was covering. I got to his office, and we quickly disposed of the matter I had come to discuss. As I got up to leave, he told me he had been to a hearing that day concerning another facet of the case we were discussing. I had been too busy that day to go to the hearing, so I asked him if he would mind telling me what had happened. As it turned out, that hearing was as important as any that had occurred in the case in months. I told him I appreciated his taking the time to tell me what happened. Then I noticed he had a Davidson diploma hanging in his office. I told him I had just graduated from Davidson. 'I know,' he said. 'I read about you in the* Update. *Why do you think I went out of my way to tell you what happened today?' After that meeting I never again underestimated the value of my degree."*

For those not attracted to graduate school or the world of work, Davidson has contracts with several programs that send graduates throughout the world to study or teach. Davidson, as well as several dozen other colleges, annually nominates four seniors to participate in the Watson Fellowship. This program awards graduates money to study abroad for a year. Two Davidson students typically win this award. If a major cash award doesn't come through, however, a year touring the globe is not out of the question, especially for students willing to teach. Kenya and Japan are just two of the countries where dozens of Davidson students have spent a year or more teaching English.

For the senior willing to spend time and energy making contacts and writing letters, no career field is out of reach. The lack of a specific professional degree does hinder careers in some fields; that's one reason many students eventually go to graduate school.

The homogeneous, upper-middle-class makeup of the Davidson student body creates a natural career triad of doctors, lawyers, and bakers. Fifth-year reunions tend to have a good many practicing lawyers and doctors at the residency stage of their educations. Banking, real-estate brokerages, insurance, and other professions also attract many Davidson graduates.

A career after Davidson is simply up to the individual graduate. The liberal arts education offered there prepares graduates with a foundation of critical thinking that will be useful in any career.

SUMMARY OVERVIEW

Davidson's liberal arts program emphasizes a core curriculum and hard work. This course of study aims to produce graduates who can analyze information critically and make original deductions as to the import of that information. Davidson's Honor Code aims to ensure that those strong thinkers are also good citizens. Most students go on to receive graduate degrees.

The highly qualified students admitted to Davidson create a campus-wide classroom. With so many intelligent people in the student body, students teaching students is a common experience. Add a top-notch faculty, and student quickly get a dose of hard work that leads to the ability to eliminate frivolous efforts and concentrate on what is important. Davidson's size creates a tight-knit student body and, with that, a loyal pool of alumni. Good friends with plenty to teach are part of the Davidson experience.

The small size can also be a drawback. Davidson students are not a diverse band. Most are career-oriented and used to having plenty of money. For the student who is a little left or right in the middle of the Davidson road, alienation can occur. The key in this situation is to find your niche. As small as Davidson is, there are innumerable contributions that can be made. Sometimes it just takes a while to find them.

Davidson's small size can also be a problem. Because everyone knows everyone, reputations are established quickly and gossip is unavoidable. The lack of a variety in social options—bars, restaurants, rock clubs—causes students to emit many a bored sigh as juniors and seniors tire of the same old scene.

"Despite never visiting Davidson before my first day of orientation freshman year, I never once felt like I had gone to the wrong school. I made friends easily, friends I feel certain I will keep in touch with for the rest of my life. The work was demanding, especially at first, but it made me a better thinker and ready for the challenges of the workplace. Not every day was a picnic. There were days, especially during exams, when I simply did not know how I would make it to the end of the term. There were cold winter days when Davidson felt like a drab, drafty cave. But the bad times are hard to remember. In fact, the problems I encountered probably are common to all college students, no matter where they go to school. For me, Davidson was the place to go to college."

Andrew Barron, B.A.

Duke University

THE PROGRAM

Duke, one of the most beautiful and easiest to spell universities, lies in the center of North Carolina. The University of North Carolina in Chapel Hill, North Carolina State University in Raleigh, and Duke are the vertices of the Research Triangle, one of the highest concentrations of Ph.D.s in the world. Duke and its hometown, Durham, have come a long way in 150 years. Back then, Durham was an ugly tobacco-and-mill town, and Duke was the tiny Brown Schoolhouse.

Today, Duke is one of the nation's premier universities, offering undergraduates both a strong liberal arts education and a fine engineering school. Trinity College of Arts and Sciences and the School of Engineering, the two undergraduate schools, together enroll almost 6000 students. Duke is a highly regarded preprofessional school, with outstanding departments—most notably English, history, and public policy studies. Duke's strong faculty, outstanding library system, and emphasis on personal achievement establish it as a leader not only in the South, but in the world.

The two main campuses, East and West, are just over a mile apart, and linked by bus lines. Together with Central Campus, North Campus, the Marine Laboratory at Beaufort, North Carolina, and Duke Forest, Duke University covers about 8500 acres in five counties and ZIP codes. Finding a quiet place to study is not usually a problem.

> *"Duke is small enough that students are more than just numbers, but big enough to be taken seriously. Students know the dean for student life, Suzanne Wasiolek, as Dean Sue (unless they're in trouble, in which case she's Dean Wasiolek), and she and your academic dean are likely to know you by name. President Brodie has regular office hours during which he will talk with anyone who cares to take the time. But if a small, comfortable*

atmosphere goes hand-in-hand with small-time thinking and facilities at many colleges, that's not so at Duke.

"Every student has access to computer facilities located throughout the university. Laboratory sciences are constantly being expanded, and a new lab sciences building is on the way. Student organizations take an active and effective role in the Duke and Durham communities. Prospective students need not fear that an intimate environment means the college experience will be 'just for funsies.' There's real work to be done and real facilities in which to do it."

Regardless of your major, the basic curriculum guarantees a wide range of study. Even for students in the School of Engineering, there's just no escaping writing an essay from time to time. And even diehard poets find themselves clamping test tubes and wearing shock-resistant safety glasses.

Duke University is a distinctively residential campus: Students are encouraged to live in the residence halls for four years. Although students at many schools take their classes and leave for a dorm or apartment far removed from the main drag of campus, Duke's residence halls offer substantial options in close proximity to the academic areas of campus. Leisure time can be spent in productive ways, too. College is four years of intense academic preparation but also a time for intellectual and spiritual growth unbridled by distractions from the outside world.

The setting certainly encourages high-mindedness. Duke's West Campus is entirely Gothic in architecture. The Chapel is more than 200 feet tall and larger than many cathedrals. Even the modest study area in Perkins Library is a full-blown English reading room. East Campus is almost entirely Georgian in architecture. East is the smaller, quieter campus and attracts more reserved and off-beat residents.

"At the head of West Campus is the 210-foot Duke Chapel, which houses a 50-bell, four-octave carillon. The bells are played everyday at 5:00 P.M. by one of two professional carilloneurs, distinguishing this music from the cheap tape recordings played from the concrete bell towers of some other nearby universities. University officials soliciting financial and other support from alumni are known to make a point of calling when the bells are being rung, to stir up fond memories.

"Memories may not be so fond for residents of the dorms just a few feet from the Chapel, whose Sunday morning hangovers are greeted by the banging of two-ton church bells, but it's always interesting to see what they'll be playing next. On national holidays, expect patriotic music. Before a Carolina basketball game, expect the Blue Devil fight song. Even Duke Transit gets into the act before the big game, displaying custom-made "Go To Hell, Carolina" messages in the destination windows."

Students come from a diversity of backgrounds. Not everyone drives a BMW, although some certainly do. Duke parents own large corporations, anchor network newscasts, and hold high government office. They also work in construction areas, take dictation, and drive trucks. Duke isn't looking for one-track achievers. Students are expected to excel academically, certainly, but also to demonstrate leadership and initiative in other areas.

Be prepared for a serious academic challenge, but not a hyper-competitive atmosphere. Your success does not depend on someone else's failure. Certain courses, notably organic chemistry, have the reputation for separating the real premeds from those who have nothing better to do; however, once you're actually *in* Duke, the faculty are generally more interested in your success than in weeding you out.

In short, Duke is looking for well-rounded achievers who can make things happen for themselves. The two campuses offer a seriously academic but always exciting environment, often described as a Gothic wonderland. There is no typical Duke student. They come from widely varying backgrounds and experience. An outstanding faculty awaits and will offer as much—or as little—as students seek out.

GETTING IN/FINANCIAL AID

One in four applicants is offered admission to Duke University's two undergraduate schools, Trinity College and the School of Engineering. But numbers like that are largely irrelevant. Many of the trade schools that advertise on late-night television have higher applicant-to-acceptance ratios, but that doesn't mean they're harder to get into.

SAT I scores are high, with the middle 50% of the freshman class scoring 600 to 690 on the verbal portion and 650 to 750 on the mathematics section. Graduating seniors also compiled an impressive record, with some 88% of the Arts and Sciences students and 92% of the engineering students graduating in the top 10% of the senior class. With academic performance like that, they could go anywhere.

Fortunately, the admissions staff knows there's more to a good student than good grades. Each application is actually read cover-to-cover and evaluated by at least two members of the admissions staff. The student is rated on a scale of one to five in each of six areas: quality of program, performance, recommendations, personal qualities, testing, and essays. If their preliminary evaluations agree, the results are forwarded to the admissions committee, which makes the final decision. If they disagree, a third reader breaks the tie.

Readers look for evidence that applicants have challenged themselves to the limits offered by their secondary schools. A recent press report about increasingly difficult college admissions standards noted the case of a student from Raleigh, North Carolina, who graduated with a 4.0 but was not admitted to Duke. What the report failed to note was that the student's school was on a 5.0 scale and that the student had enrolled in relatively unchallenging courses.

Prospective applicants should avail themselves of advanced placement and honors courses, even if they don't anticipate applying the credits toward a college degree. Don't take the shop course, take the third year of Latin.

> *"When I was a junior in high school, my father and I toured the East Coast looking closely at each of the five schools I found interesting. (I recommend that approach highly: you'd be surprised how profoundly your mind can change once you've seen a school.)*
>
> *"It's hard not to be impressed by Duke's looks alone. But closer examination reveals more than just a pretty facade. Visitors are welcome to sit in on classes or stay overnight in the dorms.*
>
> *"The admissions counselors are very helpful and freely dispense advice at the information sessions. For example: No essays about the evils of the electoral college system, we were told. Those get old. We were also advised to think carefully about our letters of recommendation. If you indicate on your application that your most absorbing extracurricular activity is competitive swimming but fail to produce a letter of recommendation from your swimming coach, the admissions committee wonders why."*

Duke boasts one of the most geographically diverse student bodies in the nation. Applicants from every state and continent except Antarctica are represented. Although Duke is proud of its heritage as a North Carolina school and a leader of southern universities, only 15% of its student body is from North Carolina.

Competition is one reason. The University of North Carolina system is the oldest and one of the best public university systems in the nation. For in-state students the UNC system is much more affordable and convenient. (For out-of-state students, UNC-Chapel Hill is harder to get into than Duke.) For a recent class, 195 North Carolina students entered the university, compared with 122 from New Jersey and 185 from New York. The other big states were Florida, 115, and Maryland, 92.

> *"Some students readily admit they came to Duke because they didn't get in somewhere else. Others claim it's the weather. As a general rule, it can be hard to convince Northeasterners that there is such a good thing as a good southern school. But while there certainly are fewer, there are some, and Duke is one.*
>
> *"Initially, the new environment can be overwhelming. When I was taking calculus in high school, I didn't worry about it if I didn't understand related rates. If I didn't understand it, the rest of the class probably didn't either, and I had nothing to worry about. The first time I tried that on a calculus test at Duke, I had a rude awakening. The rest of the class did understand, and for the first time I had to work to keep up.*
>
> *"But being surrounded by bright students, all of whom were president of the student council and Mr. and Miss Everything in*

*high school quickly offers advantages. For one thing, almost any-
one can help you with your work. Duke students have valuable
intellectual resources at their disposal 24 hours a day: each other.
As common as the late-night party binge is the late-night agoniz-
ing about the meaning of it all."*

When your application arrives at Duke, financial aid information goes one way
and admissions materials go another: The financial aid office is several buildings
down from the admissions office, and admissions decisions are in no way geared to
the student's ability to pay.

Each applicant is automatically considered for honorary scholarship packages
administered by the university, including the A. B. Duke Scholarship, a full four-
year grant that includes a summer at Oxford University. The Duke Endowment and
other scholarship funds and loans are available to students who apply to the financial aid office.

Duke estimates the current cost for an academic year, including tuition,
room, board, and other expenses to be almost $25,000 per student. Thirty-nine
percent of the undergraduates receive financial aid, and probably the most visible financial aid program is work-study. Students in the program work less that
20 hours per week in a variety of jobs. Money earned in work-study is paid directly to the student, not the bursar's office. A typical need-based package consists mostly of grants, with loans and work-study together constituting less than
25% of the financial aid package.

ACADEMIC ENVIRONMENT

Simple math will demonstrate that it's harder to get into Duke than to graduate.
Once you've made it past the admissions office, the nail-biting is over. The course
work can be rigorous, depending upon your curriculum, but the object of Duke's
game is to help you learn, not weed you out. To that end, Duke professors are
accessible almost to a fault, inviting classes over to the house for coffee, conversation about course work, and even a good party here and there. The eccentric college
professors that high school teachers warned you would "never put up with that kind
of stuff" probably exist, but happily Duke doesn't seem to be hiring them.

Duke is well known for its English, history, and public policy studies departments. Each is generously funded, recruits top faculty, and offers a popular major.
The undergraduate student-to-faculty ratio is about 12 to 1. All classes above the
introductory level are taught by the faculty. Graduate students generally teach recitation classes for lecture courses, labs, and freshman courses such as introductory
calculus.

Although each student is enrolled in either Trinity or Engineering, students in
either school may take courses in the other. There is no distinction other than

curricula on a day-to-day basis between the students of the two schools. The engineering curriculum has fewer electives than Trinity's and therefore less opportunity to "sample the other side." But defection from one school to the other isn't unheard of.

Students are not required to declare a major until the end of sophomore year, and doing so is almost as simple as filling out a card and dropping it in a box. Students have been known to change majors during their senior year — which is technically permissible — but probably not desirable, because course requirements are different from major to major.

Most Trinity College students enroll in the standard curriculum, which entails a distribution of courses in the major, a field of general study, and electives. A different number of courses is required in each field. In addition, each student has course work in five of six areas: arts and literature, civilization, natural sciences, quantitative reasoning, social sciences, and foreign languages. Three small group learning experiences, seminars, tutorials, and independent studies are required for graduation.

Engineering students have a more rigorous schedule with fewer options for defining their own course work. Even so, many engineering majors are able to double-major in liberal arts, and even diehard gear heads are required to take humanities courses. Engineering students may be segregated from Trinity students academically, but not socially or residentially. Outside the library or classroom, the distinction doesn't come into play.

Study abroad is recommended during the junior year. Duke has programs in Europe, Asia, Africa, and Canada.

The Duke faculty are a fascinating bunch. They are both strong teachers and dedicated researchers, and it isn't sufficient to be only one or the other. If your Old Testament teacher has interesting stories about Hebrew child burials, it's because she's unearthed a few of her own in Israel.

> "One of the most popular freshman courses is taught by a full professor. Every entering premed at Duke (and believe me, many enter even if fewer leave) is entertained by the fabulous Dr. James Bonk. Chemistry 11 and 12, a.k.a., Bonkistry, are daily performances by one of Duke's premier players. Bonk memorizes every lecture down to the 12-digit answers to his hypothetical demonstration equations. If he tells a joke in his 9:10 class, you can bet the folks in his 12:40 class will hear it too.
>
> "Bonk's custom-made light-up periodic chart is now guarded by a sophisticated motion-detecting security system because certain elements' translucent plates, notably uranium and other radioactive atoms, used to disappear with such regularity Bonk couldn't replace them fast enough."

Just as Duke isn't interested in admitting students who excel in only one area, the university is equally committed to a broad-based education. If your interest is chemistry, that's fine. But expect some English literature, history, religion, art, and economics along the way. The results are high acceptance rates at graduate and professional schools and high employment rates and starting salaries.

SOCIAL LIFE

In keeping with James Duke's vision of the university, West Campus is shaped like a cross, with the Chapel looming at the head. On the right arm of the cross is the academic and administrative side of the university. Perkins Library, the Allen Building, and the Davison Building highlight the right, whereas dormitories with student-selected names such as Maxwell House, FUBAR, Random House, and Stately Wayne Manor mix with Kappa Sig, Mirecourt, and House P on the left.

Less than half the students are members of fraternities or sororities, but their presence on campus is very strong. Rush for fraternities lasts the entire fall semester; pledging takes place in the spring. As a result, the fall semester is one big party after another, almost all of which are open to the entire university community.

Freshmen are required to live on campus and usually get less than great housing. After the first year, it gets more complicated.

The first major housing distinction among upperclassmen is between commitment and noncommitment housing. As compared with their counterparts in noncommitment houses, commitment house members agree to live with the group until they leave university housing, pay dues, and participate in house social and programming activities. The actual amount of participation varies from living group to living group. If you don't choose a commitment house, you simply enter the lottery and take what you get, and the pickings are usually about as choice as freshmen housing.

Commitment houses include fraternities and other selective houses and nonselective houses. Selective houses choose all or most of their residents. In addition, the university offers particular living options, such as the international dorm and women's studies dorm, for students participating in special programs.

Duke guarantees four years of housing, and most students take them up on it. At Duke, going home means walking across the quad. Weekends generally fire up at about noon Friday, much to the displeasure of religion professors, whose classrooms face the residential side of the campus.

> *"With a consistently ranked team and a stadium not much larger than most high school gyms, Duke basketball games are a social event in themselves. Duke students have the best seats in Cameron Indoor Stadium: the lower bleachers right around the court. The players are so close you could reach out and touch them, which has led to the establishment of a buffer zone between*

the crowd and the opposing team's bench. Students are admitted to varsity athletic events free of charge, and valid student IDs become a hot commodity right before key games."

Almost every fraternity and many living groups have parties once a week, each on a different night. For the most part, the parties are open to the entire university community. At a Sigma Chi party, don't be surprised to see Phi Delt letters. The university requires that all guests be carded and given an identifying hand stamp with the sponsor's name.

Recognizing that there is a difference between how students ought to act and how they often do, the university cooperates with the student government to provide such services as Safe Rides. A shuttle service using university vans and operated entirely by student volunteers makes pick-ups at bars, private parties, or anywhere students may find themselves in need of assistance. A similar program, Safe Walks, provides escorts for women who must walk back to dorms or apartments at night.

But the bulk of campus social life happens on campus. Weekend nights at Duke can be loud, especially on West Campus. East Campus, a little over a mile away, is the quieter of the two and considered by those in the "don't know" to be more boring. Less than one third of the fraternities are housed on East, but a high concentration of freshmen live there. For some, the housing lottery means waiting for the chance to escape from the perceived purgatory of East Campus.

"Having lived on East, I prefer it. East Campus offers athletic facilities, dining halls, a dance studio, an old-fashioned coffee house, and performing arts facilities. And if you need to go to West, it's only a five-minute bus ride away. But when the day is over and all I want to do is go home, there's no better place than East. Dorm rooms are about twice the size as the ones on West and cost less.

"For those who don't want either option, the university operates Central Campus Apartments between East and West. Central is the place to be if privacy is at a premium. The apartments are well maintained and served by a special Duke Transit route."

Duke's social life is uniquely free and open. Duke has a Greek life, a relatively strong one, but elitist exclusion is not part of the system. Almost every party on campus is open to the public. It isn't unusual at all for members of another living group to outnumber the hosts at a weekly gathering. And because most students live on campus, most of the social life is there as well. That means a more accessible social structure and fewer problems with drunk-driving mishaps. If you can't unwind at Duke, you aren't trying.

EXTRACURRICULAR ACTIVITIES

Duke has something to do for everyone. Intramural sports from football to track to racquetball to badminton are offered for each living group. The university offers 28 club sports, 12 varsity sports for men, and nine for women. If you're good at soccer but not good enough to play on Duke's championship team don't worry. The intramural program will give you a run for your money.

Religious organizations representing the major Christian denominations, Hillel, Baha'i, and Islam are active, and almost all of them conduct services in Duke Chapel. Many of the dorms have Bible study sessions, and religious groups are active in community service work throughout Durham.

Volunteering for community service is also very popular at Duke. A Community Service Center helps students find volunteer projects appropriate to their interests and abilities. Last year, 3000 students were involved in programs at the center. In addition, every member of the incoming class participates in Community Service Day, a project that this year involved about one dozen work sites across the city. A survey of last year's senior class revealed that 87% participated in volunteer activities, such as working at local soup kitchens, tutoring in local schools, helping out at shelters for the homeless, and working in projects run by groups like Habitat for Humanity.

The Duke University Union provides programming for the entire university community through 13 committees and media organizations. The Union is responsible for on-campus major speakers, performing artists, special events, performing arts, and art galleries. The Union also sponsors Freewater Films, an avant-garde film club bringing new and unusual cinema to campus, free to students. Cable 13, Duke's television station, and WXDU-FM, the radio station, operate under the Union umbrella and have developed a loyal following.

The *Chronicle,* Duke's student newspaper, is circulated five days a week throughout the academic year. Because Duke doesn't have a journalism school, the paper is not advised by faculty, and its $600,000 budget comes entirely from advertising revenue. Despite its lack of faculty involvement, the *Chronicle* has managed to win a number of Columbia Press Awards in the past few years and provides a hands-on approach to journalism. Students sell ads, write the news, and typeset the paper themselves, with only a few paid employees.

"The great thing about extracurricular activities at Duke is that they're so genuine. Students are not on a university-controlled leash. Funding for student groups is allocated by the Associated Students of Duke University and not the university itself.

"The point was driven home for me one night while I was working at the Chronicle. *As long as I had worked for the paper, I had wondered whether the editorial independence we perceived was an illusion. If the university had a strong enough reason to*

demand that an item be printed or withheld, would it exercise its power to censor the student newspaper?

"We found out just exactly how much editorial freedom we had when the newspaper's senior editors learned of a forthcoming and as-of-yet unannounced multimillion-dollar gift to the Capital Campaign for the Arts and Sciences. The negotiations were still in progress and releasing the information would seriously jeopardize the gift.

"Such a huge gift was indeed news, and the editors wanted to print the story. That night, the editor received phone calls from the University President Keith Brodie and Capital Campaign Director Joel Fleishman asking him to consider holding off for the sake of the gift, and after long debate among the staff, he held the story until the danger of losing the gift had passed.

"But although millions of dollars were at stake and although the president of Duke University could effectively shut down the paper with a quick phone call to our printer, that threat was never made. At no time did the university do anything more than ask the paper to use good judgment in deciding for itself. The waters were tested, and they felt fine."

GRADUATES

There was a time when a bachelor's degree wasn't something one got when finished with education. A bachelor is, after all one uninitiated into the higher pursuits. In keeping with that view, many Duke graduates go on to pursue an advanced degree.

While it may seem that almost everyone comes to Duke as a premed student, the actual figure is 20 to 30% of freshmen plan to pursue a career in medicine. Sophomore year's organic chemistry, with one of the highest failure rates of any course on campus, changes that. Only those students willing to make academics a full-time job generally stick with a premed curriculum. About 15% eventually apply, but for premeds willing to stick it out, the benefits are there. More than 90% of seniors applying to medical school from Duke are accepted.

Despite its premed reputation, more Duke students go on to business and law schools (22% and 21% respectively). Duke students often go to top business schools, especially the Fuqua School at Duke itself. Law school acceptance rate is around 99%. Finally, almost 18% of the class enter graduate schools in the humanities, natural sciences, social sciences, and engineering.

"Something strange and magical happens every year at Duke University. Guys who formerly had hair to their shoulders suddenly look like Ward Cleaver. The interviewers are coming, and like Cinderella's sisters, seniors primp and prepare.

"Shortly thereafter, the letters come back. Just as they did when

they applied to universities four years earlier, students find a thick envelope is better news than a thin one. Fraternity bulletin boards are decorated with official letterheads, beginning with messages like: 'Dear Mr. Hensley: Although your qualifications were impressive...' and a promise to keep your name on file.

"Finally, it happens, and for reasons not entirely understood by underclassmen caught in the crossfire, a senior is buying the beer that night. Someone found a job."

Duke operates an alumni program called Duke Source, allowing undergraduates access to Duke alumni advisers. The alums are always eager to meet and help out fellow Dukies and strengthen the Duke Connection.

Many cities have large populations of Duke alumni with a cohesive alumni network. In Washington, for example, alums can check in on the latest Washington Duke Club activities by calling (703) 684-DUKE. Every Wednesday night, the club gathers at a different Washington restaurant or club and relives a little of their college rowdiness.

SUMMARY OVERVIEW

In a speech to my entering freshman class, then-university president Terry Sanford told us there are a high road and a low road through Duke University, and he was right.

Duke has one of the finest faculties in the world and ever-expanding facilities. Your fellow students will have been chosen not only for intellectual aptitude but also for leadership potential and their ability to pull together Duke's resources for their best benefit.

No one makes you achieve your potential. Your behavior is not being scrutinized. Your academic plans and goals are your own. Only one course is required, and other curriculum requirements are flexible enough that you can leave Duke with a top-notch liberal education under your belt. Or you have just enough rope to hang yourself, if you so choose. But, then, that's how the real world operates.

Duke is small enough that if you don't know someone, you undoubtedly have a friend in common. The faculty are accessible and even eager to sit down over lunch and discuss the course work. Individual attention is there when you need it. But Duke is large enough that you won't be stir-crazy after four years. There are always new things to do, and with eight thousand acres there is always a place you haven't been yet.

Although there are real benefits to creating a purely collegiate and academic environment, there are drawbacks. The university is largely isolated from Durham and North Carolina. Many students make a point to get involved in community service activities, but others seem unaware that there is a real world outside the illusion college affords. Safe in their Gothic wonderland, Duke students are more likely than others to forget about the real world. There is no homelessness, no poverty, and relatively little crime at Duke University, or even within Duke's view: the university owns all the land around West Campus as far as the eye can see. But that's the price Duke students pay for being immersed in an academic environment.

Duke students are very friendly and lead an active and open social life. Private parties are rare. Most are open to anyone who happens to notice something's going on. Students on the quad are happy to help you find something or help you move that ten-ton sofa up the stairs. And they're bright. Any given sophomore can stop playing beer Frisbee long enough to talk coherently about economic theory, thermodynamics, or Gnosticism.

The new kid on the block always has more to prove. Duke is less than a century old (although it traces its roots back about 150 years) and still suffers from an identity crisis. Some administrators are perceived as trying to "Harvardize" Duke and make it more like the Ivy League schools. The opposing school of thought says, "Let Duke be Duke." But the truth of the matter is, there is little agreement about what that should be. Duke's roots are growing deeper, and very low attrition and transfer rates suggest that students are happy here.

Those who take full advantage of the Duke experience have one of the world's finest research and teaching faculty at their disposal, a variety of cultural and artistic events, one of the largest private library systems in the country, and a great place to call home.

Lane Hensley, B. A.

Emory University

THE PROGRAM

"'Turn around, you'll want to remember this,' my mother said while she snapped her Nikon at me as I walked into my freshman dorm for the first time.

"I tried to hide my face. My roommate or future girlfriend might see this spectacle. Or, I really feared, my mom was documenting the biggest mistake of my life—not going to a top-flight Eastern school.

"My high school buddies from Maryland had headed north to find ivy-covered walls, bow-tied professors, and NCAA football championships. And I wound up in Atlanta at Emory University, a school whose only assets seemed to be a fancy admissions brochure, a huge scholarship budget, and an acceptance letter for me.

"So I was shocked when more than one of my hallmates told me they had turned down Yale to come to Emory. I almost dropped my fork when my faculty advisor told me over dinner that he had resigned an appointment at Harvard to become an Emory professor.

"What secret about Emory did these people know that I didn't? The answer came in bits and pieces. Like when I found out that a CNN producer was going to teach my class about the changing world of international relations. Or when I saw a $40 million biomedical research complex rise from a patch of dirt in one semester. Or when I woke up one morning my sophomore year to learn that Atlanta (a city previously known to me as just a place to change planes) had been chosen as the site of the 1996 summer Olympics.

"I had stumbled, somewhat accidentally, onto a campus rock-

*eting from near-obscurity to the upper ranks of the nation's best
universities. And a city growing at the same pace.*

*"As graduation neared four years later, I didn't want to leave
the academic and social excitement of Emory's campus. Plenty of
people had yet to hear of Emory's success, but I was no longer
one of them. And I was glad my mom had evidence of the day I
took one of the most important steps of my life."*

Emory University—a newcomer to the ranks of America's top colleges—is engineering one of the most ambitious projects in the history of American education. In
the late 20th century, it wants to give the Ivy League schools, and everyone else, a
run for their money. So far, Emory is succeeding.

Twenty years ago, Emory was a sleepy regional school. Today full-tuition merit
scholarships lure the nation's top high school students to the lush suburban campus. Emory wins bidding wars for top-notch professors, sometimes entire departments. And new lecture halls, dorms, and science labs are springing up every
semester.

The university barely looks the same as it did on November 28, 1979, when Coca-
Cola Co. chairman Robert Woodruff gave Emory $105 million. That gift—then the
largest ever given to any school—helped build one of the nation's ten biggest en-
dowments, allowing Emory to design its own future as other colleges struggle to
maintain the past.

But the Woodruff gift didn't just enlarge Emory's bank balance. It pushed the
school's academic program and ambitions into a different orbit. After seeking advice
from hundreds of higher education experts, Emory's president set out to create "the
world's next great university."

Emory would bring together in Atlanta the finest faculty and students to create a
preeminent teaching and research university, he envisioned. Graduates from each of
its departments and schools would receive an unsurpassed and rigorous moral and
intellectual education from energetic and distinguished teachers who are committed
to setting the pace in everything from cancer research to literary scholarship. The
school should be a recognized leader in every aspect of higher education, and the
knowledge gained in Emory's classrooms, labs, and natural surroundings would enrich not only those on campus but humanity at large.

Emory isn't there yet, but the work in progress is impressive. The administration
calculates every admission and hiring decision and designs every inch of new construction to add luster to Emory's first-class liberal arts reputation. And with no im-
movable obstacles—physical or academic—to the campus' growth, Emory is a rarity
in today's world, an unfettered academic playground.

Emory professors, even those without endowed faculty chairs and international
reputations, are free to develop the university's proclaimed vision of a "community
of scholars" however they want, largely unencumbered by budgetary anxieties or
musty traditions. Everything is within reach, from offering small lectures on their favorite areas of study to buying more books and computers and creating new inter-

disciplinary research centers. Students can feast on the school's modern resources and diverse course offerings, confident that Emory will not rest on its laurels. Barely a semester passes without Emory forging another alliance with a prestigious European university or federal agency, snaring a prize-winning lecturer, or otherwise enhancing the riches it has to offer. Emory has become a place where the nation's top teachers and students want to be.

Like much of Atlanta—a city that has replaced its provincial image with dazzling skyscrapers, inviting parks, and international acclaim—everything at Emory is modern and progressive. No aspirations are really off-limits (except maybe bringing a Pepsi to class).

In addition to having bountiful academic resources, Emory is also a very pleasant place to go to school. It is located on 631 acres in a tranquil, residential community of DeKalb County a few miles from downtown Atlanta, which has quickly and deservedly developed a reputation as one of the nation's most livable cities. After years of rapid economic and cultural growth, metropolitan Atlanta is a young, bustling area larger than northern cities like Cleveland, Pittsburgh, or Baltimore, but without the harsh weather or attitudes.

The Emory campus, nestled in the tree-filled neighborhood where the movie *Driving Miss Daisy* was filmed, attracts many oohs and aahs from first-time visitors. The stately Italian Renaissance marble facades, beautiful glass buildings, and country club-like lawns are just about as clean-cut as Emory students themselves. The people and the campus are neither stuffy nor rundown.

Although the student body isn't entirely homogenous, most Emory students typically come from conservative, middle-class homes. The two largest groups—cosmopolitan Jewish Northeasterners and Christian Southern gentry—make an interesting and unlikely mix. Regardless of where Emory students come from, they sling L.L. Bean backpacks over their t-shirts and khaki shorts on the way to afternoons filled with classes, internships, and quick trips to funky record stores in Atlanta's bohemian neighborhoods.

Emory students may not have been straight-A students in high school, but they know they could have been. You won't find too many jock types or eggheads. Emory students are a hard-working bunch that doesn't take itself too seriously. They'd be happier taking a break from their late-night study session to plot a practical joke with their hallmates than they would collapsing on top of their books from exhaustion alone in the library.

Emory still has a long way to go, but the university has made great strides toward its ambitious goal: combining the academic seriousness of the North with the casual style of the capital of the New South. Wisely investing its Woodruff money in top-of-the-line buildings, professors, and students, Emory has continued to gain momentum with each passing year. It has calculated what it needs to do to join the ranks of the nation's elite universities, and it has methodically and confidently followed that path without losing its Southern charm and student-faculty intimacy. The simultaneous rise of Atlanta has only hastened the inevitable recognition of Emory's accomplishments.

GETTING IN/FINANCIAL AID

Emory's ascent has made the admission process tougher. The number of applications and the average SAT I scores of applicants have risen steadily while the class size has remained just about constant. As word of the "good life" at Emory gets around, it's becoming much more common to find the university listed as an incoming student's first-choice school instead of being behind Duke, Vanderbilt, or Georgetown.

With all those people to choose from, the admission office won't be too impressed with a 4.0 grade point average if that's all there is on the application. They're looking for students who formed their own business or club in high school, found an interesting job or volunteer position, or has followed a steady, creative path in pursuit of their interests. These days they could fill the entire freshman class with run-of-the-mill honor roll students a dozen times over, but it wouldn't make the campus too interesting a place to be. With so much growth still to come, Emory needs energetic and creative hands to build new traditions.

To maintain its Southern flavor, though, the university has made sure that Southeasterners account for about half of each entering class (the largest portions come from Georgia and Florida). Mid-Atlantic residents comprise another quarter of the student body (many students joke that Emory is really just a piece of New Jersey transplanted in Georgia), and international students and those from west of the Mississippi make up a smaller but vibrant portion of each class.

And while most colleges are struggling just to preserve their need-based scholarship budgets these days, Emory continues to have one of the largest merit-based scholarship programs in the country—a direct product of Woodruff's gift. With the Emory scholars program, the university can woo just about any high school senior it wants. About 60 students receive full-tuition scholarships each year, including more than a dozen who get the red-carpet treatment as Woodruff Scholars (or Woodies)—free tuition, room, and board for four years, a package worth more than $100,000. A host of other incoming students win partial tuition breaks along with the preferential class selection and stipends for cultural activities reserved for all Emory scholars.

"If you're remotely interested in Emory, find out about the scholars program. Competition is intense, but Emory has more to give away than most schools—especially if you don't qualify for need-based aid.

"Hundreds of high schools around the country send lists of candidates for Emory scholarships to Atlanta every fall. In addition to scholarships for the general student body, there are special merit awards set aside for debaters, Southeasterners, Atlanta public school students, and performing artists. Applying means writing an extra essay but at the very worst, you get an early, nonbinding verdict on your admission application. If you wind

up as a scholarship finalist, Emory flies you to Atlanta for a
weekend of on-campus interviews with professors and students.

"And even if you don't get one right away, don't despair. I ap-
plied for one as a high school senior and didn't get it. But after a
lot of academic and extracurricular work my freshman year, I
won a half-tuition scholarship for the remaining three years.
There aren't many of them, but you're more likely to find rewards
like that at Emory than anywhere else."

Emory scholars are usually at the top of their class, but their academic energy and
spirit rub off on the entire student body, 60% of whom receive some form of financial aid. Many students get ahead academically and financially by helping professors
with their research for work-study aid. And other campus jobs, like manning the student center snack bar, library circulation counter, or a residence hall desk, are more
social than stressful.

ACADEMIC ENVIRONMENT

"After working on Capitol Hill in high school, I thought I'd have to
wait until graduate school to learn anything more about politics.

"But Emory is the only university to have a former U.S. presi-
dent, Jimmy Carter, on its faculty. Whether you're a fan of his or
not, Carter adds a lot to the Emory community.

"As a Distinguished University Professor, Carter has lectured in
every graduate and undergraduate division of the university, in-
cluding my sophomore history class studying American politics
of the late 1970s. He's always eager to take questions, especially
at the town hall meeting he holds for the whole campus every
fall. Randomly selected people quiz him on everything from his
views on world events to what kind of breakfast cereal he eats.
And it doesn't cause a stir to see Carter, his wife Rosalynn, and
their Secret Service escorts, strolling through the student center
on their way to lead a class or symposium.

"His presidential library and public policy center (which
Emory recently absorbed as a permanent arm of the university)
are just down the street from campus. Dozens of Emory students
and professors work at the Carter Center, helping the former pres-
ident mediate Third World civil wars, international crises, and
election disputes, eradicate global malnutrition and disease, and
revitalize inner-city Atlanta. And even those who don't work for
Carter (who is a tireless Emory booster) benefit from the out-
standing lectures and conferences he brings to Atlanta.

"For example, while my friends at other schools read about

Desmond Tutu, Mikhail Gorbachev, and Eduard Shevardnadze, I covered their visits to Emory and the Carter Center for the Emory student newspaper. And I heard African generals, United Nations officials, and prominent diplomats who came to meet with Carter, discussing pressing global issues within yards of my dorm room. It's also not uncommon to find former Carter administration officials holding simultaneous Emory faculty appointments and Carter Center posts.

"Add to that Emory's faculty of nationally recognized academic experts on everything from presidential politics to post-Soviet studies—plus all the visits to the Emory area by national politicians as well as local officials like Newt Gingrich and Sam Nunn (both Emory alums)—and I think I found a pretty good political science lab more than 500 miles outside the Beltway."

The academic core of the 10,000-student university is Emory College, with its 4500 liberal arts-oriented undergraduates. Most undergrads (and even some administrators) could go years without seeing a graduate student, but Emory wouldn't be where it is today without them.

Medicine has been one of the biggest engines for the entire university's growth. Hundreds of high school seniors choose Emory each year just to be near its highly regarded Medical School, making biology and chemistry among the most popular majors. Undergrads and Med School residents alike share the resources of the booming Clifton Corridor that slices through Emory's campus: two hospitals, a state-of-the-art life sciences lab complex, and the national headquarters of both the American Cancer Society and the U.S. Centers for Disease Control and Prevention (the only federal agency with its main office outside the Washington area). Emory's strong ties to other hospitals throughout the city and the creation of a graduate school of public health (one of only 25 in the country) further enhance Emory's medical reputation. Emory's psychology department, which benefits from an on-campus federal primate research center, is also extremely popular.

Like political science, Emory's history department draws a throng of law school-bound majors. It offers a variety of exceptional courses, including those taught by distinguished scholars of the history of the American South, the Middle East, Asia, and Europe. It's a writing-intensive major, but the small-sized colloquia required during the junior and senior years are wonderful opportunities for students to develop personal relationships with faculty and complete actual research. Another solid humanities program can be found in the English department, which has always enjoyed support from the dean's office. Interest in its creative writing workshops has soared, and the program's leader is an active playwright whose works find their way onto the Emory stage. The department's faculty has more than its share of poetry fans and is justifiably proud of its scholarly resources in that area. Interesting courses in areas like Southern literature, the Bible as literature, and even the modern detective novel, spice up the course roster. A closely related department, classics, is also growing in size and reputation.

Anthropology has also traditionally been strong, but a recent multimillion dollar investment in Emory's art and archeology museum has sent it through the roof. International exhibitions of mummies and other ancient artifacts now stop at the Carlos Museum on Emory's quad, providing a great addition to the scientific resources already available for the many anthro, as well as art history, students.

As a school founded by and affiliated with the United Methodist Church, Emory's religion program is also very good. Every undergrad religion major may not want to go right into the seminary at the graduate Candler School of Theology, but Emory offers a wide variety of challenging courses on everything from Buddhism and Jewish legal thinking to Christan ethics. The university's Pitts Theology Library houses the second-largest collection of theological titles in North America, which can also come in handy for undergraduates researching an obscure philosophy paper. A number of the university's administrators are ordained ministers, so don't look for this department to miss out on the school's overall growth.

International-oriented majors have also gained steam in recent years. The Carter Center's globe-trotting agenda has helped, but many would be doing just fine without it. The international studies major, which requires a mix of classes in foreign language, politics, and other social sciences, has always drawn the college's top students. More specialized concentrations are also exceptional. Near Eastern studies has some charismatic faculty members, and many nonmajors enjoy trying their hand at learning Yiddish or the intricacies of Arab culture. Post-Soviet and East European studies boast some top-notch professors, and Emory was one of the first institutions in the U.S. to monitor live broadcasts of Moscow television in the late 1980s. Latin American and Caribbean studies has also continued to grow.

Even a lot of relatively new or nontraditional departments have established good reputations. The college has attempted to build strong interdisciplinary programs in women's studies, liberal studies, and African-American and African studies. With their faculties made up of an amalgam of professors from throughout the college, they often offer courses with broad constituencies. An undergraduate liberal studies class on Dante, for example, might be taught by an Italian scholar and a literature or history professor. The university's nine divisions are all big on interdisciplinary programs, with the most notable one being the graduate law and religion program.

A total of about 40 bachelor of arts concentrations and seven bachelor of sciences concentrations are available in Emory College. Plenty of double major combinations can be arranged, and deans really are flexible about letting students design their own majors. During senior year, students with top grades can also take advantage of Emory's honors program—a rigorous, year-long path of research and thesis writing in one's major under the direction of a professor.

Students usually take four 4-credit courses each semester plus an optional one-credit gym class (four gym classes are required over eight semesters).

In addition to completing requirements within their majors, Emory undergrads must take courses in each of the college's broad distribution requirement categories. Very few courses are mandatory (not even swimming anymore), so it's relatively painless. Students choose from big menus of courses under headings like "the In-dividual and Society" (where you could find anything from a course on modern Germany to microeconomics) and "Aesthetics and Values" (you could choose an in-troduction to theater or music). Overall, premed students can avoid most tough hu-manities courses, while those who are prelaw can duck a lot of math and lab sciences. When selecting their first courses, most students can satisfy some distribu-tion requirements with something they might eventually choose as their major.

The hardest part is navigating the complicated weight-point system to get into the needed classes before second-semester senior year (most people wipe out all dis-tribution requirements before junior year). Even undergrads who enroll in Emory's business and nursing schools—which are both building exceptional facilities and reputations—after sophomore year need to fulfill the college requirements eventu-ally. Emory students must also do their share of paper-writing each year, but most any course will allow you to satisfy that mandate.

Regardless of what you're studying, though, Emory classes are not overcrowded. Each department has one or two big lecture classes (which often break down once a week into small discussion sections led by grad students), but even freshmen can get into some classes of fewer than 15 students. The typical class has between 25 and 35 students, and the professor knows each person's name. Most professors don't terror-ize students with pop quizzes and impromptu grillings, they just want students to take an interest in the class material and show some intellectual growth with each discussion. The stereotype of cavernous lecture halls led by faceless substitutes for tenured professors is just a myth at Emory. In many upper-level classes, students really look forward to the spirited, and often amusing, lectures of their professors—who may have just finished an on-camera interview with CNN or published a text-book on the same subject. A horde of adjunct and visiting professors also add to the excitement—you could very easily have the head of the Carter Presidential Library or the Centers for Disease Control (CDC) teaching your class.

Emory also offers a variety of study abroad programs and Washington semesters. The university even maintains a campus 38 miles away in rural Oxford, Georgia, where the school was founded in 1836. About 225 students each year who don't want to plunge into the big university setting choose to attend Oxford (they must apply separately, but after two years, they usually transfer to the Atlanta campus). Es-pecially strong ties also exist between Emory and St. Andrews University in Scot-land—four students from each school switch places without cost each year as Bobby Jones Scholars, named after the famous golfer and Emory grad.

SOCIAL LIFE

Emory is not a party school. It can't compare to big state schools with their rah-rah spirit and football teams (Emory doesn't have one), but that doesn't mean Emory isn't a fun place to be.

Most people who come to Emory leave their anxiety attacks at home and enjoy relaxing. They study by the lake in Lullwater, Emory's 185-acre park surrounding the university president's home. They go rollerblading in Atlanta's sprawling Piedmont Park and wander through the city's many museums and festivals. They soak up the sun paddling down the Chattahoochee River, hiking in the North Georgia mountains, or cheering at Braves games (it's still warm during the baseball pennant race). They learn they can relax and enjoy the pleasures of college life like band parties and lazy Sunday afternoons on the quad—and still come out on top.

The university sponsors a handful of social activities, including regular band parties, cookouts, dances, and the annual Dooley's Week (named after Emory's unofficial skeletal mascot). The most successful events are those initiated and organized by students themselves, such as ones run by the Student Programming Council (SPC). The SPC has brought groups like Blues Traveler and Edie Brickell to They Might Be Giants to Emory's McDonough Field, to great reviews in recent years. Without a big stadium or theater on campus, though, the biggest names are more likely to be found performing elsewhere around town. The SPC also runs a popular movie series in the Dobbs University Center (more commonly just called the DUC) every weekend that features off-the-wall film classics and box office favorites. Admission is about the price of a big candy bar.

While plenty of dorms also have a very social atmosphere, the most popular weekend destinations are off campus. It takes a while for many non-Georgians to fully explore Atlanta, but the city offers more than just any old college town. You can hop a bus and a train to the Omni to catch the NBA's Hawks, ice hockey, a big concert, or even the circus. Emory students often shadow their favorite bands through the bars of Underground Atlanta, Virginia Highlands, and Little Five Points—which produced Emory's Grammy-winning alums, the Indigo Girls—and check out the upscale clubs and restaurants of Buckhead. The city's excellent performing arts groups also attract many Emory groups (and half the student body probably volunteers as an usher at the Fox Theater downtown to catch a free show once or twice). And if you're not the club or theater type, the suburban sprawl of restaurants, movie theaters, and miniature golf courses awaits. Or, more likely, you can just find a party at someone's house or apartment near campus.

Within this mix, though, fraternities and sororities will never disappear. Emory remains a proper Southern school. The Greek system's role has diminished since Emory began enforcing its long-ignored alcohol and hazing policies. And Emory's sororities have always been mainly large social clubs because they developed at Emory without full-scale campus mansions like fraternities. But the regular schedule of Greek mixers, date parties, and formals constitutes the bulk of the Emory social calendar. Around 40% of the student body joins, but freshmen can't rush until midway through freshman year.

> *"I never considered myself the fraternity type, and I went through rush just to see what it was all about, but joining Emory's Greek system was the right move for me. Although Emory is small enough to meet plenty of people in your dorm and around campus, my fraternity opened lots of new doors for me.*
>
> *"Emory's Greek-letter organizations push their members to take on challenges—from planning elaborate community service projects and parties to leading dozens of your peers. Being a member immediately ties you to a bigger social and academic network as you meet scores of new friends, student leaders, and study partners. My fraternity brothers were also a 45-man support network for me within the larger university. They were in my classes and clubs, beside me on the playing field and at social functions, and were always available for late-night pizza or a game of pool at the fraternity house.*
>
> *"The parties were memorable (though fraternity parties these days are more like big office cocktail parties than anything out of* Animal House), *but the friendships will last longer. My years as a fraternity brother and officer even led me to become an alumni advisor to my fraternity in another city after graduation."*

EXTRACURRICULAR ACTIVITIES

Sticking to their preprofessional goals, most Emory students seek internships during at least one of their four years in Atlanta. The vast majority of Fortune 500 companies have offices within commuting distance of Emory (Coca-Cola, Delta Air Lines, UPS, Georgia-Pacific, and plenty of others are based in Atlanta), and the city's schools, businesses, government offices, and cultural institutions all welcome Emory students as workers. CNN and the Carter Center are especially popular places to work after class.

Volunteer community service also ranks as one of the top interests of Emory students. A student-run group, Volunteer Emory, coordinates dozens of activities around campus and Atlanta each year. Its annual Playday in the Park, which exposes Boys and Girls Club members to the campus' scenic beauty, is a perennial favorite for game-playing kids and students alike. Habitat for Humanity, a Georgia-based group that helps construct housing for the needy, also attracts plenty of Emory students each Saturday morning. And Emory helped launch the Atlanta Project, former

President Carter's ambitious attempt to revitalize many of the city's forgotten neighborhoods.

Other popular activities include Emory's top-ranked debate team (the Barkley Forum, which sends its members across the country to capture trophy after trophy), campus publications (the student newspaper, the *Wheel*, has won some of the biggest awards in student journalism), and student government (which offers a host of opportunities to politic or plan elaborate festivals and lectures). Outstanding musical groups like the university chorus and concert choir bring together faculty, staff, and students—and entertain audiences on campus and throughout Atlanta. Religious and minority groups are also strong and have brought speakers like Spike Lee and Elie Wiesel to campus in recent years for standing-room-only lectures.

> *"As Emory continues to transform itself, an energetic student can create or entirely recast nearly any campus organization for the better in less than four years—an opportunity that is unlikely to exist at more tradition-bound colleges. Student activities are driven by students' ideas and not 'the way things have always been done.'*
>
> *"Emory doesn't have a journalism school, for example, but its twice-weekly student newspaper offers a valuable—and fun—extracurricular forum for the campus' aspiring writers, photographers, artists, and ad salesmen.*
>
> *"Between the first week of my freshman year, when I joined the paper, and the last late night I spent proofing an issue as editor-in-chief my senior year, nearly everything about* The Emory Wheel *had changed. Its staff still had to cope with the same crisis-a-minute pace, but the newspaper had become more aggressive and complete in covering campus crime and athletics, attracted a more outgoing and diverse staff, increased its independence from the administration, won greater respect from the student body, and even found a crisper design. I was barely able to appreciate the change before it was time to graduate. My successors continued to reshape the paper, but I didn't leave my journalism training at Emory. I used my experience covering the controversies and news events at Emory to land jobs writing for a national magazine and then a daily newspaper after graduation."*

The biggest student gripe about campus life (besides the lack of parking) is that Emory doesn't have a football team. Rumors abound that Emory promised not to start one in return for Woodruff's multimillion dollar gift. No such condition exists, administrators say, but there's little room left for a football stadium anyway with all the other construction. Emory isn't really lacking athletically, though. A brand-new gym offers plenty of swimming lanes and basketball courts, intramurals are popular, and the university helped start a nine-school Division III league that has brought an interscholastic flavor to Eagle sports. The tennis, track, and swim teams have all won a slew of titles, and a basketball program founded in the 1980s has had some good years. More than a dozen student-run clubs offer a chance to participate in other sports such as ice hockey, lacrosse, sailing, and martial arts (and if you don't see one you like, it's easy to start another). And, with the 1996 summer Olympics in Atlanta, the city isn't exactly a sports wasteland. (If your heart's really set on football, there are always games downtown at Georgia Tech or the Georgia Dome, home of the NFL's Falcons; the University of Georgia is only a short drive away in Athens.)

Plenty of people move off campus after their first year (or, if you're male, to Fraternity Row), but Emory is justifiably proud of its well-financed residence life program. Freshmen must live on campus, but it's likely to be the most enjoyable year you spend in college. Three upperclassmen (two sophomores and a junior or senior) live on each hall to help students adjust to college and to organize informal social and academic programs on the hall. These activities create lifelong friendships, and competition to be selected as a resident advisor or sophomore advisor is always stiff. Other freshmen-year activities—like the carefully crafted orientation program and informal freshman seminar class—are also very successful. The one-semester seminar program integrates students into both the university and the Atlanta communities through field trips and panel discussions.

Upperclass dorms tend to have a different sort of social energy, but most have been remodeled or air conditioned in recent years (many are new anyway). Nothing is too far from the center of campus, and most complexes have amenities like weight rooms, restaurants, computer labs, study lounges, or even patios.

But wherever Emory students live on campus, they generally feel safe around the clock. Atlanta has a high crime rate, but Emory is in a nice suburb. With a little common sense and luck, the only interaction an Emory student is likely to have with the campus police is over a misplaced backpack or drunken fraternity prank (which make for a good chuckle in the campus paper's humorous police blotter each week).

GRADUATES

The GMAT, GRE, MCAT and LSAT test dates are automatically added to the university calendar. The vast majority of Emory students have graduate school on their minds. Law school and medical school are tops on the list, and there is no shortage of forums and informal advice on the Emory campus for students following those paths. And, as Emory's reputation grows, more and more of its undergrads are getting into the top graduate schools in every discipline.

People who want to head out into the job market usually fare best when they stick to the South. Big-time recruiters are scarce on the campus itself, but Emory's name is golden in many parts of the region, especially Atlanta. You'll find Emory grads in important positions around town at places like CNN, the Olympic committee, and Coke. Combine that fact with the very livable conditions in Georgia, and it's easy to see why many lifelong Yankees see the area's rapid economic and cultural growth and never head back North.

Plenty of Emory grads, though, make their way to other cities like Washington, New York, and Miami as writers, management consultants, and researchers. Emory's national alumni network is gaining strength, but it pales in comparison to the schools Emory likes to compare itself to, like Duke and Johns Hopkins. That will come with time. Most students know that the value of their degree will steadily appreciate after graduation day with the school's continued success.

> *"Emory's name may not yet be akin to that of Harvard or Yale on the average street corner, but more people know what's going on in Atlanta than you might think. I am always surprised to mention I went to Emory to someone on a plane trip or on another campus and learn how much regard people have for the school. Maybe they knew one high school valedictorian recruited by the scholars program or read a book written by an Emory professor. Regardless of how they realized it, Emory is beginning to be perceived as it really is—a very good academic breeding ground for hard-working professionals of all stripes."*

SUMMARY OVERVIEW

Emory is a great place to go to school because it's on the way up. Buoyed by a tremendous endowment of soft-drink money, Emory has attracted thousands of top students and professors who would have gone elsewhere a decade or two ago. The school that some used to call Coca-Cola U has made a name for itself by investing heavily in its academic resources—primarily people—while preserving its earlier traditions of intimacy and moral education.

The university's lush campus is already home to some of the finest Ivy League scholars, nationally recognized medical researchers, and the globe-trotting diplomacy of former President Carter. But there are no limits to Emory's continued progress. New round-the-clock computer labs, distinguished speakers, and exchange programs with foreign universities appear at Emory every sememster—each a carefully crafted addition to the university's liberal arts tradition and luster. The quality of its students has eclipsed those at more well-known schools in the span of a decade, with more people clamoring to enjoy Emory's warm, friendly Southern setting and academic energy each year. And all this is happening on a campus sitting just outside the city limits of Atlanta, one of the most lively, yet livable, big cities anywhere in the country.

It has taken a while for people to discover that you don't need to be above the Mason-Dixon line to be above the pack in higher education. Academic excellence goes just as well with sunshine and grits as it does with snow shovels and hot choco-late. But Emory's reputation is rising as word-of-mouth—and even the mysterious an-nual rankings in *U.S. News & World Report*—begin to catch up with the reality of its rapid improvement.

Along with the growth, though, come growing pains. Some departments haven't yet reached their full potential. If you're interested in math, for example, most Emory students would suggest going to Georgia Tech. The university's largess also hasn't trickled down to economics (its faculty is stuck in a small house across the street from campus), fine arts (which has always been promised a state-of-the-art fa-cility for dance, theater, and film programs), and languages (aside from the entire French department, which was transplanted from Johns Hopkins a few years back). Most faculty advisors, who are assigned to freshmen at random, often don't know enough about all the departments to point incoming students in the right direction. And Emory lacks a general university publishing house to print scholarly books by its professors and others—an integral part of most world-class intellectual institutions.

All the hard-charging student preprofessionalism you'll find at Emory also hasn't helped to create much of a tradition of school spirit. Some blame the student apathy on not having a football team, but eventually Emory students will begin to take ad-vantage of the myriad of opportunities surrounding them. The big-name lectures, ex-citing varsity contests, and blossoming student organizations are all there, waiting to be tapped into.

Maybe Emory students are spending their time looking for jobs instead, because Emory doesn't give you that much help outside of grad school placement. To its credit, the university recently began stepping up its placement services.

Campus diversity also has room for improvement. (Disgruntled minorities win concessions from the administration every now and then (resulting in a task force or new administrative office), and everything goes back to normal. The campus re-mains a relatively homogenous place.

Emory has a lot of growing yet to do, but overall, it's not hard to see why it has gone from being a safety school to an increasingly popular early-decision pick. The university generally spends money where it's needed, works hard to improve its na-tional reputation and offers a comfortable educational environment.

For an energetic student, Emory offers the chance of a lifetime. No arbitrary tradi-tions or penny-pinching administrators hinder free thinking. No shortage of brand-new research centers, classroom materials, or playing fields exists for very long. No creative aspiration or academic goal is unrealistic. And no crushing winters take the fun out of college.

Emory's best years lie ahead, and its students will profit from—and enjoy—its ride to the top.

Adam Biegel, B.A.

Georgetown University

THE PROGRAM

"Freshman orientation week is an overwhelming experience. It consists of four days of extensive activities targeted to acclimating incoming freshmen to the city, the campus, and their new classmates. While meeting my dorm neighbors from Buenos Aires, Paris, London, Sri Lanka, Hawaii, and Idaho, I wondered what we could possibly have in common. Why had we all chosen Georgetown? Were we all basketball fanatics who wanted to call the Hoyas our very own? Was it the allure of the nation's capital that captured our imaginations? Were we a bunch of budding politicos, eager to earn our first credential on the way to Congress? Did we all hope to land an internship on Capitol Hill? Had we heard that 'Jesuits are the best teachers' and decided to find out for ourselves? Or was it Georgetown's great academic reputation we wanted? Several months passed before I began to appreciate that is a combination of all these things that endears Georgetown to its students."

John Carroll, the first American Catholic bishop, founded Georgetown University in 1789 on the Jesuit ideals of education set forth by St. Ignatius of Loyola. Although the university is guided by these ideals, students of all religious faiths have been welcomed since its inception. The Jesuits aim to educate the whole person; hence the expression "A sound mind in a sound body." This does not translate into mandatory physical education at Georgetown, but two Jesuit fathers do participate in the men's and women's basketball home games as announcer and foul-counter. Approximately 80 Jesuits live on campus. Many of them work in various offices throughout the university, such as the libraries, the university press, and campus ministries. Although only 31 out of 476 faculty members are Jesuits, their spirit of Christian humanism pervades the academic programs. The underlying emphasis on values in education surfaces in the liberal arts requirements. The Jesuits believe that an understanding of the history, literature, philosophy, and religion of other cultures, as well as our own, prepares students to face future moral and personal challenges. The Jesuit influence on the university makes these things important, but each student draws his or her own interpretation in building a program from the offerings of the university. Jesuits have historically been liberal-minded free-thinkers who encourage the original synthesis of ideas and discourage rote memorization and regurgitation of paradigms.

There are many reminders of the rich history and traditions of Georgetown; they seem to call students to the duty of carrying forward its weighty legacy. Students take pride in the university. Alumni are active in university life. Buildings are named after alumni or faculty who served the university. The massive, gothic structure of Healy Hall looms over the campus. A small Jesuit cemetery is wedged in the middle of the campus that has grown up around it. Harboring this sense of the past is a modern university, struggling to find a balance between its traditional Catholic identity and its world-class academic status.

Two of the best things about a Georgetown education are that, unlike many colleges and universities, all Georgetown classes are taught by faculty and that there is an extraordinary amount of interaction between students and faculty. The faculty is very approachable. They make themselves available during announced office hours each week and are always willing to make appointments with students at other times as well. Professors encourage students to ask questions as they go along in the lecture.

> *"Students are confident in tossing around their own ideas in class. This can be intimidating at first if you come from a high school where learning was a passive process. There is a sense that the professors are learning with you while they are helping you to develop your analytical skills and encouraging you to approach problems from various perspectives. Outside of class, many professors are involved in student activities such as the Lecture Fund and a capella and foreign language singing groups as advisers and participants. One of my professors invited our seminar class over to her home for lunch and the final class meeting. Another professor held study groups at his apartment on campus before exams."*

It is surprising that, amid all the cosmopolitan, international sophistication, political pretension, and urban chaos of our nation's capital, one can have the classic American college experience. Georgetown offers a traditional, rigorous liberal arts education with the community feeling of a small school tucked away on a serene, compact campus in a historic residential area. For most college students, that is a lot to offer.

GETTING IN/FINANCIAL AID

There is no surefire formula for a successful application to Georgetown, but certain personal attributes are especially advantageous: a record that demonstrates that a student made use of academic opportunities available in high school; good SAT I or ACT scores; original, perceptive, and sincere application essays; a sustained extracurricular interest or community involvement; worthwhile summer and/or part-time work experiences; a positive teacher recommendation; and a positive alumni-interview report. Because the admissions staff strives for diversity among the student body, being from a place with few applicants can also be an asset.

Each year a large percentage of applicants at the head of their class with lofty SAT I scores are denied admission, disproving the common suspicion that these are the only truly important criteria for admission. So don't let the ratio of 3072 acceptances to 12,652 applicants deter you from giving it a shot. Someone has to get in. Some 50% of the 1381 students who recently enrolled as freshmen are from the Mid-Atlantic/Northeast region of the United States. Every state is represented, as well as approximately 50 foreign countries. About 25% of the student body are minorities, and almost half attended public schools. In high school, more than 60% were varsity athletes, 70% performed community volunteer work, 25% were members of a religious youth group, 19% took part in dramatics, 15% in debate, and 13% participated in an international exchange program before coming to Georgetown.

> *"My high school guidance counselor discouraged me from applying to Georgetown. Maybe he thought it was a waste of time when he compared my vital statistics with those of the entering class. I had spent a lot of time with extracurricular activities, worked part-time, my grades were in the top 10% of my class, and my SAT scores were good but not great. I believed that I could handle the work and that I would like it there. I decided it would be easier to live with the temporary disappointment of not getting in than always to wonder what might have happened."*

Applying to Georgetown's early action can only be an advantage. If accepted, you are in no way obliged to enroll; you are free to apply to other schools and delay your response until May 1. If deferred, your application will be reviewed again in March. The essays on the application and the alumni interview (from which a report is written) are the two most personal parts of the whole process, where applicants have the freedom to present themselves as they wish. These documents are read at least once by each member of the admissions committee for the school to which one is applying. The admissions committees are composed of an admissions officer, a faculty member, a student, and a dean.

"My alumni interviewer had graduated just two years earlier, so he was able to give me a lot of specific details about the school. He followed up on what happened with my application and called to congratulate me. The admissions office held a reception for newly admitted students in my state during the difficult month of decision making between April 1 notification and the response deadline of May 1. They brought some faculty members, students, and local alumni to answer last-minute questions and show their enthusiasm. I cannot say whether the personal attention I received during the application process swayed me to choose Georgetown, but I know I had a better sense of what to expect once I got there than I did with any other school."

So once you get in, how do you pay for it? Estimated expenses for this year's tuition, fees, and room and board are $25,595. The good news is that since 1978 it has been Georgetown's financial aid policy to meet each student's need, as demonstrated by the College Scholarship Service Financial Aid Form analysis with an individual package of a combination of work-study, loans, and grants. The admission process is need-blind. The university expects students to cooperate with them by borrowing funds available through various student loan programs and working part-time during school. Parents are expected to take as much financial responsibility for their child's education as they can afford. Approximately 45% of Georgetown students receive need-based financial aid. Many students also receive financial aid from outside sources, including ROTC programs.

ACADEMIC ENVIRONMENT

Aside from basketball, Georgetown is probably best known for its excellent academic programs in government and international affairs. The combination of its location in the nation's capital and its distinguished faculty attract the politically minded. Among the more well-known faculty members are Madeleine Albright, Colin Campbell, John Cuddington, Michael Hudson, Gary Hufbauer, former U.S. Ambassadors to the U.N. Jeane Kirkpatrick, Donald McHenry, Ted Moran, and Angela Stent.

Students choose their school and, in some cases, their major by applying to one of the five undergraduate programs during the admissions process. They are the College of Arts and Sciences, the School of Foreign Service, the School of Business Administration, the School of Languages and Linguistics, and the School of Nursing. It seems a bit premature to ask a seventeen-year-old high school senior to make this decision; nevertheless, the large majority of students graduate from the school they originally chose. Acceptance to one school is not transferable to another, but you can apply for a transfer to another school after freshman year. The majors offered are: accounting, American studies, Arabic, biology, chemistry, Chinese, classics, computer science, economics, English, finance, fine arts (art history and studio arts),French, German, government,history, history and diplomacy, humanities in international affairs, interdisciplinary studies, international affairs, international business, international economics, international politics, Italian, Japanese, linguistics, management, marketing, mathematics, nursing, philosophy, physics, physics-engineering, Portuguese, psychology, regional and comparative studies, Russian, sociology, Spanish, and theology. The College of Arts and Sciences also offers minors in women's studies and medieval studies. Coursework is available in Modern Greek, Hebrew, Korean, and Turkish in the School of Languages and Linguistics. No matter which major you select in any of the five schools, the program includes a core curriculum in the liberal arts. Courses in English, theology, and philosophy are required for all students, as are history and a foreign language, except for those in nursing and some of the business programs. Honors and special programs are available in many departments.

> *"At the beginning of first-semester freshman year, philosophy and theology seemed somewhat amorphous, esoteric subjects, but I ended up taking some theology courses as electives. I have three friends who started off as biology, English, and international politics majors and switched to theology. Almost every student takes a theology course called The Problem of God. The uniformity of experience is in name only, however, because each professor has his or her own agenda for the course. In my section we started off by reading Freud's view of why humanity has a predisposition toward god-making in the first place then went on to learn how Buddhists, Christians, existentialists, Hindus, Jews, and Muslims solve their own so-called problems of God. The final exam for the course was to write an essay on our own personal definition of salvation, in five pages or less."*

Subsequent to the university-wide core curriculum are course requirements specific to each school, and further degree requirements follow within your major and concentration. Students in the College of Arts and Sciences have the most flexibility in choosing their courses. Students from different schools take introductory and core curriculum classes together, but most upper-level courses are open only to students of the school in which they are offered. Forty courses, or five a semester, are required for graduation. This is a heavy workload because most classes involve a midterm exam, a final exam, and either a long research or several short essay papers. A minimum C average, or 2.0 grade point average, must be maintained.

> *"One Russian history professor offers his students the option of participating in a historical theater project with classmates in place of taking the midterm or writing the research paper. Groups of about 15 students are given a time and place in Russian or Soviet history and a reading list of background books. From this they must write, produce, direct, and star in a full-*

length play. At the end of the semester the performance is open to the public, and the professor evaluates it for historical accuracy and theatrical merit. I worked on a play in three of his courses because, although it always ended up being as much work as an entire course in itself, it was great fun to make history come alive and get to know people in class."

There is a relaxed attitude toward studying, exhibited in the widespread tendency to put reading and papers off until midterms hit. Students customarily help each other out by swapping notes for classes they missed and forming study groups before exams. For all-night studying, Pierce Reading Room in Lauinger Library is open from 8:30 A.M. to 3:00 A.M. every day and 24 hours a day during exam weeks.

"I never sensed any competition between students, but a lot of kids exert undue pressure on themselves to excel. Students who come to Georgetown are generally self-motivated enough to get the work done because they really want to do it. It's just a matter of finding enough time between basketball games and parties."

Class size varies from course to course. Fifty percent of the classes enroll 19 students or less; 75% enroll between one and 40 students. Some of the liberal arts core curriculum courses such as The Problem of God, Poetry and Drama, and Short Story and Novel are limited to 20. Small seminar courses, which usually have no more than ten students, are plentiful and popular because they meet only once a week for two hours. Most of the upperclass courses are relatively small but might have up to 40 people in them, depending on their popularity. Many Georgetown professors limit enrollment for their courses to ensure that everyone in class can participate. On the other hand, there are quite a few introductory-level courses that may have up to 60 students, especially in economics, history, government, and philosophy.

About one-third of the junior class studies abroad each year, in addition to many sophomores and seniors, reflecting the keen interest in foreign affairs among the students. Georgetown sponsors many of its own programs for work and study around the globe, from Peru to Poland, including villas in Italy and Turkey. At home, Georgetown's location in Washington, D.C., is one of its greatest assets. The entire city becomes a classroom for those who seek out internships on the Hill, with trade associations, news agencies, embassies, publications, federal government agencies, nonprofit organizations, and art galleries. In addition to campus libraries, students have a multitude of research resources at their disposal, including libraries at museums, federal government agencies, other universities in the metropolitan area, the Folger Shakespeare Library, and the National Archives. The Library of Congress alone satiates anyone's research needs. Another positive influence that the city has on the university is that many professionals in the arts, business, and public service hold adjunct professorships.

"Sophomores in the School of Foreign Service take a small seminar that offers the opportunity to defend arguments and make

presentations in class and get to know a professor early on in the academic program. I took U.S. Foreign Policy-Making Process with Ambassador Smith who has had diplomatic posts in several nations in Central and South America. By listening to his policy-making experiences, I encountered the gap between ideals and the art of the possible. The Friends of the School of Foreign Service are a group of active and retired professionals from the diplomatic service, international business, and journalism who live in the Washington area and meet with interested students to talk about their careers. My friend was a retired Foreign Service officer and corporate executive for a multinational company."

Students also benefit from interesting visitors to the nation's capital who speak to audiences at the university while they are in town. Many of the U.S. presidential candidates speak on campus at some point during the campaigns, including Bill Clinton, a 1968 Georgetown graduate.

SOCIAL LIFE

In general, students have a diverse social life that centers on campus activities and nightlife in Georgetown. They have the best of both worlds. There are always a lot of parties on the weekends, thrown either by student clubs or by groups of students in their apartments. There are plays and movies on campus every weekend. And, if students feel like getting a little culture or having a good meal, all they need do is walk a few blocks from campus. There is no Greek system, but its absence is not felt.

Aside from Homecoming in October, there are many social events throughout the year. There are always a few big dances: the Business School Ball, the Diplomatic Ball, and the Senior Ball, usually held off campus at a hotel or embassy. At Casino Night, guests gamble in a "casino" with play money. The Georgetown "Chimes" invite *a cappella* groups from Georgetown, including the Phantom Singers and Grace Notes as well as groups from other schools to sing at the Cherry Tree Massacre in February. At the Senior Auction and Senior Parents Weekend dinners with deans and dream dates are auctioned off to raise money for senior class activities.

Most weekends, on-campus social life revolves around parties at upperclass apartments and visits to the student-run pub, The Basement. During the day the pub is open for students who want to watch wide-screen TV and have some pizza. At night the pub serves beer (and soda!), and there is music, sometimes live, and dancing unless the Hoyas are playing or there is "Monday Night Football." On warm days in the fall and spring people sit outside between classes on two big, grassy areas in the middle of campus, Healy Lawn and Copley Lawn, to play Frisbee or enjoy the sunshine. Lunch at New South cafeteria is the place where people come to sit around with friends, scope, read the *Hoya*, and grab a quick bite of the glop du jour.

> *"I have a group of friends who used to get to New South when it opened at 11:00 A.M. and stay until it closed at 2:00 P.M. every day, not to eat, but jut to sit around and people watch. A lot of upperclassmen who don't even like the food buy the meal plan for lunches just because it is an easy place to see their friends during the day. Georgetown is small enough that, by senior year you know, or can at least recognize, almost everyone in your class."*

Meals are a focal point of social activity freshman year, when everyone is on the meal plan. The dining halls are located in the freshman dorm and people usually come downstairs to eat with a group from their floor. Alcohol is prohibited in freshman dorms because of the D.C. drinking age of twenty-one, and as a result most parties are held at upperclass apartments on and off campus.

A few blocks from campus there are dozens of shops, movie theaters, bars, and restaurants of all varieties in Georgetown for students to enjoy. At night Wisconsin Avenue and "M" Street are packed with bumper-to-bumper cars and people strolling around.

Adams-Morgan Day in September is a huge street festival of music, dancing, crafts, and exotic foods in a neighborhood of the city where many recent émigrés live. On Halloween, probably the rowdiest night of the year, the streets of Georgetown are closed to traffic for the costume parade.

One-on-one, Georgetown students are ambitious, bright, and gregarious. Having a good time is as important to them as going to class. Going out in groups is more common than dating the first few years, but by junior and senior years people start pairing off. People tend to form their closest friendships from their freshman dorm floormates. In general, Georgetown students are liberal when it comes to social action, but conservative in their personal beliefs and life-styles.

EXTRACURRICULAR ACTIVITIES

Each September the Student Activities Commission holds an all-day outdoor fair. Each club sets up a table or booth and tries to drum up membership in whatever way it likes. The largest clubs are the International Relations Club and the Community Action Coalition (CAC), a conglomeration of many different community volunteer groups that work at soup kitchens, homeless shelters, all-night hotlines, and tutoring programs throughout Washington, D.C. There is much variety among the clubs. There are several theater groups, each with its own style: Black Theatre Ensemble, Friday Afternoon Theatre, Mask and Bauble, and Nomadic Theatre. Some have a cultural theme: Arabic Club, Armenian Club, French Club, German Club, Russian Club, and Spanish Club. Most of these clubs form choirs that compete in the annual School of Languages and Linguistics Caroling Pageant in December. Several singing groups perform on campus frequently: the Chimes, a male *a cappella* group; the Gospel Choir; and the Grace Notes, a female *a cappella* group and the Phantom Singers, a coed *a cappella* group. Church services are held in several chapels on campus for all major religions throughout the week, and they are well attended. Many of these services have student choirs.

The Corp is an extremely popular, entirely student-run corporation that operates a small grocery store, a shop with school supplies and magazines, an advertising service, a typing service, an on-campus travel service, a shipping and storage business, and a movie rental store. It is run like a professional operation and grossed over $3 million last year. Because all the accountants, managers, and employees are students, it provides an opportunity to find out what it takes to run a business.

One of the most popular organizations is the Senior Class Committee, a quasi-student government group make up of about 30 members of the senior class who plan all year long in celebration of their senior year. They also raise money for Senior Week, which is a week-long party between the end of final exams and graduation.

Because there are no social fraternities, sororities, or eating clubs at Georgetown, other clubs and activities take on an added dimension of socializing. At the same time they allow students to participate in their personal interests. Many groups have offices in the Leavey Student Center, a large multilevel structure that also contains the Student Pub, Center Café, the bookstore, the Career Center, ballrooms, large meeting rooms, and hotel accommodations for parents and university guests.

Sports are very popular at Georgetown, although only John Thompson's Hoyas can claim a large, loyal contingent of fans. Baseball, women's basketball, crew, cross country, field hockey, football, lacrosse, soccer, swimming, tennis, and track are also popular. Many students participate in intramural sports such as basketball and football. Freshman dorm floors compete for the Yates Cup, which is awarded to the team with the most points from all the intramural competitions at the end of the year. Yates Field House contains a 25-yard indoor swimming pool, indoor and outdoor running tracks, tennis, squash, racquetball, basketball, and volleyball courts, rooms for dance and karate classes, weights, rowing machines, and saunas. It is a modern, partially underground structure built about 13 years ago.

The university has several spacious and comfortable apartment complexes for upperclassmen. Some university-owned townhouses are also available to upperclassmen. Freshmen, and some upperclassmen, live in dorms. All dorms are coed; the floors alternate male-female. On-campus housing is guaranteed three out of four years. Freshmen and sophomores must live on campus. Each student chooses whether to use on-campus housing for junior or senior year. Most prefer senior year because so many people study abroad during junior year. On the other hand, parking space is not available on campus and is scarce in the Georgetown area. Luckily, you can use the Metro system, which is clean, safe, and efficient, to get around the entire D.C. metropolitan area. The Metro does not come directly into Georgetown, but there are two stations within a 15-minute walk, and Metro buses stop on each end of campus every ten minutes. The university operates a fleet of GUTS (Georgetown University Transportation System) buses, which take students around the city at reduced rates.

The main campus, which contains all the buildings for undergraduate, graduate, medical (the law school is downtown) is a compact area; it takes only ten minutes to walk from one end of the campus to the other. The school is located in a picturesque, quiet residential area of Georgetown, filled with beautiful old townhouses on shady streets. The campus feels remote from the rest of the city, and indeed it is possible to spend an entire year at school without venturing out of Georgetown except for a trip to the train station at the end of each semester. Students tend to take greater advantage of all there is to do and see in Washington during the last couple of years. Half-price student tickets are available for performances at the Kennedy Center, Arena Stage, the Folger Shakespeare Theatre, the National Theatre, and most of the other theaters in the area. Then there are all the expected tourist attractions to see at your own leisure without the crowds — for instance, Congress, the Supreme Court, the Washington Monument, Mount Vernon, and Arlington National Cemetery. For lovers of the outdoors, the C&O Canal near campus provides a convenient path for biking and jogging. There are lots of great bike paths all around the city and in Maryland and Virginia. Two outdoor ice rinks near the Mall are open from January through March. Paddle-boating on the Tidal Basin near the Jefferson Memorial is popular during the Cherry Blossom Festival in spring. The Mall has areas for soccer and volleyball, and there are polo matches and rugby games on the weekends. Canoes can be rented just a few minutes from campus.

> *"On the Fourth of July a group of us, along with about half a million other people, got together and had an all-day picnic on the Mall and listened to the National Symphony Orchestra concert. That night we fit a dozen people into a jumbo canoe and rowed down the Potomac to the monuments after dark to watch the fireworks from the water."*

GRADUATES

Twenty-six percent of a recent class reported that they planned to go straight into one of the following: law or medical school, graduate study leading to an M.A./M.S. or a Ph.D., or business school. Many others start work as accountants, bank and corporate program trainees, nurses, paralegals, and writers. Other students start working for government agencies, such as the State Department, the Defense Department, and others. Nonprofit organizations attract a lot of Georgetown students. Several years after graduation, many pursue careers in the arts, banking, industry, journalism, law, management consulting, medicine, the military, politics, and teaching.

*"Just as many of my friends went to work for the Jesuit Volunteer
Corps, the Peace Corps, or some other social service organization
for a year or two as went straight from school to grad school or
the corporate world. They have worked with people in parts of
the United States and the world that were probably the furthest
possible situation from their own personal experiences. The professors at Georgetown make students aware of what's going on in
the world beyond their own privileged community."*

Georgetown's alumni network stretches around the world. Alumni clubs in every
state and several foreign countries sponsor social events. The Alumni Admissions
Program, a separate entity that interviews prospective applicants, has committees in
all 50 states and many foreign countries. Each year at Homecoming, the Alumni Association sets up parties for graduating classes from the past ten years, and many
alumni come back. The Career Center keeps a list of alumni in every profession
who have volunteered to speak with current students and other alumni who want
to learn more about that field. Georgetown is a tradition to many alumni families;
many children and grandchildren of alumni wind up there.

SUMMARY OVERVIEW

Georgetown students take many courses that may not have any practical rele-
vance to their careers until they have to write a speech or a proposal. The first two
years are a structured, traditional liberal arts program. Most students see their time
at Georgetown not so much as a career move, but as a chance to get a broad education before eventually moving on to professional school. A lot of writing is required
of students. They give up looking for easy gut courses with multiple-choice tests
early on. The program is challenging but personal as well. It has a small school feeling even though there are approximately 6,000 undergraduates.

Above all else, Georgetown is an undergraduate institution. The Jesuit values in
education are witnessed in the professors, who are both excellent scholars and dedicated teachers. Academic strengths lie in the humanities, especially English, government, history, philosophy, and theology. Foreign languages are taught with great
tenacity; intensive basic and advanced classes meet eight or ten hours a week for
the first two years. There is a huge selection of courses in international affairs.
American studies is a strong, innovative, and popular program in the College of Arts
and Sciences. It focuses on American art, history, literature, politics, and religion.
The business and nursing schools are both excellent, comprehensive programs with
good reputations.

Academic weaknesses lie in the applied sciences. Physics-engineering majors end
up taking most of their courses at a nearby university. There are few technical
courses available. Some courses are offered in journalism, but no major is available.

A women's studies program began a few years ago. It now offers a minor, but it has far to go. The course offerings in the performing arts are miniscule in comparison with the high level of student interest and activity outside the classroom. Students can get only a minor in music theory and theater.

Among the students there is a strong sense of community within the university and commitment to social work in Washington, D.C. The largest student club is the Community Action Coalition. The flip side of this is that Georgetown students tend to take themselves rather seriously. Their nascent yearnings for politics are manifested in an air of self-importance.

Still, all in all, Georgetown gives students an excellent, well-balanced liberal arts education. Four years at Georgetown is exhausting and exhilarating. There is so much to do that you are always busy, never bored, and constantly stretching. That is the Georgetown experience.

Zoe Heineman, B.S.F.S.

Georgia Institute of Technology

THE PROGRAM

Those at Georgia Tech will tell you, "We don't fit the mold, we make it." And they seem to be right; Georgia Tech does not fit into the usual mode of a university in the southeastern United States. Georgia Tech is not the large football power-house located in a quaint rural area, nor the smug, ivy-covered university dating back to the nation's founding fathers. It simply does not fit the mold.

Located near downtown Atlanta, Tech is a mecca for top students from around the globe who are searching for a school that offers a curriculum emphasizing math and science as well as a rich history and a diverse student body. The campus is un-like most urban colleges. Tree-lined streets and large, grassy fields give visitors the impression that they are far removed from the hustle and bustle of the city, but one look to the east at the downtown skyline and the midtown skyline to the north and they are reminded that Tech is an integral part of this growing and dynamic city.

The institute recently restructured its academic programs to create an envi-ronment conducive to interdisciplinary study, to create well-rounded graduates, and to prepare for the challenges of the twenty-first century. There are three new colleges: the Ivan Allen College of Management, Policy, and International Affairs; the College of Computing; and the College of Sciences. They join the College of Engineering and the College of Architecture, which has added a Divi-sion of Fine Arts consisting of departments in three areas: music; visual arts; and theater, video, and cinema. By far, the majority of students who come to Tech do so to study in one of the 14 fields of engineering that have made the school so famous. Students in these areas will spend their academic careers concentrat-ing on mathematics, physics, and chemistry.

Another popular area of study at Tech is the basic science curriculum. These ma-jors allow students to take a base of knowledge in mathematics and the physical sci-ences and build onto it in areas such as biology, chemistry, and physics. These programs also can be used as preprofessional courses of study. Tech also offers two other areas of study that diverge from the traditional engineering and science curriculums: architecture and management.

The School of Architecture at Tech is reputed to be among the best in the country. As with most architecture schools, the program is designed to take six years, and students graduate with a master's degree. Students concentrate on basic architectural studies during their first four years and use the last two to focus on expanding their knowledge of architectural design. This is a very hands-on area of study in which student projects make up a great deal of the work that is required outside class. The College of Architecture also offers four-year programs in building construction and industrial design. At Tech, the architecture school is said to appeal to people who enjoy having little or no free time and is commonly referred to as "archi-tor-ture."

Students in the Ivan Allen College of Management, Policy, and International Affairs take the basic classes of business, including accounting, marketing, and finance as well as many of the basic math and science classes that their fellow students studying engineering take. The college is known for turning out graduates with a knowledge of business and appreciation for the technical side of things.

> *"I remember a friend of mine who had gone to high school in a small town in South Carolina. He used to tell the story of people in his hometown who weren't very familiar with out-of-state colleges. When the local townspeople found out he was going to Georgia Tech, they often asked if he was going to study air-conditioning and refrigeration. He found it amusing that in a time when Georgia Tech is helping to pioneer research in areas such as robotics, aerospace technology, and biophysics, people who didn't know of the school and its reputation were still equating it with their local technical schools. Ironically, at the same time, others were comparing it with MIT and Stanford."*

GETTING IN/FINANCIAL AID

Unlike other top colleges, Georgia Tech requires an extremely simple application. All that is needed is your name, address, social security number, desired major, SAT I or ACT score, and high school transcript. A $15 nonrefundable application fee is also required. No essays or letters of recommendation are required. Applicants are accepted based on the likelihood that they will successfully complete a degree. Georgia Tech accepts approximately 59% of all those who apply; this puts Tech in the category of selective colleges.

Sounds too easy to be true? Well, it is. The hard part is successfully completing four years. Tech does not set minimums for its entering students, but it does publish averages. The students who began their studies in a recent year had a 3.6 GPA on a

4.0 scale and an SAT I score that ranged from 1000 to 1590, with the math score approximately 100 points higher than the verbal.

The students who are accepted break down into groups that are very typical of engineering schools across the country. Seventy-three percent of the student body is male, 27% female. Coincidentally, 74% are undergraduates and 26% are graduates. Ethnic minorities make up 23.5% of the students and international students account for 9%. Most recently, Georgia Tech matriculated just over 12,000 students.

Male high school students should not let the lack of women affect their decision to go to Tech. Recent surveys in the city of Atlanta show that single women greatly outnumber unspoken-for men. A campus full of men should not deter women. In fact, I met my husband on the third floor of the student center.

Many of those officially affiliated with the college have been heard to call Georgia Tech, "one of the last great educational bargains." This statement is especially true for in-state students. Because Tech is a public college, residents of Georgia can attend for about one-third the cost of nonresidents and therefore make up about 60% of the students. In-state students most recently paid $726 per quarter for matriculation and fees; out-of-state students paid $2106 per quarter.

Anyone who completes an application for financial aid is automatically considered for all forms of aid that are controlled by the university, with the exception of the Presidential Scholarship and the National Merit/Achievement Scholarship. Last year more than 5000 students received some sort of aid through the Office of Financial Aid. The Presidential Scholarship and the National Merit/Achievement Scholarship are each handled differently. The Presidential Scholarship is awarded to students who show superior academic and leadership ability. In-state students must have an SAT I score of 1350 to be considered; out-of-state students need a 1400. They must also complete a series of personal interviews and apply separately for this award. Students who are National Merit/Achievement Finalists, designate Georgia Tech as their first choice, and do not receive another National Merit/Achievement Award, may receive between $750 and $2000 per year for the four years of their enrollment. In addition, Tech will do its best to try to meet any need a student may have beyond that. This attractive program may be one of the reasons that Georgia Tech has more National Merit and National Achievement Scholars per capita than any other public university.

ACADEMIC ENVIRONMENT

"I still remember my first test at Georgia Tech. It was calculus. This had been my first exposure to calculus, but I thought I had the material pretty much under control. Like most of the students at Tech, I had excelled at math in high school. I had been keeping on top of all the assignments and putting about the same effort

into this class as I had put forth in trig during my senior year in high school. The night before the test, I reviewed my homework and studied the material in the same manner as I had a year earlier. The next day, when the professor handed out the test and said, 'Begin,' I realized that I was no longer in high school. I remember the feeling of despair that set in as I tried my best to work the problems. I remember thinking to myself, 'So this is what it feels like to be an average student.' Two days later, when the test was returned, my worst fears were realized: I had made an F, the first of my educational career. It was a hard lesson to learn, but it was one I didn't need to experience twice. For the next test, I studied close to 25 hours and it paid off—I received a B+! From that moment forward, I knew that Georgia Tech was going to demand from me as much as I could possibly give and then some."

It is obvious from the moment you set foot on campus that academics come first at Tech. I once heard a friend of mine say that, as hard as it is to get into Tech, it's even harder to get out. In order to get in, all applying freshmen are expected to have completed four years of English, two years of algebra, one year of geometry, two years of a foreign language, one year of American history, one year of world history, and one year of economics/government. Beyond that, the requirements are more specific to the intended area of study. Students entering Tech to study engineering and science (which is the large majority of students entering Tech) also need one year of advanced algebra/trigonometry, and three years of lab sciences with at least one of them in chemistry. For architecture majors, one year of advanced algebra/trig is required in addition to the basic requirements, including three years of lab sciences. Management majors have the same requirements as architecture majors except that the advanced algebra/trig is not required. All students with the exception of those in the College of Management are expected to take calculus their freshman year, and if these students did not retain enough trigonometry from high school, they must schedule a trig refresher course their first quarter. This is considered a remedial math course. Students in the College of Management have the option of taking the calculus series or taking Math for Management. With a few exceptions, most students at Tech will study the same courses their first two years. During this time, they will be exposed to chemistry, physics, English, American history, and political science, as well as a variety of other subjects from their major field of study and from others.

Unlike a lot of universities, many of the classes that are not basic are only three hour classes instead of five. So, where students at a large liberal arts school may take only three five-hour classes a quarter, the average student at Tech may take as many as six different classes at a time. Although this requires almost the same amount of time in class, dividing study time among six classes is much more difficult. And many engineering majors require students to take as many as 19 hours a quarter in order to graduate on time.

Freshman classes of chemistry and calculus are taught in large lecture halls with as many as 150 people. A class this size will meet three times a week. On the days the large class does not meet, students are broken down into groups of about 30 to go over homework and tests with a graduate student. Both aspects of the class are equally important, and the professors treat them as such. English, psychology, and many other social sciences are taught in relatively small classes of 25-30 students. Upper-level class size varies greatly from major to major. In many of the more crowded majors, such as electrical engineering, classes could have as many as 75 people, especially if the class is required. In the smaller majors, it is unusual to have more than 20 in a class. The exact types of classes taught at Tech are as diverse as the people who teach them.

Grading at Tech tends to be on a curve. This seems to be almost a necessity, or most of the students would flunk out. In a typical freshman class, 68% stay at Tech to graduate. Of the remaining 32%, only 10% leave for strictly academic reasons.

> *"One of my most memorable professors taught by the Socratic Method. This meant that students had to be acutely in tune with every word that was spoken in class by both student and teacher. In addition, you needed to write all of the words down so that the next time he asked that question you had the answer. And you also had to have your hand in the air answering the question he was currently asking. Lord help the poor student who gave a wrong answer that someone had already given."*

It is interesting to note that almost no one ever graduates from Georgia Tech. They all "get out," as if they were being paroled from prison or discharged from a psychiatric hospital. Even at alumni functions, you can overhear the older ones say, "I got out in '53, how about you?"

SOCIAL LIFE

When I told my friends in high school that I wanted to go to Georgia Tech, many of them had the same reaction: "All you'll do is study. You'll never have any fun." Well, they were wrong. No matter where you go to college, any time you get more than 12,000 people aged 18 to 25 in the same place, you're going to have fun. The students at Tech are very serious about their education, but they also know how to blow off steam and have a good time.

In the fall the excitement at Georgia Tech reaches a fever pitch on football Saturdays. To listen to the crowds and see the preparations and alumni support, one would think that Tech's Yellow Jackets were on their way to their third consecutive undefeated season. In 1990, the Georgia Tech football team did win the Atlantic Coast Conference (ACC) and was named national champion by the United Press International Coaches' poll. While Georgia Tech may not be a powerhouse football school every year, this doesn't mean that the students or alumni are any less enthusiastic or proud when game time approaches. Many of the traditions that make Tech such a historical place are centered upon football Saturdays. There are the bright gold "rat" caps, which many freshmen wear to the games, the infamous "Ramblin' Wreck," and the hilarious antics of Tech's mascot, Buzz. An interesting note — Georgia Tech is the only school in the nation that has sent its basketball, baseball, and golf teams to the NCAA championship tournaments in each of the past eight years.

Georgia Tech is close to many of the major attractions in Atlanta and the state of Georgia. Its proximity to public transportation allows students easy access to almost all of metropolitan Atlanta. Because of the vast array of clubs, restaurants, and bars, everyone can find a place to enjoy. Georgia Tech is within a short drive of several of Atlanta's major shopping malls as well as the Georgia Dome, which houses the Falcons, and the home of the Braves. Several restaurants and bars are also within walking distance of campus.

On campus itself, Tech has a full assortment of activities to suit any taste. On most Friday and Saturday nights, there are movies that students can attend for $1. These may not be the same shows that are currently playing in the theaters, but they won't be *Killer Tomatoes* either. However, the students seem to enjoy the Bugs Bunny cartoons that are shown before the movie, sometimes even more than the movie itself. International speakers on campus have included the likes of Nelson Mandela, and concerts have featured the Rolling Stones.

There's always the usual offering of fraternity parties if that is more your speed. Tech has 32 fraternities and 8 sororities, and each of them has its own unique characteristics and ideals. Students participate in more than 170 student organizations and in community outreach enterprises.

EXTRACURRICULAR ACTIVITIES

Involvement in outside activities at Tech seems to be the norm rather than the exception. I don't know if this is because the school tends to attract students who are natural overachievers or because there are clubs and organizations of every imaginable interest. It could also be due to the fact that the curriculum is so mentally taxing that an outside diversion is essential to maintaining some sense of sanity.

Tech's organizational handbook lists page after page of groups that cater to both broad and specific interests. Most of them receive some sort of financial assistance from the Student Government Association (SGA). The SGA is solely responsible for administering the money generated from the student activity fees that each student pays at matriculation. These fees are the lifeblood of the campus organization network. They pay for the *Blueprint* and *The Technique,* Tech's student-run yearbook and newspaper, and the ever-popular Student Athletic Complex, which features four basketball courts, numerous racquetball and handball courts, an indoor swimming pool, and a weight room that would impress any health club enthusiast.

Fraternities and sororities are also a popular outlet at Tech. Approximately 25% of the student body belongs to the Greek system. And although they are by no means the majority of students on campus, they are a mighty and vocal minority. However, new students should in no way feel left out if they don't participate in a fraternity or sorority. Fraternity and sorority members are very active on campus, and there are certain organizations outside the Greek system that they dominate. There are also other organizations that attract mostly students who are not affiliated with a fraternity or sorority. This is not to say that these groups are mutually exclusive, because there are no activities on campus, outside the Greek system itself, that are restricted to fraternity and sorority members.

> *"Living at Tech was unlike anything I had every experienced in my entire life. I suddenly went from having my own bedroom and bathroom to having one room that served as a bedroom, study room, living room, and dining room and having to share that one room with another person and my bathroom with 35 others! Needless to say, it was quite an adjustment. Being thrust into a living situation with someone you don't know teaches you a lot about other people and even more about yourself. I found myself suddenly possessive of personal items that held little if no intrinsic value; I even called my mother one evening, furious because my roommate had eaten all of my cheese."*

The residence halls at Tech cover the whole spectrum. Some of the earlier ones were built during Roosevelt's New Deal; the newest one comes complete with an elevator and picture windows; and there is even one building that was once part of a public housing project. When you consider the cost of housing in that part of Atlanta, living on campus is definitely an economically sound idea, and most of the students take advantage of it. In fact, Tech usually has more people who want housing on campus than there are beds available. Freshmen are guaranteed housing if their room deposit is received by the Housing Department on or before May 1 of the year they plan to enroll. Upperclassmen and women must go through a lottery process to obtain housing after their first year. Fortunately, this is not as difficult as it sounds. The Housing Department has estimated that 55% of returning students who want to live on campus are offered housing before they leave school for the summer. Over the summer a large portion of those who were not offered housing on the first round of the lottery are given a room on campus, but by then many of them have found other places to live. This bumps the final estimated percentage of those offered housing to between 85 and 100% of those who want it. Luckily, it is by no means unusual for students to make the housing lottery every year they are enrolled.

Each residence hall at Tech (the Housing Department insists that "prisoners live in dormitories; students live in residence halls") has its own unique personality and features that appeal to people of all interests. Some of the buildings are close to the stadium and fraternity row. Others are near the Student Athletic Center, far removed from the constant hustle of East campus. Most of the halls are equipped with a kitchen for the residents to use. Those that do not have kitchen facilities allow limited cooking in the rooms. Other features offered throughout the housing system are air-conditioning, study lounges, TV lounges, semiprivate bathrooms, and loft furniture. Tech's Residence Hall Association takes an active role in planning activities.

Students at Tech are also surprisingly active in the community outside the campus. Students from all areas donate time and energy to tutoring and befriending children in a neighboring public housing project. Most recently, some architecture students calling themselves The Mad Housers gained national attention by constructing small shanties for homeless citizens in the area.

Tech's role as the Olympic Village for the 1996 Olympics has stimulated construction of eight new residence halls that will house 2700 Tech students. A Graduate Living Center, scheduled to open in the winter of 1993, will provide apartment-style living for 300 graduate students.

GRADUATES

It is said that graduating from college is second only to birth as the most shocking change in a person's life. Although this may be true, Georgia Tech does its best to soften the blow. Tech grads of every major are in demand all over the country and they usually command very good starting salaries — the average for recent graduates with a bachelor's degree ranged from $26,000 to $38,000 a year. In addition, the alumni office likes to throw around some impressive statistics: There are 138 companies in the United States that have a Georgia Tech graduate as CEO or as a vice president, and there are 146 companies that employ 25 or more Tech grads. This vast alumni network helps students twofold. First, Tech's alumni are extremely generous, and their gifts year after year help the school rank among the top in contributions per enrolled student. Second, because many Tech graduates hold influential positions in some of America's top companies, current graduates often find themselves interviewing with Tech-friendly companies.

A great many Tech graduates stay in the Southeast, especially Georgia and Florida, after graduation (which is not very surprising considering these are also the two states that supply the largest number of Tech freshmen). Outside the Southeast, California and New York also have a relatively large concentration of alumni.

"The company I worked for had a very strong Tech presence. This not only helped me in my search for a niche within the company, but I also felt that I had an instant alliance with people I had just met. The quality of graduates Georgia Tech puts out is so

well respected in this community that I have even had one person jokingly ask if he could borrow the Tech license plate from my car because he needed a raise."

SUMMARY OVERVIEW

Georgia Tech can be considered a great institution because its limited curriculum allows students the opportunity to concentrate on and excel in specific areas of study. The courses of study are offered in such a way that students know they are getting the latest information from leaders in the field. Tech's graduates use this information to become leaders in business, their community, and the nation.

Tech's curriculum concentrates in only four areas: engineering, science, management, and architecture. Although students are required to take the traditional English, history, and social science courses, most of the classes they take are in a scientific area of study. This also means that everyone else is taking classes in the same areas. Tech's faculty and staff are not only up to date on the latest advances in their fields, but they also are often creating these advances. This allows students to be on the cutting edge of technology and, in fields where new developments break daily, this can be a big advantage.

As with any public, urban campus, Tech does have its problems. Most of Tech's plights boil down to one thing: money. The school is in need of funds to hire more faculty members. This causes an inflated class size in many areas. The admissions office is doing its best to hold Tech's enrollment constant to prevent additional overcrowding. But even if they are successful, new buildings, both for research and student use, are using up much of the available land space. Although this is currently not a problem, Tech's location makes additional external expansion almost impossible. Moreover, because internal expansion is finite, Tech could be facing a difficult problem with land space in 20 years.

Even given these drawbacks, Tech still represents an excellent education at a great price. Its graduates have been able to use what they have learned in their studies to excel in every field. And tomorrow's graduates will also have an opportunity to demonstrate to the world just what an education from Georgia Tech can do.

Kelly Thomas Forlini, B.S.

Harvard University

THE PROGRAM

"'By the power invested in me, I welcome you to the company of educated men and women,' said Harvard president Derek Bok, to 1600 hung over seniors at commencement.

"There it is, in a phrase memorized by every Harvard-Radcliffe senior in the weeks prior to commencement: the pronouncement that four years at the nation's oldest, most prestigious, and, some would say, most arrogant place of higher learning—Harvard-Radcliffe Colleges—have finally come to fruition. You're an alum, crimson blood runs through your veins, and unless you choose to live or work in Cambridge, you'll never have to see another tour group gape at John Harvard's statue, or at you, as long as you live. You're ready to take on the world; rather, that's what commencement would have you believe. And you are."

Harvard-Radcliffe Colleges, the oldest institution of higher learning in North America, is in Cambridge, Massachusetts. The campus is close to Boston—four stops away on the subway's Red Line—and shares the area with over 30 other colleges and universities—Boston College, Boston University, Wellesley College, Northeastern University, and the Massachusetts Institute of Technology (MIT), to name a few. The walls of the older buildings are indeed ivy-covered, but modern buildings and facilities abound; for example, art students work in the Carpenter Center, the only North American building designed by the famed French architect Le Corbusier. The students aren't uniformly garbed in Topsiders and Polos; thanks to Boston's urban sophistication, cowboy boots, leather jackets, and black leggings, as well as sweats and sneakers, are quite popular. There are always lots of people milling about in Harvard Yard, whether they be tour groups or freshmen playing wiffle ball in front of Memorial Church; the sheer numbers counteract Harvard-Radcliffe's aura of genteel, ageless stuffiness and add a refreshing sense of youth to the 357-year-old campus.

The students defy easy stereotypes. There are liberals and conservatives, and moderates do battle with extremists; people who believe in alternative politics have to learn to work with the supporters of the status quo. The valedictorian and the football hero share a suite, and musicians do their homework with entrepreneurs; kids who have never left their hometowns party with jetsetters and publish newspapers, magazines, and journals with urban visionaries and clubhoppers. With a 35% minority enrollment, the campus has a more diverse feel than is normally associated with its image; with a growing number of women (43%), there is less a sense that Harvard, the older of the pair (Radcliffe was founded in 1879), continues to represent the male tradition of power and knowledge. Every possible viewpoint, outlook, and experience ends up at Harvard-Radcliffe; the recent number of Olympic hockey players, skaters, and swimmers proves that not only eggheads and future politicians attend the school. In some way, though, every student arrives with a passion of some sort and pursues it while he/she studies; perhaps that is the only generalization to make.

Harvard-Radcliffe is a liberal arts college in the traditional sense of the term; advisers reassure countless people that life will go on without that fellowship or cushy job offer, internationally known professors grumble about the premeds and economics jocks who crowd their courses for nonacademic reasons, and the president of the university exhorts freshmen to get involved in public service and extracurriculars so that they can function in the Real World (*always* capitalized, and with good reason). Departments hold all sorts of happy hours and meetings, campaigning for students to concentrate in their little world of knowledge; some folks tumble in by default, others already know their thesis topics. At any rate, students learn something about the world and about themselves because of their academic experiences. This is as it should be—applying what one already knows to the unknown—the hallmark of a liberal education.

What makes Harvard-Radcliffe stand out from the other top liberal arts colleges in addition to its students is the sheer vastness of academic resources available to undergraduates. The most important minds in the academic world are here—John Kenneth Galbraith, Stephen Jay Gould, Barbara Johnson, Lawrence Tribe, Bernard Bailyn, and E.O. Wilson, to name a few on faculty. Through the Faculty Assistant Program, students can conduct research with these luminaries for course and financial credit; many more opportunities to undertake individual work with a well-known scholar are gained by simply approaching her/him with an Independent Study proposal. Harvard professors are extremely eager to encourage and sponsor undergraduate academic projects. Professors rarely lecture to huge crowds and ignore the students afterwards; they love to attend sections of their courses, to argue crucial points with students, and to attend meals and special functions with them. Lifelong friendships are often initiated through the close professor-student relationship and are intellectually and emotionally enriching for both.

Additionally, Harvard-Radcliffe students have access to the world's largest university library system (Widener Library alone has over one million volumes catalogued); a fellowships and internships office, which offers to the ambitious and adventurous a wealth of travel, work, and study-abroad options (Harvard-Radcliffe typically does very well in the annual Rhodes competition); extensive career and lifestyle counseling and support; a physical plant that includes two observatories, a nationwide computer network, a research forest, artistic and performance spaces, three distinct physical recreation areas, including an Olympic-size pool and indoor track, and a host of museums, fully modern laboratories, and study space. Practically anything a Harvard-Radcliffe student would want to know can be discovered in the university's resource network by asking questions; the school provides students with a plethora of resource guides to help them in their queries.

Harvard-Radcliffe is, most importantly, learning about oneself, how to cope, how to think and to question, and how to enjoy what the world has to offer; realizing that life isn't graded and that searching for unqualified approval from one's peers, parents, and authority figures is futile, takes a lot of time, guts, and some beers with the gang. As everyone has her/his peculiar intellectual and personal interests and accomplishments, Harvard-Radcliffe, by its hands-off attitude, tries to nurture this diversity; the school thrives on the fact that not everyone votes Democratic or will go to Harvard Law School. As a result, the place is very heady and intimidating: you find yourself endlessly questioning with your friends what it really means to be here, what you're supposed to be getting out of it, and whether you can really cut it. In the end, with that red envelope in hand, you know that you have conquered the Big H in your own way. Because of the questions and the successes you've had, you know that you couldn't have done it anywhere else. And, boy, does it feel good!

GETTING IN/FINANCIAL AID

Only 14% of all applicants to Harvard-Radcliffe are admitted every year. That means you're running up against some pretty stiff competition: the valedictorians, the dancers, the jocks, the debaters, the privileged, the clever, the computer-whizzes, and the kids who did their homework, went to band practice, worked at McDonald's, and ate their carrots. These same types of people get rejected too, so how do you beat the odds? The admissions committee will admit only to looking for a combination of an eclectic student body mix with individual students who have much to offer the community and can take valuable lessons from it as well.

What helps? The best academic preparation you are able to get, plus a high sense of determination, confidence, and drive. Applicants are asked to have taken four years of English, social science, and at least one foreign language, at least three years in math and in the sciences, and a healthy dose of electives. The committee is careful to weigh the academic resources of an inner-city St. Louis resident against those of a St. Alban's graduate. Although there are a fair number of private and prep school kids at Harvard-Radcliffe, the majority of students come from public and parochial schools in the United States and abroad. Strong grades, plus proof that you challenged yourself with the resources at hand, help immensely; a record of straight As isn't impressive if you took the easiest courses available.

Although not the most important factor, standardized test scores come into play as well. Outstanding performances, especially on the achievement and advanced placement exams, often offset less-than-spectacular grades; the advanced placement exams, notably, are used to offer certain entrants sophomore standing, and course work done in preparation for these tests often catches the committee's eye. Again, a 1600 on the SAT I isn't a surefire way to get in, but it doesn't hurt to have scored it!

What really winnows candidates for the committee is the portrait it obtains from their personal essays, teacher and other recommendations, and the required alumni interview. The committee pores over every word you say, as well as how you say it; the members look for the confidence, the wit, the self-knowledge in the essay that show what sort of person you really are. The committee is attempting to find that spark that makes an otherwise typical applicant stand out from the competition. It may be a truly compassionate nature, exemplary leadership qualities, a special talent, unusual intellectual curiosity, or a highly developed sense of maturity due to personal experience. Each of these qualities counts.

> *"Everyone you know has these special traits in one way or another and will show it while in school; one of my roommates devoted much of his free time to serving food to the homeless at an area shelter, another taught English to a Chinese immigrant and served as a Big Brother to a child from a poor Cambridge neighborhood. One senior started a literacy program in his hometown, located in an impoverished nation halfway around the globe. Due to his ongoing efforts during his time in school, the program successfully spread across that country. The ones who bring you soup when you're sick are the same people who will put their energies into improving the community welfare. I learned that Harvard-Radcliffe people care about others and will seize the initiative to solve problems. They don't do it for the awards or the glory; they do what they do because they genuinely care about humanity."*

People who are exceedingly talented in some respect also populate the Harvard-Radcliffe campus. A rising young international violinist recently enrolled at the college, and Olympic hockey players have returned to lead the Crimson to national glory. Christopher Durang, class of 1970, is a respected American playwright, and Jack Lemmon and Fred Gwynne (of "Munsters" fame), graduated from the college. It has been rumored that a pipeline connects the *Harvard Lampoon* building to the writing offices of "Late Night with David Letterman" in New York City since former *Lampoon* staffers have been recent members of the writing crew. One of my class-mates has been a nationally ranked chess master, another attended a recent National Democratic Convention as one of its youngest voting delegates, and still another won election to his town council while still in school. A very close friend sparked a statewide environmental cleanup when he discovered a toxic waste dump near his home, and yet another friend defied the pundits by gaining admis-sion to the college without ever having set foot in a formal classroom. The variety of experiences and achievements Harvard-Radcliffe students have accumulated cov-ers the spectrum and makes for a lively and interesting student body.

A typical Harvard-Radcliffe class is extremely diverse: 20% come from the Northeast, 20% hail from the Mid-Atlantic region, 15% from the South, 10% from the Southwest, 15% from the Midwest, 15% from the West Coast, and the rest from Canada, Mexico, and many foreign nations. Thirty-five percent of the students are from minority groups (black, Hispanic, Asian, and Native American). The ratio of men to women is 57/43. However, when Harvard and Radcliffe merged in 1977, they agreed to admit students on a gender-blind basis, so as to achieve a 50/50 bal-ance yearly without quotas. Recent classes have come closer to that ideal. Every academic, economic, and social class is represented. Most importantly, everyone has a record of achievement and is likable, energetic, and willing to get involved.

Harvard-Radcliffe admits students on a need-blind basis as well; that is to say, any-one admitted to the college is guaranteed financial assistance to pay for the school-ing. Those with financial need are offered aid packages to finance their four years at Harvard-Radcliffe; aid is reviewed yearly and adjusted to reflect changing financial information for the applicant and family. Seventy percent of all Harvard-Radcliffe students get some sort of aid, be it scholarship, grant, loan, work-study, or a combina-tion of the above. Just as there is a lot of paperwork to be completed by January 1 for admissions, so there is a similar amount of paperwork to be completed for financial aid. If you receive aid the first year, be certain to complete and file the following year's application by April 1 of the current school year; also get accustomed to filing tax forms and learning the intricacies of your family's financial situation. If you are not offered aid when you apply, petition the financial aid committee to review your case. The admissions committee doesn't want anyone to refuse an offer of admission because of a lack of financial resources to pay the steep tuition and fees.

ACADEMIC ENVIRONMENT

Harvard has some of the best minds in the world teaching there, as well as some of the worst pendants and snooty academics ever to come down the pike. Because the talents got to where they are due to hard work and discipline and because the students are equally ambitious and demanding, the result is an intensely stimulating, if sometimes overbearing, intellectual atmosphere. The pressure the individual student feels, though, is directly linked to his/her depth of academic interest and future school plans.

Harvard-Radcliffe is a liberal arts school with a focus on three major disciplines—humanities, social science, and natural science. Harvard's faculty makes it stand apart—there are professors of international prestige teaching undergraduates. There are the Nobel Prize winners, such as chemist Dudley Herschbach and biophysicist Walter Gilbert; the most eminent of Keynesian economists. John Kenneth Galbraith, occasionally lectures in introductory economics; Stephen Jay Gould, the popular geologist-evolutionist-writer, and E.O. Wilson, another evolutionist-writer, teach introductory science courses to standing-room-only audiences. Henry Louis Gates, Jr. is the eminent African-American literature and cultural scholar, and Robert Brustein, the director of the American Repertory Theater, teaches a course on post-modern drama to aspiring actors and critics. Bernard Bailyn, the dean of early American history, Donald Fleming (European intellectual history), and Martin Feldstein, the country's most prominent conservative economist, draw crowds for their twice-weekly lectures on the American Revolution, literature's reflection in current events, and the differences between Keynesian and supply-side economics. When he isn't defending the concept of civil liberties at Harvard Law School, Alan Dershowitz is speaking out in the media on issues of the day.

Among the women, Majorie Garber (Shakespeare), Helen Vendler (poetry), Barbara Johnson (French literature and Afro-American studies), and Susan Suleiman (French literature and women's studies) have established formidable reputations both as scholars and as some of the faculty's most accessible members to undergraduates. Students can, and do, get a demanding and intellectually satisfying education at Harvard-Radcliffe, if for no other reason than that you can work with some of the brightest people in academia today.

All students must pass 32 courses, or four per semester, to qualify for the A.B.; about half are devoted to the concentration, or major, one fourth to the core curriculum, and the remaining one fourth can be used for electives and more intensive concentration work. A few honors-only concentrations require the writing of a senior thesis for the degree; most others make the thesis optional.

Students may choose to study in one of approximately 45 departments; a very few people petition to create their own unusual and rigorous concentrations with faculty support and advice. There are no professional degrees offered, such as accounting or nursing; rather, students focus on the theoretical questions of economics, government, and history. Although Harvard offers an ABET accredited degree in engineering, the sciences are taught for their own sake; people looking for research or practical experience in medicine usually find internships and jobs outside the classroom to meet those needs. Students in the larger departments, such as psychology, government, and biology, find themselves haunted by the reputations of B.F. Skinner and Henry Kissinger, and it is both an honor and a challenge to have the Harvard president advise one's senior English thesis.

Students in the smaller departments, such as Romance languages and literatures or folklore and mythology, either get lots of attention from professors or are shunted aside by aggressive graduate students; still, it is a lot easier to know your professors by name and specific interests if you head for a small department. Some concentrations, such as history and literature and social studies, are application-only (as if getting into the school wasn't enough!); others are happy to see students wanting to concentrate in something such as religion or statistics.

Class sizes and compositions run the gamut; seminars can be deadly if you are prone to skipping homework and/or dozing in midafternoon, and giant lecture courses can make you feel like a number with only an overworked graduate student to save you from grade-sheet oblivion. However, there are classes such as Justice (Moral Reasoning 22), where Michael Sandel runs through the audience à la Phil Donahue, asking members how they really feel about Kant's categorical imperative, and an avant-garde French theater course where the professor schedules a break during the two-hour session so that he can enjoy a leisurely smoke on his pipe and you can grab a cup of coffee and a muffin from Au Bon Pain. Tutorials, where most students get to pursue a topic in depth during a given semester, are where you learn just how capable your neighbor is of saying nothing, and where, just when you have given up on being brilliant, you give an insight that impresses your professor and peers. Many students find the small (one to ten) class size and undivided professor attention, as well as the discussions, to be the most enjoyable part of their concentration work. As in any venture, you get more out of it if you dive headlong into your work; if you find that you don't like your concentration, you can always switch to another. No matter how you get to commencement, it is worth the trip.

"I was a French civilization concentrator, which allowed me to study politics, history, and the arts in addition to modern literature; I had the pleasure of studying with Jean-Marie Apostolidès (now at Stanford), Susan Suleiman, and Alice Jardine, whose combined knowledge of twentieth-century literature and culture was exquisitely impressive. Having Professor Suleiman admit in a junior tutorial that Roland Barthes's approach to literary deconstruction sometimes eluded her grasp increased my respect for her as a teacher and as a person, and I found that in my papers for her course I tried to reach a higher level of sophisticated analysis than I otherwise would have attempted. During my junior year, I took five courses one semester and pored through 2000 pages of historical reading in summer school; when I returned to Harvard-Radcliffe for my senior year, I found that I had completed all of my requirements, had no thesis to write, and had only six electives standing between me and my diploma. Well, I did what any self-respecting student would do—I studied photography, Sam Shepard, surrealism, Alfred Hitchcock and Jean-Luc Godard, jazz, and women's literature! By focusing on nineteenth- and twentieth-century France for two years, I hadn't allowed myself the time to explore other

interests, as I had as a freshman; senior year was the right time to start studying other subjects that were equally attractive to me. I finally realized then what it meant at Harvard to be educated—to have a deep appreciation for a particular subject, as well as to have a healthy curiosity for everything else in the world—and I am glad that I pursued my studies as I did."

There is palpable academic pressure at Harvard-Radcliffe, probably more than at any other school; with personal, parental, and institutional expectations weighing upon the student, it can seem sometimes that the admissions office indeed made one mistake in its job the year you were admitted. Yet very few students flunk out and well over 90% of entering students will receive their Harvard degrees. Whether it is due to an ever-deepening interest in your work or because of competition with other students, you have to recognize why you study as you do and what choices you have to make in order to make your education an asset in later years. Non-Harvardians will make greater demands upon you once you enter the Real World, and your ability to cope with the pressure as a student will help you once you leave Cambridge. Those using their education as a means to an end don't fully realize the pleasures that come with academic challenge; those who balance their studies with their future plans and incorporate extracurriculars are much more fulfilled. Then there are those who are perfectly content to try all the things that couldn't be done before college and to work on friendships, confident that their work is only part of their Harvard-Radcliffe experience. Your maturity and sense of perspective will demythologize the college for you, freeing you to move on to the real purpose of college.

SOCIAL LIFE

"Social life? At Harvard? You gotta be kidding—there isn't one! You shoulda gone to Big State U, where they have frats and coeds and invented the term 'spring break.' Everyone's a wonk, or a hardcore throat-cutting s-o-b, and doesn't know how to party or dance or drink or date, and God help me the women only wear sweats and look at you funny when you open doors for them and they're not carrying anything, and the guys are socially inept and no matter how smart they are you wouldn't share a nightmare with them; and if you're lucky enough to find someone who's smart and funny and good-looking and not neurotic and thinks you're equally cool and interesting, chances are she/he is practically engaged to the only other perfect person on campus and you're literally a goner. No one has relationships here; it's all one-night stands after too much Bud and a play at sympathy over a Husky Club at the Tasty."
                                    —*The typical social life complaint*

Actually, it's not like that *at all*. Love and close friends and great times abound at Harvard-Radcliffe. It's just that people are so accustomed to planning and organizing and working on everything else in life that they end up treating personal relationships as one huge project to complete. The wise realize that life in the Real World isn't this calculated and, hence, relax during their college years. Harvard-Radcliffe people are fun and have to be enjoyed. After all, who's going to discuss biology lab at the Twenty-fifth Reunion?

The housing system provides the easiest way to meet people: you pal up with your freshman roommates and dormmates, as well as with classmates, and chances are you'll move together to one of the 12 residential houses and meet other groups of people from other dorms, as well as the seniors and juniors who already live there. Harvard-Radcliffe guarantees on-campus housing to all incoming freshmen and returning upperclassmen and is currently moving to provide immediate on-campus housing to transfer students. Allegiance to one's dorm typically lasts through part of sophomore year; by the end of the spring, though, you are ready to defend your house's honor at the annual Raft Race on the Charles River. It is in the house where your softball buddies, your paramours, and your classmates live, and most people devote considerable energy to becoming part of the community. There are clubs and public service groups to join, as well as the intramural teams, and the houses routinely hold special dinners and socials so that everyone can become acquainted. The dining hall is where upperclassmen and women check out the new crop of sophomores; once the novelty wears off, the business of planning road trips, pranks, and parties takes precedence. There are cliques, as in high school, and it seems that because of the tendency for similar people to socialize together, everyone is romantically attracted to everyone else at some point. Thankfully, there is also the crowd that heads for Fenway Park without fail in the spring and single-handedly runs the Secret Santa bawdiness every December with finesse.

Because there are no fraternities or sororities on campus (black students have joined these groups through MIT and Wellesley), the house is the social center for most people. However, it can become too insular a place, so students make it a point to keep in touch with friends made in classes and during freshman year; sharing a meal up at the quad or down at the river (the two groups of houses) is a popular route, as is attending parties and events where you know a few people. Extracurriculars bring people together from all over campus, and going out in Cambridge and Boston will broaden your perceptions of Harvard, other colleges, and the city. There's always a place to meet new people—friends are made in classes, at work, and through other friends. You just have to be aggressive and adventurous if you like variety in your social activities.

A typical social calendar may look something like this:

Late September   *Return to school, initial parties and welcoming dinners for freshmen and sophomores; Saturday football games; intramurals start*

October	*Campus-wide party, house parties; football games; Columbus Day; Halloween pranks and parties*
November	**Midterms end; many theater and musical events; The Game vs. Yale; Thanksgiving break**
December	*Major fall theater productions; hockey season begins; houses' winter formals; Secret Santa parties; winter break (through New Year's)*
January	*Hockey games; two-week reading period, two-week exam period; study breaks; intersession*
February	**Second semester begins; Valentine's Day parties; Black History Month; Radcliffe Senior Soirée; more hockey; snowball fights (maybe)**
March	*House parties; midterms; spring break (final week)*
April	*Major spring theater productions; Fenway Park opens; housing and room lotteries; houses' spring formals and parties; Boston Marathon*
May	*Two-week reading period, two-week exam period; senior dinners, events, parties; summer vacation begins*
June	*Commencement (graduation); class reunions*

Harvard-Radcliffe's reputation? The general perception is that people play as hard as they work—Trick or Drink, Stein Club, house parties, finals clubs, and golf courses are extremely popular. Alcohol is a definite part of the social scene. People will celebrate any event: a roommate's birthday, the end of fall exams, Patriot's Day, the Super Bowl. After all, college is meant to be fun as well as work!

EXTRACURRICULAR ACTIVITIES

When people aren't knocking themselves out on their homework or practicing the fine art of procrastination, they throw themselves into a myriad of activities. Sports, acting, writing, working, creating notorious personal reputations—Harvard-Radcliffe people get involved passionately and loudly.

The things one can do are endless. Political journals and papers abound, for example, as do Model Congress and Model UN; budding politicians can join the

Undergraduate Council, attend seminars at the Kennedy School of Government, and join the campus political parties. Students can step back and write about the politicians, athletes, bureaucrats, performers, and social activists who populate the campus. There are clubs for minority students that can be alternatively cliquish, political, and purely social in scope; women students also have their own student government. Issues such as South African apartheid, AIDS, gay and lesbian rights, and international human rights attract all sorts of idealists and jaded workers for the cause. Then there are the people who fervently believe that artistic expression, be it theater, film, dance, painting, or writing, is the way to confront social problems (and maybe get to New York).

For an Ivy League school, sports are taken very seriously; almost everyone will go out for crew as a freshman, and many other people wisely try out for sports where they have the chance to work out, to compete, and to meet students from both Harvard-Radcliffe and other schools. People will risk frostbite to watch Harvard trounce Yale in football every November, and the prowess of the men's hockey team has consistently drawn SRO crowd to Bright Hockey Center every winter weekend in recent years. Rugby's popularity has risen in recent times, and the men and women players live up to the "Play hard, party harder" motto. Many other students give time to aerobics, weight lifting, cycling, running, swimming, or sculling when they can fit them in; almost everyone flirts with the notion of trying out for a varsity sport at some point during her/his college career. Health concerns, as well as the search for a fit body and a sense of personal accomplishment, encourage many people to get active.

The most popular activity on campus is public service. Whether it involves tutoring Roxbury students, serving meals and providing shelter to the homeless, serving as a Big Sister or Brother to a Cambridge child, or teaching reading to prison inmates, Harvard-Radcliffe students have shown themselves to be far more sensitive and committed to others' well-being than the critics would have you believe. Yes, there are the people who belong to the Harvard Investment Club, but these are the same people who help immigrants prepare for their citizenship exams and work in Legal Aid bureaus to help the indigent get legal representation. There are people who befriend those on the heating grates in winter, showing them that someone cares about their lives and wants to be a friend.

> *"One student I knew wanted to find a way to get Leverett House residents interested in public service. She decided to try pairing interested students with both older people in need of companions and with school-age children; the students would take the children to visit the older people on a regular basis, thus giving everyone a chance to make friends with different generations. What makes the program work is that, due to my friend's commitment, over 75% of all Leverett residents participated. Because of her dedication, she was presented the Ames Award, the prize given for outstanding public service during college, at the end of her senior year."*

Most students also work part-time while in school; many do it because of financial considerations, but others have found it a good way to explore careers and to exert some degree of financial independence. Internships and jobs cover the spectrum—from library duty to film research and PR campaigns; students can enhance their academic interests with a research position under a professor or in a business situation. Many others take positions that they simply find fun or instructive, or as a diversion from their scholastic and club responsibilities. Above all, working forces people to be more organized in their habits and to appreciate their free time; it also reminds them that there is a world beyond Harvard-Radcliffe.

If there is an opportunity for something to be done, some Radcliffe or Harvard student is busy organizing the details right now. The chess team has its loyal fans, as does the WHRB radio crowd, and there always will be an interest in karate, debating, and mountain climbing. Can't find something to do? Well, don't just sit there—get involved. Start your own club!

GRADUATES

What do you do with a Harvard-Radcliffe degree? Some head for graduate school and emerge as doctors, lawyers, business moguls, and tenure-hungry academics. Although investment banking has been popular recently, almost 40% of a recent graduating class indicated that they were going to work in public service, with teaching, social work, and the Peace Corps frequently mentioned. Some travel for months at a time, some program computers and work in research labs. Others head for the theater, retail management training programs, ashrams, and industry. Over 97% of all graduates will return to graduate school for further study; by then, school has become a more personal pursuit, as opposed to a rite of passage the way college has been traditionally depicted.

> *"As I write this, I am spending a year out in the Real World before heading off to journalism school in the fall. I have been living in Boston with three classmates, and my time has been divided between news internships, a bookselling job, freelance reporting, and working as a long-term temp. I have had the time to read more, as well as catch up on international affairs, and I am diving headlong into Boston's cultural and historical offerings. I also have the time to travel, to write long letters, and to enjoy my new role as an adult. It is a decidedly indulgent year for me, one in which I can spoil myself with the skills and tastes I acquired while at Harvard-Radcliffe."*

The alumni network (over 100,000 members worldwide) is very strong; there is a central alumni and reunions office on campus, as well as Harvard-Radcliffe Clubs in most countries. The "old school" ties and connections one has are among the most coveted benefits of the degree. No matter where you go after graduation, you will meet other Harvard-Radcliffe alums; they are more than happy to help you find a job, make contact with other alums in offbeat places, and share a laugh over common memories. The feeling of community rivals that of the family, but every graduate makes room for both allegiances in her/his heart without problems.

SUMMARY OVERVIEW

Every silver lining has its cloud, and vice versa. Harvard-Radcliffe is no exception. The school will leave its unmistakable stamp of self-assuredness and open-mindedness on you, but it helps to review the lows and highs of a Harvard-Radcliffe education.

The highs are unbeatable. You have the best undergraduate education at your fingertips. The resources, the faculty's international prestige and accessibility, and the expectation to challenge existing limits in academic thought will excite your curiosity and give you satisfaction in your studies. The academic advice and support system is designed to give you ultimate freedom in creating your academic program, and the core curriculum exists to remind you of other fields of thought as you advance in your studies. The feedback you get from your classmates and friends makes for the sort of informal, relaxed intellectual atmosphere that is stimulating and enriching.

When you graduate, you are an alumna/nus of the top undergraduate institution in the world. You have access to an international network of friends and contacts, and your chances for professional success are greatly enhanced by your Harvard-Radcliffe connection. You are in a position to influence and create public opinion as no one else can; your qualifications get that extra boost from the diploma behind you. Six U.S. presidents have had Harvard degrees—you could be number seven!

Finally, you cannot beat the closeness of the ties that you will forge with other people, especially your classmates. The intensity that fills the campus atmosphere also infuses friendships; you will have a second family with whom to celebrate your triumphs and analyze your downfalls, as well as people with whom to party, to play sports, and to explore the world. The tears shed at commencement not only reflect the end of college, but also mourn the passing of some of your most important friendships. Seven months out of college, I am still amazed as to the profundity of love and respect that people have for each other; it feels wonderful to know that you had an impact upon someone's life and still inform it, even as your paths take you to different cities or countries.

The lows. First, there is a lot of competition—much more than you've ever encountered. It's the flip side of being part of the most academically talented student body in the country: everyone is driven, accomplishment-directed, and demanding. It doesn't help that your parents, teachers, hometowns, and advisers want the very best you can produce at all times. Relax! Remember—virtually everyone ends up with that Harvard diploma!

Second, exams fall after winter break—two weeks later, in fact. You will find yourself studying and writing papers while your Yale and Big State U friends are out dancing, watching the soaps, and *enjoying* their winter breaks. You can call your Princeton friends to commiserate and to proof each other's papers, or you can leave the work until reading period (ouch!).

Finally, there is the fact that being a Harvard-Radcliffe student is not a bed of roses, at least as far as dealing with nonaffiliated people goes. You have to answer to charges of Harvard as the archetypal WASP institution that perpetuates social ills or, conversely, as the institution that would single-handedly turn the United States into a rabidly socialist/communist state if it had the chance. Because of Harvard-Radcliffe's prominent spot in the media, you may find yourself caught in a heated argument with others about the schools' approach to certain problems. You have to decide how to deal with this sort of pressure, and it is to your advantage to learn the fine art of dismissal early in college. The image of the college can become a stumbling block if you aren't careful, so become well-versed in the school's problems and evaluate them for yourself. You'll be glad you did.

In sum, studying at Harvard-Radcliffe is one of the formative experiences of life (besides birth, marriage, and death). If you are offered the chance to live in Harvard Yard, don't refuse. It is an experience that truly matures and enriches you. If I had to do it all over again, I would enroll at Harvard-Radcliffe without a moment's hesitation.

Rosiland Jordan, A.B.

Harvey Mudd College

THE PROGRAM

Hey! We've hit the big time! A tiny little science and engineering school christened for a mining engineer whose name is Mudd on the same list as Stanford, Cal Tech, and the rest of the beautiful schools. I'll bet you're surprised. Well, all of us at Mudd are not surprised in the least. Harvey Mudd College is one of the very best places for bright students to hang out and get a solid technical education, and its name is starting to be associated with all that is fine and good about a college. But that's not all that Mudd has to offer. It also offers a healthy atmosphere for personal expression within and outside the sciences.

Yes, at Mudd things are done just a bit differently than other places. For example, before the college opened in the late 1950s, the first dorm was built and called, simply enough, Dorm. The second dorm was built west of the first, instantly begetting East Dorm and West Dorm. The third was built north of the other two, and thus North was born. The fourth dorm, west of North and north of West (completing the quad) simply begged to be called South even though it's not south of any bloomin' thing on campus. Later, the fifth dorm was built east of everything else, and called simply New. The sixth dorm, again further east, is known as New II.

I'm sure most of you see a certain warped logic to this process, a warped logic that beautifully typifies what it is like to attend Harvey Mudd College. You live, day by day, with the warped reality that is modern science and engineering, among people committed to personal passions including, but not limited to, science and engineering. The only common denominator of Mudders is an interest in science and math; without such, Mudd is not worth the effort. Harvey Mudd College in Claremont, California is deep down, a bastion of technical education. The college was brought about by some very clever women and men who realized that the engineers and scientists of tomorrow (which is now, of course, today) must be versed in three seemingly obvious things: their own field, related fields, and a conglomeration of other mind-expanding topics that get clumped into humanities.

And that is precisely what Harvey Mudd College assaults its students with. To make it through, no matter what you may major in (half major in engineering), you have to learn a great deal of math, chemistry, physics, engineering, biology and humanities (such as psychology, philosophy, economics, literature, history, international relations, classics, languages, and so on.) The variety of classes makes it much easier to stay interested in your academic life, and the major programs insure that you are ready for a career in academia or industry upon graduation. Mudd generally caters to the student with many interests, perhaps without a great sense of direction, but always willing to attempt to learn new things.

> *"I arrived for freshman orientation feeling like a Christian in ancient Rome, being thrust into the Coliseum packed with blood-thirsty fans wearing, 'The Christians Got Eaten and All I Got Was This Lousy T-shirt' T-shirts, and finding suddenly, instead of a lion, Rod Serling welcoming me back from 'The Twilight Zone'. The five-day orientation program grabbed me, the recent high school senior, and gently showed me what to expect for the next four years, all the while making this lesson more fun than grown-ups are usually allowed to have. I arrived that first day, shy shy SHY shy shy, absolutely afraid to step on cracks or cross someone's path, and I was taken in hand by several wonderful people. One, Suzie, was my sponsor, a person who helps freshmen (usually about six to a sponsor) make the adjustment from their high school daze to the college environment, during and after orientation. Suzie helped me find my room, find the lecture halls and bookstore and other important places, learn the tricky dance through the crowded dining hall, and just generally stood there saying, 'It's OK to be scared, The Powers That Be knew you'd be scared and gave you me to lean on.' Great people, sponsors, and their support really sets the mood for the rest of your Mudd life."*

GETTING IN/FINANCIAL AID

Mudd is not exactly easy to get into. The entire student body is approximately 600 students and there are National Merit Scholars hither and yon, so everyone characterizes the place as highly selective. But so what? If you are interested but afraid, apply anyhow. The facts looked at by the admissions department are high school grades, SAT I and SAT II (you need to take the Math Level II—Writing and one test of your choice) exam scores, activities, counselor and teacher recommendations, essays, and the personal interview either on campus or with an alumni representative somewhere else. Now, those essays can make or break you, even if you have serious strengths or weakness in the other categories, so believe in yourself, and Mudd might just believe in you.

> *"I heard about the college in what was later regarded as a fluke. Most hear of HMC via a mass mailing of its riotous 'Junk Mail Kit' to high scoring PSATers, but I wasn't on their list. I did, however, get a long letter from the head of the chemistry department, telling me about the school and about his research and about how he had to stop writing because he had to fly off to Australia to deliver a paper. I was completely impressed by such personal attention, sent off for an application, and was granted admission by the Early Decision process (i.e., I was accepted by January 1 because I got my application in before December 1). But no one on campus knows why the head of the chemistry department had mailed such a letter. I guess all I can say is fate guided me and might work for you."*

The student body is by design diverse—well, mostly diverse. Like all science and tech places, Mudd is male-dominated on paper (66% of the student body is male, most of the professors are male, most of the insects and stray dogs are male), but a lot of campus government is dominated by active and involved women. The college is under-represented in most minority groups, but it has a large percentage of Asian-American students. However, these general categories have very little to do with what I call Mudd's diversity. There are some very *original* people going to school there. Students are interested in all sorts of different things, like acting, sports, art, writing, flying, unicycling, bicycling, journalism, running, lifting weights, board games, bridge, and making eyes at each other in darkened rooms. If you have a favorite activity that you want to continue in college, I would bet your life insurance policy you can find another Mudder interested in such things.

> *"For example, I was a mathematics major who wrote a column for the school paper (*The Muddraker—cute name, no?), ran track two years, was active in dorm sports, and wrote, produced and directed a three-act, two-and-a-half-hour play his senior year (*Preoccupied in Suburbia). And, I was not particularly unusual for having done this stuff, there are gaggles of frighteningly energetic people at Mudd, which makes the campus nearly hum."*

Yes, financial aid is available. This is mostly need-based for incoming freshmen (although every frosh deserves a full ride, the college isn't that well endowed), with some honor-based scholarships available later. At present 60% of students are receiving some sort of financial aid from the college, and 80% are receiving financial aid from somewhere. A year of Mudd costs more than $20,000, but there are ways to get someone else to pay, so don't let financial considerations make your decisions for you.

ACADEMIC ENVIRONMENT

The most important thing about academics at Mudd is the Honor Code. Wait, let's try that again: The most important thing about Harvey Mudd College is the Honor Code. All students at Mudd, in all phases of campus life, fall under the guidelines of the Honor Code; in short, each student agrees upon entering the school that she/he will act towards others in a responsible manner, and then they are expected to do so. Timed take-home tests are given, and the professors are confident that the students will work alone and stop when they are supposed to. The administration trusts that each student will behave like an adult, until the student proves that she/he can't. Students lend valued possessions to one another with little to no concern. Also, the Honor Code requires that if you see an infraction, you must either reach a settlement among yourselves and report the results to the proper board, or send the information to said board for a trial. Because of the code, Mudders are trusted more than any other person, anywhere.

Now, to the classes. Your first year and a half at Mudd are pretty much structured for you by the registrar's office (staffed by three wonderful women who know everyone's names). You take physics (classical mechanics, and electricity and magnetism), chemistry (a little bit of everything), calculus (dependent on placement testing), computer science (an intro to Pascal for most people), and rhetoric (a combination intro to literature-basic composition course), plus perhaps chemistry and/or physics lab. Your longing for free will during this period is quenched by your choice of humanities classes.

> "The great thing about all these classes is that you are taking them with almost your entire class. That means that there are about 160 of you wandering the campus trying to figure out the answers to number three; you have suddenly become a part of a great, living study group disguised as a freshman class. The professors encourage cooperative learning since it helps you academically and socially simultaneously. I have never enjoyed learning as much as I did my freshman year, sitting haphazardly in a dorm room with ten of my friends, working blindly on physics or something; I really felt that I contributed to and took from the group, a feeling I highly recommend."

A sum total of six majors are offered: biology (math applied to living things), chemistry (math applied to midsize things), computer science (math applied to machines), engineering (math applied to making money), mathematics (math applied to nothing in particular) and physics (math applied to very small and very large things). The biology major was first offered in 1989-90, so having barely crawled off the drawing board it is both untested and exciting, focusing on genetics and microbiology instead of dissecting frogs. The entire school is still very young, so there are still some academic chances being taken, which makes for a more exciting college for students and professors alike.

There are, however, a couple of rather unique twists to HMC's classes. First, Harvey Mudd College is one of six Claremont Colleges (HMC, Scripps College, Claremont McKenna College [CMC], Pitzer College, Pomona College, and the Claremont Graduate School [CGS]), and students at each school can cross-register at the other schools. I took some great humanities and technical classes at the other colleges, and it gave me a chance to venture bravely out away from everyone I knew at my small school. The colleges also share libraries, giving you the benefits of a large university without stripping your individuality.

The second thing that Mudd offers is the clinic program, in both math and engineering. Projects are sponsored by companies in industry (General Dynamics, NASA, Northrop, Kodak, Coors Beer, and many others) and consist of open-ended problems to be solved by a team of junior and senior Mudders. These students are supervised by a professor and helped out by company liaisons. They learn what it's really like to really work in real engineering or applied math. Clinic is also, to be honest, the ultimate time drain, and has convinced people that either they are in the perfect major or in hell. Either way, it's best to find out while still in school.

Other than clinics and senior research projects, the main method of instruction is the classic lecture-and-test method. The professor expounds knowingly on his/her subject, and the student listens carefully and takes notes and does her/his homework and prepares for exams. A few of the humanities classes and some upper-level technical courses follow more of a seminar style, but not too many. Average class size is reported at around 20, but with an expansive standard deviation. Your freshman year is mostly spent in lectures with the rest of your class (about 150) with recitation sections of about 25 where you and the professor go over assigned problems and deal with individual questions. Then, when you reach upper-level classes, class size is a function of major. In biology, chemistry, math or physics, classes shrink below 25; some of mine were as small as four. In engineering, your lectures are still about 50-70 people, with smaller recitation sections. And, in clinic (required for a year and a half of all engineers), you get to work closely with about five other teammates and your prof and liaison. So, you get plenty of attention, whether you want it or not.

And, if you ask for help, it is there. A great majority of professors will reschedule their lives while bending over backwards to try to help you. It's hard to believe that these great wise Doctors of Knowledge would spend quality time with lowly undergrads, but that is what they do. You are never taught by teaching assistants, except for the odd day in some humanities classes. The professors are there for you, and most realize that and will work with you until time approaches infinity. Ask, and ye shall receive, from professors, fellow travelers, the dean of students office, anyone, and everyone.

Finally, there is one set of nonacademic regulations that you should know about. Every Mudder must take at least three physical education classes to graduate. One must be swimming, unless you pass a swim test. One must be Physical Fitness for Life (PE for Death) unless you compete in a varsity sport. The other one is completely up to you, with about 20 classes to choose from.

SOCIAL LIFE

Most schools that you can apply to seem to see your social life as a right written into their constitutions: thou shalt have the right to party whenever though willst and still be able to graduate. Well, HMC sees your social life as more of a privilege reserved for those who plan ahead. There are truckloads of work at Mudd—so much so that keeping your head above water can be a full-time occupation, but if you set up fun as a priority, there is time for it. And, thanks to other Mudders, it is worth the wait.

Now, Mudd (like Cal Tech and MIT) has a reputation for housing a bunch of squids (those who study until they completely forget there is anything else to do), and I'm here to tell you that's not the case at Mudd. We have fun; it's the old quality time versus quantity time question. At most colleges you have a large quantity of time to spend relaxing, but at Mudd we have to unwind quickly and then get back to work and thus have fine-tuned these skills. You can see people viciously playing pinball or ping-pong or basketball to release tension, watch out for yourself as they shoot hockey pucks down the hallway, or hear them out on the field on the outskirts of campus participating in a primal scream (my personal favorite). Relieving stress is a fine art, and there are many at Mudd who can teach you the basics so you can develop your own techniques.

So, when pressed for time, you invent fun. But with real planning, there is plenty to do in the immediate area also. There are always bands playing nearby. There is a pizza place downstairs in the Muddhole (underneath the dining hall), which serves cheap and fairly reliable slices. There are cheap movies shown on Sunday, Tuesday, Wednesday, Friday, and Saturday nights, running classic (read old) and fairly new films. There are occasional Wednesday Nighters (where Mudders have a chance to show off any talent that they possess or imagine they do) and the annual talent show. A good friend and I had a tendency to do weird renditions of Monty Python skits for Wednesday Nighters, and they usually went over pretty well (Monty Python, Douglas Adams, Bloom County [you know, thinking humor] are very popular on campus) so anyone can join in the fun.

All the dorms have TV's and VCR's, so renting movies and taking over lounges is popular on weekends. A number of people like In and Out Hamburgers, Juanita's (a good, cheap Mexican lunch place), and Mongolian Barbecue (a Chinese place, cheap for lunch and open for dinner), but these tend to require owning a car or finding a friend who's willing to drive. This is not always difficult because people usually are looking for some reason not to do their homework. Having a car can be an asset socially but a liability to academics and finances, so bringing a car may or may not be a good idea.

Speaking of cars, they have two other major purposes besides local dinner and lunch places. First, Claremont is only 30-some miles from downtown Los Angeles, so with wheels you can join in real city nightlife and/or go to the beach. These require serious advanced planning and can make Mudd even more of a challenge than it is to those who chain themselves to campus on a short leash, but everyone should do the whole Disneyland/beach/Westwood/Magic Mountain thing once while in Southern California, and there are plenty of opportunities.

> *"But the most important need for a car is to get to the world's greatest doughnut shop approximately 8.3 miles to the east in Glendora. It is called Foster's Doughnuts, and this place is unbelievable to people who've never been there. I can tell you that it has delicious, large doughnuts, but that doesn't even begin to describe their amazing taste, their debilitating smell, and their awe-inspiring presence behind the shop's windows. You simply have to go there because they are cheap and fantastic, and a run gets you away from campus for about an hour. Getting there is half the fun, a chance to talk to friends and get away from pressures and just not think about anything technical for a while."*

And there are parties on campus. Yes, drinking does take place, like everywhere else, but right now there is a new alcohol policy in effect at the Claremont Colleges: no hard alcohol can be served at parties, and you must be over 21 to drink.

So things are changing, but in general parties will stay the same and people will continue to go to them for different reasons. Some go to get drunk, period. Some go to meet the man/woman of their dreams, which can be tough because the music is a bit loud. Some go to dance with people they already know. And some go to stand around and watch everyone else.

But by far the best thing you can possibly do with your free time at Mudd is simply talk to some of the other people sharing the experience with you. As many of you have probably already found out, people become more interesting as they get less sleep (theoretically because self-consciousness is the first thing recharged when you sleep), and at Mudd no one sleeps all that much. Late-night chats with your roommate when you really should be sleeping, random conversations in doorways when you should be starting your homework, just being there for someone when they've been run ragged by the system. Harvey Mudd College sets people up to be honest and open about themselves; you merely need to be open to others and reach out to them.

> *"It is the time spent with people who understand me that means the most to me, more than anything else I learned in college. I still feel at home at Mudd because people there accepted me for what I*

am (a tall, sort of geeky fellow who likes to write). I also have a couple of good buddies on the faculty, and in the dean of students' and president's offices, people I would still call up if I needed advice on an important matter. One friend of mine, a psychology professor, has been seen on Foster's runs with varying groups of students, and been part of a group going bowling or to Star Trek V, and in short, she is just a cool person. And I know I wouldn't hang out with my profs at a large school; there, just finding your professor in his/her office is a major accomplishment."

For women reading this, it is important to note that there are many more men than women at Mudd, and this causes special problems for each sex. At first women often become the center of attention at Mudd, whether they like it or not. After a few months, however, most men and women get used to the situation and male/female interaction becomes normal.

Just remember, Mudd is like a large, extended family. You probably will love a large number of your brothers and sisters and have a few that you would like to toss off a bridge in cement Reeboks. All in all, though, it's a nice feeling to be part of a family whose members actually have some similarities to one another.

EXTRACURRICULAR ACTIVITIES

There are more extracurriculars available than I can count, so here are some of the major categories.

In intercollegiate athletics, Harvey Mudd College forms teams with Scripps College and Claremont McKenna College. These CMS teams compete in Division III athletics (i.e., no athletic scholarships are offered, period). There are all your typical sports to get involved in, plus men's water polo (which wasn't typical to me, anyhow). Rugby also is played as a club sport (i.e., not officially sponsored by the college, but run by some students interested in playing). I ran track for two years and was just terrible but had a great time, due mostly to a great and insane coach. Relatively few Mudders compete in these sports because they take a lot of time and almost certainly keep you from doing other things, but those Mudders that do go out usually find that they can be fairly competitive in the conference.

For those who don't wish to spend that much time, there are also intramural sports. Teams are made up of people in the same dorms, and the competition can be quite fierce when you get on the field. But it doesn't take any more time than the games (practices are nearly unheard of), so it is a reasonable thing to get involved in. Intramural sports include coed inner tube water polo, coed volleyball, touch football (men and women play in different leagues), coed soccer, basketball, and coed softball. It's a fun way to spend a little time. Also there are less organized games of basketball, softball, Frisbee, golf, and beer ball going on all the time.

There are all sorts of things you can get involved in if you tend to be more artistic than athletic. There is drama, both on a somewhat professional level at Pomona College (you can take classes or get involved on an extracurricular basis) or on a more fun level with HMC's own Etc. Players. These folks put on a couple of plays a year on amazingly low budgets, using mostly Mudd casts, and everyone has fun. There are many art classes at Scripps you can get into if you like drawing or sculpting. There are dance classes at Scripps and Pomona that cover modern and jazz and a little ballet. There is also a social dance class at Pomona that you can take for PE credit. There are writing classes at Scripps, Pomona, and Pitzer. Mudd has *The Muddraker*, which is a fine little paper that is always begging for writers and editors and photographers of all sorts and doesn't take great amounts of time.

There are no fraternities or sororities at Mudd, but there are less official groupings of people. Each dorm has its own specific personality. West is probably the closest family of them all, with a reputation for playing loud heavy metal and classic rock most of the time. East is also fairly close-knit, but in a quiet way (any loudness is frowned upon, even dressing loudly). North has recently become tightly knit, where the music is often loud and more progressive (i.e., dance stuff, punk, a little rap, plus classic rock). South has no strong personality, but being mostly single rooms it tends to house seniors and juniors, plus freshmen (by design there are a nearly equal number of freshmen in each dorm). New is made up of separate suites, so each suite has a unique personality, getting wilder as you get higher in the three-story dorm, and there is almost always a women's suite (women residents only), which can be a nice sanctuary among the maleness of Mudd. New II has no specific personality; it all depends on who you live near, but the walls are thick enough that people who like quiet can be fairly happy among noise.

Each Mudd residence hall has a dorm president (usually two co-presidents) who are in charge of the building itself, and of rallying the residents into a spirited group to work at parties and to compete in athletics, etc. But each dorm also has at least one proctor, who is a senior working for the dean of students office. This person has a wide variety of responsibilities, including basic first aid and knowing the quickest routes to nearby hospitals in case of emergencies. They are also the keepers of such valuable supplies as toilet paper, wall hooks, and light bulbs. However, the real job of a proctor is to be someone there to listen to you if something, anything is bothering you.

> *"I was a proctor my senior year, and I can tell you that each and every proctor I've ever met desperately wants to help each and every Mudder. Desperately. Being a proctor was the greatest experience I have ever had, due to a few really tender moments when I was there at the right place at the right time for a couple of people; that is a wonderfully warm feeling."*

GRADUATES

In a typical year, about half of Mudd grads go straight to grad school and the other half find jobs in industry. Recently, a large number of my friends went through the Find the First Job Trauma, and they all found something they really seem excited about doing. Mudd has a growing reputation in industry, and it is becoming a fine calling card for finding work.

Also, Mudd is a nice step toward grad school. Chemists, physicists, and mathematicians all place very well, as I'm sure that biologists will. Engineers, however, seem to have just a bit more difficulty because their GPA's usually are not competitive with other easier schools. But the engineers I know were accepted into fine programs, just usually not their first choices.

Five years after graduation, most Mudders have settled into a first career of some sort. A lot of Ph.D. hounds are moving into professorships, never to leave academia. Some of the people who went straight to work are reevaluating that choice, to see if they might want to jump off the technical bandwagon. Some Mudders (less than 25%) start working in less technical careers.

> *"I'm an example of the last category. I am a writer, never really intending to use my math major. I will, though, for the next four years in the Air Force and even after that if I need the money. By making me look at humanities Mudd helped me choose my life, and its other classes are helping me afford it."*

The alumni network is fairly strong and run by a wonderful person named Andy Tresowich. The alumni office sets up a number of special events every year, such as a trip to Edwards AFB to watch the shuttle land when a Mudd alum, Dr. Pinky Nelson, was aboard. They also put out the alumni directory, which can help you stay in touch with a lot of people.

SUMMARY OVERVIEW

The main points to remember about the school are its commitment to the humanities, its six majors (biology, chemistry, computer science, engineering, mathematics, and physics), its small size, its conglomeration of vibrant people, its affiliation with the other Claremont Colleges, and most of all its Honor Code, allowing you to be treated as human beings should be treated.

More specifically, there are three main reasons why I think Harvey Mudd College is an outstanding school. First and foremost are the people—faculty, staff and students. It is, perhaps, the first time that most students really feel that they are among peers and people who challenge them intellectually and otherwise, and the informal exchange of ideas is priceless. Secondly, the courses are designed to make you recheck your course in life. By taking so many classes outside your major, you get a nice snapshot of the world. Look at it all openly, and then go with what interests you. Thirdly, the attitude of the administration is commendable. Thanks to the Honor Code, they treat students like people, trusting them to live and learn in an open environment. If you like the idea of living in a society where trust is common, Mudd may be the place for you.

I call all of these strengths, but I'm sure that some see them as weaknesses, and that's OK; no college is for everyone. Of course, I can also name some weaknesses of Mudd, and will toss them out here in the interest of fairness. First, the Honor Code goes against what, in the rest of reality, seems to be human nature. I find it very difficult to trust my fellow man, and at Mudd that all changed for me. Secondly, by and large the attitude of the school is academic, and therefore stressful. To attend, you need to be able to absorb and manage major demands on your time. This can be a very difficult and painful thing to do, so set your mind in deep determination to survive before you arrive.

There it is, then. All I ask is that if Mudd sounds interesting, don't be scared off by the strange name; some people still think a Lamborghini is a pasta dish. Don't worry that none of your friends have heard of it; they probably have never heard of Polk Audio, either. Who cares if your parents think you're talking about Harvard Med, send in for that application; we're talking a quality school here, campers!

> *"As you have probably noticed, I thoroughly enjoyed my time at Harvey Mudd College. There were of course, days when I wouldn't have admitted ever liking the place one bit, but I'm confident there isn't another place that would have made me feel as at home as Mudd did. I hope someday to return, and to see some of you there."*

Kyle G. Roesler, B.S.

Haverford College

THE PROGRAM

"No, no...not Harvard. *Haverford*."

Get used to saying it. Practice in front of a mirror. Consult a speech pathologist. This is the woeful mantra of Haverfordians the world over.

If a Haverford degree is something you're considering, understand first that Haverford, a teeny little college located on Philadelphia's Main Line, is about as well known as the second man on the moon. Although often discouraging when friends are basking in their acceptance letters from the University of We're So Famous, Haverford's relative anonymity translates into an academic environment that's intense yet not overbearing, intimate with small classes, and accessible to clubs and extracurricular programs. Like ingredients in a big, fluffy educational soufflé, each one is vital. Haverford is a unique combination of ideas and opportunities that combine to challenge each student and set the college apart from its competition.

Founded in 1833 by New York and Philadelphia Quakers, the college has strong ties with its roots. Its original purpose, as stated in the charter, was to provide "a guarded education [as well as] an enlarged and liberal system of instruction." Loosely translated into modern non-Quaker language, Haverford prides itself on the classic liberal arts education. Biochemistry majors are required to take courses in literature; psychology and economics majors a foreign language. Even English majors (easy now) must take at least one or two math and science courses. Classes at Haverford even *sound* like liberal arts classes: Romanticism and the Novel, Chaucer, Metaphysics/Epistemology, and—of course—Discrete Mathematics.

Whatever your major choice, a good deal of studying lies ahead. Academics at Haverford are taken very seriously and classes are peppered with extremely well-read, intelligent students, often forcing the lesser intelligentsia (that is, the rest of us) to play catch-up. Classes that move swiftly leave little time to fall comfortably behind in the work-load, whereas others, though they aren't many, are a bit more forgiving. The feeling at Haverford abounds that students attend the college primarily to learn. All else is second to books, a possible exception being indiscriminate gossiping.

If lying, cheating, and crib notes were your tools in high school, check 'em at the door. Haverford is a remarkable example of an honor code in action. The Code, its clever alias, is an all encompassing document that addresses both academic and social responsibilities of all Haverford students and faculty members. Incoming freshmen are required to sign a card pledging to abide by it before entering. Students are at once in love with and at odds with the Code. In recent years, the social Honor Code has come under fire for lack of specificity. Several groups on campus felt that the Code failed to clearly address serious social violations—racism, sexism, homophobia—and demanded that a clause be inserted to directly address these potential problems. Such issues are broached at a biannual plenary, a paradigm of democracy, in which all students are encouraged to shape the Code as they, as a whole, see fit: all ratifications to the Code are discussed by the entire student body (affectionately known as the Community to Haverfordians who, by the way, are affectionately known as Fords). The Code also means unproctored exams, timed take-home tests, and closed book exams that can be taken in locked privacy of your own room. Yes, your own room. Amazingly, a recent anonymous survey indicated that nearly all Haverfordians live by the Code. The honor council, a group of students, handle each violation on a case by case basis.

> *"My two best friends from high school both went to the University of Pennsylvania. They both, at one time or another during my four years at college, managed to visit Haverford. If you looked hard enough at our arms, you could still see the ink from four years of high school crib notes. I told them about the Honor Code. They listened politely. I told them about the unproctored exams. They nodded. I told them about closed-book exams in your own room. They smiled. I asked one of my friends what he thought about the code. He looked at me and said, 'Mark, if I went here, I'd be tops in my class.' I smiled back a false smile, one that would have been genuine in high school. Haverfordians don't consider the Code an obstacle. They consider it a privilege. It is one of the things that sets Haverford apart from—and well above—other small liberal arts colleges."*

Haverford's campus resembles an expensive country club. Two-hundred sixteen acres of grassy splendor spotted with a duck pond, athletic fields, large common greens, and a wood skating house invite jogging, lounging, sunbathing, general frolicking, studying or just strolling. The grounds are home to an extensive arboretum (several trees have small name plaques attached to their trunks, a nice touch if that's your thing) and the Arboretum Association is always on the lookout for volunteers. Founders Green, so named because the college's original building—Founders— (Creative genius? Coincidence? You make the call) overlooks it, is the campus's center and home to frequent Frisbee tosses, outdoor parties, and snowball fights. When friends from high school visit Haverford, you can be fairly confident that your campus is much nicer and prettier than theirs. Point this out to them frequently.

Although the liberal arts are essential to Haverford life, accessible is the only way to label the entire college experience. Philadelphia is a 15-minute, $3 train ride away. Parties, if not free, generally are $1 affairs. A campus movie theater has two nightly showings, complete with popcorn and soda, for the same price. Other film organizations show weekly movies gratis. Weekend concerts are school funded and have brought the likes of Suzanne Vega, Bobby McFerrin, and They Might Be Giants to Haverford's hallowed halls. The only catch here is that Haverford tends to attract bands on the verge of fame. That is, a year or two before they hit it big (translation: when they cost less. Who do you think we are, Harvard?) The thing to remember then is to attend all the concerts because who knows, you may be missing tomorrow's Frank Sinatra.

The affluent suburbs that surround Haverford—Bryn Mawr, Haverford, Havertown, all properly pronounced with the teeth clenched and nose held high—are within easy walking distance and are chock full of pizza parlors, bars, music stores, mini-marts and other mainstays of suburban life. School clubs and activities are open to all students and most have room for nearly all applicants. Sports teams, although competitive, also extend open invitations to all those interested. The library is open-stack, and with the interlibrary loan system, nearly anything ever published is readily available.

Perhaps most important though, are the men and women who actually teach the almost 1200 undergraduates. Haverford's professors, whether potential prize-winning scholars or congressional consultants, will more than likely offer students their home phone numbers on the first day of classes, invite students to their house at least once during the semester, show up to root for the home team, applaud the guy who imitated them in the talent show, and offer at least one embarrassing story about their years as a Haverford professor.

> *"The professor I admired most was one in whose class I had fared poorly. He was an extremely literate, intelligent, witty man who taught Shakespeare with an admirable sense of humor and mirthful animation. Having distinguished myself not at all in his class in one full year (my last one) at Haverford, I felt that not only had I let myself down but that I had let him down too. I explained my feelings in a letter which I left on his door the hour before I left Haverford for the last time, a gray day in May after graduation. The summer passed; I heard nothing from the professor and was not surprised, for we rarely spoke and never socialized. I was one of perhaps 200-300 students he had encountered over the course of the year.*
>
> *"His letter arrived at my home in September. He had not received my letter until the following fall and answered it swiftly. In it, he explained his frustration with me, knowing my interests were varied and that he felt his inability to reach me in class was somehow his fault. He remembered* my *performance,* my *reti-*

*cence, my extracurricular interests. A man with perhaps 300
Johnnies and Joanies in his head remembered this individual
Johnny, one who really deserved no remembering. He even ended
the letter with a personal reference and a joke. One of Haverford's finest? Absolutely. But an anomaly? Not really."*

Intelligence, compassion for the individual, both tempered with humility and
humor. Such is Haverford. And Buzz Aldrin, a much cooler guy than Neil Armstrong—was the second man on the moon. Just so you know.

GETTING IN

Once you're in, Haverford wants you to stay. You're their investment. They
know you'll go out in the world and make a difference, so they want Haverford's
name on your accomplishments. If you want to take time off between your sophomore and junior year, Haverford will make every effort to let you do this. If you
want to finish in six years instead of four, Haverford will work something out. But
there is a catch to all this. Getting in ain't easy.

A total of 2466 seniors recently applied and 952 were accepted. Of those,
301 freshmen matriculated with a male/female ratio of 51/49. Haverford, the little teeny school in Philadelphia, is getting popular. The percentage of students
accepting a place at Haverford is increasing and, as it does, so will the standards
the college sets. The college does not release mean SAT I scores, but rumor has it
they are near the 1300 range. A perfect score on SAT I, though, won't get you in.
Haverford looks for interested, interesting people. Admission is need-blind and if
you're a financially poor, B+ student with penchants for acting, athletics, biology, and sculpting, your chances of admission are probably much better than
those of a straight A prep school graduate who's as exciting as a test pattern.

Financial aid is awarded on a need-only basis. Approximately 45% of students
receive some form of financial aid and, through work-study programs in some
pretty popular on-campus hangouts, many programs are social as well as financially
responsible. And although nearly half the students receive aid, about 40% of
Haverfordians come from private schools.

If one were to put a label on the student body, a I am getting ready to do right
now, it would best be described as very intelligent (92% of Fords rank in the top
fifth of their high school class), quite liberal (the campus Young Republican club
collected about 20 members), preprofessional (Haverford has one of the highest
graduate school applicant to acceptance ratios in the country), and fairly white
(blacks and Hispanics make up only about 10% of the community). This last statistic is a number that is of concern to many on campus. (The percentage of all minority students, including Asian and Hispanic, has been between 18% and 20%, which
is pretty good.)

The lack of diversity tends to compound the Ivory Tower feel that seems so pervasive. Haverford's minority groups are, however, quite vocal. The feeling at Haverford is that education and dialogue are the keys to equality and harmony. Students of color generally make a concerted effort to bring their cultures and values to the forefront of life at Haverford, something that is met with both receptive praise and occasional anger. And although a random survey of white Fords almost certainly reveals that each one feels Haverford is the most accepting school on the face of the earth, many students of color might say otherwise.

ACADEMIC ENVIRONMENT

"A walking tour of the college campus is a mandatory portion of any prospective student's agenda. Haverford's tour, like many others, swings past and into the library. Haverford's library though, is different from other college libraries. It's steeple-like entrance and gently flippity-flappiting fountain make it seem more like a study or a living room than a library. Once inside, any tour guide will point out different sections of the building, name them (they have nicknames, you know), and describe their personalities. 'That's what we call the boat. Freshmen study and talk up there,' the guide would say, pointing to an elevated tier overlooking the main floor. 'This is the fountain area. Nobody really studies here, people come here to see and be seen. That's the main floor,' he would continue, 'people study in there, kind of, but they also talk a lot, too. It's a pretty social library.' The fact is that the library is one of the social centers of Haverford. I met my girlfriend there. I played Frisbee there with my roommate while he worked behind the desk. Groups of people plan to have themselves locked in after dark to play tag and camp out (camp in?). The first time my mother walked in, the sheer beauty of the place literally reduced her to tears. I ask you, besides a snack bar, what more could you want from one building."

That Haverfordians treat their library as both a studyground and playground is representative of their attitude toward academics as a whole. Studying is playing and playing is often lost to studying. People spend a huge amount of time poring over books, but the environment, although intense, is almost never cutthroat. Fords are a kind breed, intent on helping others as well as themselves and tend to spend as much time talking about the amount of work they have to accomplish as they do actually working. Politcans in the making? Maybe.

One thing should be made clear. The college does not trust incoming freshmen. Correction, the freshmen they trust, their English skills they don't. Freshman

English is a one-semester, mandatory course and even if your last name is Hemingway there's no way to place out of it. It serves students well, with core readings of various kinds, frequent writing assignments, and two class meetings a week. Freshman English primes each freshman for the heavy reading and writing load to follow during the next three years. Future science majors must stay the course with future English majors, future economics majors, and future music majors. Major pain in the behind at times, but worth it.

Taught in a class of about 15, Freshman English is an average size class. Varying interest, available faculty, and course level all play key roles in determining the size of any one class. The largest introductory seminar accommodates approximately 70–80 students, whereas the smallest seminars may have room for only four or five; a good ball park average is again, somewhere around 15.

Small class size means high visibility. It's difficult to hide behind Mike or Lisa when, with the exception of the person you're desperately trying to hide from, they're the only other people in your class. Preparedness is a must as most classes are taught in round-table type discussions; participation is the key to learning at Haverford. A few professors resort to lecturing (science and math professors have to rely more heavily on the blackboard than do religion and sociology professors), but all upper level courses have small seminar classes that give each student a chance to work closely with the faculty. Most classes allow you to use your mouth—as well as your brain —fairly frequently. A favorite Haverford pastime.

Professors are generous with their grades. Some obviously more than others. If you do the assigned work and show up to class you can expect some form of a B (that is, a 2.7, 3.0, 3.3) depending again, on the professor. Because everyone is graded on the same system, grades become relative. Certain departments are known for obscene grade inflation. It wouldn't be fair to mention the departments by name but I will tell you that the most notorious one rhymes with thiology and starts with a b instead of a th. (Now don't tell anyone else if you happen to figure it out, especially not any potential thiology majors.) Professors are easily accessible and quite receptive to informal meetings, lunches, or general discussion any time of the day. Because most live on or near the campus, they're within easy walking or phoning distance should any major problems arise.

Departments usually require an introductory survey course prior to smaller, more concentrated ones. The history department's Western Civilization goes from the Big Bang to the Simpsons in one year. Sociology majors read Durkheim, Marx, Freud, and Engels before they know what hit them and economics professors make each student take one semester of micro and macro economics respectively before letting them even make change for the Coke machine. This is not to say that there are no courses that focus on specifics; they are plentiful. Haverford merely strives to give each student a full broad knowledge base in a given discipline before piling on the particulars, a system that works extremely well.

All departments, with that said, are really quite strong. History is the most popular major, the science departments are outstanding and nearly all common liberal arts majors are available and taught by top-notch professors, never TAs. However, if a student should find a deficiency in any particular department (such as a hard business course or maybe a class like Curses and Hand Gestures: Your guide to mall parking) classes at nearby Swarthmore, Bryn Mawr, or the University of Pennsylvania, which are open to Haverford students, will fill the void.

SOCIAL LIFE

College means freedom. College means parties. College should mean so much fun that even Joseph Stalin would say, "Gee, this is fun." And often for men and women, college means near death from suffocation by laundry. But before college can be any of those things, college is the unknown, and the unknown begins with freshman year.

Remember how Haverford's small size would help you land a spot on the newspaper, and how fewer people meant better chances of actually seeing playing time on the soccer field? Here again, small works to the student's advantage. Because incoming classes are relatively small, dorm hall groups are too, maybe 10 or 12 each. Two or three upperclassmen volunteer to live with a hall group (a job that is coveted) and spend the year as big brothers/big sisters to their kids. Their main job throughout the year is to help acclimate freshmen to Haverford's customs and they are therefore bestowed with the zany, freewheeling epithet Customs People. Hall groups are known as Customs Groups, orientation is known as Customs Week, the group that organizes Customs Week is known as the Customs Committee, and even parties are known as...well, they're known as parties.

Customs Groups translate into about a dozen instant friends with the same apprehensions lurking in their heads that have been keeping you up with night sweats for the past five or six weeks. For the first week or so, Customs Groups usually move in a pack not unlike a chain gang to meals, social events, meetings, almost everything, giving everyone ample time to calm down, learn the ropes, and settle into Haverford like it was a new Laz-y Boy recliner (slippers and basset hound not included). Be warned. The Customs system, although a great introduction to college, gives rise to some quirky, kinky phrases. Customs People often are referred to by their kids (freshmen) as parents, which means that if you were to meet your Customs People's Customs People, they technically would be your grandparents. Intra-group dating (often referred to as incest) generally is frowned upon for the same reason that office romances generally are avoided in the working world: the proximity to one's love interest is a blessing while the relationship lasts, but, once and if things turn sour, a failed customs group romance can make *The War of the Roses* look like a pillow fight.

> *"It was February 19. The temperature outside was hovering around 20° and the ground was covered with snow. Standing with a group of friends in the warmth of Magill Library, I was*

seized from behind, blindfolded, and forced at 'gunpoint' to exit into the cold night. My abductors barked commands at me from behind. Turn left. Walk faster. Spin around. Don't gimme any lip. Turn right. We walked for perhaps five minutes over the crunchy, icy surface of the snow down an embankment. I heard a door creak open and my captors ordered me through it. A warmth enveloped me and the smell of frosting tickled my nose. As the kidnappers removed my blindfold, I was greeted with less than melodic strains of 'Happy Birthday' from my customs group, all huddled around a stone fireplace housed in a small wooden skating house on the outskirts of campus. The "kidnappers"—my Customs People—cut me a slice of the cake they had made for me. Didn't even charge me ransom."

Haverford's social scene is unique. It has over the years developed a close relationship with Bryn Mawr College, as in the Seven Sisters' Bryn Mawr College, one mile down the road. Nearly all social activities are bi-college, as are most facets of Haverford and Bryn Mawr life. Students from both colleges have the unusual flexibility to eat, live, and even major at either school. The newspaper is a joint venture as are most dramatic productions, parties, and academic forums. A large blue bus that students have affectionately named — need I even say it? — The Blue Bus shuttles between the two schools about once every half hour making both easily accessible to all interested in accessing.

Because Haverford only turned coed in 1980 and yet still enjoys close ties to Bryn Mawr, an all women's school, the female/male ratio (including Mawrtyrs) jumps to nearly three to one. These are daunting figures if you are female, but about as hard to take as a million dollar cashier's check if you are male. (This ratio is somewhat inaccurate though as not all Bryn Mawrtyrs attend every Haverford function.)

Weekend parties practically are guaranteed and usually include, if not dancing, at least some music and general debauchery. Weekday party goers are satiated by Thursday night Lloyd Parties, named for the dorm in which they're held. Usually starting around 11 or 11:30 P.M., Lloyd parties are a precursor to the weekend's events (often concerts, movies, *a cappella* concerts, or small gatherings of friends over drinks and Pictionary) and are ideal tension releasers. Well attended, these shindigs provide even the most hard core students with an excuse to relax a little bit between bouts with a heavy Haverford work load and wear their underwear on their head.

Although Haverford's small size is often a plus, social secrets are hard to keep in a school of just about 1200 people. Show up at a party with the same person twice and get ready to see your name on page six of the local tabloid. Gossip runs rampant through Haverford so don't be surprised if someone you've never met before asks you what it's like to be dating so-and-so. Group dating is much more prevalent than one-on-one affairs and those who do engage in the latter usually wind up, at least temporarily, as a couple.

If Haverford seems a bit stifling at times, several options exist. Philadelphia, with its cheesesteaks, Phillies, comedy clubs, cultural and historic sites is a very brief car or train ride away. For those with a car (parking is cheap and plentiful) Atlantic City and New York are just over an hour and two hours away respectively. Skiing in the Poconos is also just about two hours away by car.

EXTRACURRICULAR ACTIVITIES

Haverford has the best intercollegiate cricket team in the country. Tell this to everyone you meet. Haverford has the only intercollegiate cricket team in the country. Keep this to yourself.

Sports at Haverford are extremely popular. Physical education is required to graduate and the requirement can be fulfilled in several ways. Varsity sports teams are very competitive and because Haverford has no football team, soccer is the sport with the largest spectator draw. Other popular sports include lacrosse, track and field, tennis, field hockey, fencing, squash, wrestling, cross country, swimming, basketball and baseball among others. For those interested in athletic competition without daily four-hour practices, intramural sports are extremely popular and include many of the same sports enjoyed by interscholastic athletes.

Haverford, like Reebok, lets U B U. Perhaps the best advertisement for Haverford's extracurricular program is its willingness to provide funding to anyone interested in starting any club for which they feel there is a need. You want a skydiving club? Start it. You want a croquet club? Start it. You want a sit-waist-high-in-mayonnaise club? Seek immediate professional help. If you don't see it, start it. Haverford provides the funds, you provide the initiative....

> *"A college needs a humor magazine just like a boy needs a puppy, the flowers need the rain, and a large cold sore the size of a pan pizza needs immediate medical attention. As sophomores, my roommate and I decided to start a college humor magazine. Haverford was full of bright, funny people, we decided, with no outlet for biting, cutting-edge humorous material outside the classroom. This made me feel claustrophobic. It made my roommate feel the same way. We applied for college funding and received $250. With that money we produced a crude, controversial publication that we copied, folded, collated and stapled ourselves. Positive, early feedback from peers, such as, 'Death to the infidels,' 'This is more tasteless than cardboard,' and 'I hope you get cholera' inspired us to persevere. We did. As its popularity grew, so did our funding. By the time we were seniors,* Sensitive Mail *was receiving $2500 per semester and was printed by a professional publisher. We moved about 1000 copies per issue, gained the respect of our early critics, saw a considerable drop-off in numbers of threats detailing graphic, physical harm, and neither one of us caught cholera. Life was good."*

Along with the standards—drama, an orchestra, a newspaper (its ingenious name? *The News*), a choral group—Haverford has several unusual clubs and organizations worth mentioning. *A cappella* groups are extremely popular both with participants and spectators and regularly draw crowds of several hundred people to monthly, perhaps bimonthly concerts. Campus bands get their fair share of stage time at parties, and The Eighth Dimension office, which oversees student volunteer programs, is one of the most popular, if not one of the most rewarding activities in which many students engage.

With no fraternities or sororities, Haverford houses all students in college owned rooms and suites. Freshmen are assigned rooms in one of three dorms, two on the main campus and the third, a group of two-bedroom apartments complete with a bathroom and kitchen, is a ten-minute walk from the campus's center. Freshmen often have to put up with doubles and occasionally triples, but upperclassmen will find that if it's a single they want, or perhaps a single in a suite with five or six friends, chances are they'll get it. Several suites generally reserved for seniors (rooms are assigned through a lottery system) have fireplaces and all other suites come complete with ample living rooms. Several houses are available on the fringes of the campus and their rooms tend to be quite large. Their drawbacks, however, include quiet hours and a possible sense of isolation from the main campus.

GRADUATES

Haverford students as a rule, it seems, want to make some money. One quarter of the student body pursues some sort of higher education after graduation. Of that quarter, 4.6% attend law school, 12.7% attend graduate schools for arts and sciences, 7.3% attend medical school, and 0.8% attend business schools. Haverford, it's fun to note, is also regarded as one of the schools most likely to spew business excutives from its classrooms.

Approximately 57% of graduates prefer the school of hard knocks to the school of more books. With its grime, grit, and glamour, the working world attracts over half of Haverford's graduates, scattering them over several different professions. More than 19% choose a career in business, whereas 10% go on to a job in education or recreation. The sciences attract 6.6% of the graduates and 6.1% choose a communications-related field. Graduates' interests are diverse and this also shows up in their demographics. Most graduates tend to live somewhere in the northeastern United States, after having soaked up the Philly good life for four years. The other two places you're most likely to bump into a Haverford alum are the southeastern United States and abroad, as 24% seek haven in one of those two areas.

SUMMARY OVERVIEWS

Haverford is a tiny dynamo packed with intelligent, thoughtful people, plenty of activities, and located just across town from Philadelphia, it is a terrific place to spend four years. There's a certain intimacy about it that attracts a large number of applicants for limited spaces. The intimacy is both professional and personal. There's a real sense—brace yourself, this sounds a little corny—that Haverford, both as an institution and as individual educators, really takes a personal interest in each student. Not many colleges would dare or even want to make such a claim. From day one, Haverfordians become an extended family of sorts, a giant fraternity/sorority that welcomes everyone, supports them, encourages them. Alumni are more like lost cousins than names on a list from a career development office. On the highway, Haverfordians from the class of Way Back When honk at cars with Haverford windshield stickers ferrying sophomores back from spring break. Graduates keep tabs on their kids often through three years of separation. Professors shed the aura of academia out of class and join in on the fun.

You want an education too? Haverford will give you one of the best available in this nation. The mix of bright peers, exceptional faculty members, and terrific resources makes Haverford an ideal place to explore, uncover, broaden and experience. The accessibility and initmacy only enhance the experience. Individual needs are met and no one is given the short end of the academic stick, even accidentally.

Small, intimate, cozy Haverford is all those things. But just like a small, intimate, cozy cabin in the woods, cabin fever is always lurking in the wings. Life at the college can, for some, be stifling. Casual dating is a lost concept as is any semblance of a bar scene. Groups of friends moving together, eating together, working together, and fighting together make Haverford seem like a true family. People squabble and complain and stick their nose in your business, but in a family, these are problems that occur naturally. Ignore them and they'll go away. If they don't, just ignore them until they do. If they still don't, welcome to the family.

Intense academic pressure often leaves exasperated Haverfordians longing for a chance to catch their breath. This opportunity is often elusive. The reward at Haverford, however, lies four years down the road from day one when a diploma— a diploma earned the hard way—is yours to keep forever. A constant reminder of the good times and hard work Haverford provided; it is a document that few possess but many covet.

Mark Hudis, B.A.

Johns Hopkins University

THE PROGRAM

The "the" in the formal name "The Johns Hopkins University" is the only pretension in an otherwise serious school. It's a straightforward, unpretentious university, where students don't even bother correcting the people who inevitably leave out that first "s." That's all par for the course at Hopkins, where the shadow of the prestigious Johns Hopkins Medical School has sometimes obscured the triumphs of the undergraduate program. In recent years, that has been changing. As the school's rank has risen in national surveys, people have been comparing it more favorably to the large Ivys with which it competes, and often have found Hopkins superior.

Hopkins has its own ivy, along with red brick buildings, marble columns, and stately Georgian architecture. Located 15 minutes from downtown Baltimore, it looks more collegiate than many urban universities. More telling, though, is the distribution of buildings. The vast majority of buildings on campus are used by the great percentage of students who major in the sciences at the School of Arts and Sciences, or in computers or engineering at the School of Engineering; every science has its own building (or two): biology, chemistry, physics, even geology. Hopkins is among the top schools when it comes to these sciences. Top professors and state-of-the-art equipment make the science departments gold mines for those willing to dig.

The liberal arts departments, on the other hand, are precious gems: small, but extremely valuable. Though they sometimes have only a handful of professors (and students), the liberal arts departments are among the best in the country, such as English, art history, classics, anthropology, and history. Unlike the spread of the science buildings, all the liberal arts are located in one building—Gilman Hall, named after the first university president. But it is the largest, grandest and oldest building on campus, with serpentine hallways, historic character, and a bell tower, which is the tallest structure on campus.

Johns Hopkins has a seriousness and a high level of intensity. Students complain that they work hard, but there are also those students who complain that they don't work hard enough. The school has a reputation to maintain, as the place that graduated Woodrow Wilson and Gertrude Stein, among others. With a student-to-faculty ratio of roughly nine to one, Hopkins students enjoy an unusual amount of individual attention; most classes beyond the introductory level have 25 students or less. And students are serious about their classes. Knowledge is a sought-after commodity here.

Hopkins has always been a little different. It was founded in 1876 on a bequeath from Baltimore philanthropist Johns Hopkins as the first graduate school in the nation. Based on the European model, it was devoted to research and in-depth study. Three times the school turned down an offer to join the Ivy League, fearing the rush to make its athletic program competitive would make short shrift of its academics. One hundred years later, the school retains this commitment to concentrated study. At its worst, Hopkins resembles a graduate school that happens to have undergraduates studying there. But at its best, Hopkins offers students the opportunity to pursue subjects in great depth and the time needed to do so.

> *"My friends came from all over the world and, unlike me, many knew pretty much what they had come here for. Susan gave up three years of business studies at the University of Texas for Hopkins's English department. The Cyprian government was paying for Andreas's education in engineering. Jason, meanwhile, came in as premed, switched to engineering, and wound up in international relations. We all had different backgrounds; we all had different attitudes. And I may have learned more in our late-night bull sessions than in any class I attended."*

Perhaps because it is a small school—only 3200 undergraduates—there is a tendency to form deep, strong friendships. Maybe it's because you see the same faces in the library every week, or because you know the names of everyone in your course. Hopkins as an institution can sometimes be a little cold, but the people never are.

Hopkins has an unusual number of students who come to the school knowing what they want to major in, who they want to work with, and what they want to do afterwards. The majority go on to some kind of graduate school. Even given Hopkins's reputation, it's amazing to realize that over 25% of the students go on to medical school, while over 10% go on to law school. Can this lead to students narrowing their interests too much? Sometimes, but the school actively combats narrowness. A freshman's first semester is entirely pass/fail, encouraging many to experiment outside of their majors without endangering their GPA.

As a result, many people who enter Hopkins with a major in mind come out with a degree in something else entirely. Other students come to Hopkins directionless and find themselves. Changing majors is common here, partly because each department is so good. And there's a good mix of people, from preppies to bookworms to party animals, and even jocks (Hopkins has only one Division I sport—lacrosse—and that's very good).

"I transferred to Hopkins from a state school roughly three times the size, and was at first disappointed that Hopkins didn't offer me the same opportunities. I soon realized that no one gave you opportunities at Hopkins. As in real life, you had to make your own. But because Hopkins is a small school there's always room for one more person to get involved. And if there was something you wanted that Hopkins didn't provide, you found a way to get it, join it, or start it. There was the time, for example, my friends and I were interested in starting an improvisation group. We talked to a department, reserved a room in the student union, recruited some innocent bystanders, and that was it."

Two people can go to Hopkins and have two completely different experiences. The school is more than able to accommodate those who wish to lock themselves in an ivory tower for four years, moving quietly from classroom to library and back. Baltimore is an affordable place to live, and has a small-town feel for a metropolitan area of one million. And the nearest areas of Baltimore are laid-back and residential. Others may want more of a flavor of the outside world, and for those students, Hopkins is a school that lets you grow up quickly. Dormitory housing is guaranteed (in fact, required) for freshmen and sophomores. Most juniors and seniors live in nearby apartments and become Baltimoreans as well as Hopkins students. Hopkins is in the middle of a major city, and that means the city's resources are available: films, theater, and museums; professional internships; political and community involvement; and you're an hour away from Washington, D.C.

Some people go to college to prepare for a career, and some seek knowledge for its own sake. At Hopkins there is no dichotomy between someone studying computers with an eye on a job at IBM and someone studying French with an eye on being a Renaissance scholar. Both work just as hard, both learn just as much, and both are just as serious about their fields. And Hopkins is small enough to have room for them both.

GETTING IN/FINANCIAL AID

As the reputation of Johns Hopkins has expanded, its admissions criteria have grown as well. Not only is it more selective, but—especially since going coed in 1973—it is more diverse. Once reputed to be the holding tank for Harvard and Yale wannabes, Hopkins is now considered with the top Ivys when high school seniors are choosing a university.

The school looks for more than just high averages and high SAT I scores. It looks for both students with diverse interests who will bring fresh, well-rounded personalities to the campus, and for students who will excel at their chosen field, in both class work and research. In both cases, admissions officers look for applicants who can offer the school more than just high grades.

> *"Until it was suggested to me, I hadn't thought of applying to Hopkins. I wasn't premed, so I was surprised when Hopkins accepted me and lower-ranked schools hadn't. Once I'd been at the campus for a couple of weeks, I discovered the school didn't want to be dominated by future doctors. They were very interested in people like me, people with diverse interests who were willing to take classes in various departments. It was still a premed paradise, but the admissions people were sending the message: Forget the stereotypes. We want a well-rounded student body."*

Freshman class sizes have been steadily growing. Approximately 950 freshmen are admitted each year out of almost 8000 applicants. In recent years Hopkins has tried to buck stereotypes, partly by seeking out female students (although over 60% of the student body is male), and partly by encouraging non-science majors to apply and come.

The school achieves something of a mix, though the numbers favor science and engineering majors. Most students at Hopkins are from the East Coast, especially Maryland and New York. As an international research facility, the school also attracts a fair number of foreign students. Besides the freshman class, 20 or 30 sophomores and juniors transfer into Hopkins each year from other schools.

> *"As a transfer student, my orientation experience was atypical, but it highlighted the range of students at the school. People who transferred in with me were from Texas, Cyprus, Maryland, New York, Panama, and Colorado, among other places. We were English majors, psychology majors, engineering majors, biology majors, history majors, and anthropology majors. Some were focused on their interests, others were still searching. Some wound up joining fraternities, some wound up getting married right out of school. No one looked back."*

Hopkins recommends (but doesn't require) entering students to have taken the following in high school: four years of English, four years of mathematics, two years of foreign language, two years of science (preferably three years, with lab experience), and two or three years of history. But the school stresses the quality of the course work over the number or variety of courses you've taken. Characteristically, Hopkins only gives credit for AP exams with scores of four or five.

Because total expenses are approximately $25,000 a year, financial aid is doled out with generosity and understanding. As in most schools, aid is determined by need as presented on the Financial Aid Form (FAF). More than half the students receive financial aid, either in the form of loans, grants, or work-study. Also, some 20 top high school students receive merit-based Hodson Scholarships, which provide more than $10,000 annually as long as the recipient maintains a 3.0 (B+) grade point average. It should be noted that the amount of aid a student receives usually increases slightly after the first year, if family finances remain roughly the same as at entrance.

ACADEMIC ENVIRONMENT

Although academics are obviously the raison d'etre of any university, they seem even more significant at Johns Hopkins. The school emphasizes classes, sometimes at the cost of social and extracurricular activities. But the emphasis on classes is natural, because Hopkins's academic environment has such wonderful breadth and depth. Departments are split into areas: natural sciences (N), social and behavioral sciences (S), qualitative sciences (Q), humanistic studies (H), and engineering (E). There are some 43 majors to choose from, ranging from art history to biomedical engineering. On the breadth side, there are also area majors, which allow students to focus on an entire area, such as social and behavioral sciences, or humanistic studies. On the depth side, students can sometimes pick a major with a specific concentration: for example, the writing seminars major with a concentration in film studies.

Hopkins, academically oriented, has some oft-overlooked academic opportunities. Students frequently write off an entire department because it might not seem serious, when they are sometimes passing up wonderful classes. One underused option is studying abroad: Hopkins has schools in Italy and China, and will grant credit to programs elsewhere. Another overlooked opportunity is the honors thesis. Departments often will offer their top students the chance to produce a senior project or thesis for departmental honors. In some departments, exceptional honors students can, with their theses or with one extra year of study, obtain an advanced master's degree.

Although many students come into the school with their majors already mapped out, sampling different courses and talking with academic advisors can be the best bet for others. Talking with department chairmen can be one of the most helpful routes, because there's often such a range available within one department. For example, a biology major might consist of a wide sampling of courses in the biology department, or an early specialization in genetics, with an emphasis on research.

Although there is that flexibility, there are a certain amount of core courses every undergraduate at Hopkins must take. For the B.A. programs, students must earn at least 30 credits in areas outside the area of their major (as described above). So for an English major, which is in the (H) area, the 30 credits would have to be (N), (S), (Q), or (E) courses. For the B.S. program (engineering), students must earn at least 18 credits in (H) and (S).

Plus there are requirements for each major, which often include courses in outside departments: a writing seminars major, for example, includes two history courses, two philosophy courses, and one language, besides ten courses within the writing seminars department. Almost all classes are worth three credits.

> *"At first, I took courses whose description sounded interesting. Then I began to listen to upperclassmen who were recommending professors, not classes. It's true at most schools, but especially true at a small, intense school like Hopkins: the professor makes the class. Thereafter, I sought out the best professors and took just about anything they offered. I was rarely disappointed."*

An asset of the school's small size is the consequently small size of the classes. Introductory courses, which at some colleges run to 400–500 students, rarely have more than 100 students in them. And once past those introductory levels, classes usually have favored the seminar over the lecture approach, creating classes with 15, 12, or even fewer students. For example, a class on surrealism had one student in it.

Professors are very accessible, and often hold class at their homes or find themselves being consulted on personal matters. There are those professors, on the other hand, who still believe they teach from high atop a pedestal and must reach down to teach their students. But for the most part, professors don't patronize. The flip side is that they expect the best; there is no courtesy C at Hopkins, and if you fail, you fail. At Hopkins, professors and students interact on an intimate level with professors expecting the same effort they put into the equation. And it is that kind of attention that helps engender the intense quality of academic life at Hopkins.

SOCIAL LIFE

There's such an emphasis on academics at Johns Hopkins partly because—for some—there's nothing else. Every university has its share of bookworms but, perhaps because it's a small school, they seem more visible at Hopkins. Hopkins has a reputation as a funless school and, frankly, it's partly true. There are six dorms for freshmen and sophomores. About 200 spaces there are available to the 1600 juniors and seniors, who also live in university-owned or private apartments.

Not that there isn't a social life to be had at Hopkins. Many friendships form during freshman and sophomore years, when life in the dorms places an emphasis on social life. But afterwards, students are spread out to the three or four neighborhoods surrounding campus. There is hardly a student union to speak of at Hopkins (although recent renovations have improved space for student activities), and campus dances are poorly attended. Which means that if you want a social life, you must make your own.

A large part of the social scene at Hopkins is dominated by the 15 fraternities and sororities. This happens because the frats throw the most parties, and are natural magnets for socializing. Despite a few bad eggs, the frats at Hopkins are mostly harmless, eschewing the *Animal House* image for career- and community-oriented activities. The most popular frats seem to be Phi Psi and Sig Ep.

Beyond frat life, mainstream socializing at Hopkins focuses on the Milton S. Eisenhower Library (the MSE), the four-story main library on campus. It's helpful because students know, sooner or later, everyone will pass through the MSE. There is a smaller library annex in Gilman Hall, called the Hutzler Undergraduate Reading Room, but more commonly known as the Hut, which is also a popular gathering place. Because the Hut is open 24 hours, it is usually at its most crowded at 4 A.M. before a big exam. At that point, however, the din of casual conversation usually drives most serious studiers home.

The university provides some social activity. There are dances, which dwindle after the first few weeks. Several film societies on campus show movies on the weekends, which generally find large audiences. An office of special events brings performers to campus, ranging from the Mozart Trio to Suzanne Vega. And every spring the students and administration cooperate in Spring Fair. A weekend-long celebration of fun, food, and energy that succeeds in making students forget about midterms and papers. In fact, the festival is so popular that more than 10,000 Baltimore residents attend Spring Fair each year.

Hopkins has the advantage of being 15 minutes from downtown Baltimore, plus there is a free shuttle bus from campus to the outskirts of downtown. Unfortunately, most students fail to take advantage of the city, writing it off as culturally inferior to Washington, D.C. or their own hometowns. On the contrary, Baltimore boasts a network of half a dozen amateur theater companies, one of the best regional theaters in the nation, Centerstage, and a large Broadway-type theater. There are several movie theaters, including the popular Charles, which shows foreign and independent films and is a 20-minute walk from campus. There are several historic sites, two large art galleries (including one literally next door to campus), and the new Oriole Park at Camden Yards, home of the Baltimore Orioles, only a 10-minute bus ride from campus.

Students must seek these things out for themselves, however. Unlike some larger universities, the administration hasn't tried too hard to furnish students with social activities. In fact, in the mid-eighties, a joint task force of students, administrators, and faculty issued a "Human Climate Task Force Report," which characterized the human climate at Hopkins as cold. It also described the university as very Old Boy, with few women or minorities in positions of authority. The report spoke of sexual discrimination on the campus, and noted there were few minorities on campus. The university has since created a Women's Forum to help deal with possible sexual discrimination, and its recruitment of women and minorities has noticeably improved.

> *"Because I transferred from a big state school, Hopkins seemed*
> *dead by comparison. As I met more people, though, I discovered*
> *the social scene at Hopkins was really more to my liking than*
> *those big, impersonal parties. There was an uninviting*

atmosphere at Hopkins, so people who became friends stuck rather close together. I noticed a lot of couples who hooked up at Hopkins and kept to themselves. Hopkins was an insular place; many people found their cliques and stayed in them. I'll always remember talking till dawn with my friends, or sharing sesame noodles from Uncle Lee's. We also helped each other through rough times and the sometimes 'us against them' environment of Hopkins. Because of the intimacy of our group, I think the friends I made at Hopkins will last me a lifetime."

In short, Hopkins offers a small social scene with an urban edge to it. If you're looking for a big party school, you've come to the wrong place. If you want a quiet, intimate social sphere, Hopkins will serve you perfectly.

EXTRACURRICULAR ACTIVITIES

Maybe because there is a large contingent of phantom students who shuttle back and forth between classes and the library, it seems as though there is a core of Hopkins students who get everything done on campus. It is, to be fair, a large core, and it welcomes new members with open arms.

Hopkins has more than 70 clubs, including several ethnic groups, literary magazines, a debate society, a student newspaper, a student theater group, and a band, orchestra, and chorus. Cooperative programs with the Peabody Conservatory of Music, since 1977 a full division of the University, provide ample opportunities for music enthusiasts. There are several branches of student government, from dorm councils to the Student Activities Commission, which runs the clubs, to the Intra-Greek Society, which oversees fraternities and sororities.

There are those students, of course, who join a club because they think it will look good on their records, but for the most part students are really interested in the activities they pursue after school. And extracurriculars present one of the easiest ways to meet on campus.

"I had joined the Barnstormers, the student theater group, and became more involved in the group until I was finally directing a one-act play. We rehearsed every evening. It wasn't always fun. My girlfriend complained that she hardly saw me. But then, opening night, as I paced nervously through the back of the theater, I heard laughter (at all the right spots). Afterwards, after the applause, someone asked me if it was worth it. 'I guess so,' I replied. 'But I know we could've done the good-bye scene better...'"

The activities also provide students with a chance to broaden their horizons, and do things they probably won't get to do after they graduate. One biology major said he edited the school newspaper because he knew he'd never work on a newspaper again once he became a doctor. As in many other aspects of Hopkins, activities provide room to grow.

Besides clubs, there are quite a few sports teams at Hopkins. Intramural athletics, especially basketball, are very popular. Among the varsity programs, the football, basketball, and baseball teams generate some excitement on campus. The basketball team has twice appeared in the NCAA Division III playoffs recently, and the football team has also enjoyed some winning seasons. The school has one Division I team, however: the lacrosse team. If you haven't heard of Hopkins lacrosse before you enroll, you will. The lacrosse teams at Hopkins have consistently won national championships throughout the twentieth century. Lacrosse is to Hopkins what basketball is to the Big Ten schools.

GRADUATES

Slightly more than 25% of Hopkins undergraduates go on to medical school. More than 10% go on to law school. Most others go on to graduate school of some sort, whether it's to get a Ph.D. or a master's. To say the least, Hopkins emphasizes a preprofessional outlook.

To this end, the school provides a premed and a prelaw adviser, to help prepare students for the next step. Most students take prep courses for the LSAT or the MCAT. When the time for these entrance exams roll around, a community spirit overcomes the school, and it becomes a battle of the students versus the standardized tests. Because of the large number of students continuing their education after college (more than 65%) there is a certain amount of pressure to go to some kind of graduate school. Although many students choose the job path after college, some take the GRE exams anyway, just in case.

Graduates from Hopkins tend to go on to other top schools. Hopkins also has several graduate schools that accept former undergrads, such as the School of Public Health, the School of Advanced International Studies (in Washington, D.C.), and, of course, the Medical School.

"When you get out, the Johns Hopkins name is a plus. Even if it's the Medical School they're thinking of, most people have heard of Hopkins. When I began interviewing for jobs, interviewers often said, 'Johns Hopkins? That's a good school.' And when I came into contact with other graduates, having Hopkins in common was helpful. Knowing we all went through the same intense pressure and social atmosphere, Hopkins alumni tend to be friend-

lier and more sympathetic to fellow alumni. It's not as though we all belonged to the same exclusive club; rather, it's like we all served in the same military outfit."

Unlike Boston, which is chock full of college graduates who are still hanging around the same neighborhoods, Baltimore is not filled with Hopkins alumni. There are certainly Hopkins alumni in Baltimore (in publishing, politics, business, and other influential fields), because Hopkins is very much an institution in Baltimore. But graduates tend to go off to the ends of the earth, wherever their graduate schools or jobs take them. Some tend to polarize around Washington, D.C. or New York, but there's little provincialism in the Hopkins world.

The Alumni Association is strong for a university that has seemingly little school spirit. There are alumni centers in Baltimore, Washington, and New York, and graduates can access these groups to network, for contacts or jobs. It can be an advantage to be applying for a job from someone who knows firsthand how rigorous your college education really was.

SUMMARY OVERVIEW

Although it always has had a solid reputation, it was recently that Johns Hopkins ascended to the uppermost echelon of university polls. In a recent year, *U.S. News and World Report* ranked Hopkins eleventh among the nation's universities. This was no accident. Hopkins's main assets include top-rated academics, renowned professors, and the resources of a city.

It is probably its academic strength that draws students to the school. Whether it's the biology department or the history department, Hopkins has many fields in which it excels. There are also many laboratories and state-of-the-art equipment to work with. And Hopkins offers a good range of courses for a school of 3000–4000. Courses run the gamut from science, to art, to women's studies, and to comparative religion.

Of course, the heart of the classes are the professors themselves. Hopkins attracts top professors, and demands that their faculty publish papers to stay on the tenure track. So students have the opportunity to learn from the best in their field, whether it be Michael Fried, who pioneered the "new wave" of art criticism, or Paul Dagdigian, an award-winning chemical physicist, or John Barth, one of the founders of "postmodern" fiction. Outside the classroom, students can also work with top researchers in every field, from molecular biology to stellar evolution.

As an added bonus, Hopkins has a major city from which to draw resources. Students can take courses at other colleges in Baltimore, obtain professional internships at a magazine or in city politics, or do research at the public library. Baltimore also has some terrific restaurants, offering everything from a pretentious book-store-cafe to cheap Thai cuisine. There's even a waterfront gathering of pubs and jazz clubs, called Fells Point, which has benefited from Baltimore's gentrification in the 1980s. And it's an hour away from Washington, D.C., as everyone will tell you.

There are downsides to Hopkins that must be considered if you're trying to decide which college will fit your personality and vice versa. As mentioned above, Hopkins has a sparse social scene, a rather chilly human climate, and can be competitive.

Students tend to make do with the social life as it is, throwing occasional parties, going to concerts or clubs in the city, or hanging out at the local bars (both of them). It can be the right atmosphere for some, particularly if you like quieter, smaller get-togethers. There are Saturday nights, though, when there's nothing to do but go to the library.

The atmosphere at Hopkins can be like the atmosphere of Mars—thin, and other-worldly. There is little organized resistance to this aspect of campus life, and it is an unfortunate by-product of a university built on study and research. Part of this is due to the pressure students feel, a competitive streak in the school that the faculty doesn't exactly try to temper.

There are times when a classmate will give you a dirty look if you come up with the right answer for the professor, and there's the true story of the student's mother who paid $80 for a vial of potassium so her son could come out of his experiment with the correct products. It's a competitive school, with pressure to succeed and a strong reverence for high grades. Hopkins tends to get a little carried away with success, but only because it's so good.

Despite the drawbacks, Hopkins is a university worth going to if you're interested in working hard and learning a lot, and not afraid of pressure. It's a school that demands a lot from its students, whether it's finding a place to live in after your sophomore year, or leaving it up to the student to find a suitable internship. If you're looking to broaden your perspective, or to narrow your focus, Hopkins is big enough—and small enough—for both.

Loren Fox, B.A.

Massachusetts Institute of Technology

THE PROGRAM

"MIT isn't the only place where people complain about how much work they have to do and how hard they have to work to get it done. But the difference is the scale—at other schools, staying up late to finish an assignment might mean finishing at two or three in the morning. They just don't understand finishing a problem set, turning it in, and picking up breakfast on the way back. And not just once a term, but once a week. And I can't think of another school where so many people work during weekends. It's not really an option; rather, it's a necessity."

That is the biggest complaint students here have about life at MIT. There's never, never enough time to accomplish what needs to be done. Pace and pressure have almost become buzzwords in the administration. Part of it is a sort of one-upmanship, trying to see who suffers the most. It's kind of hidden school spirit: the more someone complains about MIT, generally the more proud he is to be going there. IHTFP (I hate this [expletive deleted] place) is the school's unofficial slogan. Maybe students at some other school somewhere actually work harder, but if so, no one here will admit it. It sets MIT apart from the rest of the world, epitomized by our neighbor up the river in Cambridge (Harvard), which is seen as a playground in comparison.

If you talk to most MIT students about their experiences here, chances are you won't get past these complaints. But in a lot of ways, the atmosphere resembles that of the high-tech firms started by many of our alumni. Sure, an incredible amount is expected from the students. But the fringe benefits are substantial, and the bureaucracy goes out of its way to make sure that the 4000 overachievers who attend here are as comfortable as can be. Ask most students what the best things about life here are, and the first things that will come to mind have nothing to do with formal classroom education.

Two invaluable programs at MIT that have nothing to do with classrooms—but worlds to do with learning—are the Undergraduate Research Opportunities Program (UROP) and the Independent Activities Period (IAP). UROP offers students the opportunity to participate in the research projects of faculty, providing hands-on opportunities to experience what can only be talked about in lectures. IAP, a four-week mini-term during the month of January, gives students a chance to explore more freely than can be done within the constraints of the academic program.

These less formal activities are a welcome break from the rigors of the academic calendar, when most of the student body is engrossed in heavy-duty science and engineering. There are eight kinds of engineering, from civil to ocean to nuclear. About 60% of a recent class were engineers, with EECS (electrical engineering and computer science) and mechanical engineering the largest groups. Twenty-five percent were science majors. Twenty percent were architecture, management, and humanities majors, and the remainder were undecided.

The social sciences—economics, political science, history—as well as the management school are set apart from the engineering and science schools, both physically and philosophically. Many faculty in engineering and science believe that MIT is the preeminent school in their areas and that social sciences and humanities serve to round out an otherwise technical education. On the other hand, many faculty in the social sciences and humanities feel that they are on a crusade to see that their disciplines get equal respect at MIT. Indeed, some of these departments have already made a name of their own.

Surprisingly, some of MIT's best departments are not engineering disciplines: the biology faculty alone boasts four of MIT's nine Nobel Prize winners. Political science has a very strong faculty. The MIT School of Management (formerly the Sloan School) is one of the most highly regarded business schools in the world, especially in the areas of finance and information management. And almost every other economics professor seems to be a Nobel Prize winner. In addition to Paul Samuelson, the first American to win a Nobel in economics, MIT has (in Robert Solow and Franco Modigliani) the winners of two recent prizes in that field.

In one sense, MIT has become the world's largest educational experiment. Project Athena, which started out as an exploration of the frontiers of using computers in education, populated the campus with hundreds of high-powered workstations linked by fiberoptic cable (more than 1000 at last count). Each of these single-user workstations is approximately as powerful as a central computer that might be time-shared on other campuses.

All undergraduates get accounts—not just the computer science majors. This means that relatively few students here actually own computers because Athena workstations are always available. Although some students use the computers as computers, writing programs for CS classes, most usage is for other applications. Many students end up relying heavily on Athena machines as word processors for writing papers or for sending electronic mail to classmates to find out the answers to a problem set. By the end of the term, you can walk into the main Student Center cluster at any time of day or night and find a room full of people who have been there for a very, very long time.

There are many tales of the apocryphal student who spends the last two weeks of the term living in the Student Center library, with toiletries and an alarm clock perched at the side of the computer terminal. Although no one here fits this description exactly, there is no doubt that there are many who get caught up in the pace and pressure.

> *"One person I knew spent nearly all of his time in class, in his room, or at the library. He graduated a year early, but no one in his living group knew who he was, and he did little if anything outside of school. Another woman used to spend entire weekends working in her room because she felt that she was behind and thought that sitting in her room staring at books would make it better. What happened in reality was that after working in 24/48-hour bursts, she ended up getting sick and falling farther behind.*
>
> *"It's important to pace yourself. It is possible to do things that are fun and still do well, if you do it right."*

Rather than creating a competition among students, as pressure has been known to do at medical schools, MIT builds a sort of camaraderie, a sense that everyone is stuck in the pressure together. Very few people can get through here without relying on other people for help, whether it's to get the notes from the class they slept through or the answers to a problem set they don't have time for. It's not considered rude to ask a classmate to borrow a completed assignment; rather, it's considered rude to refuse. Some professors just request that you put the names of the students you worked with on the top of a paper.

> *"In one of my mathematics theory classes, the professor gave a take-home final exam. He warned us that the test would be graded on a curve, so if we gave other students our solutions, we would only hurt ourselves. As soon as we got out of the room, a large group of us got together and spent the night (with a very large coffee pot) and finished that exam, trading answers with each other. I got an A in that class, as did most of the people I worked with, and never could have finished the assignment by myself."*

There is definitely a certain sense of camaraderie shared among students here, like members of an oppressed class that has no choice but to stick together to face a common foe—the Institute. Not everyone is a computer scientist, or even an engineer, but many attitudes are shared. You have to have some measure of intellectual curiosity to attend MIT. You don't have to love differential equations and electromagnetism, but if you find yourself bored by a strobe photograph of a bullet passing through an apple, you are at the wrong place.

Although not everyone is a mathematician, you wouldn't know it from looking at a map of the Institute. One of MIT's quirks (whether it's endearing or not depends on how long you've been dealing with it) is that everything is numbered. All buildings and classes have names, but they're almost never used. Freshmen who are interested in majoring in Course VI (electrical engineering and computer science) might start out by taking 6.001 (Structure and Interpretation of Computer Programs) in Building 34 in room 34-101. Walking down the "Infinite Corridor" (one of the world's longest continuous walkways), one would walk from Lobby 7 to Buildings 3, 10, 4, 8, 16, 56, and finally 66. You'll appreciate the fact that you can get from almost any Institute building to any other building without ever going outside (unless you want to) during one of the typically rainy/snowy/cold Boston winters.

The buildings here are not nearly as sterile as this numbering system might suggest. There is a great range of architectural styles in evidence, and each dormitory has its own physical characteristics as well as social ones. This doesn't mean that all the buildings are attractive, but everyone has favorites.

In a lot of ways, this is an appropriate metaphor for the MIT experience. If you look at a map of the Institute, you might think that it must be a terribly uninteresting and regular place to have a numbering scheme. But if you walk down Amherst Alley, you can't help but appreciate the variety of architectural styles you won't get at a school with row upon row of ivy-covered brick. To most people, MIT is a place for narrow-minded techno-nerds who are incapable of functioning in normal society. But if you spend some time here, you will find a few thousand people who can party with anyone but who are willing to work hard, who are just plain fascinated by the world around them. MIT may not be as well known as Harvard, Yale, or Princeton, and most of its students could probably do quite well at those other schools with a lot less work, but then we wouldn't want it any other way.

GETTING IN/FINANCIAL AID

It's been said about many prestigious universities that the toughest part is getting accepted. At MIT, that's not nearly as true, mostly because it draws from a narrower range of high school seniors. The Institute accepts 30% of the students who apply, with a target of 1100 students for the incoming class.

Your chances of getting in are much better if you are female, as the acceptance rate for women is nearly 1½ times as high as it is for male applicants. Admissions officials believe the female applicant pool is more self-selected, because women get less encouragement to pursue fields in science and engineering. Programs like Campus Preview, when MIT invites all admitted women to campus for a weekend of wining and dining have also improved the yield of accepted women. The result is a male/female ratio that may not be ideal but is improving and is probably better than most people would expect—39% of a recent class were women.

The picture is not quite as rosy for other minority groups, although some 44% of each class is composed of minorities. Most of that 44% are Asians and Hispanics. Only 175 "underrepresented minorities"— the admissions office's generic classification for blacks, Mexican-Americans, Puerto Ricans, and Native Americans—were accepted last year. The problem doesn't seem to be unique to MIT because minorities don't seem to be applying to engineering institutions.

Drawing a composite image of the students who do decide to attend is a difficult problem at any world-class university that draws students from all over the world. Perhaps because of its reputation, or simply because of the requirements imposed on students, MIT attracts a special type of person. Not everyone here watches *Star Trek* or reads science fiction, or even loves computers—there are people here who can't stand them—but you do have to have a curiosity for how things work. Whether it's figuring out how people can remember Ty Cobb's batting average while forgetting their anniversary or trying to understand why people believed that the United States could balance its budget by cutting taxes or increasing defense spending, students here have to be able to ask "Why?" This includes, of course, asking how a working telephone booth could be placed on top of the great dome or a car could be disassembled and left in Lobby 10 or an exploding football balloon could be planted at the Harvard-Yale game.

> *"Having discussed the admissions process with the administration, it is clear that they don't have an image of the "typical MIT student" in mind when going over applications. Right now, the admissions office has been attempting to change the standards by which they measure prospective students, and it is not entirely clear what effects this will have on the school. Can we say for sure that by admitting fewer narrowly focused white male engineers and more women, minorities, and students with an interest in the humanities, we will not lose our status as the world's premier Institute of Technology? So far, this has not happened—no one here wants to see this school turn into just another elitist liberal arts college."*

Although many schools may claim to admit exclusively on the basis of academic merit, this is one of the few prestigious schools that lives up to that promise. People have to be willing to put in long hours of hard work—no one gets into this school because he or she is a famous name (in fact, one well-known individual, now a congressman, couldn't hack it here after one semester, when they told him he'd have to take physics and calculus). The elite just doesn't exist here.

Admissions decisions are need-blind, which means MIT guarantees to offer financial aid to those unable to afford the $22,230 tuition. Financial aid awards are totally based upon need and can be substantial—the 62% of a recent class who were deemed needy received an average of $17,050 in grants, loans, and workstudy (the other 38% received an average of $2600 from non-MIT sources).

ACADEMIC ENVIRONMENT

Learning at MIT is much more than just taking classes, and one of the most important alternatives—and one of the best things about MIT—is the Undergraduate Research Opportunities Program. Students are invited to get involved in faculty members' research projects, for either academic credit or pay. Over three fourths of the students here get a UROP at some point, and many do so as freshmen. UROPs can lead to published papers, theses, or directly to jobs in industry and academia. UROPs are a good way to get to know members of the faculty, many of them are very accessible, and they have as much respect for the ability of MIT students as the students have for them.

The Independent Activities Period (IAP), together with freshman pass/fail and UROP, is without a doubt one of the most popular things about MIT. Coming right after exams in December, it is a time for students to relax from the constant pressures of the term, a time to experience all the things there's just no time for while studying. Some students spend IAP at home, catching up with friends and family. Some stay on campus to sleep, party, and explore Boston. And others stay here to partake of wide range of seminars offered on everything from wine tasting to automobile repair. Everything is relaxed and low-key and is without a doubt MIT at its best.

Of course, students do have to attend classes as well. Most freshmen will take most of the standard Institute requirement courses their first year. All students here have to pass two semesters of calculus, two semesters of physics, one semester of chemistry, one semester of biology, eight HASS (humanities, arts, and social sciences) classes, two science distribution subjects, one laboratory class, a writing requirement, and a physical education requirement.

For those students not interested in the standard freshman program, there are several moderately popular alternatives. The Experimental Studies Group is a small group of students who do not want to be encumbered by a structured learning environment. Students work in small groups with upperclassmen who serve as tutors. The tutors teach the equivalent of the core classes and verify that the student's understanding is sufficient. Concourse is a more humanities-oriented approach and more structured than ESG, as is the Integrated Studies Program. ISP attempts to examine the social implications of science and technology while teaching the freshman core.

To ease the stress of adjusting to the high-pressure academic environment, MIT has a freshman pass/no credit plan. Back up and read the last sentence again. That's right, there are *no grades* for the freshman year. What that means is that although there are lots of adjustments to be made, you don't have to worry (too much, anyway) about getting straight As while you're adjusting. Freshman year is often the best year here, as it's a great time to get to know Boston or to meet lots of people and go to lots of parties. Of course, you can use it as an opportunity to take a lot of classes and get ahead, although your adviser will try to discourage that.

"One of the toughest things that takes getting used to about the freshman year is learning to say 'no.' There's so much to do and so little time to do it, and any time you finally convince yourself to get a good night's sleep or to catch up on the four or five problem sets you haven't done, some 'friend' will come by and invite you out to Chinatown for Ravs (Peking Ravioli) and drinks. By October, you'll be sick of hearing 'Don't worry, you're on a pass/no credit.' But by the next year, you'll wish you had gone along with them more often because you just don't have the time anymore."

A benefit of pass/no credit is that many freshmen can use the time to explore different majors without worrying that they will ruin their GPA by taking a class they may not have the background for. When you get accepted by MIT, you get accepted by MIT—not by the School of Architecture and Planning or the College of Health Sciences, Technology, and Management. This means that students can major in whatever they want and change their major at any time. In fact, one of the more harmless pranks you can play on people (more on pranks later) is to turn in a change of major form for them, which doesn't even require an adviser's signature.

Although you can graduate from MIT taking only four classes a term even without coming in with any advanced placement credit, many students will bulk up the first term to take advantage of pass/no credit.

For freshmen, most of the classes are held in big lecture halls with anywhere up to 500 students in a lecture. Typically these classes will meet in large lecture halls two or three times a week, and twice a week the class will break up into small recitations of about 30 students. All lectures are taught by members of the faculty, but recitations may be led by graduate students. Typically lectures are for the theory and background, and recitations are when you learn the material due on the problem sets. There is no required attendance in lecture, but a few recitation instructors base grades on attendance.

"I hated taking classes in 34-101 because the chairs were too comfortable. When I started falling asleep in lecture, my roommate (sitting next to me) used to wake me up. After a while, he just let me sleep. Soon after, I stopped going."

Humanities classes and upper-level science and engineering classes are the exception to this rule. The lectures are small enough that discussions can be held without recitations.

Of course, there is lots of "gee-whiz" stuff going on here, and it's not kept only for graduate students. The most popular classes at MIT are some of the undergraduate lab classes: Issues in Architecture, Introduction to [Mechanical] Design, Strobe Lab, Robotics Lab, and (surprisingly) many of the arts courses, which are perennially oversubscribed.

Introduction to Design is the design class whose final project competition is often featured on Nova. The contest is a bloody competition. Given the same parts, the same goal, whoever comes up with the most effective design and implementation wins. The class covers everything from brainstorming to technology licensing, taking you from visualization of a design to drawing it to construction.

The faculty is a Who's Who of scientific discovery. Not only do many professors teach courses based on the textbooks that they themselves wrote, but many are famous enough to be written about in other author's books as well. These faculty members, recognized as the authorities in their fields, do not just teach material that was discovered ten years ago and is now out of date — classes are kept state-of-the-art through constant change that incorporates the latest research results. Interaction with professors, which begins in the classroom and extends to UROP and beyond, is an added bonus.

There are also undergraduate classes run by many of the research labs on campus, such as the Nuclear Reactor Lab, the High Voltage Lab, the Whitehead Institute for Biomedical Research, Lincoln Labs (defense-related research), the National Magnet Lab, and the Artificial Intelligence Lab, just to name a few.

And there is tremendously little bureaucracy to fight through to register for these classes. You can take any class you want (registering for graduate-level classes as an undergraduate, if there's one that really interests you), as long as your academic adviser okays it (never a problem). Students are never dropped from classes due to over-enrollment, except for some of the arts courses and Strobe Lab, which have limits on their facilities. Registration takes only an hour or two, only one signature, and you get the classes you want to get about 99.5% of the time. Because you know months in advance what your schedule will be, it is very easy to plan things. There's no waiting in line for hours to sign up for first-come-first-served class spaces.

SOCIAL LIFE

Orientation begins just like at most other schools with a welcome speech by President Charles Vest. Last year President Vest surprised the class by falling backward off the stage into the arms of upperclass students and deans. Freshmen then do their own "trust falls" when they join upperclassmen on the athletic fields for problem-solving and trust-building games.

The second day on campus, freshmen take tests in mathematics and writing, and meet with upperclass students for advice on housing selection. Late in the afternoon they gather in Killian Court for a class picture, ice cream, and speeches. Members of fraternities, sororities, and independent living groups (FSILGs) line up on the sides of the court, behind the freshmen, and with the words, "Let the Rush begin," freshmen are off for three days of food feasts and parties.

"In some ways, Residence/Orientation Week gives freshmen a
false image of life at MIT, but in other ways it is amazing fore-

shadowing. Students have lots of freedom and an abundance of options and an incredibly short time to make their choices.

"The pressure is as great as it gets here—if you can survive R/O, you can survive anything. Freshmen don't arrive at MIT assigned a room, roommate, or even a dormitory. They show up with a suitcase (just one because they're probably going to sleep in a different place every night) and a temporary room and have about a week to choose which of the 34 independent living groups and ten dormitories they are going to live in for the next four years.

"Those students who want to join FSLIGs do so as freshmen, during this first week. About 35% of students at MIT live in the FSLIGs. Two are female, five are coed, and the rest are all male. Most fraternity houses are gorgeous townhouses donated by departed alumni—there are no Animal Houses. Right now, the fraternities are faced with declining numbers of male students, and until some more go coed, it will be a buyer's market where the men are concerned. Each FSLIG tries to outdo others in enticing freshmen to visit their houses: the "Daily Confusion" (the schedule of each day's rush offerings) lists literally hundreds of lunches, dinners, picnics, boat rides, trips to Wellesley, parties, or whatever for freshmen. If freshmen end up paying for a single meal during Rush or spending a single night in their temporarily assigned room, then they're doing something wrong."

Students are guaranteed four years of on-campus housing; although, with apartments becoming affordable again, upperclassmen are moving off campus. There are no freshman dorms; you won't be assigned a room or people to live with. Freshmen can live in singles, doubles, triples, or quads, depending on which dorm they choose. In the dorms with suite setups, three to seven people will share a bathroom and a kitchen. Some dorms are conventional college long hallways with dining halls.

There are ten dormitories; one is all female, and the rest are coed. There are no all-male dorms anymore, but some all-male sections of dorms are available. The coed regulations vary from dorm to dorm—some are coed by entry, by suite, or by room. In some dorms, males and females share bathrooms. Visitation regulations are nonexistent—it was only a few years ago that they started locking up dorms, and residents in most dormitories do not have to sign guests in. As long as roommates don't complain too vigorously, anything goes as far as overnight guests.

"For many of the freshmen in Burton House, one of the toughest parts of adjusting to MIT had nothing to do with academics—it was learning to cook. There's no dining hall in the dormitory (although residents are free to eat at other dormitories or the main Student Center dining hall) and no required meal plan. Many learn one or two specialties and end up eating those two or three times a week, with canned soup and macaroni and cheese

*inserted in between for variety. When one of the girls on another
floor finally mastered the exotic art of spaghetti after many
failed attempts, her entire floor celebrated."*

There is a variety of architectures and cultures in the dormitories. When you
decide to move into a dorm, you should look at the people who live there and not
the architecture. Some of the more interesting dorms are the most run-down as
they allow you to have a lot of freedom and creativity in designing your surroundings. Any given year, about 95% or more of the freshmen get into one of their top
three dormitory choices. If you don't like where you wind up, you may be able to
switch dorms between terms and during the summer.

Choosing which dormitory to live in is not enough; in many dormitories, each
floor is a separate living group. Social life in the dormitories is organized by living
groups, which are generally about 50 people who live together, socialize together,
and participate in intramural sports together. Even within a single dormitory, all the
different living groups can have very different characteristics.

Visitors from other universities usually are surprised to find out how much there
is to do during the weekend at MIT. Believe it or not, MIT—ranked twenty-fifth in
a recent poll of party schools—is one of the major social centers for Boston college students. Campus parties' popularity can be attributed to two factors: the fact
that there are fewer regulations covering parties held at MIT's living groups than
there are at nearly any other university in the metropolitan area and the attraction
that a 65% male student body has for the many all-female colleges in the area.
There is a bus that runs between MIT and Wellesley every hour. Fraternities and
MIT sororities often party together, with fraternities postering the dorms and corri-
dors to get MIT women to come to their parties. Dorm parties attract men and
women in equal numbers.

EXTRACURRICULAR ACTIVITIES

There's much more to MIT than all-nighters; MIT has more recognized student
activities (206) than any other college. Because there are so many different activities, ranging from the Assassins' Guild to the Arms Control Study Group, and
from the Students for the Exploration and Development of Space to the Society
for Creative Anachronism, membership in these groups tends to be small. This
gives one lots of opportunity to get very involved in a short period of time—
there are no trials you have to pass to get on the newspaper staff, you just have to
be willing to write once in a while. This doesn't mean that the groups aren't
good—the *Tech*, the student-run newspaper, is independent of any administration control and currently owns the most advanced composition and typesetting equipment of any college newspaper. There isn't much activism on campus,

which in a way is good because the administration reacts to protests by arresting the demonstrators.

> *"A friend of mine and his adviser had an ongoing battle about whether he was spending too much time on activities like the newspaper and the theater group. This became an important question for him after his sophomore year, when he received a letter from his department expressing concern about his grades and his decision to study electrical engineering.*
>
> *"After being a bit scared by that letter, he took classes a little more seriously, but the time spent on other things wasn't the problem. He actually found that doing other things helped him concentrate on school when the time for that came. Just from other people I knew at the paper and the theater group, I decided it was possible to spend far more time than I did on outside things and still do very well academically. Activities are a key part of the education here."*

MIT also has an extraordinary reputation for music for a school known mainly as a haven for technocrats. John Harbison, the Pulitzer Prize-winning composer, is on the faculty here, as is composer Peter Child. John Oliver, conductor of the famous Tanglewood Festival Chorus (the chorus of the Boston Symphony Orchestra) teaches at MIT, too. David Epstein, a music theorist and conductor who has guest-conducted well-known orchestras around the world leads the MIT Symphony Orchestra. Marcus Thompson, winner of prizes for his viola playing, heads up the MIT Chamber Players. There are also many lively course offerings in music (the Introduction to Music class has one of the highest registrations in all of MIT) and it is even possible to major in the subject.

Although there are some 40 intercollegiate sports at MIT (the admissions office will proudly tell you that's more than at Oklahoma or USC), varsity athletics just doesn't play a big part in student life here. When the football team became Division III this past year (they were a club team), all the news media made a big deal about it (Pat Summerall butchered the MIT cheer on national TV, and CBS recruited George Carlin to do a little routine about the Beavers). Nevertheless, we still draw about 250 people to games on sunny days. This does have its advantages—how many students at Duke University can go to a game and have a picnic on the sidelines? Actually, MIT fields excellent teams in some of the less visible sports: track, cross country, women's and men's volleyball, fencing, and rifle.

> *"The Beavers had an away football game on a Friday evening a little while ago. They were extremely flat and lost a game they should have won, 12-7. After the game, one of the team's stars complained that they had no business playing on a Friday night. The team's entire backfield—coincidentally all majoring in aeronautics and astronautics—were up until all hours of the morning on Thursday night completing a problem set and were*

too exhausted to play well. Somehow I can't imagine Michigan losing a game and Bo telling Brent that the Wolverines were too drained from doing homework the night before.

"A friend of mine, who is from Michigan, ran into the basketball team's star center in one of his classes. They were both worried about getting a microprogrammed circuit to work. Having grown up next to a Big Ten university, he always associated college basketball stars with some kind of magic aura or mystique. This kind of thing just doesn't exist at MIT. You're a dedicated student first, and if you have the time, you can also be a dedicated athlete. College sport here is not supposed to be an exploitative institution; sports are just for fun."

Although intercollegiate sports are no big deal, intramural athletics certainly are. Last year there were over 1150 IM teams competing in 20 sports, with football, basketball, and softball leading in popularity and hockey and soccer not far behind. Most people compete on four or five teams, which are organized around the living groups. IMs are not for the athletic type only; they are organized into four leagues based on ability. A-League is everyone who could have played on the varsity but didn't have time, B is for serious amateur athletic types, whereas C and D are for people who have never played the sport before (or prefer their football to be coed).

"One of the first times I had ever been on hockey skates came in a D-League hockey game my freshman year. The day of the game, my roommates and I drove to the sporting goods store to get skates and a stick. It was considered an accomplishment to reach the puck without falling, and to actually hit it (with or without falling) was worthy of a commendation. After the game, we all went to Twenty Chimneys (a now-defunct pub on campus) for a few pitchers of beer, reminiscing over exploits worthy of the "Agony of Defeat" segment in 'Wide World of Sports.' The videotape of that first game still exists, and we occasionally pop it into the VCR for laughs."

GRADUATES

"It's hard to believe how much the 'Brass Rat' means to employers. One firm came to campus intending to hire over 100 MIT graduates in the coming year—after a five-minute interview, I had a flight to California, a week's stay in a hotel, and a rental car. And with many firms, I didn't have to write and set up interviews—they wrote letters, or called, to ask seniors please to come and meet with them. And it's not just engineering firms; many

acquaintances have gone on to law school, medical school, places that recognize that the work ethic and quantitative skills imbued at MIT mean success no matter what the field."

It should come as no surprise that the majority of MIT students become engineers and scientists after graduating. Go to a research and development laboratory at a blue-chip American company—AT&T, IBM, Hewlett-Packard, Xerox—and you're guaranteed to find creative, top-notch engineers from MIT. Visit any university that's at the forefront of scientific research—in electronics, superconductivity, biotechnology—and you'll probably run into folks from MIT as well. Some of the largest and most influential companies in America were started by MIT entrepreneurs—Digital Equipment Corporation, Texas Instruments, Hewlett-Packard, Lotus. The dream of starting and expanding a company is widespread.

But enough Institute graduates have gone on to other walks of life to dispel the notion that all MIT graduates become bench scientists or entrepreneurs. MIT graduates have increasingly gone into nontraditional disciplines—management consulting, Wall Street, law, politics, journalism—and have plenty of role models to follow.

John Reed, the chairman of Citicorp, graduated from MIT. So did George Shultz, secretary of state under the Reagan administration, who studied economics at MIT. John Sununu, former governor of New Hampshire and now George Bush's chief of staff, received three engineering degrees from MIT. Reid Ashe, publisher of the *Jackson Sun*, also studied electrical engineering there. MIT grads have succeeded in any area that requires heavy intellectual firepower and a touch of creativity.

SUMMARY OVERVIEW

If you are interested in science, technology, and their effects on society and the opportunity to work with some of the world's best professors and most brilliant students in a very supportive academic environment, MIT is the school of first choice. The Institute is unique in providing financial incentives to professors who involve undergraduates in their research projects, a program that attracts the vast majority of students here.

And excellence at MIT is not limited to the traditional hard sciences. Although most students major in engineering, the Institute's best-kept secret is that some of its best programs are the smallest ones—the social sciences, such as economics and political science, and architecture are all first-rate.

For those who are concerned about the pace and pressure of academic life, the Institute tries hard to smooth the transition from high school to the rigors of college life here. All incoming students are graded on a pass/no credit basis for their entire freshman year, and the Independent Activities Period gives continuing students a chance to unwind and explore some of the more esoteric facets of MIT and its surroundings. And the social advantages of living in one of the most liberal colleges in terms of party regulations in the world's largest college towns are considerable.

The downside is that the pressure that so concerns the administration is very real. Life at MIT is not a picnic. Students here can expect to work long hours on a seemingly never-ending stream of problem sets, papers, and exams. Although it sometimes will be necessary to make a conscious effort to put aside the books and enjoy life, many live in fear of falling behind and getting caught in an avalanche of overdue assignments.

And for all the attempts at educational reform, the academic program is still narrow in focus. The humanities just do not play an important role here in comparison to the sciences and engineering. Just take a look at the freshman core requirements—two semesters of physics, two semesters of calculus, and a semester of chemistry. A school that features a Department of Humanities is no place to major in Mesopotamian literature.

MIT may not have the name recognition of the Ivies. It is not the right school to go to if your biggest concern is impressing others. And the toughest thing here is not getting in, but surviving once you get here. But for students who are willing to put up with an occasional all-nighter or two in return for exposure to the leading edge of science and technology, there's no better school anywhere.

> *"MIT is a perfect opportunity for those who take the initiative.*
> *There's so much to do. So many possibilities. So little time."*

> *Harold A. Stern, B.S. and M.S.*

Middlebury College

THE PROGRAM

Tucked into Vermont's lovely Champlain Valley, where Holsteins and hay bales fleck the landscape, Middlebury College is defined largely by its size and location. Middlebury, with fewer than 2000 students, feels cozy and intimate. Yet the campus spreads out along a hill at the base of the Green Mountains and New York State's Adirondack Mountains to form a sweeping blue panorama. It's difficult to find a room *without* a view.

Because Vermont's winters call early and are reluctant to leave, and because darkness can often seem to set in shortly after noon, Middlebury students quickly become adept—with the help of a virtually bottomless supply of lectures, concerts, and movies—at inventing their own diversions, intellectual and otherwise. And, oddly, the same seems true of Middlebury's rigorous, eclectic, and poly-cultural academic offerings. It's as if the college pieced together its strong, internationally flavored curriculum to compensate for its stark ruralness—all those cows, and that cold.

Middlebury was founded in 1800, and its core of gray limestone buildings exhibits a solidity—a tenacity in the face of the elements—that the college works to echo in its course offerings. Although Middlebury doesn't hug the shore of a rigidly conservative Great Books curriculum, it does have a nucleus of require-ments that argue for the broadest possible education, a spectrum of ideas. In addi-tion to having a major and a concentration (similar to a minor), students must complete a distribution requirement consisting of a minimum of two courses in each of four areas: humanities, natural sciences, social sciences, and foreign lan-guages/area studies. In other words, the college isn't looking to hone narrow-minded careerists.

Middlebury looks to equip students for the long haul, right down to its emphasis on life sports, like swimming, tennis, and cross-country skiing. And students are expected to give as much as they take. Middlebury is fond of quoting the poet Robert Frost, a long time friend of the college, to make its point that students won't profit from the Middlebury experience unless they are willing to offer "the gift outright" of their own vitality and talents.

> *"When I arrived at Middlebury I barely had time to get my course schedule straight before I was encouraged to get involved in all kinds of extracurricular activities. So much of what you learn at Middlebury happens outside the classroom—there's so much going on. At an activity fair, an editor of the campus newspaper talked me into writing an article for him, and someone from a community service organization invited me downtown to talk to her about volunteer work. I was a pretty confused freshman, but I quickly met a lot of people. It was a nice introduction to Vermont."*

What makes Middlebury's academic program distinctive? Quite a bit. Like other good northeastern colleges, it zealously covers the basic liberal arts bases, and the most populated majors are English, history, and political science. But there's a lot of international spice. Middlebury's summer language schools, where the use of English virtually is banned for three months, are internationally famous and fun, in a Tower of Babel sort of way. What's more, the transcultural energy the summer programs kick up spills over into the general curriculum.

The language and international politics programs at the college are very popular, and every year hundreds of Middlebury juniors go abroad to study at one of five Middlebury schools scattered across Europe. Language majors at Middlebury may choose to live in dormitories where use of their language is encouraged, and they occasionally can eat together in special dining halls. Foreign food, films, magazines, and ideas abound—it's not uncommon to hear dining hall conversations that are laced with puns (and oblique insults) in two or three languages.

During the summer many Middlebury students also attend Middlebury's Bread Loaf campus—located high in the Green Mountains, near the college's ski area—which plays host to the Bread Loaf School of English and Bread Loaf Writers' Conference. The School of English conducts a six-week graduate session each summer at the mountain campus (students may also attend the Bread Loaf at Oxford Program or the one at Santa Fe), and then the Writers' Conference moves in for a few weeks. At the Writers' Conference, students work with established writers on everything from the mechanics of their manuscripts to negotiating the professional world of editors and literary agents. The conference is also known for its high-powered social scene (networking is the operative word here); the parties are *almost* as legendary as the lectures.

Contrary to the college's (largely valid) proclamations of ever-increasing diversity, it *is* possible to color in, if only broadly, the outlines of a typical Middlebury student. Most noticeably, he or she more often than not tends to be both athletic and, well, kind of all-American. As one freshman put it: "When I first arrived here, I felt lost in either an L.L. Bean pop-up book or a Beautiful People Convention. I couldn't tell which." (Money is everywhere in evidence, as well: there are a lot of Saabs at Middlebury, and a lot of ski racks perched atop them.) Students appear to be in perpetual motion: they ski, they hike, they jog. It's chic to turn up at supper in (ragged, mismatched) sweats. Although tattered jeans and worn sweaters are also everywhere in evidence, true sloth is frowned upon.

Besides being fit and fetching, Middlebury students also happen to be predominantly white. Only 11% of its students are from minority groups, although the college is trying very hard to attract more. (The effort is paying off: 13% of a recent freshman class were minorities.)

Although *Big Chill* types tend to dominate the landscape at first glance, Middlebury students aren't quite that easily labeled. For one thing, almost everyone is into something. The arts community, with its attendant black-clad sophisticates, has a very high profile, as do many political and environmental groups. Many in these groups expend a lot of energy cultivating their alienation from the "homogeneous and apathetic" student body—it's what keeps their juices flowing. Although there is a lot of talk at Middlebury of a schism between jocks and social house members on one hand, and the politically correct and artists on the other, the social boundaries are actually quite fluid.

> *"I don't think there's much pressure to conform at Middlebury, even though there do seem to be a lot of Yuppies, for lack of a better word. A lot of people tend to identify themselves loosely with some group, like the environmental people, but my friends weren't of any type. People aren't that closed-minded. I didn't feel I had to change my image to fit in anywhere. On many nights I'd go with friends to a play or dance performance—at Middlebury, these are considered fairly artsy, leftist activities— and then meet downtown later with people who'd spent most of the evening at the social houses."*

Socially, four years in Middlebury, Vermont—where registered cows almost outnumber registered voters—means attending to certain realities. Much of the state of Vermont seems to close at about 8 P.M., and the closest major city, Montreal, is more than two hours away. That said, Middlebury students seldom have trouble outpacing cabin fever.

A few years ago, when Vermont was one of the few states with a drinking age of eighteen, students flocked to downtown bars on weekends to dance, drink, and shoot pool. Because the downtown area was so close, there was no problem with drinking and driving; students simply walked. With the drinking age now twenty-one, many of those bars have closed, and students tend to remain on campus.

Middlebury's five co-ed social houses (formerly fraternities) continue to attract large crowds, but smaller parties also abound, and the college offers social options that touch a broad spectrum, from student-run nightclubs to poetry readings in a campus cafe. Students also make their own fun, like borrowing cafeteria trays to sled down nearby hills.

Having a car isn't a necessity at Middlebury, but it helps. Road trips to Burlington, Vermont's cultural hub, are common. Burlington is only 40 minutes away, and it's the closest place to catch first-run movies, among other things. Downtown Middlebury's one cinema gets movies about three months late, and runs them out of focus.

At Middlebury, you quickly come to appreciate winter's flip side: that is, the best part about being cold is devising worthwhile ways to get warm again. Social activities at Middlebury tend to begin outdoors (skiing, sledding, running) and then move inside, where there's a lot of camaraderie at the close of the day.

GETTING IN/FINANCIAL AID

Middlebury has worked feverishly in the past ten years to improve its national profile along with its programs, facilities, and endowment. The hard work is paying off. Middlebury has become a hot ticket. More students are applying each year, and getting in isn't easy. Last year 3871 students applied to Middlebury and only 1238 were accepted—that's about 32%.

As with all good liberal arts colleges, a strong academic record and good standardized test scores are probably the surest ticket to admission. Middlebury no longer requires SAT I scores, but if you do well it's certainly to your benefit to submit them. ACT or SAT II exam scores may be substituted for SAT I. Sixty-three percent of Middlebury's most recent class graduated in the top 10% of their secondary school class, and 85% in the top 20%.

Don't let the numbers daunt you, however; there are many roads to Middlebury. The college looks beyond statistics—it wants a broad, talented, intellectually adventurous community, not a clutch of pale grinds. They get those, too. A promising writer, painter, computer programmer, or musician may well be chosen over another candidate in order to add some countercurrents. The college plans for a 50/50 ratio of men and women.

"My high school GPA was only so-so, but I'd done quite a bit of photography and writing, and I was encouraged to send some samples to the admissions office. I sent some fairly bizarre stuff. Not only did I get in, but they allowed me to defer my enrollment twice—once on very short notice—in order to travel. When I returned from abroad, I found several letters from Middlebury, inquiring about my travels and with updated information enclosed. There was always a lot of personal attention."

The largest percentage of Middlebury's undergraduates (41%) are from New England, but 50 states and 66 countries are represented. The college doesn't discriminate on the basis of race or religion, and all major religious faiths and racial groups are represented.

Financial aid at Middlebury is entirely need-based. No student is denied admission on the basis of financial need and the college works to guide students through the maze of forms and applications necessary to secure proper Middlebury and government aid. Students gripe anyway. Last year approximately 700 Middlebury students—35%—received some portion of the $9.2 million the college made available.

ACADEMIC ENVIRONMENT

What are *The 10 Biggest Lies at Middlebury College?* That's the pop quiz posed on the back of a T-shirt—a takeoff on talk-show host David Letterman's ubiquitous Top Ten Lists—that was popular on campus last year. Although most of the lies explored universal collegiate themes (beer and sex, that is), at least one prompted some knowing glances: *"Oh, take it...it's a gut."* At Middlebury, the ultimate gut— the undergraduate's Holy Grail—simply doesn't exist. Here's why: with a student-to-faculty ratio of approximately 11 to 1, the classes are most often small and top-heavy with reading assignments.

Middlebury is by no means an academic *gulag*, but the Club Midd tag doesn't fit, either. As one senior put it, "You're on such close terms with your professors that there's not much room to coast. When you do poor work you feel guilty, as if you've let not only yourself (but them) down." In other words, there's plenty of time for skiing (your professors may even come along), but it's prudent to have an eye out for stray academic avalanches.

Middlebury students, on average, tend to work hard. Another of the Biggest Lies: "I barely studied for the test." Although it's nearly impossible to flunk out of Middlebury—you'd have to be obscenely neglectful, and maybe even live in another state—it takes real effort to do well. The college's Starr Library is routinely packed on weeknights—arrive early, if you want a seat—and the buzz isn't just social. Students also form their own small study groups.

> *"My major was history, which is one of Middlebury's largest. In some of my larger classes and discussions it was possible to hide in back and sort of coast through if you did well on papers and tests. But more often the classes were small, and to do well you really had to apply yourself. Many of the students in the classes were very bright, and the give-and-take—sometimes heated— between them and the professors made the classes constantly interesting.*

"One particularly busy semester I took a very large course, hoping that I could tuck myself in a corner and get by without expending a lot of energy. That didn't happen. The professor made sure not only that everyone attended discussion sections, but he made sure that everyone talked and that everyone had read the material. It was frightening if you weren't caught up. But it was a great course."

Although the three most popular majors are English, history and political science, Middlebury has any number of other noteworthy majors. To mention just a few: the languages, international politics, Northern studies (students may elect to study at various Arctic or Subarctic Research facilities, or Middlebury's own, 75 miles northeast of the college), and American literature. There are also art, music, theater, dance, and film/video majors. Many students can't decide, and opt for dual majors — or independent study.

Middlebury operates on a 4-1-4 calendar: two 12-week terms (the normal load is four courses) that sandwich a one-month winter term, during which students take one intensive course. Traditionally, the winter term is a time for faculty to branch out, kick back, and devise courses that normally couldn't squeezed into a regular term. In the past, some of these courses have seemed slightly *out there*. For example, Middlebury took a ribbing six years ago when *Esquire* magazine bestowed a "Dubious Achievement Award" on a winter course on Brigitte Bardot films. And another course featured wine-tasting sessions. Students saw winter term as a month-long ski party, sans academic stress.

Not anymore. The courses are still innovative (two examples: Politics and the Network News, and a jazz course taught by New York musicians), but they've gotten tougher. Reading loads can be heavy. "Remember the 'I Love Lucy' episode where Lucy's in the candy factory and can't keep up?" one sophomore said, "That's the way I felt during my first winter term." Winter term courses tend to be small (10–20 students), but so do virtually all of Middlebury's courses. Students most often get to know their professors quite well, and many professors occasionally will host a course meeting in their own homes. In the more populated majors, larger courses can't always be escaped, but smaller discussions, led by the professor, virtually are always required.

There isn't any one predominant teaching style at Middlebury. Some professors give earnest, straightforward lectures (à la John Houseman in *The Paper Chase*) while students thoughtfully scribble away in their notebooks; others like to circle the desks and engage in some nonlinear Q and A. The average Middlebury professor—whose average age, by the way, is 42, and who is more likely to have studied at Harvard than anywhere else—does a little of both. There are few brittle bones among them: questions are always encouraged, and they're most often accessible after classes.

"The trick, I think, to getting the best education at Middlebury— as it probably is anywhere—is to choose your courses on the basis

of the professors. There's a difference between brilliant men and women and brilliant teachers, and Middlebury has many of both. It's worth your while to ask around and seek out the professors who really care about teaching and provoking, even if they're not in your major. I made a list in my junior year, and I still missed far too many of them. One literature professor, while a brilliant scholar, also gives lectures that are absolutely entrancing. At the end of one lecture, during a course on the 1960s in America, he'd done such a remarkable job of making politics and literature applicable to the students' lives that many of them left in tears. They talked about nothing else for days."

SOCIAL LIFE

Although Middlebury students used to be told that almost 60% of them would go on to marry other Middlebury graduates, the true percentage is currently only 17; however, it still remains the theme of a number of running jokes. When the subject of dating comes up, many tend to roll their eyes in frustration.

The most common complaint is the so-called fishbowl effect. Middlebury is small enough—and gossipy enough—that it can be tough to have much privacy (more and more students are now opting for single rooms) or to keep romantic secrets. Many budding relationships wither, students say, under the glare of relentless observation.

But this doesn't stop anyone from trying. Standard dates at Middlebury include skiing or hiking, dinner in downtown Middlebury, and drives to Burlington. More often, however, students tend to travel in groups.

"A friend of mine related her experiences: During my first year I did what most of the women did, which was go to house parties. We went and stood around and drank beer and kept close together. It wasn't that much fun—we just didn't know what else to do. It wasn't until later that I learned how many other options there were, and now I feel like I wasted a lot of weekends. There's a definite maturing process that happens to a lot of students at Middlebury: they grow more confident and meet more people, and they tend to wean themselves off the house parties. Every weekend there are so many smaller dinner parties and other things, you wonder why you ever went to those huge parties in the first place."

The social life at Middlebury has radically changed in the past couple of years. In an effort to create more diverse social activities, the college has endeavored to create structures and organizations that will expand, compliment, and strengthen student life. In the fall of 1991 the college completed the new Student Center, which now holds the mail room, student activities offices, several social spaces, and a cafe; the $16 million Center for the Arts opened in the fall of 1992; and a residential life system was instituted in 1992 that seeks to enrich Middlebury's social life by arranging all campus residences into one of the five Commons and giving each Commons autonomous control over its social, athletic, and cultural activities.

A restructuring of Middlebury's social life was necessary in order to compensate for the loss of the college's six fraternities. Since the college forced the fraternities to become coed social houses in 1989 and therefore lose affiliation with their nationals, five of these former fraternities have become coed living facilities whose members involve themselves in social activities and occasional community service projects. (The college has no sororities.) Parties at the social houses still make up a significant part of the drinking scene at Middlebury. For the most part, the campus has seen a smooth transformation since the fraternity system was removed (approximately 120 women and 120 men are members of the coed social houses), especially for the incoming classes unfamiliar with the all-male social clubs of recent years.

Not all of Middlebury's social life revolves around the social houses, however. The Middlebury College Activities Board (MCAB), a college-funded organization led by students, sponsors diverse programs of interest that try to appeal to all groups in the college community. They hold an annual Casino Night and other semiformals, a student/faculty/staff talent show on Parents' Weekend, student/faculty dinners, weekly comedy and DJ nights, films, and concerts. Some activities sponsored by the MCAB or other college organizations have included concerts by Michelle Shocked, Poi Dog Pondering, Blues Travelers, Arlo Guthrie, The Village People, The Samples, Boogie Down Productions, Phish, Pato Baton; performances by hypnotists, magicians, dancers; fashion shows; international food festivals; and intramural sports. Homecoming weekend (usually in the middle of October) always promises crowds of alums who come back to see old friends and the Panthers play football at home. In February, Winter Carnival weekend includes four days chock full of intercollegiate ski races, a Winter Carnival Ball, ice-skating performances, student-performed nightclub skits, and a big name concert.

Whether students attend social house parties or not—and many never do—drinking is part of most social activity. Most students don't often drink to excess, mind you, but alcohol is always around, whether you're reserving dorm lounges for a registered student party, hosting dinners (almost all dorms have kitchens), or gathering at a local restaurant. Vermont's large counterculture population—all those aging hippies—have to gather somewhere.

> *"One thing I noticed about Middlebury's social scene is how much of it is based on sports, as well as parties. I played racquetball with my friends, and people were forever going skiing together, or playing squash or jogging. I met a lot of my friends that way, and sports are also a popular form of dating. I even began playing racquetball with the curator of the library's spe-*

cial collections room—he whipped me regularly—and through him I met a lot of people in the Middlebury community. At the college, sports bring together a spectrum of people."

EXTRACURRICULAR ACTIVITIES

The Middlebury experience by no means ends in the classroom or at campus parties. The college and the surrounding area offer hundreds of opportunities to become involved in other activities, and most students take full advantage of these options.

Middlebury students involve themselves with the community to an extraordinary degree. Each year more than 500 students do volunteer work with one of the many programs with which the college is affiliated. Perhaps the most popular is the Big Brother/Big Sister program, where students spend several hours a week with a young friend. It's not uncommon to see a group of students—along with a few six-to-twelve-year-olds—out eating pizza or tossing a Frisbee.

Clubs of all varieties meet regularly on campus, from political and religious groups to film and environmental clubs. The Middlebury Gay/Lesbian/Bisexual Alliance strives to raise consciousness on campus by sponsoring lectures and relevant films, as well as provide a place of community for its members. The Women's Union is dedicated to strengthening the diverse voices of all women on campus, to creating an environment in which women can feel safe to express their opinion, and to heightening awareness of women's experiences on campus and in society at large. The African American Alliance (AAA), the Alianza Latino Americana y Caribena, and the Asian Student Organization represent just three of the numerous cultural organizations that provide a forum of support for their members and for the exchange of ideas and concerns specifically dealing with their cultural existence on campus and elsewhere, and at the same time seek to share their knowledge with the college community.

Students interested in theater and music will find plenty of opportunities at Middlebury, as will aspiring writers and journalists. There are several notable student publications at Middlebury: the weekly newspaper *The Campus,* which has been among the best small college weeklies in the last few years; *Artemis,* a bimonthly gender issues magazine with a feminist approach publishes articles focusing on politics, health, academics, sports, culture and welcomes opinion and fiction pieces from the college community; *Frontiers,* a semiannual literary magazine that takes itself pretty seriously; and *Section 8,* a willfully weird and left-of-center journal. Other widely-varied publications, including *The Stamp,* a nonpartisan political forum open to the written opinion of college community members, and *Wham and Slam* (a.k.a. *The Crampus),* a student humor magazine, appear on an irregular basis.

Middlebury also operates an FM radio station, WRMC, and there's almost no kind of music its wide-ranging format can't embrace. It's not hard to get your own weekly show (if you're willing to start with a 3 A.M. to 5 A.M. shift, that is), and many students stick with the station for all of their four years. WRMC is also popular with many in the town of Middlebury, where mountains can block reception of some more distant interesting stations.

There are also any number of athletic options at Middlebury, including 21 intramural sports each for men and women. These include everything from touch football to badminton and hockey. Club sports include men's and women's rugby and volleyball, polo, scuba, and martial arts.

The college also provides an 18-hole golf course and two ski areas. The Middlebury College Snow Bowl has two double chair lifts and a triple chair lift serving 14 trails and slopes—this gives students a total of 20 miles of skiing, dropping 1200 vertical feet. (There is also snowmaking equipment.) The college's cross-country ski area at Bread Loaf is supplemented on campus by a 3.5 kilometer trail that is the longest lighted course in the country. With so much skiing going on, many students turn up in the spring wearing leg casts—they're a kind of badge of honor.

Middlebury, a member of the NCAA, the Eastern College Athletic Conference, and the New England Small College Athletic Conference (NESCAC), has many varsity and junior varsity sports for both men and women. Men's intercollegiate sports include: football, track, lacrosse, soccer, cross country, hockey, basketball, Alpine and Nordic skiing, tennis, baseball, golf, and swimming. Women's intercollegiate sports include: field hockey, tennis, soccer, cross country, hockey, basketball, squash, Alpine and Nordic skiing, swimming, track, and lacrosse. There's something for everyone, and then some.

RESIDENCE LIFE

Recently, the college has reorganized its residential life by forming the Middlebury Commons System. The purpose of the system is to enrich social and residential life and to help improve the quality of social residential life. In their residences, students create structures for self-government. By organizing the campus dormitories into five groupings or commons (a sixth will be added later to include social houses, academic interest houses, and block draw houses), the system will provide for the creation of smaller communities on campus and promote interaction among students from all four classes, faculty, and staff. Each commons has been assigned one or two faculty associates, each of whom will eventually live in a college-owned house on the perimeter of campus, and will have a number of faculty and staff affiliates.

The college hopes that, by the end of this year, each commons will have established its own identity. Whereas each commons may establish unique characteristics, traditions, special interests, colors, flags, or songs, students will not be limited to one commons for four years; in fact, students will have the opportunity to live in a different commons each year, depending upon where they draw rooms.

As far as actual living quarters are concerned, Middlebury's diverse range of dormitories leaves several options for students to explore. The social houses, as the fraternities once were, remain a popular activity at Middlebury, but there isn't room for most members to live in a house. The college has spent millions of dollars in the past several years renovating its dormitories, but housing at Middlebury remains a mixed bag. If you're lucky (i.e., if you're an upperclassman with a good room-draw number) you might end up with a huge, beautiful space, quite possibly with more than one room; if you're not, you could spend a year in a dimly-lit shoe box. But those are extremes; in general, most rooms are quite livable.

Freshmen and sophomores have little or no choice about their housing although many good rooms are open to them. The least popular dormitories on campus are the so-called New Dorms (although newer ones have since been built), which are towering concrete slabs that look like industrial tombstones with windows. And they don't look much better from inside. There has been some talk this year of a renovation, but the architects have only recently finished drawing up the plans — try to stay away until the buildings are completely renovated. Many of the older dormitories on campus are quite lovely, however, and Middlebury also owns several small houses around campus that are made available to students, usually seniors with good draw numbers.

Middlebury is serious about being a residential college. Roughly 98% of its students live on campus, and the college wants to keep it that way. Only a limited number of students are allowed to live off campus, and refunds for room and board are paltry. Quite a few students, mostly juniors and seniors, do elect to live off campus, however, and there are some wonderful houses and apartments available close to the campus. Students with cars often find places farther out in the countryside.

GRADUATES

Middlebury likes to think of its students, faculty, and employees as something of an extended family, and nowhere is this more apparent than in its career-counseling program and alumni network. Middlebury doesn't like to lose touch with any of its graduates (it's financially prudent, for one thing), and many use these career and alumni programs later in life, when making a career change or moving to a new city.

What do most Middlebury students do after graduation? Anything and everything. There are no standard professions for Middlebury graduates. Although many students interview with large companies and explore investment banking, just as many seek out the Peace Corps and social work—and everything in-between.

Many Middlebury graduates fall in love with the state and elect to stay around. Middlebury people in Vermont, like Middlebury people everywhere, work in a huge variety of fields, from banking to pottery and from architecture to farming. Many Vermont journalists, also, are Middlebury graduates.

Middlebury's career-counseling center does more than help students narrow their career options and compose résumés. There's also a computer file of graduates, listed by profession, and students are encouraged to write exploratory letters to these graduates asking for advice.

> *"I wrote tens of letters to Middlebury graduates in journalism before I graduated, and almost all of them wrote me back lengthy letters full of advice, some of it painfully honest. Some offered to take a look at my work; others suggested magazines and newspapers worth sending my résumé to. Their advice opened my eyes to a lot of options I'd never considered. One recent graduate managed to persuade an editor to look at my résumé, and, soon after, I was on my way to New York for an interview."*

Middlebury's alumni network is quite strong. Among the alumni programs is Middnet: groups of alumni in most large cities across the country that can give advice to other graduates about job prospects—or just tips on everything from good schools and housing to restaurants and cultural events in the area. Alumni groups also hold frequent parties and other get-togethers in their areas. Most Middlebury graduates, for any number of reasons, tend to seek each other out.

SUMMARY OVERVIEW

The Middlebury experience is valuable in any number of ways, and these include the college's small size, its rural location, and its energized, poly-cultural intellectual atmosphere.

Middlebury is small enough that there's no way to become lost in the shuffle. Everything is on a personal scale. Classes are small and intimate, and you'll get to know your professors (and even the deans and other administrators) quite well. By the end of four years, there won't be many unfamiliar faces.

Middlebury's campus is located in Vermont's rolling Champlain Valley, and is surrounded by mountains and gorgeous farmland. Students take full advantage of the setting. Hiking and skiing are particularly popular. Even a short walk can have you feeling that you've left most of civilization behind; it's difficult not to feel some exhilaration in Vermont's stark natural beauty.

Although Middlebury is tucked into a rural setting, however, there's nothing hayseed about its intellectual climate. Classes are both challenging and demanding, and students constantly are pushed to press out their boundaries. Middlebury also has a spicy international flavor, thanks to its popular language programs. Foreign ideas and enthusiasms abound. And there is plenty of intellectual and cultural stimulation in the form of lectures, concerts, and films.

No college is perfect, though. Middlebury's drawbacks include a certain homogeneity in its student body and a social scene that is perhaps too dependent on alcohol and the social houses. For some, the college's rural location also can become claustrophobic.

Middlebury students tend to be white and well-heeled, and many students complain about the lack of diversity. Middlebury students are tolerant of cultural differences, but the sheer lack of students from minority groups is apparent to everyone. The college is trying to attract more minorities, however, and their numbers are rising every year.

Fraternities have occupied a dominant position in Middlebury's social scene since Vermont's drinking age rose to twenty-one and downtown bars became off-limits to students. The house parties tend to be too large, and drinking is heavy. Middlebury is committed to the restructured social house system, the Commons System, and an ever-changing and expanding range of diverse social activities available on campus.

Although many students rejoice in Middlebury's rural location, others feel they've been exiled to Siberia. Students accustomed to brighter lights and bigger cities often miss the higher energy levels that more urban locations offer. One student, suffering from urban withdrawal, wondered aloud if she could have some smog sent up by Federal Express. Her case was more acute than most.

Overall, though, most students come to love Middlebury's natural environment, just as they become enthralled with the college's bright intellectual, cultural, and social atmosphere. Middlebury expects students to give of their talents and energies in a huge variety of ways, and the rewards are always plentiful. To the student willing to explore and become involved, Middlebury offers an embarrassment of riches.

Dwight Garner, B.A. and
Stefanie Hirsh, B.A.

Northwestern University

THE PROGRAM

"I didn't discover what Northwestern had to offer in a lecture hall, fraternity house, or campus bar. I found my Northwestern at the end of a 30-minute elevated train ride, inside Chicago's venerable City Hall. I was taking a freshman journalism class in which an old news hound drilled us on the basics of the business. 'If you can't handle the pressure, then you ought to pick another field—like janitorial services,' he was fond of saying with a scowl. He lectured us on crime stories, obituaries, and all the other tenets of journalism. But there was more than classes. I didn't learn to put it all together until I covered the Chicago City Council for the campus newspaper, The Daily Northwestern. *A freshman journalism student, there I was, reporting about one of the country's greatest stages for political theater. Just two quarters into school and with only one journalism course under my belt, I was doing what many newspaper veterans would never have a chance to do. And my experience wasn't out of the ordinary. It was exactly the kind of opportunity Northwestern offers its students: a solid academic background and the chance to put that background to work."*

Northwestern has the standard fare of many universities, including boisterous parties and late-night bull sessions over Domino's pizza and beer. But what makes the school more than that is its ability to combine the theory of the classroom with the practical know-how of the professional world.

At the heart of this approach is NU's philosophy that real world training begins with a broad-based liberal arts education. Though requirements among the six undergraduate schools vary, students must take at least some courses in all general academic fields. Engineering majors, for instance, must complete writing and humanities courses. Journalism students can't get away without taking a class in statistics. The approach works because NU's faculty includes noted professors in a wide range of disciplines who are committed to applying both research and teaching to the real world. As a result, students enjoy that most uncommon of academic blends: rigorous scientific and liberal arts training combined, simply put, with the skills needed to get a job.

Students at Northwestern then are able to utilize this approach to education through a variety of real world opportunities:

• Students at the McCormick School of Engineering and Applied Science can go on co-op, in which they spend a quarter working as engineers or researchers for industrial firms as part of the school's Cooperative Engineering Program.

• Journalism students spend a quarter actively working for daily newspapers across the country through the Medill School of Journalism's Teaching Newspaper Program, or they can choose the Teaching Magazine or Teaching Television Program.

• Political science majors work as staff members on election campaigns.

• Other students complete internships or field-study programs in archaeology, theater, and urban affairs. I even know of a School of Music student who wrote a jingle for Wrigley's chewing gum while interning at a Chicago firm that writes music for radio and television ads.

This emphasis on careers has some predictable results. The most popular major in the College of Arts and Sciences, for instance, is economics. And many journalism students end up more interested in the bigger salary fields of marketing and public relations than in newspapers, which are Medill's roots.

Still, the ability to mix the theoretical and the practical inside the classroom and out gives Northwestern an edge. And it is an edge that is sharpened by the school's connection to Chicago. Whether it's the city's cultural cornucopia or its professional opportunities, Chicago provides NU with an intellectual laboratory that few other colleges can match.

> *"I remember writing a paper for an art history course in which we were supposed to compare the forms of landmark buildings that had the same function, such as two government buildings with entirely different designs. There was no need to scour the library stacks to complete the assignment. The professor simply sent us into the city to examine any pair of Chicago's many architectural icons. Even introductory engineering courses in the Technological Institute take students into the city for field trips."*

Regardless of what part of the university they're enrolled in, or where they come from, NU students arrive with some common interests. Chief among them, of course, is a serious attitude towards learning. And, judging from their decision to attend a school next to America's third largest city, they have a keen curiosity about the world outside college.

A natural extension of this is the determination that demanding course work shouldn't stifle one's social life. NU students relish their intramural sports, their campus publications, and their campus parties. Many also relish the city next door and often travel into Chicago. NU, situated in the northeastern part of Evanston, a Chicago suburb, is far enough from the inner city to offer relative safety from the higher crime levels there. But Chicago is so accessible by el that a student with nothing but a few bucks can be strolling Michigan Avenue in no time. Moreover, Evanston provides a beautiful, tree-lined campus on the shores of Lake Michigan (albeit, the winter transforms it into an icy, wind-whipped campus on the shores of Lake Michigan).

> *"When I was deciding which college to attend, I was told that Northwestern had one of the top journalism schools in the country. The best one I could pick, supposedly, was located in a small town in the center of Missouri. From the time I took my first el ride through the heart of Chicago, I didn't regret my decision."*

GETTING IN/FINANCIAL AID

By most measures, Northwestern University is a highly selective school: The College of Arts and Sciences, the Medill School of Journalism, and the School of Speech are the most selective, taking 43% of those who apply. But apparently it is getting tougher. Despite a national drop in the number of high school seniors, a record number applied in the most recent year for admission. In general, those who do get in are a pretty sharp bunch. More than two thirds ranked in the top 10% of their high school classes (half in the top 5%), and they had a median combined SAT I score of 1260 and more than 28 on the ACT.

The majority of students are from the Midwest, with 56% of undergraduates from the region, exactly evenly split (50/50) between males and females. Afro-Americans, Asian-Americans, and Hispanics make up 22% of the student body. A sizable number of students come from the Middle Atlantic states and the West.

> *"An Irish Catholic, I grew up in a small conservative town in southern Idaho. My freshman-year roommate was from a wealthy suburb of Washington, D.C., and became a Dead Head while we were at NU. My best friends then were a black guy from Queens who wanted to be a newspaper reporter, a Jewish guy from Buffalo who was going to law school, and a WASP from Houston who dropped his biomedical engineering major to study English."*

A quick but key note to students and parents: For the most recent school year, it cost undergraduates $15,075 for tuition, $5,079 for room and board, and $1710 for personal expenses. Still, Northwestern is quite generous with the financial aid to help pay these big bills. Sixty percent of undergraduates get some form of aid; half get need-based grants from NU. Other forms of available aid include outside grants, work-study, federally guaranteed student loans, and NU-sponsored loans.

> *"The amount of financial aid, of course, varies with a student's (and his/her parents') income, but consider this: Coming from a single-parent home that had an income of about $28,000 a year, I wound up taking out $6,000 in loans and paying about $6,000 out of pocket over four years. Not bad for an education that cost some $68,000. In fact, financial aid made it cheaper for me to attend Northwestern than it would have cost me to attend the other school I was considering, the University of Oregon."*

ACADEMIC ENVIRONMENT

Historically, NU is known as a maker of actors and journalists, the school that produced Ann-Margret, Charlton Heston, and countless newspeople, including *Chicago Tribune* syndicated columnist Bob Greene. To some degree, this is still is true. NU prides itself on the quality of its School of Speech and Medill School of Journalism. It also has several other bright spots, including nationally ranked departments in the School of Music, economics, anthropology, chemistry, political science, and several areas of engineering.

Underpinning all of these is a demanding liberal arts foundation. CAS, which enrolls the majority of students, requires at least two courses each in natural sciences, formal studies (such as linguistics and logic), social and behavioral sciences, historical studies, values, and literatures and fine arts. Students may select a major from an individual department, create an ad hoc major with approval from a faculty committee, or choose one of eight programs that encompass several departments, such as American Culture, Integrated Science, and Urban Studies. CAS students also must take two Freshman Seminars and show proficiency in a classical or modern language and in writing.

The grade average for degree requirements may not be lower than C. In addition, no more than six classes may be taken P/N (pass/no credit), and none of those may be used to fulfill requirements for a major. Students may be placed on academic probation if they receive final grades below C in two or more courses in a single quarter or if they have a cumulative record after freshman year that is below a C average.

The McCormick School of Engineering and Applied Science, NU's second largest school, includes fields ranging from applied mathematics to environmental engineering, but all include the same basic components: six math courses, six basic science courses, six basic engineering courses, seven social sciences/humanities courses, two communications courses, one computer programming course, five unrestricted electives, and 16 courses in the student's major.

Class sizes in all six undergraduate schools vary from large introductory-level courses to small advanced seminars. Sometimes the biggest classes are the best. One Slavic languages and literatures professor closes few people out of his popular class, Introduction to the Soviet Union. Despite a class of more than 800 students, he keeps students entranced with his method of explaining Soviet history through novels and poetry.

There are great professors in other departments as well. The economics department boasts a former president of the American Economic Association who manages the improbable: he gives maddeningly difficult multiple-choice exams. His introductory macroeconomics course is a must for anyone who wants to know who really controls this country and how they do it. In the political science department, a student can take a class called Latin America, taught by a professor who once trained CIA agents for work in South America. Another professor, a former department chairman, is a member of the Palestine Liberation Organization's legislative arm. The engineering school's faculty, meanwhile, includes nine members of the prestigious National Academy of Engineering and a nominee to the National Academy of Sciences.

These noted professors, like most of their colleagues, are very accessible to students and quite willing to spend time with them after classes, which typically meet two or three times a week for lecture and again for discussion. Although graduate teaching assistants lead many of the discussions, it is not uncommon for professors to do so themselves. In the liberal arts departments particularly, faculty aren't just there to do research but genuinely are interested in teaching undergraduates in challenging ways.

> *"Perhaps the best class I took at Northwestern was called Problems of Contemporary American Cities. The course explored everything from race relations to public housing. And the professor's provocative way of teaching sparked emotional debate among students, many of whom came from disparate economic and ethnic backgrounds. His exams were like nothing I'd seen before. One sample question: "You're the superintendent of an inner-city school that is torn by racial strife, low morale among faculty, and a rapidly declining tax base to support it. What do you do?" He was expert at encouraging students to learn from each other."*

At the engineering school, the emphasis is on hard work and research. Some students express frustration over the quality of basic science classes, such as physics and math (which actually fall under CAS). Still, engineering administrators and faculty are considered accessible and helpful. The massive engineering building, called the Technological Institute, is part way through a complete reconstruction, costing more than $100 million. Additionally, there is a new catalysis building, and a material and life sciences facility that opened in the fall of 1992. Also, computers are incorporated extensively into the curriculum of courses, and each engineering department has its own computer bank.

To all of this, add Northwestern's ability to attract professional part-time faculty to many departments. Whether it be a prominent Chicago antitrust attorney or the bureau chief of a major news magazine, NU is able to draw on the city's many talented professionals to teach courses from a real-world perspective that longtime academicians sometimes don't have.

> *"In a magazine editing course I took, a man who redesigned the* Washington Post *magazine spoke to us about changing trends in graphics and design. A columnist for the* Chicago Tribune *taught my freshman-level journalism course. And my Law and Ethics of Journalism class was taught by a former libel attorney for NBC News."*

This effort to bring in people who work outside academia augments the university's already strong faculty and liberal arts base.

SOCIAL LIFE

Northwestern splits the difference between a party school and one too academically serious to have some fun. One good illustration of this: Students pack the library many nights, but they also pack the library's main lounge for another NU tradition, the nine o'clock study break in which everyone drops his or her books for a half hour or so of gossip and snacking.

Perhaps the highlight of NU social life is Mayfest. It's a week-long party late in spring quarter that includes musicians, dance troupes, and outdoor movies capped by Dillo Day, a campus-wide time warp back to the late 1960s.

As for entertainment, the most popular campus event is Waa-Mu, a variety show that mixes skits and musicals. Regardless of how good any preceding Waa-Mu is, students camp out for days in advance just to buy tickets. It's a matter of pride for Greek houses and dorms to see who can secure the spots closest to the front of the line. Also popular is Waa-Mu's irreverent cousin, the Mee-Ow Show. This is improvisational comedy at its funniest. Many students consider it more entertaining than the tradition-bound Waa-Mu show, partly because it gets the audience involved.

NU's two big annual dances are the Pumpkin Prom and A&O Ball (sponsored by the Activities and Organizations Board), which are held during fall and winter quarters, respectively. Both draw some of the best musical talent, from Ziggy Marley to the Violent Femmes. A&O Ball is followed closely by Dance Marathon, NU's biggest philanthropic event, in which more than 200 students pair up to boogie for 30 hours straight—all in the name of charity.

> *"It was chaos. Early in my sophomore year, several dorms pooled their funds and rented an el train for a night, packed it with liquor, munchies, and students and proceeded to throw, as the commemorative sweatshirts boasted, 'One El of a Party.' For two hours, we rode the el tracks from one end of Chicago to the other. Once we ran out of mixers to temper the effects of the alcohol, one car soon had to be designated the 'sick bay,' but the rest of us continued to enjoy the thrill of barreling down an el track, beer in hand, with no need to worry about who was driving."*

One notable exception to what you might expect from other Big Ten Conference schools: don't count on athletics playing a big part in social activities. Until Columbia University's football team mercifully went on extended losing streak, Northwestern held the Division I record for most consecutive losses (34). Now, that doesn't mean Wildcat fans don't enjoy a good tailgate before home games, but the big-ticket sports simply don't mean as much at NU. The positive corollary, though, is that there isn't the inevitable friction on campus that comes when athletes are treated as quasi-students. The win/loss percentage of many NU teams doesn't come close to matching the school's graduation rate for its athletes, but they sort of like it that way here.

Dorms and fraternity houses are fertile grounds for parties. (Virtually all of the frats are on the north end of NU's long, skinny campus; hence the oft-heard underclassmen's call of, "Let's go north.") With about 40% of the student body in Greek houses, fraternities and sororities often have dominated the social scene. But this imbalance is likely to change for two reasons: one, underclassmen recently were prohibited from rushing a house until winter quarter, which could make freshmen and sophomores more likely to look to their dorms for entertainment; second, the university has a strong and growing network of residential colleges, that is , smaller dorms with programmatic themes such as communications, international studies, and humanities. These residence halls offer an alternative to fraternity parties and sorority formals. About 20% of the student body lives in off-campus housing (less than 5% commute from home), and the apartments they most often rent are close enough to each other to make finding a party an easy task.

Some NU students, particularly upperclassmen, seize every chance to spend time in Chicago. And there's a good reason: Evanston is simply far from anyone's idea of the perfect college town. It says much that the most popular student bar, the PM Club, isn't even in Evanston; it's across the street from the city's southern border with Chicago. This North Shore suburb of Chicago is, after all, the birthplace of the Women's Christian Temperance Union.

Any student with sufficient ID and curiosity has Chicago's countless offerings from which to choose. Blues bars, reggae joints, and dance clubs are scattered across the North Side of the city, virtually all of them near el stops. World famous blues artists, such as Koko Taylor and Sugar Blue, who draw thousands to outdoor concerts, can be seen in one of the city's intimate clubs for a $6 cover charge.

The city's many theater companies, perhaps the cultural offering most over-looked by students, have something for everyone from the professional actor to the theater neophyte. And the fare ranges from major musicals, such as *Miss Saigon,* to small off-the-wall productions.

Chicago's museums have to be seen to be appreciated. In addition to the Art Institute of Chicago, other major institutions include the Museum of Science and Industry, the Shedd Aquarium, the Adler Planetarium, and the Field Museum of Nat-ural History. If you can avoid being trampled by little kids, all of these make for a great break from books. Finally, there are the Chicago Symphony Orchestra, and the Lyric Opera of Chicago, both of which are world renowned. Just as with the university's academic program, Chicago enhances what NU's social scene has to offer.

EXTRACURRICULAR ACTIVITIES

Never mind Evanston's nasty winters and too-short springs. There's enough on campus to keep you busy for several seasons. In addition to the standard fare of intramural sports, students can pick from mini-courses held in the student union building that range from wine tasting to ballroom dancing. For the health-conscious undergraduate, NU recently finished a new sports and aquatic center that features tennis, basketball, and racquetball courts, a top-quality fitness room, a running track, and an Olympic-size lap and diving pool.

For a little intellectual exercise, many students also become involved in campus publications and broadcast stations. WNUR-FM, tucked in the basement of Annie May Swift hall, is the nation's largest student-run radio station. The station, whose playlist ranges from classical to punk, prides itself on its alternative programming, and consequently has surprising national influence.

Two newspapers serve NU, giving student journalists of all political stripes a chance to practice their craft. The *Daily Northwestern* is the university's paper of record and is open to anyone interested in learning about newspapers, not just journalism students. The *Northwestern* Review is NU's conservative weekly; it serves up a more ideological brand of journalism. For the lover of prose and poetry, there is *Helicon*, the quarterly literary journal. For the lover of puns and punch lines, there is *Rubber Teeth*, the campus humor group that publishes a quarterly magazine and puts on its own variety show.

> *"As a first-quarter freshman, I was reluctant to get too involved in any extracurricular activities, at least until I could gauge how much time my classes would take. But the minute I walked into*

the newsroom at The Daily Northwestern, *I knew I'd found a second home. I started drawing editorial cartoons for it once a week, and by winter quarter I was a staff reporter on the paper's city desk. Soon after, I was covering the Chicago City Council, attending raucous council sessions and interviewing some of the city's most powerful people. At* The Daily, *I found a whole new group of lifelong friends."*

Those students interested in television can try NSTV, the student-produced television enterprise that airs on Evanston's cable channel. It features talk shows, game shows, and public affairs presentations. Many other students are involved in the numerous theater productions that are staged each quarter. And for those more intrigued with producing than performing, there's the Arts Alliance Board, which sponsors several plays each year.

Student government at NU has something for budding politicians (Associated Student Government Senate), business managers (Student Activities Funding Board), and entertainment executives (A&O Film Board). Other campus organizations include the Interfraternity Council, the Gay and Lesbian Alliance, and For Members Only, the main black student group.

Recently, more and more students also have become involved in the Northwestern Volunteer Network, which was established a few years ago and now sends dozens of students to help social service agencies and other groups across the Chicago area. NVN, as it's called, has done much to combat the perception that NU students are merely job-hungry, self-centered individuals.

As for housing, incoming students should be forewarned: Quality and comfort vary widely. The type of living units for underclassmen range from large, noisy dorms to secluded, apartment-like rooms. If you like to study in your dorm on most nights, for example, try Chapin Residential College. If you enjoy a game of hallway hockey now and again, pick Bobb-McCulloch Hall.

The same holds true for the various cafeterias: Some serve food that's quite edible, whereas the offerings at other cafeterias aren't exactly mouth watering.

The point is, check before you fill out your housing application.

GRADUATES

Whatever you say about NU's curriculum, social scene, or football team, you have to concede: these people get good jobs. Fifty-three percent of seniors immediately went to work full-time after graduation, 35% attended graduate/professional school, and 11% had plans for military service, travel, or other pursuits, according to university statistics.

"While some Northwestern students inevitably suffer the trauma of not knowing what in the world they're going to do come graduation, most find that an NU degree does more than look good in a picture frame. Among my closest friends, one is working as a reporter for The Los Angeles Times, *another writes for* The Orange County Register, *and yet another got a reporting position at the* St. Petersburg Times. *My sophomore year roommate, meanwhile, works for a Big Six accounting firm."*

The university's alumni network is quite strong, and it shows in the school's fund-raising efforts. In a recent school year, NU alumni and friends donated $61.7 million, up from $36.3 million one year earlier. The same Chicago connections that make NU an enjoyable place to spend four years make it easier for students to meet the right people when they're hunting for jobs. It's no coincidence that many NU students end up working in Chicago, for instance, at Arthur Andersen as analysts, Amoco as engineers, and Apple as computer programmers.

SUMMARY OVERVIEW

Northwestern sets itself apart from virtually all Midwestern schools because of a strong liberal arts foundation that is able to combine theory and practice in a way that makes students more discerning and more perceptive. This foundation is enhanced by Chicago, a great intellectual laboratory. And the range of social activities—both on campus and in Chicago—make Evanston's bitter winters more than bearable.

Each of Northwestern's six undergraduate schools—College of Arts and Sciences, Music, Speech, Medill (journalism), Education and Social Policy, and Engineering and Applied Science—provides a broad-based curriculum that forces students to consider issues and ideas outside of their areas of interest. In addition, each of them makes a point of offering internships and field-study programs that allow students to apply what they've learned.

Many do so in one of the best possible classrooms, Chicago. The city and NU play off each other—academically, culturally, and professionally. The Art Institute of Chicago, for example, gives an art history student studying French Impressionists a chance to see one of the world's best collections of those artists. An urban studies major has Chicago's troubled public housing projects to see if what his textbooks claim about poverty and crime is true. Moreover, NU's faculty is sprinkled with professionals who bring a fresh perspective as part-time instructors, augmenting an already strong staff of professors.

NU also offers students enough extracurricular activities to make them forget they're living in Evanston, the birthplace of Prohibition. From student publications to theater productions, there are organizations to satisfy anyone. And, just an el ride away, is the City of Big Shoulders—home of the blues, the Bears, and countless bars.

Those advantages notwithstanding, Northwestern does have its weaknesses. For instance, many students go through four years of school in Evanston and still view Chicago more as a tourist than a resident. They don't realize the city is too good to pass up. Although making an occasional trip to Rush Street, home of many a club without character, they miss the smoky blues bars on Halsted Street. They hit the trendy restaurants, but neglect to check out the Ethiopian, Thai, and other wonderful little places to eat.

This shortcoming, however, detracts little from the university's greatest strength: a demanding academic program that combines theoretical and practical knowledge to develop thoughtful, successful graduates. And they're graduates, by and large, who had a great time along the way. NU's mix of top-quality faculty, challenging courses, and active social scene—all enhanced by Chicago—is tough to beat. Imagine attending a high-powered urban university that just happens to be located in a tree-covered burg next to a lake. That's Northwestern. And it even has its own beach.

Flynn McRoberts, B.S.

Pomona College

THE PROGRAM

"Coming from a monstrously large public high school I didn't even seriously consider a small private school when first applying to college. Berkeley, UCLA, and Stanford were at the top of my list, then there was a safety net school. At the last minute, I added Pomona College.

"I didn't even know Pomona was a difficult school to get into until after I had decided to go there.

"Once there, my first writing intensive class at Pomona freshman year was my initial clue that I had made the right choice. There was a lot of writing. Only 14 people in the class, and the professor actually cared whether or not I could write. After having difficulties with the first drafts of my final project for the class, I went in to see him.

'Try to write like you're writing a newspaper story,' he explained. 'What's your scoop in this paper?'

"First, I didn't even realize he knew I was into newspapers. Second, I didn't expect this from an economics professor. And third, he managed to put his message into a form that I could understand.

"But what appealed to me most was the idea of a discussion class with a real professor who knew me by my first name and understood my weaknesses and strengths."

Pomona College, a small, liberal arts college in the finest tradition of many distinguished New England institutions, has one asset that its East Coast rivals lack. It is on the West Coast. Sun-filled skies all year and proximity to the Pacific Rim gives Pomona students an educational atmosphere not found elsewhere. This asset, however, is also Pomona's liability when it comes to name recognition. The mention of its name is frequently met by blank stares and mispronunciations (Ponoma?).

Pomona, to be sure, has its share of superb faculty, creative curriculum, and educational resources. The streets are tree-lined (a term that has been applied to all but 20 streets in the United States), but the fact that these trees are of the palm variety and that they border not just the streets but also the volleyball courts are just some aspects that make it so iniviting.

The one hundred-five-year-old coeducational institution is the founding member of The Claremont Colleges, a consortium of five undergraduate colleges and one graduate school. Each school is autonomous and has distinctive purposes. The other five members are Claremont McKenna College, Harvey Mudd College, Pitzer College, Scripps College, and The Claremont Graduate School.

Although each school is unique and independent of the others, the schools share a few centrally located facilities and, in some cases, faculty. This gives students the individual attention characteristic of a small college while making available resources often found only in larger universities. Students are also able to enroll in most of the courses at the neighboring institutions, including the graduate school, at no extra charge.

Pomona has a broad educational philosophy. Its purpose is the "pursuit of knowledge and understanding, whether scientific or aesthetic, historical, ethical, or social." In addition, Pomona tries to "prepare its students for lives of personal fulfillment and social responsibility."

Fair enough.

At least part of the educational philosophy at Pomona is not what to think, but how to think, preferably with independence and criticism. "Think for yourself" may have been advice from your mother, but learning how not to let others think for you is more difficult than your mother would let you believe. To say that Pomona molds men and women into critical thinkers may be giving it more credit than it deserves, but then again, the college cannot be held responsible for all the molding.

Success at Pomona College is determined largely by the students, and their levels of responsibility and ambition. The college acts as a catalyst to achieve the educational goals created by the student, but not as a protagonist. The phrase "Your mother is not enrolled here" may be appropriate.

Perhaps the most overused phrase in college catalogs is the college experience, and although no two experiences are quite the same, it is only because no two persons are exactly the same, not necessarily the college. Pomona tries to allow the student to create the experience by providing the most accommodating atmosphere in which to do so.

International relations, history, politics, economics, and psychology are the most popular majors. About one-third of the degrees awarded are in the social sciences. A significant minority of the students major in the natural sciences.

The school is not the sweatshop that other small liberal arts schools have the reputation of being, but it certainly is not the vacation paradise that the palm trees may lead one to expect. The academic requirements are designed to give students a sample of a variety of disciplines. A large degree of self-motivation is assumed, and there is a heavy emphasis placed on writing well. (I think half my classes had *The Elements of Style* as required reading.) Above all, asking questions is encouraged.

The front entrance to Pomona has an ivy-covered gate, just like every other self-respecting liberal arts institution in the Western hemisphere. The gates read "Let only the eager, thoughtful and reverent enter here." Later, the author of those words, former president James Blaisdell, had second thoughts about the word "only," noting that it may be a little much to ask of all eighteen year-olds to have all three characteristics.

But the back entrance to the college is used more often because it has better access to Interstate 10, and, like most back entrances, is much more telling of the nature of the place. To the left is what until recently was Veggie House, a Victorian house informally reserved for students pledged to vegetarianism. It has been restored and is now used as a college guest house. To the right lie a volleyball court and a softball field that are well used, year-round. Go on for another block, and the Carnegie Building, formerly used as a library, now the home of the politics, economics, and sociology/anthropology departments sits in a stately manner on the left. Across the street is an expanse of grass the size of two football fields called Marston Quad, which is the center of the school. Grass for the sake of grass, and no other reason. Southern California has enough concrete. The atmosphere is relaxed, and people sunbathing on the quad in the middle of winter is not an uncommon sight. After all, it's not hard to be relaxed when it's 75° and sunny in late January. Eating outside on a grassy field or in a sun-drenched square can't help but loosen people up a bit. The people at Pomona are politically liberal (for conservatives, see Claremont McKenna College), economically conservative, and socially loose.

What about the pictures of sunny California with mountains that can be found in Pomona's catalogs? Well, those are real pictures, albeit rare, because generally the view of the mountains is not that clear. Smog is a big problem in Los Angeles, as bad as everything that you've heard. Not unbearable, but it can be annoying.

Looking at Pomona, one finds the qualities of a small, East Coast liberal arts school 2500 miles removed. Trade in the elm trees for palm trees, snow tires for skateboards, and a Western European outlook for a Pacific Rim orientation, and you have Pomona.

GETTING IN/FINANCIAL AID

"This is what a college is supposed to look like," one girl said to me when we were on a group tour of Pomona before I had decided where to go. And she was right. Grass everywhere, ivy-

covered buildings with impressive names like Carnegie and Millikan, students lugging books, and kids shooting pool in the student union."

While sitting in on a politics class (which had seven people in it), the professor asked a question having to do with the founders' conception of democracy. I sheepishly gave an answer, to which he responded with another question. I felt impressed that he would take *real* class time to treat me as a *real* student. If professors take me this seriously when I'm just a prospective student, I thought, how will they treat me when I'm actually attending?

That's when I decided to find out.

Is it difficult to get in? In a word, yes, and like everywhere else, it's getting harder. A few numbers to think about: The most recent freshman class had 380 members, about evenly divided among men and women, and a combined median SAT I score of 1320 (630, verbal; 690, math). More than three-quarters of the class graduated in the top 10% of their high school class and 92% graduated in the top 20%. Slightly more than two out of three applicants were denied admission, a rate that has been increasing recently.

But grades and test scores aren't everything. Unlike public schools, which generally rely on grades and standardized test scores, Pomona also takes into consideration extracurricular activities, class rank, and the rigor of the course load taken. And, of course, everybody is looking for that something special, which could be anything from an interest in medieval art to opening a venture capital firm. Also, there is luck. For example, if you happen to be a resident of a state from which Pomona re-ceives very few applications, there may be hope despite, say, only moderate test scores. The reason for this is that the college values diversity, which means geographic as well as racial and cultural diversity.

Like most schools, Pomona looks for the creative as well as the intelligent and hardworking. This is not a place of diligrinds where graduates are the only thing. Pomona recognizes that there is more to school than grades, and more to learning than essays and tests. Pomona has made a concerted effort to attract minority students and, to a large part, has succeeded in doing so. With diversity on campus being one of the most pressing student issues, focus on diversity in the admissions process has become more intense. Forty percent of the freshmen classes over the past three years have been nonwhite. Forty three percent are from California, and another 22% are from other western states.

"This is a small school, and that fact is reflected in just about every aspect of the system. At one point, I was having difficulty with my financial aid package, and so I telephoned the financial aid office. Expecting a secretary to answer the phone, I asked for the director of financial aid, Pat Coye, with whom I had spoken once before. However, it was Ms. Coye who answered the telephone, and before I even said my name, she recognized my voice and said, 'Hold on, Jonathan, I have your file right here.'"

Getting into Pomona College is hard, and once you get there, it's hard on the pocketbook, too. Nothing worth having comes cheap, and Pomona is no exception. Tuition for a year runs $17,000 plus $8000 for room and board. Toss in miscellaneous fees, and you're looking as $25,140 a year. And you haven't even bought your books yet. Books will run around $275 per semester.

There is, however, some relief in sight. The ever-so-helpful people at financial aid, and that is written with the utmost sincerity, say that more than half of all students receive some sort of financial aid. The average aid package awards $16,820 in grants, low-interest loans, and part-time employment. The average grant is $12,800. There is no family income ceiling to receive financial aid, so if you feel you need it, by all means apply for it.

To apply all applicants must file an Application for Federal Student Aid and Supplemental Financial Aid Form. Both are available from the College Scholarship Service or from Pomona College. California residents are required to apply for Cal Grants and should contact the California Student Aid Commission, P.O. Box 510845, Sacramento, CA 94245-0845, for application instructions. Early decision candidates must file a special early version Financial Aid Form available upon request from Pomona. Things are tough all over, so federal grants like the Pell Grant and the SEOG are hard to come by. State-funded Cal Grants are a little more common. Pomona administers a variety of loan programs that are interest-free until six months after graduation at which point a modest rate is charged. Pomona also has a monthly payment plan to make the college more affordable.

Rule to live by: APPLY EARLY.

ACADEMIC ENVIRONMENT

The work is tough and demanding. This isn't Romper Room, and people won't hold your hand, although there are those who will be more than willing to shed their guiding light. Part of that guiding light is the faculty adviser who is assigned to each student. Certainly, some of the faculty are more involved with their advisees than others, but students do have the option to change advisers, and most do if their adviser is not in their field of study.

Thirty-two courses, four courses per semester, are required for the degree of Bachelor of Arts, the only kind of degree Pomona offers. Most people don't stick to the four courses a semester routine, but still, most graduate in four years. The general education requirements are designed to give students exposure to a variety of subjects, although at the same time not confining students. Students must satisfy requirements in three areas: foreign language, English language, and breadth of study.

Students must demonstrate knowledge of a foreign language by one of three means: passing the third semester of a foreign language course at Pomona; scoring a four or five on the advanced placement examination; or scoring 600 or better on the College Board Achievement Test. The English language requirement has two parts. First, there is a writing proficiency test administered to all freshmen. Second, every student must pass courses deemed writing intensive. One of these courses is a Freshman Seminar, which is a small, discussion-oriented class with frequent writing assignments. Topics vary from year to year, with past topics including the Economics of Poverty, Biological Determinism, and the Baby Boom Generation. The breadth of study requirement asks the student to take nine courses, three each in the humanities, social sciences, and natural sciences.

Students are, at least on paper, required to "make a definite choice" as to their concentration by the end of their sophomore year. In actuality, they won't kick you out if you haven't declared a concentration until your senior year. No concentration requires more than 16 courses, but some require some advance planning, especially some of the natural sciences and international relations because often there are many prerequisites for required courses. Concentrations are offered in 38 fields in the natural sciences, social sciences, and humanities.

Students also can apply for a special concentration if regularly offered concentrations don't meet the student's needs. It looks easy in the catalog, but some students say that faculty and administrators discourage the practice. Still, in my class, 19 students graduated with special concentrations, just behind the number of people concentrating in philosophy, psychology, and international relations, and more than the number that concentrated in mathematics and biology. For premeds, life can be particularly difficult, especially in the beginning of the program. General chemistry, a required course for concentrations in chemistry, biology, and molecular biology, is somewhat of an endurance test where only the dedicated survive.

Enrolling in classes at the other Claremont Colleges is a simple process with only a few exceptions. First-semester freshmen normally enroll for the entire program at Pomona. Second-semester freshmen and sophomores are limited to one course per semester at the other campuses. Juniors and seniors may enroll up to half of their program in any one semester outside of Pomona. Limits on cross-registration for specific classes are sometimes imposed by the host college, but those times are rare.

The average class size is 14, and there is a student-to-faculty ratio of 9 to 1, a major selling point for the college. All classes are taught by professors. There are no graduate teachers' aides lecturing to an auditorium of 400. Because of the small class size, most classes involve plenty of interaction between the students and professors. Then, of course, there are the tests, the papers, the lab work and the problem sets. The usual.

"Thesis. The very thought sent shivers down my spine like fingernails against a blackboard. The semester that I worked on my government thesis, I stayed away from the government offices for fear that one of my readers would see me and ask me how it's going.

"I had three readers, and I had a specific use for each one. One was well equipped in the technique of writing a thesis. Another was the faculty's expert in the field my thesis was discussing. And the third reader was the one I worked best with and understood me the most. Put together, they made a great team, although I produced only an average thesis. Despite the input from my profs, it took me nearly three months just to erase the idea that a thesis is just a big essay and to actually figure out what a thesis was for.

"But in the end, there's a satisfying feeling involved in turning in a 64-page bound manuscript. You get to reflect on the hours of sitting in front of a computer and count the number of pizzas and gallons of coffee you consumed. And although the thesis itself wasn't great, the process of researching and writing, with the counseling from professors, was an invaluable experience."

Pomona also sponsors a wide range of study-abroad programs in which about half of the student body participates at some point in their college career. Programs are located in Athens (Greece), Berlin (Germany), Cambridge (England), Edinburgh (Scotland), Glasgow (Scotland), Harare (Zimbabwe), Kathmandu (Nepal), Kyoto (Japan), London (England), Lund (Sweden), Madrid (Spain), Marburg (Germany), Moscow (Russia), Nairobi (Kenya), Nanjing (China), Oxford (England), Padua (Italy), Paris (France), Queensland (Australia), Quito (Ecuador), Rome (Italy), Santiago (Chile), St. Petersburg (Russia), Santiago (Dominican Republic), Seville (Spain), Strasbourg (France), Tel Aviv (Israel), Tokyo (Japan), and Toledo (Spain).

Freshmen, first-semester sophomores, and second-semester seniors normally are ineligible for study abroad programs. Students who study abroad pay tuition, fees, and room and board to Pomona, which includes all instruction, room and board, and an allowance toward round-trip airfare between Los Angeles and the program site. Also open to Pomona students are semester-long programs in Washington, D.C. and Sacramento. Both programs offer internship experience as well as course credit. The Washington Semester Program is operated by nearby Claremont McKenna College and is said to be a lot of work, but well worth it.

Combined programs in engineering with the California Institute of Technology and Washington University in St. Louis offer qualified students the option to earn a Bachelor of Arts degree from Pomona College. The programs take five years, the first three of which are spent at Pomona and the last two in Pasedena or St. Louis. Semester-long student exchange programs with liberal arts colleges are also available. Qualified students may study as exchange students at Colby College, Maine; Fisk University, Tennessee; Smith College, Massachusetts; Spellman College, Georgia; or Swarthmore College, Pennsylvania. Generally, these are programs that are relatively easy to get into. Participating colleges must trade with Pomona on a student-for-student basis, and usually there are plenty of people that want to come to sunny California.

The Oldenborg Center is a dormitory and foreign language center devoted to promoting international education. Students living at the dorm choose which language section they want to live in, and there are formal and informal opportunities to learn the language and culture of another country.

I have found the library facilities particularly lacking, especially when it comes to needed periodicals. Having concentrated in government and taken relatively few science classes, I can only write about my library experiences in that area, but I have heard similar remarks made by those in other fields. The UCLA and Cal Poly Pomona libraries are good supplements to the Claremont Colleges' Honnold Library, although a car may be needed to get to either one.

What you can't find at Pomona College in the way of academics is certain to be available at the other Claremont Colleges or other nearby institutions. The courses are demanding, the teachers are both your friends and instructors, and the only limits are the amount of energy the student is willing to invest.

SOCIAL LIFE

Pomona is located 35 miles outside of Los Angeles in a suburban community called Claremont, a conservative town of about 35,000 that doesn't even allow fast-food restaurants within the city limits. No, it's not much of a college town.

The Pomona campus, however, provides some relief from the town. There are some limitations, but only inasmuch as they affect other students. For example, alcohol is allowed on campus, but it is strictly controlled. The administration recognizes that they are not surrogate parents to students who are placed here by their parents to be taken care of. Much of the responsibility as to whether or not Pomona remains a wet campus lies with the students and whether or not they treat alcohol responsibly.

Because the school is so small, about 1400 students, there is very little difference between the social opportunities for upper and lower division students on campus. It's just a matter of knowing where to go. The sponsor group system for first-year persons helps ease new students into the college environment, giving them a chance to meet people in an otherwise difficult atmosphere. Sophomore and juniors head groups of six first-year persons and show them the college ropes. Few things can be more daunting than to enter a huge dining hall for the first time and not have anyone to eat with. Sponsors help the transition from high school to college.

> *"By the end of the first year, most have grown out of the sponsor system and found niches of their own within the colleges. Mine were the Nu Alpha Phi fraternity and my poker group. Go to a small, Friday afternoon get-together in the Wash, an open-air amphitheater where the grass melts into trees and bands*

*are invited to strut their stuff, invite your government prof who
just gave you a C— on your midterm, and throw a frisbee around.
Friday night would be determined by your mood."*

And about the dining halls.... well, it's a little better than high school, but not
much. A mural by Orozco of the Greek Titan Prometheus bringing fire to mankind
dominates Frary Dining Hall, which adds to or detracts from one's dining experience, depending on the experience being sought.

Because the campus is wet, there is no lack of weekend on-campus activities. A
variety of annual and weekly parties are well-attended. Formal and informal dance
parties on Fridays and Saturdays playing funk, pop, and rock music make it easy for
students to stay on campus and not be bored.

Those who do go out generally hit the big city, but a car is a necessity in that case.
For those with the transportation, Westwood and Los Angeles offer every major
music performer, from rock to pop to jazz to funk, a large variety of traditional and
experimental theater, and a host of museums and artistic attractions. Then, of
course, there's Disneyland, a close 40 minutes away in Anaheim.

One of the aspects of the six-college arrangement at Claremont is that, in theory,
the students of the different colleges can interact and learn from each other. And, of
course, relative to the other colleges, each college has its own reputation as to the
kinds of students that go there. Pomona students have the reputation of not interacting with the other colleges, and to a large extent it is a true perception. Although
the student government seems to acknowledge the role of trying to facilitate six-
college activities, the students as a whole do not. And there are at least two reasons
for that. First, Pomona is the largest, oldest, and wealthiest of the six undergraduate
and graduate schools, and many students find no reason to go to the other campuses. Second, the other colleges themselves have reputations, which are mere
self-perpetuating stereotypes of past students, that discourage Pomonans from
traveling north to the other campuses.

But the distinctive atmospheres of the different campuses are assets of the Claremont College system and can be taken advantage of easily. Simple things like eating
dinner or going to parties at the other colleges (Harvey Mudd throws some of the
best parties around) can be welcome departures from the Pomona habit.

As far as nightlife outside of the college campuses go, forget it. There are movies
and bars and whatnot, but unless you have a car, they are pretty inaccessible. Even
things like supermarkets are a fair walk away. Downtown Los Angeles is 35 miles
away, a 45-minute trek by car (when traffic is good, and that isn't often). However,
a new commuter train has made Los Angeles more accessible—only an hour away. In
addition, the college offers weekly junkets to cultural entertainment centers in L.A.

For midnight snacks, there are the local favorites. A bicycle will get you to Ben-
jie's, a 24-hour cafe, which on any given weeknight looks like a library with a lot of
onion rings. You can spot sweatshirts from all of the Claremont Colleges there, and
if it's not run over with local high schoolers it can be a great place to study. Foster's
Doughnuts changed its name to Donut Man, and as corny as the name may be, it

makes great doughnuts all night, which Claremonters take advantage of at all hours.

All in all, most of the nightlife adventures take place on campus and for the foreseeable future, things will stay that way.

Pizza is delivered until 2 A.M.

EXTRACURRICULAR ACTIVITIES

"We were on deadline at Student Life, *the student newspaper at Pomona College, and there was a late-breaking story. I wanted to talk to President David Alexander to get a comment from the administration on the situation. He wasn't in, but returned my call an hour later. At the end of the five-minute conversation, Alexander asked me if we shouldn't arrange for regular meetings between him and some of the editors at the newspaper so that we could have better communication. Access to the administration was never difficult, but I didn't think it would be that easy."*

Pomona has most of the comforts of home, and then some. There are the ususal extracurricular activities that can be found in every other college: a student newspaper, a radio station, fraternities, student government, concerts, art openings, lectures, films, rugby, lacrosse, water polo, and the list goes on. In fact, there are almost 80 student clubs and organizations.

And the activities that you can't find often can be arranged for. The student government has been more than generous in funding student interests and activities that cannot be provided for by academic means. Student projects, such as two recent films on date rape, have been funded in whole or in part by the student government. Sometimes, all you have to do is ask.

Even the traditional extracurricular activities found at most schools are just a little bit different at Pomona. The newspaper, for example, is *The Student Life*, which is a weekly published by the student government. There are, however, at least three other newspapers that are available for students. One, *Collage*, is a six-college newsmagazine. The *Re-View*, a feminist publication formed in 1988, was begun by a group of Pomona women and receives most of its funding from the student government.

Intramural sports, such as rugby and lacrosse, have traditionally held active recruiting sessions, along with the usual array of athletics, such as football, baseball, basketball, swimming, water polo, soccer, and tennis. Pomona College recently unveiled a multimillion dollar gymnasium, complete with weight room, squash and racquetball courts, basketball courts, and volleyball courts. Also completed in the last few years were new track and field and tennis facilities.

The radio station, KSPC, is the most powerful student-run radio station in the Los Angeles area, with a broadcasting radius of 35 miles. It has an alternative music format, with nearly half of the playing time dedicated to alternative rock music. There's no real definition of alternative rock, just as long as it's not commercial. The Cure is not alternative; Salem 66 and the Butthole Surfers are. The idea is to give airtime to bands that don't have big record corporations pushing airtime for them. About 100 students spin the vinyl, put the news on, and basically run the show. The station is funded in part by the student government, but mostly by the college administration.

Political clubs and social conscience clubs have a great presence in the college community, often bringing the Claremont Colleges together or fracturing them apart. Pitzer College has traditionally been one to lead the way in areas of social concern, such as the environment, but lately Pomona and Claremont McKenna have been taking the helm in such issues. Institutions such as the Women's Union, Central American Concern, Pan-African Students Association, MEChA, and Asian/Pacific-Islander Awareness Committee are among the many student organizations supported by the students of the Claremont Colleges.

The fraternities at Pomona like in many colleges in the country, are in danger of extinction, partly due to their own misadventures and partly due to a rejection of all-male social groupings on campus. At last count, there were seven fraternities, none of them national, on campus that appeal to a significant number of people. There are no sororities. Four of the seven fraternities have become coeducational, and the three that are all-male are being pressured by a significant group of students either to become coed or to disband.

Although the fraternities' alumni ties are strong, support for the fraternities has been weakening, especially for the all-male ones. Unfortunately, the good ones will die with the bad, and there is a strong possibility that there will be no fraternities at Pomona by the end of the 1990s.

There are choirs and orchestras to be joined, and campus bands generally can find parties to play, and vice versa. Additionally, ethnic, gay and lesbian, and women's organizations are exceptionally active on the campus.

GRADUATES

About 70% of all Pomona College graduates go on to graduate or professional schools within a few years of graduation, the administration says. And Pomona students have won their share of Marshall, Watson, Mellon, Fullbright-Hays, National Science Foundation, Luce, Truman, and Rotary scholarships and fellowships. About one-third of Pomona graduates are in business professions. Education and medicine are the next two largest fields that graduates have entered, with 20%

and 14% respectively; 10% have gone into law, and 5% each have gone into journalism and government service.

The career development office offers a library of alumni contacts, literature on various fellowships, scholarships and internships, listings of graduate schools, and job hunting techniques. Although these resources are helpful in getting a general idea of what is out there, specific information on jobs is something the student has to dig for. The office also offers individual counseling to students on how to find jobs, how to prepare résumés and cover letters, interviewing skills, and the basics on making contacts. For many students in liberal arts colleges, just deciding on the kind of job they want to do poses problems, and the career development office offers help in that also. There are over 1200 alumni in a network who are willing to talk with students and tell them about careers and contacts.

The on-campus recruiting by various companies, mainly insurance, finance, and retail companies, is an option taken by many students. The career development office also has developed a variety of summer and term-time internships in various fields, from government and law to sciences and the arts.

> *"Who said a liberal arts education doesn't teach you anything productive? Well, they are only partly right. Three of my friends who graduated with degrees in economics formed their own computer consulting firm in nearby Orange County. As a start-up company, it's doing a brisk, but growing business. At least one of them was hired away by a San Francisco investment firm. On the other hand, a friend of mine who graduated with me planned to be a lifeguard in Barcelona, Spain, until the 1992 Olympics. He ended up in Costa Rica, and Lord only knows where he is now. In any case, Pomona graduates are spread far and wide."*

SUMMARY OVERVIEW

Pomona College combines the personal advantages of a small college with the resources of a larger university, culminating in a well-endowed liberal arts institution with a tradition of excellence. The classes are small, the faces are friendly, and the sun is ever shining.

The size of Pomona implies limited. But on the contrary, it also means flexible. If it's not here, it can be developed with a little time and effort. Create your own major, design your own thesis, plan out a summer reading course with your professor. If it's not done on a formal level, it can be done informally.

The other five colleges in the Claremont system give Pomona College the depth and resources of a much larger university. Classes and course schedules for just about every need are available, and the extensive exchange programs with institutions both domestically and abroad make Pomona an ideal place for those wanting to stretch their horizons.

The sun is a powerful force, even in education, and it is little wonder that the Aztecs worshipped it. Here, it means a calm and inviting atmosphere to concentrate on whatever the student decides is important. The ocean is 35 miles away; the snow in the mountains is maybe an hour away. The skiing isn't like Aspen, but it is skiing.

But the school is small, and there is no escaping it. You know everybody and, for better or worse, everyone knows you. It's hard to get away from it all and start anew.

The cost of the college can be prohibitive. They say that cost should not be a factor in choosing your education, but when you're looking at the thousands of dollars in loans to pay off at the end of four years, it can be a little daunting. They say it hits the middle class the hardest, and being from the middle class, I would say it's true.

Finally, despite how wonderful Pomona College looks on paper and in pictures, it is relatively unknown outside southern California, and somewhat unknown even within the region. If it's a reputation you're looking for, Pomona is not the right choice. Still, about 60% of the student population come from outside California.

Pomona College lets the students create what they want, to a reasonable extent, with the option to do nothing. The relative freedom allowed at the college, the abundance of educational and cultural opportunities, and the time, space, and setting given the students make the Pomona diploma a very valuable one.

Jonathan Gaw, B.A.

Princeton University

THE PROGRAM

"For me, Princeton was an easy school to fall in love with. The first time I ever went to Princeton was during the university's colorful June reunion weekend. I was immediately struck by Princeton's sheer beauty. Covered with Gothic architecture, grass quads, and even black squirrels, the campus could be described only as idyllic. Then there were the reunions—5000 alumni, clothed in orange and black, faithfully returning to their alma mater—the spirit and happiness radiating from campus was enough to make any teenager feel very comfortable.

"The Princeton I attended was even better than the one I first visited. The beautiful campus was only a cosmetic preview of the astounding academic program to be found inside the ivy-covered walls. Reunions, meanwhile, proved to be the first of many wonderful Princeton traditions; these traditions did not bog Princeton down in the old-fashioned; instead, they did a lot to enhance everyday college life."

Unquestionably, Princeton remains one of the finest academic institutions in the world and one of the most challenging. The faculty is first-rate, and the student body of roughly 4500 is drawn from one of the most competitive applicant pools in the country. At the heart of a Princeton education lies the university's total commitment to its undergraduates. At Princeton, you really believe that the university and the professors are there for you because there are no law, business, or medical schools, and the graduate school, although quite strong, remains small and relatively hidden.

"I remember that during my first semester at Princeton, I took a course on political theory. Our first paper was on Plato, and I was completely lost. However, not only did I have the professor as

*my teacher for precept, but I was also able to go in and see him
one afternoon and discuss Plato and my paper with him. I never
really mastered Plato or any of the other great theorists for that
matter. However, thanks to that professor and Princeton, I got
much more out of that course than I ever thought possible."*

Princeton is academically very difficult. Professors expect a great deal, and students are there to work (you would be amazed at the number of hours some people are willing to devote to their courses). In comparison with other schools, the Princeton course load for A.B. candidates is surprisingly light—only 30 courses over eight semesters (B.S.E.s are not as lucky; they need 36 courses). Nevertheless, Princeton's emphasis on independent study more than compensates for this lighter course load. In addition to writing one or two junior papers (JPs), every candidate for the A.B. degree (and many in the engineering school) must complete a thesis. Theses usually run between 80 and 100 pages, and the project unfailingly becomes the obsession of every Princeton senior.

Although many schools move towards more structured and practical majors, Princeton continues to be a firm believer in the well-rounded liberal arts education. A.B.s are required to take two courses in each of four broad areas in addition to demonstrating proficiency in a foreign language; meanwhile, they are required to earn only ten credits in their major, and even this number can be reduced by taking related courses. Students have 32 majors to choose from, but, not surprisingly, the standard liberal arts majors—history, politics, English, and economics—remain the most popular. Engineers, who make up 15% of every class, are also required to branch out into other areas; they must take seven courses in the humanities and social sciences in addition to their engineering work.

The social life at Princeton essentially revolves around the university's eating clubs; they are as much a part of Princeton as Nassau Hall, the thesis, and the legendary Bill Bradley. The system itself consists of the 13 privately-owned clubs that line Prospect Street directly adjacent to the university. Created over a century ago, these clubs—regular mansions complete with dining halls, libraries, pool and television rooms, and bars—are similar to fraternities and sororities except that they are responsible for feeding over 75% of the junior and senior classes. For many, club life is the best part of Princeton.

For the first half of the twentieth century, Princeton was seen as being very elitist. Nevertheless, the Princeton of today is a long way from the Princeton of yesteryear. This is not to say that Princeton can be seen in the same light as a Brown or a Harvard; Princeton's alumni and board of trustees remain quite conservative, and the university still recruits roughly 40% of every class from private schools and 15% from the genes of its alumni.

Nevertheless, Princeton today is dominated by a student body that truly comes from all walks of life. There are students from all 50 states and over 50 foreign countries. Minorities make up 18% of the undergraduate population; roughly 6% are black while over 4% are foreign citizens. In addition, a liberal left-wing group has rooted itself on campus in recent years, leading protests on everything from apartheid to the CIA to sexual harassment. Yes, there remains on campus a strong, social, Yuppie community, largely centered on the selective eating clubs and the major athletic teams. However, there also has emerged on campus a more artistic, more liberal community. Finally, the backbone of the university is really a more middle-class, hardworking circle of students. All of these groups coexist smoothly, and they are in no way mutually exclusive.

Princeton is a school that has continued to improve tremendously with age. Life at Princeton is enhanced by many wonderful traditions, such as the academic Honor Code, but Princeton is not dominated by tradition. Princeton is truly a great place to spend four years. Most students are able to get out of it both socially and academically largely what they want, and they would quickly vote to attend again if they were given the choice.

GETTING IN/FINANCIAL AID

As difficult as Princeton is, perhaps the hardest part is actually receiving that acceptance letter. Princeton received well over 14,000 applications last year, but only 2043 candidates were offered admission. Average SAT I scores for a recent entering class were 650 verbal and 700 math, and 90% of the students were in the top 10% of their class. A recent class consisted of no less than 205 high school valedictorians.

Princeton's only true admission requirements consist of the SATs, three achievement tests, and the application. Nevertheless, it is recommended that a student complete four years of English, math, and a foreign language, and two years each of history and science. Like all colleges, Princeton has an admissions process surrounded by a haze. No one really knows how the office determines whom to take and whom to reject. According to admissions officer Spencer Reynolds, though, one can continue to expect "the strongest emphasis to be put on the academic component — the kinds of courses students take and how they do."

Princeton is one of the few schools that offers an early action program (E.A.). As with any early decision plan, if you apply by early November, you are informed of the committee's decision just before Christmas; however, with E.A., if you are accepted, you are not required to reply before May 1, and you are also not required to withdraw your other applications. The advantage of going E.A. is that if you are successful, it can make the entire college admission process a whole lot easier. E.A. is not recommended for the person who is counting on showing improvement in the senior year, but if you have a consistently solid record, give it a shot. One advantage of E.A. is that very few candidates are rejected; most are simply deferred into the regular applicant pool.

There are of course, intangibles that can play a significant role in the admission process. Legacies receive special consideration as they do at many schools (47% of the 389 alumni children who applied for the class of 1995 were admitted). Furthermore, athletics are also carefully considered. Athletic talent, especially in Princeton's traditional sports such as football, basketball, and hockey, combined with competent grades and board scores can be a ticket in.

Princeton is very proud of its financial aid program. Admissions are completely need-blind. Financial aid from the university is also given only on the basis of need; that is, no scholarships are conferred for either academic or athletic prowess. The university paid out almost $14 million in pure financial aid in the most recent year to roughly 42% of the undergraduate population.

> *"Perhaps the most comforting part about Princeton's financial aid is that it is kept very confidential. Even after four years of Princeton, I have almost no clue who of my friends received aid and who did not."*

At Princeton, there are ample student jobs on campus for scholarship and non-scholarship students alike, and most pay well. In addition, the Student Agencies give a handful of students the opportunity to run their own businesses and make a significant amount of money in the process. There is also a thriving ROTC scholarship program.

Overall Princeton admissions are not very obliging, but if you get in, the university is very accommodating in helping finance your education.

ACADEMIC ENVIRONMENT

Academically, Princeton surely will not disappoint; it might frustrate you and it might make for sleepless nights, but you will learn.

With the largest endowment per student of any school in the country, Princeton has at its disposal some of the finest facilities, and it continues to expand. Firestone Library, already one of the largest open-stack libraries in the world with over 4 million books and 40,000 current journals, has recently added an entire new wing. The university's art center and its art museum have also both been completely renovated. In 1986, Princeton opened a new $29 million molecular biology building that will help the school move to the forefront of that field. Students also have at their disposal an ever-expanding computer network. Princeton's main system is an IBM 3081 with 32 million bytes of main storage. Perhaps more significant, though, there are micro-computer clusters all over campus stocked with hundreds of IBM PC's, Macintoshes, and laser printers for the student who just wants to write an English paper.

More important than the facilities, though, is that Princeton has a world-class faculty. Three current faculty members are Nobel laureates, and 12 have won Mac-

Arthur Foundation "genius" grants. The faculty includes such luminaries as Joyce Carol Oates, Toni Morrison, John McPhee, Paul Volcker, and Stephen Cohen. Princeton is considered to have the finest math and philosophy departments in the world, and its French, German, history, physics, biology, art history, and political science departments also rank right up there with the best of them. The engineering school is also very well regarded, especially in the areas of mechanical and aerospace engineering. The only areas where Princeton is considered somewhat weak are in some of the social sciences, such as sociology and anthropology.

For people who want a more flexible academic slate, Princeton also has 20 interdepartmental programs ranging from Afro-American studies to creative writing. In addition, a student, with the backing of two professors, can create an independent major. Be warned, though; Princeton is not nearly so flexible away from campus. Students can go abroad, but it is not nearly as encouraged as it is at other schools. Furthermore, it is almost impossible to take a semester off and get credit unless you have advanced standing.

Perhaps Princeton's most unique program is the Woodrow Wilson School, designed to prepare students for leadership in public affairs. The school emphasizes the concept of problem-solving in such areas as urban affairs and economic policy. The school limits enrollment to 80 students per class, and the competition for the spots is fierce. The school is also full of budding politicos, which can be a real turnoff to many students.

The true greatness of the Princeton education comes from the close contact between top professors and undergraduates. The student-to-faculty ratio at Princeton is an impressive seven to one, and you can take a course from virtually any professor on the faculty. All those things you are told before you get here about being able to work with this professor or that professor are completely true. The trade-off is that because Princeton's faculty is smaller than those at many other top research universities, its course curriculum tends to be less sizable, and occasionally class enrollment is limited.

Courses at Princeton generally consist of two lectures and a class per week. Engineering and science courses might meet more than this and usually include a lab period. A great source of pride for Princeton is the small classes, which meet along with the lectures in social science and humanities courses. Known as preceptorials, these small classes (usually six to 15 students) were begun by Woodrow Wilson when he was president of the university with the idea of encouraging more in-depth discussion of specific topics.

> *"I can remember some precepts I had that were taught by professors: They were so inspiring and informative. I can also remember precepts taught by inexperienced grad students: They were boring and added nothing to the course. Unfortunately, the problem is that you have no control over who you get, and you only get lucky a little more than half the time. Be assured, though; those times when you get a quality preceptor make the whole system incredibly worthwhile."*

Professors are readily accessible to Princeton students. They regularly set aside a couple of hours each week when students can go to their offices and talk. Students undoubtedly will have their closest contact with a professor during their independent work. In writing the thesis and the junior paper (sort of a practice run), students not only research both primary and secondary sources, but they also discuss their theories and strategies at length with their adviser. Independent work really allows a student to rub elbows with a professor as a peer, not as a student.

Comparing the JP and the thesis is like comparing a quiz to a final exam. The thesis is a legend; as the deadline approaches, every senior receives (and expects) total sympathy from every underclassman. Obviously, some students work diligently on their theses throughout the senior year. Most, though, sort of casually think about it the first semester then go into high panic second semester (this is almost another tradition at Princeton).

> *"For me, the thesis truly was the most academically rewarding part of Princeton. Before I finished I had always heard this and never once believed it. Working on my thesis was at times a nightmare. I had my moments writing and talking with my adviser when I would become enthusiastic and thrilled about what I was doing; however, these were outweighed by the instances of panic and stress when I felt like my ideas made no sense or when I could do nothing but stare at the blinking cursor on the blank computer screen. Nevertheless, something happens when you finally turn the thesis in. I have never had a greater sense of accomplishment."*

Professors at Princeton expect a great deal, and unlike standard procedure at many schools, late papers really are not tolerated. Furthermore, most students at Princeton are very driven; thus, there is sort of a peer pressure to work that does not exist at many other universities. Nevertheless, one can get by at Princeton without working very hard, especially if one uses his or her gut courses and six pass/fail options judiciously. Furthermore, Princeton is very lenient when it comes to levying academic suspensions. Finally, Princeton has its own built-in safety mechanism for people who are lax about their work: reading period. At the end of every semester, the university has a two-week period without classes when students are supposed to study for exams; however, students can, and many do, use this time to catch up on all the reading that they somehow "forgot" to do during the semester. However, before you get too excited about the reading period, keep in mind a couple of things: a) professors know you have all this extra time, and most assign an extra paper; b) with so much time to study, the pressure only builds. For instance, reading period for the fall semester doesn't begin until January; hence, you'll be expected to take an exam at the end of January for a course you have not actually attended in over a month. This exam, and possibly a paper too, will loom over your head all through the holiday season.

"Overall, I found the work load at Princeton to be tough but not backbreaking. There are times, such as during exams and when JP and thesis deadlines are bearing down, when stress just radiates from the campus, and the pressure is quite a bit to be reckoned with. However, the whole rest of the time things are very manageable. Yes, there is always a lot of reading. However, you only have weekly assignments, and outside of the occasional problem set and paper, the assignments can be put off if necessary. (I should add that the engineers face an exception here. Most engineers have numerous daily and weekly homework assignments, and thus the work load is much more constant.) Ultimately, at Princeton, the work is there, but you still have plenty of spare time to have fun. If you're successful enough to get into Princeton, you can bet you can handle the work load."

SOCIAL LIFE

To talk about the social life at Princeton is really to talk about Prospect Street and the eating clubs. The clubs go a long way beyond their purpose of merely feeding upperclassmen. The clubs essentially provide juniors and seniors with a small, tight-knit community where they can go to escape and be with their friends. Upperclassmen not only eat all their meals at their clubs, but they often also study, party, and watch television there.

Membership at most of the clubs is based on a lottery system although five of the clubs remain selective and choose their members through a system similar to rush (known as Bicker). The Bicker system continues to create controversy. Some people see Bicker as an unnecessary selection process and criticize the pain it causes when inevitably some sophomores get turned away. Nevertheless, the clubs still remain one of the most revered elements of Princeton.

"For me, my club was definitely one of the best parts, if not the best, of my Princeton experience; outside of my roommates, my closest friendships came from my club, and I spent a significant part of every day (and weekend night) hanging out there."

The importance of the clubs also goes far beyond the role they play in the lives of club members. The clubs are where all Princetonians do by far the majority of their drinking and partying. Usually, two or three clubs have parties each weekend, and most students, even freshmen, can get in by obtaining a pass from a member. Prospect Street has become much stricter since an incident of alcohol poisoning. Nevertheless, the Street is still quite active. If you are looking for a hard-core party scene (huge parties and endless drinking games), you can find it at Princeton; it is not the scene of choice for a majority of students, but for a very significant minority it is a way of life.

Not joining a club has become a popular alternative for a large number of students, especially seniors. Non-club members can in their senior year live in Spelman Dormitory, which has fancy four-person suites complete with kitchens. Junior year, though, there are fewer options. In terms of a meal plan, one can eat either at Stevenson Hall, a university dining hall located on Prospect, or back with the freshmen and sophomores. The only other alternative is to cook for oneself in the very limited student kitchen facilities located in some of the dorms.

The social life away from the clubs is not great. First, 96% of the students live on campus, so there isn't much action off of it. In terms of a college town, Princeton is a long way from Georgetown or Cambridge. There are only a handful of night spots, and they are strict on age, not very crowded, and close sharply at 1 A.M. University-sponsored social events are poorly attended, and Princeton lacks a big student center. If you hate the clubs, perhaps the only saving grace is that New York and Philadelphia are both pretty close. There is a train station on the Princeton campus from which both cities can be reached in an hour. I did not know many students who went into either city frequently. However, when it is done, it can definitely offer a nice change of pace.

In order to improve the quality of life for freshmen and sophomores, the university five years ago implemented a residential college system similar to Yale's. These colleges are sort of mini-universities, complete with their own dining halls, libraries, and computer centers. The system has been easily accepted, and it has done a lot to bring freshmen and sophomores closer together and provide them with a greater sense of security. Perhaps the only drawback has been that it has led to further social fragmentation between younger students and upperclassmen; it has essentially split the college career into two parts: the college and the club.

Despite its reputation for academics, Princeton has a pleasant social environment. There is a substantial student population that is very active socially, and Prospect Street is just as alive as any fraternity row. More important, both the clubs and colleges do a great job of promoting strong social interaction and comfort. As with much of Princeton, the social life can cater to many different kinds of people.

EXTRACURRICULAR ACTIVITIES

For a university of its size, Princeton offers an extensive number of extracurricular opportunities. Despite its academic reputation, almost 40% of the student body participates in varsity or club sports. Although Princeton will never be thought of as a sports factory, athletes are just as serious and spend just as much time practicing as they would at a top athletic school. The Ivy League provides excellent balanced competition for Princeton, and in a number of men's and women's sports—crew, squash, swimming, lacrosse, softball, basketball, hockey—Princeton can play on the same field with just about any school in the country.

In addition to a large array of varsity sports, Princeton also has a number of teams that participate at the club level. Club sports, which range from ultimate Frisbee to power-lifting, receive minimal funding from the university and are usually taken less seriously, but they are just as popular. Princeton also has a wonderful intramural sports program. The university has a full-time intramural director, and the residential colleges and clubs make for a perfect system of teams. Sixty percent of the student body participates in intramural sports which range from the normal—flag football, softball, hockey and volleyball—to the more exotic—inner tube water polo, broomball, and wiffleball.

Of course, Princeton's extracurricular activities go far beyond athletics. Perhaps Princeton's most famous activity is the Triangle Club. Triangle, whose members have included Joshua Logan, Jimmy Stewart, and, yes, Brooke Shields, annually produces and takes on tour a musical revue. The club also performs a Broadway musical each fall. The university has eight student-run *a cappella* singing groups, which not only perform weekly on campus at arch sings but also travel extensively during school breaks. Other musical groups include the University Orchestra, the Glee Club, the Jazz Ensemble, and the University Band, which performs musical marching skits at all of the football games. Theater Intime, the Expressions Dance Company, and the Mime Company provide other performance options.

Princeton offers a number of opportunities in the area of communications. The *Daily Princetonian* and the *Nassau Weekly* are Princeton's two big newspapers. In addition, there are both conservative and liberal papers and a press club where students work as stringers for local papers. Princeton not only has its own radio station (WPRB) but also its own syndicated radio program ("American Focus"). Lastly, students produce two yearbooks and a humor magazine.

Princeton has a large student government, the USG. The Whig-Cliosophic is the oldest college political and debating society in the country; it regularly brings prominent speakers to campus, and its debate team remains one of the best in the country. The Student Volunteers Council recruits students for social service work, including the Big Brother/Big Sister program and the New Jersey Special Olympics. Additionally, Princeton's Outdoor Action program not only offers students the chance to participate in a wide variety of outdoor activities, but it also sponsors a number of very popular trips for incoming freshmen. There are hundreds of other clubs and organizations on campus ranging from the chess club to the soaring society.

There are also organizations at Princeton dedicated to improving the quality of life on campus. In addition to a number of religious groups and ethnic societies, Princeton has an International Center designed to help foreign students adjust to campus life and American culture. In addition, there is the Third World Center, which serves not only as a place for conferences, courses, and social events but also as a place where students can go to relax and study. The TWC plays a huge role in the lives of many foreign and minority students. Finally, the Women's Center tries to provide a more comfortable setting for the exploration of gender issues. Run by a more liberal faction of women, the Center has done a lot in recent years to raise campus awareness and improve the quality of female life.

Overall, opportunities abound for all different kinds of students. If something interests you, chances are you can find it at Princeton.

GRADUATES

There can be no question that a Princeton degree provides a great starting point for a career. The Princeton name carries a lot of weight in scholarly and corporate circles alike.

Graduate school is a popular option for many students. In a recent class, 32% of the seniors continued their education right after graduation—7% went to med school, 6% to law school, and 15% to graduate school in the arts and sciences, whereas almost another half reported they had definite plans eventually to return to the classroom.

Straight out of school, a significant number of Princeton students go through corporate recruiting and take analyst or marketing jobs. Another group of students take advantage of a program known as Princeton-in-Asia, which provides students with jobs (usually teaching) in China and Japan for one or two years.

In terms of long-range planning, close to half (39%) of this class listed employment in the profit-making sector as their ultimate career objective. Meanwhile, the rest of the class was almost evenly divided amongst the fields of law (10%), medicine (10%), education (9%), government and nonprofit employment (14%), and the arts (11%).

Depending on one's field, the university can be very helpful when it comes to gaining employment. Career Services does a great job of organizing and helping students with corporate recruiting and with applying to graduate school. In addition, its résumé and interview workshops receive strong praise. However, if you plan to go into a less popular, less glamorous field, Career Services cannot do a lot for you.

One needs to look no further than the size of Princeton's annual giving (over $20 million) or the popularity of its June reunions (over 5000 alumni return each year) to see the strength of its alumni network. Reunions must be seen to be believed; planning goes on all year long, and the weekend is culminated by the P-rade in which all alumni and their families (the P-rade usually totals well over 10,000 people) march across campus decked out in orange and black costumes.

"Upon arriving at Princeton, you quickly realize that the alumni hold the university in great esteem. There really seems to

be a genuine bond that exists among Princeton alumni, and they are quick to help each other out. The alumni network is extensive. Personally, in looking for a job, I received an interview from a company solely, I believe, because the person I wrote to happened, without my knowing it, to have gone to Princeton."

Ultimately, one cannot beat the postgraduate opportunities that are opened up by a Princeton degree. In addition, Princeton's incredible alumni network provides not only comfort and security but also occasional assistance and connections.

SUMMARY OVERVIEW

Princeton University is truly an outstanding place to go to college. It offers a top-notch academic program, wonderful facilities, a surprisingly good social life, and a student body that is both diverse and gifted.

The strengths at Princeton are clear. Few schools can match Princeton when it comes to facilities. Furthermore, social, athletic, and extracurricular opportunities abound. Finally, Princeton's greatest strength will always be the education it is able to give. At no other institution in the United States is such a top-quality faculty so accessible to undergraduates. Through precepts and independent work, especially the thesis, you, as a Princeton student, will receive a rare opportunity to mingle intellectually with some of the finest minds in your field.

Obviously, like all schools, Princeton has its drawbacks. The university's biggest problem remains an unbalanced male/female ratio that continues to hover at 56/44. Students almost unanimously want it evened out. The administration has acknowledged the problem; however, it sees the ratio, according to Reynolds, "as a recruiting problem" and steadfastly refuses to adopt any kind of quota system to balance it. The backwards ratio ends up having a negative effect on the social system. First, there is almost no casual dating at Princeton. More important, the ratio in many cases leads to a kind of male bonding that leaves some women uncomfortable within the community.

There are also some other areas of controversy. The Bicker system is criticized as elitist and unnecessary. For some, the board of trustees remains too conservative and too slow to adopt new policies such as divestment. Finally, some minorities complain that they are not fully integrated into the community.

In the end, Princeton University remains a very special place to go to college. It represents a school that has many wonderful things to offer many different kinds of people. And, most important, for all there is an academic experience that is really second to none.

David Grumbaus, A.B.

Reed College

THE PROGRAM

"Reed changed my life. If you stop and think about it, any college will do that to you in some way or another, even if the most memorable part about the experience is just leaving home for the first time. But at Reed I was exposed to the possibilities and problems of questioning , talking, reading, writing, thinking—the life of the mind, I suppose. And now I'm always probing the world, asking questions, wondering, looking, figuring, It's a pretty confusing world, really. I wonder sometimes if it would be easier to just float through life— 'Hey, that's just the way it is.' But I've got the tools now to probe, ask, wonder, look, and figure in some intelligent, meaningful way. And even if I wanted to, I'm not sure that I could package up my experience at Reed and take it out with yesterday's trash. What I learned there has become an inextricable part of me."

If you really want to know what Reed is all about, ask a Reedie. Better yet, ask several. If there's one thing they share, it's a propensity for reflection and opinion about the place, what it does, what it should do, why it is good or bad (or both), what it should be. (Rumor has it that if n is the number of Reedies in a room, the number of opinions about a given topic will be $n + 1$.) This preoccupation with questioning the purpose and structure of the college says as much, if not more, about Reed than anything else. It's a place where questions are at least as important as answers, a place that thrives on thinking. This preoccupation is evidence that Reed does very well what it intends to do: teach people how to think about themselves, the world, what makes it tick, and what others have to say about it.

Reed is a small liberal arts college in Portland, Oregon. It is well known for its commitment to undergraduate teaching, its disregard for divisions between disciplines, and the quality and rigor of its curriculum. The low student-to-faculty ratio and the college's belief in the effectiveness of conference-style teaching encourage debate and interaction both inside the classroom and out. Socially, individual expression is valued highly; stifling expectations are not. Any extracurricular activities exist as an opportunity to participate, not spectate. It is a community of apparent opposites, where traditional educational theories mix with a unique social atmosphere in a way that is all Reed's own.

The Reed Institute, as it was first known, was named after a successful Portland businessman, Simeon Reed, whose estate provided the initial financing. (It was not founded by or named for, as various tales have it, Portland journalist John Reed, most recently portrayed in the movie *Reds*.) From the outset, the college was markedly different from existing institutions. Reed's first president, William Foster, and the original faculty successfully established a community where the life of the mind—not intercollegiate athletics, fraternities and sororities, or the quest for top spot on the dean's list—was considered most important. They were successful. Although the winds of higher education and American society have shifted repeatedly the last 75 or so years, Reed stubbornly has maintained its belief and practice that the life of the mind is both an important and a noble pursuit.

Reedies have long had a reputation as eccentric geniuses, hippies, radicals, or just plain nerds who lock up in the library night after night hunched over a pack of Camels, a thermos of coffee, and Kant's *Critique of Pure Reason*. Whatever names one assigns, Reed has always attracted people who are interested in and sensitive to the world around them, whether the focus of their attention is intellectual, cultural, social, or political. They expect a lot from each other, not just academically, but ethically as well. There are few hard and fast rules at Reed; the freedom to choose how you will interact with others is prized. One tie that binds is the Honor Principle, a statement that, loosely paraphrased, amounts to "you have your space, I have mine, let's respect both."

Academically, Reed has long had a reputation as one of the top liberal arts colleges in the country, both in academic (i.e., graduate and professional schools) and nonacademic circles. Several departments—biology, English, history, and chemistry—have been singled out in recent years as among the very best in the country. It's no surprise then, to find biology and English leading the list of most popular majors. Psychology, physics, and history round out the top five. And unlike many institutions, traditional divisions between students and disciplines—scientists on one side, humanists on the other—are more the exception than the rule.

One of the centers of campus is the library. It's unique in that it's open from 8 A.M. to 2:30 A.M. every day but Friday and Saturday (and then from 8 A.M. until midnight) and all day and night during finals week. Equally important, the local Domino's Pizza crew know exactly where the lobby is. With the exception of the science majors, who usually have thesis desks and lab space in their respective buildings, and psychology majors, who often receive offices in the basement of Eliot, most seniors have their thesis desks in the library. Assigned by lottery, these desks are theirs to keep for the year and often become a home away from home. Other desks are spread throughout the library, available for use by all, although the shelves above each can be claimed at the beginning of the semester by placing assorted books and papers on them. Although you can't evict someone from a desk, you can have a shelf and, usually, a place of your own to study. Equally important, it's a place where friends can find you to take you away for a break—perhaps another cup of coffee, a good concert, or dinner.

Several years ago, a new name was coined for the college: MacReed. Apples are everywhere. This is a result of Reed's participation in a nationwide consortium of colleges and universities, all of whom receive hefty discounts on Macintoshes from Apple. Forty-five Macs are housed in the Information Resource Center (IRC) in the library and are available 24 hours a day. From the IRC, you can look up books, send electronic mail, or just get down to the business of writing. A classroom with 15 more of the little boxes is made available to seniors when IRCs are too crowded. Laser printing costs ten cents per page. Twenty-four Macs are dispersed via lottery to groups of seniors and students receiving financial aid and in groups of three to everyone else. The Macs are theirs to keep and use for the year in return for a $250 deposit, $200 of which is refunded. The college also has a DEC system 5500, two Sequent S27 parallel computers, and a variety of workstations available around the clock for those interested in more serious number crunching.

When students are not working on their computers, they often are battling the elements, which in Portland is rain. It's no secret that it rains a lot in Portland, so much so that in mid-February T-shirts and bumper stickers that proudly proclaim, "Oregonians don't tan, they rust," cease to be funny. Actually, rain is too strong; it doesn't often pour buckets as in some places—it drizzles, sometimes for a few minutes, sometimes for days. Mostly in the winter, too. This requires that one always knows where the umbrella is (and, more importantly, how to use it), and keeping one eye on the lookout for puddles deeper than the sole of your shoe is thick. The alternative is to adopt the state of mind attitude embraced by many longtime Portland residents. That is to say, "rain is a state of mind; ignore it." Try it; it really works.

The benefits of rain far outweigh its negative aspects, however. First of all, winter and spring rains make summer vacation a welcome and anticipated event. Moreover, when classes start in August, reading outside on the front lawn just makes more sense than reading at a desk in the library, watching everyone else read outside. Also, if it weren't for the rain, the campus would wither and die. As it is, the grass is always green, the trees never die, and the air always has that clean, just-washed smell most people have only heard about in laundry commercials.

Portland usually heads the list, or is close to the top, in a number of America's most livable cities polls, and with good reason. One recent study conducted by the Palo Alto-based Collagen Commission for the Study of Beauty and Aging determined that Portland is easier on the complexion than any city in the United States! In Bridgetown (so named because of the many bridges that span the Willamette River, joining the east and west sides of town), summers are warm, spring and fall are pleasant, and winter snows are rare. The largest city in Oregon, Portland is unpretentious and accessible, yet possesses a big city feel and offers an abundance of activities: lectures and exhibitions, professional and semiprofessional sports, and an especially active theater, music, and arts scene.

Reed isn't for everyone. But for those with the desire to learn and to participate in their own education, and for those who seek an energetic, reflective community, Reed can be a welcome surprise.

GETTING IN/FINANCIAL AID

"Reading and evaluating applications is hard work, the evaluating part much more so than the reading part. Once you're past the name and address, you tread the ground of someone's personal history. High school transcripts, SAT scores, recommendations, essays, interview summaries—all fall under your scrutiny. You have ten to 12 pieces of paper with which you try to get to know someone you've often never met, develop opinions about them, and decide if they are a good match for the college. It's a process with few, if any, fixed rules, minimums, or maximums, and therein lies its beauty."

Every application for admission to Reed is evaluated by at least three people, sometimes by as many as ten, including admissions professionals, student interns, and faculty. Approximately 2000 people apply for one of about 300 places in the freshman class. The male/female ratio is 52/48, and about 18% are ethnic minorities. Reedies come from all over the United States and from around the world, but more than half hail from the Atlantic and Pacific costs. The majority of admitted students rank in the top 20% of their class and have combined SAT I scores of 1270, but Reed has no GPA or high school course work requirements and no minimum SAT I cutoffs. Essays, recommendations, and interview reports are evaluated with transcripts and test scores in an attempt to gauge both an applicant's enthusiasm and seriousness about learning, and his or her ability to succeed academically at Reed. Ultimately, each reader tries to answer the question: Will this person be a successful member of the Reed community?

The bad news is that Reed's tuition, room and board, and student body fees recently totaled $25,600 a year. The good news is that more than half of the student body receives some form of financial aid, assistance that is guaranteed in successive years as long as a student maintains satisfactory academic progress and demonstrates need. The familiar Financial Aid Form (FAF) and Reed's own financial aid application are the primary sources of information used in determining need, but the financial aid director always is willing to discuss individual circumstances.

ACADEMIC ENVIRONMENT

"I don't think I really appreciated some of the distinctive things about Reed's academic character—conferences, professors who are accessible and interested in talking after class, written comments instead of letter grades, even lots of reading and papers— until I left Reed for a semester to attend a university on the East Coast. The differences were immediately apparent. Large lectures were standard fare, exams (I wrote no papers) were returned unmarked but for a grade on the booklet cover. My professors were surprised when I came to them with questions or an argument. As for my classmates, the majority were interested only in absorbing and regurgitating whatever information was necessary for a good grade. I returned to Reed the following fall, feeling lucky, and eager to get back to the grind. With a context in which to place my academic experience at Reed, it finally dawned on me what education can and should be."

Two adjectives come to mind when describing the academic environment at Reed: enthusiastic and rigorous. Teaching is the college's primary mission; teaching people how to think, its primary goal. Accordingly, both professors and students are serious about and interested in learning. Tales of scholars barking down from the ivory tower to a numb, faceless mass aren't told at Reed. The professors listed in the back of the college catalog are scholars *and* the same people who lead discussions, give lectures, explain and assist in labs, read papers, and assign grades—there are no graduate students or teaching assistants. Likewise, Reedies are anything but numb and faceless. If it is possible to characterize the academic personality of Reed students, it would not be inaccurate to say that they like learning, that they want to learn more about the things that interest them and discover new interests, and that they take an active role in the whole process because doing it any other way just doesn't make much sense. Besides, it would be boring.

With such emphasis on academics, one might think that intense competition among students is not only expected, but inevitable. Fortunately, neither is true. This is due in part to the college's de-emphasis of grades. Papers and exams are returned with comments and questions, not letters and percentages. And although grades are assigned, recorded by the registrar, and given to a student's adviser, they are not posted, or sent to students or parents (students and advisers are notified, however, if a grade of C- or below is assigned at midterm or at the end of a semester). Some students check their grades frequently, others not so, and some never do. The emphasis throughout is on learning as an ongoing process, not an event whose passage is marked by a letter or summed up in a transcript.

Classes at Reed typically are conferences of 15–20 people or combinations of lectures and conferences, providing an interactive forum for discussion, explanation, agreement, disagreement, and reasons why. The goal is not simply to absorb information (although that happens, too), but rather to think critically about things, to form opinions and shape ideas—often different from traditional or accepted positions—and to learn how to defend them. Clear, effective writing is emphasized from day one, so frequent papers and lab reports are the rule. Individual interaction between faculty and students is frequent and encouraged, from scheduled paper conferences and thesis meetings to impromptu hallway stops and office visits. There is, quite frankly, a feeling (indeed, a belief), that students and professors are partners in a mutual, exciting intellectual enterprise.

The cornerstones of the Reed curriculum are Humanities 110 and the senior thesis; each is required by all for graduation. Taken in the first year, Humanities 110, known simply as Hum (pronounced H-yoom) investigates the civilizations of ancient Greece and Rome and proceeds through the Middle Ages to Dante and the threshold of the Renaissance. Lectures, conferences, frequent writing assignments, and individual paper conferences with professors introduce students to Reed's academic approach, and strengthen writing skills. The thesis, though, brings it all together.

> *"The thesis parade was the end for me; graduation paled in comparison. Sure, I still had orals and three papers to write, but after I handed four copies of my thesis to the registrar 15 minutes earlier, in my mind this was the grand finale. It was another December day in Portland: wet. Drenched and delirious, I stood on the library steps, a bottle of champagne in each hand, screaming and hollering for all I was worth. Thirty or 40 of us marched to the cadence of kazoos and clapping hands from the library to the registrar's office, whereupon we received our congratulatory lollipop, ran back outside, and screamed and shouted and drank some more.*
>
> *"I suppose I took the whole project to the extreme: reading, thinking, talking, blabbering, writing until I was drunk with ideas, opinions, confusion. I didn't pay much attention to my other two classes that final semester. I'm not sure if that kind of single-mindedness is a particularly good way of going about it, and I'm fortunate that it was a good experience for me; it isn't for everyone. And sure, I'm romanticizing some: grinding it out, tapping the keyboard, and checking the* MLA Handbook *a zillion times was tiresome, frustrating work. But I felt I'd really found something new to say, and it all seemed so important, so terribly important. I thought big and little thoughts, said big and little things, some of them good, some of them silly, some of them downright horrible. In the end, though, they were my thoughts, my words. When was the last time you said that about anything?"*

The senior thesis is a year-long independent project in the student's major field undertaken with the advisement of a faculty member in the department. Projects run the gamut from artistic, musical, and dramatic creations to scientific experiments to research and interpretation in any number of areas. A few students know exactly what they want to do, some have an assortment of possible ideas, and still others haven't a clue. Not to worry, though: two to four weeks into the first semester of the senior year, most departments require that a summary statement be filed. Thereafter, a variety of deadlines ensure some sort of orderly march to the final draft. Theoretically, the brunt of one's research and/or experimentation should be completed during the first semester, the majority of the writing, during the second. However, the thesis is not complete until the orals. Convened during Reading Week, the oral is an opportunity to discuss and defend one's ideas and conclusions with four or more faculty members. Food and drink are customary (some hold that the quality of the thesis is in inverse proportion to the extravagance of the spread) and reactions vary ("They liked it" or "I got crucified"), when it's done, your thesis is bound, cataloged, and added to the thesis shelves in the art tower of the library.

Reed is organized into five divisions, each with numerous departments. Students can select from the following majors: anthropology, American studies, art, biochemistry and molecular biology, biology, chemistry, chemistry-physics, Chinese, classics, classics-religion, dance-theater, economics, English literature, French literature, general literature, German literature, history, history-literature, international studies, linguistics, literature-philosophy, literature-theater, mathematics, mathematics-economics, mathematics-physics, mathematics-sociology, music, philosophy, philosophy-mathematics, philosophy-religion, physics, political science, psychology, religion, Russian literature, sociology, Spanish literature, and theater.

Reed has a number of requirements for graduation. Besides Hum 110 and the senior thesis, there are general distribution requirements met by courses chosen from four groups: literature, philosophy, and the arts; history, social sciences, and psychology; the natural sciences; and mathematics, logic, or foreign language or linguistics. Two units from each group *in the same discipline* are required. In addition, each division and department has its own requirements, some of which may satisfy the general distribution requirements, some of which may not. Finally, everyone must complete six quarters of physical education. It seems like a pretty confusing system. Thankfully, everyone is assigned an adviser and given a catalog at registration; among the three of you, you'll make some sense of it.

Reed also offers special programs, including off-campus study (both foreign and domestic) and 3–2 programs, wherein students spend three years at Reed and two at another institution, and receive degrees from both. Reedies have opted for off-campus study at, among others, Howard University (Washington, D.C.), Tübingen University and the University of Munich, University of Costa Rica, Beijing Teachers College (People's Republic of China), and St. Petersburg University and the ACTR/Pushkin Institute in Moscow. The 3–2 programs include applied physics and electronic science with the Oregon Graduate Institute; art with the Pacific Northwest College of Art; computer science with the University of Washington or Oregon Graduate Institute; engineering with Cal Tech, Columbia University, Washington University, or Rensselaer Polytechnic Institute; and forestry with Duke University.

SOCIAL LIFE

"A friend of mine once said that the social life at Reed is whatever you choose to make it. That's the best answer to the question, 'What's the social life like at Reed?' It's not difficult to plunk down in the library, the lab, or at a desk at home and spend most of one's waking hours trying to get ahead, trying to stay even, or trying to catch up. And it's not difficult to hang out, study a little, and get by. Most important, a person can be whomever and can do whatever they choose without running the risk of ridicule or exclusion. There simply aren't any fixed expectations about what people should do with their time. That may frighten people who are looking for some sort of defined or regimented social life in which everyone participates in a specific manner, but for those who seek spontaneity, who value whatever you choose to make of it, Reed is a wonderful place to be."

To the casual observer, social life at Reed may not appear particularly exciting. Reedies do what students at other colleges and universities around the country do: drink coffee, hang out with friends in the coffee shop or library and talk about politics, what happened in class, or the weather; they go to dinner, movies, concerts, parties, lectures; they eat, drink, and make merry with one's dormies; they play rugby or tennis or softball or Frisbee. What is exciting, however, is the idea that one can have a social life on one's own terms. There are no fraternities, sororities, or exclusive clubs; there is no expected or normal social life. Reed is a collection of people doing what they want to do when they want to do it.

Off campus, there is all of Portland, a friendly, inexpensive city. There's an abundance of dinner-for-$5-or-less eateries and for the all-nighter crowd, it's tough to beat the Original Pancake House for a 3 A.M. cholesterol and caffeine boost. Thursday night (or any other night for that matter) at the Lutz is the perfect pool, pinball, and blitz thesis break. Fifteen minutes away is downtown, and all that downtown stuff: concerts, movies, restaurants, and dessert and coffee shops. It is also home to Powells, one of the best bookstores on the West Coast, if not the country. A city block big, the City of Books is a potpourri of new and used books (and the place to find all those paperbacks on next semester's syllabus dirt cheap complete with notes in the margins from four or five years ago).

With the Cascade Mountains to the east and the Coast Range to the west, a variety of outdoor recreation is on Portland's doorstep. To the east, skiers hit the slopes on Mt. Hood and Mt. Bachelor, and boardheads sail in the Columbia River Gorge, one of the world's premier windsurfing hotspots. And a bit more than an hour to the west lies the rugged and beautiful Oregon Coast.

EXTRACURRICULAR ACTIVITIES

The operative word in any description of extracurricular activities at Reed is participation. From the student newspaper, *The Quest*, to team and individual sports, students begin, organize, perform, and fund a variety of goings-on. What this boils down to is an opportunity to participate in over 100 organizations and activities, from Amnesty International to yoga. In recent years, the list of organizations and activities has included such diverse ones as aikido, the Collegium Musicum, Environmental Coalition, Gay Lesbian Bisexual Union, Cultural Affairs Board, Music Listening and Lending Library, Poetry Forum, rugby, *Rude Girl Press*, sailing, and Volunteer Tutoring Program.

Two annual events (they are no mere activities) deserve special mention. The first, *Paideia*, is a two-week period in January before the beginning of spring semester set aside for students and faculty alike to dabble in those things that just can't be squeezed into a busy semester. Calligraphy, cooking, dance, massage, computers, fitness, even underwater basket weaving—the classes are offered by students, faculty, staff and numerous imported experts, so the sky's the limit. The other is Renaissance Fayre (or just Ren Fayre), a weekend of fun and frivolity that begins with the thesis parade on the last day of classes. Whatever else one may call it, Ren Fayre is, quite simply, a knock down, drag out party to celebrate the near completion of another year. Thankfully, Reading Week falls between Ren Fayre and final exams, ostensibly for reading up and preparing for exams. In practice, however, it's the time to sleep it off, complete thesis orals, write those overdue (or soon-to-be-due) papers, *and* prepare for finals.

> *"I was a quasi-jock in high school: enough talent and enthusiasm to make the team, but a far cry from being able to play seriously at the major college level. Upon graduation, I thought my days of competitive sports were finished. And they were sort of: I played on and coached the Reed basketball team. We had a schedule, uniforms, referees, and a scoreboard. That's where the similarities to big-time college sports end. We practiced only once a week (and at the end of the semester, there was a telltale glassy-eyed look), tried to run plays, argued strategy during time-outs and took great pride in our irreverence. But we got a chance to compete, usually against some pretty talented teams. Most importantly, though, we all played and, I think, all had a hell of a lot of fun."*

Sports at Reed may be a contradiction for those who want to know where the stadium is, what league Reed belongs to, and why there are no box scores in Sunday's paper, but for those who like to *do*—not watch and wait—it makes perfect sense. Reedies stream into the Sports Center daily to work on their squash game, swim a few laps, take a fencing lesson, or learn how to dance. If something isn't offered, a suggestion may find you teaching. For those seeking team competition, team sports include basketball, soccer, and men's and women's rugby, to name a few, and are often organized and coached by students. The emphasis throughout is on learning and doing, not winning and losing—a breath of fresh air for those who want to compete *and* have fun.

As there are only enough rooms on campus for a bit more than half of the student population, housing at Reed sometimes can be an adventure, depending on your viewpoint and experience. Frosh are guaranteed a room (although they are not required to live on campus); the rest are assigned by lottery: seniors first, then juniors, then sophomores. Needless to say, most people end up living off campus for at least a year, either by choice or bad luck. There, you are introduced to the realities of rent, housemates, the phone and power companies, cooking and dishes, and paid and unpaid bills—in short, what life is like after college. As Reedies have been living in the neighborhood for years, there are a number of Reed houses—big, multibedroom places that have been rented to students year in and year out forever.

On-campus housing, on the other hand, is ready-made: roommates, heat, meals in Commons. Some dorms, though, are better than others. The newly restored Old Dorm Block (Ladd, Abington, Kerr, Eastport, Westport, Doyle, Quincy, and Winch) and Anna Mann (almost all of its rooms are singles; its occupants, mostly seniors) are great. Both are older and quaint. They're tops, unless you have some fluency in Russian, Spanish, French, or German, in which case you can apply for a space in one of the cozy language houses, faculty residences from the college's earlier days. The Cross-Canyon dorms are next on the preference list, occupying a middle position between quaint and cell-block. Last and certainly least are MacNaughton and Foster/Scholz. Several theme houses also exist, each with a different slant, depending on the interest of current students: an Asia house with a resident Chinese scholar, a greenhouse, for people interested in environmental issues, and for those interested in bits and bytes, a computer house, and others.

GRADUATES

"Trying to categorize what it is that Reedies do after graduation is difficult at best. Trying to assign careers or jobs to majors is, as fast as I can tell, nearly impossible. One friend of mine, a history major, worked in the admissions office and now teaches English to Japanese schoolchildren. Another, an international studies major, is at Berkeley studying law. Two buddies that I still play basketball with, one a French major, the other an English major, play in a successful rhythm and blues band here in Portland. Another friend of mine, an economics major, worked as a financial analyst in Portland for several years and now lives in St.

Louis where she is pursuing her M.B.A. and helping run the family wholesale produce business. Three friends are in graduate school, one in classics at Princeton, one in religion at Brown, one in rhetoric at Berkeley. Another, a biology major and avid fisherman and hunter, runs his own guide business. I guess it is safe to say that Reedies do, and are prepared to do, whatever they damn well please."

Yes, Virginia, there is life after Reed. Or, more accurately, there are lives after Reed, for the highways and byways that Reedies explore are as numerous and diverse as the interests and desires of each individual. More than one third of the graduating class continue in their major or related fields in graduate programs at some of the top schools in the country. (Are they prepared? A few report that their graduate program is easier than Reed. Go figure it.) About the same number of grads begin law school, business school, and medical school, to name a few professional programs, also at many of the top schools in the country. A bit more than one-fourth successfully test the job market, from teaching to research assistantships to internships to a variety of positions with nonprofit organizations and businesses worldwide. Many travel and there are those, of course, who just plain hang out.

For many, if not most, life after Reed begins sometime during the senior year with a visit to the Career Advising Office. All the essential job-hunt and graduate school admissions information is available here, from handouts and advice on résumés and cover letters to GRE and fellowship applications, and graduate school catalogs. Here, too, is where job hunters get the names of alums to contact.

Down the line a few years, or more than a few, the picture doesn't change drastically. Reedies are everywhere: more than one third are in academia; about one fifth are in business; another third pursue careers in a number of areas—law, medicine, computer science, government, journalism, the arts. Some are traveling and many are raising families. If it is possible to distill a common denominator or lesson about life, or lives, after Reed, it would be that being able to read, write, and think critically and effectively—in short, to solve problems of all shapes and sizes—has not gone out of style.

SUMMARY OVERVIEW

"What's good and what's bad about Reed? Depends on who you ask. Everyone has a different opinion, experience, attitude, or idea. And for all the good and bad things that people find, there are at least as many suggestions and theories about what should be changed and what should be left alone. That's the kind of place Reed is, I suppose: it grows on you, for better or worse. You become attached to the place, spend time thinking about it, and

end up extolling its virtues or pointing out all its faults, often in the same breath. It can be a magical, frustrating, happy, depressing, crazy place.''

What's remarkable about Reed academically is not that its faculty is committed to, and very good at, undergraduate teaching, nor its emphasis on conference-style teaching, nor its belief in breadth and depth in undergraduate education. Many good, small liberal arts colleges can and do make the same claims. What is remarkable is the enthusiastic attitude that pervades the place, a kind of naiveté, a belief in the power and intrinsic value of education. Hanging out in the library reading Kant all night or putzing around the lab running some fascinating (or not so fascinating) experiment are not only OK; they're even worthwhile; they're deserving of time and energy for their own sake. You don't have to be a rocket scientist to go to Reed, just enthusiastic about learning.

At Reed one doesn't have to contend with the silly posturing or elaborate fashion shows that dominate some places, or endure the fraternities, sororities, and exclusive clubs that foster specific conventions about social life at other places. Idiosyncrasy is welcome. In fact, although generalizations are notoriously dangerous, it might not be far from the truth to say that idiosyncrasy is the one thing Reedies have in common socially. It is, in short, a community inhabited by independent spirits.

Participation is one buzzword that probably is overused in this chapter, but it hits the nail on the head: participation in extracurricular activities at Reed is a very real phenomenon. You don't have to be good at or even knowledgeable about something in order to participate in some organization or activity; curiosity is enough.

The downside to academics at Reed is not intensity or too much work, though both are at the heart of the matter. It's work anxiety, that peculiar affliction wherein perfectly intelligent and capable people are immobilized by F.U.D.: fear, uncertainty, and doubt. Fear, because they're afraid they'll never get done whatever it is that's due; uncertainty, because they're not sure they can get it done; and doubt, because they're wondering what the hell they're doing there in the first place.

Reedies are such an independent, interesting group of people that the illusion of diversity is persistent and tempting. But the Reed population is remarkably homogeneous: it's a lot of smart, liberal, white, upper-middle-class children of intellectuals and professionals who for the most part live on the East and West Coasts. In other words, it's not Berkeley. If you're looking for racial, political, economic, and/ or cultural diversity, look elsewhere. Given those limitations, Reed's an exciting place, but it does have its limitations.

Within Reed, the stifling traditions of ivory towerism—like professors talking at students, not with them—are, by and large, extinct. Yet how students perceive Reed in relation to the outside world can be stifling. There's an arrogance that seems to say to the rest of the world, "Hey, look at me, I'm an intellectual and you're all morons." Interestingly enough, the net result of this preening around is a condition that most Reedies openly detest: ivory towerism. In this case, Reed is the ivory tower, the rest of the world, the madding crowd. For many, Reed is an island. That's too bad, because the rest of the world is a very real, very fascinating place to discover and explore.

There it is, the good and the bad. In short, Reed can be a wonderful place to go to college. Its philosophies about education translate into practices that liberate, not inhibit, the power of questioning and answering, reading and writing, thinking and wondering. The people that come to Reed do so not only because they like to read and think and ask and talk and write about ideas and people and books, but also because they want to be in a place where they can live life on their own terms. Reed is a place that allows, indeed, encourages, both. In an age where education often is viewed solely as a means to an end, a prelude to a lucrative meal ticket, getting excited about ideas "just for the hell of it" may not be particularly fashionable or necessarily lucrative (although sometimes it can be both), but it is unquestionably a pleasant, invigorating change of pace.

Brendon Reay, B.A.

Rice University

THE PROGRAM

"When I first considered Rice, I kept asking myself: if it's so good, why haven't I heard more about it? The answers I've found are these: it's small; it's in Houston, away from the media-saturated coasts; and at seventy five it's young for a major university.

"Rice is going to stay small, going to stay in Houston, and will never be older than Yale—but it is a top university, and it is becoming better known. When I applied to Rice a few years ago, people usually compared it to Emory and Duke. Now they're more likely to compare it to Harvard."

Lovett Hall, the centerpiece of Rice's academic quadrangle, isn't the model of ivy-covered austerity one expects from an institution of higher learning. Instead, the building is Italianate and overwhelming, replete with columns, wrought iron, and hand-carved marble. The building's carvings place the great thinkers of Western culture cheek-to-jowl with football players, nerds, and flirtatious coeds.

The building's symbolism fits Rice to a *T*. Like the building, Rice students bring foreign styles to Texas soil: the accents one hears on campus are about as likely to be from India or New Jersey as from Waco. And like the building, Rice students combine the solemn fruits of academia with a quirky sense of humor: tough class work doesn't stop them from turning around a 2000 pound statue of the university founder or electing a male homecoming queen.

Rice's 2700 undergraduate students are almost evenly split into S/Es (science and engineering majors) and academs (humanities and liberal arts majors), with a few handfuls of archis (architecture majors, pronounced AR-kees) and music majors. Of Rice's departments, the engineering and architecture programs have the strongest reputations. Though its programs in the humanities and social sciences are strong, they are not as well-recognized outside the Southwest; and Rice's Shepherd School of Music is still too young to have earned much of a reputation one way or another.

As an institution, Rice aims to combine the strengths of a small liberal arts school—small classes, approachable professors, and the feeling that one is a person, not a number—with the high-caliber research and faculty of large research universities. The combination works: most classes *are* small, usually with seven to 30 students; students often meet their professors outside the classroom, in relaxed settings such as the lunch table or the intramural soccer field; and top-notch researchers, not graduate students, teach introductory classes.

> *"Most of my professors knew my name. Some made heroic efforts to learn it: spending a few minutes of the first classes so each student could tell the class his or her name and a few personal things; calling random names from the class roll to answer questions; or even photographing the class so the professor could, in the comfort of his/her own home, practice matching our names to our faces. Knowing that my professor would notice that I'd skipped class was a powerful incentive to show up; and when I didn't do my best work, I sometimes felt guilty for letting the professor down. Few things in my academic career inspired me as much as knowing that a professor cared whether I—Lisa Gray, a sophomore in the third row back—understood the material."*

When flying over Houston, it's easy to see that the Rice campus—300 acres with 4000 trees—is only a few miles from downtown's postmodern high-rises. But inside the Rice hedges, students find it easy to forget they're in the fourth largest city in the United States. Students who do venture out find that Houston's problems are those of any large city: pollution, rush hour traffic, and crime. (Rice is in one of the city's richest, safest neighborhoods, so students needn't worry much about the last.) Houston's good points are also those of a large city: a lively nightlife, a varied population, and abundant entertainment, restaurants, and shopping.

Admittedly, Houston doesn't have the concentration of high-octane schools that Boston does, and it lacks the college town feel of Chapel Hill or Austin. But the necessary college student amenities—bookstores, bars, and bike repair shops—are easy to find here, and the city's diversity of thought easily rivals that of the biggest college towns. In Houston (as on the Rice campus), the art scene, the Republican Party, the gay community, and the Baptist church are all alive and well.

And a last word about Houston: winters are warm here. Forget about brilliant fall colors and drinking hot chocolate at football games. Rice students wear shorts until late November. Even then, Houston's winter is warmer than a northeastern fall. Birds migrate to Houston for the winter. The hundreds of oaks on Rice's campus rarely lose all their leaves, and the grass is greener and softer in January than in June. That's the good news. The bad news is that summer is unbearable. The brave students who stay and weather it out do so with air-conditioning.

GETTING IN/FINANCIAL AID

"My heart was set on Stanford. Not only did it have strong academic programs, but it also had a national reputation, a California-perfect campus, and (alas, the things that swayed me when I was a high school senior) a recruiter who made good eye contact. I filled out only two other applications: one for Duke because my parents wanted me to apply to an in-state college; and one for Rice because my guidance counselor suggested it and (I repeat, alas) because the application was free.

"Rice offered me more than twice as much financial aid as either Stanford or Duke: if I went to Rice, I'd get a one-year Rice University grant, two renewable merit scholarships, and work-study—enough to cover all but my plane fares and a few hundred dollars of room and board; if I went to either Stanford or Duke, I'd have to ask my parents for thousands and pay back hefty loans after graduation.

"Financial aid alone didn't convince me to go to Rice, but it did convince me to consider the university seriously. I liked what I found: no barriers to double majors in different disciplines, good faculty, fellow students at least as smart as I, and a high energy social life. In fact, had Rice sent a recruiter with good eyes, I might have had my heart set on it in the first place."

Getting into Rice isn't easy. Recently, the university accepted 22% of its 7779 applications. The 620 who make up a recent Rice class are an impressive lot: their average SAT I score was 1370 and 462 of them had ranked in the top 5% of their high school classes. But fear not: Rice doesn't admit on the basis of scores and grades alone but weighs applicants' extracurriculars, essays, recommendations, and required personal interviews.

What sort of people go to Rice? Though Rice no longer favors Texans in its admissions policy, almost half of Rice's typical classes hail from the Lone Star State. Roughly 57% of the incoming freshmen are male. And African-Americans, Mexican-Americans, and Native Americans make up 15% of the class—a percentage that Rice hopes to raise with new scholarships and a recently opened Minority Affairs Office.

"It's my impression that, while I was at Rice, the students were, in general, from poorer families than students of most other top colleges. Not that the average student has a family below the poverty level, but that Rice students' families are more likely to be middle class. Many of my friends were accepted by the Ivies, but their families couldn't afford Ivy League tuitions."

Rice's Texas-sized endowment has helped keep the school's tuition low for a top college ($10,400 most recently), and it allows Rice to give generous financial aid. About 85% of Rice students receive some form of financial assistance, the average award being $6500.

Rice offers several kinds of financial aid that its Ivy League cousins don't. For instance, Rice gives merit-based scholarships to the deserving, regardless of their financial need or lack of it. Such aid includes university-sponsored National Merit and National Achievement scholarships—important, no doubt, to the third of the student body who hold those scholarships. Other merit awards can cover as much as full room and board. Rice gives athletic scholarships in sports including football, volleyball, baseball, basketball, golf, tennis, swimming, and track. The Tuition Equalization Grant, available to Texans and out-of-state students who receive any merit scholarships, can be worth up to $1800. For minorities, in addition to National Achievement Scholarships, Rice offers 16 four-year awards ranging from half tuition to full tuition with room, board, and fees. And of course Rice offers the standard packages of loans and work-study available at most colleges.

ACADEMIC ENVIRONMENT

"Sociology 421, The Craft of Sociology, looked awful, but I signed up for it because it was the last class I needed to finish my double major. The subject of the course—the methodology of sociological studies—left me cold. The course syllabus showed long, dull readings in the first weeks. And to make matters worse, the seminar class was scheduled for a windowless, antiseptic room. I could only hope the class would be less painful than I expected.

"It was. On the third class meeting the dozen or so of us students mutinied, leaving a note for the professor that we'd moved class to the campus pub. She followed us there and liked the place. From then on, we met there once a week for three hours, settling into a dimly lit circle of couches and fat chairs to discuss questions such as whether Nancy Chodorow's feminist interpretation of Freud was methodologically sound—and to drink Cokes and beer, eat cheese goldfish, and swap gossip. To my surprise, by midterms I found myself as interested in methodology as I was in the goldfish."

That class shows Rice academics at their best: allowing a small group of bright undergrads to explore a topic with a first-class professor, with an emphasis on student participation and independence.

Though the Rice atmosphere is relaxed—the typical student outfit consists of shorts and a T-shirt—most classes aren't as low-key as that sociology class. In fact, some say the Rice state of mind is a lumberjack mentality: work hard, play hard, and rarely the twain shall meet.

The work hard part of the statement is obvious. Students are not surprised to find that a one-semester class will cover an introductory text intended for two semesters. S/Es recognize weekly all-nighters as de facto requirements for some courses. And Rice's 15 week semesters—among the longest in higher education—make getting a Rice degree a test of endurance as well as intensity. Rice academics are not for the faint of heart.

Nor are they for the narrow of mind: Rice recently tightened its distribution requirements. Freshmen are required to take foundation courses in the discipline opposite their planned majors: that is, students in the social sciences, arts, and humanities must take a two-semester course in the physical sciences; science and engineering majors must take two foundation courses: a two-semester course in the humanities and a one-semester course in the social sciences; and architecture and music majors must take all three courses. In addition to fulfilling foundation requirements, students must also complete 15–21 hours of courses outside their majors.

Rice offers formal undergraduate degree programs in a wide range of subjects. In the humanities, students can major in art and art history, English, French, German, and Slavic studies, human performance and health sciences, history, linguistics, philosophy, religious studies, Spanish, and classics. In the natural sciences, they can choose from biochemistry, biology, chemistry, geology and geophysics, mathematics, and physics. In the social sciences, they can pick anthropology, economics, political science, psychology, sociology, statistics; in engineering, they can choose chemical engineering, civil engineering, computer science, electrical and computer engineering, mathematical sciences, mechanical engineering, and materials science.

Rice also offers undergraduate programs in architecture and music and interdepartmental majors such as ancient Mediterranean civilization, behavioral science, chemical physics, managerial studies, and policy studies. Students may also design their own area majors in subjects such as Asian studies.

At Rice, as at most universities, no single teaching method predominates, though differences in the teaching of different academic areas are obvious. S/Es are reckoned to have the roughest academic schedules, especially in their freshman and sophomore years. Freshman year is boot camp for S/Es, who face "the big three": large, impersonal introductory classes in calculus, physics, and chemistry. Large classes in these subjects are a fact of life almost everywhere. But at Rice, where freshman English classes have 15 people per section at most, we resent large classes more. Though tutorials and study groups pull through the intro classes, a prospective student would be well-advised to substitute a four or a five on the advanced placement test in those subjects. And after the freshman year? Though classes get smaller, they're just as hard. But by then, according to my S/E friends, you're used to it.

To say that S/E classes are thought the hardest is not to say that other majors have it easy. Archis are known for staying up all night to meet deadlines, and academs often must do staggering amounts of reading and writing. In one two-week exam period, for instance, I took two three-hour exams and wrote papers totaling more than 70 pages.

The two ugliest by-products of academic rigor—cheating and cutthroat competition—are rare at Rice. The university's Honor Code takes care of cheating: the code works so well that many professors give take-home exams, to be completed wherever and whenever (during the exam period) the student chooses. Infractions of the Honor Code are few and are usually punished severely by the student-run Honor Council.

Why cutthroat competition doesn't surface at Rice is harder to explain. Perhaps the college system can take credit, because few people are as anxious to claw their way to the top when they have to claw people they'll live with for four years. Or perhaps credit should go to the study groups so many find necessary, or to students' commitment to extracurriculars, or to Houston's warm winters. After all, who cares about clawing your way to the top on a balmy day in February?

SOCIAL LIFE

"'Brown College?' people would ask when they saw one of my T-shirts. 'But I thought you were going to Rice.'"

To understand social life at Rice, you have to understand the colleges, the units of social and residential life on campus. Fraternities, sororities, eating clubs, and the like don't exist; and, truth to tell, no one seems to mind.

Each freshman is assigned to one of the eight coed colleges, where he or she will live with the rest of the college's 220 or so on-campus members for as long as he or she lives on campus. Except for a few special requests, assignments to the colleges are random, guaranteeing that no college has all the athletes, all the S/Es, or all the well-groomed blondes who wear pearls. After a year on campus, a freshman is likely to know nearly all of the diverse group who live in his or her college, many of the off-campus members (O/Cs), and dozens of people from other colleges.

Most Rice students like life in their colleges so much that they choose to live on campus after the freshman-year requirement is up, in spite of the bargain rents in oil-bust Houston. Unfortunately, wanting to live on campus is no guarantee that one can. In most years each college has more people who want to live on campus than can be housed and must bump some of them. Once bumped, you can never be bumped again—so if you really want to live on campus, you'll be an O/C for a year at most.

The colleges are at the heart of social life at Rice, so much so that O/Cs often feel they miss out. Most of the organized social activities on campus—parties, TGs

(Thank-God-It's-Friday gatherings with free beer and Coke), movies and plays—are sponsored by individual colleges, and even unorganized activities have college affiliations. Yell wars, yogurt throwings, and large-scale toothbrush theft take place in the name of college rivalry. And a final example: Club 13—whose sole raison d'etre is to run through campus on the thirteenth of most months, clad only in shaving cream—is often called Baker 13, in honor of the college where the runs begin and end, and where most of the runners live.

Members of all eight colleges patronize Willy's Pub, the place where my Soci 421 class met, a dark, comfortable place to exchange views on love or politics or to chug in a boat race. Bohemian undergrads favor Valhalla, the dank, smoky center of graduate student life and home of some of the cheapest beer in Texas.

The social event of the year at Rice? The Archi-Arts Ball, the Lovett Casino Party, and Wiess's Night of Decadence are strong contenders, but first place belongs to Beer-Bike, a peculiar rite of spring that brings college competition to its pinnacle. The race itself is a ten-person relay, in which male, female, and alumni teams from each college alternate bike sprints with chugging 12 ounces of water or beer. (No, don't worry: the iron man who does both is rare and always chugs *after* he bikes.) Bikers train seriously for the competition—many riding 200 or 300 miles a week—but the hoopla surrounding Beer-Bike is at least as much fun as the race itself. Recent college entrances to the track have included fire engines, Hell's Angels, and a 60-foot helium-filled battle sow. Rondolet, one of Rice's two annual formals, always caps the evening.

With so much happening on campus, most freshmen and sophomores rarely venture into the world beyond Rice's hedges for entertainment. Upperclassmen, though, find the trip outside Rice's hedges worth facing Houston traffic. The club scene here is active and varied, with venues for everything from folk to speed metal. The offerings of Houston restaurants range from good, cheap burritos to good, expensive dim sum. Two major art museums—the Contemporary Arts Museum and the Museum of Fine Arts—are an easy walk from Rice, as is the city's largest park. The Oilers and the Astros play regularly at the Dome; the symphony, opera, and ballet play regularly downtown.

> *"Most of the Texans I've met know two things about Rice: (1) that if you go there, you must be smart; and (2) that the Owls don't have a prayer of making the Cotton Bowl. No such consensus exists on the social lives of Rice students. Ask a Texan what Rice students do when we're not studying or losing football games, and you'll hear one of two things: that all Rice students are geeks and that an exciting weekend at Rice is studying German instead of differential equations; or, conversely, that all Rice students are party beasts—wild, perverse, and maybe a little dangerous.*
>
> *"The truth? A little of both. Most of us have our geeky side, and most of us like to have a good time—and that doesn't mean studying German on Friday night."*

EXTRACURRICULAR ACTIVITIES

"In my four years at Rice, I did lots of things: was assistant direc-tor of a play, served on a few committees, advised groups of fresh-men during Orientation Week, wrote occasional letters for Amnesty International, was O/C rep to my college cabinet, was part of a women's group, and played intramural soccer and soft-ball. All of them were good experiences for me: I either had a great time or felt as though I'd done something for the good of the world at large."

So many extracurriculars, so little time. If you want to write for the student newspaper, try the *Thresher*. Fiction or poetry are your specialties? The *University Blue*, the Rice literary magazine, begs for contributors twice a year. Photography a hobby? The *Thresher* and the *Campanile*, Rice's yearbook, will welcome you with open arms and free film. Love music, especially progressive music? KTRU (91.7 on your FM dial) can teach you to be a deejay or run a radio newsroom. Want to exer-cise your sense of humor, meet a lot of people, and maybe play an instrument? Join the Marching Owl Band, better known as the MOB. The band doesn't march—who has time?—but instead runs from formation to formation, satirizing current events, the opposing team, and other bands. Want to be president someday? Interview or run for a place in your college's government, the Student Association, the Honor Council, the Rice Program Council, or any of the dozen or so student-and-faculty committees. Like sports, but can't make it as a walk-on? Rice has intramural foot-ball, soccer, baseball, softball, volleyball, basketball, Laser Tag, and more. Inter-ested in acting? bridge? Japanese culture? fencing? women's issues? black or Hispanic issues? stopping torture? crusading for Christ? square dancing? being a Republican, a Democrat, or a Libertarian? nude sunbathing? shouting rude things at football games? There are clubs custom-made for you. And if you can't find a group already doing something you want, it's not hard to form your own.

"None of my other extracurriculars caused me to pull regular all-nighters, to argue with professors about the mission of the university, to curse at a phototypesetter, to drink too much coffee. Working at the Rice student newspaper did, and I loved it.

"Actually, 'and I was obsessed with it' might be more accu-rate. I started at the Thresher *as a typesetter, eventually became editor-in-chief, and at one time or another did most of the jobs in between. I learned what inverse-pyramid style means, what an emspace is, how to delegate work, and how it felt to see sunrise through the window beside my Macintosh.*

"When I matriculated at Rice, I'd planned to get a Ph.D. in English after I graduated. Working at the Thresher *showed me that I'd rather be a journalist."*

Let us not forget the most visible extracurricular of all: sports. As any sports-literate person knows, the Southwest Conference means the big time. Rice is competitive in most sports: our baseball, track, swimming, basketball, soccer, and cycling teams are not to be sneezed at. But—at the risk of understatement—our football team leaves something to be desired. At most football games, a sizable percentage of the student section shows up to see the band.

That doesn't mean that Rice is a bad place to be an athlete. Rice is the only school in the SWC the NCAA has never placed on probation. Instead, Rice wins NCAA awards for the high percentage of its scholarship athletes who graduate. Rice's graduation rate is all the more impressive because, except for free tutoring throughout their undergraduate careers, athletes get no special academic breaks. Of course, it helps that Rice's admission standards for athletes are tough: the university's athletic adviser estimates that the average scholarship athlete has an SAT score of 1050 and graduated in the top 17% of his or her high school class.

GRADUATES

Rice's football stadium, built back when the Owls were a power to be reckoned with, is huge. Huge enough to hold the 1974 Super Bowl. Huge enough to hold the 1988 Monsters of Rock concert. Huge enough that the Astrodome will have as many seats only after its latest round of renovations. Or—my favorite illustration—huge enough that if every one of Rice's 28,000 living alums showed up for Homecoming, they wouldn't fill it. In fact, they wouldn't even fill the Rice half.

Of course, as Rice often points out, it's quality, not quantity, that counts. That 28,000 includes a high percentage of people who make important decisions and don't answer their own phones. The lieutenant governor of Texas, an editor-in-chief of *Newsweek*, a Wall Street millionaire, several Silicon Valley millionaires, and at least one honest-to-God hermit have been eligible for Rice senior rings in the last 30-odd years.

But what, you ask, do new graduates do? More than half of my friends are now doing graduate work, most at the university of their choice. Of those who decided to work after graduation, about half took high-tech jobs such as computer programming, most in Silicon Valley and Boston. The other half, mostly academs, have taken a wider assortment of jobs: for instance, one friend taught English in Japan, one is a congressional aide, one is a paralegal, another is a an actuary, another works for a Big Six accounting firm, and so on. Many who are now working intend to go to grad school eventually.

> *"For the most part, Rice alumni are accessible and will take your having been admitted to Rice as introduction and recommendation enough. When I wanted an internship in magazine work, I*

matched up names on the masthead of Texas Monthly *with
names in the Rice alumni directory, and found that the editor-in-
chief is an alum. I called him, traded a few stories about professors we'd both had, and became the magazine's first intern in
Houston. One of the senior editors I worked for was an alum
herself."*

SUMMARY OVERVIEW

Intense is the watchword at Rice, where nothing—not academics, not social life,
not extracurriculars—takes place at half speed. Most Rice students thrive on the
breathless pace.

Rice's college system and its small size are assets; students know each other, and
faculty know the students. Low tuition and solid financial aid are points in Rice's
favor, as are Houston's warm winters and lively nightlife. Teaching is another of
Rice's strong points: though a few introductory classes may be less than sparkling in
their presentation, a four-year Rice education prepares a student to handle almost
anything.

Rice's weaknesses? Let's not talk about the Cotton Bowl.

Rice's greatest weakness is that outside the Southwest, it lacks the reputation of
Yale or Stanford. Rice's lack of cachet is clearly one of its weak spots: for instance,
though a major weekly newsmagazine ranked Rice in the top ten American colleges
overall recently, Rice didn't even make the magazine's list of the top 25 in reputation. A graduate, especially a liberal arts or social sciences graduate, may have to
defend or explain Rice to potential employers and grad schools, especially those
outside the Southwest. If nothing else, this lack of reputation hurts students'
pride.

But Rice is a school on the make, with plans to break into the first rank of higher
education. These plans seem to be working: in the last five years, the applicant pool
has grown, the reviews have been more and more glowing, and the changes in
curriculum seem to have been for the better. Though Rice isn't a household word
yet, it soon will be.

Lisa Gray, B.A.

Stanford University

THE PROGRAM

"During freshman orientation, the weekend before regular classes began, one of my classes met for the first time in the main lounge of my dorm. A large, bulking, intimidating history professor, who, I later found out, is a Jewish Marxist, led the discussion on Homer and the morality of war, modern or ancient. 'We aim to systematically challenge or dismantle every value, every preconception, every faith you brought with you to Stanford,' he said, scowling at us. Like the 70 other peons scattered on the couches or seated on the floor before the lectern, I cowered before him at that first class, scared and a little disoriented. Over the course of the year, though, as we traveled from Greece to Renaissance Italy to the end of modernism at the Holocaust, I developed a distinct fondness for Professor Mancall, and I got to the point where I argued with him about our readings after hours in his nearby apartment and challenged his values. The class was great. It blew my mind, tossed out the whole notion of culture I had been spoon-fed in high school textbooks, and readied me for my remaining years on the Farm."

Because Stanford, affectionately known as the Farm, has risen so quickly in the rankings of the nation's top schools, there is a vacuum of real information about the place, as well as plenty of well-intentioned but misguided myths. Here's a catalog of some of them:

- Stanford is laid-back.
- Stanford is the Harvard of the West.
- Stanford is the Disneyland of the North.
- Stanford is nirvana.
- Stanford killed Western culture, from Socrates on down.

All of these capture yet distort some aspect of the university. The key to understanding Stanford is that it has no fixed identity. Its mascot is Cardinal, for pete's sake. Not the bird, not the Catholic official, not the sin, but the color. In the abstract. (You can't refer to the sports teams as the Cardinals.) There is a school song, but no one learns it. The school doesn't even know when its birthday is. Its centennial celebration lasted *four years*, from 1987 to 1991.

But the search for identity is endlessly fascinating and consumes an enormous amount of energy on campus. The search, the ferment are probably the best reasons to go to Stanford. An example of the introspection is the recent great debate over Western culture, which attracted national attention and brought comment and even a visit from then Secretary of Education William Bennett. For two years, the university went through a tremendous upheaval deciding how it should teach culture to entering freshmen. There were many protests by minority student groups and several factions of the faculty demanding a reevaluation of the accepted canon of Western culture. After a lot of civilized, and at times uncivilized, debate, the university moved to broaden its base of reading and teaching to include Malcolm X alongside Socrates. The former Western culture course is now called Cultures, Ideas, and Values, with an emphasis on the plural.

Stanford is about one hundred years old, younger than any Ivy. Along with UC/Berkeley, it is the only university of Ivy caliber that faces the Pacific rim, which gives it several cultural and technological advantages. It is known first for its science and engineering, second for its social sciences, and third for its humanities. The school's founder, U.S. Senator Leland Stanford, wanted the school to produce graduates who would do something useful in the world, and by and large that emphasis on utility and preprofessionalism has stuck, or at least the reputation has stuck. The business, medical, and law schools, along with several other graduate programs, are among the best in the country.

In practical terms, the school's educational maxim is "Breadth and Depth," meaning a mandatory survey of several large fields of knowledge and a concentration of at least one fourth the total number of units in one specialty. Most students tend to dabble in the smorgasbord of departments and programs—more than 70 in all—before choosing a major. In the School of Engineering, computer science and industrial engineering are the most popular majors. In the School of Humanities and Sciences, the majors of choice are biological sciences, English, economics, history, political science, human biology, and international relations.

People at Stanford often speak of a "techie-fuzzie" dichotomy, in which half the students are engineering or science nerds, studying 24 hours a day with problem sets, whereas the other, supposedly cooler half take it easy and write a few papers each quarter in between volleyball matches and tanning on the lawn.

Again a grain of truth, but not much more than a grain. There is considerable overlap in the living environment, social environment, and academic schedules of most students in either category. If there is any generalization to be made about the Stanford experience, it is that all students like to *look* like they're having a good time, engaged in several recreational or extracurricular activities at once while effortlessly carrying a maximum load of courses. Secretly they all study like hell.

Despite this, national rankings in football, basketball, baseball, swimming, and gymnastics are realistic goals at Stanford, and national championships are almost the norm in a host of other wildly diverse sports like tennis and water polo, where Stanford has few peers. Making friendly sport of the University of California/Berkeley, known on campus as the Weenies, is a favorite pastime, and pictures are regularly taken of Stanford students around the globe hanging "Beat CAL" banners in famous places, like the Eiffel Tower and Leaning Tower of Pisa. In November, at the time of the Big Game, CAL vandals reciprocate, regularly stealing every Stanford sign in sight and spray-painting Bear paw marks on campus landmarks, among other dastardly pranks.

Stanford is best known to outsiders for its beautiful campus, with thousands of acres of open space, Spanish-style architecture, palm trees and tennis courts, where you can play outdoors in January. Really. Wintering at Stanford, where only the occasional rainstorm clouds the skies, enables you to lord it over your friends who decided to shiver for four years at a prestigious school in the Northeast. Reading assignments and problem sets are as likely to be finished outdoors, with a beach towel and sunglasses, as in the libraries.

Any way you look at it, Stanford, on the San Francisco Peninsula, halfway between San Francisco and San Jose, is unlike any other school in the country. It is top-notch academically, number one or thereabouts in just about everybody's poll. At the same time, it seriously pursues everything top academic schools are not known for, i.e., fun in the sun, a relaxed approach to studies and extracurricular activities, and big-time college sports. Think of Stanford as a hybrid of the Pac-10 and the Ivy League.

GETTING IN/FINANCIAL AID

"One day during the fall of my senior year in high school, when I was applying to Stanford, I received a note from the admissions staff. 'There are times when it is nice to be able to have an image of the person one is hearing from, writing to, talking with, or reading about,' the note said. 'Because we think it helps to make the admissions process more personal by being able to connect names with faces, here are the mug shots (for better or for worse) of the members of the admissions staff.' Next to the note were ten smiling somewhat goofy faces of admissions officials, just as I had sent them a small photo of my smiling face on my application. It was a nice touch, and it made me laugh. Of all the reasons that made me want to come to Stanford, not the least was the casual, humorous approach taken by members of the admissions

staff, who were far less uptight than staffs from other schools where I applied and had interviews. I had no interview with a Stanford official, but I nevertheless felt a more personal connection with Stanford than with the other schools."

More and more people apply to Stanford every fall, but the goal of a class size of about 1600 remains the same. Only about 2600 applicants are accepted once a year, at the beginning of April, from a pool of about 14,000. Thousands of those applicants routinely come with straight-A credentials, but not all get in. Thousands get in without straight As, too.

It's difficult for all of those 4.0, 1400-SAT I folks out there to come to grips with an arbitrary admissions process. But the admissions staff at Stanford is pretty straightforward, caring, and sympathetic, and gives the tough answers to any and all questions, no matter if you write or call. What you see is what you get with admissions. There are no early admissions programs, no extra letters to be solicited from friends or alumni, no interviews (unless you really want one for your own benefit), and no rules for judging. The admissions staff says there are no quotas, but the number of minorities admitted every year has risen steadily: about 8% of the most recent class was black; 11% Hispanic; and 24% Asian-American. Women are barely a minority at 48% of those admitted. People from all 50 states and several foreign lands are generally admitted, with Californians of course constituting the bulk of the students admitted at more than 30%.

Although the admissions staff hates saying that any particular type of student is characteristic of Stanford, there are clear generalizations about what the staff is looking for: overachievers, who have done a lot of things, academically and otherwise, and done them well. Once in a while a Stanford student is admitted for having a special talent, without an especially broad list of other activities.

Applications are due by December 15, although some Stanford students have boasted of sneaking theirs in just after deadline. There are the standard résumé-type questions on the Stanford application, and admissions officials say they least look forward to reading these sections. Although you shouldn't be modest, remember that everyone was class treasurer and president of the Honor Society. Blatant résumé-packing, with no clear commitment to any particular activity, is not the way to get your ticket to Stanford. The application also includes three short essay questions, calling for a third of a page each and you can't go overboard and use more space. This year, applicants are asked to jot a note to a future roommate relating a personal anecdote. They are also being asked to describe the best conversations they have had. In addition, a longer essay is required. The questions can be off the wall. One year, applicants were asked to write a fable, drawing on a personal experience.

They're looking for humor, honesty, and a spark in the essays, and, like it or not, that usually decides who gets in, among otherwise equally qualified applicants. There's also the factor of the special talent, and the admissions staff is open to hearing a tape of a violin concert by a budding young musical star or knowing of athletic or artistic prowess. A concerted effort is being made to lure mathematical and scientific geniuses, too.

But generally the applicant is not a genius or superstar in any one thing, just possesses all-around excellence, with a commitment or two to something interesting, be it public service, sports, drama, music, or class leadership. Maximizing advanced placement courses in high school is a must, and taking as many years as possible of one or two foreign languages also helps. In general, Stanford wants to know not just how well you did in high school, but how well you took advantage of the resources that were available to you. The two teacher recommendations also give some idea of how well you achieved in those areas.

Lastly, get the SATs or ACTs (mandatory) and achievement tests (optional but highly recommended) out of the way as soon as possible. Stanford officials disdain these tests but consider them a necessary evil.

> *"Before I came to Stanford, I won a $4000 scholarship from the Pacific Gas and Electric Company in San Francisco. It was a regional competition among dozens of high schools in Northern California, and I was ecstatic. Every year I would get a $1000 check from the company. I thought that would go a long way toward meeting my bills and making the margin of error in my budget that much less."*
>
> *"I also sought and won awards from the Elks Club, the National Honor Society, the Bank of America, and a host of other places. In fact, half my senior year in high school was devoted to searching for outside scholarships, half to getting into college. The scholarships were useful, I got lots of nice plaques, and Stanford appreciated the fact that I had the extra cash, but in my case the whole exercise turned out to be unnecessary because many students I knew who had similar financial backgrounds simply went to Stanford with no outside scholarships and received just as much aid as I did. The lesson was clear: outside scholarships aren't necessary for a middle-income student to go to a school like this although they can help a bit. And they certainly help the school."*

Like students at any school costing more than $20,000 a year, Stanford students require a lot of financial aid, and the university generally has a good attitude toward helping them. But the financial aid office is still a mystery to many students at Stanford and sometimes the cause of severe headaches. Stanford gives as many as three fifths of its students some kind of aid package and guarantees that those packages are not a consideration in any admissions decisions.

But that's where the straightforward part ends. A bewildering variety of government-subsidized loans, through Stanford or private banks, are generally offered in some form or another to pay the total yearly bill, along with a scholarship grant and a federally subsidized work-study program to make up the rest. Usually students can elect to work more and have less loan debt, or the other way around. The student loan staples are called the Guaranteed Student Loan and the Perkins Loan and can be augmented by university loans. Some loans are available for families who don't qualify for any financial aid but still need some help, like the Parent Loan for Undergraduate Students (PLUS) and the Stanford Parent Loan Plan (PLP), at variable but not exorbitant rates of interest.

ACADEMIC ENVIRONMENT

"In the second quarter of my sophomore year I decided to major in English and showed up one day for a seminar on the Romantic Age. There was one other sophomore in the class of 12; the rest were seniors or graduate students, an intimidating bunch. Because it was my first class in the major, I was more than a little out of my league. In the first few weeks, the names of obscure poets and German Romantic philosophers flew over my head, and I made simplistic and, well, sophomoric contributions to the class. But I stuck it out and learned not to be in awe of the grad students; most of them were simply name-droppers, it turned out. The professor, a kindly man named George Dekker, whom I later learned was chairman of the department, wasn't at all impatient with me. 'You keep the discussion grounded in the text,' he told me one day after hours, with a smile. One of the best compliments I ever got."

By and large, Stanford has made its academic reputation through its engineering and science faculty, with facilities like its world-class medical school and the Stanford Linear Accelerator Center. But there are also well-known humanities and sciences faculty at the school, like poet and English professor Adrienne Rich, economics professor and presidential adviser Michael Boskin, and a host of others. In addition, the Hoover Institution, technically separate from the university, is located in a prime spot on campus and has unrivaled historical archives. This controversial right wing organization, named for Stanford alum and U.S. President Herbert Hoover, is housed in a famous campus landmark, the Hoover Tower.

The academic environment at Stanford is relaxed, governed by an Honor Code that prohibits proctoring of exams. Students end up pushing themselves more than teachers push them. One truism about the university is that it's almost impossible to get in, but once you're there, it's (nearly) impossible to fail. That's literally true: there are no F grades at the school, and students stop out rather than drop out. Other signs of a relaxed grading policy:

• being able to drop a class up to 24 hours before the final exam;

• a grading scale that hovers between Cs and As generally, although some profs dip regularly into the Ds and are unafraid to give a no-credit grade; and

• the no-credit grade's being omitted from the transcript.

This is not to say that things are easy at Stanford. There are three ten-week quarters in the academic year (an eight-week summer quarter is also available). That means that three times a year, rather than twice a year as at other schools, finals frenzy hits the campus. Professors exacerbate the situation because they tend to treat an academic quarter as they would the longer semester. They cram as much information into the shorter time period as possible, and the reading load can be immense. There is a Dead Week before final exams, when things are supposed to slack off to give you time to study, but that is rarely the case. Most profs just keep piling it on, and the masochistic students don't often complain.

The university-wide requirements are broad. One course each is required in literature and fine arts; philosophical, social and religious thought; human development, behavior, and language; social processes and institutions; mathematical sciences; natural sciences; and technology and applied sciences. On top of that, there is a year-long course called Cultures, Ideas, and Values that is mandatory for freshmen, a two-quarter freshman writing requirement, a foreign language requirement, and a requirement to take a course studying a non-Western culture. Passing the AP test with a four or a five doesn't get you entirely out of the writing requirement; you still have to take a one-quarter advanced writing course. That's good because you learn quickly that writing at Stanford is nothing like the writing you did in high school, no matter how much your teachers loved you there.

Once all of those requirements are out of the way, there is still the task of somehow securing 180 units (units are generally three to five per course, 15 for the average quarter) and completing a major requiring anywhere from 50 to 100 of those units.

Extreme flexibility marks academics at Stanford. Studying for a quarter or two overseas in Europe, Asia, South America, or Africa is a very real possibility because the university has outposts all over the world. About one third of Stanford students go overseas at some point in their careers, even engineering and science students. Another sign of flexibility is the option for a self-designed major. If you don't like what's offered from the 70 or more departments or programs, you're free to make your own proposal. There's also an optional honors program, which matches you with a faculty adviser to do research on a proposed topic during the junior and senior year, winding up with a 50 to 80 page paper.

Mention must also be made of the Residential Education program, which serves as a base for classes and hosts talks in the dorms. Education, it turns out, goes on around the clock at Stanford, at meals or in the student lounges after dinner. Res Ed, as the program is known, is said to be a model for schools around the country. The Res Ed office sponsors first-year civilization classes in many student houses, arranges for other alternative classes or workshops in evening hours after dinner, coordinates counseling and a network of upperclass advising associates and residential assistants, organizes academics for language and cultural theme houses, and generally organizes and dominates your life during freshman year and probably for most of the years afterward. It helps design the liberal but sometimes toughly enforced alcohol policy, for example. Much of the education Res Ed gives you has a unit value attached and shows up on your transcript, but most of it is intangible—simply the nurturing of a creative, stimulating, tolerant living environment.

Class-size statistics and faculty-student ratios are seductive and misleading. Basically, in your first two years, you can expect a lot of lecture halls with 100 students or more. Those years are interspersed, though, with plenty of opportunities for small-group seminars with 15 or fewer students. As you move through your major and specialize, classes should get smaller and smaller. Generally there's enough faculty to go around, and they're likely to know your name.

A word about the faculty. Sometimes you can be misled into thinking they're great because they did award-winning research decades ago. There's a lot of talk about all the Nobel laureates around the campus. Don't be fooled. They're good, but you need to push them and challenge them to maximize their teaching skills. They appreciate it because they don't like overawed students who are afraid to open their mouths and say something original.

SOCIAL LIFE

"Trips to Mazatlan, the beach, Berkeley, San Francisco, and Yosemite were the offerings of my freshman year. Going to Berkeley for the Big Game, we packed the subway and sang crude and rowdy fight songs, which I'm not sure I'm terribly proud of. Going to football games at home we didn't have enough Chapstick to go around and got burnt like lobsters. Going to San Francisco for an all-night pre-Big Game rally, we got drunk as skunks in the bus we chartered for the occasion. Then Stanford students packed the city's marina and marched for a mile to the waterfront, where the band held a wild, ornery pep rally. Mild-mannered library jocks were transformed into a maniac mob. It was hellacious fun, but I never did anything like it again. I'm not sure I was myself freshman year, but neither was anyone else, really, and whatever I was or wasn't, I had a great time being it. I met most of my closest Stanford friends in that year, and I won't forget it."

The social life on campus starts always and forever with freshman year. There's pressure to do everything at once, and the first-year requirement to live in the dorms creates social bonds that linger during the remaining years at the school.

Parties at fraternities are the most visible lure for freshmen. During those first couple of months, all fraternities advertise their social events heavily in the freshman dorms to take advantage of the initial peer pressure to party and drink heavily. Alcohol, by the way, is pretty much available anywhere on campus although in recent years campus police have made a token, sometimes earnest effort at cracking down on underage drinking. Equally attractive nonalcoholic beverages, tagged EANABs, are a requirement at all parties.

Fraternities are by no means the only social option. There are other parties at all kinds of houses, offered by all kinds of groups. There are ethnic and language theme houses that have their own flavor. There are cooperative houses that offer some of the wildest parties on campus, and, though popularly rumored to be the meeting place of holistic hippies on campus these houses are actually populated by all kinds of folks, from the normal to the spaced-out.

A perennial complaint about the school is the dating scene. The school's reputation is bad, and in truth the scene is pretty bad. For whatever reason, it's tough to find a casual date on campus although serious relationships proliferate in abundance. There is a standard joke on campus, especially among freshmen, about the modest attempt at a date that, no matter how great the effort, winds up being an intimacy-killing group outing, with a dozen or so friends from the dorm along for the ride.

Off-campus social life is pretty nonexistent. Almost everyone lives on campus, and nearby Palo Alto doesn't have much social life to offer. Mass transit is available to San Francisco or Berkeley, where the real off-campus action is, but it's not terribly convenient and involves a lot of bus and train transfers, along with at least an hour or two or three to kill.

So you're stuck on campus, unless you can snag your roommate's car for the 45-minute drive north to the city, where there are clubs, bars, dance spots, restaurants, and performing arts to please any taste.

To generalize about the social scene at Stanford: there are no generalizations, just a thousand niches. You can find whatever you want at this school if you look around, from the raunchiest, bawdiest fraternities to the most studious academic clubs, to the sophisticated, somewhat European crowd that mingles in the Coffee House, the main hangout and pub on campus.

Specific social events are headlined by the annual Viennese Ball, a hot ticket seller, which brings together top university officials, faculty, students, and anyone else brave enough to learn how to waltz. Really, they teach you before you go out there in your tux or evening gown and make a fool of yourself. It's a kind of prom, happening every winter, and it comes with a whole host of Austrian/German activities the week before. For those who don't get tickets, other formal dances are often sponsored on an ad hoc basis by individual student residences, and these can be quite lavish, depending on how much effort the dorm puts into it.

EXTRACURRICULAR ACTIVITIES

"After three years of procrastinating, I finally got around to walking into the editorial offices of the Stanford Daily, *a wholly independent, million-dollar paper staffed by more than 100*

> *manic students. The paper started in 1893, two years after the university granted its first degrees. My worldly editors ripped up and rewrote my first tepid inside-page stories, but within weeks I had written several front-page lead stories and was intimately acquainted with most significant campus events. I covered a two-month trial in San Jose between Stanford and the NCAA that was a national precedent-setting case in the area of drug testing, the surprise closure of a popular dorm due to earthquake hazards, and protests at the law school over affirmative action programs for minorities and women. I spent more time at the* Daily *during my senior year than on any other activity, with the exception perhaps of sleeping and certain other bodily functions. I was there even when I had no assignment and any sane person would have been studying like mad for midterms or finals. I became a newsaholic. My editors were my friends and accomplices to the disease."*

Any list of extracurricular activities on campus wouldn't be exhaustive because new ones sprout up all the time. There are hundreds of student organizations, ranging from the dozens of periodicals to music, theater, dance, debate, government, politics, environment, and athletics in intramural, club, and varsity formats. There are intercollegiate, nonvarsity club teams in ultimate Frisbee, rugby, ice hockey, and other sports. There are black, Hispanic, Asian-American, Native American, Jewish, and other ethnic student organizations, as well as women's groups and an active gay and lesbian culture. The Gay and Lesbian Alliance at Stanford is a major student group that helps destroy myths about the 10% culture by conducting discussion groups in dorms and other campus-wide awareness activities.

Extracurriculars are fostered by the weather, too, which makes you make want to get out and do something. It's nearly always sunny, or else the clouds are breaking. There is a golf course on campus that you must see to believe.

The most popular extracurricular activities are probably intramural sports and journalism of some sort. Politics runs a close second and, of course, is sometimes intertwined with the journalism. The Stanford College Republicans and Stanford Democrats hold spirited debates and sponsor dozens of campus speakers.

Politics on campus are overwhelmingly liberal, which is a bit surprising, considering the broad range of classes and backgrounds drawn to Stanford. There is, however, a quite vocal, persistent band of conservatives on campus who are quite unafraid to say what they think. Their flagship publication is the *Stanford Review*, a recently organized publication that styles itself in the tradition of the notorious *Dartmouth Review.*

There are fraternities and sororities, and about one-fifth of the students join in the annual spring rush. Many of the fraternities and all of the sororities are unhoused. Those fraternities that are still residential, and they grow fewer all the time, have some of the most gorgeous houses on campus. The Greek groups have come under pressure in the last couple of years to become less homogeneous and reactionary and more in tune with the ethnic diversity and progressive politics on campus.

One such progressive movement is Stanford's Rape Education Project, which holds talks in fraternities and other residences to increase awareness of recently publicized phenomena such as date rape and acquaintance rape.

RESIDENCE LIFE

Meal plans are based in all residences and are expensive for the middling fare offered although some cooks have been known to rise to the occasion in some houses. A computerized system is in the works to give all students meal/library/ identification cards, and that may increase the quality and accessibility of the university's food service. Those students who by chance live off campus or for whatever reason don't live in university housing can join many houses as eating associates and thus get a hook into an alternative social life. Eating is the definitive social experience for many at Stanford. Where you dine, whom you chat with, and whether you cook yourself are all, naturally, main features of the daily routine.

The quality of the university's housing varies wildly although, on the plus side, the university guarantees housing for all four undergraduate years. Nine-tenths of all undergraduates live in university housing on campus, which includes two relatively new dormitories.

If you're a freshman, be forewarned: you're likely to get stuck in an ugly concrete cement-block dorm. The majority of freshman housing, built 30, 40, or 50 years ago, is definitely not palatial. It crowds two, three or four students into close, in some cases tiny, quarters. This may be what is known as freshman camaraderie, or it may be too close for comfort. But all freshmen suffer more or less equally, which provides some solace.

However, some housing built by the university for upperclassmen in recent years is quite nice, and sophomores, juniors, and seniors have a very high probability of obtaining large, semiprivate or totally private rooms. On the west side of campus, near the golf course, is Governors' Corners, for instance, where upperclassmen can get apartment-like suites or single rooms. Nothing's for sure, though, because an annual spring housing lottery places people almost randomly, and it's not unheard of for a student to get stuck in one of those crowded cement blocks for two or three years in a row. The Draw, as the lottery is called, is fickle and provides the lucky person who draws number one instant, brief celebrity and an obligatory picture in the *Stanford Daily*. For the month of April and some weeks afterward and beforehand, the Draw is the subject of most campus small talk and speculation.

GRADUATES

"I didn't get a job until late May, four weeks before graduation, when I was hired, to my surprise and delight, as a general assignment and city hall news reporter at a local newspaper. Being an English major, I expected a hard time, but I wasn't that worried. People at home seemed to care more about the job situation than I did, in some ways, and they sometimes had an annoying tendency of linking my major to the problem. I said, 'Hey, I don't care about what kind of job my major's going to get me after school. I care about learning something.'

"Sometimes, though, the elaborate career planning bureaucracy at Stanford bugged me. There were lots of career days for the engineers, lawyers, doctors, and investment bankers in my class, but where was the information table with recruiters avidly seeking someone in my position, who wanted a job in mass communications? In the end, I had to get my own job, but the Stanford degree helped."

After graduation, Stanford students go in a zillion different directions. There are no hard statistics on where Stanford students end up, but some hit the Peace Corps, some hit California's computer-happy Silicon Valley, some join the Wall Street pinstripe brigade, some take time off and travel in Europe, some invade Capitol Hill. Many go straight into law or med schools or other grad programs.

There is a Career Planning and Placement Center on campus that has job listings, counselors, resume coaches, and events designed to wean students from the Farm. Most students visit the CPPC starting junior year although it's a good idea to go earlier than that because there are incredible opportunities for summer internships there too. If the CPPC can't give you a listing, it can tell you where to get a listing. It also hosts interviews year-round for those giant corporations and investment banks that recruit Stanford grads in economics or other social sciences and engineering. The interviews are granted on a competitive bid system.

To generalize grossly, most Stanford graduates are not expecting to settle into a lifetime career immediately, and many switch jobs or just bounce around for a while before settling on something they want or like. Stanford officials and faculty, from the university president on down, exhort students to major in whatever they like and have great expectations about their peers and superiors, no matter where they go. It can be a rude shock to discover it's not the same idyllic situation in the outside world. These and other factors lead to high career mobility.

Stanford's alumni network is vast and pays great sums of money annually to the university endowment, sports, and other programs. With outposts in cities across the country, the network is a good place to make initial contacts in the job market, too. Many students find summer or permanent jobs with the help of alumni, and there are special programs that bring undergraduates together at coffee or dinner with local alumni families, who can have valuable advice for nervous job seekers.

A final note about the older alumni: they tend to be a little more sentimental about the school than recent grads and yearn for the pre-1970s days, when the football team was still called the Indians and the fight song was common knowledge.

SUMMARY OVERVIEW

Stanford's strengths are many. Academically, the school has something for everyone—engineering, liberal arts, and social sciences. Stanford's reputation has been built on the sciences and engineering, but the school is making vast strides in other disciplines, and its breadth of cross-disciplinary studies is unmatched among the top schools. Individually designed majors, freedom from the fear of failure, overseas campuses, and several other factors combine to make Stanford relaxing and stimulating at the same time. You won't be suffocated by the academics at this school; you can go your own way, at your own leisurely speed.

Academics here don't stop with the classroom. A highly charged multicultural political environment, with activism from diverse minority groups ranging from gays and lesbians to blacks, Latinos, and Asian-Americans, is bringing about profound changes in the campus social and academic scene. Those changes haven't been accomplished easily—the revision of the Western culture course toward a pluralistic view of culture upset many traditionalists—but they have been for the better. They have made the campus a hotbed of ethnic, racial, cultural, and sexual debate, an inherently good thing at a university.

On the flip side of things, despite this debate, Stanford remains undeniably somewhat elitist. It probably always will be so, being an astronomically expensive, insulated school with world-class pretensions. The country club atmosphere of the school can be unnerving and difficult to adjust to for a student from an urban background. Financial aid is no easy trick here although it is available, and there are occasionally undue pressures on students to try to succeed in everything—materially, socially, and academically.

An important consideration before deciding to come here is the isolation of the campus. Neighboring Palo Alto isn't known for much of a nightlife, or day life for that matter. The town closes up at 11 P.M. Period. San Francisco and Berkeley are alluring, rewarding places to be, but they are relatively inaccessible to the student who can't afford a car. Mass transit is poor on the San Francisco Peninsula. So the immediate question, of course, for someone who wants the vitality and energy of those two cities is "Why not go to school there instead of here?" There is a strong case to be made for that suggestion. Ask those at UC/Berkeley. Stanfordians some-times snidely suggest that Berkeley is the school of second choice, but the more thoughtful students on the Farm may think otherwise.

Taking everything into consideration, though, Stanford is an inherently satisfy-ing and stimulating place to spend four years of your life. The fact that the school is so desperately searching for an identity as it turns into its second century is disarm-ing and even endearing. The upshot is that it's your Stanford, not theirs. The place is what you make of it, which is the ultimate challenge. Take a great school, with great resources, great faculty (and, let's not forget, great weather), and ask a kid to make a little history there. The kid can't help but oblige.

Nick Anderson, A.B.

Swarthmore College

THE PROGRAM

"When I was considering Swarthmore as a high school senior, I scoured the various guides to the colleges for information about this small, selective, slightly mysterious place. In my Virginia town, known primarily as the home of the CIA, good students went to UVA, great students went to the Ivy League, and the only people I knew who had gone to Swarthmore were a libertarian Mormon who left high school without a diploma and a slack-faced woman who claimed to be a witch. Not much to go on, so I checked the guidebooks, which told me that Swarthmore was intense and liberal, that students were passionate and earnest, that the campus was gorgeous and that whether a student was a soccer-playing psychology major from a local Pennsylvania town, an engineer from Pakistan, or a libertarian Mormon from Virginia, she or he was likely to be bright, interesting, and open-minded. All that was true, but what they didn't tell me was this: it's impossible to feel lukewarm about this tiny liberal arts college that looks like an arboretum and comes to feel like the world by the end of your four years there."

Swarthmore was founded in 1864 in a suburb of Philadelphia by members of the Religious Society of Friends, and though you won't find many students at the Quaker services, which are still held in the Meeting House on campus, the school does promote traditional Quaker values—an appreciation of diverse viewpoints and a commitment to making the world a better place. For a small—make that *tiny*—college, Swarthmore has done pretty well on the diversity front: In a recent year, the 1325 Swarthmore students hailed from 40 countries and 49 states; extracurricular activities ranged from an informal ice-hockey club called Mother-puckers to HOLA (The Hispanic Organization for Latino Awareness) to the Chester

Community Improvement Project (a student-run organization to rebuild low-income housing in nearby Chester, Pennsylvania); classes focused on everything from Russian folklore to American foreign policy to aeronautics. And social life involves more than partying; it includes social change. In fact, student-run political organizations outnumber fraternities by about eight to one, and—maybe more important—many people belong to both. Only at Swarthmore, I suspect, would you find a woman active in the Women's Center rooming with a cheerleader or a football player wearing a red armband over his uniform to protest the school's investments in South Africa (Swarthmore did agree to divest its holdings over a multiyear period). There *are* little mini-Swarthmores: clusters of people who do different things, take different classes, live in different dorms, eat in different parts of the one dining hall, and probably have dramatically different ideas about what it means to be a Swarthmorean; what these groups share, for the most part, is the school's open-mindedness.

Not that day-to-day life at Swarthmore revolves around anything social. This might be true for the first semester, when courses are graded pass/fail, but after that it's academics that bind this strange collection of people together. The two major libraries, McCabe (for the humanities/social sciences) and Cornell (for the sciences), are—after the dining hall, which is without a doubt the Meeting Place Extraordinaire—the biggest hubs of activity. Swarthmore's reputation for mile-long reading lists and almost unmasterable work loads isn't unwarranted; most professors expect their students to be motivated, interested in the material, and able to think critically about the issues involved. It's not that Swarthmore is impossibly difficult, though; contrary to popular belief, it *is* possible to get by without studying 12 hours a day or late into the night; there *are* classes considered easy A's. But here's the thing: most students don't *want* to take the easier route, to get by doing minimal reading or taking easier classes. Most students *choose* to challenge themselves, to take advantage of the low student-to-faculty ratio of nine to one and to get to know professors by name, often striking up friendships with them. And about 20% opt to enter the External Examinations Program—informally known as Honors—for the last two years of study, foregoing regular classes and grades for weekly seminars at professors' houses and a barrage of exams from visiting experts at the end of the senior year.

All this strenuous self-challenging takes place, believe it or not, within a relatively open academic framework. Swarthmore requires students to take at least three classes in each of three areas—humanities, social sciences, natural sciences/engineering—and to satisfy a foreign language requirement, but that done, students are free to concentrate on whatever they like while they satisfy the (usually bendable) requirements for their majors. The regular course load is four classes (or, within the External Examination Program, two seminars) per semester—and even in the last year of study, it's not uncommon to find a chemistry major taking sociology just for the fun of it.

"A few weeks before my first year at Swarthmore, I received a letter from the Orientation Committee, telling me that on September 5, I would check into my dorm and begin to meet the women and men who would be my classmates. My first impres-

sion was that I had mistakenly enrolled in an adult education institute; my peers were girls and boys, surely, not women and men.

"But this language was intentional, and important. Swarthmore treats its students as mature, able individuals, not as children or even young adults. Whatever else I felt there— overworked, harried—I always felt respected. Students lead discussions, as often as professors; any organizations may receive college funding as long as Student Council approves it; the college regularly grants lengthy leaves of absence. President Alfred Bloom holds a weekly open office hour for students to ask him about anything. Friends from other schools have told me horror stories about transcripts sent home to parents, domineering professors, movies banned from campus because of offensive content. I can't help feeling that by treating me as an adult, Swarthmore helped me become one."

GETTING IN/FINANCIAL AID

As perhaps the top liberal arts college in the country (it's been voted number one twice by *U.S. News and World Report*), Swarthmore maintains tough admission standards, accepting only one-quarter of the applications it receives. Median SAT I scores are high, between 600-700 for verbal and 620-730 for math. But Swarthmore doesn't seek out the average overachiever. Sure, good grades don't hurt—but Swarthmore courts students who have something more, be it an extracurricular interest (athletic, intellectual, political, or spiritual) or a unique background in another country or culture. There are a lot of high school valedictorians wandering around Swarthmore, but there are certainly some people who didn't do that well in high school, people who were too busy programming their computers/writing poetry to really apply themselves to algebra and composition. More often than not, Swarthmore chooses students with stellar SAT I scores—or a stellar interview, or stellar talents—over students with flawless grades.

An average Swarthmore class consists of approximately 330 students (from an admitted pool of about 1000), with a male/female ratio of 51/49. The larger number of students come from the Mid-Atlantic states, with healthy chunks from New England, the South, the Midwest, and the West, and about 5% from overseas. Minorities currently comprise 18% of the student body, and the college is trying to increase minority enrollment.

"My Swarthmore application included an essay question that I still have committed to memory: 'Imagine that you have the opportunity to travel back through time. At what point in history

*would you like to stop and why?' After considerable delibera-
tion, I decided to write about the Gilded Age, the 1890's, a time
fresh in my head from recent discussions in my history class. I
remember thinking proudly that I was being pretty original, that
everyone else was probably going to write about the Renaissance
or ancient Rome. In retrospect, I was pretty conservative:
Friends at Swarthmore later told me that they wrote about everything from the 1960s (one woman even included a tape of herself
singing an unaccompanied version of 'Blowing in the Wind') to
the moment of the Big Bang."*

In addition to the essay, Swarthmore requires applicants to provide an information sheet, a transcript, recommendations, and a fee (waivable if need be), and have
an interview—either on campus or with an alumni representative in their area.
(Visits to the campus are the way to go, if possible, because students willingly house
prospectives, as they're termed, in their dorm rooms overnight—a great way to get
a bird's-eye view into college life.) The school also encourages applicants to submit
additional materials: anything from videos of performance art to poems written to
letters of recommendation from former employers.

Swarthmore maintains a need-blind admissions program, which accepts qualified students regardless of their financial status. Of course, need-blind admissions
won't help you pay for tuition once you're in, so it's good that Swarthmore also
boasts one of the nation's most generous financial aid programs, with about 46% of
the student body receiving some sort of aid (average amount: $14,500), and many
receiving out-and-out awards rather than loans. They need it, too, because Swarthmore's pricey—$22,160 for a recent academic year, of which $17,460 goes to tuition. Once you're on campus, though, almost everything's free—performances,
dinner at a student-run restaurant called Served Meal, and admission to college parties. Because of changes in the Pennsylvania alcohol laws, alcohol may no longer be
served free of charge, but in the good old days before restrictions set in, the going
expression was "Swarthmore College—$19,000 cover charge, all you can drink."

ACADEMIC ENVIRONMENT

Swarthmore's academics have won it worldwide recognition as one of the best—
and toughest—schools in the country. (This notwithstanding, the wisdom among
alumni is that no one you meet will ever have heard of the college.) There's truth to
Swarthmore's reputation for toughness. Depending on how seriously you decide to
take your work, there's a good chance you will spend much of your four years
peering out of a library window, down the mouth of a test tube, or into the screen of
a word processor.

Swarthmore offers both a B.A. degree in the arts and sciences and a B.S. in engineering. The most popular majors are English, political science, and economics, but the sciences and engineering boast impressive departments, too—in fact, Swarthmore ranks second only to Cal Tech in per capita production of students awarded National Science Foundation fellowships. Particularly strong departments are English, history, religion, political science, and economics. You can major in almost anything; if what you're interested in isn't offered, it's possible to create your own special major. You also can earn a concentration alongside your major by taking enough courses with a particular slant—black studies, women's studies, public policy, international relations, computer science, Asian studies, theater studies, environmental studies, and so on.

Swarthmore requires students to take two Primary Distribution Courses (PDCs) in each of three areas—humanities, social sciences, and natural sciences/engineering. Like most schools, the point is to acquaint students with fields they may not choose to focus on later; what's different at Swarthmore is the emphasis on methodology in the PDCs. In a biology PDC, for instance, you might learn more about how scientists interpret data and draw conclusions than about the ins and outs of lipopolysaccharides. And the PDCs have writing requirements, too, that regular courses — especially in the sciences — may not, designed to encourage students to become lucid, thoughtful writers even if they go into a traditionally nonwriting field.

After two years of distribution satisfying and general playing around (Swarthmore encourages students to sample as many departments as possible), students plunge into a major. Many take the plunge several times, in fact; Swarthmore is notoriously flexible in its understanding of the "Well, I *thought* I wanted to do art history, but maybe I'll try physics after all" type of crisis. Spring-semester juniors must also decide whether or not to enter the External Examination Program, two years of intimate, ungraded seminars culminating in three weeks of terror-laced exams given by visiting experts.

"My decision to go into the Honors Program was almost a reluctant one. I didn't like the elitist ring of the name, and wanted to be able to take a lot of different courses rather than only two seminars a semester. But in my department—English—there was unfortunately, a real slant toward the Honors Program; if you didn't go Honors, you simply didn't receive the personalized attention that those in seminars did. So I backed into the program—and, to my surprise, loved it. Seminars were a strange mixture of the very critical and the very supportive; they got me to think analytically about every common sense truth without feeling my own confidence undermined. Occasionally, they were the sites of humiliation (a woman in my Modern Comparative Literature class was rebuked for an interpretation that another student said was stupid—really stupid) or of boredom (a numerical analysis of Romeo and Juliet *springs to mind), but much more often they were interesting and inspiring.*

"The mythology and horror built up around the External Exams is mind-boggling. There were stories of a visiting professor who hurled a book at a student during her oral exam; of one panic-fraught student long ago who wrote her entire history exam over and over and over on one line of her exam book. After this buildup, my exams were anticlimactic—but still rewarding. Having to consolidate two years' worth of learning into six essays helped me place my thoughts in a broader frame, a more global perspective than I ever would have had otherwise. It's probably the closest I've come yet to articulating a sort of philosophy of life."

Seminars usually range from five to ten in size; classes usually hover at 15–20. Although as a first-year student or freshperson (as they're called), you might expect to be in a few large lecture-type courses, most professors incorporate regular discussion into their classes — and when they don't, students often protest. In an effort to provide even more personalized attention, the college instituted a Writing Associates Program, which trains students as peer counselors and then pays them to work in specific courses, helping students to revise and edit papers.

Swarthmore's commitment to helping its students, though, does not extend to grade inflation. A Swarthmore T-shirt reads, "Swarthmore: Anywhere Else It Would Have Been An A," and although that snobbism is for the most part untypical of the school, the sentiment is not. Grade inflation has passed Swarthmore by (leaving some angry students in its wake: a recent student movement tried—unsuccessfully—to require the registrar's office to enclose letters explaining Swarthmore's rigor when sending transcripts to law schools), and although there are a few easy As, there are also a lot of not-so-easy Bs and Cs. But if Swarthmore is tough on students grade-wise, it certainly won't kick them out: students who fail classes generally stay for the extra year or so they need to finish up.

Despite its best efforts, though, Swarthmore's college (as opposed to university) status sometimes will take students by surprise. Some semesters, it's not easy to find four courses you're ecstatic about taking; some semesters, you find them and they're all offered at the same time. That's when students take advantage of Swarthmore's liberal exchange and study-abroad policy. Swarthmore sponsors a semester-long exchange program with Pomona, Mills, Middlebury, and Rice colleges; it also runs a semester-long program in Grenoble, France, and awards credit for several other programs in places from Bogotá to Sri Lanka to Madrid. Ironically, the cost of a semester in any of these places — including airfare, substantial travel, and gifts for friends back home — usually totals several thousand dollars less than a semester at Swarthmore. The college's commitment to international education and, specifically, foreign study has increased substantially in recent years. Students are strongly encouraged to undertake study abroad as an integral part of their degree programs. Many programs have been added to the credit-worthy list in the last few years, advising for foreign study has been much expanded, and financial aid, as needed, is available for virtually all study abroad.

SOCIAL LIFE

If the academic atmosphere at Swarthmore can be intense, the social atmosphere is doubly so; after all, studying is at least done *alone*. At its best, Swarthmore is positively familial. Wander into its one great dining hall, and you'll find most of your friends; traipse across the vast expanse of lawn between McCabe Library and Tarble Social Center, and you'll be invited to join any number of Frisbee games, political arguments, or plain old gossip sessions. The same goes for nightlife: Because there tends to be a limited number of parties, concerts, or anything else on any given night, it's probable that you'll run into just about everyone just about everywhere. If you don't, you'll doubtless see them in Sharples—the aforementioned dining hall and gossip center par excellence.

Sharples, microcosm of Swarthmore social life, sports self-imposed distinctions between people who eat in its Big Room (jocks, economics majors, and other members of Swarthmore's more mainstream crew), its Small Room (poets, religion majors, and science-fiction aficionados) and its Middle Room (just about anybody). These distinctions matter mostly to freshpeople and sophomores, though; once past your second year at Swarthmore, chances are you know a wide enough range of people to bypass these divisions. But no matter where you sit and what your year, you know about the Swarthmore Swivel: a quick glance at the people around you to make sure it's safe to talk to your dinner partner in confidence. For if Swarthmore students can study hard, they can gossip harder.

"I never really understood Swarthmore's reputation as, well, socially dead; it always seemed to be that there was a lot going on. Freshman year socializing took place mainly in my Howard Johnson-style dorm; it consisted in large part of sitting on the floor outside someone's room drinking beer, or sitting on someone's bed eating pizza. Not exciting fare, but many of the people I lived near became—and still are—my best friends. The things we did together changed as the years went on, though: By senior year, we were going to less of the jam-packed college-sponsored parties and freebie concerts that we loved freshman year. Instead, we held cocktail or late-night parties in our own—and by then quite spacious—rooms, went to divey local bars, danced at parties in the Old Club or the Black Cultural Center. When people say there's not much to do at Swarthmore, that's not what

they mean. There's a lot to do—whether your definition of social-izing is going to a free sitar concert or dancing on a table to 'Louie, Louie.' It's just that after your first month there, you're probably not going to meet anyone new doing it."

When life in the Quaker sardine tin gets particularly confining, students take to nearby pizza places and cheap bars, and to Philadelphia for its upscale offerings. Though not many spend as much time in the city as they tell themselves they will, there are a few popular Swarthmore hangouts in Philadelphia: Dalek in West Philly for Ethiopian food, the Marrakesh restaurant off South Street, the Roxy movie the-ater for its great films. Other off-campus hotspots include the you-have-to-see-it-to-believe-it tackiness of Pulsations, a local nightclub with Chippendale dancers, and the Springfield Mall, home of everything a mall should be home to.

EXTRACURRICULAR ACTIVITIES

Swarthmore boasts an unbelievable number of extracurricular organizations and activities—over 200 groups ranging from the musical (there is an orchestra, a gos-pel choir, several *a cappella* groups, and any number of bands) to the journalistic (the newspaper, *The Phoenix,* always has a good debate going about something) to the social (the school has two fraternities; sororities were banished in 1933 by for-mer National Organization of Women president Molly Yard, then a Swarthmore senior). A new Intercultural Center provides a home and support for Asian Ameri-can, Hispanic, and Gay/Lesbian groups; a Black Cultural Center has been around for more than a decade; and a new community Resource Center offers meeting space and office equipment for a dozen minority groups. No matter who you are and what your interests, there's probably a group doing something that appeals to you. If not, start your own — Student Council is generous about funding.

"New groups pop up at a dizzying clip at Swarthmore. During my four years there, the debating society went from a four-person group to a monstrously popular team that was garnering prizes across the globe and filling Tarble Social Center to the gills with its 'pub rounds,' in which members of the team would debate college administrators while the student body drank beer and watched. Two students turned an unused lounge into a popular weekly showcase for student performers. And a passing comment that my roommate made sophomore year about how she'd like to play rugby metamorphosed into a hugely popular—and success-ful—women's rugby team."

Despite the school's reputation as anti-athletic (in 1984, the "Tank MacNamara" comic strip spoofed Swarthmore with a feature about a school where the students were embarrassed when the football team won), sports may well be the most popular extracurricular activity. About one third of the student body plays varsity sports, and more are involved with junior varsity and intramurals. Forget visions of grueling tryouts and ultracompetitive cuts, though: If you're interested in a sport, chances are you can get on the team. Particularly good teams are tennis, cross country, lacrosse, and swimming. Music, dance, and theater are also popular at Swarthmore, and the students' longtime complaint that the school doesn't support the arts as much as it could has been answered by the brand-new Lang Performing Arts Center.

Much of Swarthmore life revolves around the dorms, at least for the 90% of students who live on campus. Though freshpeople often are crowded into small doubles, the school's housing system after that is relatively fair. A harrowing lottery—fraught with almost as much nervous tension as Honors exams—controls the room-choosing process every year: You get a good number, you and your roommate pick a spacious two-room double in ivy-covered Wharton or modern Mertz; you get a bad number and the two of you are living in frosh-ridden Willets or out-of-the-way Mary Lyons. For the most part, though, students are satisfied with their housing, and different dorms come to suit the tempers of the people that fill them. Mertz houses athletes, Palmer, Pittenger, and Roberts house those who want peace and quiet. Worth houses seniors who want silence by day and the Grateful Dead by night. The school's two fraternity houses offer no living quarters; they basically serve as party space for weekly bashes. In fact, these bashes are the raison d'être of Swarthmore's low-profile Greek system, which attracts the school's brawniest contingent.

GRADUATES

Swarthmore alums are a tight-knit bunch. Not literally—they're sprinkled across the globe working everywhere from the Peace Corps to the White House—but in a more cosmic sense. A full 16% of the school's graduates marry other graduates (this, coupled with a fire in the 1980's that leveled the social center, earns Swarthmore the nickname the Quaker matchbox) and many of the 15,500 living alumni maintain strong ties with the school and with each other. Even those who don't keep up any actual connection with the college will talk animatedly to a stranger on a train when they find out that person attended Swarthmore.

> *"After graduation, I launched a mammoth job hunt. The Swarthmore career planning and placement office gave me a list of all the alumni in publishing, and I wrote letters and sent my résumé to at least 15 of them, expecting to get one or two replies at the most. What I got was incredible: interviews for choice jobs at great publishing houses, long letters from executive editors listing names of people I might contact. The rest, of course, was up to*

me—but the extent to which Swarthmore alumni are willing to help one another was a heartwarming introduction to the supposedly cold, impersonal working world."

Though about 60% of Swarthmore students take jobs right after graduation, within five years about half of them have gone to graduate school. Swarthmore ranks second among all colleges for the number of students who go on to earn doctorates, and there are an inordinate number of National Science Foundation, Mellon, Fulbright, and National Endowment for the Humanities fellowships awarded each year. Among students who choose to go back to school the going rumor is that "it's never as hard as Swarthmore." Among those who don't, there's a lot of diversity. Many students go into politics—working either for the government or for small, public-interest organizations—and many into publishing, the arts, and business. Lots do more interesting, innovative things, though. One recent graduate helped found a company that makes boxer shorts with college logos on them; another founded a school in Thailand. Alumni include former presidential candidate Michael Dukakis; author James Michener; Victor Navasky, editor of *The Nation*; philanthropist Eugene Lang; Neil Austrian, president of the NFL; Michigan Senator Carl Levin; and an impressive list of others, including three Nobel Laureates, 36 members of the National Academy of Sciences, and nine members of the National Academy of Engineering. Oh, and a 1972 graduate and former associate dean of the college, Cigus Vanni, competed in "Jeopardy's" 1989 Tournament of Champions.

SUMMARY OVERVIEW

In short, Swarthmore is a difficult, intense place you'll probably either love or hate. You'll meet people who are bright, inventive and funny. You'll take classes that challenge your assumptions, stir your imagination, and make you passionate about issues you never even heard of before. You'll spend four years wandering through 330 acres of lush greenery. And you will suffer occasional, but serious, claustrophobia, brought on by the knowledge that everyone knows everything about you.

The people you'll meet at Swarthmore probably will stay with you forever—either literally, as friends and future colleagues, or figuratively, as murky but inspiring memories. It's hard to say which is more important; it's hard to say when you'll again meet a group of people at once so eccentric and so sane, at once so serious and so funny. The chance to share a small, tightly woven community with intelligent, motivated people—people whose paths may well keep out of your sight for the rest of your life—is invaluable.

Couple the people you'll meet with the classes you'll meet them in, and Swarthmore becomes a deeply challenging, provocative place. Professors are serious, work loads are heavy, but the real focus of a Swarthmore education is on the way you learn, on—to coin a terrible cliche from campus brochures—learning *how* to learn. This also means coming to think critically, to question your most fundamental assumptions in an effort to find your most personal values. Finally, the education involves beginning to respect other people's philosophies.

But the kernel of the Swarthmore experience may be the school's emphatic commitment to diversity, to helping everyone from introspective poets to ebullient athletes share the same small green campus. Swarthmore knows that it, like any campus, isn't *really* diverse—it's mostly white (though less so than other schools), mostly upper or middle class (ditto), and by definition educated—and so it encourages its students to look past the campus to local communities and the world in order to see what *real* diversity—of color, wealth, and perspective—looks like.

Swarthmore's great blessing, though, is its great failing—a tiny community bound to stifle you if you're set on the spaciousness of a big university, on the anonymity that's possible at a larger school. There's no hope for anonymity at Swarthmore: Even the quietest, most reclusive students find themselves the meat of mundane meal time conversation. And although spaciousness exists in the figurative sense (there's always something new to do), it doesn't mean much literally (there's never anyone new to do it with).

And Swarthmore's size means measly reputation in the eyes of those for whom a well-educated person is necessarily Ivy-bred. That may not sound important, but the fiftieth time you hear, "*Where* is it again?" you'll feel like impaling the speaker on your Swarthmore umbrella. Comfort yourself with the knowledge that among many academic and professional circles Swarthmore is known as the best college in the country; if that's not enough for you, choose another school.

Finally, if full- or most-of-the-time socializing is high on your list of college objectives, Swarthmore — with its single party a night and meager two fraternities — will be a difficult, frustrating place for you. And if cosmopolitan living ranks up there, think again: Despite the quick train ride into Philadelphia, the college's immediate surroundings are far from metropolitan.

So will it be worth it, this four-year-stint in suburban Pennsylvania? Will luxurious greenery, quick intellectual wit, and small size redeem backbreaking work, rampant gossip—and small size? That depends on who you are. If the school's commitments to tolerance and diversity are *really* what you want; if the chance to work hard at things that interest you sounds like privilege, not punishment; and, finally, if the idea of a small, intimate community filled with what will come to be very familiar faces intrigues you, then go to Swarthmore.

Cindi Leive, B.A.

Tufts University

THE PROGRAM

"My first memory of Tufts is of walking onto campus on a cold rainy day in February to take a tour as a prospective student. By the end of the half-hour tour around the hilly campus, I was soaked to the skin and convinced that I wanted to go to Tufts.

"That may sound irrational, and I can't exactly explain it; but somehow, Tufts University looked like everything I had ever thought college would be. The student who guided our group through the tree-lined campus couldn't say enough about the place.

"That was the best part about Tufts, the feeling of being a part of a community. I could sense it even on the tour. Looking back, I became part of that rich academic community. And that was enough for me."

To get an idea of what Tufts is like, you must understand the people who go there. Students are opinionated, motivated, and outgoing. If there are more than five Tufts students in a room at once, you as easily could have a party as a debate or a heated political discussion. If you are a visitor on campus, don't hesitate to ask a passing student what he or she thinks about the school, but be prepared to spend some time; the student probably will give you a personal guided tour to show you around.

The Tufts University undergraduate campus sits on a 150-acre site five miles northwest of Boston. The location means that Tufts has the best of both worlds. It offers the relative quiet of a suburban residential campus, while being only a 15-minute bus or train ride away from the biggest college towns in the country: Boston and Cambridge. Going to school in the Boston area is like no other experience. There are more than 40,000 college students in and around Boston, and at least that many recent graduates. It is a community that caters to young people.

The neatly placed red brick buildings of the academic quad originally housed most of the academic departments but as the university grew, the campus expanded down the hill to provide more space for academics and housing. One of the unique aspects of Tufts is that it can be so many different things to different people. University President John DiBiaggio says that Tufts combines the complexity of a large university with the camaraderie of a small college. Therefore, Tufts students can take a diverse array of classes on campus or explore the wide resources in the Boston area. At the same time, students receive individualized attention from faculty that is often unavailable at a large school. This combination gives Tufts its distinctive educational advantage.

A salient feature of this individualized yet broad-based education at Tufts is flexibility. If there is a subject you want to study and you can't find the course, you can design an independent study course to fill the gap. If you want your major concentration to combine two or three disciplines, figure it out and present it to your adviser as a plan of study. You can do almost anything. But don't think you will graduate without studying the basics. You won't. In addition to whatever you decide to major in, the university requires all students to fulfill a set of distribution requirements that are designed to round you out in areas you might miss otherwise.

The style of education at Tufts is best described as friendly yet demanding, or that is to say the professors are friendly but demanding. Almost 100% of the classes are taught by professors, not graduate students. Because professors make this commitment to hands-on teaching, they demand that students put in the same kind of effort. If you end up at Tufts, you may just find yourself sitting in the campus center drinking coffee one evening discussing with your professor your rewrite of a paper on Emily Dickinson or American foreign policy. At the start of every term most professors will ask for their students' home phone numbers, and don't be surprised when they give you theirs in return. And they expect you to use it.

Students at Tufts earn either a Bachelor of Arts degree or a Bachelor of Science degree after finishing 34 courses over eight semesters. At least ten of those courses should be in a major. The most popular majors are (in order) English, economics, political science, international relations, and history.

The most popular courses at Tufts cover the range of disciplines from culture to classics and several things in-between. The fact that most students take either Greek and Roman Comedy or Greek and Roman Tragedy, doesn't mean that the entire school is made up of classicists. What it does mean is that the school encourages students to get a diverse background. But don't think that the popular classes are only in the classics, because they're not. Introduction to Yiddish Culture, German Expressionism, West African Dance and Drum Ensemble, Classical Mythology and Introduction to International Relations also make the top of the Tufts University hit parade. This range of classes affords students the opportunity to do things that they never have done before and probably never will do again. You haven't truly laughed until you've seen six football players dressed in Roman togas, and high-topped sneakers perform a scene from *Antigone* in front of a group of 150 students.

"I only realized how much Tufts had to offer academically when I was organizing my classes for registration for the first semester of my senior year. Because I was abroad at the Tufts program in London, I was sitting with five or six other students in our professor's office, and we were talking about what we were taking.

"Because I was almost done with the requirements for my major, I had some flexibility. Therefore, I started to take suggestions from the group about good elective courses. When all the suggestions were in and I had made some choices myself, I looked at the list before me and realized I needed to spend another three years there just to take the classes I was interested in.

In every department from engineering to chemistry, with the possible exception of math (a personal dislike), I had classes that seemed pertinent and appealing for one reason or another."

GETTING IN/FINANCIAL AID

The undergraduate community at Tufts is made up of the College of Liberal Arts and Sciences, with 3900 students, and the College of Engineering, with 760 students. The student population is slightly more than half female. In the engineering school, 19% are women. Tufts received 7880 applications for a recent class and accepted 3010. The average freshman class size at Tufts is 1170.

Applications to Tufts are read by at least two of the school's 12 admissions officers and evaluated on the basis of academics, school activities, and outside activities. As part of the academic evaluation, a prospective student's course selection and the level of courses taken, a student's grades and class rank, and standardized test results are reviewed. In the area of extracurricular activities, the admissions officer looks for an indication that a student participated and was involved.

"My freshman year, I lived in a coed dorm with students from all over the United States and from France, England, and Italy. Since I grew up in suburban New Jersey, living in the same dorm as a guy from Utah and a woman from Rome was as exciting as any of my classes. To be perfectly honest, the late nights sitting up comparing our lives and making fun of the regional and foreign accents and mannerisms that we all had were probably as educational as any class I could have taken in comparative cultures …yet with no exams to study for."

School stats show the diversity of the student body. In a recent class, 30% of the students were from Massachusetts, 15% from other New England states, 32% from the Mid-Atlantic states, 6% from the North Central states, 7% from the South, 6% from the West, and 4% from foreign countries. Foreign students from over 60 countries enroll each year. In addition to being regionally and nationally diverse, Tufts tries to create an ethnically diverse environment as well. Roughly 16% of the students are people of color, mostly black, Asian, and Hispanic.

The cost for attending Tufts is not cheap; tuition and fees for a student in residence total more than $26,000. To help meet these costs, Tufts students are eligible for the full range of financial aid from university, state, and federal loans and grants, and federally subsidized campus employment. Approximately 50% of the students receive some kind of financial aid. All financial aid at Tufts is based on need and usually is awarded in packages that combine loans, grants, and campus work.

ACADEMIC ENVIRONMENT

The best way to describe a Tufts education is "multidisciplinary." Tufts's faculty insist that every well-educated individual should be exposed to many different areas of knowledge. In order to accomplish this, the school offers flexible and innovative programs that allow students to pursue almost any conceivable course of study. Although 80–85% of the student body at Tufts choose a liberal arts education, there are certain requirements that every student must fulfill in order to graduate.

These distribution requirements, as they are called, mean that every student must complete a two-course sequence in each of the five major areas of the curriculum: humanities, arts, social studies, natural sciences and technology, and mathematical science.

"As an international relations and history major, I couldn't understand why it was necessary to take a science class. I put it off until my junior year and then realized I had better get it over with. I didn't enjoy science in high school, but I was determined to get through my choice of reproductive biology with a minimum of problems. Something like swallowing castor oil, simply because it is good for you.

"The class was taught by an energetic biologist who was doing ground-breaking work in the area of fetal development. I became entranced. The science she was teaching was actually interesting. Studying genetic engineering and the creation of new animals wasn't just technical mumbo jumbo; it was really fascinating. The class also dealt with one of the touchiest subjects of our time, abortion. But by keeping discussions to the scientific processes and the medical facts, intelligent dialogues came out.

"The class didn't make me want to be a biologist, but it did open my eyes to the world of science. More than learning about biology, I learned about learning."

The academic atmosphere at Tufts is conducive to learning anything a student could want to learn. Essentially the program guarantees a student the basics and a lot of options. The easiest way to exercise those options is through the extensive independent study program. In addition to the traditional classes, more than 900 independent study arrangements are made each year for students to work directly with faculty members and create a curriculum for study or research.

Tufts offers 42 different major areas of concentration and the option for students to develop their own plan of study that combines two or more disciplines not usually thought of as related. These plans are developed by a student and his or her adviser and are approved by a faculty committee. Plans of study in recent years have included Environmental Effects of Urban Development, Nutrition and Population in National Development, and Bilingual Education.

Perhaps the most unusual class options come from the Tufts Experimental College. Having just celebrated its twenty-fifth anniversary, the Ex College, as it is known, offers classes in everything from freshman explorations, which serve as advisory groups, to an introduction to Caribbean music. In the Ex College, students and faculty together evaluate course proposals. The classes offered are programs that do not fit well in the regular curriculum. Currently, the Ex College offers 60 credit-bearing undergraduate courses and enrolls more than 1100 students every year. Examples of Ex College classes include Latino Poetry, The Kibbutz, Filmmaking, Discrimination and Its Remedies, Commodities and Futures, and The History of the Women's Movement.

Going beyond the classroom options available on the Tufts campus, students can take advantage of opportunities at other colleges and institutions in and around the Boston area. This makes Tufts home to several combined degree programs. Working with the New England Conservatory of Music, students can enroll in a five-year program leading to a Bachelor of Science or a Bachelor of Arts from Tufts and a Bachelor of Music from the conservatory. A similar program exists with Tufts and the School of the Museum of Fine Arts. This five-year program allows students with interests in studio art to receive a Bachelor of Arts or Bachelor of Science from Tufts and a Bachelor of Fine Arts.

Within Tufts itself, students can combine bachelor's and master's degrees in liberal arts in five-year programs or combine a liberal arts and engineering degree and receive both a Bachelor of Arts and a Bachelor of Science. A final combined six-year degree program involves the College of Liberal Arts and Sciences and the Fletcher School of Law and Diplomacy, Tufts's graduate school of international relations.

Most Tufts classes offer the opportunity for an active exchange of ideas in the classroom, so class format usually is more of a running dialogue than a straight lecture. Beyond the introductory level, most classes are relatively small. The average class size is 25 students. More than 60% of classes have 20 or fewer students, many are as small as 10–15. The student-to-faculty ratio is 14 to 1. Professors are very accessible to their students and encourage students to see them outside the classroom for additional discussion. Grades are done on a standard A through F scale.

In sum, the Tufts academic program allows students to do intensive study in a wide variety of areas, yet still have the intimate atmosphere of a small college. One can get individualized attention from faculty and not just be one of thousands. The Boston location with all its academic resources and the flexibility of the academic program at Tufts add to a student's education. Although Tufts may not be the absolutely best academic program in the country, it offers one of the best total educational experiences around.

SOCIAL LIFE

Tufts's location, just a short train ride from Boston and Cambridge, gives students the opportunity to explore those cities for their social and cultural offerings. But being a predominantly residential school, Tufts provides entertainment and social activities on campus as well. Students can and do take advantage of both. People with all kinds of interests can find things to do at Tufts. Weekends mean concerts and dance performances, athletic events, and parties of all kinds for students of all ages.

The university sponsors several special-event weekends every year that include concerts from well-known performers and special performances and parties on campus. The biggest social event of the year is Spring Fling, held the last weekend of classes every spring. Spring Fling is the last big blowout of the year, giving students the chance to let off steam before putting their noses into their books to study for finals. The festivities kick off on Thursday with a block party featuring a local band. Students by the thousands swarm onto Professor's Row to dance, talk, and hope to enjoy balmy New England spring weather. Things wrap up Saturday afternoon with a concert from a nationally known band. In recent years, Stevie Ray Vaughn and the Busboys have graced the outdoor stage.

> "Sophomore year, the weather didn't hold, and Spring Fling weekend was soaked with the April showers and unpredictable weather Massachusetts is known for. Concert organizers worked all weekend arranging to move the whole event into a club in Boston. They succeeded, and many Jumbos piled onto chartered busses and headed for town. A few of us, however, felt it wasn't Spring Fling if we weren't at Tufts, so we stayed in soggy, cloudy Medford and had our own Spring Fling.
>
> "We rigged up a barbecue on the balcony of a friend's dorm, hooked up a stereo, and partied our hearts out. Except for the chance to catch some sun in early April, we didn't feel like we'd missed a thing. Even the weather couldn't keep Fling away."

That is not to say that Tufts students are tied to campus. With the Davis Square "T" stop only a short walk from campus, you can be in Boston in a matter of minutes, and that means access to some of the best cultural and social sites in the country. From the somewhat touristy Faneuil Hall and its shops, restaurants, and bars, to the Museum of Fine Arts and the dance clubs in Kenmore Square, Boston offers a neverending supply of cultural and not-so-cultural things to do.

As if Boston didn't offer enough options, there is also Cambridge with its bohemian air, just over the Somerville border. The array of ethnic restaurants can keep you busy for your four years at Tufts and more. There are jazz clubs and comedy clubs and shopping galore in the streets of Harvard Square. If you are on a tight budget, you can just walk around the square and enjoy the array of street performers who sing, dance, juggle, and entertain the passersby on any day when the weather permits.

There are plenty of organized events at and around Tufts to keep anyone busy, but one of the best things about the students here is their ability to be spontaneous. Though an outsider might think that Tufts is a grunt school where people study all the time and the social life is weak, this reputation is far from accurate.

It is true that Tufts students are conscious of their grades and their academic performance, but they also like to have a good time. Often a group of Jumbos just standing around can develop into a party or game. The quad, a grassy area between dorms, is often the sight of impromptu snowball fights in winter and Frisbee matches in the spring and summer.

Because Tufts students study particularly hard during exam periods, several Jumbo traditions have developed to help ease the tension. A winter exam highlight is the midnight ice cream social where students come and gorge themselves at a make-your-own sundae bar. For students who prefer a more physical form of tension release, there is the quad run. Dormitories compete to amass the greatest number of total laps over the course of exams and are rewarded with a party paid for by the dormitory council.

EXTRACURRICULAR ACTIVITIES

At Tufts, the motto governing student activities always seems to be if you can't find a group doing something that interests you, start one of your own. Most student activities are funded through the student activities fee that everyone pays each year. These funds, approximately $450,000 per year, are administered by the student senate.

The activities available to students include groups that work in the arts, athletics, the media, academic areas, and more. In all there are more than 150 student organizations on campus.

"In my four years at Tufts, I probably spent more time working on the shows I did with Torn Ticket II (the musical theater group)

than I did in class. Some of my best memories from Tufts are of the time I spent up to my elbows in sawdust and paint at 2 A.M., building a set and painting it. How can you not become friends with a person when you are standing two inches away from his face with your finger practically in his nose putting makeup on him for the upcoming performance? I can't say I have as many great memories about writing papers or studying for exams."

Student activities are just that at Tufts, *student* activities. Though every group has a faculty adviser, the idea is to sink or swim on your own. That means everyone has to work together to get the job done or the play doesn't go on, the paper doesn't come out, the blood drive or Kid's Day doesn't happen. Being a part of an organization at Tufts can mean long hours and tiring work, often more time-consuming than class work, but the results are amazing. There isn't much that a group of Tufts students can't do if they put their minds to it.

At the start of every semester, the student organizations get together and hold an activities fair where groups practically compete with one another for the students' attention. Some of the most popular activities on campus include the theatrical groups like Torn Ticket II and Pen Paint and Pretzels; singing groups like the Third Day Gospel Choir, and the three *a cappella* groups, the Beelzebubs, the Jackson Jills, and the Amalgamates; the school's several newspapers including *The Tufts Daily* and *The Tufts Observer* (a weekly); the intramural sports programs that involved over 3110 men and women last year; and the concert board that has arranged for performers such as the Pat Metheny Group and comedian Steven Wright to come on campus.

Fraternities and sororities also compete for students' attention at the start of every semester. There are 11 fraternities and three sororities active on the Tufts campus. About 19% of the students join them. The Greeks' houses are owned either by the organization itself or by the university. Most of the houses sit along Professor's Row in the center of campus. Because the Greeks are a minority on campus, many of the events they host are open to the rest of the student body, making their activities important to the school as a whole.

Although fraternities and sororities offer housing for some upperclassmen, most students live in school dorms or houses. Freshmen and sophomores are guaranteed housing in one of Tufts's 18 dormitories. The dorms range in size from 40–260 people and have rooms that vary from singles to quads. There are no all-freshmen dorms at Tufts, so students from different classes live together in the same building. In addition to the dorms, Tufts owns 26 small houses where students with similar cultural or special interests live together.

GRADUATES

Ninety percent of students who enter Tufts as freshmen graduate from the school, a figure higher than most universities and one of which Tufts is very proud. After graduation, Tufts graduates tend to continue their education. Roughly 40% of graduates go directly to graduate school. Of that group, 12% go to law school, 10% go to business school, 8% go to medical school, and 1% go to dental school. An additional uncounted group go on to pursue graduate degrees in the arts, sciences, and engineering. Of the graduates who do not go directly to graduate school, 78% indicate that they have plans for graduate studies in the future.

Each year, approximately 11–12% of the class apply to medical school, of whom 75% are accepted. About 15% apply to law school, with more than 80% accepted. With business school applications, Tufts, which does not offer an undergraduate business degree, has its best record. One hundred percent of the graduates applying to business schools are accepted.

Five years after graduation, most Tufts alums are pursuing their respective careers. Tufts alums occupy positions in business, the arts, medicine, law, and almost every other field you can name. And the best thing about it is that once a Jumbo, always a Jumbo.

Tufts alumni are a friendly group that stays connected with the university. They have formed various networks to celebrate the Tufts spirit around the country. The New York Tufts Alliance hosts a homecoming touch football game in Central Park for the people who can't make it back to Tufts for the event. Groups like the New York Alliance exist in most major cities in the United States, and there even are several around the world.

SUMMARY OVERVIEW

There is very little that a student can't find at Tufts University. Although the university is small in size, Tufts students have a large number of options both academically and socially. The flexible nature of the academic opportunities at Tufts means that, if you can't find a course you want, you can get together with your professor and create a course that meets your needs. The social and cultural options for Tufts students abound in the Boston and Cambridge area, which lie at the feet of any student willing to explore them.

The students at Tufts don't tend to explore alone. You are more likely to see a group of 12 than a solo Jumbo out on the town. Outgoing and vivacious, the energy is almost contagious when the mood is festive. Tufts students are friendly and outgoing, and the university prides itself on making everyone feel welcome. It is not unusual for freshmen to be friends with seniors at this school, where all four classes mix in academic and social settings.

The drawbacks to Tufts include some paranoia about life in the shadow of some of the most prestigious universities in the country, if not the world. With both Harvard University and the Massachusetts Institute of Technology just down the road, Tufts sometimes can feel forgotten. Despite ranking just below the Ivy League in many polls, some students who didn't make it to the Ivies may feel that they settled for second choice. However, this Ivy Wannabe syndrome usually disappears after freshman year, when students discover the strengths of a Tufts education.

The cost of a Tufts education can be seen as another drawback. With prices so high, the student body has an upper-middle-class tilt to it. Despite university efforts to keep it mixed, Tufts can look like a parking lot for fancy cars at first glance. The university administration is making efforts to offer more financial aid and improve the mix of students, but some changes are slow in coming.

Another downside to the Tufts experience is the weather. If you don't like the cold and you want to keep your tan year-round, maybe a small New England college isn't for you. Despite all the advantages of being in Boston, you have to remember that it is cold and rainy and snowy, unpredictably so from October through April some years. To some people, the Tufts campus looks beautiful after a winter (or spring) snowfall. To others, the campus's rolling hills look like treacherous Himalayan cliffs.

Still, Tufts offers students a chance to get one of the best well-rounded educations in the country and the opportunity to go to school in Boston, the country's biggest college town. In the end, if asked would they attend again if they had it to do over, every graduate I know would say "yes" in a second. And that is the best endorsement a college can have.

Amy Resnick, B.A.

University of California at Berkeley

THE PROGRAM

"I can still remember my first day of school at UC/Berkeley. As I walked through the campus, I was amazed at the heterogeneity of the people before my eyes. There were old people with backpacks, young people, people with shorts on, people in business suits (seniors on their way to interviews), and people from all minority groups. These students were all here because they were different from the average high school student and had excelled in some area. To be a part of this group is a feeling that is exciting and scary at the same time. Feelings of inferiority came over me in my classes the first day as I sat next to two people who both had been valedictorians at their high schools. But I realized that there were skills that I possessed that they did not, and that was why I was here."

The University of California at Berkeley prides itself on its "excellence and diversity." The students at Cal have ceased being sponges that absorb certain knowledge and regurgitate it on command for a test. Rather, they are a sounding board for new ideas from both their fellow students and the faculty. Berkeley is an institution known as a place where students can come and discuss any academic endeavor, and the discussion and learning will not stop in the classroom. It is because of this attitude towards academic freedom and tolerance of new ideas that Berkeley was the birthplace of the Free Speech movement of the 1960s.

This philosophy of academic freedom and challenging faculty has also attracted thousands of students from overseas to the Berkeley campus. Because of the number of foreign students attending Cal, it has developed the reputation of an international academic center. To foster this sentiment, the university maintains a residence known as the International House. Not only does it serve as home to many foreign students, but many cultural, social, and recreational events are held here to promote understanding among different nationalities. This attitude symbolizes the open-mindedness and unquenching thirst for knowledge that prevails on this campus.

> *"My first encounter with this peculiar trait was after an anthropology discussion section my freshman year. After class had finished, some upper-division students said they were going to grab a cup of coffee and wanted to know if I would like to join them. Feeling a little tired from a long day of classes, I figured why not. First they introduced me to a drink that would enable me to take part in many cram study sessions, the double cappucino, or double cap, as it is fondly referred to. This large cup of extra-strength coffee is the student's best friend come exam time. We then proceeded to engage in a lengthy discussion about anthropology and its application to human behavior. What really impressed me was that these students really cared about anthropology and did not just forget it when the class ended. That is what Berkeley is about, whether it is having a double cap at Cafe Roma while discussing anthropology or doing chemical research in the bowels of Latimer Hall, the Cal student is always learning."*

All this learning takes place in the middle of a college town, Berkeley, California, which is like a garden oasis. Some of the buildings look like they came right out of ancient Greece with their pillars and stone carvings, whereas others almost look like skyscrapers as they rise above the beautiful lawns and trees. With a creek running right through the middle of campus and several groves of trees, it is quite easy to find a nice peaceful place to sit and think only a few blocks from the noisy streets of the city. The Campanile Clock towers over the campus reminding us all of splendor and tradition as well as the fact that we are late for class again.

Although Cal is a large public institution with approximately 22,000 undergraduates, the quality of education it offers is considered among the best in the nation. It is able to compete with the top private colleges at only a fraction of the cost. Because it is a large university, the student body is more diverse than at most colleges. The academic freedom and the differing ideas expressed at Cal attract the best faculty, who in turn challenge the students. You can't get a better education for the price.

GETTING IN

One of the hardest things about UC/Berkeley is actually getting into the school. There are over 21,000 applicants for approximately 3300 spots every year, so the university can afford to be picky about whom it accepts. The excellence and diversity of the university carry over to the student body. Factoring in advanced placement grades, most of the incoming freshman had GPAs approaching 4.0 on a 4.0 scale. So, then, how does one get into Cal?

In the admissions process there are the "A-to-F" requirements. These are 15 high school courses that must be completed with at least a C grade. These 15 courses consist of one year of history, four years of English, three years of mathematics, one year of a laboratory science, two years of a foreign language, and, finally, the equivalent of four years of additional elective academic courses. The grades received in the A to F courses are the only grades taken into consideration in calculating your GPA for admission.

Approximately 50% of the applicants are offered admission on the basis of their academic index score alone. This score is calculated by indexing the A-to-F GPA and adding the scores of five tests: the math and verbal portions of the SAT I (or the ACT) and three SAT II exams.

For the balance of the incoming class, university readers not only evaluate grades and test scores, but also review the entire application looking for other academic accomplishments and extracurricular activities. This allows the students who were really involved in extracurricular activities, such as student government, the chance for admission, although they did not achieve the very top on tests and grades. In this second review process, the university also pays particular attention to an applicant's life circumstances such as enrollment in rural or nontraditional high school, special talent, disability, reentry status, socioeconomic background, athletic talent, and ethnicity. This ensures that, for 50% of the class, students are more broadly evaluated for evidence of intellectual and creative ability, honors, commitment to work and community, and factors that contribute to student body diversity, rather than for a numerical score alone.

Because of the admissions policies, I met a range of students who helped me understand different cultures and different attitudes. Through its minority recruitment efforts, Berkeley has become one of the first top-ranked academic institutions in the United States to crack the 50% barrier. No one ethnic group now makes up a majority in the undergraduate student population. The current undergraduate study body consists of 38% whites, 31% Asians, with blacks, Hispanics, and American Indians making up the rest. There is also a fair number of older students who enroll at Berkeley.

"I was very surprised one day to look up and see a friend of my mother's sitting in the first row of my paleontology class. I have also had the pleasure of sharing a class with royalty from a European country. However, the incident that really brings to mind what Berkeley is about involves a black woman. I was invited to a luncheon to honor outstanding students. There was the usual group of 3.8 GPA Phi Beta Kappas who were involved in almost every activity and were on their way to medical or law school. But there was also an incredible woman from the ghetto who had not only achieved a 3.9 GPA but had done so while raising two small kids by herself. The crowd rose in unison to applaud

*this woman and her amazing efforts. All these different kinds of
people help enhance the portion of your college education that
occurs outside the academic realm."*

FINANCIAL AID

The university prides itself on the diversity of its student body. Although the in-state expenses are relatively low, $11,378 total for a recent year including $3248 for fees, and $8130 for room, board, and personal expenses, financial aid must be available to all who need it if Berkeley is to remain diverse. Approximately 48% of Berkeley students receive financial aid in some form or another. A total of $42.7 million is awarded each year to students who have demonstrated a financial need. This need is ascertained from the information provided on the federal financial aid application. Students are offered a financial aid package that may consist of a combination of funds from various sources from which financial aid is drawn.

Scholarships, which do not have to be repaid, include the Regents Scholarships, Alumni Scholarships, and University Scholarships. Even if you do not think you are eligible for financial aid, I encourage you to apply for the many scholarships that are available. Although I was not eligible to receive any financial aid, I was awarded an Alumni Scholarship. This award carries many benefits besides the monetary value. For example, the Alumni Scholars program has a number of dormitory rooms set aside for scholarship winners who need housing.

Grants and loans are awarded on the basis of financial need only. Grants available include the Pell Grant and the Cal Grants A and B, among others. These grants do not have to be repaid. The loans that are available carry below-market interest rates and must be repaid over a period of years.

The university also offers special programs to assist underrepresented minorities and students from educationally disadvantaged and low-income backgrounds. The Educational Opportunity Program (EOP) offers assistance to those students who would be otherwise unable to attend Berkeley. EOP is open to students who meet regular admission requirements as well as those who require special admission.

In short, if the only thing holding you back from attending Berkeley is the finances, then do not worry. It has been my experience that the financial aid office will do all in its power to help any qualified student attend Cal.

ACADEMIC ENVIRONMENT

Although it is very hard to get into Cal, it is almost as hard to stay in. The competition is very intense, and unlike some schools there is the very real possibility of flunking out. The old joke is that in Chemistry 1 the professor asks you to look to your left and then to your right. Then he tells you that only one of the three of you will graduate from Cal. There may be more fiction than truth to that statement (more than two-thirds of freshmen graduate in five years), but, it has some applicability. There were many times I left a lecture hall in a daze wondering what the professor was talking about or where he got the question for the final. However, this is the beauty of an education at Cal.

Berkeley has a reputation for academic excellence, and it didn't earn that by providing easy answers or letting students slide. Although the professors may ask tough questions, they give the students the necessary tools to ascertain the answers. Professors challenge you and in return expect you to challenge them. I have rarely found a teacher that is not impressed with a student who is willing to offer an argument contrary to the one being presented. You do have to be prepared to back up your arguments because the faculty will challenge you.

This can be quite a task because the faculty consists of the best and the brightest. Berkeley has eight Nobel laureates on its staff. There are also 107 members of the National Academy of Sciences, and 64 members of the National Academy of Engineering, as well as more Guggenheim Fellows and Presidential Young Investigators teaching on the Berkeley campus than at any other university in the nation. Chances are that no matter what field you choose, your professor will be a renowned and honored individual. I personally had the pleasure of learning physics from Owen Chamberlain, a man who was involved in the creation of the original atomic bomb in 1945.

Berkeley carries its philosophy of excellence and diversity into its academic program. Its undergraduate program is one of the best in the nation, and although it is especially noted for its science and engineering programs, Berkeley offers something for everyone. Undergraduate majors are offered through colleges, such as the College of Letters and Science or the College of Chemistry. Most majors are designed to be taken over a four-year period although you do not have to declare your major until your junior year. There are over 100 majors from which a student can choose. These literally range from *A* to *Z,* as one can major in African American studies or zoology and everything in between. If, however, there is not a major that suits you, you can design your own.

If you find that you need to get away from the Berkeley campus for a while to continue your studies, there are excellent programs abroad, which many students take advantage of. The Education Abroad Program (EAP) has over 60 study centers located in Africa, Asia, Australia, Central America, Europe, the Middle East, and South America. Students generally go abroad their junior year, a plan that provides an excellent opportunity to see a different country while earning credit toward a degree at Berkeley.

Thirty units of successfully completed work per year is considered normal progress toward a degree. Although requirements vary from major to major and from college to college, the university does set two general requirements: Basic English and American History and Institutions. These requirements can be completed in high school, at Cal, by scoring well on the English and U.S. history achievement tests, or by the advanced placement tests. In addition, all Berkeley undergraduates must complete a requirement in American cultures.

Because of the high caliber of students at Berkeley, there is intense competition for grades.

> *"I can still recall my first midterm at Cal. The class was Mathematics 1A, and after I took the test I was sure I had failed. What would my parents think when they found out? How was I going to stay in school? How could I face my friends when they found out how stupid I was? These and other questions were dancing around in my head as I walked home. Like most students at Cal, I had done well in high school and was not used to the idea of failing tests. What I did not realize was that most of the class had walked out of the test feeling the exact same way I did. When it came time to hand the exams back, the professor, who was obviously experienced in dealing with freshman, told us not to worry. Most of us had done better than we had expected, he said, but this test would teach us a few things.*
>
> *"First of all, almost everyone in the room was an A student in high school, so the competition was fierce. No longer could we afford to slide by. If we wanted a good grade, we were going to have to work hard for it. Second, he added, this test exemplified the kind of test we would be taking for the next four years. Gone were the tests that required rote memorization. Professors in college wanted to know if we could use and apply their teachings rather than regurgitate them on a piece of paper. Because of the curve, I was able to get a C+, which was above average. This gave me tremendous confidence. I was competing against all these smart students and doing OK, and I was actually using the information taught to me. I ended up getting a B+ in the class."*

The upper-division courses tend to have a mean of B. Although a grade higher than a B+ is hard to achieve, a B is considered very acceptable because only a C average is required for continued enrollment. Some of the professors do grade on a straight percentage. The classes that do this tend to be the ones with larger enrollment. In the upper-division courses, competition between students is de-emphasized and a cooperative spirit is fostered as classes examine problems in depth.

> *"Everyone always told me that the classes at Berkeley were big, but nothing anyone said prepared me for my first class my freshman year. The building the class was held in was both beautiful and imposing. It was a huge three-story building that looked like it belonged next to the Parthenon in Greece. The class was Economics 1. I knew the class was going to be big when I heard it was held in an auditorium. In high school, only two thing happened in the auditorium: pep rallies and basketball games, so I was interested to see how an academic class was going to be*

taught there. Approximately 900 students filled the classroom that day, and much to my surprise I not only learned a lot, but I enjoyed the class so much I became an economics major. However, I do remember looking at this room, which contained as many students as were enrolled in my entire high school, and thinking that the professor would never know if I showed up or not."

This is entirely true. With the big lectures one can be totally anonymous. The big classes are broken up into smaller sections of 30 people or less twice a week. It is here that the interaction between student and professor occurs. The ideas are presented in the professor's lectures; then section leaders expand on the ideas and clarify them for the students. However, there are only a handful of classes that are that big, all lower-division courses. Berkeley also offers a number of seminars limited to 20 people for lower-division students. These classes are mostly discussion and writing seminars. The upper-division courses are different in that they are usually very small classes that allow for individual expression and the exploration of complex issues. The average class size for the upper-division courses is around 30 students although this will vary according to the department in which the class is offered.

In short, Berkeley offers an unparalleled education experience. Top professors, an excellent and diverse student body, and an atmosphere that encourages learning combine to make Berkeley stand out even among the best. It is the model for what an educational institution, public or private, should be.

SOCIAL LIFE

"Berkeley's never really been known as a party school. In fact, before I came to Cal, I anticipated that having a social life would entail going to the library in a group rather than alone. That fear was quickly put to rest my first week of school when I was introduced to the adage Berkeley students seem to live by: 'We work hard and we play hard.' I discovered that Moffit Library was more of a pick-up scene for lower classmen than the local bars (though I soon discovered the local bars as well). But the greatest thing about the social life at Cal is that it's as diverse as the students who go here."

I seriously doubt that any other major academic university could boast as wide a range of social activities as Berkeley can. Making friends is relatively easy in the dorms, Greek houses, theme houses, or co-ops. If group living isn't your thing, there are literally hundreds of student organizations to join. The atmosphere among students is relatively friendly, so with an open mind and some insight to share, finding people to hang out with is easier than most expect. And, if you're not a joiner, just try studying in one of the multitude of cafes; before you know it you've put your book aside to discuss politics over *cafe lattes* with the stranger who asks to share your table.

Although the cafe scene is quite unique to Berkeley, the bars are of equal character and popularity. The south side of campus is spotted with a mix of places to hang out with buddies or make new friends. Traditional pubs offer premium beer, pool, and shuffleboard, while others offer quality live blues music or funk dance parties nightly. Cheap beer and a Friday afternoon of sun attract a regular crowd to the Bears' Lair, a campus pub. Wednesdays at that same bar you can catch Comedy Night, while on weekends the place hosts some great local bands.

Music has always been an integral part of the Berkeley night life. Blues, punk, funk, and rock bands can be caught just about every night at one or more out-of-the-way establishments. Bigger bands play on campus in Zellerbach Auditorium or the impressive Greek theater on the east end of the university. The Bay Area traditionally both hosts and produces the best in musical talent. But if you're on a college student's budget or dancing is just fine with you, there's always a DJ spinning tunes at a fraternity house on Friday or Saturday nights.

> *"Cal has more than 30,000 people. I couldn't help wondering where to begin meeting people without getting completely lost in the crowd. So I rushed a sorority my freshman year. Four years later, the friends I met so casually through the Greek system that first week of school are still here. We laugh about the bad date party set-ups, the time we rented a Winnebago to road trip to the USC game, and the late night/early morning talks we couldn't put off until a decent hour. My social life extends beyond the adventures at the bars, the wild nights in San Francisco, or 'studying' in cafes. . .it's mostly about the friends I've made and the people I've met."*

Believe it or not, the liberal bastion of Berkeley hosts the "largest Greek system west of the Mississippi," with 42 fraternities and 17 sororities. Commonly used as a source for cheap housing, Greek membership also offers a support system and a social life. Be warned, however — the days of free-for-all keg parties are long gone. Strict guest lists and a "bring your own" policy are in effect to manage risk. Don't let that change be a deterrent though; being Greek means more now to those within the system, as the focus on alcohol, hazing, and elitism is being replaced with an emphasis on academics, diversity, and survival in general.

Despite the on-again, off-again athletic teams, football and basketball games always draw large crowds. One of the oldest college rivalries, The Big Game brings out the pride for the Blue and Gold and the hatred for Stanford's Red. Big Game day begins with hours of tailgating, cheers, and pranks that tend to extend into the game. Characterized by fierce competition on and off the field, the Game generates a strong desire to bond with every Cal fan with a "Go Bears." The area around the stadium becomes one big party. Suddenly, in this large university we are all friends for one week, just as long as you hate "Stanfurd." Basketball tends to stir the same excitement in what's been called "the most rockin' gym in the PacTen Conference." Once again, you instantly become best friends with whomever's sitting next to you — as long as they're cheering for the Bears.

If the campus or the city of Berkeley isn't exciting enough, a twenty-minute drive gets you to San Francisco, one of the great cities in the world. Bars, dance clubs, theaters, museums, and other unique things to do make the short trip to "The City" well worth the effort. Take a day trip to wine country just an hour and a half away, or cruise over to Lake Tahoe for some late night gambling or world-class skiing. The more adventurous travelers or die-hard Cal fans road trip to Southern California for the USC or UCLA games, or to Mexico for spring break.

So, I suppose if your idea of a social life in college is catching a movie, drinking and dancing 'till dawn, or just kicking back with some good friends over coffee or beer, Berkeley can't possibly fail you. Diverse is often an overused word at this university, but there could be no other word to more appropriately describe the social scene in Berkeley and the Bay Area.

EXTRACURRICULAR ACTIVITIES

The number of activities that are available to the student is simply amazing. There are over 550 registered student organizations. These clubs range from the UC Men's Octet and the Marching Band, to the Cal Hiking Club, to a number of professional organizations, such as the Undergraduate Business Association. Many times students have started their own clubs when they have not found what they want in an existing club. The campus is governed by the Associated Students of the University of California (ASUC). This provides a great training ground for those people who want to get into politics or for those who just want to get involved.

By far the most popular activity is intramural sports. Approximately 15,000 students take part in a variety of sports ranging from football to coed innertube water polo. For those people who are frustrated high school athletes, the intramural program gives them a chance to continue to compete. In intramurals I competed against athletes who were not quite good enough to play intercollegiate sports and athletes who went on to compete at a professional level in sports such as indoor soccer. The intramural program features three different divisions for students of various skill-levels. The recreational league is for those interested in noncompetitive activities. For those interested in the thrill of victory, there are both A and B level comp leagues. With so many students participating, it is quite a thrill to win a championship in the intramural program. Often these championship games are watched by as many as 75 spectators. The Recreational Sports Facility that houses most of the intramural events is a modern building well equipped for any sport or athletic program.

For those athletes who want to compete at a higher level, Cal belongs to the PacTen Conference, which consistently ranks among the nation's best in terms of national championships won. There is a full spectrum of intercollegiate sports available for both men and women. The men's water polo and rugby teams and the women's soccer team are almost always competing for the national championship.

Finally, on-and-near-campus housing at Berkeley is always in high demand. However, there are many alternatives available to students. Cal has 5200 spaces in on-campus residence halls with plans for more in the near future. There are also co-ops, fraternities and sororities, married student housing, private apartments, and the International House.

GRADUATES

More students who earn their undergraduate degree at Berkeley complete Ph.D.s than graduates of any other university in the country. Berkeley students have a special ticket in their hand when they hold a Cal diploma. Cal grads go on to succeed in every field ranging from Supreme Court justices to executives of Fortune 500 companies. Friends of mine who recently graduated are currently attending law school, selling insurance and commercial real estate, working as stockbrokers, teaching in Australia, and working in Africa for the Peace Corps. There is a great concentration of Berkeley graduates in centers of finance and trade such as New York and San Francisco.

One reason for the success of many Cal graduates is the California Alumni Association, one of the largest such groups in the country with a network of 100,000 former students stretching from San Francisco to Japan. The association sponsors career programs and maintains the Alumni Career Resources file, which contains listings of all alumni in various fields. There is an especially strong young alumni network, referred to as Young Blues, which helps recent graduates stay in touch with the university and offers them assistance in their job search.

> *"When I was looking for a job, I contacted numerous alumni. Most of them agreed to meet with me, whether they themselves had job openings or not. They were more than happy to share their experience and thoughts with me and put me in touch with other alumni who did have positions open. There is an amazing network of Cal graduates out there who are more than willing to help."*

SUMMARY OVERVIEW

The program at UC-Berkeley is based on excellence and diversity. In its academic program and social life, Berkeley prides itself on being able to offer something for everyone. And if on the odd chance there is not something for a particular student, there is the freedom to create something new.

The academic program is one of the strongest in the nation with a faculty that is world renowned. There are almost as many Nobel Prize winners at the University of California as there are in the former Soviet Union. Known for its science and engineering departments, Berkeley gives students a chance to work with the best and brightest minds while they live in the shadow of San Francisco, one of the most beautiful and interesting cities in the nation.

Many people feel Berkeley's greatest drawback is its size. It can be an impersonal place where you feel like a number rather than an individual, especially when you are sitting in a big lecture hall, for instance. While it has been difficult in the past for lower-division students to get access to the brilliant professors one hears about, the university recently addressed that problem by setting up a series of small freshman seminars taught by professors.

Other complaints I have heard stem from having to deal with the administrative side of attending college, such as getting the classes you want or spending two hours trying to unblock your registration. But these problems are associated with attending any big, public university. A related complaint sometimes heard is that Berkeley can be so diverse that there is no real unifying factor. It is almost impossible to get a large percentage of the student body together for any event. A bond, the feeling of true connection, is sometimes missing among students.

Still, Berkeley is the best deal going in higher education. The school consistently ranks at the top in the quality of education offered, yet it costs a fraction of what most top private universities do. Being a large public school also allows Cal to offer admission to a wider range of students. What sets Berkeley apart, though, is that this diversity is not achieved at the expense of academic excellence. The University of California at Berkeley is truly a great international educational institution.

Scott Elliot, B.A.
and Kate Sardou, B.A.

University of California at Los Angeles

THE PROGRAM

"I plodded across the 419-acre campus in search of my first class at UCLA. I was sweaty, anxious, and void of any sense of direction. My feet already hurt, my heart frantically pounded. Hundreds of strangers walked, jogged, skateboarded, and cycled by me, all seeming to know exactly where to find Dodd 100. Clutching a map in one hand and a schedule of classes in the other, I worried about feeling alienated, feared the curriculum, and dreaded the unknown of a large public university with more than 36,000 students. Then I saw the Bruin Bear. Standing steadfast amidst the Central Plaza, nose pointed toward the heart of campus, the massive statue inspired me to embrace rather than cower at the university's large size. During my years as a Bruin, I grew to cherish its vastness as its wealth. I found my niche at UCLA within its rich social diversity, prospered from the challenge of a rigorous academic program, and relished the excitement at one of the prominent public universities in the nation."

Consistently ranked as a top research university, UCLA is synonymous with Nobel laureates, Olympic champions, and legendary filmmakers. Established in the twentieth century, UCLA has emerged as an academic, athletic, and artistic powerhouse in less than 75 years. Donald Cram, 1987 Nobel Prize winner in chemistry, is one of three Nobel laureates serving on the university's faculty, and Jackie Joyner-Kersey, 1992 Olympic gold medalist in track and field, is among dozens of Olympic champions who've competed in Bruin jerseys. Alumni of UCLA's Theater, Film and Television program include internationally-renowned director Francis Ford Coppola. Excellence in not one but all facets of higher education distinguishes UCLA from other institutions.

Housed in one of the most influential cities in the world, UCLA offers a metropolitan flavor unparalleled by other academic meccas. During the 1988 presidential campaign, the debate between candidates George Bush and Michael Dukakis in UCLA's Pauley Pavilion drew the attention of thousands of politicians, journalists, and scholars from around the world to the Westwood campus. The 1984 Olympic Games, held in Los Angeles, brought scores of world-class competitors to the UCLA residence halls and sports facilities. Pauley Pavilion served as the site for gymnastics competition, and the campus's Los Angeles Tennis Center hosted tennis events.

In addition, the university's Center for the Performing Arts schedules performances on an ongoing basis by artists such as mime Marcel Marceau, avant-garde composer Philip Glass, and the Los Angeles Philharmonic Orchestra. Celebrities—ranging from talk show host David Letterman and comedian Billy Crystal to actor Jimmy Stewart and author Alice Walker—frequently address UCLA audiences through the Campus Events noon speakers program.

With more than 35,000 undergraduate, graduate, and professional students, UCLA has the largest student population of the nine University of California campuses. Students come from all 50 states and approximately 100 foreign countries, although most are native Californians. People at UCLA tend to divide the university into two distinct regions, identifying themselves as North Campus liberal arts majors sporting fashionable clothes, a California tan, and Ray-Ban sunglasses or as South Campus science gurus wielding pocket calculators and portable computers. Yet whether they're in the chemistry lab or on the Sculpture Garden lawn, students almost always have an experiment in their hands or a textbook on their laps.

Academics at UCLA are rigorous and challenging, and the curriculum gives students the tools to analyze and interpret what they learn. A UCLA education seeks to provide students with a well-rounded perspective on the issues that confront society, equip them for problem solving and inquiry, and teach them to write analytically and critically.

> *"Working alongside major metropolitan newspaper and national network television journalists as a staff writer for the* Daily Bruin, *I realized my education at UCLA enabled me to tackle any assignment at a professional level. Although the university lacks a journalism department, my job at the paper filled my portfolio with stories I never would have written at another college paper. As a student journalist, I covered the March for Women's Equality/Women's Lives in Washington D.C., the Presidential Debates, gang violence in Venice, vivisection protests, the Fifth Annual Los Angeles Marathon, Comic Relief III, and the premiere of the movie* Batman. *Regardless of the subject, I was able to research an issue thoroughly, prepare intelligent questions, think quickly during interviews, and recognize the human angle of a story—skills that have made me a better reporter today."*

Despite the large enrollment, UCLA students rarely feel lost or alienated as the richly varied population has resulted in more than 400 social, political, and service organizations. Unlike huge impersonal campuses that turn students into numbers, UCLA is a mosaic that offers a place for everyone to express his or her own unique identity while still remaining part of the total ensemble.

> *"Since UCLA seemed like a city within a city, I expected to constantly drown in a sea of unfamiliar faces. Surprisingly, however, seeing a familiar smile was far from rare and by the end of my first quarter, 419 acres seemed no bigger than my own backyard."*

Even the physical structure of the campus exudes this mosaic feeling. Just eight miles east of the Pacific Ocean at the foot of the Santa Monica Mountains, UCLA mixes traditional structures with contemporary buildings to create one of the most beautiful college campuses in the country. Flowers, broad lawns, and tree-lined walkways blend the Tudor Gothic Kerckhoff Hall, the visionary Medical Plaza, and the cinnamon-color brick of Kinsey, Haines, Powell, and Royce into a harmonious whole. Patterned after the basilica of San Ambrogio in Milan, Royce Hall has grown to symbolize UCLA more than any of the other 220 buildings. Murals in the exterior loggia depicting the 12 professions and seals of the universities of the Middle Ages exude prestigious academia, whereas an elaborate Romanesque style was chosen as especially appropriate to southern California's Mediterranean climate. Once surrounded by 400 empty acres, Royce Hall now embodies the strength and grace of one of the world's finest institutions. All in all, UCLA offers an educational experience unlike that of any other school in the country.

GETTING IN/FINANCIAL AID

Top-notch academics, champion Pacific Ten Conference athletics, and a beautiful southern California location have made UCLA one of the most popular campuses in the nation as well as one of the most selective. As its popularity continues to escalate, admission standards become increasingly stringent. With more than 24,000 applicants vying for about 3650 slots, admission is highly competitive. Applicants to UCLA demonstrate academic excellence as evidenced by high school GPA and test scores (the SAT I and ACT and three SAT II exams are required). The comprehensive admission process includes a review of GPA; test scores; the overall quality, content, and level of courses (including the number of college preparatory courses taken); and the strength of the senior year program.

UCLA, and all the University of California campuses, have minimum academic subject requirements for freshman applicants: one year of U.S. history, or one-half year of U.S. history and one-half year of civics or American government; one year of world history, cultures, and geography; four years of college preparatory English; three years of mathematics (including second-year, advanced algebra); two years of laboratory science; two years of the same language other than English; and two years of college preparatory electives. (Requirements for transfers are basically the same. Older students, however, have more options to satisfy the academic subject requirements and must have satisfied some prerequisites for anticipated majors.)

To be competitive, applicants should take more than the required courses in science, language, and math. Although academic achievement is the main selling point of any application, it is not the only one.

> *"After being accepted to UCLA with a 3.6 GPA and an SAT score of about 1200, I was shocked to learn that classmates with 4.0 GPAs and equally solid SAT scores were turned down. While I rationalized that my job as editor of the school paper, position in student government, and membership on the swim team gave me the edge over my book-oriented classmates, I secretly worried the university made a mistake. Within a year, however, I realized those extra high school activities taught me the organizational and social skills I needed to cope with college life and that my admission to UCLA was not a clerical error."*

UCLA's selection criteria are designed to admit students who demonstrate the capacity for high academic achievement and who have a variety of other qualities that contribute to the strength and diversity of the campus community. A portion of the class (55 to 60%) is admitted solely on the basis of academic criteria. The balance of the class is admitted on the basis of the academic criteria listed above and supplemental criteria, which include California residency, membership in an ethnic group historically underrepresented in the University of California eligibility pool, low income status, presence of a disability, hardship, special talent, leadership, and extraordinary achievement.

UCLA is committed to serving the people of California and the needs of the state. Its mission as a public institution is to achieve a student body that reflects the cultural, racial, geographic, economic, and social diversity of California itself.

> *"Interacting with Bruins from ethnic, religious, and socioeconomic backgrounds different than my own showed me more about life and human nature than any sociology, psychology, or political science textbook. During my freshman year, late night pajama talks about everything from school and parents to politics and love taught my female roommates—a Korean, an Irish-Catholic, and an African American—and I, a Mexican-American, to recognize our similarities and appreciate our differences. Filled with cramming sessions, junk food binges, serious discussions, and pillow fights, those countless nights are among my fondest memories at UCLA. Over and over, the campus's diversity fostered close friendships with people I would never have met elsewhere."*

Recognizing that students come from the wealth of Beverly Hills as well as the poverty of inner-city ghettos, UCLA offers financial aid options to suit everyone's needs. Hundreds to thousands of dollars in aid are available through scholarships, grants, loans, and work-study programs. Athletic, regents, and alumni scholarships are the most well-known, although other scholarships have been established through private gifts. The university's Financial Aid Office calculates need based on the resources available from the student's family.

> *"When a crisis drained family finances, I suddenly found myself with tuition expenses, housing costs, parking fees, and an empty wallet. Until my senior year, I had been lucky enough to have parents who could afford to foot my bills. Faced with an unexpected money problem, I turned to the financial aid office where I got help obtaining a student loan at below market interest rates and finished my education on time."*

ACADEMIC ENVIRONMENT

Because UCLA is one of the country's most outstanding research universities, the same faculty members who transmit knowledge also create it. Taught by scholars dedicated to research, students learn the latest findings on every front and exchange ideas with professors who are authorities in their fields.

High caliber instructors, however, demand top quality pupils. Success at UCLA means discipline, hard work, and most important, self-motivation. Professors rarely badger students to study for tests or hold their hands on the way to class. Yet the pressure to succeed inspires rather than discourages. Although UCLA professors really push students to the limit, their high expectations bring out everyone's personal best.

> *"Groping my way through the incomprehensible language of* Beowulf *and other Old English poetry convinced me not only that I should drop my English 10A class, but that I'd chosen the wrong major. The slow, grueling material was merely a sample of increasingly tough assignments and what I understood was typical of prerequisites for all upper-division English courses. Yet before I could switch into the History of Rock Music or the Development of the American Motion Picture, the professor made me realize I wanted the easy way out. Of course he knew the class was hell, since the professor said he designed it that way. English 10A is a 'weeder' course for goodness sake, intended to sift out people who have no business majoring in English. Feeling challenged, I decided to grin and bear eight more weeks of purgatory. Naturally I hated every minute of it, but by the end of the quarter I could translate Old English with relative ease, knew*

> *I hadn't selected the wrong major after all, and felt proud that I never gave up."*

UCLA has one college and 13 professional schools. Undergraduate programs are offered in the College of Letters and Science, the School of Engineering and Applied Science, the School of the Arts, the School of Theater, Film and Television, and the School of Nursing. Graduate programs are offered in the College and all 13 professional schools: architecture and urban planning; arts; dentistry; education; engineering; law; library and information science; management; medicine; nursing; public health; social welfare; and theater, film and television.

Specific requirements vary from department to department, although all undergraduates must follow a curriculum that reflects a broad spectrum of knowledge with an emphasis on a major field of study.

> *"Earning a bachelor's degree in English left me with much more than an understanding of Shakespeare, Victorian poetry, and twentieth century British literature. As a student in the College of Letters and Science, where general education requirements include physical science, life science, social science, and humanities, I also learned statistics, marine biology, human anatomy, and the history of Chicanos in education. Previously unaware of the alarming dropout rate among Latino high school students, it was in an introductory sociology class that I first began tutoring 'at-risk' youth. Although the course lasted only ten weeks, my dedication to Hispanic issues and volunteer work within the Latino community will last a lifetime. Exploring a wide variety of academic subjects rather than focusing solely on English not only enhanced my education and helped shape my perceptions of the world, it also introduced me to interests and causes that I have continued to incorporate in my purposes and goals today."*

Regardless of the program or academic discipline, obtaining a degree from UCLA is a guaranteed challenge. Because analyzing written materials and reading and writing critically and correctly is stressed in most course work, polished English skills are a must. Furthermore, the rigorous pace of the ten-week quarter system leaves few moments to catch a breath and no time to recover after falling behind. Despite the quarter system's voracious speed, students repeatedly refuse to switch to the longer semesters. Ten-week courses offer more concentrated learning, increased self-discipline, and less pain for the more grueling subjects. The option to drop a course without penalty up to the end of the fourth week or to change the grading basis to pass/no pass as late as the sixth week also keeps the quarter system fiercely popular.

Class sizes vary from as small as 15 to as large as 400. Yet large classes don't mean less individualized instruction. Introductory lecture courses in popular areas such as psychology, chemistry, and economics divide enrollment into weekly discussions sections or lab groups of about 25. Although the required sections are usually led by a graduate student teaching assistant, professors also always schedule weekly office hours for students to ask questions or discuss material.

> *"What I loved most about UCLA was that I could sit in the back remaining virtually anonymous or visit the professor so often he knew my mother's maiden name. Bored by the intricate details of a cucumber's life cycle, I did the minimum work necessary for a passing grade and never said a word in my Biology lab class. Yet while my science professor wouldn't recognize me if we passed on the street, my Advanced Journalism instructor still sends Christmas cards and calls to say hello. With this journalism professor, two hours of lecture almost always seemed too short and after being the most outspoken student in class, I'd invariably wind up in his office discussing everything from media ethics to the impossibility of purely objective journalism. Whether I preferred to remain nameless among a class of 300 or stand out above the rest, at UCLA, the choice was mine."*

Free tutoring in many subjects is also available in the residence halls, at the Academic Resource Center, and through the Academic Advancement Program. Lecture notes taken by a paid scribe are available at the professor's request, but work better as a supplement than as an excuse to skip class.

Ranked among the top five research libraries in the United States and Canada, the UCLA library system includes 15 separate branches and houses more than 6.1 million volumes of books, periodicals, manuscripts, maps, audio recordings, slides, photographs, and films. Key features include an on-line information system called ORION; an outstanding Department of Special Collections containing rare books, manuscripts, and papers; and a Public Affairs Service for government and official publications.

But Bruins are not limited to studying in libraries, student lounges, and outdoor nooks. Numerous student field projects offer hands-on experience and can be arranged in most academic disciplines. Through the Education Abroad Program, students may study at more than 90 institutions in 33 countries throughout Africa, Asia, Australia, Canada, the Middle East, New Zealand, South Africa, and Western and Eastern Europe. Local, state, and federal government internships as well as international business opportunities also are offered through the Extramural Programs and Opportunities Center (EXPO) and the Placement and Career Planning Center.

> *"Lacking specific career goals, I decided to apply for a media internship since I loved reading, writing, and working with people. Working for a quarter at KTLA Channel 5, I realized my passion was for news reporting, but I didn't want a job in television. After that one four-unit internship, I immediately enrolled in the journalism course that convinced me more than any other class to pursue my current career in newspapers."*

Despite a highly theoretical approach to education, UCLA's curriculum provides students with valuable classroom experiences that translate directly to the working world. The vast selection of courses, wide variety of class sizes, and infinite educational resources allow students not only to develop at their own rate, but also to dabble in an assortment of subjects or explore one area in-depth.

SOCIAL LIFE

Bordered by the Pacific Ocean, Hollywood, the Santa Monica Mountains, and downtown Los Angeles, UCLA offers a cornucopia of cultural treasures, outdoor recreation, and exciting nightlife.

Within a five-minute walking distance, Westwood Village offers a variety of specialty shops, restaurants, dessert parlors, and first-run movie theaters. The Los Angeles County Museum of Art, the Music Center, Chinatown, Olvera Street, Little Tokyo, Hollywood nightclubs, and the downtown business area lie a few miles to the east. A trip west offers the palm tree-lined jogging paths of Santa Monica, the roller-skating, bicycling, and suntanning of Venice Beach and the boating, windsurfing, and jetskiing of Marina Del Rey.

Whether it's a Saturday afternoon or a Tuesday night, this socially rich habitat suits any student thirsting for grog and good times after arduous hours of studying. A 24,000 undergraduate enrollment may mean 24,000 different ideas of fun, but one thing's for sure: at UCLA, the students work hard and play hard. Known as a hybrid between bookworm and party animal, UCLA students never miss a chance to celebrate a hard earned accomplishment.

> *"Ridden with midquarter anxiety, my roommates and I loved to spend Monday nights studying until 10 P.M. and then ditch the books to go dancing. Knowing we'd done some work kept us from feeling guilty and getting out for some fun kept us sane for the library the rest of the week."*

Although no single definition captures UCLA's campus life for everyone, students do share a number of distinctively Bruin experiences. Year after year, students line the streets of Westwood for the annual homecoming parade, flock to the intramural field for the three-day Mardi Gras carnival (the largest student-run event in the country), and jam the Rose Bowl for the big USC-UCLA rival football game.

Wearing anti-USC buttons on "University of Spoiled Children" T-shirts, waving credit cards or money at every Trojan in sight, and chanting derogatory slogans toward the USC side of the stadium are only a few favorite Bruin pregame, halftime, and postgame activities. Following the footsteps of tradition, daring UCLA students also sneak onto enemy territory to deface Tommy Trojan with blue and gold paint.

Such boisterous Bruin spirit, however, isn't limited to the annual USC-UCLA confrontation. Keg-toting buses and caravanning students to football and basketball games typify campus life in the fall, whereas suntanning on campus lawns and splashing about the Rec Center pool characterize the social whirl of the spring.

Although many students prefer Happy Hour at Baxter's Bar and Grill or dollar-drink night at Mom's Saloon to the official dry campus policy (UCLA has no student pub and restricts those twenty-one years or older to drinking behind closed doors), the on-campus party scene is far from dead. Weekend dorm parties, fraternity shindigs, and holiday dances rage nearly every week throughout the year.

Those opting for a quieter time enjoy sharing a pizza with friends at the Cooperage, listening to live jazz and drinking cappuccino at the Coffee House in Kerckhoff Hall, or watching hit movies at the student union.

> *"After three years of pranks, parties, daiquiris, and dancing, meeting a friend for a noontime concert in Central Plaza, a weekly comedy show at Ackerman Grand Ballroom, a free movie at Melnitz Hall, or an ice cream sundae at Tout de Suite became the thrust of my social life. My idea of fun may have slowed down to a simpler speed, but I still never had to leave campus to enjoy my free time."*

Those who crave entertainment beyond the boundaries of Sunset Boulevard and Le Conte Avenue, however, can find tickets to concerts, art shows, and professional sporting events within an order form's reach at an on-campus ticket agency. A full-time travel service on campus includes a staff of professional travel agents who can book spring break in Mexico or write tickets for a flight home during the holidays. By combining the spirit of a large college campus with the excitement of a cosmopolitan city, UCLA offers a rich social life to any student regardless of wallet size or personal interests.

EXTRACURRICULAR ACTIVITIES

Extracurricular activities at UCLA range from running for student government to tutoring prisoners in reading to joining an intramural sports team to writing for one of eight student newspapers. As the third largest daily in Los Angeles, The *Daily Bruin* flies sports writers across the country with Bruin athletic teams, assigns staff reporters to major local, state, and national news events, and is the only college paper permitted at the Academy Awards.

Among the student publications are several special-interest newsmagazines that focus on specific populations, such as *TenPercent*, which focuses on gay and lesbian community; *Pacific Ties*, which targets Asian-Pacific concerns; and *La Gente*, which concentrates on Latino issues.

With more than 400 officially registered clubs and organizations to choose from, everyone from politics enthusiasts to avid rock climbers can find something to do besides homework. On any given day, Bruin Walk, a major campus thoroughfare for pedestrian traffic, is filled with students promoting community service projects, environmental concerns, student government elections, fund-raising activities, and the like.

Bruin Democrats, Bruin Republicans, and the UCLA chapter of the National Organization for Women are among the strongest political networks, and Bruin Belles, Peer Health Counselors, and Mortar Board are some of the more active service organizations. Groups such as Black Student Alliance and MEChA work toward increasing ethnic diversity and cultural awareness, whereas the ski, cycling, and hockey clubs devote their time to the enjoyment of sport.

Students swim, picnic, and barbecue at the Sunset Canyon Recreation Center, play squash and racquetball and lift weights at the John Wooden Center, and play tennis at the Los Angeles Tennis Center. Extensive courses in sailing, windsurfing, and other water sports, offered at UCLA's Aquatic Center in Marina del Rey, also are fiercely popular. Graduates of all sailing classes need only a reg card to check out a craft and sail with friends during free time.

Whether students want to learn how to play basketball or face the challenge of lacrosse, the UCLA intramural program can fill the need. More than 45 individual and team sports are available each quarter at all levels of competition. Rugby, chess, dance, and several martial arts clubs also offer everything from intercollegiate competition to lessons for beginners.

Lining the east and west sides of campus, Fraternity and Sorority Rows offer an extracurricular activity that's actually an entire way of life. UCLA has more than 50 different sororities and fraternities in its Greek system, making them an integral part of Bruin life. Between rush parties, winter formals, and Greek Week competition, sorority and fraternity members find more than their share of fun and friendships.

Fraternities and sororities also provide about 2300 students, primarily upperclassmen, with a place to live. Nevertheless, with the opening of the new Sunset Village undergraduate residential development, which has living space for 1260 students, UCLA now offers on-campus housing to the entire freshman class each year.

UCLA's five residence halls, two residential suites, and three Sunset Village facilities offer coed accommodations, dining halls, game rooms, and other amenities that make residential life at UCLA one of the most rewarding experiences college has to offer. Living in the dorms is one of the easiest ways to meet study partners or exercise buddies. Lifelong friendships often begin in the Reiber Hall cafeteria or the Hedrick Hall lounge.

Although most freshmen tend to live on campus, upperclassmen most often live off campus. Students rent apartments, board in guest houses, and commute from home. The high-rent district surrounding UCLA is tough to afford, but sharing a two-bedroom house or renting apartments a few miles farther out are the most common ways to dart expensive housing costs.

Brunis who hate to cook or grow tired of cafeteria food frequently feast on fried chicken from the Treehouse, soup and salad from LuValle Commons or a pita sandwich from the outdoor Campus Corner. UCLA's menu includes everything from

Mexican food to gourmet cheesecake and its eateries offer ambience to suit any diner.

> *"Since my schedule was so wacky and I hated cooking for one, I bought a Bruin Gold Card and ate breakfast, lunch, and dinner on campus for most of my college career. Accepted at every campus restaurant just like cash, the card was easier to use than money and kept me from spending my dinner allowance on video games and magazines."*

GRADUATES

A Bruin remains a Bruin even after turning the tassel over the mortarboard. Naturally, a campus as socially and economically diverse as UCLA is bound to produce graduates with divergent beliefs, goals, and pursuits. Sure, the classes of '75, '85, and '95 have dispersed into the world of business, politics, entertainment, scientific research, social work, community service, and professional athletics. But regardless of their differences, UCLA alumni bleed blue and gold.

According to a recent survey, two thirds of the university's baccalaureate recipients go on to graduate school. No matter where they continue their education, however, UCLA grads always retain their Bruin identity and never stop rooting for their Westwood alma mater.

> *"Even after spending two years in USC's graduate school of education, my friend Frances still preferred to tell people she graduated from UCLA and couldn't bear to root for the Trojans. Her loyalty to the Bruins may have made her the most unpopular fan in the USC stands, but she chanted that UCLA fight song until the bitter end of every crosstown rival football or basketball game."*

Although the majority of the university's recent graduates continue educational pursuits, the final career paths of UCLA alumni run the gamut.

> *"Lumped together as undeclared freshmen in the fall of my first year, my friends all wound up going in drastically different directions. Nobody had any concrete goals that freshman year, yet Nan is now a social worker in Monterey County, Jay was an executive story editor for the 'Tracey Ullman Show,' Ron is a law student at the University of Chicago, and Flipper is an emerging football star for the Los Angeles Rams."*

Despite the university's youth, its alumni network is strong enough to offer extensive opportunities for past as well as present students. Career development programs, great health insurance plans, custom-designed credit cards, Extension class discounts, and UCLA library access are only a few of the 59,000-member Alumni Association's benefits. Through the association's Career Network Program, students are paired with alumni who are willing to share their professional experiences either through brief talks, a day-on-the-job tour, or part-time internships. The program not only helps younger Bruins branch into the real world, it also keeps alumni in touch with the ever increasing world of learning.

For many, life after UCLA is a bittersweet taste of economic freedom and burdening responsibilities. Relishing the excitement of college life, UCLA graduates from as early as the 1930s still attend football games in droves and even play for the renowned UCLA Alumni Band, whose wacky leader is a favorite among current students.

SUMMARY OVERVIEW

Endowed with a diverse student body, a vast array of academic options and a rich social environment, UCLA's strength is that it is a school of choices. The variety provides something for everyone and, more importantly allows each student to create his/her own unique college experience.

Unlike expensive private schools, where most of the student body comes from a similar socioeconomic background, the Westwood campus brings together people from all walks of life. Only at UCLA could a woman who watched her brother get shot and killed in a gang fight teach something about life to a European boarding school debutante who once thought tragedy was a broken fingernail; or could a seventy-eight-year-old man hang out with twenty-year-old sports fanatics who love listening to play-by-play memories of legendary football heros.

Although great socioeconomic diversity means some students will begin their academic careers better prepared than others, numerous tutorial programs, computer labs, and learning workshops allow everyone the opportunity to succeed. UCLA's immense variety of classes gives people time to explore many subjects before choosing a major and helps students maintain a good GPA. For example, all students must complete the same number of general education courses, but they can choose among dozens of courses to satisfy the general education requirement.

Couched within a rich social environment, UCLA affords students the opportunity to enhance their creativity and to learn to mix with people in a relaxed atmosphere. Although academics and business ethics are of utmost importance, social flexibility is still a must for success in nearly any profession. At UCLA, students not only know how to get the job done, they learn how to do it with flair and style. They've learned also to explore their own unique individuality through art, music, comedy, sports, volunteer work, political activism, and, of course, relationships.

But a campus adorned with lavish opportunity and resources also is bound to have a few drawbacks. Just as UCLA's size often is its source of strength, the campus's huge enrollment also occasionally is its weakness. At time 35,000 (total) students, 419 acres, and 220 buildings translates into long lines at the bookstore, a hassle to get all the right classes at the most convenient times, and waiting to get parking. Enrolling in classes has been greatly simplified, however, with the implementation of the UCLA Telephone Enrollment System, which allows students to directly access the enrollment database by using a touch-tone phone. Students can use the system to enroll in, add, drop or change classes without leaving home.

The large student body also can mean occasionally not getting a ticket to a popular sporting event, having a housing application turned down by a lottery ball, and getting tangled in a web of red tape when a computer suddenly decides not to record those five summer school classes.

All in all, however, the benefits, services, and opportunities at UCLA far outweigh an occasional day of aggravation. Lines generally disappear after the first week of classes, not getting the right schedule usually means not having all Tuesday/Thursday classes, and parking problems are solved easily by free shuttle buses, mopeds, and one of the country's most efficient van pool, car pool transportation programs. In sum, UCLA combines incredible resources with maximum opportunity, making it one of the world's finest educational institutions.

Marlene Casillas, B.A.

University of Chicago

THE PROGRAM

"Do you want to hear one of our most popular football cheers? a
U of C cheerleader asked my roommate and me on the eve of our
freshman year. We had wandered into Henry Crown Field House,
a huge athletic complex a block from our dorm, looking for
rumors, gossip, and information. 'Sure,' we agreed, but won-
dered how a cheer would answer our question about the atmos-
phere of the University of Chicago. She laughed and shook her
head. 'OK. You asked for it. Thucydides. Herodotus. Peloponne-
sian War. X-squared, Y-squared, H-2-S-O-4. Who for, what for,
who the hell we cheerin' for! Go-o-o Chicago!' We got the
picture."

The U of C's reputation as the home of a lively and pervasive intellectual life is
well deserved. The Great Books, the Great Ideas, and the Great Conversation find
their way into daily events and ordinary conversation in just about every part of the
university community, even football games. You can find students discussing ideas
and issues important to them in dorm rooms, coffee shops, restaurants, the quads,
tennis courts, and almost anywhere else. If you're looking for a school where you
can talk about your classes and ideas with other students and with professors, you
won't find a better place than the U of C.

The atmosphere and traditions of the U of C encourage people to share their
intellectual concerns. The university has a long and proud tradition of reflecting
upon the value of education and the meaning of its motto, "Let knowledge grow
from more to more, and so let life be enriched." Every year freshmen are welcomed to the school in an address by a distinguished faculty member on the
Aims of Education. Periodic conferences and seminars on liberal education are
well attended. Education is taken seriously because people think that ideas are

important, that they shape the way human beings act and feel, and that new ideas can make the world a better, or a worse, place.

> *"It's not easy to question the worth of your education while you're studying. The following exchange is not, I think, uncommon. U of C student: 'I'm discovering all these things about myself, Dad. It's great. I think I'm learning that I'm really a Trotskyite at heart. I've found this cool socialist jazz club. Learning to ask important questions about myself and the world is invigorating, but it's hard for me to concentrate on genetics.' U of C parent: 'Listen, goddammit. I'm not paying $25,000 a year for you to find yourself. You're supposed to be doing your work.' Opening up new ways of thinking and of seeing the world can be hard, even burdensome. New insights challenge your own longheld beliefs and the values that others want for you."*

U of C students, like anyone else, can't endure that kind of seriousness indefinitely. So the social life at Chicago adapts to accommodate the strong intellectual life. How? A friend of mine had a simple motto that a lot of U of C students have taken to heart: "Study hard. Party hard." After a full Saturday of Regging (studying at the Regenstein Library), students often go out for dinner and then head to a typically late-starting (and late-ending) U of C party. College-wide major events are often designed to turn the intellectual atmosphere on its head. My sophomore year, the annual Festival of the Arts brought a very loud cow onto the quads next to an outdoor performance of a Greek tragedy. The famous (though currently more-or-less defunct) Lascivious Costume Ball encouraged, and subsidized, lasciviously creative attire. The intense intellectual life helps create an intense social life.

> *"After a long and difficult candidacy for fellowships, one friend threw a big party. Over a hundred people came to his place and danced and drank into the early morning. Outside the door to the apartment was a picture of this normally polite and restrained senior swinging a chain. Under the picture, a quote, the theme of the party: I'd rather be a Road Warrior than a Rhodes Scholar."*

Students from the U of C come from all parts of the United States and from several other nations. They're a very diverse group with all kinds of interests. There are musicians, poets, punkers, gymnasts, Dungeons and Dragons groupies, and investors. Most come from middle-class families, they're fairly serious and, for the most part, do not mind working hard. That's not to say that they don't like to have fun. A group of 3400 eighteen-to twenty-two-year-olds will create zaniness and mischief anywhere in the world. The U of C has its share.

The heart of the U of C consists of gothic-style buildings collected in squares, or quads. The science quad is more modern, as is the Regenstein Library. Most dorms are within a ten-minute walk to the quads. Shuttle buses run regularly to the more distant dorms. During the spring and summer, the main quads are a popular spot for playing Frisbee, strumming guitars, and catching some rays.

Hyde Park, the neighborhood of the university, is a quiet, residential community on Chicago's South Side. Near campus, Victorian-style houses line the streets. A bit farther away six-flat apartment buildings, often filled with students, are the norm. Hyde Park has a movie theater, several bars, and many restaurants and stores. It is located on the edge of Lake Michigan, and students often walk or ride to the lake to swim, play, run in the park (which is called The Point), or catch more rays.

All in all, the University of Chicago is an outstanding academic institution set in an exciting and comfortable city. The university challenges its students to discover and enjoy the life of the mind and, at the same time, recognizes the need to offer its students more than books and learning.

GETTING IN/FINANCIAL AID

Although the percentage of applications accepted has been falling in recent years, it is still not as hard to get into the U of C as it is to get into some of the other top colleges. Recently, about 50% of freshman applications were accepted. The reason behind this figure is a process of self-selection. The U of C is not well-known to the general public. People who've heard of Yale or Princeton are not aware that the U of C is a school of the same caliber. (Sometimes people asked me: "The University of Chicago. Let's see. Is that a state school?" or "Oh, you mean the University of Illinois at Chicago?") In certain circles, however, the U of C is very well-known, and its reputation is clearly defined as a serious and intellectual school. Almost all of the people who apply to the U of C, therefore, know what they're getting into. They understand the school for what it is and choose to apply because they see that they are suited to it.

Who are the students that go to the U of C? In general, they're intelligent, motivated, and willing to work hard. Some statistics might help you get a feel for the student body: about two thirds of the students are from the Midwest or Mid-Atlantic United States; about 30% are minority students of one sort or another; about 57% are male; about 70% are from public schools; and about 60% were in the top 5% of their high school class. There isn't really any one type of individual who is attracted to the U of C. The personalities, interests, career plans, and backgrounds of the students are remarkably diverse. Here are some of the people who were in my dorm freshman year:

> *"Within a week I met a very good physics student who was born in Hungary and who went to high school in Ohio, a girl from Scarsdale, New York, who loved theater but who majored in history, a punk rocker from Missouri, a biologist and future Rhodes*

Scholar from Vancouver, a fiercely competitive swimmer from Toronto, a chemistry major from Florida whose house can be seen in episodes of 'Miami Vice,' a high school cheerleader from south Chicago, and a politically conservative humanities major from Kansas who would eventually have a giant spider tattooed onto his shaven head."

What can you do to improve your chances of getting in? Pay close attention to your written essays. The admissions staff reads them diligently. Don't try to give what you think is the right answer. Be bold and take chances. The staff likes to read original, creative essays. (Wouldn't you, if you had to read 6700 applications?) The questions on the U of C application are usually peculiar or provocative, so you won't be tempted to recycle your essays from your Podunk University application. If you have an interview in the admissions office, try to relax and simply have a good conversation. The admissions staff is, for the most part, pretty laid-back. Talk about anything you want—what it is like to be choosing a college, your high school, quantum mechanics, AIDS, or your family—but try to give the interviewer a sense of what you like to do and of what things are important to you. Off-campus interviews with alumni have less impact on your admissions decision than do those on campus. They can help if you do well, but they're not counted against you if you don't.

About 66% of U of C students receive financial aid. The average size of an aid package is somewhere around $15,005 a year. That consists of loans, work-study jobs, and outright gift aid. The U of C also grants around 40 College Honor Scholarships each year based on merit alone. These range from $10,000 to full tuition. To apply for these scholarships, you need to write an extra essay or two and get additional teacher recommendations.

The work-study jobs can be interesting. Some students work in coffee shops, clean up on campus, or count light bulbs; others find jobs working as computer programmers or in scientific labs. It's not hard at all to find work in a field you are interested in. I know many students who really enjoyed and were challenged by their work-study jobs. Some people worked on creating a cure for AIDS, others studied mating in salamanders, and still others helped put satellites into space. Many of these opportunities are also open to those students who do not qualify for financial aid.

"For my work study, I worked in the Laboratory for Astrophysics and Space Research. My Lab was next to the office of Subrahmanyan Chandrasekhar, the world-famous Indian astrophysicist, Nobel Prize-winner, and the 'inventor' of black holes. I always wanted to meet him. One day I ran into him outside our building and, gathering my courage, introduced myself. 'I'm Varun Gauri, a physics student in the College,' I declared. 'Hello,' he said. 'I've read about you and your work for a long time and have always wanted to meet you, I chimed.' 'Yes,' he said. I couldn't think of anything else to say, so that was the end of our

*conversation. Eventually I did get beyond Hello. We discussed
black holes and kinship in India. I learned a lot and enjoyed
those conversations."*

ACADEMIC ENVIRONMENT

The most significant aspect of academic life at the U of C is the way students share their academic experiences. They talk about their classes a lot. Conversations (and arguments) about books and ideas are common in coffee shops, in restaurants, in dorms, under trees, and at street corners. If you meet someone at a party, it's safe to start talking about what courses you're taking and how they're going. You won't seem nerdy. Even if you go beyond describing and complaining about all the work you have to do to discussing the substantive arguments of a paper you're writing or a book you're reading, it won't be extraordinary. The great majority of U of C students care a lot about the quality of their education, and many are positively captivated by the questions and problems they're engaged with.

The centerpiece of the curriculum is the Common Core. One of the legacies of Robert Maynard Hutchins, the famous and controversial fifth president of the university, the core is an object of great pedagogic pride and considerable historical tradition. The custodians of the school refer to it constantly. The justifications for it are usually one or more of the following: the core provides the materials with which students become educated citizens in our culture; the core teaches the basic vocabulary and methods of the fundamental academic disciplines; the core promotes critical thinking, careful reading, and clean writing; or the core gives U of C students a shared academic experience, a basis for further and deeper conversation.

Whereas the first three justifications are arguable, the last one is, if you want to graduate, indisputable. So here's your shared academic experience: three quarters of humanities, one quarter of music or art, three or four quarters of a foreign language, two quarters of math (beyond pre-calculus), six quarters of social science, three quarters of civilization studies, and three quarters of physical education. That adds up to 21/22 quarters (not counting phys ed.), or about half your college career. You can place out of everything except humanities, art/music, social science, and civilization on the basis of high school AP test scores, the international baccalaureat, or freshman placement exams. Many students do place out of several parts of the core.

"My approach to the core, and, in fact, to most of my U of C education, was to get into the classes with the best teachers without too much concern over what they were teaching. I took around ten classes with ten or fewer students in them, most with less than

> *seven, and had several opportunities to work with full professors one-on-one. The professors were generally very good and available. (Over 65% of them live in Hyde Park, the immediate neighborhood of the university.) Here's a sampling of interactions I had with some of my teachers: I remember discussing pierced noses and tattoos at a teacher's apartment, Nietzsche in Morry's Deli, Michael Dukakis at a reception, the Lakers over the phone, Eliade over pizza, the history of Swarthmore College while barbecuing on the quads, cosmic ray experiments at the Fermi Institute, psychoanalysis in the library, and Beethoven in a thunderstorm."*

Although U of C professors work at a major research university under the publish or perish regime, a large number of them are very committed to teaching. They work hard in and out of the classroom to help their students learn. Perhaps my most important lesson from them was about thinking. I learned that thinking is work, but that if you're persistent, it sometimes becomes very pleasurable work. I learned to enjoy working on my own and really to appreciate good classes.

> *"On a cold winter morning of my sophomore year, we began working on* Hamlet *in Common Core humanities. We read Act I, Scene I aloud. When a student read Francisco's line 'Stand, ho! Who is there?' the teacher jumped in. 'No, that's not right. You try it, Peter.' Peter said, 'Stand, ho! Who is there?' 'No,' she responded. 'Ingrid, try that line.' Five people read the line, and no one got it right. Finally, the teacher said, 'Listen. That line repeats the first words of the play, Bernardo's 'Who's there?' You have to see that, understand it, emphasize it. Things get increasingly murky in this play, and the characters begin to realize that they don't know who they're talking to, who's out there, and who they themselves are.' The teacher had captured our imagination. Thereafter we talked about the play a lot with her and among ourselves."*

In humanities and social sciences classes, including the core, a typical class has 20–25 students and is designed as a discussion class. Some are larger or smaller, and some are set up as lectures. In the natural sciences, lectures are more common than discussion classes, and the class sizes are larger, typically ranging from 40–80 students. The natural science courses all have labs and discussion sections, however, which are much smaller.

It is rumored that Charles H. Percy, the former U.S. senator from Illinois, was the last senior at the U of C to graduate with a 4.0 GPA. That may or may not be true. No one during my four years at Chicago, however, had any reason to challenge that legend. Classes are tough. Professors expect a lot of you. One result is that GPAs are noticeably lower at Chicago than at other top schools. Most graduate programs and employers are aware of that. In science classes the mean scores tend to be low. In humanities and social sciences, everyone is expected to work with some of the most challenging and influential texts ever written. The high standards and the quarter system, which requires you to prepare for final exams about every ten weeks, together create a high-powered academic atmosphere.

The U of C conducts college registration every spring on a first-come, first-serve basis. i.e., the longer you wait in line, the more likely you are to get the classes you want with the teachers you want. (It's kind of like getting tickets for a show.) Registration begins at 8 A.M. Monday morning. Last year students started camping out for classes on Friday night, and by Sunday evening 600, or one out of every four freshmen, sophomores, and juniors in the college, were in line. As far as anyone knows, it was an all-time record.

> *"When I was a freshman I waited in registration line all night with a bunch of dorm friends. However, I had a physics problem set due the next morning, which I had planned to finish, but instead I got caught up in a movie the film society was showing. After two long conversations about relationships, a huge pillow fight, and singing at 4 A.M. I gave up. By the time registration opened in the morning, I had only half the problems done. But I did get the classes I wanted."*

SOCIAL LIFE

The most important fact about social life at the University of Chicago is the setting: Chicago. I mean this in two ways.

First, Chicago is a no-nonsense, tough-minded city in the American Midwest: the "city of the big shoulders." Although it is home to the Magnificent Mile on Michigan Avenue and carriage rides on the Gold Coast, Chicagoans like to emphasize the rough-and-tumble more than the glitz. They'll tell you that their city is the home of Mike Ditka and Mike Royko, that Chicagoans eat the least quiche and work the hardest, that the only thing they know about high society is what they've seen from the top of the Sears Tower.

The University of Chicago adopts some of these social values for itself. Students are serious and hard working. Social classes and cliques are not well-defined. Your dress and social niche are much less important than at many of the schools on the coasts. You're more apt to hang out somewhere and go out with a guy or girl than to attend a social event or have a dinner date. It's curious that an elite institution like the University of Chicago can adopt prairie values and a blue-collar ethos for itself, but it tries to do just that.

Second, Chicago offers an exciting and diverse social and cultural world of its own. I won't describe the many interesting museums, jazz clubs, ethnic neighborhoods, cinemas, theaters, and other social attractions in the city. Everyone has his or her own favorites. (One of mine was midnight bowling at Miami Lanes.) Some students complain that the action is too far away or that they're too busy to take advantage of Chicago. It might be true that they feel that way, but every year there are a number of students who really explore the city and adopt it as a second home. It's a question of what you want for yourself. Some people are looking for a second home; some just know how to entertain themselves. They plan ahead, take the initiative, and go out. Some students don't feel the need to explore the entire city because the social life in Hyde Park is so easily available. Hyde Park has a movie theater, four bars, all kind of stores, many restaurants and coffee shops, and the three best pizzerias in the world. (If you've never had Chicago-style stuffed pizza, the opportunity to try it should perhaps be a significant factor in choosing your school.) On campus there are always one or two films playing every night, plays on weekends, concerts, and a whole slew of university-sponsored, student-organized activities. You can probably find five or six parties every weekend.

People sometimes ask about safety in Chicago's South Side. Hyde Park is fairly quiet (outside the dorms), residential, and secure. The U of C has its own security cars, which patrol the area, but neighboring sections of the South Side can pose threats if students wander into the wrong place at the wrong times. Students at the U of C need to remember that they're in an American urban environment and that prudence is important. If you're cautious, however—lock your bike and your door, walk in groups late at night, don't leave valuables in your car—you should be fine.

The social life at the U of C is what you make of it. There's virtually no pressure to participate in a certain activity, to make an appearance at a given event, or to seem to be a member of any in group. You can socialize any way you choose. For some, this is a mixed blessing. It means that they have to initiate and organize their own events, and the academic work load sometimes makes that seem difficult. It's not, really. If you decide that an active social life is important to you, you'll find plenty of people who feel similarly and a lot of interesting, fun places to go.

The college sponsors many campus-wide social events. Apart from sports events and lectures, of which there are several almost every day, other social events of note include: Kuviasungnerk, a week-long winter festival; Festival of the Arts, a spring gala for more than artsy types; end-of-quarter formals; the annual registration sleep-out; and many, many plays, concerts, movies, and trips to ball games.

> *"One Friday night I went with a group of people to a Mexican restaurant in Chicago's Pilsen neighborhood to celebrate a friend's birthday. Afterwards, we drove up to the North Side to see Second City's comedy improv. When we got back to Hyde Park, we heard about a 70s party at a nearby apartment. We put on bell-bottoms and sideburns and danced to Earth, Wind, and Fire till morning."*

EXTRACURRICULAR ACTIVITIES

"Whenever I have an itch to exercise, I lie down until the itch goes away."

—Attributed to Robert Maynard Hutchins,
Fifth President of the U of C

The U of C football team once dominated the sport in middle America. It won six Big Ten championships. Hutchins disbanded the team in the middle of the century and changed the character of the school for good. Although several U of C athletic teams, including the football team, are competitive in their NCAA Division III conferences, they are not important as spectator sports. Although the U of C has cheerleaders, it's not a rah-rah school.

"I came to Chicago from a traditional, Midwestern public high school that loved its teams with pep rallies and parades. So I was stunned to learn my freshman year that the U of C was going to have, instead of a Homecoming Dance, a Homecoming Barbecue. Unable to figure out who an appropriate date for a barbeque would be, I skipped it and just went to the game. The team lost, but we had fun. We did the wave. A few people pretended to calculate its period and amplitude."

Recently the U of C wrestling, fencing, swimming, tennis, and track teams have done well. I've known several athletes who, despite rigorous academic lives, were motivated, fiercely competitive, and very talented. A lot of college students (over 70%) who, like me, love to play but don't have the time or the talent for varsity sports, participate in intramurals. There are also a lot of interesting club sports, including crew, Shotokan karate, aikido, and lacrosse.

On the whole, U of C students spend more time and energy on their academic and intellectual lives than on extracurricular activities. There are many exceptions, of course. Some individuals spend countless hours volunteering at the university hospitals, editing the *Chicago Maroon*, choreographing a dance, working on a guitar solo, or rehearsing a scene from a play. Two of the most successful and popular groups are DOC Films, which brings good movies to campus seven days a week, and the Major Activities Board, which during my stay sponsored campus performances by Spyro Gyra, Run-DMC, Jimmy Cliff, Jay Leno, Philip Glass, Miles Davis, and the Beastie Boys. The U of C chess team and the College Bowl Team recently won national championships, and the debate team (parliamentary, off-topic) is competitive at the national level. Student government, involved in continual scandals or controversies, was ineffectual during my college career. There is hope, however. A well-organized, apparently capable, and politically progressive group recently won control of the government.

RESIDENCE LIFE

The housing system at the U of C is moderately successful. Each house is made up of rooms and has one or two resident heads, who are faculty or graduate students, and a resident assistant, an upperclassperson; each dorm building, composed of houses, has a couple, always faculty, who serve as resident masters. The resident assistants, heads, and masters lead cultural events, host famous visitors to the U of C, help organize student parties and outings, establish house government, and provide counseling and emotional support. They're generally well liked. The dorm rooms range from your basic 10 x 12 double to the spacious apartments with lake views in Shoreland Hall, which was once a luxury hotel. Non-commuting freshmen have to live in dorms for their first year. After one or two years, many students move into off-campus apartments, which are generally cheaper and always more private.

> *"My most enjoyable dorm activity was an overnight cross-country skiing trip to Michigan. It was exhilarating to be outside in a sprawling park. I didn't know how to ski before I went, but a few veterans led a class for the beginners before we went out. I learned that there are two tricks to good cross-country skiing: (1) learn to glide; and (2) avoid a certain group of friends who insist on throwing off your rhythm by tackling you whenever you come within 15 feet. After skiing we sang songs, drank wine by firelight, and fought endless snowball battles. It was like being in an idyllic winter camp."*

If you're looking for communal living, there are nine frats with houses on campus. (Two sororities are looking for houses, which are hard to come by in Hyde Park.) The Greek movement is growing: at least five new groups sprang up during my four years. Several student co-ops sprang up and died during my career as well. A new one is slated to try its luck.

GRADUATES

> *"I went to a Halloween party in New York City attended by recent U of C graduates. It was interesting to learn what people were doing and to see what they were wearing. My friend, who works at the ACLU, and I went as The Blues Brothers. One guy, a weight*

lifter who is going to join the Army before going to graduate school, came as a bumble bee. His girlfriend, who works for Levi-Strauss, was a flower. One girl came—it had to happen—as the stereotypical U of C geek, complete with floods, runny nose, and a calculator."

Of the 590 members of my graduating class, about 40% went on to full-time employment. Thirty four percent started graduate school right away. In a survey, over 95% said that they would eventually go on to receive an advanced degree. The most desired advanced degrees were: Ph.D. (54%), J.D. (18%), M.B.A. (7%), and M.D. (12%). U of C graduates go into a variety of fields. Many become academics. Many others go into law, arts, journalism, business, government, medicine, and social service. The U of C is a good place to prepare for almost any profession. Some famous U of C graduates include Kurt Vonnegut, Jr., Ed Asner, Susan Sontag, Carl Sagan, Philip Glass, and Robert Bork.

The alumni network is pretty strong. There are a number of graduates in influential places. The Career and Placement Services office on campus is helpful. They help many students find employment and give out the names of alumni in various fields. A degree from the University of Chicago, even if it is not a household name like a Harvard degree, will carry you a long way.

> *"At the beginning of my senior year, I routinely ignored announcements from the office of Career and Placement Services (CAPS) about upcoming recruiting visits of major firms. I finally decided to attend a meeting in February about opportunities at a Boston-based financial consulting firm. The day before the meeting, I received a call from an acquaintance who had been in a class on* The Odyssey *with me. He was now working for this firm. He remembered me from the class and encouraged me to attend the recruitment meeting. In the end, the firm didn't interest me, but I was pleased to know that one U of C grad would look out for another."*

SUMMARY OVERVIEW

The U of C is an academic school top to bottom. College guidebooks, alumni, admissions staff, and a personal visit will all confirm that for you. If you're looking for a school with a challenging intellectual atmosphere, where being a student is taken seriously, and where conversations and ideas create a sense of community, look no further

The U of C will offer you an undergraduate academic program and intellectual environment as solid and stimulating as any in the country. The faculty is excellent.

They're committed to undergraduate teaching. The students are intelligent and actively engaged in their classes. The curriculum is demanding. The environment encourages students to pursue and express their intellectual interests in and out of class.

Social life at the U of C is informal. There's no pressure to belong to any particular social group, and all kinds of people, whether unusually eccentric or peculiarly normal, are welcome. You can be editor of the school newspaper even if you didn't write for your high school paper and can join a theater troupe even if you haven't acted before. The social life at the U of C does not take place primarily at social events, like formal balls. U of C social life emphasizes informal social interactions, like conversations and trips to movies and restaurants.

Some of the disadvantages of the U of C are the flipsides of the advantages. The academic pressure is often intense. The quarter system means that exams are always right around the corner. The emphasis on academics leaves less time for extracurricular activities.

Other disadvantages are related to the financial state of the university. Although no one worries that the U of C will go under, a few committees have recommended temporary austerity measures. As a result, class sizes have crept upward in recent years, and it has become more common for graduate students to lead undergraduate classes. The U of C has stood by its commitment to need-blind admissions and to meeting the full financial need of students, but it has considered reducing the number of merit scholarships.

The U of C is a unique community. There aren't many communities, even among colleges, that place as much emphasis on the life of the mind. If when you ask yourself "Why am I going to college anyway?" a desire to learn is the first thing that comes to mind, the U of C is a good choice. You'll probably have a good time there. I certainly did.

Varun Gauri, B.A.

University of Illinois at Urbana-Champaign

THE PROGRAM

"Choices, choices, choices! I was stunned by all of them at the University of Illinois. During my four years as an undergraduate, I took courses in news reporting, differential equations, Shakespeare, computer science, sociology, and voice. The professors had won the Nobel Prize and Pulitzer Prize, and I remember one semester I tried to decide whether to study under a former New York Times *correspondent, a Broadway and Hollywood star, or a world-renowned expert in artificial intelligence. I started my own magazine, joined the Oriental Cultural Organization, and listened to speakers invited by the British history club. Never again will I have the supermarket of choices that were available to me at the U of I."*

That's a far cry from the spring of 1868, when 50 students—most of them farmers' sons—sloshed through acres of muddy prairie to attend the newly opened Illinois Industrial University. The school was housed in a single five-story brick building, surrounded by dirt roads and ragweed. The Green Street of campustown was nothing more than a cow path.

A century later, the Illinois Industrial University had grown into the University of Illinois, a world-class institution with 200 buildings sprawling over 785 acres. It is home to one of the nation's four supercomputer centers and to the third largest academic library after Harvard and Yale. To this day, the U of I is heavily oriented towards science and industry. The College of Engineering is second only to MIT, according to a recent *U.S. News and World Report* survey. And the accounting program was ranked number one nationally in a survey done by *Public Accounting Report.*

Theory and practical application work side by side at the U of I. Two professors in mathematics used computers to develop the Four Color Theorem, solving a puzzle that had stumped intellectuals for more than 100 years. Psychology students counsel each other through paraprofessional programs, run experiments on thousands of other students, and crunch data on thousands of university computers.

With 150 majors to choose from, and 4000 courses, students drool over the course catalog as if it were an all-you-can-eat buffet. What usually ensues is a search for one's self. Students try out a number of student activities as freshmen, use the free counseling service, and utilize the computerized career search program. On average, they switch their majors two or three times before they graduate.

> *"I started out as a math and computer science major, and later switched into journalism. This confused people in both fields. In the dorm cafeteria, my C.S. buddies urged me to come to my senses: 'At least get a science degree as a backup.' In my creative writing classes, my teacher and classmates would tease me for being too rational: 'Where's your sense of romance?' There's no way to get only one perspective at a school as large as the U of I. That's what I liked about it—hearing these different opinions all the time."*

The University of Illinois is located in Urbana-Champaign, a 100,000 population town located in central Illinois, between Chicago and St. Louis. More than 35,000 students attend the U of I in Urbana, taught by 2700 faculty members.

There are ten colleges in the U of I, the smallest ones being the School of Social Work and the Institute of Aviation and the largest being the College of Liberal Arts and Sciences, enrolling 45% of the undergraduate student body.

There is no typical Illini person. Some students come from farms a few miles away, others from Iran and China and India. They live in the wealthiest suburbs in Chicago and in the poorest neighborhoods of East St. Louis.

However, most of the students are from Illinois — something that has worried school administrators who see rival Big Ten schools actively recruiting students nationwide. In fact, 93% of the undergraduate students are in-state residents, 53% of whom are from the Chicago area. Urbana-Champaign townies brace themselves each fall for the invasion of Chicago kids and suburbanites who, after three hours of driving through cornfields and soybeans, are itching for some excitement.

And they'll get it from more than 700 registered campus organizations, whether it's the Student Government Association or the Sherlock Holmes club. They can write for the *Daily Illini,* an award-winning newspaper and one of the best student publications in the country. And if they're adventurous, they can learn how to fly airplanes and join the parachuting club.

The U of I has the largest Greek system in the world, with 53 national fraternities and 27 sororities. And that's not counting the dozen or so professional fraternities that house people of a specific major, like chemistry, veterinary medicine, and architecture.

About a quarter of the campus's 14,427 men and 11,419 women undergraduates belong to fraternities and sororities. Greeks and non-Greeks tend to make stereotypes about each other, and most of them simply aren't true. Several sorority cheer-leaders bouncing on the field are on their way to medical school. And far from being a nerd, a straight A, non-Greek female mechanical engineering student became Homecoming Queen.

During the summer, students head for the tennis courts and two Olympic-size swimming pools in the Intramural Physical Education Building. Inside, they can play squash and volleyball and dozens of other sports. In the wintertime, the ice arena opens and along with it, free skating lessons. When it snows, fraternities and dorms split into teams for all-out snowball fights, and when the excitement cools off, they bundle up for some cross-country skiing.

Urbana-Champaign is a town similar to Ann Arbor and Ithaca: it is a peaceful academic community in the countryside. All kinds of students go here, from the professional partyer who lives on beer and football to the quiet scholar who hides in the libraries and labs. The U of I has so many programs, housing possibilities, organizations, and people—every student can find a place here he or she can call home.

GETTING IN/FINANCIAL AID

"My letter of acceptance from the University of Illinois was a computer printout of a form letter, a contrast to the friendly acceptance letter signed by deans from smaller, private universities like Cornell.

"But I decided to go to the U of I because it was (a) inexpensive and (b) close to home. I wasn't alone. To save money, most of my high school classmates turned down offers from schools like MIT and Brown to go to Illinois's public Ivy."

It's becoming more difficult to get into the University of Illinois. As costs at private institutions push towards $25,000 a year, students have been fighting to get into the best public schools. The U of I offers prestige and a world-class education—all for $9864 a year in-state.

The University of Illinois is the top choice for one out of every four valedictorians in the Chicago area. It is also a favorite at the Illinois Mathematics and Science Academy (dubbed hi-tech high for attracting the brightest young minds in the state); one-quarter of its most recent graduating class enrolled in the U of I last fall.

In the Big Ten, only Northwestern and the University of Michigan can rival the University of Illinois in attracting top-notch students. The average Illinois freshman last year scored a 27 on the ACT and graduated at the top of the class.

A recent freshman class in the College of Commerce had a median high school percentile ranking of 93 and a median ACT score of 27. The median high school percentile ranking of the most recent freshman class in the College of Engineering was 95%, and the class median ACT was 30.

Besides the usual bunch of National Merit scholars and Westinghouse science winners, engineering students are exceptionally talented in computer science, many of whom have worked as computer consultants for businesses and hospitals while still in high school.

The U of I admitted 11,843 of its 15,616 applicants last year. Although that may not seem selective, the criteria for admission is charted out so clearly in terms of college board scores and class rank that most high school students who can't meet them don't bother applying. For instance, let's say you want to major in electrical engineering. If you scored a 32 on your ACT, you only have to be in the top 20% of your high school class. But if you scored a 25, you'd better be in the top 5%.

Some students major in the liberal arts or go to a local community college for two years and then try to transfer into the more competitive departments. For instance, they may major in economics to break into accounting or finance, study math and chemistry to edge their way into engineering, or major in speech communications to later find a spot in the broadcast journalism program.

Sixty-eight percent of all U of I undergraduates get financial aid. The average award to a freshman is $3800, and the most common student scholarship is given by the Illinois State Scholarship Commission, which gives students anything from $300 to nearly full tuition and fees. Students must be residents of Illinois and demonstrate financial need.

Forty percent of all students work part-time. Whether they are shelving books in the library or helping a professor write a book, the university is bulging with job opportunities.

Many students are accepted into prestigious cooperative programs with high-tech corporations like IBM and AT&T. During summers and some semesters, the science and engineering majors write computer software, help design aircraft engines, and do research for the companies. Not only do the students earn enough money to pay for school but their work experience almost guarantees them high paying jobs after graduation.

"Sometimes you have to be creative to finance your education. One Illini student did it without working or taking out loans or receiving any scholarships. Mike Hayes, a junior from Rochelle, Illinois was broke when he finished high school and didn't know how he was going to pay for college.

"Hayes wrote a letter to Bob Greene, a columnist at the Chicago Tribune. If everyone in Chicago gave him just one penny, the boy wrote, he could easily go to the U of I for four years. Greene announced the 'Many Pennies for Mike' program and soon pennies, nickels, dimes and $100 checks from all over the world started pouring into Haye's hometown post office. Hayes received tens of thousands of letters a day and accumulated a mountain of coins that added to about $30,000. He even got a letter and a $25 check from a former Miss America.

*"I probably would have run out of money if I hadn't thought
of this and I would have had to drop out and work a few years,'
says the grateful twenty-one year old Hayes. He is majoring in
food science, although he probably should be in finance."*

ACADEMIC ENVIRONMENT

*"Every year, the University of Illinois holds an Engineering Open
House. Students display their inventions and research within a
row of engineering buildings along Green Street. I never know
what to expect. I have seen a robot that solved a Rubik's cube with
its steel fingers in less than five minutes, a computer that recognized faces at a glance, even a huge metal monster of an insect
that crawled down the hall.*

*"I knew many of these inventors: they were my classmates, my
boyfriend, my roommates at the University of Illinois. These students, now in jeans and sweats, will be the future leaders of science and technology."*

You can't go through four years of the University of Illinois without being bombarded with reminders of research and new discoveries. Everywhere you go, professors are hunched over computers or discussing superstring theory or cold fusion
over lunch. They may be simulating a tornado on a Cray supercomputer or trying to
read your thoughts by measuring your brain waves.

Your classmates won't be much different. Your roommate might be on the street
handing out questionnaires for a psychology experiment or decorating your apartment with bones, rocks, and fossils from an archeological dig. Your other friends
may disappear for a semester and then come back to talk about their co-op experiences helping to design million-dollar computers for Hughes Aircraft, program
software for IBM, or work on a NASA space shuttle.

Every college has different requirements. The College of Liberal Arts and
Sciences, which enrolls 45% of the student body, requires that students have the
equivalent of two college years of a single foreign language and several semesters of
various subjects like math, English, computer science, biology and history. Engineering students have to choose a cognate field in the humanities or social sciences
while taking a heavy load of calculus, physics and technical courses.

After hearing accusations that "engineers can't spell" and "English majors can't
add," administrators have drawn up a new set of requirements that will force every
student to take more courses in English, math, the humanities, the natural sciences,
the social sciences, and non-western civilization.

Because the U of I is such a big university, opportunities for undergraduates to do
independent research are unsurpassed. Students can even design their own major.

In every department they can sign up for courses to work closely with a certain professor. In such classes, ambitious students can go to Africa and Asia, produce their own television shows and write novels. One professor even sends his students to the South Pole to do engineering research.

Of course, students have complained that the university is *too* big—that they have to wait in line for everything, that they feel like a number in an impersonal learning factory. Freshman year *can* be overwhelming. You cram into a lecture hall with 800 other students. The smaller discussion classes are taught by teaching assistants. You do see the professor, yes, but he looks more like an ant because he's so far away.

Freshman year is the time when students end up doing their chemistry experiments by computer. By pressing buttons, they can mix solutions into a beaker and watch test tubes and bunsen burners flicker on the screen. (If they make a mistake, the beaker explodes.) But after the first year, classes shrink to as small as ten to 25 students. And sometimes even smaller: one girl learned Swahili in a class of three. Such classes usually are taught by professors, who get to know each student well.

> *"I heard all the horror stories about journalism professor Robert Reid, before I took his in-depth reporting class. A man of inflexible deadlines, he was known to flunk people who stumbled in class a few minutes late when handing in their 40 page papers.*
>
> *"I was pleasantly surprised when I sat with 14 other people on the first day of class. Reid wanted us to be more than reporters. He wanted us to be writers. Creative nonfiction writers who, like novelists, would capture details and make a story so real a reader could see it and smell it and taste it. Reid hated reporters who insisted on punching facts into a cold new formula. 'If I had any such robots in my newsroom, I'd fire them,' he liked to say, cracking a piece of chalk onto the ground for emphasis.*
>
> *"Later in the year, Reid became my mentor. I would spend hours with him after class to discuss writing techniques, journalistic ethics, and the works of literary journalists like Tom Wolfe, Lillian Ross and John McPhee. And since he was convinced that each student in his class would do something important one day, he told us to quit worrying about our grades and start trying to do our best."*

The professors at the University of Illinois are some of the top researchers in their fields. In the journalism department, you will find award-winning faculty members who write for the *New Yorker* and the *New York Times*. On the other side of campus, you will find people like Nick Holonyak, who developed the light-emitting diode (LED), and Paul Lauterbur, whose pioneering research led to magnetic resonance imaging, now used extensively in medicine to view internal parts of the body without the use of X rays.

Competition is intense at the U of I and some departments are more demanding than others. Most of the time, however, there is a sense of camaraderie. Students do their homework together, compare experimental data to make sure nothing is way out of wack, proofread and critique each other's writing, work past midnight and sleep in their friends' rooms. Frequently, they will have cram parties in which about 20 students will squeeze into a single dorm room the night before an exam to quiz each other about the material.

During finals week, some of the computer rooms and libraries are open 24 hours a day. Students can be found staring into NOVAnet terminals, a computer system that tutors students in subjects ranging from physics to Chinese. Some devoted bookworms live in the undergraduate library for several days, surviving on a diet of soup and candy bars from the vending machines. If the pressure of final exams is too much, the U of I will provide free counseling and even offers emergency workshops that will give some strategies on last-minute studying.

There are increased efforts to make the new student feel at home. The campus honors program allows exceptional freshmen to do independent research and pairs them with professors who will act as mentors and advisers. Also, some courses have moved out of the classroom and into the dormitory. Students living in those dorms can take the elevator and stroll into a small class of ten or 15 people, some of whom may live on their floor.

SOCIAL LIFE

Most students enjoy a rich social life at the University of Illinois. That's not surprising, considering that the campus has 23 undergraduate residential halls, two graduate student halls, 19 certified private housing units, and 71 sorority and fraternity houses.

The dorms are the center of social activity and prime dating grounds for some undergraduate students. Hall residents can meet new people during meals and also through floor exchanges, when the gentlemen from one floor visit the ladies on another floor, or vice versa. The residential halls sponsor free movies, parties and dances several times a month, and once a year many dorms have a spring formal; a serious and extravagant affair, judging from the number of students who hire limousine drivers to carry the tuxedo-and-gown couple from dinner to dorm.

Dorm dwellers also can sign up for a number of activities like horseback riding, canoeing, cookouts and picnics at nearby parks. Lake of the Woods and the university Allerton Park are favorite weekend spots. Often, they sign up in groups to go to events at Krannert or Assembly Hall, such as REM concerts, student musicals, or Second City performances. Even if a student spends most of his time within his dorm room (definitely not recommended), he won't be able to dodge people who will try to recruit him to join dorm newsletter committees, bible groups, blood drives, massage seminars, ping-pong games, and so on.

"At least once a week, I would get together with some of my buddies and—over Chinese food and pizza boxes in our dorm

rooms—we might talk until three in the morning. The subjects of conversation ranged from boys to comic books to thermodynamics, depending on the group I was with.

"I especially liked being with journalism friends—we would read each other's writings, suggest changes and toss around story ideas. We swapped books and discussed John Steinbeck and Guy de Maupassant and Franz Kafka; we slammed on bad articles in the local newspapers, sometimes highlighting key paragraphs. These nightly chats were some of the best times I had at the U of I and what I learned from them was as valuable as anything taught in the classroom."

Most people live in the dorms their freshman year and later move into apartments or fraternity houses. The housing surplus in Urbana-Champaign makes it easy for a student to find a large, inexpensive apartment on campus in one afternoon.

Members of the Greek system don't have to worry about finding something to do on Friday night; they usually worry about how to worm OUT of social activities so they can find time to study. They have barn dances and spring and fall formals. On weekends there are dozens of exchanges between sororities and fraternities, as well as fraternity-sponsored street parties and theme parties like Pee-Wee Herman, Carribean Cruise, the Wedding Game and Revenge of the Nerds. That's on top of their annual parties on Halloween and Valentine's Day.

The campus is more traditional than most. Fraternity men give their girlfriends lavalieres, pins, or engagement rings, which results in a tearful candlelight ceremony at the sorority and a wild one at the fraternity that promises to leave the victim drenched or gooey with chocolate sauce.

There also are preprofessional fraternities, like the veterinary, chemistry and agriculture houses. Students usually share the same major and same career goals. In the French and German houses, students try to speak as little English as possible. Members of the architecture fraternity, Alpha Rho Chi, work on blueprints together and live in one of the most beautifully designed houses in town.

Every student has his/her own idea of a fun time, whether, it's poetry reading or cheering for the contestants in the Foxy Lady contest or dancing at the Gay and Lesbian Prom. But the whole campus gathers together at Homecoming, a national college tradition that, incidentally, was started by two University of Illinois students.

In 1909, C. F. Williams and W. Elmer Ekblaw sat on the steps of the YMCA and thought, why not have a day for U of I alumni to visit the campus and see their old friends? After all, it would be good for school spirit and publicity. They worked out the details, talked to the university president and dean, and the first Homecoming took place on October 15, 1910.

So every fall, alumni descend on Urbana-Champaign, wearing orange and blue striped sweaters and run to check their old rooms in dorms and fraternities. Thousands of people watch the Homecoming game and a parade of memorable floats, such as one of a dragon breathing fire onto the effigy of a Michigan football player.

EXTRACURRICULAR ACTIVITIES

"The University of Illinois is a haven for the entrepreneur. During my four years as an undergraduate, I have seen fellow students start an advertising agency, a silk screening company, a humor magazine and a new cable television sitcom. I watched one group of business students devote 20 to 40 hours a week to found a new credit union on campus. And one of my friends started his own computer company that, among other things, gives the campus police better technology to issue parking tickets to student violators."

The U of I is such a big institution that any student who starts a club or business is sure to attract others. There are more than 700 registered students organizations at the University of Illinois, and that doesn't even include the hundreds of nonregistered groups floating on campus.

Each fall before the first day of class, the University of Illinois hosts Quad Day, when hundreds of organizations put on a circus to recruit the new flock of freshmen. Booths and tables form a ring around the quadrangle, encircling student gymnasts who do triple twists over the grass.

Like a marketplace, it is noisy and exciting. The marching band pounds the eardrums with the Fighting Illini cheer song, together with the chattering deejays for WPGU, the campus radio station. The *Illio* yearbook committee, the underwater hockey team, the science fiction club, the Hare Krishnas…too many clubs, too little time! Dazed freshmen remember Quad Day as a blur—a day of repeatedly scribbling down their names and telephone numbers in exchange for an armful of pamphlets and flyers.

Students learn that not only are there enough ethnic, religious, and political organizations to go around, but there are special interest groups within each of them. Besides general groups like the Ukrainian Student Association and the Irish Illini, you will find the Chinese Dance Club, the Iranian Cinema Club, the Korean Scientists and Engineers Association, the Jewish Law Students Network and the Islamic Committee for Solidarity with the Palestinian People—among countless others.

Which organization is the most popular among students? It's hard to say, if you were to judge by sheer size, then the Greek system on a whole is the champion. Block I is another biggie. Its 250 members are football fans who wave pompoms and hold colored cards to form giant pictures on one side of the Memorial Stadium.

Some organizations are smaller but more prestigious. Thousands of students try out for the Marching Illini every year, but only a few will make it in the team of 300 band members, two dozen Illinette dancers and 30 Flag Corp women. The people who do make it—typically those who were the heads of their high school pompom squads and leaders of their bands—spend up to 20 hours a week practicing their routines.

The Student Government Association can be even more demanding. Groups of students spend thousands of dollars each fall to get elected on the 15-member executive board: They place ads in the *Daily Illini,* pass out buttons, layer the bulletin boards with posters, hold fund-raising parties, and give speeches in dormitories and fraternities and on the quad. The *Daily Illini* devotes three weeks of campaign coverage before the two-day elections, during which more than 5000 students turn out to vote.

The SGA, which consists of about 120 active members, appoints students on university committees to work with administrators to decide school policy. It also forms its own committees to deal with social issues, like alcohol abuse, hazing and date rape, and tries to provide new services for the campus, such as printing a new course evaluation book.

More than 600 people are involved in Volunteer Illini Projects, an organization that sponsors a wide variety of community service programs. Volunteer Illini members tutor grade school children, assist the elderly, organize blood drives, work in hospitals, and perform many other duties. There are also several independent groups on campus that devote their time to help the homeless, volunteer at local soup kitchens, and read to the blind.

Students who want to learn more about their fields of study can find a preprofessional club in every department, whether it is hybrid microelectronics or home economics. These organizations also give students a chance to sample a major before deciding to go into it.

Journalism students can practice their skills in the *Daily Illini*, run entirely by students without sponsorship from faculty or administration. The daily paper sweeps up national awards each year. Many of its staffers win summer internships and permanent jobs at metropolitan dailies, like the *Washington Post* and the *Wall Street Journal.*

"I remember the first article I wrote for the Daily Illini, *I was assigned to do a feature about Pop Rocks, the candy that allegedly killed Mikey, star of the Life cereal commercials. After experimenting with ten packs of Pop Rocks—sprinkling them on my tongue, feeling them sizzle and explode in my mouth—I tried the candy out on my friends, carefully researched the history of the candy, and typed the story in the DI computer system.*

"A few days later, I snatched up the DI that was thrust under my door. There it was, a full-page article next to this cartoon of a man with his mouth shattered open from a volcano of Pop Rocks! I did it! I had broken into print! My stomach felt as if all ten packs were bursting out at once. An hour later, my phone was ringing off the hook from excited friends who had seen the article. Although I was later writing for bigger newspapers like the New York Times, *nothing could match the thrill of seeing my first byline in the* Daily Illini. *"*

THE GRADUATES

"I was a junior when I first wandered into Professor Stegeman's office. He was the placement officer for the journalism department and I asked him for some advice about breaking into the newspaper business. Stegeman smiled, stroked his white beard, and told me about his first job as a reporter in a coal mining town in southern Illinois, his adventures in Africa and even his investigative reporting crew in East St. Louis.

"Stegeman was the one who suggested that I apply to 50 newspaper and magazine internships; he gave me a big batch of application forms and even proofread my résumé and cover letters to make sure they were free of typos. He gave names of U of I alumni to contact and frequently stopped me in the hall to tell me about new job opportunities. Unlike the machine-like career placement center I expected of a Big Ten university, the journalism placement office was very personal."

The University of Illinois has an exceptional reputation in placing its students in high-paying jobs and prestigious graduate schools. Between 80 and 90% of all applicants from the U of I are admitted to law school and 95% of the students receive offers of employment within eight months of graduation.

Recruiters from top firms and graduate programs flock to the U of I—over 40,000 interviews are conducted on campus every year. There are also special job fairs for seniors in computer science, law, business and other fields. During the spring, it is typical to see fellow Illini students decked in suits—backpack in one hand, portfolio in the other—running to meet the interviewers between classes.

Where do U of I graduates work? All over the world, although they tend to cluster in big cities like Los Angeles, New York and Chicago. Students who were born and raised in the Windy City tend to go back after graduation, spend a few years living downtown to work before buying a home in the suburbs. Engineering graduates who go to Chicago are moving into the fast growing DuPage County. Plenty of opportunity awaits them; Argonne National Laboratory, Fermilab, AT&T, to name just a few landmarks in Chicagoland's high-tech corridor.

U of I alumni are household names. The *Chicago Sun-Times* film critic Roger Ebert and the *New York Times* columnist James Reston are two of the 15 Illini graduates who are Pulitzer Prize winners. Nine graduates are Nobel Prize winners. Former Illinois students stand out in every field, such as television (Gene Shalit of the Today Show), comics (Lee Falk, creator of the Phantom and Mandrake the Magician), and magazine publishing (Hugh Hefner, founder of *Playboy*.)

Although many Illinois graduates are chief executive officers at Fortune 500 companies, many more are successful entrepreneurs, such as the Flying Tomato Brothers. Ralph Senn and Joe Ream were two rockin' and rollin' hippies who started a tiny pizza place that grew into the multimillion dollar empire.

Fun loving as ever, the two of them use cute advertising gimmicks to tempt the tummy; cars and hot air balloons shaped like tomatoes, heart-shaped pizza on Valentine's Day.

One of U of I's wealthiest alumni is Arnold O. Beckman, who was born the son of a blacksmith in a small town in central Illinois. He financed his education by playing in dance orchestras and movie houses and graduated from the U of I with a degree in chemical engineering. After becoming an inventor and professor at CalTech, he founded the mega-corporation of Beckman Instruments and donated $40 million dollars to establish the U of I Beckman Institute, a leading center of artificial intelligence and robotics. At the time, it was the largest gift ever to a public university.

Although most loyal Illini graduates aren't near Beckman's level, they donate more than $9 million to the university each year. The University of Illinois has the largest alumni association in the world, with 115,000 members out of 404,000 surviving graduates. More than 90 cities have Illinois alumni clubs—some which are as far away as Hong Kong and Turkey.

SUMMARY OVERVIEW

Few schools can rival the University of Illinois in academics, size and price. Its world-class status and excellent faculty attract the brightest students everywhere, many who cross oceans to get an education at Illinois. The school boasts of such things as having the third largest academic library in the country, the biggest alumni network, the biggest Greek system, the best centers for science and technology and all for low, low, state university tuition.

The University of Illinois has a rigorous academic life, admitting only those students who rank in the top few percent in the nation in terms of high school grades and College Board scores. With several National Medal of Science winners and many other prize winners and inventors on the faculty, students have a chance to work with some of the best experts in their fields. A leader of new technology, the U of I is in the midst of a building boom—already the home of two supercomputing centers. The university is known for its work in engineering, robotics, and artificial intelligence.

More than 35,000 students attend the U of I, which provides the school with diversity, an active social life, and a wealth of extracurricular activities. There are more than 150 majors to choose from and more than 700 student organizations. As a student you would have the opportunity to try anything you want, whether it's acting or Zen Buddhism. Throughout the years, enterprising Illini students have started a number of traditions, such as the first Homecoming and the first college concert band in the nation.

Many top students who couldn't—or didn't want to—pay the soaring costs of private universities come to the University of Illinois. The U of I costs only $7388 (in-state) a year for tuition and room and board, compared to price tags of more than $20,000 a year at other schools. No wonder people call Illinois one of the best buys in education; it offers a matchless education at a matchless price.

However, there are a few drawbacks to attending the U of I. The school is isolated, surrounded by cornfields and farm communities. A road trip to Chicago or St. Louis takes at least two hours, and is a pretty monotonous ride at that. (A popular T-shirt sold around campus displays rows of corn, cows and barns above the line "You gotta love the drive"). Without the university, the twin cities of Urbana-Champaign wouldn't have much entertainment to offer besides a few bars, movie theaters and playhouses.

Another thing students have to endure is the weather. At least once every winter, students brace themselves for the 40° minus blast that needles through four layers of sweaters and coats. On those days, snow doesn't fall, it comes sideways, scratching eyelids like sand. Of course, the summers make up for the coldness, boiling the population as the mercury crawls past the 100° mark. There is the consoling thought, however, that all of it builds character.

Although the enormous size of the school is a dream come true for some people, it can be a nightmare for others. Some students have complained that they have to wait in line for everything, especially during the mass confusion of fall registration. They feel intimidated by the sheer numbers of other talented students as well as by professors who seem cold and distant. This is not a school for those who need a lot of coddling and personal attention, unless they are aggressive enough to find a support system immediately, such as in the Greek system or in a club.

Indeed, the University of Illinois is not for everyone. But it's a great place to go to school, especially if you are an independent person who needs a fast-paced college, a person who takes the initiative to explore new things, a person who wants competition and who makes friends easily. If that description fits your personality, you will thrive at the U of I.

Iris Chang, B.S.

University of Michigan at Ann Arbor

THE PROGRAM

When you think about the University of Michigan, you might want to dismiss it as just another one of those big state schools located somewhere in the Midwest. Yes, Michigan is big and it is located in the Rust Belt, but the school also is one of the best academic institutions in the nation. With a distinguished faculty, talented students, and the resources of an exciting city, learning comes alive at Michigan.

The school is not only large in size, about 23,000 undergraduates and 13,000 graduate students, but grand in the scope of academic opportunities it offers those students. Although many students elect traditional majors, like psychology or English, others take a different path and choose nontraditional majors. At Michigan you can major in everything from Caribbean Studies to an ICP — an individualized concentration program in which a student selects a series of courses to create his or her own major. No matter what courses you select, you can't make a bad choice because all academics are excellent at Michigan. The core of this academic excellence is a commitment to both history and progress. Students benefit from a traditional education, but they are taught to consider all knowledge within the context of an ever changing modern world.

Although the primary focus at Michigan is academics, several features of the school make all of its fields of study exceptional. Rated as one of the top five faculties in the nation, Michigan instructors offer superior skills in teaching, research, and scholarship. Many faculty members participate in research projects in conjunction with teaching. As a result, they bring modern day applications of academics into the classroom and give students knowledge that goes beyond theory. By serving as a research center, Michigan always is moving toward the future. The Institute for Social Research (ISR) is one of the best psychological research centers in the nation. At Michigan, students have access to the center and the institute's faculty, who are shaping the future of academic thought and science.

Michigan also has a history of graduating a diverse group of talented people. Former president Gerald Ford and congressman Richard Gephardt attended the school, as well as the former president of Radcliffe, Matina Horner. Playwright Arthur Miller, novelist Judith Guest, the author of *Ordinary People*; and comedienne Gilda Radner also graced Michigan with their presence.

Aside from the school's list of academic programs and esteemed instructors, you can't help but notice the school's campus. The "diag" is a series of concrete walkways that meet in the heart of the campus. Perhaps the one central point among 2600 acres and 220 buildings, the diag extends in directions of the old and the new, espousing the educational philosophy at Michigan. In one direction lies the graduate library, just one of the 23 homes to the six million volumes of text at the university. Next door sits Angell Hall, a building where students attend classes. Although its facade is made up of classical columns that represent history, the school has a microcomputing center inside. Filled with Macintosh and Zenith computers, it's one way Michigan is preparing students to meet the challenges of the future. Campus buildings pay homage to both history and progress, mimicking the school's ideology.

The Michigan Union is a building that houses many student activities and functions. Located within the union's basement, the Michigan Union Grill (MUG) is a favorite meeting place for students and faculty. When first erected, the union forbade entrance to women. In response to the discriminatory policy, a group of women established the Michigan League, a campus building that now boasts a coffee shop and a theater. Today Michigan is much more progressive in its attitudes toward women. One bit of evidence of that progressiveness is its Women's Studies program for students.

Although Michigan is a large school, it's a comfortable walk from one end of central campus to another. To get to north campus, just hop on one of the free maize and blue buses that regularly circle the campus.

Interwoven into the university setting is the life of the city of Ann Arbor. If you're on campus long enough, you're bound to spot a man called Shakey Jake. A street musician and an Ann Arbor institution since 1957, he's one of a cast of characters who give the city and the campus its distinctive style. Within the community, there are several storefront businesses, shops, theaters, and restaurants. On North University you'll find Drake's Sandwich Shop, an old-fashioned candy store and cafe with a history all its own. Just down the corner and across the street there is a modern coffee shop that serves espresso and cappuccino. The two cafes mark the distinguishing characteristics of Michigan. Again, the old and the new complement each other.

Aside from architecture, Ann Arbor is home to Nichols Arboretum, informally known as the Arb. Located slightly out of the way of campus, next to Mary Markley Residence, students can wander through the Arb's trails of trees and meadows for the best in nature Michigan has to offer.

> *"It was sometime in mid-February and in Michigan that means snow. Late one night, a few friends and I decided we'd hit the Arb for some late night sledding. We geared up with all the essentials: long underwear, down coats, wool socks, and hot chocolate. Now*

all that was left was the fun part, stealing the trays. Those beautiful orange plastic things that make good sleds when used properly. We sneaked into the cafeteria through the dorm's kitchen entrance and quickly spotted the trays. We each grabbed one and bolted out the door. When we got outside there was six inches of white stuff on the ground. It was chilly and wet, but we pushed on to the forest. It took us about a half hour, and one rest stop for warmth, but when we got to the Arb, we were glad we'd made the trip. At least 50 people were out that night, trays in hand, rolling down the hills. I just hopped on my tray and held on tight as I sailed across the snow. The adventure would soon become a seasonal ritual among my friends.''

Another complement to Michigan is its excellence in sports. Each year the Michigan Wolverines consistently rank among the best of Big Ten football and often head for the Rose Bowl. Michigan's basketball team also showcases a lot of talent. In a recent year, Michigan won the NCAA championship, and last year, with five freshman starters, Michigan went as far as the NCAA Final Four, before falling to Duke. The school's sports teams embody the energetic spirit that is so much a focal point at Michigan.

With its academic excellence, an incredible campus life, and the resources of an exciting city, Michigan introduces students to almost everything they could want in an undergraduate education. Founded in 1817, the school is one of the oldest public universities in the nation. Over the years, Michigan has developed into a world of possibilities and demands of its students that they work hard and dedicate themselves to their own educational evolution.

GETTING IN/FINANCIAL AID

Gaining admission to U of M is difficult. In a recent academic year, 19,393 students applied and 13,276 were accepted to the freshman class, with 5068 enrolling. Each year more and more students apply to Michigan—what is hailed as a public Ivy. About 70% of undergraduate students are state residents; the rest come from outside the state and foreign countries. Because Michigan is a state school, residents have an advantage over out-of-state applicants who face tougher admissions standards.

Compared to other schools, Michigan's admissions policy is highly competitive. There are no specific numbers that will guarantee acceptance, but generally in-state students need a 3.6 GPA and an 1100 SAT I to be considered seriously for admission. Michigan also accepts the ACT in lieu of the SAT I. The ACT is considered an achievement test and admissions counselors say it measures what you have learned, whereas SAT I measures aptitude, or your potential for learning. Whether or not these tests measure anything is debatable, but, like it or not, they are required.

When reviewing applications, counselors consider a student's grades, the difficulty of his or her course work, and test scores as the primary indicators of the student's abilities. Recommendations from counselors, an essay, and extracurricular activities are reviewed.

Unlike many private schools, Michigan places little importance on extracurriculars when reviewing applications. Acceptance is pretty much a matter of numbers. At such a large school, it's difficult to review each application with the consideration you might get at a smaller school.

> *"Given the size and variety of the school, it is impossible to point out the specific type of person who goes to Michigan. People come to the school from a variety of backgrounds and bring with them many different talents. But a common thread of intelligence weaves through all of the school's students. All Wolverines share a great capacity for learning and a curiosity about life that makes Michigan such an exciting university. Michigan students engage in an active kind of learning, acquiring knowledge not only in the classroom, but through all the activities and opportunities afforded them by the school and surrounding city of Ann Arbor."*

Michigan promotes the idea of a diverse student body, but over the years many protestors have argued that admissions policies favor students who come from white, upper-middle class background. Recently, administrators have made a good faith effort to increase minority enrollment. Last year, minority enrollment increased to 20%, and the university regularly cancels classes on Martin Luther King's birthday. Many student groups set up educational programs and workshops in an effort to combat racism and to increase student awareness.

In terms of costs, tuition at Michigan is very high for a public school. In fact, it's one of the most expensive public universities in the nation. For an in-state student tuition is $3830 a year, and $12,938 a year for those from out-of-state. Although a Michigan education is expensive, it's far less than the cost of an Ivy League college or other private schools. Considering room and board, books, and other expenses, in-state students pay about $11,650 per year and out-of-staters pay about $22,350. A year at one of the Ivys can exceed $20,000, so comparatively, Michigan is a wise investment, especially for Michigan residents.

In an attempt to compensate for high tuition and living expenses, Michigan's financial aid department gives aid to about one-third of all undergraduate students, in the form of grants, loans, and work-study jobs. The school tries to help students cover the difference in cost between the price of their education and what they can afford to pay.

The best way to ensure that you are considered for aid is to submit the necessary application materials each year. Waiting in line is a pain, but if it will put some dollars in your pocket, it's definitely worth it. Although aid is based on need primarily, in some cases merit scholarships are available. To be eligible for aid, students must carry a full load of academics throughout the year, a minimum of 12 credits per semester.

ACADEMIC ENVIRONMENT

Michigan is made up of 11 undergraduate schools, but the majority of the students, about 80%, enroll in the College of Literature, Science and the Arts (LSA). The second most popular program is engineering.

Academic requirements for LSA vary depending on the particular degree program a student elects. The three degrees offered by the college are the Bachelor of Arts (A.B.), Bachelor of Science (B.S.), and Bachelor of General Studies (B.G.S.). Basic requirements include 120 hours of course work, proficiency in a second-year level foreign language program (ouch), and the successful completion of two English courses: introductory composition and the junior/senior writing requirement. B.S. students must complete half of their course work in the areas of physical science, natural science, or math. In addition to these requirements, Michigan attempts to expose all students to a variety of subject areas through a distribution program, whereby students are required to take credits in the social science, natural science, humanities, and other areas.

In your junior year, you declare your major. At Michigan it's called an area of concentration. Different majors vary in terms of requirements, but generally students must take between 24 and 48 credits in a particular subject.

The LSA offers 47 different fields of specialization. Traditional majors—like English, political science, economics, and psychology — are popular, but Michigan also offers nontraditional majors that are not available at other schools. Where else can you major in Scandinavian studies, spend a semester at the world's largest geological land station, or take courses in Ojibwa (the language of the North American Indian tribe that originally occupied the Lake Superior region)? Along with the size of Michigan comes a long list of academic choices, all of them excellent.

> *"When I first came to Michigan, I planned to major in biology. I had always been interested in the subject, so why not continue on doing what I enjoyed and what I had excelled at in high school. At freshman orientation I soon realized that choosing a major so early in the game was foolish. There were so many courses, so many ideas just waiting to be explored. If I stuck with one subject now, I would be cheating myself. I had to try a little bit of everything. My first semester I took a variety of humanities courses, including logic, religion, literature, and anthropology. To my surprise, I found all of them interesting. The teachers were all good, and because of the way the material was presented, I began to consider a broader and more diverse course of study than I had originally intended to take at college.*
>
> *"I remember sitting in my dorm room one night composing my first essay. So many ideas fell onto my paper I couldn't believe it. I felt like I was being introduced to learning all over again."*

The size and diversity of Michigan does have its drawbacks. Classes generally are very large and can seem impersonal. Although teaching methods and class size varies, courses are taught primarily in large lectures coupled with smaller recitation sections led by instructors. Students meet in sections to discuss and comment on material presented in lecture. Sections are about 15–40 students per class, whereas lectures are much larger, they can run from 50–500 students. Advanced courses tend to be smaller, but introductory 100 level classes are big lectures.

> *"When I first walked into Econ 101, I looked around the room and thought about walking out. There were so many people, at least 300. The students looked weary, all of them draped over the furniture staring as if lost in Michigan's vast universe. I slouched into an aisle seat and wondered what I had gotten myself into. I sat close to the door so when class was over and the stampede came, I'd be able to exit quickly. I had to be in there for an hour and a half but so far my watch had only passed five minutes. Out of the blue, a woman sitting next to me remarked, 'This is the most insane thing I've seen yet at this place.' We exchanged our names and other seemingly superficial information, but to this day, I'm still thankful for that moment of conversation which made the chaos of that morning a little more human. Even though Michigan is a big place, I soon began to feel like I wasn't just one student floating in a sea of strangers."*

The lecture/recitation method of teaching is good and bad. If you're not prepared for class, chances are you won't be put on the spot. On the other hand, large scale teaching leaves a great deal of responsibility for learning up to students. You have to make sure you complete your work and take part in your education. If students want to discuss materials outside of class, they can meet with instructors one-on-one during office hours. If you make an effort to talk to instructors, they're usually pretty good about meeting with you. Just remember, professors are people. Some you'll like and some you won't. If you go out of your way to meet with them, they'll appreciate it. There is nothing an instructor likes more than an interested and interesting student.

In addition to having one of the most talented faculties in the nation, Michigan professors are a diverse group of individuals, each bringing something unique to the classroom. Many profs work jointly on research projects and academics, providing students with theoretical knowledge as well as the benefit of their hands-on experience in a particular field. For example, Professor Carl Cohen teaches logic and philosophy in the Residential College, but frequently works and lectures in other areas of the university, such as medical ethics and arbitration.

In addition to the variety of academic resources at Michigan, the school also has some programs that make the university a little smaller and more accessible. The Residential College (RC), the Pilot Program, and the Honors College all make Michigan easier to manage through programs that pay more attention to the individual student. The RC is a smaller college within the LSA that offers students the benefits of a learning and living community. RC students spend their first two years living in East Quad and take smaller, seminar classes that approach nontraditional subject matters. When I was a freshman, and a member of the RC, I took a seminar called Anthropology of Black Fiction instead of the more traditional introductory composition requirement of LSA.

The RC requires students to take a course in creative expression and three RC courses a year to graduate from the college. Another plus of the RC is that students have the option of receiving written evaluations instead of grades. The school's philosophy centers on the importance of an undergraduate education. The program began in 1967 and enrolls about 800 students each year. The two other programs, the Pilot Program and the Honors College, are similar in orientation and philosophy and enroll 300 and 1700 students respectively.

SOCIAL LIFE

Although the social life at Michigan is as broad and diverse as the school's student body, the one driving force in almost every student's life is the importance of the Michigan Wolverines (the football team to you laymen.) During the fall and early winter months, football reigns supreme on the social calendar of a Michigan student. The idea of football is more than a three-hour event; its social ramifications can encompass an entire weekend for those students up to the challenge. Several fraternities, sororities, and student groups host pre-game, kick-off, and post-game parties centered around the sporting event. Any mention of football at Michigan stirs the social consciousness and gives students a reason to party.

Michigan is tough academically, and aside from the predominance of football frenzies, the main focus of most students' lives is their studies. Though academic life is demanding, rarely do students let their schoolwork keep them from having a good time. It's not unusual to walk into a library on the weekend and see a mass of students studying until the late hours of the night, but after work, there is always time for play.

Perhaps the greatest demand on the incoming freshman is the need for an endless supply of energy. At Michigan, students work hard, but they play hard. There are a variety of bars, clubs, and campus events for any student who feels a well-developed social life is an essential part of the college experience.

There are three popular bars located on campus that cater to the undergraduate mentality.

Rick's American Cafe (no, it's not the same one as in *Casablanca*) offers live bands, pool, and a good time for those who want to kick back, relax, and listen to good music. Rick's hosts local bands and even some imports.

The Nectarine Ballroom has more of a neon New York feel to it. With a bopping dance floor amd different types of music featured nightly, it's a favorite among undergraduates seeking the club atmosphere.

Good Time Charlies, located at the center of campus, largely caters to the fraternity and sorority crowd. Unlike other campus bars, it doesn't charge a cover, and in warmer months offers an outdoor cafe.

The University Club, or U-Club, is a restaraunt open to U of M students and faculty. The club appeals to all students; grads and undergrads alike, and has regular comedy shows, dance music, and an outdoor patio. Dominick's, a local restaurant and bar, is the hottest spot in town during the warmer months in Ann Arbor. On Friday afternoons, hordes of students embark on happy hour, sitting in the bar's outdoor area. Sometimes professors will hold classes at Dominick's to get away from the stuffy classroom setting.

> *"It was the weekend before my first set of exams when I discovered Dominick's. The bar sits across the street from the law school library and offers quite a departure from the local grind found within the esteemed walls. I was studying on a Friday afternoon when I got the calling. It was a warm, sunny, April day and I soon realized any attempt at logical thought was foolish.*
>
> *"I walked outside and was greeted by sun worshippers scattered throughout the lawn just outside the library. They were all pretending to study, but I knew better. With just a few steps and a little initiative, I left my mind in the library and moved to the other side of the street. I spotted a group of friends right away and joined them on the outdoor patio. One friend handed me a daiquiri and I slid back into a chair, escaping the worries of exams and other pressures, if only for a sunny afternoon."*

Although, like any university, bars are a popular form of entertainment, there are a variety of other things to do on campus. Dorms usually have social events ranging anywhere from dinners to overnight excursions and small hall parties. Some dorms host annual events, like East Quad's Halloween Bash. Almost all dorms sponsor movie nights where everyone can gather around the VCR, munching popcorn and taking a break from the day's classes.

Thirty-seven fraternities and 20 sororities are on campus, and they make up a great deal of the social life on campus. About 23% of students join the groups. Although some are part of national chapters, each has a different focus: some perform community service, whereas others participate in competitive athletics and other activities. On any given weekend, there is always a fraternity party, especially during football season. Each chapter has traditional rush ceremonies at the beginning of the semester. Some offer housing to members as an alternative to life in the dorms.

Although students attend various clubs and parties on campus, some lead quieter lifestyles. Just as there is no typical Michigan student, there is no typical way to spend a Friday or Saturday night. Some students like the bar scene, whereas others spend time at the movies, plays, or talking with friends.

Off campus you'll find downtown Ann Arbor. The area serves an older crowd and caters to the community as well as to students. Downtown offers bars, restaurants, movies, and whatnot of a typical college town.

Students can find almost anything they want on campus and in the downtown area. Michigan sponsors a variety of lectures and readings. One of the greatest resources of Michigan is the list of esteemed scholars who come to town to speak with students. When I was in school, I heard Toni Morrison, John Irving, and Kurt Vonnegut speak, just to name a few.

EXTRACURRICULAR ACTIVITIES

As far as extracurricular activities, there is a lot to do at Michigan. With its enormous student body, Michigan has over 400 clubs and activity groups. Whatever you like to do, you can find it here. And if there isn't a club that sponsors your favorite activity, chances are you can round up enough people with similar interests to start up a club of your own. Many local clubs have community members as well as students for members. Some of the more interesting clubs on campus include Friends of Siddha Yoga, the juggling club, and a variety of political organizations such as Amnesty International.

There are 35 sports clubs and a number of drop-in sports like basketball, swimming and racquetball. If you don't own and can't borrow the proper equipment, you usually can rent it for a small fee. There are also classes in aerobics, dance, and even scuba for students as well as Ann Arbor residents. The classes aren't free, but fees are reasonable. If you like the outdoors, you will want to take advantage of the school's fully equipped outdoor recreation program that rents camping equipment, skis, and even boots. Michigan, known for its four seasons and ever changing weather, is a great school for the outdoor enthusiast.

In terms of religion, most traditional and even lesser-known faiths are represented on campus. The Guild House, home of the ministerial alliance, provides weekly beans and rice dinners and nonsectarian poetry readings. Members of the Jewish community in Ann Arbor recently completed work on a new Hillel building. Jewish students are welcome to meet there and attend religious services along with various social events.

Although Michigan is not recognized as a film school, like UCLA or NYU, it does sponsor several student-run film groups. The groups coordinate film showings in the various university auditoriums. Campus films include a variety of movies, including recent releases, classics, and cult favorites. The costs to see the movies are about half the price of commercial theaters.

Michigan has a variety of facilities for the performing arts. Hill Auditorium, located in the heart of the campus, sponsors student and professional concerts. Noted for its exceptional sound system, performers from around the world and classical artists choose to perform at Hill. Other theaters, like the Performance Network, the ornate Michigan Theater, and the modern Power Center provide students with many opportunities to experience theater on campus.

RESIDENCE LIFE

Almost all incoming freshman choose to live in residence halls, or dorms as they're called on campus. It may sound trite, but the dorms are a great place to meet people. Living in the dorm, you'll find the university a little more accessible and friendly. When you start your life at Michigan, you're thrown into a completely new situation, but in the dorms you'll find hundreds of people in the same predicament. Everyone is new.

> *"After my parents dropped me off, I didn't know what to do. Here I was at Michigan with a million opportunities, all just waiting for me, and I couldn't move. My roommate walked in and we exchanged a few words. She was a sophomore and a freshman orientation leader. She zipped in and zipped out, explaining she had to go help out the freshmen who didn't know where they were going. Who did she think I was?*
>
> *"I decided to walk down the hall to check out if there was any sign of life around. It was a few days before classes and I didn't know if anyone had arrived yet. I walked into a little alcove and noticed a few people milling around and talking. Someone came up to me, a short blonde woman, and said, 'Hi, I'm Debbie. Welcome to the Quad.' All of a sudden my anxiety lifted and I felt a whole lot better."*

There are ten dorms on campus and each one comes equipped with a cafeteria, study and TV lounge, and distinct personality. Over the years, dorms at Michigan have acquired certain reputations. The hill dorms generally are known for their socially-minded attitudes, whereas West Quad is called the jock dorm. Although Michigan acts to enforce alcohol and drug regulations, the greatest amount of alcohol on campus reportedly is consumed in South Quad. East Quad is known for its artsy, more liberal attitude. Bursley, located on north campus, is slightly out of the way of central campus, but it's convenient for art, music, and engineering students who take classes there. Although each dorm may have a certain stereotype, from year to year dorms change, depending on the students who live in them.

Co-op housing is an alternative to the dorm. Co-op dwellers live in large houses with other students where they share a variety of household duties. Co-op living is cheaper than the dorms and it appeals to some students, but isn't right for the person who doesn't like close quarters. There are more people per square foot in a co-op than in any other housing situation. Usually students who elect to live in co-ops do so after their first year in the dorm.

The third option for students is off-campus, privately-owned housing. Most students move into apartments or houses in their junior year. Off-campus housing is great because it gives you more privacy than the dorms. On the other hand, Ann Arbor is known for its high housing cost—a two-bedroom apartment typically runs $750 and up a month, depending on where you choose to live.

GRADUATES

Students who graduate from the University of Michigan go on to do a variety of things with their lives. The school is known for producing alums who continue their education in graduate and professional school. Michigan has the highest law school acceptance rate, 86%, of any undergraduate program in the nation. Similarly, more students are accepted into U.S. medical schools from Michigan than from any other school in the country.

Although graduate school is a popular choice, many graduates choose to travel, if their pocketbooks allow, or to enter the working world. Just as there is no typical Michigan student, there is no particular course through life a graduate chooses to take.

> *"When I graduated from school, about a third of my friends went on directly to graduate school. One went to New York University Law School and another enrolled in the oceanography program at the University of Rhode Island. These friends knew what they wanted to do, in terms of the career sense of the word, and needed to get additional degrees. The rest decided to travel, go to work, or hang out in Ann Arbor, soaking up the aftermath of an incredible college experience. One took a teaching job in Michigan and one friend left for Europe with no permanent destination or return date in mind. I, along with a bunch of people, settled in Ann Arbor for a while. It's a great community and one that's difficult to leave."*

In terms of economics, Michigan graduates traditionally make up an affluent community. About half of all graduates go on to make a minimum of $40,000 a year during their peak earning years. Most alums stay in Michigan; the next most desirable locales are California, Illinois, Ohio, and Florida.

The alumni network at Michigan is odd. In terms of size, there are more living graduates from Michigan than from any other school in the nation. About 50% of alums show financial support for the school through donations, but the university does very little to help graduates keep in touch with each other. Aside from football games, rarely do alums come together in any organized and formal way. Make no mistake, however, Michigan alums show their true Wolverine spirit during football season. The alumni club, the one alumni organization at Michigan, sponsors bus tours to the Michigan/Michigan State game when the teams fight it out in East Lansing. Hundreds of fans gather to cheer on the maize and blue.

> *"After you leave Michigan, you are bound to run into alums all over the country. When I traveled to Los Angeles a few years ago, I met a couple who graduated from the university 50 years ago. I got on the plane and noticed the man sitting next to me wore a maize and blue cap. When I asked him if he went to Michigan he laughed and said, 'Oh yes, a long time ago, but I'm still quite a fan.' He introduced me to his wife and I learned they were enroute to the Rose Bowl. She asked me how I liked Michigan, had it changed, along with a million other questions. Even though I didn't know these people, I immediately felt a warmth between us. We continued talking and before I knew it, the plane touched down in L.A. Thinking back on it, I'm not surprised at how quickly we got to know each other. I had spent an afternoon with a couple with whom I had a common bond. We shared a part of history."*

SUMMARY OVERVIEW

Life at Michigan allows students to explore a myriad of possibilities both educationally and culturally. In terms of academics, the school provides a wide range of studies to choose from including 124 fields of specialization for undergraduates and an impressive faculty of teachers, scholars, and researchers. For a broad-based, liberal arts education, no other university can give you as many excellent choices as Michigan. Faculty members encourage students to learn the basics, like math and history, but also allow them the freedom to develop their own interests and to take advantage of the many educational opportunities available to them.

The 110,000 people of Ann Arbor, half of whom are in some way affiliated with the university, make up a city that is socially, culturally, and politically aware. Student life interacts with the community and together, the two generate an energy like that found in a big city. Unlike many universities, a few of the Ivys included, life at Michigan does not exist in isolation of the world around it. Instead, the school and the city interweave to give students an education rich in culture and in life. And for those who still want the resources of a large metropolitan area, Detroit is just a 45-minute car ride away.

For students who want to pursue their studies beyond the undergraduate level, Michigan serves as an excellent springboard. Because of its outstanding reputation, many graduate schools rank Michigan students highly when they consider applications for admission.

The size of Michigan, however, can create problems for students. The enormity of the school can be overwhelming, especially if you're from a small town. With the large student body comes a lot of hassles and red tape you wouldn't find at a smaller school. When you have to make an appointment, you have to make many phone calls to finally get in touch with the right department—the hazards of large institutional learning. It's impersonal and at times you might feel like no one really cares about you as an individual. The important thing to remember is you're not alone. Everyone else is coping with the same problems and frustrations.

At a big school like Michigan, another drawback is that no one looks over your shoulder to make sure you are fulfilling your graduation requirements. You meet with counselors occasionally, but you pretty much are on your own. Michigan promotes a policy of self-advocacy and asks that you take the course of your education into your own hands. It's a good lesson to learn for life. A Michigan education will not pamper you; it may not be easy, but it's probably the best prep course you can get for entering the working world.

Michigan, and any college for that matter, is what you make it. You may encounter the problem of excess—too much and too many good choices—but once you learn a few survival skills, you will welcome the challenge. Find out what you want to do, what you want to get out of your education, and throw yourself into it. Michigan can provide you with the raw materials to build a fantastic four years. The school gives students a basic history of knowledge to work with and allows each student to integrate that information into his or her own life with a look toward the future.

Judith Abrams, B.A.

University of North Carolina at Chapel Hill

THE PROGRAM

"The University of North Carolina at Chapel Hill is the essence of diversity. My first day on campus I met a fraternity guy whose paisley boxers hung down below his shorts, a young activist who had been fasting for five days, a student poet laughing hysterically at something he had written, a religious fanatic preaching the gospel between twin trees in the pit (central campus), and Michael Jordan—the one, the only, the famous basketball star.

"Each person fit perfectly into the Carolina puzzle. Did I? At the time, I didn't feel like it. I didn't fit those categories. But soon I realized I embodied my own category. Everyone does. To each, his own; all make up the UNC whole."

At Carolina, there's no way to avoid different cultures and ideas, personalities and perspectives. Diversity permeates social life, classes, and curriculum and paces academic excellence. Often called the public Ivy of the South because of high standards and relatively low cost for North Carolina residents, UNC has an atmosphere of academic rigor mingled with an unpretentious, friendly lifestyle. Some 15,000 undergraduates fill Chapel Hill during fall and spring semesters. Graduate students boost the numbers to nearly 24,000 students. But you're not the number you imagine yourself to be. Even the largest lecture classes are comprised of small discussion groups; professors believe in freedom of thought and expression.

In fact, Carolina's philosophy of liberal arts secures free thought, speech, and actions. You could be wrong, but still you can voice your opinion, knowing that another student or the professor may rebut. It's been that way since 1795, when the school, the nation's first public university, was founded with a vision for "all-useful learning." Later, Edwin Anderson Alderman, university president from 1896–1900, described his dreams for "a sound and various learning... where [students] are trained to observe closely, to imagine vividly, to reason accurately, and to have some humility and toleration." Today, UNC professors and educators applaud the liberal arts curriculum as do the students.

Most students major in history, English, political science, or psychology, although the professional schools — journalism, education, nursing, and business — attract their share. Students heading for medical school cling to the most popular major — biology. The common threads are interesting, qualified instructors and a heavy workload.

> *"Almost every UNC professor seems to think his/her class is the most important class at the university and that, surely, you will spend all your time studying the subject. At the beginning of the semester they roll out the words, 'For each hour in the class, you should study three hours outside of class.' By the senior year you figure out how to read chapters and more chapters in just a few hours, absorbing the important points, computing and analyzing and writing. And writing. And writing.*
>
> *"One semester, I wrote 18 papers, not including the essay exams where for a solid three hours you scribble all your learning into a couple of standard blue books. When it's over, you have to massage your fingers to straighten them. But if you have prepared, there's nothing like the feeling that you knew what to write, that you could have written more and more if you had to. Unless you didn't study enough or drew a blank. You have to prepare well to do well. You have to read and think and write and think. And when you leave Carolina, you know you earned that degree and you rejoice that you persevered."*

Classes are but a part of the rich, educational experience offered at UNC. Most students say they learn life outside class, beyond books and grades—in other people, in extracurricular activities, such as student government and Greek life, and in the classic, village-like ambience Chapel Hill has worn through the years despite the metropolitan growth in surrounding cities. Nestled at the top of a hill in central North Carolina, the town, however, does constitute one corner of the steadily growing Raleigh-Durham-Chapel-Hill Triangle. You'll find everything in the area: lakes, businesses, hospitals, restaurants, shopping malls, movie theaters, playhouses, and opportunities for internships, among various other things. But you can always retreat back to your own corner of the world, tucked away like a vintage oasis preserving time.

The Triangle is also a territory of archrivals because Duke and North Carolina State universities are just 10 and 30 minutes away. Chapel Hill can hardly contain itself on game days. Whether it's football in Kenan Stadium or an explosive basketball game in Dean E. Smith Center, Tar Heel fans, students, and alumni bleed Carolina Blue. Fans painted the streets blue in 1982 when the Tar Heels won the NCAA basketball title, and Coach Dean Smith grew as popular as God. Crowds still cluster around television sets and wring their fists and cuss out the officials and throw streamers and toilet paper off balconies into trees, all the while hoping that the Tar Heels, *this* year, will edge their way to the top again, which they did in 1993.

Essentially, the Carolina experience connects people. You may not look or dress like your roommate or hallmates or the people in your classes. You may not talk or walk or think like the people from New York, New Orleans, California, or the small towns of North Carolina. You don't have to. The university is big enough to grant your individuality yet small enough for you to find your niche. And no matter how different, everyone is a Tar Heel, from the fifty-five-year-old alum who gives annually to the university and shows up weekly for games, to the college grad just making his way in the world, to the befuddled freshman searching for his next class or major. Each person, in some way, helps mold the school. And, undoubtedly, Carolina days and friendships have a lasting effect on those who have traveled its course.

GETTING IN/FINANCIAL AID

Because of the school's outstanding reputation, both socially and academically, the road to acceptance is difficult, the competition keen. Already more people attend than the university can house, and most upperclassmen live off campus although freshmen are guaranteed dorm space. The fact is, greater numbers are applying to the university, so the percentage of admitted students is shrinking. A recent class, for example, arrived on campus 3331 strong, selected from an applicant pool of nearly 15,041. Although annually one in three applicants is accepted, it's much harder for out-of-state candidates to get in due to the limited number of spaces available to them. Most recently, only 600 out-of-state students were chosen from a record 10,200 out-of-state applicants.

The figures could suffocate a person, so it's better to ignore them. If you're a hardworking, dedicated high school student, you have the potential to get into Carolina. The university celebrates a student body with varied interests and talents. Of the more than 17,000 undergraduates, for instance, 59% are women and about 9% are black, a number Carolina hopes will grow. You may have that extra ingredient admissions officers are looking for. Be specific on your application, and when you reach the part that says "optional: write a personal statement,"—by all means, write an essay whether or not you believe you need to. That plug can't hurt.

"You will find that your application is the only true hint of who you are. Beyond SAT I scores, it reports what you've done and allows room for your voice, so don't limit yourself to the printed lines and small, blank spaces. One admissions officer said the essay and a good description of extracurricular involvement sometimes are the deciding factors, when test scores and class records begin to run together. Applicants have

> *sent work résumés and videotapes, artistic photographs, newspapers, and short stories. Anything to grab attention. Some even send recommendations from people who know them well, although that's not required."*

Personal interviews aren't used in the candidate's evaluation. Yet, if you plan to major in music or drama, you should contact the department chair concerning an audition, which could qualify you for a scholarship.

Still, you wonder whether your application will stand out against some valedictorian/student body president/yearbook editor's application. What exactly are admissions officers looking for? How do you get in?

Carolina seeks individuals with a history of achievement, those who have challenged themselves as much as the local context would allow—those who, in effect, will take advantage of the total educational community that is UNC. The selection committee requires the following minimum number of high school courses, all of which should be college preparatory:

- four years of English;
- three years of mathematics (one geometry and two algebra or a higher math course with algebra II);
- two years of the same foreign language (modern or classical);
- three years of natural science (one biological, one physical, and at least one laboratory course);
- two years of social science (one must be U.S. history); and
- two additional years of electives in the traditional academic areas listed above, for a minimum of 16 traditional academic units (most students present more).

Although SAT I/ACT scores are a consideration, the average SAT I being about 1120, UNC emphasizes more the student's classroom performance and the difficulty of courses taken, as well as leadership and involvement in extracurricular activities. The net result is an interested and active student body and a highly stimulating atmosphere.

> *"Most people, their freshman year, wonder how they made it to Carolina. Sure, you worked hard in high school, but so did the people sitting on either side of you, so did the bright students who are answering all the questions and have done all the reading for class and have already aced the first few quizzes. Suddenly, you realize that someone had enough confidence in you to invite you into the system. Now, it's your obligation to prove yourself, which isn't quite the breeze that it was in high school. Yet, with the challenge, you go for it. And soon the minds you believed to be so great look to you for your contribution. Everyone has a place and something to give. That's why you're there."*

Cited in several recent publications as one of the best educational bargains in America, equal to richly endowed Ivy League schools, one of Carolina's advantages is cost. For a top-notch university, educational expenses are exceptionally low. Residents of North Carolina paid less than $7000 in costs for full-time enrollment in a recent year, and nonresidents less than $13,500. Of course, these charges are subject to change yearly. If you need financial assistance, the Office of Scholarships and Student Aid may help. More than 7800 students receive approximately $35 million in financial aid each year from scholarships, grants, loans, and part-time jobs. On payday, the financial aid building overflows with students collecting checks. They could not have afforded school without help.

ACADEMIC ENVIRONMENT

"The crowd grew numb as Eudora Welty, the brilliant author from Jackson, Mississippi, stepped to the podium on stage and began speaking, her deep, liquidy voice filling the stillness. It was her voice that held us, that gently pulled us through her words. It was the same—I should say force—which drove me through her stories, her fiction, her truth: 'A Worn Path,' 'Why I Live at the P.O.,' 'Golden Apples,' 'The Wide Net,' 'The Wanderers,' and others in my literature classes. She was my favorite writer, and there I sat, in awe, three rows back from the aged Welty, her purple gown flowing down to her calves, her shoulders rounded from years of hunching over a typewriter. She was the text personified.

"Carolina often attracts speakers and writers who excite and stimulate the learning atmosphere. Students have the opportunity to meet and talk with outstanding personalities, which, in the past, have included Kurt Vonnegut, Coretta Scott King, Maki Mandela, David Brinkley, Bill Clinton, Toni Morrison, and George Bush. The list continues. And when you shake the hands and face the eyes that have touched and witnessed experiences you have only imagined, you somehow feel connected to the past, and your perspective begins to unfold."

UNC's academic program is designed to broaden and expand perspectives. Students take four to six courses per semester during the two-semester year, totaling at least 120 required units for graduation. Two basic components structure the system: the general education requirements common to all programs and the more specialized major field of study requirements. Before declaring a major, all freshmen and sophomores enter the General College and must complete general education courses, such as English literature, art, psychology, history, philosophy, or biology, along with approximately seven free electives and two physical education classes.

"At times the requirements seem outrageous, and you wonder how in the world you'll cram them all into your schedule and why you have to take geology when your major is English. But then

you remember the liberal arts philosophy, the diversity in the curriculum—you're there to learn about what you don't know, and surveying as many topics as possible will surely sharpen your perspective."

During the spring semester, sophomores declare a major and transfer to the College of Arts and Sciences or to one of the professional schools in either the Division of Academic Affairs or the Division of Health Affairs. There are 2245 full-time faculty members. Not all are advisors, but every student has a faculty advisor.

The areas of undergraduate study at UNC are: accounting; African studies; Afro-American studies; American studies; anthropology; applied sciences; art; art history; astronomy; biology; business administration; chemistry; classics; clinical laboratory science; comparative literature; computer sciences; criminal justice; dental hygiene; dramatic art; East Asian studies; economics; education; English; French; geography; geology; German; history; industrial relations; international studies; Italian; journalism and mass communication; Latin; Latin American studies; leisure studies and recreation administration; linguistics; mathematical sciences; mathematics; medical technology; music; nursing; peace, war, and defense; pharmacy; philosophy; physical education, exercise and sport science; physical therapy; physics and astronomy; political science; Portuguese; psychology; public health; public policy analysis; radio, TV, and motion pictures; radiologic science; religious studies; Russian and East European studies; Slavic languages; sociology; Spanish; speech communication; speech and hearing sciences; and statistics.

The Honors Program adds a deeper dimension to the system. Each year, about 175 incoming freshmen are invited into the Honors Program, which enables academically gifted students to structure their freshman-, sophomore-, and junior-year curricula around special seminars and honors sections of departmental courses. Selection depends upon factors including SAT scores, academic performance, and course selection in high school, but if your UNC grades are good enough—at least 3.0, you may participate. Seminars vary from term to term, and each term's offerings include a variety of disciplines, taught by outstanding professors and limited to just 15 students. The seminar experience is an invaluable means of fostering critical thought and encountering the values central to the liberal arts.

"Honors courses skip the survey. One semester I took a class on Ernest Hemingway, where we read everything he had written and everything written about him. The Old Man and the Sea came to life right there in the classroom. The seven of us sat around a circular table in a small room in Greenlaw, the English building. But it seemed that we were everywhere but that room. The professor challenged us with reading and paper assignments. We challenged each other with questions and opinions and lived the days of Hemingway. And no way on earth would anyone dare not show up or not prepare for class. It was like running on a treadmill—stop for a breather and you'd fall off."

You don't have to be an honors student to take small classes. At UNC, classes range from seven to 450 students, with the opportunity for independent study. Even the big classes retain the small-class atmosphere in discussion sections, where the professor divides students into groups of about 15 people. Small classes and discussion sections personalize the Carolina experience.

It also helps to know the professors, who make themselves available to students. Large lecture classes are set up in the speaker-class mode, so the only true way to meet the professor—and make yourself known—is to introduce yourself. By simply attending class, taking notes, studying, and taking exams, you miss out on the human voice behind the course. Instead, you can step into the professors' offices and understand them as real people. They laugh and speak of things other than the Romans, *The Iliad,* the supply and demand curves, and the pros and cons of apartheid in South Africa.

The university also offers study-abroad programs that may complement language study or an interest in international affairs. Year, semester, and summer programs include study in China, Denmark, England, France, Germany, Italy, Japan, Mexico, Russia, and Spain.

It isn't difficult to enjoy studying at UNC, that is, if you pace yourself. Some students choose to read 30 chapters the weekend before an exam. Needless to say—but I will say it anyway—that doesn't work. To avoid the crunch, it's best to pace yourself. Students pack the libraries during midterm and final exams. They cram at 2 P.M. and midnight and 3 A.M. They report to the language, reading, and writing labs to learn more efficient ways to study. When papers are due, they crowd into the computer labs and pound the keys, the green words staggering across the screen, or they hover over typewriters in their rooms at home. Everyone is reading and writing. And when they finish and hand in their work, it's the professors' turn to read and write.

SOCIAL LIFE

While the academic side is strenuous and challenging, Carolina's social life still abounds. Somewhere along the line, the university topped the party-hardy lists, with 29 fraternities, 15 sororities, and several bars lining Franklin Street alone. The first few weeks of each semester seem the perfect time to procrastinate about studying and concentrate on playing. That's when you fall behind, terribly behind, because you forget you're at school and think you're at camp. Then the exams hit and snap you back to reality.

Social life at UNC is as diverse as the people who live it. From fall's football games and fraternity parties to winter socializing in the library at exam time to spring sunbathing, frisbee, and volleyball, to long summer evenings on the patio at He's Not Here, there's an event for every season in Chapel Hill. And everything is within walking distance.

Sporting events, especially football, provide a rallying point for students. From pregame tailgate parties to postgame social activities on Franklin Street and in dorms or apartments, there is always something happening. Other sports, such as the NCAA record-breaking women's soccer team, women's field hockey, and the perennial top-ranked men's basketball team, draw a large following.

Because Chapel Hill is a college town, small and colorful, it's a hot spot for entertainment. The Smith Center (The Dean Dome), which seats nearly 23,000 people, presents major concerts year-round, including recent appearances by David Bowie, Eric Clapton, Lionel Ritchie, Billy Joel, James Taylor, Amy Grant, and Bruce Springsteen, among others. Several plays and musicals take the stage at Playmaker's and Paul Green theaters, and the Morehead Planetarium features interesting specials, such as "The Star of Bethlehem," which presents a scientific explanation of the Star of David. Also, there are ten movie theaters in the area, in addition to free flicks at the Carolina Student Union.

The Student Union sponsors a variety of events, such as concerts, craft shows, art exhibits, and lecture series, blending with UNC's social life its crisp intellectual atmosphere. The Carolina Athletic Association plans the activity-filled Rampage homecoming week, which culminates with a parade and a football game.

Underclassmen at UNC have just as many social opportunities as upperclassmen. They populate parties and spice up dorm life with mixers, ice cream socials, formal dances, cookouts, movie nights, and other parties. And even the libraries, during any season, heighten social life for everyone.

> *"It's a funny place, the library. When you first arrive at Carolina, people tell you the library is the hottest spot for scoping, checking out the opposite sex, and collecting tidbits on the latest couples. Seldom will lasting relationships develop at a mixer. But in the library you can stake out your spot near that person you want to know and, eventually, strike up a conversation.*
>
> *"One UNC graduate said he and his wife met at the card catalog at the Undergraduate Library. They have two children now and live in Durham."*

EXTRACURRICULAR ACTIVITIES

There are endless chances for extracurricular involvement at UNC, more than you could ever hope to touch. Find your niche, find your specialty, and you've discovered your personal Carolina experience, one which no one else will ever totally comprehend. Of 300 student groups, here are some of the more popular ones.

About 20% of the undergraduates pledge sororities or fraternities, social organizations that also serve the community and spark interest in other activities. Greek life offers involvement in intramural sports, social programs, government, faculty-speaker programs, and most importantly, lasting friendships.

"Through a sorority or fraternity, you gain leadership skills and an invaluable perspective on people. Most sororities have 150 members, all different, from different regions of the country and world. Each person brings to the chapter another perspective, another dimension of campus life.

"Members of my sorority included Morehead Scholars, who received full-paid, four-year tuition, a senior class president and vice president, the president of the Student Union, the Panhellenic president, program coordinators for the Campus Y, the literary magazine editor, the yearbook editor, student television and radio broadcasters, newspaper writers, members of various varsity teams, and other people who served on different campus committees.

"With diverse group interests, you can't help but learn from people. And if you ever want to try something new, just ask someone."

At Carolina, few moments lag. Some people fill every waking hour with activities, which is a plus for developing memories, friendships, and leadership skills, but it definitely throws the study life off balance. Most organizations require a chunk of your time. Take the student newspaper, for instance. The *Daily Tar Heel,* among other student publications, is a perfect starting point for aspiring journalists; nothing beats hands-on experience. Charles Kuralt often tells of his own affiliation with the paper—how he quit classes when he became editor because the work load was so massive. Journalists live at the DTH.

"I was a freshman rookie writer, and my editor, a senior, sent me out to cover the Young Democrat/Young Republican debate. It was election year, and debaters hurled words like rotten eggs. I scribbled nervously—pieces of sentences—just enough to get the gist back at the office.

"'You want it when?' I thought as the editor glanced at his watch and gestured toward the old manual typewriter. Thirty minutes, he said. Thirty minutes to recapitulate four hours. Thirty minutes on a donkey-of-a-typewriter. I had never written straight onto a typewriter, especially a manual. But I did it. And the guy stood over me—literally breathed down my neck and ding-donged every five minutes until midnight, when I finished. It took just over 30 minutes to type three pages, the print barely legible. From there, the editor darted to the productions office.

"Compact, pressure-filled moments, when the adrenaline is flowing and people are counting on you, build you up and give you a glimpse of the real world. For every committee, for every leadership position, there are moments like these."

There are also great moments in sports. Name the sport: lacrosse, rugby, soccer, football, golf, swimming, basketball, cross country, field hockey, and so on. Carolina has all. Events flood Kenan Stadium, Carmichael Auditorium, the Dean E. Smith Center, Boshamer Stadium, Fetzer Gym, and Fetaer Field. The Carolina Athletic Association recently made cheering an extracurricular activity. Many students now join Carolina Fever, the rowdy group at the center of the crowd.

Carolina students love to play sports, too. The university currently fields 13 intercollegiate teams for women and 13 for men. Approximately 75% of undergraduates participate in at least one intramural activity. Also popular are the 29 club sports, such as rugby, with games played against other colleges and universities.

Student government, the Black Student Movement, the Student Union Building, and the Campus Y are other highly popular organizations. Members of the Campus Y serve the community and wear the slogan, "Think Globally, Act Locally." They build homes for the poor, work in soup kitchens, walk for humanity, visit rest homes, handicapped children, and prisoners, sponsor UNICEF, and become big brothers and sisters to underprivileged children.

> *"There's nothing like the feeling that you're giving something. The greatest gift is time and energy, and the rewards are manifold. Sometimes you see a child's faint smile; other times you just trust that your small contribution reached a person. And always you work with other students, building relationships that don't crumble. Relationships which enrich the Carolina experience. And years later, when you glance back, you remember Carolina not just for excellent classes and all-night study sessions, but more for the people and outside activities that challenged you and made you grow."*

After a day of classes and committee meetings, you go home, either to your dorm or to an apartment or house off campus. All freshmen are guaranteed housing in one of the 30 dorms, which are all male, all female, or coed. Continuing students usually enter a random drawing for an assignment after freshman year. Campus is divided into three regions: North, South, and Mid Campus. Most people choose North Campus because these dorms, which are some of UNC's oldest buildings, are closest to classes, libraries, and Franklin Street. However, Mid and South Campus are within walking distance, and for the days you don't feel like hiking to class, you can just hop on the bus. Because the Smith Center now hosts ticket sales for concerts and games, more people are moving South. And Mid Campus is comfortably between the two. Granville Towers, a privately owned residence hall on East Franklin Street, has a separate dining hall and maid service. Most seniors live in houses or apartments off campus.

GRADUATES

"The senior class president, my graduation day, spoke of the construction of our minds and lives and the firm foundation that is UNC.

"It is upon the foundation that we build our future and savor our past, that we accept our shortcomings and eagerly press ahead.

"Graduation marked a beginning, not an end."

Some people are so ready to graduate that they skip the ceremony. Most, however, relish Carolina days and dread The End. Of course, nothing has to end. Certainly not friendships, memories, intellectual stimulation, or connections to Carolina. And no matter what your major, the opportunities, too, are endless, although it's difficult to chart the paths of UNC students after graduation. Still, follow-up surveys report a few trends.

About 18% of the graduating class goes straight to graduate school. Biology, chemistry, and arts and science majors are the most likely candidates, including half the biology and chemistry majors. Within five years, a greater percentage, although undetermined, have enrolled in programs to earn advanced degrees. Law school, M.B.A. programs, and medical school are popular. Students also continue studies in their undergraduate fields.

Most graduates enter the work force, whether or not the job is in their field. In fact, because Carolina is a liberal arts school, only about 300 members of the graduating class are business majors. Almost anyone, though, may drop résumés and interview with over 200 companies that recruit on campus through the University Career Planning and Placement Services (UCPPS). Among recent graduates who reported using on-campus interviews, 84% said they were useful, and 38% responded that the service helped them identify and obtain their current position. The UCPPS can help every job-seeker in some way, whether through interviews, résumé referral service and critiques, practice interviewing, career and employer literature, workshops, career and professional school days or individual sessions with counselors. Also available for journalists is the School of Journalism Placement Office, which has been used for many years by newspapers in North Carolina, South Carolina, and Virginia, among others.

"Senior year, everyone wears navy blue or gray suits and rushes from class to interviews to interviews to interviews. One of my friends had interviews almost every day for a month, company

dinners and cocktail parties during midterm exam week, and job offers seeping from her pores. By Christmas, she chose her favorite, made top grades and looked forward to relaxing the next semester, not a worry on her mind. After all, she could actually see her future.

"The process wasn't that simple for most people, though. Most people still were freaking out the week before graduation because they didn't know what they wanted to do. But you learn not to worry. You realize that everything works out, and that your Carolina degree, through time, only increases in value."

Recognized nationally and internationally, the Carolina degree is one of excellence. No wonder students are proud; no wonder graduates return again and again to build upon the foundation of a remarkably strong alumni network and university endowment. People come and go, but the Carolina bond remains, linking together years and classes and generations.

SUMMARY OVERVIEW

In summary, diversity and excellence describe the Carolina way. Steeped in the liberal arts tradition, UNC is a large public university—the first state university—located in the ever-expanding, yet still village-like Chapel Hill, North Carolina. With approximately 15,000 undergraduates, 7000 graduate students, and over 1600 professional students, the university is known particularly for social, cultural, and intellectual diversity, outstanding faculty, academic excellence, and the Tar Heels that people either love or love to hate.

Diversity permeates every aspect of the program. Academically, course offerings and curriculum range from women's studies and civil rights to the New Deal to the Romantic poets to land before time. And that's perfect for such a culturally diverse student body. Students come from every state in the nation and 75 foreign countries. Socially, there's something for everyone, whether it's Greek life, student government, activities committees, newspaper, intramurals, or any of over 300 student groups campuswide.

Characteristically, UNC embodies a tradition of academic excellence. Its liberal arts philosophy encourages critical, analytical, and creative thinking and writing and freedom of expression. Courses are difficult and challenging, with strong faculty. Professors teach, research, and publish, and generally are excited about their subjects. They take a genuine interest in the students, too, whether the class has seven or 500 people. It's harder to get to know them in large lecture classes, so they suggest you visit them in their offices and introduce yourself.

Sports are another strength. You know you're in Chapel Hill on football Saturdays, when fans flood the streets and cars sit still, idling for a chance to move.

Whether Carolina wins or loses, sports are a major part of student, faculty, and alumni life.

Although the classes and curriculum are intellectually stimulating at Carolina, there is a downside to the stringent course requirements. Administrators say that, in order to get the best liberal arts education, students need to take a core curriculum of classes, divided into basic skills and perspectives. Yet there are so many requirements that, sometimes, you feel you are majoring in perspective requirements instead of your true field of study. If you don't take them all, you don't graduate. But then, although a few classes may weigh you down, many others present interesting ways of seeing the world.

Parking on campus is extremely limited. Students, faculty, and staff can park on campus and in remote lots. Fortunately, there is a good bus system, subsidized by the university, to alleviate the need for driving for off-campus students.

The Carolina experience is your own, rich and stimulating. It links together days, sparks ideas, and fosters within you a deep desire to learn. Upon its foundation, we build our future and live for now; we glimpse gently behind and, enlightened, celebrate what's ahead. I couldn't have imagined a more rewarding and satisfying college experience—one that seems to transcend time.

Joan Clifford, B.A.

University of Notre Dame

THE PROGRAM

Located in South Bend, Indiana, five minutes from Interstate 80/90 and less than two hours from Chicago, the University of Notre Dame is a medium-sized school (7600 undergraduates) situated on a beautiful campus. Given the prominence and tradition of Notre Dame's football team, many people are surprised to hear how small it is. It may have become famous because of its success on the gridiron and the legendary Knute Rockne and George Gipp, but over the past 25 years Notre Dame has gained a national reputation as a top-notch university. Its academic prestige is derived from a uniformly strong undergraduate program. Though its four divisions—arts and letters, business, science, and engineering—are all first-rate, its particular strengths are preprofessional studies, the humanities, accounting, and chemical engineering. But academic excellence is not enough to make Notre Dame unique—what distinguishes it from other top schools is a profound interest in its students' moral development.

Notre Dame's philosophy of education flows from its perceived mission as a Catholic university. Viewing the human as an intellectual and moral being, Notre Dame seeks to educate the mind and the heart. Because knowledge confers power, the university believes that intellectual development should be accompanied by heightened moral discernment and action. Notre Dame holds that it is not enough to turn out competent professionals; it is successful only if it manages to educate its students to recognize this moral dimension of knowledge and to use their talents to serve others. Such idealism would be hypocritical if Notre Dame did not display such interest in its students' intellectual, emotional, and spiritual health. This concern for its students' overall well-being is reflected in the sense of community and the impressively low rate of attrition that distinguish the university. At a time when less than 25% of the nation's students complete their undergraduate education in four years, only 2–3% of its freshman class leave Notre Dame. Most students enter with career aspirations in medicine, business, law, or engineering, and though many change their majors and career plans along the way, it is accepted as a given that you will graduate on time. And nearly everybody does.

> *"It's reassuring to feel that the whole university community has a genuine interest in you, an interest that most students come to realize is actually a deep affection. There is an atmosphere of outgoing hospitality that, as I discovered my freshman year, extends to the university's president. During first semester finals my roommates and I went to the bookstore to do some Christmas shopping. Near the checkout counter we noticed the president's book,* The Hesburgh Papers *and Chris jokingly said that it would be cool to buy a copy for his dad and to have Father Hesburgh autograph it. I had heard stories about kids coming back from the bars and climbing the fire escape to Father Ted's office window, just to say hello at 3 A.M. These stories usually ended with Hesburgh coming outside to talk for a while. 'Why not?' we figured. 'We're not drunk, and it's three in the afternoon.' So two freshmen with no appointment soon stood in the anteroom of the president's office, looking at all the pictures of Hesburgh with popes and presidents and getting more and more sure that once he got off the phone ('Be with you in a minute,' he had shouted from behind a closed door) he'd be annoyed at the interruption. Much to our relief, quite the opposite happened. Father Ted ushered us into his office, autographed the books, and chatted with us for over ten minutes about our first semester at Notre Dame. Hesburgh's successor, Father Edward 'Monk' Malloy, is even more accessible to the student body. Not much has changed since Monk became president in 1987; he still lives in his two-room apartment in Sorin Hall, still takes all the freshmen in Sorin out to dinner, still puts a 'Welcome' sign on his door when he's in, and still plays basketball with guys from Sorin on Monday and Wednesday nights in a ritual called Monk hoops. This willingness to set work aside and spend time with people, not so much out of duty as pleasure—it characterizes Notre Dame and is what you come to appreciate even more after you graduate and enter the real world."*

In many ways walking onto campus is like stepping out of the real world. The statue of Mary atop the Golden Dome overlooks tree-lined quadrangles and two serene lakes, giving the campus a quality of self-contained separation from the rest of the world. One road encircles the campus, and footpaths crisscross the quads from building to building. Notre Dame is a pedestrian's paradise until winter snows turn these cement walks into skating rinks. It can take upwards of 20 minutes to walk from one end of campus to another, but most common destinations—the library, dining halls, classroom buildings, and most dormitories—are less than ten minutes away from wherever you happen to be. Because most students live on campus for four years, it becomes a home for a fairly close-knit community. After you've been there a while, it's unusual to walk anywhere without running into someone you know.

GETTING IN/FINANCIAL AID

Like any competitive school, Notre Dame is difficult to get into. Present trends show four applicants for every freshman class position. Median SAT I scores for a recent entering freshman class were 580 verbal and 670 math. Over a third of this class graduated as one of the top five people of their senior class. Eighty percent graduated in the upper 10% and 94% of the freshmen finished in the top fifth of their high school class. Yet numbers do not comprise the only admissions criteria. Obviously it's important to have an impressive high school record and high SAT I scores, but a 4.0 GPA and 1400 boards do not ensure admission. In an effort to promote an atmosphere where students with varied interests and talents can learn from one another, Notre Dame's application requires an activities list, a personal statement, and an essay—all of which enable the admissions staff to get a fuller portrait of the prospective student. A special talent in music, for example, or evidence of outstanding leadership qualities can distinguish an applicant with lesser numbers. Remember that half of the freshman class has SAT I scores below 1250. On the other hand, don't feel that you have to have written a novel or organized a drug awareness program in your community in order to demonstrate special talents or leadership.

Notre Dame attracts students from Florida to Alaska as well as about 65 foreign countries, yet in spite of their diverse origins most students share one thing in common: 87% are Roman Catholic. Religious preference has absolutely no bearing on admission decisions, though an optional section of the application is used for statistical purposes. As its name suggests, Notre Dame is unabashedly Catholic in its policies, personality, and image. But its Catholicism is peculiarly American in its comfort with pluralistic ideals. Current president Father Malloy, continuing the policy established by his predecessor, Father Hesburgh, has quietly insisted on the need for the Catholic university to serve as a forum for free exchange of ideas.

> *"When I first arrived at Notre Dame, constant reminders of Catholicism, such as a chapel in every residence hall, made me wonder whether the religious atmosphere was overbearing to non-Catholics, and even some Catholics. I still think some people would not be entirely comfortable at Notre Dame. Yet two of my roommates weren't Catholic, and they said that they never felt excluded from the Notre Dame family or pressured in any way."*

Though it sees its coherent religious vision as a strength, the university continues efforts to improve the more problematic homogeneity of a student body that is largely white, middle to upper-middle class, and male. Notre Dame first admitted undergraduate women in 1972 and has steadily increased the percentage of women since that time. When I was a freshman, only 28% of the undergrads were women, but recently, with the completion of two new women's dormitories, the ratio has jumped to 42% women and is continuing to increase appreciably. Given the proximity of St. Mary's, a women's college across the street from Notre Dame, the male/female ratio for the overall community is virtually 50/50. Proclaiming a recent school year the Year of Cultural Diversity, Father Malloy made explicit the need for Notre Dame to attract more minority students. To this end, minority enrollment has jumped to 15% of the undergraduate population. This commitment to diversifying the student body is reflected by a recently announced $12 million minority scholarship fund.

Located in an area with a low cost of living and blessed with an endowment of more than $700 million, Notre Dame is able to keep its tuition, room, and board ($21,240 for the most recent year) well below levels of most comparable institutions. About two-thirds of the undergraduates receive some form of financial aid from sources as diverse as ROTC awards, scholarships, loans, and campus work. No exception to the increasing cost of higher education across the country, Notre Dame's tuition continues to rise steadily. However, the university has made financial aid its number one priority. A recently completed $463 million capital campaign—the largest and most successful in the history of Catholic higher education—a five-year contract with NBC for the television rights to home football games, and other development efforts are expected to generate more than $6 million annually in new scholarship support by the year 2000.

Notre Dame's reputation as a jock school may derive largely from its highly visible athletic program, but it's also a fairly accurate generalization of the student body. Most students played one or more sports in high school, and the Fighting Irish football and basketball teams are a natural rallying point. Students tend to be more concerned about the game on Saturday than upcoming cultural events. On the other hand, don't think that these sports fanatics aren't intelligent or hard working.

ACADEMIC ENVIRONMENT

Notre Dame's remarkably low attrition rate suggests that financial aid is rarely stripped or substantially lowered from initial awards. Of course, finances are not the only problems faced by college students—academic and emotional health are equally important. The university traces much of its success at keeping students in school once they have enrolled, to its Freshman Year of Studies, an academic program that provides special support and guidance to all first-year students. Each freshman has an advisor who closely monitors his or her progress and can prove helpful in suggesting possible majors toward the end of the second semester.

Beyond offering special attention to anxious students, the Freshman Year of Studies is designed to ease the pressure involved in choosing a major by delaying the choice until the end of the first year.

> *"The idea that you can pursue any major after the freshman year is only partially true. I soon discovered that those intending to major in engineering have a fairly structured curriculum even during the first year, with two semesters of physics, chemistry, calculus, and an introductory course in engineering. These courses fulfill university requirements and may be applied to degrees in other majors. But lower-level science and math courses generally taken by freshmen looking to major in the colleges of arts and letters or business are of no use if they decide later to major in engineering. So if you the slightest interest in an engineering major, I'd recommend that you take the appropriate courses from the outset. Better to find out early that it is not for you than to have to retake calculus again at a higher level. There's no reason to be embarrassed if you leave engineering. It's the one major dominated by emigration, most of which occurs after the freshman year before you officially become an engineering major. Scrawled on desks around campus is a bit of graffiti that neatly conveys a common decision:*
>
> $$\lim_{GPA \to 0}(ENG) = A \,\&\, L \;(Arts\;and\;Letters)\;or\;Business.$$
>
> *Loosely translated for those who've forgotten their math, this means that as grade point average approaches zero, it's time to get out of engineering and into arts and letters or business."*

After their freshman year, students enter one of Notre Dame's four colleges: arts and letters, business administration, engineering, and science. Course requirements are divided into three categories: university, college, and major. Regardless of major or college, all students must fulfill certain university requirements, among them two theology and two philosophy courses. Different for each of the four main divisions listed above, college requirements ensure that the student has acquired essential knowledge of the field in which his or her major lies. In the College of Engineering, for example, every student must take, among others, introductory courses in computer science and thermodynamics. Major requirements provide the most specific exposure to a fairly focused branch of study. These vary widely in terms of number of courses and flexibility of choice, from the highly structured curriculum of any branch of engineering to the relatively open selection available to a major in the College of Arts and Letters.

One advantage of Notre Dame's academic program that appeals to many students is the opportunity to take up a diverse combination of majors. If you find it difficult to make a decision that closes off alternatives, Notre Dame is the place for you. It is fairly painless to change your major (one friend of mine spent time in all four colleges before getting her B.A. in English...and she's now in a top-five M.B.A.

program, so it didn't hurt her!). But it is equally painless to satisfy widely scattered academic interests. This is particularly common within the College of Arts and Letters, where double majors (history and economics, for example) are commonplace. Even triple majors are not unheard of.

In keeping with its desire to educate the whole person, the university offers several creative and well-received programs aimed at preventing single-minded careerism. The Arts and Letters Program for Administrators (ALPA) is a popular sequence that augments a focus in the humanities with a sequence of business courses. Many of my friends saw this as a way to make their English or government major more immediately marketable. Thinking about medical school but reluctant to plunge into a science curriculum? I have several friends in top medical schools who went Arts and Letters/Pre-Med, a sequence where they took the requisite science courses to qualify for medical school but majored within the College of Arts and Letters.

> *"One reason I decided to go to Notre Dame was its combined arts and letters/engineering program. Set up as a five-year course of study that yields both a B.S. in engineering and a B.A. in one of the humanities, it was ideal for me because I never had to decide between my interest in science and technology and my love of literature. You can even complete this program in four years with enough advanced placement credit, careful scheduling, and a summer or two at Notre Dame (where the tuition for summer session is less than $125 a credit hour and campus jobs are fairly easy to come by)."*

Though most students work hard, I'd describe the academic atmosphere as far more cooperative than competitive. In four years I never had anyone refuse me help. Whether it's a new boyfriend/girlfriend or a reputation for cutthroat behavior, news travels quickly on campus. Certainly there are disadvantages to such an efficient grapevine, but it tends to discourage misplaced academic zeal. Academic success is valued and admired, but unbalanced obsession with grades wins few friends in a community where people tend to downplay their accomplishments. Sometimes it can get ridiculous, as in the case of a good friend whom I knew for a year before learning that he was a brilliant pianist who had studied under a pupil of Rachmaninoff. Simply put, people work hard to succeed but don't want to be seen as unbalanced or too intense.

Another strong point of Notre Dame's academic environment is its emphasis on foreign study as an invaluable learning experience. It runs year-long programs in Innsbruck, Mexico City, Dublin, Tokyo, and Toledo, Spain; semester programs in Jerusalem, Mexico City, Santiago, Fremantle, and London; and a summer engineering program in London. Architecture majors go to Rome for the third year of their five-year program. Past success with its foreign-studies programs has prompted the university to initiate new programs for majors who typically have no opportunity to study abroad, the summer session for interested engineers being a prime example.

> *"Perhaps the most popular program, and one about which I can speak from experience, is the semester in London for juniors organized by the College of Arts and Letters. Living in one of the world's major cities and traveling throughout Europe on two ten-day breaks was without question the most exciting and enjoyable time of my life. All 80 students agreed that London became our home over the course of the semester; we got a far richer appreciation of Europe by living and studying there because we came to see ourselves as more than tourists in search of landmarks and local color."*

Back on its American campus, Notre Dame has made some significant additions in recent years. Formerly a gaping deficiency, the computer systems have been dramatically expanded during the past 10 years with two completely computerized classrooms and some 500 workstations in 11 public clusters across campus. A space crunch was addressed in the fall of 1992 with the opening of DeBartolo Hall, a 150,000-square-foot building with 84 classrooms and state-of-the-art audiovisual and computer equipment that makes it one of the most technologically advanced classroom facilities in the country. Hesburgh Library, a 14-story structure in which more than half the 7600 undergraduates can study at one time, and seven other university libraries contain more than 1.9 million volumes and 1.4 million microform units. An area of concern several years ago when it was low rated, the library system has gotten much better and continues to improve as the university seeks to keep and attract first-rate faculty.

The student-to-faculty ratio is 12 to one, but this can be a deceptive statistic in any college description, especially at schools where the best professors are so caught up in their research that they haven't taught undergrads in years. With very few exceptions, every professor at Notre Dame must teach at least one undergraduate course a year. This is not to say that you won't have large lectures, particularly in introductory courses in science, engineering, and business. But you'll never have anyone less than a professor after freshman English and calculus.

> *"I never had an English class with more than 30 students in it, nor did I ever have a paper parceled out for a TA to grade. Teaching methods vary from lecture to discussion, depending on the course objective and the professor. Dedicated and approachable, the faculty complain more about short rather than long lines of students outside their offices. They frequently criticize an attitude of careerism among many students, recognizing that it is a national phenomenon but lamenting it nonetheless. So students enthusiastic about intellectual issues invariably find their professors eager to talk. I am currently in graduate school in English, not so much because I've always loved books but because I had professors whose enthusiasm for literature and teaching was nothing less than inspirational."*

SOCIAL LIFE

For most college students, social life is tied in one way or another to alcohol. When I entered Notre Dame as a freshman, it had a reputation of being a school where students worked hard all week and partied hard all weekend, especially on weekends with home football games. Kegs were banned from either dorm or room parties, but that did little to slow down alcohol consumption. Concerned about liability and alcohol abuse, the university changed its alcohol policy several years ago, ending the infamous and beloved dorm parties and curtailing the size of room parties. Though Notre Dame is not a dry campus (you can drink in your room), many students see the administration as moving in that direction. Beer remains the beverage of choice for most; really sophisticated drinkers are those who have a favorite brand beyond the special of the week. A recently expanded student union with a nonalcoholic nightclub/dance floor is fairly popular with underclassmen. Yet a typical Friday night for freshmen and sophomores consists of trying to have as big a party as possible in a dorm room without having it broken up by the hall staff. Hall formals and hall-sponsored dances where your roommate is in charge of selecting your date are highlights in the social calendar, especially when your roommate bears you no ill will and finds you a compatible date.

Dances aside, casual dating (movie/dinner/whatever with a different person every week) is probably not as common at Notre Dame as it is at other schools. One reason for this is a limited number of places to go without a car. But this alone does not account for a certain undercurrent of tension between men and women. Both men and women complain about the unbalanced male/female ratio. Men argue that the women have it made with so many more guys to choose from; women claim that they must struggle against a traditionally masculine atmosphere. One positive note is that this tension decreases markedly from freshman to senior years. Moreover, the situation continues to improve as the university brings the male/female ratio closer to equality.

Aside from its low cost of living, South Bend offers little as a college town from a cultural or really any standpoint. Restaurants, bars, and shops are beyond walking distance from campus, and most students complain that South Bend has all too few places worth driving to. Still, social life improves when you or your friends have a car to get off campus now and then. There is a fairly spacious bar on campus and two bars about a mile away where most upperclassmen hang out unless they decide to go to one of the many off-campus parties on a given weekend. Perhaps the best thing about South Bend is its proximity to Chicago (less than two hours from this oasis of the Midwest, with its restaurants, bars, museums, and sporting events). The Freshman Year of Studies usually sponsors a bus trip to Chicago at least once a semester, and visits to the Windy City (both planned and impromptu) become more frequent for upperclassmen.

"One thing I took for granted about the social life, until I came to graduate school and sometimes felt as though getting people together was like pulling teeth, was the way students at Notre Dame tend to go out in large groups. Even if you go to the bars with one or two people, you are guaranteed to run into plenty of familiar faces. Even couples who have been dating for a while often start the evening by going to the bars or a party with a large group of friends."

Intercollegiate sports, especially football and basketball, are a huge part of the social life at Notre Dame. They are a major source of the school's spirited and unified student body—in the student section everyone stands for the entire game. Major college competition is entertaining in its own right, and Notre Dame perennially schedules many of the nation's top teams. It's a great feeling, especially when you're home on break visiting friends from other schools, to know that your school and eventual alma mater has a high profile in the national limelight. It's an even greater thrill to have a student ticket to a football game where general admission tickets have a market value over $100. For those indifferent and those passionate about football, home game weekends are the high points of social life at Notre Dame, especially with the resurgence of the Fighting Irish under Lou Holtz.

"I'll never forget that first home football game of my freshman year, as alumni flooded the campus, came to see their old rooms, and showed that age hadn't dampened their eagerness to party. By Saturday morning the fields surrounding the stadium are packed with RVs and cars with thousands of people tailgating in one central location. I never fully appreciated this arrangement until I returned after graduation and ran into dozens of friends, from as far away as Arizona and Florida, as we wandered from tailgater to tailgater. Football put Notre Dame on the map, and though the university has since grown into a prestigious academic institution, football remains special as a magnet that draws people back to campus and back together."

EXTRACURRICULAR ACTIVITIES

If football weekends are the peak of the social life, it should come as no surprise that sports are common topics of conversation and participation. Twelve outdoor basketball courts (lighted for use at night), spacious grassy quads, and several playing fields on the edge of campus provide ample space for outdoor activity when the weather obliges. An indoor tennis facility and Olympic-size pool augment numerous indoor basketball, volleyball, racquetball, and squash courts. Two lakes on campus have a scenic shoreline trail that makes running as pleasant as possible. In addition to informal football and basketball games so popular after classes, organized athletics are a major focus of extracurricular activities. Most students participated in high school athletics and want to continue some sort of involvement on the nonvarsity level at Notre Dame. There are 10 club sports, with rugby, boxing, and crew (both men's and women's) being quite popular. These clubs offer nonvarsity athletes a chance to join a team and to compete with other schools.

> *"Depending on the attitude of members, club sports are approached with varying degrees of seriousness. Competition can be difficult, but they are also social organizations where you get to know a lot of people. Many times I used to dread the thought of crew practice, especially when foul weather or a test made the prospect of getting up to row at 5 A.M. seem insane. But the exercise, my teammates, and the parties—not to mention the thrill of racing—made those early mornings worthwhile."*

Intramurals involve even more people than club sports, with more than 50 different events. They are organized on an interhall basis where each dormitory fields a team, a setup that gives teams a natural identity that heightens spirit and interest. Football (full equipment tackle for men and flag for women), basketball, soccer, and ice hockey are the most popular, receiving regular coverage in the student newspaper and widespread interest from the student body.

> *"The highlight of the annual spring fling, the Bookstore Basketball Tournament, reflects this sports-minded atmosphere. Touted as one of, if not the, largest single-elimination basketball tournament in the country, Bookstore involves over 600 teams, whose frequently creative names add to the spectacle. For instance, a friend of mine who is legally blind got some visually impaired students together to form a team called Blind Ambition. There is a separate women's division, but women are also free to play with the men. Open to any employee or student, including Monk Malloy, onetime member of the varsity hoop team and now university president, the two-week tournament goes on regardless of weather conditions until a champion is crowned."*

With two student-run radio stations, a daily newspaper, a weekly newsmagazine, a biannual literary magazine; a yearbook, and some 100 campus clubs, Notre Dame offers a wide range of extracurricular activities beyond athletics. It's a great way for new students to find out what is available outside the classroom, and if you have an idea for a club or organization that doesn't exist, start one — it's as easy as placing an ad in the *Observer*.

With more than one-sixth of the student body participating in the many programs sponsored by the Center for Social Concerns, volunteer service is easily the largest extracurricular activity at Notre Dame. Political activism is fairly dormant on campus, but social activism is alive and well. Some of the more popular programs include volunteer service at the Center for the Homeless (a facility the university helped establish in downtown South Bend), Christmas in April, Big Brothers/Big Sisters, and work with the mentally retarded at nearby Logan Center. Many students spend their breaks away from school engaged in the Summer Service Projects, an eight-week program in which they work with social service agencies in impoverished areas across the country, and Urban Plunge, a 48-hour live-in encounter in the nation's poorest neighborhoods. By encouraging commitment to community service the university hopes to instill in its students a lifelong sense of social concern and responsibility, one that extends beyond their years at Notre Dame and carries over into their careers.

> *"My involvement in the Big Brothers program was a direct result of this emphasis on social concern; my decision to participate probably originated from a healthy type of peer pressure, from a desire to imitate people I admired. 'What a great guy I am,' I thought to myself—until I began to realize that I was probably getting more from the service in terms of learning and pure enjoyment than I was able to give back. With its green quads and generally content students, Notre Dame can be an unrealistic oasis from the world. Being a Big Brother was an invaluable growing experience that made me aware of a community beyond the campus."*

RESIDENCE LIFE

Notre Dame's strong sense of community derives in large part from its emphasis on residence life as a central part of collegiate experience. Though there are no fraternities, sororities, or eating clubs, more than 80% of the undergraduates live on campus. Students are encouraged to remain in the same residence hall for four years if they choose to remain on campus, though nothing prevents them from transferring to another dorm. This gives residence life a continuity, as each hall develops an identity based on the personalities of its members and its particular traditions. There is no coed housing, nor are any residence halls limited to athletes or freshmen. Dorms vary greatly in size, from two 550-capacity towers to a few small halls with fewer than 200 residents. The procedure for dorm assignments has recently changed from one where new admits could indicate a preference to the present system of arbitrary lottery. Each hall has a rector who heads a staff of one or two assistant rectors and several resident assistants. The hall staff is there to enforce rules like visiting hours (midnight on weekdays and 2 A.M. on weekends). But its more important function (ideally) centers on developing a happy community.

"I think that Notre Dame's residence system offers many of the advantages of fraternities and sororities without potentially hurtful drawbacks like rush and hazing. The hall provides you with a communal identity from the first day on campus. Each dorm tends to congregate in a certain part of the dining hall, so you can go directly from class to lunch without worrying about having to eat alone. This is especially comforting the first few weeks of freshman year. I remember being surprised at how readily most upperclassmen accepted us; without hazing I felt welcome from the moment I arrived. The juniors who lived across the hall gave us naive freshmen advice on building lofts, suggested professors to take and to avoid, and regularly invited us over for a beer to watch a game or Letterman. Upperclassmen in the dorm provide visible models of how to succeed (or fail) at learning and living at Notre Dame. This is not to imply that residence halls are utopian communities. They're not. Rules like restricted visiting hours (parietals at Notre Dame) can seem outdated when you hear stories from friends at other schools. Personality conflicts occur as they do anywhere else. But the four-year continuity helped me form incredibly close friendships and, perhaps more important, taught me a lot about tolerating people whom I may have written off under different circumstances."

GRADUATES

In addition to preparing you with a first-rate education, Notre Dame does its best to help launch your career. The Career and Placement Center brings in numerous companies that conduct on-campus interviews, which can make landing that first job a more convenient process. Most accountants get offers from at least one Big Six firm. Business majors and engineers generally work for a few years after graduation, even if they plan on getting an M.B.A. Notre Dame traditionally maintains a high ratio of placement to applications for professional schools. Medical and law school are popular destinations, and an increasing number of students are deciding to enter graduate school. Many graduates elect a third option beyond work or further education—devoting a year or more to community service through volunteer organizations. The Center for Social Concerns has information on and contact with a wide range of service programs spread out from New York City to Chile. The university encourages service projects as an opportunity to help others, to gain exposure to problems that otherwise are ignored or abstracted, and to learn more about oneself.

"I stayed in the Midwest for graduate school in English, and I suppose in many ways I haven't really left Notre Dame, returning each fall for two or three football games and spending my summers on campus working as a dorm manager—a job that allows me plenty of free time to do my required reading. When I came to graduate school, I was shocked that some of my new classmates had written senior papers 50 pages or longer, especially since my longest paper up until that point totaled 15 pages—with stretched margins and large font. Slightly intimidated at first, I came to realize that our senior design project in chemical engineering was almost 50 pages. Notre Dame had indeed prepared me with a well-rounded education. If I had to do it all over again, knowing what I do now, I'd do it all over again!"

Notre Dame's extensive and spirited alumni network can help to ease the departure from campus and friends after senior year. Alumni clubs can be a lot of help when you move to a new city, occasionally with your career but more often with your social well-being. The clubs, which can be found in most American cities (or geographical areas in sparsely populated parts of the country) as well as in 18 countries around the world, help continue the sense of community away from campus and more recently have engaged in social service programs in their local communities. If fund-raising is an accurate gauge of alumni involvement, Notre Dame's 88,000 alumni, having contributed $23.4 million to their alma mater last year, exhibit a level of participation that is among the best in American higher education.

SUMMARY OVERVIEW

The real strength of Notre Dame cannot be captured in rankings and statistics; it lies in the familial spirit among administrators, faculty, students, and alumni who care deeply about one another and the school that unites them. Strong in most areas, Notre Dame's undergraduate program also provides a range of interesting combinations of majors, allowing students to combine both a technical and a liberal course of study. From a financial standpoint—always a major consideration in this era of the escalating cost of higher education—Notre Dame's tuition, though by no means cheap, remains one of the lowest among its peer institutions. The popularity of sports—whether varsity, club, intramural, or informal—is only one example of the university's effort to develop more than the minds of its students. More importantly, the high level of participation in service projects through the Center for Social Concerns illustrates Notre Dame's emphasis on its students using their talents and energies to help others.

This is not to say that Notre Dame has no weaknesses. Lamenting an intellectual atmosphere that could be more highly charged, many professors complain that their students are more concerned with achieving than learning, more intent on having a good time and landing good jobs than on taking up intellectual challenges. South Bend is far from being the ideal college town, but there is also a general feeling that most students fail to take advantage of cultural opportunities on campus. Complaints over nothing to do and a repressive administration generally dwindle as underclassmen move toward senior year. As a Catholic university that went coed only in 1972, Notre Dame is struggling to move beyond its paternalistic tradition. Efforts to increase the percentage of minorities and women promise to improve a still largely homogeneous student body. Some 20% of the professors are women, a significant improvement over just a few years ago.

Nevertheless, a building boom is one indication that Notre Dame is a university on the move. In addition to the massive DeBartolo Hall classroom facility, other recent additions to the campus are the Hesburgh Center for International Studies, the Fischer Graduate Residences, Loftus Sports Center, a new band building, Pasquerilla Center for ROTC units, a support services facility, Eck Tennis Pavilion, two undergraduate residence halls, and the Hessert Center for Aerospace Research. A new complex for the College of Business Administration and a performing arts center are scheduled for construction in the next couple of years.

Yet this expansion is a reason some people see Notre Dame as a university at a crossroads. Its undergraduate program has been excellent for years, and much of the latest effort is aimed at improving its graduate programs. Some worry that this reflects a shift in emphasis from teaching to research and publishing, the most important criteria used to rank institutions. Others see no inherent conflict between research and teaching, pointing out that exciting research can actually enliven a professor's classroom performance. With this tension out in the open, it is highly doubtful that Notre Dame will sacrifice the unique qualities of its undergraduate program but will instead improve it along with its graduate and professional schools.

If you hate cold weather, love the excitement and cultural opportunities of a big city, are indifferent to sports, crave a highly intellectual environment, are a free spirit who would be stifled by so much emphasis on community, and feel uncomfortable with the thought of being educated in a religious atmosphere, then Notre Dame is not for you. But if you think a gorgeous campus compensates for severe winters, love to play and/or watch sports, can live without urban bustle and excitement, think you would like to become a member of a close-knit family, want a strong academic program, and can at least accept a Catholic environment and value-oriented education, then send for an application. It could be the start of an experience you will treasure forever.

John Staud, B.S. and B.A.

University of Pennsylvania

THE PROGRAM

Benjamin Franklin was a practical man, and he founded a practical school. For years, the University of Pennsylvania has been known for the strength of its professional programs. But today, a few years after celebrating its 250th anniversary, Penn has hit its stride and is firmly established as a hot school among college bound students.

A university with more than 9000 undergraduates and 9500 graduate students defies a singular characterization. Penn is a complex organism, occupying its own corner of Philadelphia, and embodying four separate undergraduate schools—the College of Arts and Sciences, the Wharton School, the Engineering and Applied Science School, and the School of Nursing—as well as 12 graduate and professional schools, a hospital, a research center, and a hotel. Because of its size, there is no common Penn experience. Instead, students find their own direction from the university's limitless possibilities.

Perhaps the most surprising thing about Penn is that it feels like a much smaller school. It may be a bit bureaucratic at times, but it is never impersonal. You hear few complaints from students, and hardly anyone transfers out of Penn, whereas there seems to be a constant influx of transfer students from every school in the country. A college whose promotional material begins with a quotation from its founder stating that good education is the "surest foundation of happiness" knows how to please its students.

> *"Freshman week begins with the unforgettable Philadelphia And You tour, in which specially chartered trollies transport 2000 or so freshmen around the historic and scenic areas of the city, allowing them to visit at their leisure until they jump on another trolley and proceed to the next site. Not only does this familiarize*

students with the city, but it also enables them to do things they would otherwise feel too silly to do—I never did make it back to the Liberty Bell. Many an enduring friendship has begun as freshmen make their obligatory Rocky-run up the art museum steps. I made one of my closest friends in college when we discovered a common affection for Woody Allen while waiting for a trolley outside the Bourse building."

On the whole, Penn students are laid-back, friendly and very social. Despite the competitive admissions process, the academic environment is seldom intense. And going to school at Penn means you are rarely alone: no matter what your academic interest, there is someone at Penn who is an expert on the subject. Whatever you enjoy doing in your spare time, probably 100 others enjoy exactly the same thing. Clubs for everything from comic book lovers to philomatheans attract enthusiastic groups of students.

Penn is difficult to pigeonhole academically. The Wharton School tends to overshadow the College of Arts and Sciences. With the recently constructed Wharton Executive Education Center sitting like a medieval manor in the center of campus (all it lacks is a moat), the business school's conspicuous presence serves as a constant reminder of the university's practical-minded roots. The stereotypical Wharton student—entrepreneurial, conservative, and relentlessly in pursuit of a Wall Street job—prospers at Penn. Some Wharton students also enroll in the college, giving them more exposure to the liberal arts than the typical business student.

As several humanities departments have been foundering in recent years, some have questioned Penn's dedication to the liberal arts. But recent college fund-raising efforts have ensured a secure future for the humanities, and top-notch professors and students are attracted to the College of Arts and Sciences because of its fine reputation. After all, the bulk of the university does not attend Wharton, and even without it Penn would be among the top schools in the country.

Penn combines a suburban campus setting with the advantage of the fifth largest city in the country. Astonished visitors have often remarked that they have never seen a city school with as nice a campus, and despite the recent proliferation of new buildings, the College Green area seems miles away from the city streets. In good weather, the grassy areas overflows with students sunning, socializing, and trying to elude assertive campus dogs in search of lunch.

Downtown Philadelphia is a five-minute subway ride from campus. The city is in the midst of a revival, with numerous new residential and commercial developments in progress. The South Street area, where green-haired punks hang out in front of quirky stores, has often been compared to Greenwich Village. Vibrant ethnic neighborhoods have charmed many an adventurous Penn student who has taken the time to trek beyond Center City. Sports fans may attend professional baseball, football, hockey, and basketball games. And concerts, dance clubs, restaurants, movies, theater, and lots of stores provide endless distractions from studying.

GETTING IN/FINANCIAL AID

Getting into Penn is not as easy as it used to be. *Time* magazine reported recently that an overwhelming number of applicants with SAT I scores above 1400 were rejected by Penn in an earlier year. This does not mean that you should give up if you don't have perfect scores. Penn claims to be aiming for a varied, geographically diverse class. The bulk of each class still hails from the Northeast, but the demographics are rapidly changing. California, Florida, and the Midwest are well represented, and because of strong recruiting in once weak areas, so is much of the rest of the country. There are also many foreign students.

The undergraduate population is 49% female and, according to university literature, 20% racial minorities. Some racial difficulties, perhaps magnified by impassioned student leaders, have been well publicized in recent years. The administration, however, always takes racial problems seriously and recently established a minority resource center.

"In the midst of one of these racial controversies, a friend remarked to me that the small college that his sister attended did not have problems like this—they didn't even have a Black Student League. (I seriously doubt that's true.) I asked him if he would prefer to be sheltered from such real-life problems so he could pretend they don't exist. A large university is a microcosm of the real world, and there will be times when unpleasant situations develop. Some students respond by ignoring what goes on; others jump into the fray, either looking for solutions or aggravating the problem. As a newspaper editor, I dealt with all types of students and was interested in finding solutions. The process was often frustrating, but no one who took a constructive approach to these emotional issues ever concluded that it was a completely futile endeavor. I believe this was as much a part of my education as my classes. As a result of a dispute about Louis Farrakhan speaking on campus my sophomore year, one professor even offered a course on black-Jewish relations which allowed students to draw on their own experiences to examine a societal problem."

Penn's application allows students a great deal of creativity and freedom to present themselves as they wish to be perceived. On recent applications, questions have included: "If you could spend an evening with one person, who would it be and why?" "Take a piece of paper 8 inches by 11 inches and do anything with it," and "If you could take three things to a desert island, what would they be?"

The admissions office has also received a deluge of video tapes displaying applicants' skills. Unless you have something that can be conveyed only on video tape (and this doesn't include a personal plea to admissions officers), you should probably stick with paper. Wherever you apply, avoid anything overly contrived—in writing or on video tape. And whatever you do, don't lie or even exaggerate. Admissions officers read enough applications to spot insincerity when they see it.

The admissions office is not seeking any one specific quality. Almost everyone who applies was a newspaper editor, class president, or debate champion. The challenge is to separate yourself from the masses without seeming arrogant. If you are certain that Penn is your first-choice school, then consider applying for an early decision. This may prevent you from getting lost among the thousands of applications, and it will show that you are willing to commit yourself to attending the school if admitted.

Penn requires SATs and three achievements, including English composition. Although no specific high school courses are required, the admissions material states that Penn "recommends a thorough grounding in English and foreign languages, social science, mathematics, and science."

Like all Ivy League schools, Penn has need-blind admissions, which guarantees that aid packages will be provided to those who require help. Also like all Ivy League schools, Penn is extremely expensive. Sixty percent of all students receive some form of financial aid, and most people graduate with loans to repay. Nevertheless, the loans are manageable, and few would say that their education wasn't worth the price.

ACADEMIC ENVIRONMENT

The curriculum of the College of Arts and Sciences, instituted a few years ago, covers the spectrum of academic areas. Although the new program is more stringent than the previous requirements, it is hardly oppressive and allows students freedom to choose their course of study. Proficiency in a foreign language is necessary, although students may waive the Penn exam by scoring well on the achievement test. They may also receive class credit for high scores on most AP tests.

There are more than 40 majors in the College of Arts and Sciences, covering almost every conceivable subject. History, biology, math, and English are among the most popular majors, and each is a top-rated department, with internationally acclaimed professors teaching undergraduate courses. Nobel Prize winner Lawrence Klein teaches in the economics department, and the psychology and anthropology departments are among the best in the country. Being at a major research university allows undergraduates to work with professors on projects and to be taught by those on the cutting edge of scientific development. And opportunities for students to work individually with professors abound in the liberal arts, as well as in science departments.

In addition to the common majors, students may also choose from some unusual ones: folklore, environmental studies, history and sociology of science, architecture, linguistics, urban studies, women's studies, and South Asia regional studies. One specialty area is the Biological Basis of Behavior, a unique program that allows pre-meds and others to take an array of science courses from various departments. The Annenberg School for Communication offers an undergraduate major. Individualized majors are also popular and not too difficult to get approved. Penn also awards credit for some internships and encourages students to spend time studying in a foreign country.

Many departments take advantage of the city by incorporating Philadelphia's resources into their courses. Students may visit the art museum, take a tour of historical architecture, or meet with city leaders as part of a class. The steady stream of important and famous people into Philadelphia also enables student and university groups to attract interesting speakers to campus.

Students are permitted to take courses in the other undergraduate schools. Many College of Arts and Sciences students, for example, take marketing or legal studies in Wharton. The college also permits undergraduates to take graduate-level classes with special permission from the professor. And independent studies are a convenient way for students to work closely with a professor in an area of particular interest to them.

The requirements in the Wharton, engineering, and nursing schools are quite different from those in the college, although each school requires its students to take some liberal arts classes. Wharton students must take finance, accounting, management, and marketing, and they do a lot of group projects. Because there are so many required Wharton courses, a major is actually a concentration of six or so classes.

The Engineering School has struck a good balance between technical requirements and electives. The administration there believes that students need more than a smattering of nonengineering classes, and this appears to work nicely. However, engineering students seem to work harder than anyone, and they are notorious for spending all night in the computer lab. A few enterprising students enroll in the management-technology program, which enables them to obtain degrees from both the engineering and Wharton schools.

Penn is the only Ivy League school with a nursing program. The Nursing School, affiliated with the Hospital of the University of Pennsylvania, has rigorous requirements for its students.

Almost no Penn classes are taught by teaching assistants, a rarity at a large school. Professors are accessible: they are not there solely for graduate students and research. After freshman year, when college students take upper-level courses, most classes have fewer than 40 students. I had one class with only six other students. Several of my professors held parties for their smaller classes at the end of the semester, and one or two even invited us to their homes.

One way to avoid feeling lost at a large school is to pick a major in a small department. Instead of majoring in history, which I planned to do until the end of my sophomore year, I decided to be an American civilization major. This meant that I knew most of the professors in the department, as well as most of the other majors. Because Penn doesn't force students to choose a major until the end of the sophomore year, one can make such decisions, which would be late by many school's standards. Actually, I didn't declare my major until the end of my junior year. (One advantage of being at a large school is that there is no way for the administration to know what each student is doing, providing a bit of stretching room.)

The flip side of this is that academic advising in the College of Arts and Sciences is not great. Not only must one actively seek it out, but many people also do not feel the overworked advisers provide much guidance. Once you declare your major, you will be assigned an adviser in the department, which helps. However, college students are largely left on their own. Ultimately this may not be bad, but people who need to be nurtured, who want someone telling them that they're taking the right course and that they're on the right (or wrong) track, may feel a little neglected.

Is registration at a large school a nightmare? Yes and no. Preregistration, which occurs in the middle of the prior semester, is simple and involves few lines, unless a course requires approval. I admit that on a few occasions I dragged myself out of the house at 8 A.M. to get in line at the English department, but I always got the course I wanted. This is the price one pays for variety: small schools offer only a few classes. At Penn, if you don't get your first-choice class, there are still hundreds of others to choose from. Juniors and seniors receive registration preference, so freshmen may have to wait to take a very popular course. Sometimes a rewarding academic experience occurs when students ignore their elaborate planning the prior semester and instead take a course because it sounds interesting although they know nothing beforehand about the subject or the professor.

SOCIAL LIFE

People who may initially be intimidated by the idea of a large school shouldn't be discouraged by the numbers. Of course, if your dream school is an idyllic country paradise with a total of 2000 students, Penn may be a difficult adjustment. But many people find that they appreciate the variety and stimulation a larger school offers.

To compensate for the size of the freshman class, the university has adopted a college house program in some dorms, although not on the scale of other schools. The Quad is a massive, ancient structure that houses several thousand students in separate (but connected) dorms. Now completely renovated, the Quad has lost some of its charm, but not its appeal to hundreds of freshmen who thrive there each year. Some people never leave, taking advantage of the limited Quad spaces for upperclassmen. If college means loud music, beer, and lots of community spirit, the Quad is the way—though not the only way— for a freshmen to go. Those who choose or are assigned to other housing seem just as happy with their environment.

Although the drinking age is strictly enforced on campus and off, freshmen need not sit in their rooms waiting to turn twenty-one. Freshman dorms are naturally social places, with parties spontaneously erupting on weekend nights. Student groups show movies on the weekends, and there are also two first-run movie theaters within a block of the campus. Some students get symphony or theater tickets, attend professional sporting events, or go out to eat on South Street.

Upperclassmen live primarily in one of the three high-rises, which consist of two-, three-, and four-bedroom apartments with living rooms and kitchens. Because of the impersonal nature of these buildings, more and more students are choosing to live off-campus. (As a result, on-campus housing is essentially guaranteed for four years.) Abutting the western end of the campus is a residential area inhabited by faculty and students, as well as people unaffiliated with the university. Within ten blocks of campus, there are countless apartments and houses available for yearly rental. The popularity of 41st Street between Spruce and Walnut—known as the Beige Block because of the drab color of the houses—has spawned a burgeoning student neighborhood farther west of campus.

> *"By far the best living situation of my college career was the two years I spent in a ten-person house off campus—well, across the street from campus, actually. If you think being in a dorm with a few hundred strangers teaches you about communal living, try living in a house with nine other people. It means tolerating other people's dirty dishes, annoying musical tastes, thesis deadlines, job searches, and pets (my tenth housemate one year was a snake). But it also means huge parties, group cooking, constant study breaks and company for* Letterman. *So what if we had a few leaky faucets and a hole in our bathroom ceiling? We also made popcorn every night and engaged in pointless arguments about everything from Philadelphia politics to football."*

One way students deal with Penn's size is by gravitating to smaller groups—fraternities and sororities, campus organizations, upperclass college houses, and the like. The approximately 30 fraternities and seven sororities (about 20% of students join) provide the basis of social activity for freshmen and some upperclassmen, but they are not the only option. Philadelphia has movie theaters, dance clubs, concert halls, and countless bars. Off-campus parties are a popular activity, and occasionally the university organizes a social event that attracts a few people. The planned $10 million student center, which will replace the outdated Houston Hall, the oldest student union in the country, may provide a more suitable place for student gatherings. Smokey Joe's is the main campus hangout, attracting hoards of students every night of the week in search of fun, relaxation, and beer.

Restaurants near the campus are inexpensive and varied. The Shops at Penn building, which bring the spirit of suburbia to the heart of University City, boast a food court with every type of fast-food imaginable, including famous Philly cheese-steaks, pizza, hamburgers, hot dogs, and deli. Those who take the time to explore the area to the west of campus, will discover beautiful old houses, as well as wonderful restaurants and stores. Quiet neighborhood bars provide a more colorful and interesting background for a beer than some of the noisy campus establishments.

Although Ivy League sports may not fulfill every sports fan's desire for extraordinary competition, football and basketball games are attended by enthusiastic crowds who sing traditional songs and shout nasty comments at opposing teams. Penn's football team, which has a new coach and is making a strong comeback after a couple of disappointing seasons, draws throngs of students to every home game at historic Franklin Field. The Penn Band, one of the most popular student activities, keep the fans singing. Some diehard fans make road trips to other schools to cheer for Dear Old Penn. After title-clinching games, students pour onto the field, tear down the goal-posts, and throw them into the Schuykill River. (The administration has tried to discourage this practice, with little success.)

Like all old schools, Penn has its share of traditions, some of them rather ridiculous. At the end of each spring semester, the juniors officially become seniors on Hey Day, the most joyous of Penn traditions. Led by the class officers, the seniors-to-be march from the Quad to the library, wearing Penn red and blue, carrying canes, and taking bites out of each other's styrofoam hats. By the time they reach the library to hear a brief speech by the president of the university, most people are in such good spirits (so to speak) that they don't remember much of what he says.

But everyone's favorite tradition is Spring Fling. Each April, the entire Quad becomes one gigantic carnival, with games, food, music, food, an air-band contest and more food. Local vendors set up stands selling everything from sushi to funnel cakes. A fraternity runs a dunking booth where campus celebrities plunge into freezing cold water. At the Community Outreach service auction, students can help local charities by bidding on a tennis game with the dean of Wharton or pancakes cooked by a popular professor. Fling invariably involves three days of too much food, beer, and music and leaves students in less-than-perfect shape to study for finals.

EXTRACURRICULAR ACTIVITIES

"Why, a friend asked me recently, did we do it? Why would anyone choose to spend almost every night of her college career imprisoned in a windowless office, sitting in front of a computer terminal while the partying hours drifted away? It was called the Daily Pennsylvanian—*also known as that rag by a skeptical few—and it was the best experience of my college career. Newspaper reporters and editors are universally considered crazy for spending so much time churning out a product that inevitably ends up on the floors of classrooms and hallways. But so are student government types, who spend hours trying to fulfill such pressing needs as on-campus mail folders for college students,*

and performing arts nuts who spend 1000 hours in rehearsal to have it all over in two nights of playing to unappreciative crowds."

Extracurricular activities are an obsession among many at Penn, who form communities of individuals with common interests. Not only are the aforementioned activities extremely popular, but so are varsity and intramural athletics, singing groups, and political organizations. Show me a school where extracurricular life is limited to one weekly newspaper, a few intramural sports, and one show a semester, and I'll show you a place where the library is crowded during the Super Bowl. Penn students have boundless energy that they devote to all sorts of non-academic endeavors—sometimes at the expense of their academic work.

Being in Philadelphia also enables students to take advantage of the city's abundant opportunities by interning at a government office, a publication, or a business. Many Penn students volunteer to work with children at local schools, with homeless people, or prisoners. I have a friend who spent three summers rebuilding dilapidated houses with high school students in the heart of West Philadelphia.

Of course, just as being at Penn often gives students a startling introduction to real life problems, living in Philadelphia means adjusting to urban realities. The fifth largest city in the country is not without its problems, homelessness primary among them. Students from small towns may be shocked the first time a homeless person asks them for money. It is a difficult adjustment, but the homeless do not present a threat to students—they just want some change.

At the same time, many students from less populated areas have legitimate concerns about safety in a large city. Like all city schools, Penn has occasional security problems. The university has its own police force, which patrols the campus, and the Philadelphia police watch the off-campus area. Students must develop some street savvy, and, most important, they must use common sense to avoid potentially dangerous situations.

Ultimately, being at a large city school means that there are a lot of distractions. The library loses a lot of battles for a student's attention, which may be a problem for someone who views college as an opportunity to spend most of his or her spare time discussing the meaning of life and reading Sartre. Of course, Penn has its share of workaholics who spend every waking moment studying, but the library is more famous as a social center than as a center of intellectual activity. Intellectual debate exists, but, like everything at Penn, it often occurs on a very practical level.

GRADUATES

Sometimes it seems as though everyone at Penn is looking for a job in business. The annual senior job search is marked by the appearance of hundreds of suit-clad students eager to spend 80 hours a week working on Wall Street. And because of the presence of Wharton, business placement is what the Career Planning and Placement Office does best. Hundreds of interviewers from banks and businesses come to campus to recruit students—from the college as well as Wharton. An overwhelming number take jobs in business and industry.

A substantial number of students (more than 30%) go straight to graduate school—law and medicine are the most popular. The rest of the class uses career planning's resources and their own research to find jobs in other areas or to apply to master's or doctoral programs. Many Penn students eventually go to graduate school of one form or another.

Having a degree from Penn definitely makes getting a job or getting into graduate school easier. For example, career planning tells students applying to graduate schools that their Penn degree will help them to be admitted to top schools, even if they did not get straight *A*s. My experience at law school seems to bear this out: my GPA was lower than that of people who did not attend top schools. I doubt I would have been admitted to many of the law schools that accepted me if I had not attended a top undergraduate college. The degree is worth something. The rest depends on you and what you have to show for your four years.

SUMMARY OVERVIEW

Although it is the second largest undergraduate college in the Ivy League, Penn combines the advantage of a small, friendly school with the resources and variety of a large university. Located in a residential area of West Philadelphia, it is a five-minute subway ride from Center City, which offers vast opportunities for relaxation and education.

Penn cannot be easily classified. Students on the whole are easygoing and social, and the atmosphere is seldom intense. Academically, there is a wide variety of majors, professors, and courses. Students may take classes in any of the undergraduate schools, which include the College of Arts and Sciences and the Wharton engineering, and nursing schools. The Wharton School's prominence sometimes overwhelms liberal arts majors, but the College of Arts and Sciences is far larger and offers as many, if not more, opportunities for its students. Renowned scholars teach undergraduate courses in every field.

Extracurricular activities attract large numbers of students. Among the most popular groups are student government, service organizations, publications, the performing arts, including the Penn Band, and varsity and intramural sports. Many students also take advantage of opportunities to work with businesses and organizations in Philadelphia.

No matter how friendly the university may be, it can never approximate the intimacy of very small colleges. There are frustrations that go along with being at a large city school, ranging from the merely annoying registration lines to the seriously troubling problem of homeless people around campus.

Being at a large school means that personal attention is not guaranteed and that, yes, sometimes one must wait in line during preregistration. Most students feel that on balance, the advantage of diversity and variety outweigh the annoyance of having to wake up early to get a popular course.

Living in a major city also has some drawbacks. Students must learn how to conduct themselves in an urban area to avoid potentially dangerous situations. The best way to remain safe is to use common sense. The university's police force and the Philadelphia police patrol the area around campus, and the overwhelming majority of students graduate from Penn without ever having been a victim of even a minor crime. Of course, students must take responsibility for their own safety by not doing careless things such as walking alone off campus at night.

Such are the realities of being at a large city school. But many students believe that facing and addressing such issues enhances their education. A student-run escort service provides rides for students who need to travel off campus late at night. In addition, the student government has often attempted to come up with better registration methods, and many Penn students volunteer at local soup kitchens or with organizations that help the homeless.

Penn is a large and diverse school that provides endless opportunities for talented students. The students and graduates are uniformly pleased with their college experience—a more devoted group of alumni would be hard to find.

Laura Shaw, B.A.

University of Texas at Austin

THE PROGRAM

What makes a top flight college? Most literature that trumpets the virtues of a university will cite the number of Nobel laureates employed as professors, the number of National Merit finalists, and the school's research capabilities. Compared to these criteria, the University of Texas at Austin certainly excels. It attracts Nobel laureates and many other outstanding professors from the National Academies of Sciences, Engineering, and Arts and Sciences. One recent fall semester, the university enrolled 207 National Merit finalists, making the campus third in the nation. About 49% of the entering freshman came from the top 10% of their high school class. Moreover, the school offers more than 100 undergraduate degree programs — literally everything from architecture to zoology — though most students opt for the liberal arts and business majors. The university's stature in research was a key factor in attracting the superconducting super collider to Texas.

But that's not all. The university's graduate programs in law, education, and public affairs are ranked among the top ten of all public schools. The library system, which includes its own law library, is the country's sixth largest. Also located on campus are the Barker Texas History Center, one of the world's largest Latin American collections, and the Lyndon B. Johnson Presidential Library and Museum. Also, UT is proud to own an original Gutenberg Bible at its Harry Ransom Humanities Research Center.

UT stacks up well against these measures, but what really makes the University of Texas stand alone is that this academic excellence is offered at a price that almost everyone can afford. Who can argue with tuition and fees under $1400 per year to attend one of the top-ranked schools in the country? Surprisingly, most students seem to discover this cost benefit after the fact.

It's no secret that lots of freshmen choose UT because for Texans, it's just the place to go. It attracts just about every prototype—jocks, brains, activists, moneyed frat boys and average Joes. One unifying element to note is that about 80% of them are Texans. Most students from the big cities find themselves in classes with people they knew in high school. The University of Texas has something of a party reputation and Austin is arguably the best college town in the United States. So the tradition runs high to attend the school where parents and siblings attended, the place where friends will go, a university with a great reputation for football, extracurricular activities, and of course a superb academic environment.

Many chapters describing a university or college include some discussion about "green, rolling hills and gardens nestled"...Not the University of Texas. The UT campus, situated in the middle of a major city, is fairly devoid of rolling hills. And it certainly doesn't do any nestling. In keeping with the old maxim that everything is bigger in Texas, the UT campus sprawls over 357 acres. Nonetheless, one of the best things about attending the university is the placement of the campus in Austin, the capital of Texas, which is the ultimate college town. Still populated by some 500,000 people, Austin doesn't pose the same traffic and congestion problems so familiar to those from Houston, the Dallas/Ft. Worth metroplex, and San Antonio. You are never too far from anything in Austin, including downtown.

The city of Austin is populated with innumerable dance bars and small hole-in-the-wall places with cheap pitchers of beer and pool tables and bad singers trying to break into the Austin music scene. There are hip restaurants that stay open all night, quiet places for picnics, sporting events all year long, lakes for boating and sunbathing, and lots of cheap apartments that cater specifically to college students.

The students in Austin are as groovy, weird, straight, gay, political, fraternal, and diverse as any town I've ever seen. Although the home to conservative Texas politics quite a bit of the time, Austin also seems to be the birthplace of every liberal ideology or rally, and often attracts national attention for some new stunt pulled on the steps of the Capitol.

But strangely, it isn't the Capitol building in whose presence students and faculty draw themselves up just a little bit taller. Rising high above the UT campus is the tower, which truly represents Austin and the university better than any single structure. It can be seen from miles around the city, and is a familiar sight on Welcome to Austin postcards. The tower's official name is the Main Building, the hub of all official workings, home to the president and other upper echelon administrators, a magnetic unifying force on the 40 acres, or the original expanse of campus when it opened with one building in 1883. You never have to ask what time it is at UT, just check one of the four huge clocks on any side of the tower. At noon, the chimes play a number of tunes and end with "Happy Birthday." Every UT student loves to see the tower lit orange, which means one of the teams has won a sporting event or someone has received an award. An orange tower with the office lights burning in a #1 configuration means the school has won a national championship.

One of the university's two mottos is emblazoned across the front of the Main Building: "Ye shall know the truth and the truth shall make you free." The other is to make UT a "university of the first class." The second, sometimes, seems to be the more powerful of the two. Texas is fiercely proud and protective of this flagship of a

15-component system. The state has provided the system a large trust fund that, ironically, it shares with its arch rival, the Texas A&M University System. The UT system, however, is entitled to the earnings from two-thirds of the money—perhaps part of the reason that disgruntled A&M advocates feel that UT gets all the attention from the legislature. That Permanent University Fund, whose book value surpasses $3 billion, is rooted in oil profits—the stuff that makes Texas legends.

The colleges of liberal arts and business far outweigh the other nine schools in terms of enrollment, a combined 16,500 undergraduates out of a total 36,000. Nonetheless, UT doesn't really fit the clichéd liberal arts college, it's too big. It isn't an Ivy League sort of driven atmosphere either. In short, UT is Texas—big, grand, innovative, well-funded—everything you ever thought about the state and more.

GETTING IN/FINANCIAL AID

"Filling out the application for the University of Texas did not send chills of expectation up and down my spine. The form is so simple, some friends joked about 'signing up.' Not only that, but about 100 students of my high school class of 550 would be joining me. It didn't seem like an auspicious start in life to attend college with everyone and his second cousin whom you knew in high school.

"But I sought a school with a great journalism department that would not mire me in red ink. Northwestern was too cold and Missouri meant well, being in Missouri. UT, which, as a top-ranked journalism school and one of the cheapest state schools around, fit the bill."

In recent years, the subject of admissions and enrollment at the university evokes for both students and the administration the same response as running fingernails across a chalkboard. Being a state institution means that UT legally cannot keep anyone out who meets official requirements. And by virtue of a flagging Texas economy in the mid-1980s, more students tended to look at the value of an excellent education in their own state rather than choose private schools in faraway corners of the country.

Now, more than ever, the school's requirements seem to be getting more and more stringent, to keep enrollment in check. Most recently, 49,253 students were enrolled at UT. Of those 49,253 students, 35,914 were undergraduates; Texas residents comprised 80% of total enrollment.

"I covered the UT administration for the university newspaper, The Daily Texan, *when the total student population crossed the 50,000 mark. Remember, that number usually refers to*

populations of cities, not a student body. The students felt the pinch in terms of their ability to get classes. The administration was pitched into a frenzy, screaming metaphors like 'stretching the rubber band to the limit' when referring to space, money, faculty, and resources. Drastic efforts were required to open new sections and reallocate funds to pay for more instructors. Studies were conducted to seek long-range planning to cut down enrollment. The 40 acres, they said, are best served at 46,000 to 48,000 people.

"The administration hoped that recently implemented stiffer standards would cut enrollment, but it didn't. In fact, enrollment actually rose the following fateful fall. Raising the standards seemed to raise prestige, making the school more attractive to a higher-quality student."

You almost need a college degree to understand the "standards for entering freshmen." UT has three in-state admission categories—regular, subject to review, and provisional. Regular means automatic admission. Subject to review means deferred until May 1 when you either will be offered regular or provisional. Provisional means there is no way you'll be considered unless you take UT summer school before your freshmen year and meet certain criteria in thoses courses.

For regular admission, you can be in the top 10% of your class with any SAT I score; the next 15% with 1000 or above; the second quarter with 1100 or above; the third and fourth quarters, 1200 or above. Nonresidents in the top quarter must have an 1100 SAT I score or a 27 ACT score for regular admission. Anyone else is ineligible, and the provisional and subject-to-review categories do not apply.

One problem with UT is its image as a white school. Of the more than 50,000 students, blacks comprise 4%; Hispanics, 12%. Many minority families remember the not-too-distant 1960s when black students entered the academic buildings through different doors. Nonetheless, UT administrators work diligently on this problem of recruitment and retention probably more than any other. Almost 140 programs exist on campus to assist minority students. UT is working with Texas A&M in coordinating outreach centers in six Texas cities to prepare minority junior and senior high school students for college. The university awards almost $4.5 million in merit-and need-based minority scholarships each year.

"Probably the university's biggest coup in minority recruitment was hiring Earl Campbell, former football player for the UT Longhorns and the Houston Oilers, as a special recruiter. My cynical reporter friends questioned his $40K salary to go on occasional junkets representing the University of Texas and to serve as a role model for our football team of mostly academic flunkies. I was skeptical until I went on one of those trips with UT President Bill Cunningham, his wife, several key administrators, and Earl on the university's private plane. We flew to a number of little towns in the Rio Grande Valley (the region south of San Antonio to the Mexico border) and visited elementary school chil-

*dren in predominantly Hispanic schools. They listened politely
to the president, but went crazy to meet Earl and get his auto-
graph. He told them about how important it is to go to college,
and I saw some of those kids' minds clicking. In fact, it appears
Earl is a bargain after all."*

Typical charges for in-state tuition fees, room, board, and books at Texas are
$6885, out-of-state, $11,175. But whereas these figures dwarf in comparison
with most other schools in Texas's class, both public and private, financial aid is
available through several sources.

Grants, scholarships, loans, and work-study jobs can be obtained through the
Office of Student Financial Aid. Aid packages are devised based on students' and
parents' income tax returns. About 23,000 students take advantage of these opportunities and receive assistance totaling $121 million. Be warned, however, that to
get help you have to be persistent. Existing on a campus with 50,000 others means
being a little aggressive, unlike at smaller schools where all students get lots of personal attention.

I cannot stress enough the true economic value of UT. In the fall of my senior
year, tuition was still $16 an hour. Not $160 an hour, not $16,000 a year. My yearly
tuition and fees cost about $900 when you threw in the yearbook package, sports
sticker, and parking permit.

*"A word about those last two items. I remember thinking during
summer orientation before my freshman year that as a self-pro-
fessed sports hater, I would find it profoundly difficult to plunk
down $50 for the privilege of attending ANY school sporting
event for free. A kindly upperclassman must have pitied me and
talked me into buying it. That sticker was the key to my whole fall
social calendar, which everyone knows centers around when the
Longhorns will play in town. With no sticker, you pay $15 to sit in
the nosebleed zone at Memorial Stadium (which soon becomes
even more expensive than the original investment). No sticker
means no tickets in the student section, hence, no dates and I
think we all know where that leads. Moral: buy the sticker, even if
you hate football. You can always people watch or keep your eyes
on Bevo, the live Longhorn steer mascot. Bevo will still occasionally eat oats or break loose, which provided much more entertainment for me than the actual game.*

*"Oh, and about that parking sticker. They issue about a mil-
lion for every one student spot so it really just gives you the
RIGHT to park if you ever could find a space. Additionally, you
can't drive on campus, so if you found a space behind the stadium, you probably will only have a 20-minute hike to your next
class. A paradox, I know, but one that plays a role in every UT
student's life."*

ACADEMIC ENVIRONMENT

The outstanding academic program, in my opinion, is tied directly to the low cost of tuition. A University of Texas graduate has taken courses from a wide range of disciplines, often because the classes are so inexpensive and the choices are so varied. Such an arrangement provides students a little time to play around and try a number of different departments to decide what they really like. I mean, could students justify six changes in their majors when tuition costs $20,000 per year?

To hear my father tell it, in *his* day, students attended college for four years or less and graduated. No monkeying around. Well, Dad, times have changed. Although the school does not directly encourage students to stay longer than four years, Texas has such a wealth of resources, a student would be foolish not to take advantage of them.

> *"My parents pushed me to graduate in three years. What better way to get started in your career sooner, they said. I used a semester in Monterrey, Mexico as a delay tactic. Ostensibly, I was attending a Mexican university in the pursuit of higher education. Actually, I was going to school in pursuit of the caramel-filled pastries that they sold at the cafeteria. Nonetheless, the experience was handy in that I became fluent in Spanish from living with a wonderful family. I also learned that if your suitcase tears and you see your undergarments taking a ride around the luggage carousel, you probably won't have to open your bags at U.S. Customs.*
>
> *"My parents then wanted me to graduate in three and a half years. And as the time approached, I realized that I never took a course in religion or any interesting English classes. So I spent some time taking a punk rock-oriented literature class, judo (more on this later), and a Judaism course. And I stayed four years. You're only an undergraduate once, so it's important to make the best of it, especially when the price is right."*

The academic program is hard to define, mainly because each college establishes its own requirements for a general lower-division course load before students move into courses geared toward their major. Students may study in the college of architecture, business administration, communication, education, engineering, fine arts, liberal arts, natural science, nursing, pharmacy, or social work. Naturally, the individual departments within those school are diverse and again are subdivided with their own degree requirements. For example, a student enrolled in the communication college may study in the department of journalism, radio-television-film, speech communication, or advertising.

Some general rules do apply. For example, most students must take some English, math, science, foreign language, and fine arts, though the number of hours vary among colleges. Every student must take six hours of government and six of history, as required by Texas law. It is in these general 101-type classes that attending a large university sometimes becomes difficult. It is not unusual for a lower-division government class to have 300–500 students enrolled, which makes professor-student contact limited, although most of my professors tried to make themselves as accessible as possible. Some even encouraged us to call them at home with questions. Additionally, the tremendous class size usually lends itself to the bubble-sheet method of testing. I rarely suffered through an essay exam, although I couldn't swear to any rule of thumb here. Most major classes, however, are scaled down in size and teacher assistants are available for study sessions and private assistance.

For the most part, students must maintain a 2.0 GPA or risk scholastic probation. Also, UT tends to be much freer with credit by exam than private schools, which means if you fare well on standardized tests, you can start college with most of your basic core classes already out of the way

The university does offer a small, intense, specialized degree program for exceptional students seeking the diversity of a large university combined with the advantages of a small liberal arts college. The Plan II Honors program creates a challenging curriculum for students to learn in a small, intimate environment. Some of the top professors teach freshman level courses and seminars. Admission is competitive and separate from admission to UT-Austin.

Part of being a university of the first class means offering a wide assortment of courses, and I believe UT rates with the best on this count. Although the rest of my semesters tended to be less exciting, and certainly less physical, I always was impressed with the options.

> *"All through college, I had a close friend who reveled in selecting the most outlandish classes and then trying to get me to take them with her. I eschewed the Sanskrit, a dead Indian language that neither is spoken nor used in the modern world (on the advice of my father who threatened not to let me return to the homestead if I signed up). I did the same with Turkey and Social Change, Music of Oceania, Arabic, and some other motley assortment of courses. Finally, our last semester we took judo together. So we wore some goofy outfits that felt like large paper towels and were told by the instructor that we reached new lows in skill level for the martial arts. The experience was a blast—always good for a laugh from our friends—and we can throw people five different ways."*

SOCIAL LIFE

As I mentioned before, one of the best aspects of attending UT is the fine extra-curricular atmosphere. Dave Barry, the *Miami Herald* newspaper columnist, has said that if Communists tried to take over the United States, they'd first have to win Texas, using such psychological ploys as "promising to extend the football season." This assessment, I assure you, is completely accurate. The fall season, for a huge percentage of students, is dominated by football. Every year, 20,000 students fight for tickets to the Texas-Oklahoma University game in Dallas. The night before the game against Texas A&M, thousands of students gather in front of the tower to hex the school by carrying red candles and singing "Texas Fight" and "The Eyes of Texas," the fight song and the alma mater.

Few students have graduated from the University of Texas without making at least one trip to the infamous Sixth Street. Ask any UT student where to eke out a social existence, and nine out of ten will tell you about the three or four blocks of clubs and bars that thrive on college students looking for a good time, a place to dance, and of course, alcohol. All clubs have their own personalities, from all reggae to hard rock to new wave, and you usually can find a good band somewhere. Austin, nationally known as a music capital, has produced such entertainers as The Fabulous Thunderbirds, and Tim Buk 3.

The street is legendary, especially on Halloween night when an estimated 50,000 people show up in costume, and you always run into someone you know there. Of course, it can get obnoxious and parking is sometimes impossible, so I recommend it only in moderation. When you get tired of it, you always can go a little further down the block for breakfast to Katz's, a New York-style deli that stays open all night. Be prepared to wait, however, because the place is packed from about midnight to 6 A.M.

Texans guard their right to tanning with a vengeance. Hey, if we're going to live in a state where you only get to wear sweaters for about three days in February, we might as well be brown the rest of the year. So prime tanning spots are important, and Barton Springs probably outranks any other locale. Basically, Barton Springs is a reservoir of water that never gets warmer than say, 41°, so any sane person gets in a raft so no body parts actually touch the water. The land surrounding it is a big hill, so when you lay out, you're always on an uncomfortable incline. The flat concrete side is for families, avoid it. Still, the sun is great and the social climate is even better, so it can't be passed up. Also, if you have a young looking face, you always can trick the guy at the gate into believing that you are in high school and only pay 50 cents to get in.

Tanning also can be accomplished by taking tubing trips down the Guadalupe River, located about 45 minutes away in New Braunfels, a town whose sole function is to promote the river. Tubing is wonderfully enjoyable and relaxing—made better if you get a group together—even if it means bouncing your rear end along some rocks while in your tire. The trips take about three to five hours, depending on how fast the river is running, and most folks bring a cooler of beer along in its own tire. But don't volunteer to be responsible for dragging the tire with your friends' beer behind you. It's too much trouble.

One additional benefit to living in Texas is the proximity of Mexico for beach purposes. I spent three out of four years on Mexican beaches during spring break frolics, but the idea is not a novel one. Most UT students run into about 300 other classmates at any given beach resort town. Those who don't go to Mexico converge on South Padre Island, where a conservative estimate would place the spring break student population at 100,000.

Although Greeks may be fodder for admiration, scorn and/or lively debate, their presence at the university should be duly noted. About 30 fraternities and sororities play large roles in UT events and university life. Some of those events include Texas Independence Celebration on March 2, when students gather at noon in front of the Main Building for a state birthday party and salute to the Texas flag (Texans are heavy into state pride).

Many students are attracted to the university's thriving Greek community. However, monthly dues can run upwards of $100, an extremely conservative estimate, which means it can be an expensive way to make friends. UT Greeks attracted national notoriety a few years ago when one fraternity succeeded in using what a grand jury termed "friendly pressure" to get a pledge to drink between 16 to 20 ounces of rum, which caused him to die of alcohol poisoning. Most of the Greek houses are located in the West Campus area, so the noise and parties there can be a problem for serious studiers.

RESIDENCE LIFE

Choosing a place to live becomes one of those wonderful side benefits to living away from home. As a three-year veteran of dorm living, (and I don't recommend more than two years), I really can speak with authority about the Division of Food and Housing. About 5500 students live in the 11 residence halls.

The coed housing, called Jester Dormitory, merits a word on it own. More than 3000 students inhabit this high-rise monstrosity that has its own two-story cafeteria, classrooms, movie theater, general store, and study lounges. It is infamous for parties, noise, disregard for the rules, and well, more parties. It also is notorious for the presence of UT athletes, all of whom are required to live on campus. But don't worry about them mixing with you. The football team lives in its own wing and eats in a special cafeteria, which word has it, serves real food.

Speaking of food, dorm residents may eat at any of the three cafeterias on campus and may buy packages of 20, 13, or 10 meals weekly. Sunday nights, you're on your own.

"The eating situation requires some special attention, particularly for the women. I won't be going too far out on a limb here if I say that unless you're a big fan of chili-mac or fried anything, dorm food could pose some problems. In Texas, Mexican food is a staple along with bread and water, so residents live for the taco, enchilada, and fajita days. At Jester, sandwich, pizza, baked potato, and hamburger bars were installed that serve said items every day, in addition to the daily entrees. But the walk from the women's residence halls and the long lines rarely made the trip worth it for me. Thus, I probably was deficient for three years of every nutrient except carbohydrate-related vitamins."

When you are ready to move out of the dorm, the city begs for your apartment rental dollars. I've already mentioned the West Campus area directly adjacent to the campus. Housing there is relatively expensive, but if you are willing to move anywhere from two to ten miles away from the campus, housing prices are extremely reasonable. Some complexes cater to students exclusively. Also, UT offers a free shuttle bus service throughout most of the city and it runs until 11 P.M.

EXTRACURRICULAR ACTIVITIES

Many freshmen imagine that finding friends in a sea of 50,000 students will be a formidable task. Actually, it's easy. The residence hall advisers plan activities for residents on their floors and with other halls. Most dorms organize advisory boards that plan parties, semiformals, and fund-raisers. Students interested in getting involved in dorm life often participate on these governing boards.

On campus, clubs are so numerous, I really don't know where to start. Hundreds of clubs—political, social, religious,—are listed in the campus directory. More than 400 organizations make finding companions with similar interests simple. All clubs registered with the Campus Activities Office and list themselves in the campus directory. Here's a sampling: American Helicopter Society, Data Processing Management Association, Hispanic Business Students Association, Longhorn Singers, Orthodox Christian Campus Fellowship, Students Ending Hunger, Texas Mountain Recreational Club, University Folk Dance Society.

The Texas Union, which serves as a community center for intellectual, cultural, and social events, also sponsors a number of clubs. I served on the Student Issues Committee, which brought Dr. Ruth Westheimer to the Performing Arts Center and set up monthly crossfire debates on hot topics, among other activities. The Union houses a movie theater, game room, bowling alley, restaurants, and study areas that are open all night.

Young, budding politicians rarely miss their chance to learn about swaying public opinion and representing their college constituents through involvement in the

Students' Association. The association deals with policy making, lobbying efforts, and student issues.

The multimillion dollar student publication budget provides for production of the *The Daily Texan,* an award-winning newspaper run entirely by students (and the positions are paid). Of course, I could go on and on about the paper, but that would bias my completely objective account of the university's extracurricular activities. Students also run and contribute to *Cactus,* the yearbook.

A budget of more than $1 million funds recreational sports. About 2150 students participate in sports clubs, which receive money, a place to practice, and the right to call themselves UT sponsored. Some of the teams, like lacrosse and soccer, compete in NCAA competition. Aerobic dance, crew, cycling, water polo, sailing, running, and tennis are a few of the many sport clubs available for serious athletes. Those a little less inclined toward long-term commitment join intramural athletics teams. These informal teams, usually comprised of groups of friends, play together against other teams of similar skill levels for short seasons of sports, such as softball, basketball, or football. Rec sports also runs an outdoor recreational department that sponsors hiking, kayaking, or rock climbing trips, to name a few.

GRADUATES

Anyone who has ever heard of the "good old boy network" understands the nature of the Ex-Students' Association. Texans make it their business to associate, negotiate, and coordinate with other Texans. Fierce loyalty to the state, its residents, and the university makes the Exes unique. Even in states far from the Southwest, people with alumni stickers on their back windshield get honks and the "hook 'em horns" hand signal while driving on the freeway. I recently heard of a magazine for people living in other states who are homesick for Texas. You get the picture.

> *"I offer myself as an example of someone who used the state networking to land my first job out of school. My boss, the managing editor of the newspaper outside of San Diego where I work, graduated a few years ahead of me. He needed an editor, so he flew back to Austin for a round of interviews with recent journalism graduates. We had some friends in common who recommended me and I got the job. After I arrived, I discovered that not only did the managing editor come from Texas, but so did the publisher, his wife, who works as the composing room manager, and the circulation manager. Subsequently, I hired a friend from UT as a reporter. We call ourselves the Texas Mafia.*
>
> *"UT graduates may choose a number of paths. Thankfully, all of my friends from the journalism department went straight to*

jobs on newspapers across the state. My judo buddy decided to continue with graduate school. Another friend took post graduate courses in preparation for study of occupational therapy."

On the whole, I would state that UT alumni are well-rounded and probably more prepared for the real world than graduates of small schools, primarily because they are used to fending for themselves in a big, fairly impersonal environment, The Ex-Students' Association as a whole, however, is a 47,000-strong network of friends who love UT. Old alumni may come to football games in burnt orange polyester wear, but they operate a multimillion dollar budget for programs, projects, and scholarships like nobody's business. Once again, these are the cattle ranchers and oilmen for whom Texas has become famous.

Texas alumni work for the benefit of the university in a big way. Not content with their alumni center (used for pre-game drinking parties), the Exes raised $6.5 million to renovate the building. Some nice folks donated $1 million apiece for rooms, but quite a bit of the money was raised by the sale of $100–10,000 tiles to line the new walkway, which donors could have engraved with their names. For the ground breaking ceremony, a bulldozer was painted burnt orange and white and large horns were attached.

The alumni throw a football banquet every year to honor the team. In May, Texas Exes organize a senior send-off party, called the Great Texas Ex-it, where seniors come in to toast their commencement with about 50 cases of champagne. Former Longhorns also give annual monetary awards to outstanding professors in every department, as well as to exceptional high school teachers in the state.

Though people in the other 49 states might consider Texas Exes a bit drawn to excess, the alumni also are regular people who really care about the school. Case in point: one legislative session, the alumni believed UT might not be getting as much money from the state as it wanted. Through phone calls and fax machines, alumni contacted each other about their concern. Then about 3000 telegrams and calls poured into legislators' offices within 96 hours. This effort prompted formation of the Legislative Information Network Contacts program, with a chairperson in almost every local club who mobilizes the Exes to contact legislators regarding UT funding.

SUMMARY OVERVIEW

The University of Texas at Austin is a huge educational and research institution. In addition to the main campus, UT administers the Institute for Geophysics, Marine Science Institute, McDonald Observatory, Balcones Research Center for science and engineering laboratories, and the Winedale Historical Center. The Lyndon B. Johnson Presidential Library is located on the campus. Research capabilities at the university played a large role in the decision to locate the superconducting super collider in Texas.

The university's strengths lie in its size and financial stability. UT offers many interesting and stimulating courses, taught by outstanding professors. With about a dozen schools to choose from, the degree options are tremendous. A school backed by lots of money can provide more scholarships, services, amenities, and academic advantages. It also means the weight of funding the school doesn't lie on the students' shoulders. Texas has been named a public Ivy, meaning that it is one of about eight elite public schools whose standards match those of the famous cost inefficient colleges on the East Coast.

Even if you never attended a class, living in Austin would make attending UT worth your time. The eclectic and unique city, a strange mix of politicos and students, always provides some sort of entertainment. The city offers a myriad of nightlife, which can be sorely missed by living in a small town.

However, too much of a good thing can be overwhelming. Whereas being one of 50,000 means attending a state school with a lot of academic, political, and financial muscle, it also means learning lots of independence. Students at UT can't relax and let the administration and staff take care of them. Classes, resources, scholarships—they won't come to you, but they can be mastered with a little perseverance and practice.

Attending the university also requires accepting large classes and the struggle to get into them. (They don't take attendance in large classes—a plus in the students' favor.) The occasional troubles getting classes probably will pose the greatest frustration to a UT student, but the administration is taking steps to rectify the problems. These steps, however, seem to be leading to further limiting the number of students that will be allowed to enter and raising the standards even higher.

The university's size helps attract the best professors, but it sometimes means sharing them with a lot of people and often only learning from a distance. Most freshman and sophomore classes can be monstrous in size, but upperclassmen enjoy the smaller classes with more individual attention.

A commitment to excellence in academia and low tuition make UT the bargain of the century. There is a lot to be said about attending one of the largest schools in the country, but as the adage goes, "You've got to see it to believe it." UT-Austin, in keeping with its promise, truly is a university of the first class.

Linda Beth Milch, B.A.

University of Virginia

THE PROGRAM

"I was a northern boy in Mr. Jefferson's court.

"In picturesque Charlottesville, I spent my first few days learning the local lingo and traditions of this academical village. There were no freshman, only first-year students, second-years, and so on. And it wasn't a campus. Here in Virginia, I was on the Grounds of the University. We also have no professors because ol' Tom Jefferson didn't believe in such titles. An early mistake was not rescheduling the 8 A.M. class I was saddled with that first semester. Spanish with a southern accent was weird enough to these ears (como esta usted, y'all?) *without the additional burden of rising near dawn. Still, passing the Rotunda on the Lawn every day helped make the early morning trek more bearable."*

Many classes are near the Lawn, the university's focal point. Anchoring the Lawn is the Rotunda, a neoclassical marvel modeled on the Roman Pantheon and epitomizing UVa's dual love of tradition and progress. Founded by Thomas Jefferson in 1819, the university seeks to enhance its national reputation by attracting the best faculty and students while maintaining its roots in the Old Dominion. UVa's stated purpose is to enrich the mind by stimulating and sustaining free inquiry to better understand the world. A strong liberal arts education is at the core of the educational philosophy and forms the basis for each of the six undergraduate schools' curricula.

Part of the sense of tradition is the student-run honor system in place since 1842. Any lying, cheating, or stealing that meet certain criteria warrants permanent expulsion under the system. Much justifiable criticism has been heaped on the system in recent years. But it does allow for some exams to go unproctored and for extended check-writing privileges in Charlottesville, particularly the area of shops, restaurants, and bars nearest the Grounds known as the Corner.

> *"I didn't expect to meet one of the deans standing on the Lawn when I had a beer in my hand and was standing next to a keg (in the good old days when that sort of stuff was allowed on the Lawn). It was early in the first semester, and I was excited about being invited to a Lawn party. Anyway, the dean nodded, and someone even offered him a drink. He declined, but I was beginning to get a sense of how we all shared this community."*

UVa has been dubbed a public Ivy, meaning the academic quality is outstanding but the price won't force parents to take out a triple mortgage. Because the university is a public school, the Board of Visitors has to deal with the state's General Assembly when making out the biennial budget. UVa and Charlottesville officials traditionally have been at odds about the school's continual expansion because it means the loss of taxable revenue for the city. But for students, the most tangible aspect about the university's public side is its lower prices.

Then there's the Ivy part. It's not just quality education—it's some of the country's best. The English, history, and modern language departments all are nationally ranked, and many of the departments attract top-flight profs. The best part is that those outstanding teachers typically are very committed to their students. UVa has also placed very high in recent national surveys.

Most students apply directly to the College of Arts and Sciences, commonly called the college. The engineering, architecture, and nursing schools also accept first-year students and transfers. Because these three schools are much smaller than the college, some find it safer to apply to the college and then try transferring over to the other schools. The School of Commerce accepts students only in the third year. The Education School has a five-year joint master's-bachelor's program with the college that students begin in the second year.

> *"I guess I had expected to be the only northerner in my dorm, but I was wrong. There was a good mix of North and South in my suite, which held ten people. To my surprise, there were even a few fellow Philadelphians around. Many of the in-state students came from Washington, D.C.'s exciting suburbs of northern Virginia, and they all seemed to have gone to the same high school. Yet they were as eager as everyone else to meet new people. The main geographic differences ended up as friendly rivalries over sports teams and local lingo."*

There are approximately 11,500 undergraduates and 6500 graduate students on Grounds. Known officially as the Cavaliers, the other main nickname is the Wahoos (or 'Hoos), which stems from the school's "Good Ol' Song" sung at sporting events and other festive occasions. (Incidentally, a Wahoo is a fish that can drink twice its weight.) Saturday home football games are big party events where, after every

UVa score, everyone joins in a chorus of the "Good Ol' Song." It's all part of the UVa experience, where balancing academics, extracurriculars, and social activities is the key to getting the most out of a public school excelling in all three areas.

GETTING IN/FINANCIAL AID

UVa has benefitted from a slew of national attention lauding it as one of the best colleges in the country, providing quality education at significantly less cost than private schools. That publicity contributed to record-breaking numbers of admission applicants to an already very selective school.

About 65% of those accepted come from Virginia itself. It is the school of choice for many Virginians, and they know the odds are in their favor. Out-of-state applicants face stiffer competition. But minority students from any area are highly sought after. Approximately 10% of the undergraduates are blacks. Women comprise about half of the student population. Outside Virginia, states sending many students include Maryland, Pennsylvania, and New York. A fair amount have gone to private school before entering the university, but that doesn't make a difference in the classroom. They just drive nicer cars.

> *"UVa was always my first choice for college. Coming from a sharp, suburban-Philadelphia public school, many of my friends were going to the Ivies. But that route seemed like an extension of high school to me with the same people and classes. UVa had a great academic reputation although it was not as well known around my area at that time. What sold me was my first visit to the Grounds. The Lawn's beauty was simply overwhelming, the curriculum first-rate. I knew this was where I belonged, and it was a choice I never regretted, especially when I was chosen to live in one of the 54 Lawn rooms."*

Application factors considered by the committee include: high school record; standardized test scores; the application itself and how it conveys the person's writing ability in expressing his or her goals, background, and extracurricular activities; and reference letters from guidance counselors and teachers. Personal interviews are not used. The regular decision deadline is January 15, with a $40 nonrefundable application fee. April 1 is the Big Day when applicants receive their answer. About 20% of the first-year class are admitted through the early decision plan that has a November 1 deadline. Those not accepted when letters go out on December 1 are reconsidered in the spring. About 70% graduate in four years, and 90% of the incoming students eventually graduate.

The college and the Engineering School run honors programs known respectively as Echols and Rodman. The honor students live in their own dorm in the first year.

Rodman scholars get to take four special courses during their first two years. Echols don't have to complete area requirements or declare a major. They also get all the classes for which they preregister. The Jefferson Scholars program is sponsored by the university's alumni association and awards full four-year scholarships to about 18 outstanding applicants each year.

> *"I did my research on the school before trying to convince the admissions-powers-that-be that they couldn't live without me. In the all-important essays, I sprinkled in samplings of my knowledge of the university. Any little advantage helps. That I didn't get in early only redoubled my efforts to succeed during the regular admissions timetable. Besides, I'm sure they really wanted to read those periodic updates on my high school activities and achievements."*

About 33% of the students annually receive some form of financial aid. The university also operates affirmative action and equal opportunity programs. Entering students must complete the College Scholarship Service Financial Aid Form in order to be considered for need-based assistance. Students have to apply for the aid before being offered admission since they are notified about the financial aid situation shortly after learning the admission committee's decision. Financial aid usually is a combination of grants, loans, and employment for full-time students.

ACADEMIC ENVIRONMENT

The college has 36 departments and interdisciplinary major programs, offering such options as study abroad and honors programs. Achievement and advanced placement tests may satisfy some of the following requirements: two courses in the humanities, social sciences, and composition; three classes of math and natural sciences; and competence in a foreign language through the second-year level.

When taking these classes, students will study anywhere and at any time: at the library, on the Lawn, in a cafeteria, waiting for laundry, in the dorm. Of course, most people tend to procrastinate at times. But they know what they have to do to get the job done. Like it or not, they usually do. For instance, 40 UVa graduates have been Rhodes Scholars so far, among the highest number from a state institution. And 25% of the students end up on the dean's list with a 3.4 GPA or better.

> *"One of the fellas in the suite next door came back very excited after an intro German class. He had learned how to say the magical German phrase, 'Your grandmother has flowers on her wallpaper.' Soon, several of us in the dorm became experts in this particular piece of Prussian prose."*

The average course load is five three-hour classes per semester. The challenge to succeed derives not so much from competition against other students but from individual motivation and desire. One of the nicest aspects about UVa is that most professors are eager to get to know students. Office hours are kept for help on classwork as well as talking about career advice, how the 'Hoos are doing in sports, or whatever. Faculty are very accessible if students make an effort and prove there is much to be learned outside the classroom. Two residential colleges, one opened last year, feature faculty living and dining with students.

Top profs teaching introductory-level classes is another plus that students should try to explore—learning early from the best. Some of the finest educators in the country have chosen UVa. They are the ones who help keep the school an academic powerhouse. Still, some good advice is to take the prof, not the course, because there are no guarantees that the class that sounds like it would be paradise couldn't turn into the semester-from-hell with the wrong teacher.

Class size includes small seminars, medium lectures of up to 100 people or so, and large lectures. In the larger courses, there is often a weekly discussion seminar led by a teaching assistant. These TAs are graduate students who usually have to teach as part of their own training. Because no two TAs are alike, it's smart to ask around about reputations. Large lectures don't have mandatory attendance, and if you come in hung over from Thursday night activities, the back of the auditorium looks mighty good. Seminars offer direct contact and interaction with the teacher. Participation is a must because there are so few people there. Medium-size classes are usually run as lectures, with the professor talking the whole time.

The add drop process generally works well. You preregister for classes the semester before and find out what you got shortly before classes begin. If visions of supply-side curves fill your worst nightmares after a day of economics, dropping the class near the start of the semester probably is a good plan. Many people revel in telling about the all-nighter they pulled for the latest midterm, problem set, or term paper. The labyrinthine stacks of Alderman Library are popular, especially during finals time. Clemons Library is more social and laid-back.

Academic advising in the college had long been a rare weak point at the university, but the school has made efforts to improve this situation. First-year students in the college meet an assigned faculty advisor during their first day on Grounds, and receive encouragement to make personal contact with instructors and other faculty early on. Some insist on going it alone, and critics of the system are sometimes heard, but no one can preregister without first seeing an advisor. Students declare majors at the end of second year and then transfer to an advisor in that department. Older students are a great resource. It never hurts to grab a syllabus and sit in on the first lecture if you are unsure about what to take.

"Intense panic, utter despair. Devastation of biblical proportion—I'm talking thesis time. History majors are the only ones in the college required to write a thesis regardless of whether they were in an honors program. Lucky us, lucky me. Since one of my favorite profs was teaching the Constitution during the Civil War era, I

quickly signed up. We spent several weeks researching primary sources for our topics and meeting individually with the professor. (I didn't go out much during the entire month of November.) Finally, I finished the paper, which weighed in at about 42 pages. We spent the last two weeks of the semester critiquing everyone's work, and the prof had us over for a spaghetti dinner. I had never written anything like it before, nor have I since. It sharpened my skills in research, writing, and organization of material. I was actually glad I did it, proud of the A– I received and probably grew as a person somehow. But as a famous southerner once said, 'As God is my witness, I'll never do a thesis again.'"

SOCIAL LIFE

Work hard—play hard. It's as simple as that.

Wahoos will find any reason and any place to have a good time. This tendency balances equally with academics and extracurriculars. Certain events are such ingrained traditions that many feel their university experience is lacking without them. Take the aforementioned football games. Day games are usually met with some sort of pregame gathering, preferably with alumni who are notoriously generous with their food and drink. Night games are even better because there is little time after the game to rest up before going out.

Charlottesville itself presents a diverse offering for a small-town social scene. Aesthetically, you couldn't ask for a more gorgeous environment than a town nestled in the bosom of the Blue Ridge Mountains. The quality of life there is very high. Because it's a small town, students make the most of the available hangouts. First and foremost is the Corner, probably the university's favorite all-around gathering place. Its proximity to Grounds helps its popularity, as do the late hours of most of the restaurants. The downtown mall area provides a more diverse crowd where students mix with the locals, or townies. For road trips, Richmond is about an hour away, and Washington D.C., about two-and-a-half hours. Many people also like to escape to the nearby Skyline Drive, visit Monticello, or tan at Chris Greene Lake.

"The first exhilarating rush of total freedom I felt at the university was during the Friday after my first week of classes. A realization dawns on the seventeen-year-old from Philly that he does not have to report in at a set time, that he does not have to answer to parental authority, that he does not have anyone else making choices for him.

"So naturally I asked my suitemates what their plans were. Like many first-years on their first weekend, they wanted to head to Rugby Road and the fraternities. Kegs, tunes, and partying

with the opposite sex was quite an enticing combination. While I eventually tired of the fraternity scene, that initial thrill was something else."

Many first-year activities are designed by the resident student advisers in the dorms or occasionally by the first-year council. One perennial favorite is the stranger dance, where you get a friend to ask a stranger to the dance for you. Usually, the stranger has been the subject of some serious scoping in the O-Hill dining hall. The drinking age in Virginia is twenty-one. UVa has been reexamining its alcohol policy after upperclass students rebelled at plans to ban alcohol at university facilities where underage students were present. Drug use is not tolerated at all. Alcohol is no more prevalent at the university than on any other major campus. It's simply there if you choose to seek it out. Most people have a good time with or without it.

Several key events dominate the social scene. Midwinters is the largest school-wide bash tossed by the fraternities. The semesterly Foxfield steeple races provide some of the more preppy-oriented students the chance to sip G-and-Ts in a more traditional southern setting. Two major formal balls, Commonwealth and Restoration, are held each year. Fraternity and sorority formals abound at certain times as well.

Many on-Grounds activities are programmed by the University Union student association. Grad Social Hour, a weekly social/drink function, is popular with upperclass students. Union also runs the movie theater in the basement of Newcomb Hall, a student activities building that doubles as one of the main cafeterias. The theater draws good crowds and is a popular date place following dinner on the Corner.

Although the Charlottesville area may be small, there is enough room for people to find a group or lifestyle with which they feel comfortable. Although some students party six days a week and sleep on the seventh day, others don't. UVa has long held the reputation of a party school. To an extent, it's accurate. But most students are committed to getting the most out of their education as well as their leisure time.

EXTRACURRICULAR ACTIVITIES

A wide range of activities provides a vital outlet from classroom rigors. It is an escape that many students readily take advantage of and can spend as much time with as their studies. Sometimes more. People really find their niche in groups varying from political interests to polo. The university experience is not complete for many students without these activities. They balance off academics and social life on a consistent basis, sometimes combining the elements of the other two. Long-lasting friendships are forged, and it is often the people in these groups that are the reason students keep returning. Areas covered include the arts, sports, communications, service, ethnic culture, religion, academia, and student government.

> *"Nap time ended for the 30 preschoolers. It was my first time on the job as a day-care helper for Madison House, UVa's largest volunteer program. The kids began to stir, and it didn't take long to realize that this job would require as much energy as my other activities. It's not easy trying to rationalize to a four-year-old why she must wait in line before climbing back up the slide. But it also didn't take long to realize the intangible rewards involved. When they started calling me Mr. Adam later that day, it struck a chord somewhere, and I knew that this job wasn't really work after all."*

Almost half of the university students become involved with one of Madison House's programs during their stay at UVa. Its community service programs range from helping underprivileged kids to working in the university's health-care facilities. Other perennial favorites include groups like the Young Democrats, College Republicans, and Student Council's numerous committees. University Union's groups also attract a large number of people.

> *"You get some sense of the importance of activities in university life during registration first year. Seemingly hundreds of groups bombard you with information on your way out. Just to shut them up, you probably sign up for half a dozen groups. Not knowing what was in store at registration, I had wandered up the day before to the offices of the student paper, the* Cavalier Daily. *It was a thrill having 14,000 people read my byline that first week of classes. There were many great times along with many 40-hour weeks. I learned a lot about life from the people there, several of whom are now my closest friends."*

The university is one of only two in the country with two daily student newspapers. There are also two radio stations, a weekly news magazine, a yearbook, and numerous other specialty publications. Groups like the Black Student Alliance, the Indian Student Association, and the Chinese Student Society offer outlets for minority students. Several honor and secret societies on Grounds recognize contributions made by outstanding students as well as aid the university. And their ubiquitous symbols adorn many buildings around Grounds. For those interested in the fraternity system, there is ample opportunity to experience Greek life, which began at the university in 1852. At last count, there were nearly 40 fraternities (whose membership included some 28% of the men on Grounds) and about half as many sororities (with around 30% of the women), including several black Greek service organizations.

Athletics represents another popular area. There are 12 intercollegiate sports for men and 11 for women. The football team won both of its bowl appearances in the

1980s, marking the first two times they saw post-season action. The men's and women's soccer, basketball, and lacrosse teams, and men's polo teams have been strong national contenders in recent years. Intramural teams and club sports also attract many eager participants.

RESIDENCE LIFE

All first-years are required to live in the old or new dorms. The old ones are a little closer to Grounds and have rooms linked by halls. The new dorms have suites of five double rooms each. Students generally like whichever arrangement they end up with. After first year, many choose to live in an apartment, rent a house, or live in a fraternity or sorority, but the upperclass residential colleges have become popular. With the opening of 500 new spaces this year, the university can now house all students who want to live on Grounds. One of the most prestigious UVa honors is being selected to live in a Lawn room your final year. These single rooms were part of the original university, flank the Rotunda, and come complete with fireplaces. Bathrooms, however, are outside, and it's common on the way to classes to see Lawnies running around in bathrobes.

GRADUATES

The Office of Career Planning and Placement is an invaluable resource for many upperclass students. More than 75% of the university degree candidates turn to OCPP each year. It assists students in realizing career and educational goals, such as résumé workshops, externships, and preprofessional advising. Some 600 companies participate in recruiting and career fairs throughout the year. The career office also has an extensive library including catalogs of graduate schools, material on career planning, and information about government service and national companies.

There exists a very strong alumni network. OCPP has a list of more than 3000 alumni willing to offer their advice. Alumni participate in job seminars at the university and in their own regions. There are many local chapters, and the alumni association recently celebrated its centennial. Among the more famous university alumni and former students are: Edgar Allan Poe, Woodrow Wilson, Ralph Sampson, Dr. Walter Reed, Louis Auchincloss, Katie Couric, James Rouse, and most of Virginia's top politicos, including Charles Robb.

According to a recent survey of college alumni, nearly 60% eventually completed graduate degrees. Some 70% of those who entered the work force found jobs within three months after graduating, the survey stated. A look at the Engineering School showed that about 60% were employed after graduation or had job offers and 30 percent went on to graduate school. Some of the more popular industries for commerce students were accounting, consulting, and investment banking.

> *"The job search proved to be almost as tough on my ego as dating. Was it possible that so many papers thought I just wasn't right for them right now? One particularly gloomy day, I was nuked by papers in three different time zones. But I plowed on, sending out more résumés and cover letters. And my day finally came in the spring when I found out I had landed a job with one of my top choices."*

SUMMARY OVERVIEW

UVa offers a brilliant combination of academics, extracurricular activities, and social life in one of the most beautiful settings in the country. The college's English, history, and modern language departments are ranked among the best. Rhetoric and communication studies has developed into one of the hottest majors on Grounds. Friendly competition among schools and students does not add up to an intense, pressure-cooker environment. Rather, motivation to succeed stems mainly from individual desire. It is buttressed by top-flight professors who generally take a genuine interest in the results.

The concern for a liberal arts background is one of Jefferson's many legacies. Another is the university's heart and soul—the Rotunda and the Lawn. Its neoclassical features serve to emphasize UVa's continual balance of continuity and change. It is a school steeped in tradition that wants to lead the way into the future. That is why new facilities such as the Balfour Addition to the Commerce School resemble in design other buildings on Grounds.

There is a bond between university students of having shared a common experience. It could be Sunday afternoon laundry runs. Or struggling to find parking spaces in a town that is better suited for horse-and-buggies. Or late-night snacks on the Corner after polishing off the latest term paper. And on certain spring days the Lawn readily changes into UVa Country Club as people relax with music, toss Frisbees, and just hang out.

The places where the university could be stronger, such as academic advising, it is trying to remedy. And students make themselves heard on issues concerning them at the moment even if the administration is usually slow to react. Recent controversy has focussed on administration policy regarding alcohol use, dorm lockups, graduation exercises, and faculty tenure. Students have criticized the university's apparent emphasis on research over teaching in its tenure decisions, and some very popular profs have been axed. Student Council has been trying to get more student input into that process.

Some other topics of concern include fraternity relations with non-Greek students and neighboring communities, the honor system, minority concerns, emphasis on athletics or academics, expansion, and the Board of Visitors' divestment policy. The honor system always seems to reap its share of controversy. Questions regarding the single sanction of permanent expulsion, faculty involvement in the student-run system, and a disproportionate number of blacks being investigated are among the recent issues of concern about the system. Changes in attitude and policy are slow to come to a school so steeped in tradition. But perhaps it is the university's sense of its mission as a public school that allows it to grapple openly with these problems.

Yet there is much more to commend the university. It is a school encompassing a diverse range of views, personalities, and lifestyles. You are just as likely to see someone go to class in a pressed shirt and tie as in tie-dye and cut-offs. Alumni are a constant sight throughout the year, and students know they will be in the same position in the not-too-distant future. The yearbook likes to end with words written by its 1903 editor-in-chief, James Hay, Jr., whose feelings are just as appropriate today: "Remembering the purple shadows on the Lawn, the majesty of the colonnades, and the dreams of your youth, you may say in reverence and thankfulness: I have worn the honors of honor; I graduated from Virginia."

Adam Bell, B.A.

Vassar College

THE PROGRAM

"Vassar.

  'Isn't that a women's college?'

  "Whether you're a woman or a man at Vassar you are asked this question many times by people outside the college and eventually you start to develop creative answers.

  "A man, president of the Vassar Student Association (VSA) attending the Seven Sisters Conference referred to the illustrious group as the Seven Siblings in order to include his coed college.

  "A member of the men's soccer team attending a game away from home replied to the question by simply saying 'yes.' When the inquirer looked hopelessly puzzled, the Vassar student explained that Vassar has not lost its roots as a women's college, but men now attend in practically equal numbers as women (44% of the student body is male).

  "Vassar is a women's college that has built a reputation for academic excellence, but it is also a coed institution in which both men and women benefit from a unique coeducational experience."

Vassar has always been an innovator. At a time when women's access to the advantages of higher education was severely limited, master brewer and Poughkeepsie businessman Matthew Vassar founded what he called a "magnificent enterprise." His enterprise, Vassar College, opened in 1865, the first women's college of academic merit in the country. His goal was to provide a college for women that would offer an education equal to that of men's colleges like Harvard and Yale. The first students—some 350 women from all over the United States—were attracted by the idea of showing the world that this was possible.

In order to obtain his goals, Matthew Vassar set the highest intellectual criteria for his students and within only ten years, Vassar's admission standards were as rigorous as those of its male counterparts. Vassar quickly developed a reputation for being not only a pioneer in women's education, but in the liberal arts as well. Maria Mitchell, the first woman to be elected to the Academy of Arts and Sciences, was one of Vassar's first professors. Vassar had the first chapter of Phi Beta Kappa at a women's college. Vassar became an academic innovator by breaking down the rigid boundaries between disciplines. Believing that understanding can be increased by learning many different perspectives, Vassar has been a leader in developing interdepartmental concentrations.

Finally, Vassar led the coed revolution among prestigious all-women's colleges. Yale University proposed a merger with Vassar, with whom they'd had a long-term relationship. Vassar, independent as always, turned down the offer to merge. Instead, Vassar decided to go coed on its own terms. By being the first of the prestigious group of all-women's colleges to go coed, and the only one to go coed without merging with another school, Vassar offers its students a unique coeducational environment. Men have not overshadowed women at Vassar, but have come in as equal partners. The faculty are evenly divided between men and women. Many of the major student leadership positions are held by women. Unlike many other coed schools where women's status is less than equal, neither men nor women are faced with an oppressive and lingering boys club mentality that limits people to perform only in stereotypical roles. Going to Vassar still involves the excitement and challenge of knowing that its students are expected to develop independence of thought.

This independence of thought is cultivated through a program where students develop their own curriculum. The close contact students have with their faculty advisers is crucial to the success of this flexible program. These advisers help students to distribute courses over four broad curricular divisions and to choose a major. A major can be in any field, or in a multidisciplinary program, or students can design their own independent major integrating different disciplines with their overlapping topics and concerns.

Access to educational opportunity is deeply embedded in the life of the college. Twenty-two percent of its student body are minorities, placing it well above the 15.3% average for four-year private schools cited in *The Chronicle of Higher Education*. Vassar students are from every state and many foreign countries, but what they have in common is a degree of independent achievement.

This student body of risk-takers becomes a central part of Vassar's informal education, which occurs outside the traditional classroom setting. The students, coming from every type of cultural, religious, and socioeconomic background, form the backbone of this informal education, but it gains its significance through the *interaction* of these groups.

"I didn't get a chance to visit the Vassar campus until I had been accepted and was trying to decide what school I wanted to attend. This visit made all the difference. Many other schools I'd visited had figures that represented the geographical diversity of

their student body, but the Vassar campus felt different. Groups
of students weren't so easily identified because everyone hung
out together. The lack of tension was the first signal that this was
a place where the informal interaction between the students
would be an education in and of itself. The student I was staying
with used a powerful phrase to describe my observations: 'We
don't tolerate intolerance.' "

Vassar is not a school that expects this interaction to happen automatically. There are many formal and informal means for students to become actively engaged in struggles to create movement. Students sit on almost every college committee, including the Board of Trustees, and develop their own groups. Some of these recent movements have resulted in the development of an Intercultural Center and a kitchen for kosher dining.

The informal interactions that make up this education outside the classroom happen all over the campus, but the College Center is the most frequented spot. Located in Main Building, the oldest and largest building on the campus, the College Center contains the post office, faculty and student mailboxes, offices for many of the student-run organizations, the college store and computer store, along with the Cafe, Matthew's Mug (the campus bar), and, most notably, the Retreat.

The Retreat is a snack bar that is open every day until midnight. Tables sprawl out among potted trees. All day the tables outside the Retreat are buzzing with activity. You'll find professors and students studying, talking, eating, and smoking. Around 11 o'clock many Vassar students take a break from studying and meet in the Retreat for sustenance in the form of a huge pile of french fries or a mound of ice cream. Passing through the Retreat at least three times a day is practically unavoidable. You're sure to see someone you know (not difficult, when with 2335 students, you'll know almost everyone's face, if not the name that goes with it.)

But should you wish more room to think, the Vassar campus sits on 1000 acres in the Hudson River Valley, which include two lakes, 200 species of trees, gardens, streams, a natural outdoor amphitheater seating 3000, and a 280-acre ecological preserve and field laboratory. Furthermore, Vassar is only two hours away from New York City, the epicenter of things to do.

As Vassar leads the way for other colleges, it provides for its students a flexible curriculum with an innovative approach to multidisciplinary study and a diverse student body whose interactions with one another add a crucial dimension to the Vassar education.

GETTING IN/FINANCIAL AID

Vassar received 3760 applications for its most recent freshman class of 612 students. Along with high school grades (over 75% of Vassar students were in the top fifth of their high school graduating classes), and standardized tests (average SAT I scores of admitted students are 610 in verbal, 625 in math), Vassar's admission policy includes a close assessment of personal strengths, talents, goals, and potential.

Forty percent of the incoming class held major leadership roles in their high schools: 26 were student body presidents and 19 vice presidents; 67 were captains of athletic teams; 96 were editors of their school publications; and 67 held leadership roles in a myriad of clubs and organizations. Forty-four percent of the class is male, and 25% are people of color; 73 students come from multilingual households and speak 31 different languages.

> *"When I returned to campus as an alumnae class representative at Fall Council, I heard the director of admissions speak. He painted a much more vivid picture of the incoming class than the traditional statistics would allow. 'Vassar is more than a series of statistics', he said. He told us that the most important question he faced when he evaluated prospective students was: 'Has this student made a difference and will he or she continue to make a difference once part of the Vassar community?' The current class shows how closely he paid attention to the answers to these questions: 'Vassar has students who have been recognized for excellence in pursuits as diverse as martial arts, flamenco dancing, horsemanship, comedy performance, and restaurant management.'*
>
> *"These people not only make a difference, they become the Vassar community."*

Vassar maintains financial aid assistance for every student who demonstrates need. This is especially noteworthy at a time when many schools are being forced to determine admission by the student's ability to pay. Sixty percent of Vassar students receive some sort of financial aid, and 43% of these students receive financial assistance directly from the college. The financial aid package includes a choice of campus jobs to help the student in earning money for daily expenses. These jobs are available in all areas of the campus from faculty assistantships in academic departments to cooks or cashiers at the Retreat or bartenders at the Mug. Students can be confident that if they continue to perform well academically, financial aid that is received in the first year will be renewed.

Vassar's generous endowment (nearly $250 million) and annual giving to the college subsidizes every student's education as well as providing for the recruitment of talented faculty members and up-to-date facilities.

ACADEMIC ENVIRONMENT

The Vassar student is the architect of his/her own education. Vassar, itself, was developed through experimentation and risk-taking so it stands to reason that the educational philosophy encourages the student to take advantage of the flexibility and breadth that mark the Vassar curriculum. With nothing pre-ordained, students become personally invested in their choice of courses and majors. The independence that marks the academic environment results in a personal drive to excel. Fellow classmates don't ask each other about their grades on papers and exams. Students work together on projects and help each other on assignments. Direct competition for grades is frowned upon by one's peers and professors.

At Vassar you won't have two or three years of requirements to fulfill, but you'll probably graduate wishing you had more time to explore its extensive offering of over 1000 courses. Today, Vassar's curriculum is broader, richer, and more varied than ever, mirroring its diverse community with over a hundred courses being taught from an explicit third world, cross-cultural, or feminist perspective.

Each first-year student (the term freshman is being phased out at Vassar because of its inherent sexism) is required to take an introductory course, which is offered in a variety of departments and is limited to 19 first-year students. These courses put heavy emphasis on oral and written work and are characterized by frequent individual meetings with professors. The only other general requirement outside of the major is proficiency in a foreign language.

By the end of the sophomore year, students at Vassar have to declare their majors. Again a broad range of choices are available to serve the varied interests of the student body. There are four paths to the A.B. degree: a traditional discipline, a double major (which requires the student to complete all the requirements of the two departments), a multidisciplinary major, or an independent major.

Vassar has been in the forefront of developing the multidisciplinary course of study. These courses are taught by two or more professors from departments that have different points of view on a shared topic (e.g., Africana studies, American culture, women's studies). Vassar was the first undergraduate college in the country to offer a major in cognitive science, integrating the fields of psychology, computer science, biology, mathematics, and philosophy. These multidisciplinary courses of study are meant to prepare the student for the complicated interconnections they will face in their professional lives outside the college.

The independent program allows the student to design his/her own major with the help of faculty members from any number of fields. Many students choose to submit detailed proposals for admission into this program. Their majors span a wide spectrum and have included such examples as international political economy, history of the British satire, the family, Soviet studies and computer science, and the theater.

Students are not left on their own to make important decisions about what courses to take. Close ties between students and faculty members make the system work. All first-year students are assigned pre-major advisers and student fellows who help to choose courses and chart out a plan of study that will involve course work distributed over four broad divisions of the curriculum: arts, foreign languages and literature, social sciences, and natural sciences. Frequent meetings with advisers, rather than a rigid core curriculum, help the student to keep in mind the broad range of fields that combine to create a strong liberal arts education.

The comprehensive system of advising is possible because Vassar's faculty members are highly accessible. There are no teaching assistants and the professors spend their time teaching only undergraduates. As a student, you'll soon realize that the faculty is one of the college's most valuable resources. Over 90% have Ph.Ds and are looked upon as experts in their fields. It is not unusual to see one of your professors quoted in the books you'll be studying in class.

The professors not only teach, but become engaged in the life of the college. Eighty percent of the faculty live within a two-mile radius of the campus. Many of these professors live in the dorms as house fellows, helping to plan activities with the dorm officers as well as supporting peer counseling and referral services. It is not unusual, then, that relationships with professors often become more relaxed and informal.

> *"One of my Vassar professors needed someone to house-sit for her family over spring break. She invited me to her house for dinner to go over the details I would need to know about the house and the care of their dog. That evening we discussed our common academic interests over dinner, and campus issues while washing the dishes. Now, two years after graduation, we have become even closer friends. I helped her son when he moved into New York City, and I look to her for advice in my professional life. I took these relationships for granted at Vassar, but now I know how lucky I was to develop relationships with my professors outside the classroom."*

Classes are small, even at the introductory level, with the average class size just 14 students and a student-to-faculty ratio of 11 to one. The small class size means that class meetings are intense with a high level of student participation. There is an expectation that a Vassar student will come to class having done the required reading and will be ready to speak about and reflect on what he/she has read.

Strong academic facilities support the student's class work. The main library has over 700,000 volumes with a rare book room that includes holograph manuscripts and papers of Mary McCarthy '33, Elizabeth Bishop '34, Mark Twain, and Ruth Benedict '09, among many others. Vassar also has auxiliary libraries in art and music (the music library is considered one of the finest in the nation with first editions of published scores of Haydn and letters of Mozart, Verdi, and Wagner).

At Vassar the five most popular majors are English, psychology, political science, art, and history. The English department, with the largest number of student majors, is known for its rigorous enforcement of standards. The faculty and graduates of the English department include an impressive list of published writers and poets. Although grades are not the important goal in any department, English is a department that does not give grades on papers. Papers in English classes are given extensive written comments, and professors usually meet with students midsemester to discuss their progress and the emphasis is put on the degree to which students are fulfilling their potential.

The art department, another of the most popular majors, has a strong national reputation. It has one of the oldest museums in the nation. Started in 1864, it is eight years older than the Metropolitan Museum of Art. This year, ground will be broken for the $15.6 million Frances Lehman Loeb '28 Art Gallery, a center designed by Cesar Pelli. In addition to teaching and lecture facilities, it will provide extra display space for approximately 9000 art objects.

> *"Art History 105 is one of Vassar's most popular courses. Even though I was one of the few who made it through Vassar without actually taking the course, I learned very quickly that the times to avoid the dining hall were directly after introductory art history was let out. Students make flashcards to use as study guides for exams in art history. In the library, dorm lounges, and the dining hall, these flashcards displaying the works of artists like Praxiteles, Caravaggio, and Monet became part of the campus landscape."*

Vassar's drama department launched the college's most famous graduate, Meryl Streep '71. The Powerhouse Theater is an experimental theater on campus that allows for over 100 different stage sets. This capacity makes it especially useful for trying out different arrangements for new plays. It is this capacity that has made the Powerhouse the setting for one of Vassar's most successful summer programs. The Powerhouse Theater summer program attracts up to 50 apprentices from colleges across the country. The apprentices receive academic credit and Actor's Equity points for their work with a company of 150 theater professionals, performing and producing both new scripts and established works. The members of the professional company also teach and lead workshops in acting, directing, and stage design.

The breadth of Vassar's curriculum extends to strength in the sciences, as well. Nearly one third of Vassar students major in the natural sciences division (which includes psychology). Vassar offers these students small classes and close contact with faculty members and their research in addition to facilities that are state-of-the art. The Olmsted Hall of the Biological Sciences is equipped with both scanning and transmission electron microscopes, and the newest building on campus, the Seeley G. Mudd Chemistry Building, makes instrumentation available for such techniques as high-performance liquid chromatography, nuclear magnetic resonance spectrometry, and single-crystal X-ray diffraction.

The sciences, as well as almost every field, are strengthened by the opportunity students have to become involved in faculty research. The Undergraduate Research Summer Institute (URSI) pays students a stipend to work with faculty members in the sciences on ongoing research projects.

> *"I was one of only two freshmen involved in URSI. The summer I worked with three psychology professors developed into three years of involvement. Although I came in midway in an ongoing study, I was given a great deal of independence and responsibility. I worked alone and in one-on-one situations with my professors. One of them even took time out to teach me the basics of statistics and data analysis, because as a freshman I was not qualified to register for these upper-level classes.*
>
> *"The URSI students made up quite an intellectual community that summer. In weekly lunch seminars we heard about the work of our peers involved in research on such important topics as obesity, and the development of AIDS drugs.*
>
> *"The summer culminated in a symposium where the students summarized their own part in the research and presented their findings. Many of the students went on to publish and present professional papers on their work. One of my friends, the only other freshman in the program, described to me how people at these meetings assumed that she was in graduate school because she looked younger than the other presenters, and how surprised the professionals were when they found out she was able to know so much about her field while only an undergraduate."*

SOCIAL LIFE

A residential community like Vassar, with 98% of it students living on campus, integrates social life into part of every day. Time between classes, in the dorms, and at dinner are an integral part of the student's social life, as well as the more traditionally social times like weekends. Social life at Vassar is made up of a wide variety of student-planned parties on weekends, as well as lectures, exhibitions, films, and concerts scheduled on almost every night of the week.

The hot spot on weeknights is likely to be the 24-hour room in the library. Studying is serious stuff here. Vassar students set a tone of working hard during the week, and then enjoying themselves when the work is done. VICE, the student-run entertainment programming group, brings big-name concerts and comedians to campus, provides free first-run and avant-garde movies on campus every night of the week, and sponsors the annual fall and spring formals.

The dorms offer many opportunities for socializing and epitomize the integration of the diverse student body. Eight of the nine dorms are coed. The friends you make in your dorm will be from all classes (there are no freshman or exclusively upperclass dorms), and from all parts of the world. The dorms are regal buildings (one is referred to as the Gingerbread House) and the rooms are spacious. The common rooms have televisions, Steinway pianos, fireplaces, pool and ping-pong tables, as well as vending machines and laundry facilities. Two thirds of the rooms are singles, so after the first year, almost everyone has a single.

All of the dorms on campus are run by a student senate and sponsor frequent parties, lectures, and athletic competitions. Dorm parties are campus-wide events. There are no exclusive social events, no sororities or fraternities, and no eating clubs. All dormitory students eat at the All-Campus Dining Center (ACDC).

ACDC offers a wide variety of meal choices including vegetarian entrees, and even dishes made from recipes students bring in from home. The dining hall has two distinct sides to it—one is much more sedate than the other (translation: you can escape with a book and not be seen by any of your friends). The left side definitely is one of the most social spots on campus. Dinners here easily can last for two hours with dinner companions changing as the evening progresses. This is one of the key places to catch up with friends and hear the latest campus news.

Upperclass students can choose to brave the supermarket and cook for themselves when living in Vassar's apartment complexes. Each unit houses either four or five students. These on-campus apartments are called Town Houses (THs) or Terrace Apartments (TAs).

The weekends usually start off on Thursday night with a long but active wait on the Mug line (Matthew's Mug is the official name of the campus pub) with other Mug rats, as those who frequent the Mug are affectionately called. The weekend calendar always includes all-campus parties, with pre-parties held in individual THs or TAs.

There are many nonalcoholic spots on campus including the Cafe where you can relax to live jazz, classical, and blues music over coffee and desserts while studying or socializing. The Aula is a popular alternative dance spot where campus bands frequently perform against a backdrop of huge video screens.

Many long-held traditions mark the year socially. Serenading is the first big event of the school year and that's when the senior class gets to strut its stuff. The seniors march around to each of the dorms where the freshmen sing them songs and then are told to kneel as a show of respect.

> *"During my freshmen year, the buildup for Serenading was much more fun than the actual event. The freshmen in my dorm first started to get to know each other as we contrived a song that would say something witty and characterize the spirit of our dorm.*
>
> *"'And no matter what,' we were told by our fellow students, 'don't kneel. This dorm has a reputation to uphold'.*
>
> *"This somehow lost its sparkle on the evening of Serenading when our irreverent freshmen were doused with beer by seniors unappreciative of our rebellious spirit.*

"The next year the tradition was reassessed and it was decided that Serenading would be held during the afternoon. This made the festivities much more enjoyable for all, less like a drunken fraternity party (a model no one at Vassar is interested in). The presentations for the seniors and college administrators in the outdoor theater were lively and creative, complete with loud music and elaborate costumes. Our dorm, still harboring an attitude, won the distinction of being the most offensive."

At the beginning of second semester, trays start disappearing from the dining hall. They're used as sleds on Sunset Hill during Winter Weekend, another of Vassar's long-held traditions. The weekend includes a full slate of activities to welcome students back to the campus including an Air Band contest, dorm tug of wars, and the Motown party.

No student can escape the most raucous of Vassar's traditions, Founder's Day. It's Vassar's closest thing to a Homecoming (minus the big football game; Vassar has an intramural football league that does not compete with other schools), with alums coming back in large numbers to join in the festivities. In April the entire campus comes out to celebrate Matthew Vassar's birthday with a full-scale carnival complete with rides, lots of food, beer, dancing to a top-name band, all ending in an evening fireworks display.

The campus is surrounded by small sets of shops and restaurants. Poughkeepsie is a small city of 72,000 in the heart of the Hudson River Valley. Few students graduate without packing a picnic and seeing the Roosevelt or Vanderbilt mansions in nearby Hyde Park, or taking advantage of skiing and sight-seeing in the nearby Berkshires or the Adirondacks. They also get involved in the surrounding community through field work placements and campus outreach programs, such as Hunger Action and an annual all-campus event that benefits many of Poughkeepsie's nonprofit and social advocacy organizations, called A Step Beyond.

Some Vassar students use their weekends to take advantage of their close proximity to New York City (less than two hours by train), exploring museums, parks, and unlimited entertainment opportunities like dance clubs, concerts, and Broadway plays.

EXTRACURRICULAR ACTIVITIES

There are groups formed for virtually every extracurricular interest at Vassar. And if there isn't one for your special interest, you are encouraged to start your own. There are at least nine campus newspapers covering many different topics, a literary review, and the yearbook, the *Vassarion*. The campus has its own 1000 watt radio station where student and faculty DJs cater to literally every musical taste.

Jewish students, gay, lesbian, and bisexual students, as well as Latino, Asian, International, and African-American are just some of the students that have formed their own social, religious, and political groups. These groups plan a wide variety of events for the whole campus centered around increasing awareness of these groups and their concerns.

A variety of student performance groups are active on campus. Students can perform in a drama production of the Philaletheis Society, dance with the Repertory Dance Theater, or sing with formal choral or *a cappella* groups. Musicians enjoy a similar range of options with a campus orchestra, band, jazz band, and chamber music ensembles.

Athletics are an integral part of the extracurricular offerings whether the student is looking for serious competition or simply a wide variety of options for physical exercise. On the interscholastic level (NCAA Division III), there are 18 varsity teams, nine for men, nine for women. Vassar does not give any athletic scholarships, but seeks to develop in its students a lifelong commitment to fitness and the enjoyment of athletic competition.

Recent highlights of the success of these interscholastic teams: women's tennis received a national ranking for the third year in a row; men's squash ranked twelfth in the nation for *all* schools including Divisions I, II, and III; men's soccer won the ECAC Division III title in the New York/New Jersey region; and the women's volleyball team had its best season ever with a ninth place showing in the New York state tournament.

Walker Field House, built in 1982, contains 42,250 square feet of uninterrupted playing space, conditioning and weight rooms, with Eagle and Nautilus equipment, and a six-lane, 111-foot swimming pool with separate diving well. Kenyon Hall includes squash and racquetball courts as well as two floors of dance studios. Also on the campus are 14 outdoor tennis courts, a nine-hole golf course, playing fields, a quarter-mile all-weather track, and a baseball diamond.

More than 70% of Vassar students participate in intramural sports. Innertube water polo is one of the most popular. Coeducational teams compete in a league whose teams are comprised of groups of friends or members of the same dorm.

"Our team was called Silver Streak, and we competed against the Rubber Duckies and many more teams with inventive names that must be censored here. I often swam in the pool when it was open for night lap swim from 8 to 10 P.M., but during the time of year when innertube water polo was in swing, the pool came alive with activity. Expert swimmers and novices alike looked equally silly trying to maneuver around the pool with their inner tubes sliding around on their stomachs. We weren't out for a division title, after all. This was a great way to be social and get in shape, simultaneously."

GRADUATES

Vassar graduates continue to excel after they leave the college. Pursuing advanced degrees is the most common goal of Vassar graduates. Eighty percent enter advanced degree programs within five years of graduation. Law is the most popular degree pursued followed by medicine, business, and education. In a recent year, 100% of those who applied to medical school were accepted. Clearly, the Vassar degree is well respected in graduate programs across the country.

Vassar graduates going on to employment use the Career Development Office, which maintains detailed files on alumnae/i and their respective fields. The Career Advisory Project (CAP) lists alumnae/i by profession and location who are willing to have students contact them for information and advice in job hunting.

> *"When I started my career in public relations, I had never taken a course directly related to it like Press Release Writing or Marketing 101. In talking to many willing alums, I found out that the broad background I had had at Vassar both in academics and through the experiences I had in event planning would prepare me well for my chosen career path. One of these alums helped get me through the door at one of New York's largest public relations firms where I got a job.*
>
> *"Since working there, I constantly run into Vassar people. By serving on the Career Services Committee of the Vassar Club of New York, I now try to help graduates moving into New York City. We have held panels on many careers including business, nonprofits, and television. I didn't realize how much it would matter when I chose Vassar or even when I graduated, but this tie to a college with distinguished alumnae/i leaders in every field will be an invaluable resource as I continue to develop my career."*

SUMMARY OVERVIEW

The Vassar education combines the contrasting elements of its traditional excellence with a desire to retain the pioneering spirit that gave it its strength.

Traditional excellence in the liberal arts involves a broad-based education with strengths in the basic building blocks of education—an understanding of the English language, arts and literature, laboratory sciences, languages, as well as quantitative studies in mathematics and other related fields.

The pioneering spirit results in many advantages for the Vassar student. You are challenged, in every arena, to develop individual strength of conviction. You choose your own courses. You are expected to develop your own thoughts and express them effectively. Whatever you end up majoring in, your focus will be different from anyone else's. The level of responsibility you are given tests your individual strength in a way that rigid structure cannot.

The coeducational environment is a strength for both men and women. It draws men and women with a desire to create a unique relationship between the sexes. Vassar is not a melting pot where individual differences of gender or anything else are wiped out, rather the diversity is a central part of the strength of a Vassar education.

The physical campus strikes you from the moment you enter underneath Main Gate. The 1000 acres that used to be Matthew Vassar's farm provide tranquility and plenty of room to explore. Because it's not in a major city, the campus location works to unify the independent and varied student body. But, all of this is enhanced by the fact that in less than two hours the Vassar student can be in the middle of New York City with unlimited opportunities for entertainment.

However, Poughkeepsie is also the most often cited negative of Vassar College. A major IBM hub, 75 miles north of New York City, it is hardly a draw to Vassar's cosmopolitan student body. The main attractions are two shopping malls, both of which you must have a car to reach. There is a public bus system in Poughkeepsie but very few Vassar students take advantage of it. Generally speaking, Poughkeepsie is not a college town.

There also are down sides to the independent nature of the college and the student body. Communal life can be hard to come by. Connections are not based on easily identifiable qualities like members of a fraternity or athletic team, but are formed around more esoteric factors such as issues of common concern. If you want structure—academically or socially—it is possible to find it at Vassar, but you'll have to make an effort to seek it out.

The privileges of responsibility and independence have their costs. You should be ready to spend a lot of time and energy making choices. You won't be supplied with easy answers. You will be expected to develop insightful questions. If you feel less challenged than you'd like to be academically or socially, it is your responsibility to help create greater challenges. There are many avenues, but no one is going to force you to take advantage of them.

The balance of traditional ideas of excellence and the drive to be on the cutting edge of thought come together to form the Vassar experience. Being a student at Vassar means being part of an environment concerned with doing it first only when you can do it best. As its past history demonstrates, Vassar often is in a position to do just that.

Jana Rich, A.B.

Wake Forest University

THE PROGRAM

"At dinner, the committee members' inquiries were not unlike those I had encountered at other scholarship competitions and campus interviews. The dean of the college asked the applicants seated at my table a rather general question about our high school experiences. Each of us, with visible anxiety, answered in turn, just before the evening's program began. Three days later, I was shocked to find a handwritten note from the dean in the mail at home. He said that my comment at dinner had left him thoughtful, and asked that I explain further what I meant. Never did I expect the dean to recall our conversation from that awkward evening, much less to take a continuing interest in my thoughts. In astonishment, I wrote a careful reply, to which he promptly responded. That initial dialogue, which evolved into a good friendship, is typical of what set Wake Forest apart from other schools I was considering at the time. Frequent contact between faculty and students at Wake is more the rule than the exception. My friendship with the dean, which started with the interview, was typical of the support I received from many faculty members during my undergraduate years."

Wake Forest University, according to many of its students, curiously combines the best qualities of a small, liberal arts college with a larger university. With a student-to-faculty ratio of around 13 to one, access to professors and to personalized instruction is phenomenal, in the admirable tradition of many smaller institutions. Unlike those schools, however, Wake Forest offers full graduate programs in the arts and sciences, as well as professional degrees in law, medicine, and business management. The school fields teams of Demon Deacons at the highest level of intercollegiate athletics against many major universities. Yet all of its buildings lie within easy walking distance across familiar and beautiful grounds. The idea of community has been important since Baptists founded the school in 1834, and the university's president still greets all incoming freshmen in a single afternoon. But fear not—with about 3500 undergraduates (50% men, 50% women), everyone does not know you, nor what you did last weekend.

Wake maintains a passionate commitment to the ideal of a liberal education, which is the open pursuit of learning for its own sake. This does not mean that none of its majors has any practical import—in fact, the most popular field of study is business. But even future accountants and physicists must grapple with courses in religion and philosophy. No specialized technical degrees exist—to graduate in engineering, you have to spend two years studying elsewhere. The classical roots of Wake's educational philosophy run deep. Although almost no one pursues them, Latin and Greek still are offered as majors. Undergraduates who examine power and policy in society study politics, not political science, betraying that department's partiality to ideas over statistics. In the undergraduate college, outside the School of Business and Accountancy, the strongest academic programs traditionally are English and history. Many other fields also attract a significant number of majors, including psychology, biology, economics, politics, communication, and theater arts. In general, the student body is spread rather evenly across a range of disciplines, most of which are very strong. No single department is known as the place to be.

> *"I came to Wake Forest from only two hours away. Several other students from my high school traveled that short distance with me, and I had some concerns that the road might be too easy, the company too familiar. Wake Forest, after all, was a known commodity, or so I thought. I had always considered it a North Carolina Baptist school, and I assumed the student body would reflect this. Yet in many ways, it did not. When I arrived, my roommates were from West Virginia and Florida. There were more students from New Jersey than South Carolina, and as many Catholics as Baptists. This diversity surprised and impressed me, and it seemed only to increase over the years—my younger sister's roommate was from El Salvador."*

Wake Forest's roots are in the South, and signs of its North Carolina Baptist heritage live on, some in reality, some only in folklore. Magnolia trees still grace the campus, and friendly greetings abound, but "you guys" is almost as commonly heard as "y'all." The steeple of Wait Chapel, home to a local Baptist congregation, still towers over the central quadrangle, but attendance has not been mandatory for decades. Campus officials still keep a somewhat watchful eye over parties, but students today protest keg limits, not a ban on dancing, as they did in the 1950s. Images of fraternity guys, sporting Ray-Bans, khakis, and blue blazers, and flocking to football games with their carefully dressed dates, describe what some consider the typical Wake Forest student of old: white, southern, upper-middle class. Though still accurate in corners of the campus, these stereotypes no longer fit as comfortably as they once may have. Wake Forest today is a place of increasing diversity—students from 48 states and 28 countries stroll along the Magnolia Court, enjoying the school's relaxed, southern atmosphere.

Like much of the populace these days, many students tend to be politically conservative, perhaps more so than at some larger universities. When Wake hosted the most recent presidential debate, for example, Republican signs outnumbered Democratic ones in dorm windows. Students organized and participated actively in that national political event, but the prevailing attitude toward politics tends to be one of indifference. Perhaps in reaction to this general apathy, a number of students actively seek to build alternatives, and a plurality of associations exists, lobbying for causes as diverse as the pro-life movement and South African divestment.

The campus itself is set among the woods and meadows of North Carolina's Piedmont, on an expansive tract of land dotted by trails, streams, and gardens. The administration takes great (and some say excessive) pride in the harmony of the School's Georgian architecture and the natural beauty of its meticulously landscaped grounds. Many were surprised a few years ago when a memorial service was held for the towering trees of the quadrangle, which, after 40 years of majestic beauty, fell victim to Dutch elm disease and were removed. In sincerity, a handful of students and administrators offered poems and personal tributes to the great elms under their canopy, just before they were replaced by puny, hopeful saplings. All of this attention to the appearance of the campus may seem odd, but the net effect can be stunning on a beautiful day, especially with the colorful blooms of spring or brilliant leaves of autumn.

The university is located in Winston-Salem, a city of 150,000 residents. As its name suggests, Winston-Salem is best known as the original home of the R. J. Reynolds Tobacco Company. The generosity of the Reynolds family was instrumental in bringing the school to Winston-Salem in 1956 from its original location in the small town of (you guessed it) Wake Forest, North Carolina. Winston-Salem is not the reason most students choose to attend Wake Forest. The city does, however, offer numerous attractions, many of which go undiscovered, because little is directly adjacent to the campus. All students can have cars, and those who venture beyond the grounds enjoy a decent variety of clubs, parks, shops, and restaurants. For its size, Winston-Salem also has a thriving arts community, with a major performing arts center, The North Carolina School of the Arts, a city symphony, and two excellent art museums. The city also is located conveniently within easy striking distance of North Carolina's fantastic beaches and mountains, both of which are popular for weekend jaunts.

In this suburban setting, Wake Forest unites the best attributes of a small college and a large university. The combination is unusual, even in comparison to other southern institutions that claim many of the same advantages. Like Davidson, for example, Wake provides incredible access to an excellent faculty, but does so with well over twice the number of students. With its strong regional roots, Wake claims a southern tradition of friendliness and community, not unlike Washington and Lee, but it also offers the excitement of ACC sports. Like Duke, Wake Forest has graduate and professional schools, but none of its faculty in the arts and sciences escape their primary responsibility—to teach undergraduates—behind mountains of research. With superior facilities and a beautiful campus as well, Wake Forest's blend of big and small is difficult to surpass.

GETTING IN/FINANCIAL AID

Wake Forest recently has enjoyed a considerable amount of positive publicity, ranking first in its category for seven consecutive years in a *U.S. News and World Report* survey, and being favorably evaluated in several college guides and reviews, based on student selectivity, academics, and overall value. As a result, the number of applications received has grown steadily, and currently stands at more than 5900. Out of this pool, slightly over 40% are admitted, and roughly 35% of those decide to enroll. Average SAT I scores also have climbed. The middle 50% of the freshman class achieved a combined score of between 1150 and 1300. Admissions counselors stress that SAT I scores are not their primary yardstick of academic ability. High school performance is extremely important, as is the relative difficulty of courses taken at that level.

Administrators and faculty members alike note with pride that the academic potential and preparedness of each freshman class seems to rise as the school's reputation improves. Admission is most competitive academically: approximately 80% of all applicants rank in the top 10% of their high school classes. Yet in making its decision, Wake's admissions staff looks for a broad range of qualities, including leadership, extracurricular activities, and musical or artistic ability. Students come to Wake from across the nation, and because the school is private, those from outside North Carolina are at no disadvantage. In fact, the school has announced its intention to continue seeking geographical diversity, and international applicants are welcomed. On average, 30% of the student body does not call North Carolina home, through a deliberate decision of the university. The administration has decided to work actively to increase the number of minority students at Wake Forest. This move was called for and applauded by many members of the university community, and efforts have begun to pay off: black students made up 8% of this year's freshman class.

> *"Wake Forest has always prided itself as a bargain among schools of comparable quality. My suitemate from Pennsylvania, for example, chose Wake over Bucknell and Lehigh because it then cost almost half as much. I went to several administrators with my concerns, and was reassured at every turn that the school's commitment to meeting the financial need of any admitted student was firm, and that all revenues above costs*

from the tuition hikes were reserved for financial aid and faculty pay. They showed me how financial aid expenditures had risen more rapidly than tuition in recent years. I must admit their case was convincing. I tried to find students with aid packages who feared that the cost increase would jeopardize their position, but encountered few complaints. The aid system seemed solid, and the silence on tuition increases seemed to make sense."

Even with rising tuition, Wake Forest is still a bargain. Few private liberal arts institutions of similar reputation can match its price tag, which is currently $18,115. Tuition is comparatively low in part because of Wake's extraordinary endowment, which subsidizes the cost of educating each student. The university controls assets of over $336 million, and is one of the wealthiest schools of its size in the nation. Though Wake is inexpensive in comparative terms, its fees still exceed the means of many families. Any regularly admitted student who demonstrates financial need will receive assistance commensurate with that need. Roughly one-quarter of the student body receives need-based aid. A number of generous academic and honor scholarships also are available, several of which include exciting opportunities to obtain summer grants for individually designed study and travel projects. Overall, awards for merit and need range from $500 to $16,000. In short, the admissions office claims that any admitted student who wants to come to Wake can do so: its admission policy is need-blind.

ACADEMIC ENVIRONMENT

"As an alternative to introductory courses, Wake offered a few classes each semester in interdisciplinary honors, designed to encourage independent and critical thinking in a way that survey courses cannot. Like most freshmen, I was hesitant to venture too far from the standard curriculum, unsure of what I might find. My faculty adviser, however, convinced me to give honors a shot—it was, he said, one of Wake's most innovative and exciting programs. I chose a class that examined three figures from different fields and historical periods and searched for common threads. Twice a week, two faulty members and 16 students gathered informally to discuss Thomas Jefferson, George Eliot, and Igor Stravinsky in unusual depth. In turn, every student wrote one paper on each of the three figures. We were completely free to develop our topics. The only suggestion was to be provocative, since class time was devoted almost solely to the presentation and critique of our papers. The discussions, often invigorating, were led by the students as much as the professors. Never had I been so stimulated by the open and informal exchange of ideas— it felt like what college should be."

Though not all students participate in it, the interdisciplinary honors program symbolizes what is best about the overall academic environment at Wake. Students are encouraged to think creatively and independently in small class settings. Faculty members are expected to emphasize teaching as much as, if not more than, personal research. At Wake, no teaching assistants stand behind the lectern, struggling to balance the demands of undergraduate instruction and graduate study. Even tenured faculty members teach introductory surveys, and many attempt to learn the name of each freshman in the class. During its long relationship with the Baptist Church, which officially ended in 1986, Wake Forest fiercely defended its academic independence. The school protected what it found most admirable in the Baptist tradition: the principles of intellectual freedom and local autonomy. This spirit endures in the classroom, where open inquiry still is prized. Wake's commitment to academic excellence goes beyond the admission brochure. Faculty expectations are high, and students work hard. Rarely are there parties or other social events on weekdays—there just isn't time. Standards are tough, and grade inflation is nonexistent. A number of students do excel. Four have earned Rhodes scholarships in the past seven years.

The strength of the academic program lies in the diversity of its requirements. All Wake graduates receive a liberal education, no mater what their major. In addition to one course each from history, religion, and philosophy, everyone must select three courses from each of the following categories: literature and the arts, the natural sciences and mathematics, and the social and behavioral sciences. The school also places an unusual emphasis on foreign languages. Students must complete courses in one language through the literature level. This, of course does not mean that everyone achieves proficiency, but even the premed student who slides through literature in silence worrying about organic chemistry gains valuable exposure. Japanese, Chinese, and Russian are all offered, in addition to more standard lingual fare. Overall, the requirements are rigorous and take up most of one's freshman and sophomore years. They are not, however, inflexible. Advanced placement credits are accepted by many departments, and interdisciplinary courses in honors or the humanities can substitute for certain requirements. Students of exceptional ability with an exceptional sense of purpose can apply for and design an open curriculum with faculty consent. At the end of the road for everyone is a liberal arts education, but there are a variety of ways to get there. Consistent with the school's ideal of personalized instruction, all freshmen are assigned a faculty and a student adviser to guide them through the maze.

Wake Forest is a very wealthy institution, and its students benefit from this. The school's educational facilities are excellent. The library contains over 1.1 million volumes, far more than most universities of comparable size. A new wing on the library has increased its capacity by 40%. The school recently has taken significant steps to improve the natural sciences by renovating the chemistry building, adding on to the biology hall, and putting up a new physics laboratory, complete with a laser lab of superior quality. Construction is, however, ending on the campus. The Graduate Schools of Law and Management soon will move to a new professional center, the largest building on campus and the first joint facility of its kind in the nation. In the process, their old locations will be left to the undergraduate college for additional office and classroom space. All of this will happen without an increase in enrollment.

Outside the classroom, the library, and the lab, students enjoy a number of special academic events sponsored by faculty and friends of the university. Lecture series regularly bring distinguished academics, poets, politicians, and business leaders to the campus, and scholarly symposiums on a range of topics are not uncommon. If all the offerings on campus are not quite stimulating enough, go abroad—the school encourages you to do so. International studies is a burgeoning field at Wake Forest, and an unusual number of foreign study programs is available. Wake owns incredible houses in the Hampstead area of London and on the Grand Canal of Venice. Each semester, a different faculty member selects a small group of students to go to each of these centers. At both locations, the art history instruction is exceptionally strong, and a long parade of Wake students has taken advantage of these proven programs. Faculty members also direct semesters in Dijon, France and Salamanca, Spain, where students live with local families. Recently, the school has arranged direct exchanges with Moscow University in Russia and Tokai University in Japan. Students who prefer to study abroad independently can do so with some effort. Though strict, many departments will allow transfer credits, and independent study projects can be designed. In a foreign country, learning is experiential as well as academic, and Wake encourages students to gain invaluable exposure to one of many cultures.

SOCIAL LIFE

"Like many of my classmates, I spent my freshman year checking out the social scene on campus, trying to decide if the advantages of Greek life were worth what I feared might be the costs. To encourage friendships in the dorms, no freshmen were allowed to rush during their first semester, but many of my friends did pledge in the spring. I decided to sit tight, still hesitant to isolate myself to one group of people and to carry the labels that often seemed to come with Greek letters. During that spring semester, however, I saw that at Wake, Greek life does not at all imply a distance from campus activities and diverse friendships. Fraternities and societies are not isolated away from campus. Their houses are merely the corners of the dorms, and all students eat together in the main cafeteria, known as the Pit. In the fall of my sophomore year, I pledged and until graduation enjoyed time with friends both within and without the fraternity."

Greek organizations at Wake Forest have an unusually high profile, and much of the most visible social life on campus revolves exclusively around their activities. By reserving lounges for them in the residence halls, the school is able to monitor fraternities and societies and keep them in the mainstream of campus life. In general, Greeks live next door to independents all over campus, and relations between the two are relaxed. Roughly 40% of undergraduate men belong to fraternities. A slightly larger percentage of women are Greeks, but at Wake, most belong to societies, not sororities. Four national sororities are active, and are growing each year. Instead of Kappa Delta and Chi Omega, Greek women at Wake wear sweatshirts reading Fideles, Lynks, Strings, and Sophs, among other unrecognizable (and inexplicable) names. On a typical weekend, there are several fraternity parties. Most are open to all students, and many are good, with dancing for all and beer for those over age twenty-one. Students tend to stay on campus for the weekends and make the rounds, often going to three different parties without walking more than a few hundred feet.

Because most of it is concentrated on campus, Greek life is misleadingly visible at Wake. Huge letters are plastered across the dorms, and on nice days, groups of fraternity guys hang out on their respective walls along the central Quad to catch some sun, or just to see and be seen. Most of the students that pass by, however, are independents. Frats and societies seem to be everywhere, but are in fact a minority. Independents sometimes complain that social life on campus is monopolized by Greeks. In response, the school has tried to offer alternatives, such as open residence hall parties, complete with bands and beer. These initiatives have met with encouraging success, but breaking established patterns can be difficult.

Because all their activities are planned, social life for Greeks may be easier, but not better. Wake Forest and Winston-Salem both offer no shortage of exciting activities to students who look for them. Excellent movies, concerts, and theater productions all are available regularly on campus. Winston-Salem itself is dotted by a variety of good nightspots for students and locals, offering everything from honky-tonk to progressive music. Along with Duke, North Carolina, and N.C. State, Wake Forest sits on tobacco road, the name given the region in recognition of its devotion to college basketball, a devotion that often borders on obsession. Scores of students turn out for ACC basketball and football games, wearing gold and black and screaming "Go Deacs!" Wake is the second smallest school competing in Division I sports, and its teams' records sometimes reflect this. Perhaps because they are unexpected, all wins in basketball and football are celebrated by blanketing the campus with a sea of toilet paper. Whatever the outcome, student and alumni enthusiasm remains strong in all seasons, and games are a regular part of the community's life.

EXTRACURRICULAR ACTIVITIES

At Wake Forest, as at most schools, the number of extracurricular activities is limited only by the imagination and drive of the students. Those at Wake have set up an impressive array of organizations and clubs, offering something for almost every taste and inclination. Suffice it to say that whatever your interest—be it dance or rugby, rock climbing or singing, theater or journalism—you can find, or if need be create, a niche at Wake Forest.

Many of the activities resemble those at other schools. Scores of undergraduates participate in the Student Union, a conglomerate of committees that manages lectures, films, concerts, and a variety of special events. Residence house councils organize life in the dorms and sponsor numerous social functions, especially for freshmen. The *Old Gold & Black,* a weekly student paper, focuses on campus news but often is a forum for broader debates. Concert bands and choirs practice and perform regularly, and students act in a series of major stage productions each year.

Established organizations such as these are standard fare at most schools and form the core of extracurricular activities at Wake Forest. Yet more unusual and in some ways more exciting are the small, less visible groups that dot the campus. Some, like the Anthropology Club and Circolo Italiano, evolve out of academic pursuits, whereas others, such as the Volunteer Student Corps, reflect a commitment to community service. Some, like Amnesty International and College Republicans, are grounded in politics, others, such as Intervarsity and the Wesley Foundation, in spirituality. The roots of still others remain obscure, but all are connected by the sparks of interest that create and sustain them.

One quality that may distinguish Wake Forest from other larger institutions is the extent of student input into the governance of the school. The university places a consistent emphasis on open consultation among faculty, students, and administrators. At its best, student input is active and influential. At its worst, such participation is for appearances only. Whatever the outcome, the opportunity for meaningful participation is undeniable. Students serve on the Board of Trustees, faculty committees, and advisory commissions. A group of presidential aides accompanies the president to official functions, representing the student body and serving as a channel of communication. The principle of self-governance is at the core of the system of student government. Students elected to judicial boards enforce the honor system and rules that govern campus life, often judging and sentencing their classmates in the process. Representatives in the student government legislature and its officers control the funds available to organizations on campus and issue regular policy recommendations to the administration, most of which are subsequently executed. Some students are skeptical about the amount of influence they hold, but on a range of issues—as narrow as visitation policies and as broad as race relations—students have voiced their opinion and shaped the course of change.

In extracurriculars as in academics, Wake Forest's superb facilities are an advantage for its students. Construction in 1990 of the Benson Student Center, described by some faculty as the pleasure dome, created an unprecedented amount of space for student activities. Films are shown nightly in its cushy new theater. Bands perform in the Food Court (a welcome alternative to the traditional cafeteria, the Pit), while students munch on the fast food pizzas and burritos they can now purchase on their meal plans. Several major student organizations have moved their offices into the Benson Center and now enjoy equipment and space to which they never before had access. Athletic facilities are magnificent for individual students and teams at the varsity, club, and intramural levels. In addition to an aging, but adequate gym and numerous playing fields, the school recently has built tennis and soccer stadiums, as well as a new exercise and weight center open to all students, not just the varsity athletes.

RESIDENCE LIFE

"When I visited friends at Chapel Hill and other large universities, I found most were living in apartment complexes somewhat removed from the central campus. I soon realized that this kind of distance was typical at most schools, especially among upperclassmen. Nonetheless, I was always surprised by how far most of my friends lived from campus, and by how few students they regularly saw, despite the size of their enrollments.

"At Wake Forest, by contrast, almost everyone seems to live on campus. All undergraduates are guaranteed housing, but only freshmen are required to take it. Everyone else chooses to do so. The immense popularity of on-campus housing is not due to any shortage of apartments in the area. Students have a good time in the residence halls. Few want to give up the constant contact with friends or the convenience of proximity. Whatever the rationale, Wake students enjoy life on campus and are hesitant to leave it. To me, this always seemed to capture the best of the community."

University housing at Wake is overwhelmingly popular. Some 85% of all undergraduates live on campus for all four years. Unfortunately, this is not because of the size of the rooms. Most are comfortable, but rather small; some singles can be tiny, and are aptly named the cracker box. Many residence halls are divided into suites of four or five rooms, one of which often is left open as a lounge. Others are organized into halls or floors in more standard fashion. Many of the residence halls are now coed, and visitation policies have been relaxed over recent years, much to the delight of students who are tired of breaking the rules. Cable television outlets are provided to all rooms across campus. Students voted for cable installation in a referendum, defending all the educational ends toward which such equipment could be used, and then, predictably, turned into the movie channels and ESPN.

The university offers a variety of alternatives to standard housing arrangements, most notably in the form of theme houses. The school purchased homes that surround the campus and invited groups of students to create themes with the informal sponsorship of a faculty member. The responses have been imaginative. In addition to several well-established language houses, themes have included religion, culinary arts, African American, and women's studies. Students are free to design and submit their own themes, reflecting their academic or extracurricular interests. Many participants have enjoyed the experience, and the popularity of such programs will likely continue. On campus, one alternative residence hall exists. This is Huffman House, the so-called academic hall, where many scholarship students and others choose to live. In the words of its residents, Huffman is a community unto itself, known around campus for being enthusiastic and a bit eccentric. There is an increasing trend toward a substance-free living environment at Wake Forest with approximately 400 first-year and upperclass students selecting this living option.

GRADUATES

"When deciding among different schools, I paid unusual attention to subtle impressions. After investigating a range of possibilities, I finally narrowed my choices to Wake Forest and Duke, two institutions I had long admired. While visiting Winston-Salem and speaking to alumni, I was struck at once by the enthusiasm with which Wake graduates described their alma mater and encouraged me to become a Demon Deacon. Their emotional link to the university was immediate, their ties to area alumni strong. I noticed the same was not true at Duke, where several North Carolina alumni, though proud of their school's accomplishments, felt distanced during Duke's drive for national prominence. Wake Forest graduates evoke a sense of family, a sense of having shared something special. This, at least, was my impression, and I realize now that it shaped my decision to attend the school."

Deacon alumni return to Wake for reunions from all walks of life. The school has no comprehensive record of what professions its graduates pursue in what numbers, but any such list certainly would be varied. Liberal arts training prepares students to do almost anything, and over the years, Wake alumni probably have covered the spectrum.

Immediately after graduation, over half of the students enter the business world directly, typically pursuing careers in banking, accountancy, sales, or consultancy, in cities such as Charlotte, Atlanta, and Washington, D.C. Approximately 300 companies and organizations recruit Wake students every year. Seniors smartly dressed in dark suits and skirts stroll nervously toward Reynolda Hall for interviews, conspicuously trying not to appear conspicuous. Another third of the graduating class relies on a solid liberal arts background to pursue advanced study in graduate and professional schools. Wake Forest is a good place to prepare for a career in law or medicine, and many students enter the fields of education and government/social service. And of course, there is always the remainder of undecided graduates. Some career paths are traditional, others are not. The point is that you have a real choice, because a Wake Forest diploma prepares and enables students to do what they want.

SUMMARY OVERVIEW

Wake Forest, in short, is a fantastic school—its strengths are numerous. The university is in many ways a caring community. Even visitors comment regularly on the school's friendly atmosphere. Students interact in a close-knit environment, with social life and housing arrangements both centered on the school's beautiful grounds. Contact with faculty and administrators often is personal, and access to their offices virtually is unlimited for students who seek to know their professors outside of the classroom.

These are the advantages of a small school, and students at Wake appreciate them. Yet Wake students also have access to excellent facilities unusual at an institution of this size. The library, the student center, the science labs, the athletic facilities, and other buildings all contribute to the quality of life on campus, both academic and extracurricular. The school's enrollment is small by many standards, but its students enjoy the resources and activities of a larger university, including the excitement of Division I sports.

The real reason to come to Wake Forest, however, is for the education it offers. This is not just the advice of earnest, naive parents. Every student at Wake graduates with a solid background in the liberal arts, with exposure to a range of disciplines, each of which perceives the world through a different lens, a different set of assumptions. Understanding how these fields relate to each other, how they diverge and connect, is the essence of a liberal education. At Wake, with initiative, one can achieve it. Professors are eager to teach—that, after all, is their primary mission. This commitment to quality instruction makes the faculty Wake's greatest resource. Expectations are high and work loads heavy, but the doors to professors' offices always are open. The result is an intense, personal academic program with an incredible amount to offer students who are eager to learn.

A few of Wake's apparent advantages may constitute negatives for some prospective students. The school has the feel of a small campus, a self-contained community. Students who seek a broader environment, a place to be anonymous and independent, may find Wake a bit restrictive in terms of size. Despite increasing diversity in the student body, Wake remains today a predominantly southern institution. This atmosphere accounts for part of the school's charm but students who seek a university of unlimited diversity with no discernible regional identity may prefer to look elsewhere.

Wake is a caring community, where administrators and faculty often take an interest in the development of students. Yet at times, their concern has been viewed as excessive. Students have taken exception with certain regulations, especially in the social sphere. Although many rules, such as those governing visitation, have been revised, several unpopular regulations remain in place. Among these is a rule which forces all parties in the dorms to close officially at 1:00 A.M. Conflict over such issues perhaps is inevitable, because so much of social life is centered on campus. Despite the regulations, students tend to do exactly what they want, and rarely do they get in trouble for it. Yet those who value freedom over community may prefer a larger institution where social regulations are nonexistent.

Social life is dominated by fraternities and societies, and students who seek to escape that scene have some difficulty doing so on campus. In Winston-Salem, however, there are a number of alternatives to campus activities, but a city of 150,000 will never have the cultural diversity of Manhattan or San Francisco. If a big city environment is important to you, don't come to Winston-Salem.

If, on the other hand, a beautiful campus with first-rate academics and a friendly atmosphere sounds interesting, do come to Wake Forest. There you will find a rigorous liberal arts curriculum, personalized instruction, and superior facilities, all within a vibrant, close-knit community of students and faculty. The school joins the best of both larger and smaller institutions in a remarkable mix. If this combination seems exciting, give Wake Forest a visit—you won't be disappointed.

Jay Smith, B.A.

Washington and Lee University

THE PROGRAM

Washington and Lee University, a small liberal arts college nestled in the middle of Virginia's lush Shenandoah Valley, is something of a schizophrenic place. Not really quite one thing, nor another, W&L (that's pronounced "Dub' yun ell") really is two things at once. The school benefits from a fortunate and fruitful tug-of-war between a faculty that emphasizes broad-based, liberal arts learning and a pragmatic student body interested in utility and preprofessionalism. Thus, via a system of mutual give-and-take, a W&L student gets the best of both worlds. Here's what I mean.

First, the school offers a rich and exciting curriculum of more than 800 courses and 42 possible majors. If you can't find a major to your liking, you're free to design your own—hey, it's your education. Moreover, the school's flexible yet inclusive general education requirements guarantee that every W&L student learns at least something about basically everything. Because that's what liberal arts education is all about—*liberal*, as in liberated and free of constraints.

And yet, placed harmoniously in the middle of all this, is the School of Commerce, which really is just a business school with a funny name. Then again, being one of the top 25 business schools in the country (the whole country, period), it is hardly just a business school. The C-School, as we call it, offers preprofessional degrees in economics, business administration, and marketing, and boasts a faculty that is as distinguished as it is approachable.

There's more. Robert E. Lee, in his short but influential tenure as college president, established the country's first School of Journalism, and to this day the J-School has managed to maintain its first status in more ways than one, offering degrees in both print and broadcast media. Even if you don't major in journalism, make sure you take a class from Edwin P. Yoder, Pulitzer Prize-winning journalist, syndicated columnist for *The Washington Post* writers' group.

"Due to the fact that I was working on an honors thesis my senior year, I scored a locked study carrel in the university library. I was the only person on campus besides the library custodian who had a key. Not that that mattered much—Washington and Lee's Honor System pretty much renders all keys, save those for your car, obsolete. In my carrel I had a desk, a lounge chair, a spitoon, an endless stack of books, and a personal computer. That's right: I kept my computer in the university library. What's more, I left the door open most of the time—a friend might come by while I was in the snack bar, or someone might need one of my books. I used to spend entire nights in my carrel, either at the computer or asleep in my lounge chair. Entire nights.

"Did I mention that the library was open 24 hours a day?"

When he came to the school after the Civil War, Robert E. Lee tossed out the rule book and replaced it with this one admonition: Every student will conduct himself as a complete gentleman. That means a W&L student does not cheat, he does not steal, and he does not lie. Of course, the term W&L gentleman has been rendered a quaint anachronism: these days, honor no longer is gender specific. But otherwise Lee's ideals hold true today. If a student commits an honor violation and is found guilty, he/she is quietly and confidentially released from the school. It's that simple.

For the overwhelming majority of W&L students, however, the Honor System makes for positively ideal living conditions—virtually unique on college campuses in this country. Students schedule their own exams and take them unproctored. All buildings, including the library, are open 24 hours a day. You can leave your books in the dining hall and return the next day to find them exactly where you left them. And a W&L student's honor is good all over town: I once wrote a check for $1.50 at a local convenience store.

This feeling of implicit trust and openness influences every aspect of student life. The school has a student-to-faculty ratio of 11.5 to one and it is nearly impossible to go four years without ever eating a home-cooked meal at a professor's house. Moreover, not a single facility at W&L is closed to you—you have free access, at virtually any time, to an indoor swimming pool, racquetball and handball courts, and outdoor athletic fields. More than 130 computers are available 24 hours a day; you don't need an access card, you don't have to pay for computer time—hell, you don't even have to pay for paper.

It's true that a lot of students are from the South, but what do you expect? The school *is* in Virginia. On the other hand you'd be surprised by how large, say, is the Pennsylvania/New York delegation. But here's another schizophrenic thing about W&L: despite the fact that people come from all over and possess a diverse jumble of interests, the student body as a whole is remarkably unified. Everybody basically knows everybody else. One reason for this is the fact that even the most buttoned-down business student will end up in the English department at least once. And every diehard English major will at one point wander through the C-School. Everybody has something to teach everyone else.

But what really inspires this unity is the school's warm sense of community. Imagine being able to trust *everybody*. With anything. You can bet barriers come down. And because everything is open all the time, the campus bustles round-the-clock. At 4 A.M. you're likely to find economic majors in the English department pouring down jugs of coffee and pages of Keynes, biology majors reconstructing weird viruses with a Grateful Dead bootleg blaring in the background, and journalism majors losing their marbles in the video editing lab.

The campus is situated in the middle of the Shenandoah Valley and is framed by an absolutely gorgeous stretch of mountains. To get to the campus proper, you have to go by foot, behind the freshman dorms. There you'll encounter the front campus which, to the rest of the country, is a National Historic Landmark and, to the W&L student, is simply the Hill. A breathtaking stretch of eighteenth century red-brick buildings adorned with stately white columns, the Hill is where all the learning gets done. More importantly (depending on your priorities), the Hill looks out upon a broad expanse of grass that on fall afternoons is the site of Frisbee football games and sack tournaments and in the spring becomes Sunbathing Central for sun worshippers of all walks of life.

All this, and great weather to boot: Fall will take your breath, winter is, well… *winter*, and spring is sheer heaven. Your best bet is to do as much of your partying as possible out-of-doors (uh, yes: W&L students do their share of partying): Not only can you enjoy the beautiful surroundings, but you also can let everyone know you are a true W&L Mink—a term I never quite understood exactly, but one that seems to mean, "A person who knows a good time and never lets on that he/she studies like hell." It's all there—academics, social activities, extracurriculars—and every facet characterized by openness, trust, and a powerful sense of community. It's like no other school in the country.

GETTING IN/FINANCIAL AID

Washington and Lee always has been a first-rate school; the only problem was, no one seemed to know it. The Best Kept Secret of the South is a dubious honor, I suppose. But when the doors were opened to women, the secret got out and now the university is far and away one of the hottest tickets in the country. Applications have soared. So have test scores. But W&L remains pretty much the same place it's always been.

Of course when applications are high, that means W&L can be selective. In fact, W&L is one of the choosiest schools in the country. Just about everyone who gets accepted was a high school class leader, a student athlete, or a newspaper editor; everyone is plenty smart. High school rank is in the top 12% and grade averages clock in at A to B+. Two-thirds of the students graduated from public schools and one-third are from private schools. None of this seems to matter after about a semester or two; by the time you become a sophomore, you'll find that everyone has pretty much forgotten what high school was like.

The admissions office receives about 3600 applications a year; a little over 1050 of these prospects get accepted, out of which an estimated 440 actually will attend. That's pretty stiff competition. So how do you set yourself apart from that stack of 3600 hopefuls?

At the bare minimum, you need to get your application in by January 15. In addition, you also must take SAT I and three SAT II exams, including Writing. Normally, you want to get these out of the way no later than December of your senior year. As an alternate method, you can take the ACT and that will cover both the SAT I and SAT II requirement. Your choice.

> *"I wouldn't advise this for anybody, but I arrived at W&L for orientation week having never seen the place. My parents borrowed a van from a friend and we made a little family trip of the whole affair, but I was terrified, no way to get around it. As we drove onto campus, however, all I saw were young people unpacking books, tennis rackets, record albums—each of them with the 'my scared look' on their face. And one look at the Hill dispelled any fears I might have had that I had been sold a bill of goods.*
>
> *"In the space of two weeks I had dinner with my advisor, got recruited for the newspaper, stunned myself by joining a fraternity, spent a Friday night in Washington D.C., acquired a girlfriend, got swamped in schoolwork, and put on a couple of pounds. Sometime in the middle of September, my parents somehow tracked me down and wondered why I hadn't called. 'Golly,' I said, sincerely astonished, 'has it been two weeks already?"'*

Washington and Lee won't mean that much to you if you don't get involved in a wide variety of campus activities—and the admissions people know that. On the whole the admissions office looks for leadership and *chutzpah*—they want people who take charge and get involved. They also want people who will thrive in an environment geared for high achievers. For instance, did you take advantage of all the academic opportunities offered at your high school—this includes AP programs, honors programs, and so on? Did you get involved in a *variety* of extracurriculars? Have you distinguished yourself as a leader? These are the kinds of things that will count.

About 35% of the student body are on some form of financial aid, and each case is decided on an individual basis. A typical package might include a loan, a grant, or a scholarship, some work-study, and so on. The school's financial aid budget exceeds $2.2 million, which simply means if you really need financial aid, you'll get it. But remember: with $18,700 a year tuition, Washington and Lee is a low cost private school, one of the best college values in the country.

Virginia residents only make up about 14% of the student body—people literally hail from all over. The school strives for, and steadily is achieving, broad diversity. Women, who only have been at the school for seven years, already make up 40% of the student body. And the percentage of minority students is increasing at a favorable rate.

ACADEMIC ENVIRONMENT

As you know, you cannot cheat, steal, or lie at Washington and Lee. But other than that, everything else basically is free game. A relatively small school of about 1600 undergraduates, W&L is committed to the ideals of a liberal education—i.e., knowledge for *knowledge's* sake—so usually it's a good idea to keep your mind open when you arrive. If you have it closed, however, the professors will be happy to open it for you.

> *"First paper for my first English class of my first semester: I figured, hey, piece of cake. I mean, I was editor of my high school newspaper, for Pete's sake. The paper was on Mark Twain's* Pudd'nhead Wilson *and I chose to examine, in five pages, Twain's attitude toward the South at the time of the book's publication. I had quotations, a footnote or two, the word 'textuality' in the opening paragraph—I was set. When I dropped the paper on Professor Duvall's desk I think I winked, conspiratorially.*
>
> *"Severn Duvall was a sixty-year-old sage with a shock of longish gray hair, eyes that could bore a hole through granite, and an aristocratic southern accent fresh out of* Gone With the Wind. *Put simply, I was terrified of the guy. But I thought I had it made it with my* Pudd'nhead Wilson *paper, what with my keen understanding of the southern* milieu *(a new word I had just learned). Next class period I got the paper back and Duvall's comments read roughly as follows: 'Too poorly written to really assess your argument, what there is of one.' Grade: D.*
>
> *"Welcome to Washington and Lee."*

W&L boasts an 800 course catalogue—an astonishingly rich offering for such a small school. From there, you can choose from 42 majors, many of them cross-discipline. Basically, students follow one or more of three paths: liberal arts, commerce and business, or the natural sciences. The school of journalism and mass communications, moreover, is the oldest as well as one of the best of its kind in the country, offering degrees in both print and broadcast media.

The first thing pretty much everyone takes is freshman composition. Although a four or five on your AP test can test you out of English comp, you still have to take two more literature classes before you leave, so don't assume you can escape writing papers. For high school you probably *can* write, but college is a different story entirely. And it doesn't matter what you major in—if you're a history, biology, journalism, or economics major, you are going to have to formulate ideas clearly and concisely at every juncture.

Those two literature classes are part of your general education requirements, one of the hallmarks of W&L's liberal arts emphasis. All told, you have 30 GERs, scattered all over campus. The lineup goes something like this:

two years of a foreign language (During freshman orientation you can try and test out of part or all of the first year);

12 credits from at least two of the following: fine arts, history, philosophy, and religion;

ten credits in math and natural science, including a lab;

nine credits from the social sciences: economics, politics, psychology, and journalism.

Around 90% of the faculty hold doctorate degrees (that's just about everybody, by the way), but that does not at all mean these people are unapproachable. Sure, W&L snags their share of luminaries—Pulitzer Prize winner Ed Yoder, award-winning poet Dabney Stuart—but every one of these luminaries is at Washington and Lee for one thing: to teach. You'll never encounter a graduate assistant in any of your classes because there are no graduate assistants. Department heads even take their turn teaching introductory and survey classes. By *choice.*

And because the place is so small, you can get to know every one of your professors personally: rest assured, each of your professors will get to know *you.* Classes hardly ever exceed 20 members—most clock in at ten or 11 people. It's no surprise, then, that a deep sense of camaraderie develops between teachers and students. Drinking with profs, for instance, is a time-honored tradition at W&L, exuberantly upheld by both parties.

> *"After that* Pudd'nhead Wilson *paper, you can bet Duvall had my attention. I attended his class with religious devotion, white-knuckling the side of my desk, trying to take it all in. Duvall was the most exhilarating teacher I had ever encountered—he seemed to have read everything, made me want to read everything, pulled stuff out of me in class I didn't even know I had. A senior English major who was close friends with Duvall pulled me aside during the writing of my second paper and pointed out everything I was doing wrong. I was stunned on two accounts: one, why was this guy wasting his time on me, a lowly freshman; two, how does one become friends with…well, Duvall?*
>
> *"My grade for that second paper: A. That's how one becomes friends with Duvall."*

You don't have semesters, you have terms: three of them, as a matter of fact. Fall and winter terms are both 12 weeks apiece, and you take four three-hour classes each term. Then, from mid-April to the end of May, you take two six-hour classes—and enjoy the weather. Thus, you can concentrate on your studies throughout the year and then experiment a bit in the spring, when the study-abroad program kicks into high gear. Want to study in China, Denmark, Germany, the Soviet Union, or the Galapagos Islands? As they say on the tube, "Just do it."

No one admits to studying hard, but everyone does. It's the only way to remain afloat. If you want to major in the liberal arts—English, philosophy, history, and so on—most of your grades come from papers; on the average you can bet on about 20 pages per class. Foreign language majors find themselves in much the same boat, but only after a few years in the language lab. C-School majors face all sorts of nifty headaches—tests, group projects, computer exercises, papers. As for the natural science majors, they pretty much live in the lab, although they would deny it if asked.

The university scholars program is designed to challenge the school's best prepared and most able students. This independent honors program supplements your normal class load and is an invitation only affair. The program starts winter term freshman year, in which you read a selected list of texts and discuss them informally with faculty. During spring term, you take an honors seminar arising out of the previous reading. You then have a choice of special seminars during your sophomore and junior year, culminating in an honors thesis in your major during senior year. Perks come with all this hard work, of course: not only are private tutorials made available to you, but—and get this—faculty members are *encouraged* to relax course prerequisites for well-prepared university scholars.

In general, classes are pretty laid-back. You can bring in food, your dog, a visiting friend, whatever. The small class size provides a wonderful setting for discussion, so that's the way most classes are conducted. Stenographers need not apply: You're there to contribute. The university has no policy on class attendance (the Honor System is usually all the policy the school needs), nor is there anything like an injunction against late assignments or the like. You're an adult, it's your education, no one's going to hold your hand.

The week prior to finals is when you schedule your exams. The process is simple. You have six days, two test periods per day, in which to take your four final exams, so all you do is give your professor a manila envelope with the desired date scrawled on the outside, and when the time comes to take the exam, you simply go pick up your envelope from the department secretary. Your exam will be inside. Find yourself a quiet spot on campus and start writing. Chances are, your professor won't even be on campus that day.

> *"Senior year: It is a Tuesday night, I've been accepted to graduate school, spring has arrived, life is groovy. Some friends and I are eating our bimonthly meal at Professor Duvall's house—he and his wife are not only good friends of ours, but killer cooks to boot. After a little wine (okay, a lot of wine) and hours of dazzling talk, nostalgia sets in. We all start swapping freshman year war stories and when my turn comes I remind Duvall of my* Pudd'nhead Wilson *experience, to which he reminds me of the help I received from his protégé. As I went home that night I had a crazy thought that I've never quite been able to shake: maybe, it occurred to me, Duvall sent that guy to my dorm room way back when."*

SOCIAL LIFE

The on-campus social calendar bustles year-round, so much so that your first real battle that freshman year will be figuring out when to stay home and study. Fraternities and sororities provide the lion's share of the social life, and every house on campus throws a full-tilt party at least once a week. Friday and Saturday night the whole campus is alive with music, drinks—alcoholic and otherwise—and an abundant gathering of both sexes. All you have to do is dive in. Moreover, women from the neighboring women's colleges roar into campus sometime around 9:00 P.M. Friday, immediately readjusting the male/female ratio.

> *"I had barely set my parents on their way when W&L's rather aggressive party scene reared its smiling face. Rush was set to start the next day and so all the houses were wide open, on their best behavior. Of course, in the Greek world, best behavior is a loaded term. Some new friends I had made that day from my hall were my companions, and I guess we hit every house on campus, although my recall of events after 11:30 P.M. is a little shaky. I woke up in my clothes with red grain punch in my hair and two illegible phone numbers scrawled on my wrist. Slightly disoriented I stumbled to the bathroom down the hall only to encounter my roommate, who had chosen to sleep not in his bed but on the linoleum floor of the shower stall. He had to have been insanely uncomfortable, but I swear he was smiling in his sleep, so I left him where he was. Just a typical Saturday morning in the dorms."*

W&L is located in a little rural town called Lexington, and there's not much in the Big Lex except W&L and the neighboring Virginia Military Institute. Everything pretty much happens on campus, which is why the fraternities and sororities are so integral to the school's social life. But if the fraternity/sorority scene starts to get a little old, you can always go road tripping. You are three hours away from Washington D.C., an hour away from the University of Virginia, and 40 minutes away from any of the five surrounding women's colleges. In the fall and spring you can go swimming and rafting at Goshen Streams, and in the winter you can go skiing in Snowshoe, West Virginia. The latter is about a two hour drive—the perfect road trip distance. In the world of road tripping, half the fun is getting there.

Despite the lack of a Lexington nightlife, W&L has its tentacles all over town. A great many party barns provide perfect settings for bands and special affairs, and all of them are open for easy rental by just about any group on campus. And the school's social calendar is rich and busy, including the Superdance for muscular dystrophy, the annual Christmas concert, Homecoming weekend, and the Fancy Dress Ball in March. Fancy Dress is a formal dance that has turned into a weekend-long marathon that must be experienced to believe. A splendid time is guaranteed for all.

That's the way it works at W&L—the partying is intense, and so is the pressure to participate. And make no mistake: although new drinking laws have made things a bit calmer than in the old days, alcohol still is more than prevalent. Also, this no-holds-barred, fraternity-based system makes it hard to date casually. You spend most of your time shouting over the live band of the fraternity stereo, and you'll very rarely be without a keg in sight. In the end, you simply have to take it all in stride—you'll soon realize that it's no big deal if something goes on without you.

EXTRACURRICULAR ACTIVITIES

"My second day on campus, one week before classes were set to begin, I was sitting in my dorm room drinking with my hallmates when I got a visit from an upperclassman I'd never seen before.

"'I hear you're interested in journalism,' he said, settling himself into an available chair and popping open a beer someone had given him. 'I read your profile, but don't panic. I'm the editor of the school newspaper and just wanted to know if you'd be interested in doing some writing for us'

"I attended a meeting that night, met the staff, and was given my first story assignment. I walked home wondering, how can I write this piece when I don't even know how to get back to my dorm room? But somehow I got it written, then got it rewritten by the editors, and then found the thing on page three of that week's edition, with my own byline. What the hell: I was hooked."

The possibilities for extracurricular activity will steamroll your way as soon as you arrive. Fraternity rush begins the first week of classes and lasts an exhausting two weeks, and before you even take your first test, chances are you might already be in a house. Sorority rush is at the beginning of the winter term. There's no real fraternity row, as the school's 16 houses are scattered throughout town. Dorms only house freshmen, and except for Gaines Hall and Wood Creek Apartments, the university offers no other additional on-campus housing, so fraternities offer you a roof over your head and a meal plan for a year or two. By your junior year, however, you'll probably find a house in the country with some of your friends and live the life, as we say.

Fraternities and sororities certainly are not the only social groups on campus. A plethora of drinking societies and the like abound, as well. Actually, just about any organization on campus, from the Women's Forum to the Cold Check Committee to the Minority Students Association, becomes a social group at least once a year. Any excuse to have a good time.

But it's not all fun and games. You can work on a variety of publications, all of which are run completely by students. Moreover, the school has radio and television stations, both also student-run. WLUR 91.5 FM plays a wide variety of music, from reggae to Rachmaninoff, so you're sure to find your niche somewhere; positions at Cable Nine include everything from on-air anchoring of the news to cinematography.

> *"The whole campus was buzzing: The Student Activities Board had booked R.E.M. for the annual Christmas concert. The opening act, the Minutemen, were on the verge of national attention as well. As music director of the radio station, I received a press package from the Minutemen's P.R. people; as features editor of the school newspaper, I received a duplicate of the same package. One phone call later and an interview was set up. I ran a tape of the interview on the radio, ran the accompanying story in the paper, and made friends with the group's bass player in the process. After their performance, in fact, the whole group, including the manager, showed up at my fraternity house for a party. 'We usually sleep in the van,' the drummer told me. 'Would it be all right if we crash here for the night?'"*

W&L is a member of the Old Dominion Athletic Conference, Division III. In other words, academics come first. On the other hand, W&L teams consistently compete in post-season competition, and all sports are open to everyone. If that level of competition is a bit too intense, you can play on a variety of club sports (rugby, lacrosse, fencing) or dive headlong into intramurals.

If you are musically inclined, you can worm your way with no trouble into the university glee club, the chorus, or Southern Comfort (an award-winning *a cappella* group). Special instrumental ensembles are prevalent as well.

Student government is the real McCoy at W&L: The executive committee not only proposes and enforces student policy, but also handles the mechanics of the Honor System. Disciplinary matters are handled by the Student Affairs Committee, and fraternity affairs are the domain of the Interfraternity Council. In all cases, the administration basically keeps its bureaucratic little hands off.

GRADUATES

Washington and Lee's Career Development Center is a fairly new addition, but its newness hardly has affected its effectiveness. The people there start getting you ready for the job market as early as your junior year—even if you don't quite know what it is you want to do. Early in your senior year you are then free to attend their Career Training Workshop, which includes sessions on résumé writing and mock interviews. The year proceeds with job fairs, various Career Day events, and the like.

Hot spots for W&L grads include Washington D.C., Atlanta, Richmond, and New York. Not only are these great places to live, but they also feature strong alumni chapters. W&L's alumni are in fact one of the school's best strengths; what some might pejoratively call an Old Boy setup is in fact a vast, sincere, and absolutely effective network of influential contacts. Not only have they endowed the university up to its ears, but alumni literally will bend over backwards for W&L grads. The Alumni Career Assistance Program is a case in point. ACAP is a network of 83 alumni chapters, the strongest of which include D.C., Atlanta, and Richmond; each chapter features a career placement support program, including placement sheets, job openings, and contacts.

Generally W&L grads jump directly into the real world, whatever that means. A little over half hightail it immediately into the private business sector or local government. With Washington D.C. so close and so full of W&L alumni, national government is a pretty popular draw as well. About one fourth of graduating seniors head into postgraduate school, with law school being the most popular route. Favorite law and medical schools include the University of Virginia, William and Mary, Vanderbilt, and little old W&L itself. Business school is of course popular as well, but most W&L grads opt for a two- or three-year training program first, in hopes that some company will foot the bill for school. All told, at least 60% of all W&L grads eventually earn advanced degrees.

> *"Hard as it was to believe, graduation finally arrived. Despite the vast number of great people I had met in my four years, my greatest affection was reserved for four friends—the best friends I had ever had. One was going home to the Republic of Panama to try her hand at painting; another was off to Chicago, armed with a new job and no place to live; the remaining two were gearing up for law school. As for me, St. Louis and an M.A. in English literature were calling my name. 'Look at us,' one of the future lawyers said. 'None of us has a damn thing in common. How'd we become such good friends?' It's simple: Washington and Lee."*

SUMMARY OVERVIEW

Washington and Lee lets you have a big piece of cake and then lets you eat the whole thing. Long considered one of the best colleges in the country, it is now also one of the choosiest. Offering every academic, cultural, and social benefit of colleges twice its size, W&L allows its students to explore knowledge in a setting based on openness and honesty. And all of this at a tuition of approximately 25% less than just about any prestigious liberal arts institution. *Barron's 300 Best Buys in College Education* selected Washington and Lee as "one of the most affordable selective colleges in the country." Period. Don't forget that the school's small size allows for close, intimate contact between students and faculty, and involvement in campus affairs isn't just encouraged—it's inevitable.

Moreover, W&L offers one the opportunity to pursue a pragmatic, preprofessional curriculum tempered by a rich liberal arts base. And the school's vast alumni network is eager to help a W&L grad in any way possible. The enthusiasm of the alumni is understandable—so unique is the W&L experience that anyone who goes through it emerges with a characteristic *something* that simply says, W&L. Part of it is the honor system, part of it is the close-knit environment that extends beyond graduation, and part of it is a shared sense that people who went to W&L are in on a secret the rest of the country just won't understand.

As strong as the school is in the humanities, however, a sizable number (22%) herd themselves through the commerce school with dollar signs in their eyes and fail to fully appreciate the free exchange of ideas (a market where numbers don't count at all). The schizophrenia mentioned earlier has its drawbacks as well. One easily can sense a rupture between the expectations of the faculty and the rather pragmatic demands of many of the students, and the university as a whole suffers from it. Moreover, the general political slant of the student body is unswervingly toward the right, which isn't bad in and of itself, but does present problems in the area of change and growth. A great many fresh, innovative ideas fail to get a fair hearing at W&L.

And, like I said, Lexington is a small town—not a college town at all, but rather a sleepy community full of warm, friendly people. Washington and Lee is never boring, but one must dive into the fraternity fray full tilt to really enjoy what is offered socially. If you tend toward the fringe or the avant-garde, you might run into trouble.

But what might be a drawback on one hand is a plus on the other. Lexington is small, but it also is gorgeous. Washington and Lee may be conservative, but by the same token it is powerfully unified. Speaking from my own experience, the fact that many of the students miss out on the school's broad spectrum of course offerings simply means there's that much more room for the likes of me. And I can't think of another school in the country that can boast an Honor System as effective as W&L's—which simply is saying that no other school in the country can guarantee you four years of complete honesty and integrity. In the end, the worst thing about W&L is leaving the place. Four years down the road and I still haven't gotten it out of my system. My father, who went there 30 years ago, has the same problem.

Marshall Boswell, B.A.

Wellesley College

THE PROGRAM

"Wellesley? Isn't that a girl's school?"
"WOMEN'S COLLEGE!!!"

You already may have received some stereotype of this prestigious women's college from a relative or friend. You may think of Wellesley as a finishing school with a beautiful campus that is teeming with plaid, pearls, and BMWs. You may think of it as a haven for leftist feminists. There just may be a shred of truth in both impressions. However, at Wellesley, you are not bound to be like someone else, you are given the opportunity to shape your experience and call it your own.

Wellesley probably is the best small liberal arts college in the United States today. It is widely known for its tradition of academic excellence and the achievements it has made in the name of higher education for women. Wellesley women, at least by the time they graduate, are some of the most confident and self-assured women you ever will meet. They also are some of the most daring. They dare to strive continually for more. They dare to question and discover. Wellesley offers women the chance to gain an invaluable experience and an excellent education.

Wellesley is completely committed to its undergraduates. There are no graduate programs diverting the focus from you or graduate students teaching you. The college prides itself on a workable nine to one student-to-faculty ratio. Classes normally will be quite small. Within this environment, you have the opportunity to face the greatest academic challenge of your life. You will study, argue, question, and really get to know some fascinating professors. You will go to the library on weekends. You will hate it then, but you will love it for the rest of your life.

"I was sitting by Lake Waban with a friend who went to one of those Ivy League schools one summer when Ifeanyi Menkiti, a professor of philosophy, walked by. He greeted me with a huge smile and a

hug and began to ask me why I wasn't at home in Vermont with my family. He then asked how my friend Martha was doing in Minnesota and whether or not my other friend Buvana was around for the summer. We briefly chatted about what I might take the next fall and what I was currently reading. When he left, my companion's mouth and eyes were wide open. 'That's a professor of yours? My professors barely even knew me, let alone cared about my family and friends! That's incredible! You're so lucky!' I hadn't really even thought about it before, but he was certainly right."

Wellesley is not a party school, even though it is in a suburb of Boston, the ultimate college town. Wellesley's 2300 students are not serious all the time, but their studies come first. And everyone on campus knows that. During exams, the food service presents you with special study food, coaches let you out early, professors hold extra office hours for you. The campus world revolves around you.

"During my very first exam time, our professor held a review session for us. I thought it would be exactly like a class, but when I got there the prof was in his ripped T-shirt, sitting on the desk, eating his sandwich and drinking a beer. I guess nothing was unusual about this except for the beer. It was then that it hit me that he was putting in long hours along with the rest of us. This was no stuffy Ph.D. He was there to know us so he could really help us. And he did."

Many Wellesley students are heading toward business, law, or medical schools. Economics is one of the most popular majors, along with political science. A large number of students double-major, most likely because the requirements for a major are not great. Fairly new to Wellesley's academic program is the minor. Because languages are popular choices to double up with one's major, they are a popular choice for minors as well.

Wellesley is the type of school where you can do whatever you want. Studio art and sports medicine exist at Wellesley. You can take five classes, two of which are labs, and three of which are for AP credit. You can study in the college libraries and in the MIT, BU, BC, and Harvard libraries. You can work for food service all four years or get internships in downtown Boston. The opportunities are there.

Wellesley values racial, ethnic, and religious diversity in its students. But it values diversity of thought and is committed to protecting and tolerating it.

"My first year at Wellesley I was able to debate in our House Council such issues as whether or not ROTC should be on campus and whether or not it was OK for people to hang a pink triangle in the middle of the Quad in a show of support for persecuted homosexuals. And these were real *issues. And these were* important *issues to everyone at Wellesley. And my first-year student voice was heard and valued."*

Because Wellesley values it students' opinions, it lets you make your own decisions. For this reason, every student develops her own individuality at Wellesley. The school really helps you decide who and what you want to be. The school's open, caring atmosphere not only tolerates individuality but embraces it. In the end, it is this development of the individual that sets Wellesley apart and makes for a rich college experience.

GETTING IN/FINANCIAL AID

Admission to Wellesley is most competitive. With applications to women's colleges in general on the rise, Wellesley has the luxury of being choosey. About 39% of all the applicants are accepted. Their median SAT I scores are about 620 verbal and 660 math. But diversity is a priority. If your scores do not illustrate your intelligence, demonstrate it through your essay and interview by explaining why you are different and how this difference can add to the richness of life at Wellesley. Show off your intellectual ability, strength of character, and willingness to assume leadership roles.

A vast majority of students have a story about why they ended up at Wellesley. There certainly are those who come because of its fine reputation. There are some who come because it is close to Boston and quite pretty. But there are many who never even considered a women's college.

Wellesley prides itself on trying to maintain a diverse student body. Once accepted, about 72% of the students will be Caucasian, 17% Asian, 7% African-American, 3% Hispanic, and 1% other. In a recent year, 151 women from 46 different countries were enrolled.

Wellesley also is expensive, but about one half of the students receive need-based financial aid from the college. About 20% more receive aid from other sources. Anyone who can successfully fill out forms should apply for financial aid. A parent contribution is considered in the analysis that is done. The student will be expected to contribute from summer and holiday earnings. On- and off-campus work is available. Besides work, there are loans and grants. There are all sorts of special cases and special arrangements that can be made.

ACADEMIC ENVIRONMENT

Wellesley has outstanding professors and is committed to being a teaching college. Add students who are absorbed with their studies and fine facilities, and you will understand the pervasive atmosphere of excellence. Wellesley women share a common experience and as a result bond together.

Because Wellesley does not offer any graduate programs, almost all your teachers most likely will be full professors. Most professors will lecture for the majority of the class time though active student participation almost always is encouraged. Professors are very accessible, have frequent office hours, and often have students to their homes for informal gatherings.

> *"A wonderful scent met me at the door of the basement of my dorm where I was going to cram in a little reading before class. Two of my good friends were down there using the kitchen. 'Baking instead of studying, huh? Won't your parents be thrilled to learn that their money is being so well spent!' I teased. 'We're studying!' They retorted. 'But see if we give you any of this!' It turned out that they were preparing for class. They held their seminar in their professor's home, and everyone took turns bringing snacks each week. So they actually discussed Women in Medicine while baking banana bread with chocolate chips. Now that's what Wellesley is all about."*

Such an atmosphere is supported by the college's Honor Code, which serves to reiterate trust and the community feeling at Wellesley. According to my experience, it works quite well in most areas. The biggest difference between Wellesley's Honor Code and that of other schools is that you schedule your own exams during finals. This means that you can wake up one morning and decide to take your math exam. Or you can hit your snooze button and take it that afternoon or the next day. Wellesley has faith you will take responsibility for your own education.

Graduation requirements are minimal. Students rarely have difficulty fulfilling any but the physical education requirement! (Students are required to take eight points of P.E., which equal about one academic year of P.E. classes or sports. Options are available for those less athletically inclined. Students must fulfill distribution requirements, which are in place to ensure that everyone takes courses in diversified disciplines to validate receiving a liberal arts degree. Three courses must be completed from each of the three disciplines, which includes the humanities (such as literature, foreign languages, art, and music), the social sciences (such as religion, philosophy, psychology, economics, and education), and the natural sciences (such as biology, chemistry, physics, and mathematics). There also is a first-year writing requirement. Other than these few restrictions, the choices are up to you. You even can design your own major.

The requirements are reasonable because it can be difficult to find the classes to fulfill them. Many classes beyond the introductory level are only offered every other year, so planning must be done quite carefully. For a college of its size, Wellesley's offerings are remarkably varied. You can take anything from astronomy to sports medicine.

The academic year at Wellesley consists of two semesters. Final exams for the first semester take place before the winter break begins in December. Classes don't resume again until late January. There is the choice to stay on campus during January to take optional seminars, participate in activities, or work at a job. The second semester ends by the middle of May. Seniors enjoy a full two weeks of sun and fun before commencement.

The average class size is about 15–18 students, though those taking astronomy to fulfill requirements sometimes find themselves in a class of about 50! However, a low student-to-faculty ratio allows for small classes. In the future, given the expense of running a college like Wellesley, cutbacks are beginning to take place and changes are being made. Hopefully the student-to-faculty ratio will remain small in the future.

"Don't you miss having guys in your classes?"

No matter how much we want to talk about other (more important!) aspects of Wellesley, we can never escape the questions from prospective students regarding the fact that it is a women's college. There are quite a few men in the classes at Wellesley. About one half of the professors are men which means, of course, that Wellesley may brag about its almost 50% female faculty. Students from MIT may take classes at Wellesley through cross-registration, and Wellesley students may take classes at MIT. Wellesley also is part of the twelve college Exchange program, which enables its students to attend one of the participating coed schools and for other coeds to attend Wellesley for a semester or year. In short, there *are* men around, but not enough to compromise this fine women's college.

SOCIAL LIFE

Let me repeat, Wellesley is not a party school. However, there are certainly many parties and partyers. At Wellesley, a good social life takes effort, for Wellesley is not its own little social entity. A large part of the social life occurs off campus, which is a welcome change from the same old beer-drinking keg parties week after week. You certainly can go to keg parties every weekend, but the other alternatives look great after two weeks!

By being near Boston and its numerous colleges and universities, opportunities exist for virtually anything and everything. Wellesley students go to functions at numerous schools in the area. The choices range from jazz concerts at Tufts, to singing groups at Harvard, to the movies at MIT. Of course there are also all of Boston's restaurants, theaters, clubs, bars, concerts, and operas. The fact remains that many events occur off campus. But leaving campus often seems to be the objective on the weekend.

You certainly can and will stay on campus and go to a variety of parties. Or you can attend a student production—plays, singing groups and so on. You always can go to campus movies, but people rarely do. Many dorms now have VCRs, so people often rent movies, buy food and drink, invite a few friends over and spend a quiet night in. Such nights invariably end with a rushed trip trying to beat closing time at White Mountain Creamery for homemade ice cream. (Oreo with a Reese's mix-in is the favorite.)

> *"I'll never forget when we all got together for a spontaneous party in Fordo's room in the middle of the week sophomore year. We thought they were going to call Lake Day the next morning—which is supposed to be a warm, sunny day in the spring when classes are called off—so we partied late into the night. We had lots of beer, and these guys from some international programs at Babson showed up. We just drank and laughed all night. When we woke up the next day, there was snow and ice on the ground and no Lake Day! We were the laughing stock of our dorm."*

With a car, and now with the new express bus, the infamous Route 9—packed with Chinese food and pizza places, movies, and bars—is a popular place to go. The Senate bus and the T (the Boston area subway) provide access to Harvard Square, Boston clubs, and MIT parties. Not to exclude anyone, students often frequent Tufts, Northeastern, BU, BC, Babson, and Brandeis, though it may be difficult to get there without a car.

The Wellesley social life is different for everyone. Some Wellesley women date men from five different schools so no one will know about the others. Other Wellesley women enjoy each other's company so that they often have more fun staying in on the weekends. Many claim that only first-years and those who have to get up early go to dorm parties. Some students must have a car. These are the ones who think the thing to do on the weekend is *leave*. You will find Wellesley women at Indigo, the bar for women, and at the Boathouse Bar, a notorious pick up joint frequented by Harvard Law School guys. Your Wellesley friends will at some point date balding Harvard B-school (business school) men. Finally, most will recommend that you get a fake ID.

Although Wellesley is a relatively small school, it is not so plagued with the everyone-knows-everything-about-everyone syndrome common to schools like Williams and Middlebury. This can be credited not to lack of gossip but to the fact that many students leave campus on the weekends, whereas at the same time many women and men from other schools come to visit. Whether you like to go to fraternity parties and beer bashes, dance clubs, fancy restaurants, pizza pads, the symphony, or the movies, you can do it at or near Wellesley.

EXTRACURRICULAR ACTIVITIES

Some students play pool in their spare time, others jog, others shop on Newbury Street in Boston, and some Reserve Room geeks claim that there is no spare time at Wellesley! The activities you enjoy will lead you to meet many people, though friendships usually are established initially in the dorms. About 98% of the students live in the dorms for all four years. There seems to be more dorm spirit than class spirit at Wellesley. Almost all of the dorms have a mixture of women from all four classes, which gives one a sense of equality and sisterhood. Seniors often don't feel a great distinction between them and the younger students. In the dining halls, tables often will hold a wide range of students.

Almost every dorm has its own small dining hall, although this may be changing within a few years. (Plans are being discussed to create a more efficient, centralized dining hall.) Most schools complain about the food. This holds true at Wellesley although there are alternatives. With the meal plan, students may use their magnetized IDs (when functioning properly) for meals in any of the dining halls, at Schneider (the snack bar offering pizza, deli sandwiches, salad bar, and ice cream) or at the Convenience Store (which functions as a small grocery store). On weekends, many students stock up on soda, frozen pizza, Smartfood, and pretzels. There are a few great places for snacks on campus, too, including Cafe Hoop (which specializes in coffees, teas, frozen yogurt, and bakery yummies), Bedrock Cafe (an up-and-coming enterprise), and the Candy Store (an exam time favorite). You won't starve.

Activities range from varsity, club, and recreational sports to dorm and college government. In between are *a cappella* singing groups and choir, the newspaper(s) and other publications, theater and dance groups, the debate team, the film club, the French club, WOLF (Wellesley Organization of Lesbians and Friends), the chamber orchestra.... The list goes on.

> *"Of course, as a former two-sport, four-year, eight-season Wellesley varsity athlete, I want to begin by telling you all about sports at Wellesley and what I think about them. (I can mention what others have said, too, if I must.) They're great!!! The coaches are a dedicated group of fantastic people, though some are known to be more wonderful than others. However, the coaches are quite overworked. Wellesley has yet to fit assistant coaches into its budget. The varsity teams, which include basketball, varsity and novice crew, cross country, fencing, field hockey, soccer, lacrosse, squash, swimming and diving, tennis, and volleyball, are still quite successful. Most teams at Wellesley develop an extraordinary camaraderie. Coaches are often viewed as both mentors and friends. OK, OK. You want to know if we win. Well, we are now able to beat Smith in quite a few sports. We are*

ashamed on the day that we lose to Vassar. And Mount Holyoke is strong here and there, but we can often crush them! In other words, we're usually pretty good for our league.''

Other athletic opportunities include club teams, intramurals, and instructional athletics. Clubs that have been popular recently include rugby, skiing, and softball. Sailing and ultimate Frisbee are up and coming. Other than dorm and class crew, intramurals at Wellesley are lacking, if nonexistent. Basketball, field hockey, soccer, and volleyball, usually end up being comprised of the varsity athletes because they are the only ones who show up. Don't expect to come to Wellesley and participate in numerous pickup games every evening. Crew is the big exception to this. There is a certain romanticism about getting up at 5 A.M. to row through the early morning mist rising from the lake. It has been a favorite among Wellesley women for years.

Students are into individual athletics these days. Running around the lake or on the track, aerobics, weights, rowing machines, and, of course, stair master are very popular. This interest can be attributed to the fact that the sports center (or Sport Palace, as we so affectionately call it) is such a wonderful facility. It first opened in 1985 and quickly has become one of the top 21 facilities in the country. It contains a great pool and weight room, tennis, squash, and racquetball courts, basketball and volleyball courts, a track, a sauna, and so on. They even pipe music into the locker rooms. (Unfortunately, the same tape has been playing since 1985.)

I obviously have overemphasized athletics at Wellesley. There also are singing groups, such as the Tupelos, Widows, and Blue Notes (the *a cappella* groups). Here you have the opportunity to sing and/or clown around on stage, travel to other schools, and go to their parties. There is college government in which you can discuss and argue controversial issues ranging from ROTC and racism to parking lots and dining facilities on campus. Even if the activity isn't offered at Wellesley, being near Boston, you most likely can find it.

GRADUATES

"The majority of employers who hire Wellesley women return to recruit more."—Marcie Schorr Hirsch, director of the Career Center.

Wellesley women show up everywhere. A recent Wellesley brochure quotes economics professor Marshall Goldman as saying, ''Wherever I go, *The New York Times*, *The Boston Globe*, the networks, I find former students as correspondents, economic reporters, and producers. And they're succeeding in the business world as well, as investment consultants, financial analysts, vice presidents, CEOs.'' Wellesley alumnae can be found in colleges, hospitals, museums, banks, board rooms, and courts of law. There are over 33,000 Wellesley alumnae all over the world.

Wellesley graduates are as diverse as the students. There probably are successful Wellesley women in every field imaginable. Wellesley women develop the capacity for continued learning with their liberal arts education and carry it with them throughout their lives. They are self-confident and willing to make changes in the world.

The admissions office states that immediately after commencement, 67% of the graduates are in business (have jobs), 19% are in a professional school (business, law, or medical), and 13% are in graduate school (If my math is correct, that leaves only 1% in the floating around/hanging out/traveling category.) After about five years, Wellesley alums are doing various things: 42% are in business, 40% in professions, 8% in education, 6% in arts, and 4% in other. Most of these women and others comprise the Wellesley network, which is known to be quite strong. There are Wellesley women all over the place who are ready and willing to help fellow undergrads and alums.

Some famous Wellesley graduates are First Lady Hillary Rodham Clinton, journalist Diane Sawyer, actress Ali McGraw, and Harvard law professor and former presidential campaign manager Susan Estrich.

SUMMARY OVERVIEW

Wellesley College is one of the finest colleges in existence today. And for women seeking a liberal arts education, there is no place better than Wellesley. Its reputation for excellence is based on its commitment to learning, which is highly esteemed through the academic community. Its students are highly motivated individuals who continually challenge themselves and those around them.

One of the best things about Wellesley is the relationships that develop between faculty and students. Because classes are quite small and the professors are very willing to meet with the students, close relationships are inevitable. The faculty are dedicated to the opening of minds, which is invaluable to learning. If you are personally encouraged and inspired by only one professor in your time at Wellesley, it will be both unusual and unfortunate.

The commitment and excitement demonstrated by the faculty is contagious and spreads quickly to the students. You will be surrounded by students who will open themselves up to different experiences. Wellesley women gain the confidence to take control of their learning, and they are invigorated and empowered by it. You will be able to attain a complete education at Wellesley.

The diversity that Wellesley embraces and inspires only adds to the positive atmosphere conducive to learning. You will have the appropriate surroundings to be free to find and express yourself as you wish. Come to Wellesley if you want to grow in ways you never before imagined possible.

If, however, you are looking for that fun college that you see portrayed in movies, Wellesley may not be the place for you. It doesn't have fraternity parties or tail gates before the big football game, although you can participate in such activities without much effort. Wellesley is not known to be a big drinking/party school, nor do her athletic teams ever appear on national television (well, they once showed the swim team smiling and waving at the beginning of "Good Morning America").

Because Wellesley is not a large college, the students sometimes are apt to complain about the availability of classes. If you choose to go to Wellesley, there inevitably will be a time when the class that you wanted to take is not offered again until the following year. And some of your top choice classes will have conflicting days and times. It also could be that your favorite department is quite small and your choices seem to be more limited than they might be at a large university. Of course, this is mainly because Wellesley is a small liberal arts college.

Wellesley women are forever plagued by girls' school and lesbian questions because Wellesley is a women's college. It certainly makes for a different atmosphere than most of us are used to, and not everyone likes this completely. Many argue that one's college experience is only enhanced at a women's college, but other disagree.

Still, all in all, Wellesley offers you both the finest education and the finest location. Its academics are outstanding—from professors to courses. Its bright students complement the campus. Wellesley will offer an unparalleled opportunity to learn. Whether your affinity is toward the country or the city, Wellesley is the perfect place to be.

> *"I found myself in a place where there was no social pressure inside the classroom, where you might as well be smart, and where there was a sense, at least within the Wellesley world, that women could do anything."*—Susan Estrich '74

Linda Sommers, B.A.

Wesleyan University

THE PROGRAM

"One of my friends from high school wondered why I would want to go to Wesleyan: 'I visited that school,' she said. 'The buildings don't match.' Well, I had to give her some credit. Anyone who visits Wesleyan's campus in Middletown, Connecticut, will attest to the variety of architectual styles, ranging from College Row's brownstone administration buildings to the motel-like dorms on Foss Hill and the spare elegance of the 11-building Center for the Arts. The combination of styles is unexpected, but somehow it suits Wesleyan."

Wesleyan University intends to be an intellectual adventure for its students. At this small liberal arts college of about 2700 undergraduate students and 340 professors, you will learn *how* to think. No one tells you what to think. Wesleyan takes the position that the only way to learn to think is by thinking for yourself and making your own decisions and that the struggle of thinking and making decisions is, in and of itself, exciting.

Wesleyan is peculiar in that it is a small university. It aims to offer university-caliber variety couched in a small and comfortable setting. The 2600 B.A. bound undergrads choose from 35 departmental majors, 12 interdisciplinary majors, and nearly 1000 courses plus the possibility of creating self-designed university majors and tutorial courses. The average class size is 20, and professors are expected to be teacher-scholars. They all write books, do research, or choreograph and pursue their specialties outside of class as well as teach undergraduates.

There are nearly 1 million volumes in the university's library, graduate programs in the sciences, social sciences, and music, university-level scientific research facilities, high-tech computerized sound and light systems in a theater worthy of Broadway, over 200 student organizations, 29 varsity sports, and 5 newspapers. And, best of all, Wesleyan attracts sharp, bright, interesting people into its student body. With all this available and with no Big Institutional Voice telling students what to do, Wesleyan can be both exhilarating and confusing, but it is always interesting.

Wesleyan's philosophy of education could sound like an intense series of struggles and epiphanies. But in reality the diversity is balanced by the comfortableness of the Wesleyan community. Twenty-seven hundred students is not a large number—at least not so large that students get lost in the crowd. You will know people wherever you go, yet at commencement many of your fellow marchers may be total strangers. You will know physics majors and French majors, filmmakers and statisticians, students who conduct their own research and who perform their own dances, subscribers to the *Wall Street Journal* and to *Mother Jones*, soccer players, flute players, Javanese gamelan players, rowers, writers of satire. In short, Wesleyan is many kinds of people with different interests, talents, and backgrounds.

With such diversity in this small community, opinions vary greatly. Students see issues from all sides of the proverbial fence and realize how unusual this situation is. One year, there was an unusually high number of student political protests. Several students organized a rally, chanting "No more, no more," while carrying blank placards. To me, that's typical, wonderful Wesleyan humor.

There is no dress code, behavior code, opinion code at Wesleyan. Yet members of this community *do* have certain traits in common. They are tolerant, energetic, and really like to learn. These shared qualities draw together the different elements of the community and create a noticeable Wesleyan spirit. Because of this, many different kinds of people find the campus community to be an incredibly comfortable and supportive environment for them.

> *"My best proof of Wesleyan's educational philosophy at work is how it affected me when I was a student. Change is difficult to measure in yourself. But I did notice somewhere during my sophomore year that I spent more time laboring over my papers. I had begun to read books not as storylines but as texts written and shaped in deliberate ways. When meeting people, I wanted to go beyond just learning about them. I wanted to understand them and why we are different. I wondered what I might be like if I were of a different race or family or gender or economic class or nationality or religion. If I hadn't gone to Wesleyan, I would still be curious and fairly tolerant, but I don't think I would be making connections in the same way."*

GETTING IN/FINANCIAL AID

Getting into Wesleyan is difficult, but so is anything worth doing. Most students who apply to Wesleyan won't get in. This is true for the majority of top colleges.

What then is Wesleyan looking for? Wesleyan's admissions office tries to create a class of bright and capable students who not only want to use their talents but also represent as wide a range of backgrounds as possible, so that each student contributes his or her perspective to the community.

There are lots of Neat Kid stories—recent freshman classes have included blacksmiths, blueberry-pickers, female firefighters, department store Santa Clauses, students who grew up on sailboats, and a kid who lived in such a remote corner of Alaska that he took a Snow Kat to school each day. But you don't need to do something wildly funky to be admissible. What you need to do is show what you are committed to and why. You need to show that you like to learn. You need to show what kind of mark you have made on your high school and the people around you.

The most recent class (727 students selected from 5482 applicants) has students from almost every state in the country, including 14% from the Western states, 8% from the Midwest, 7% from the South, 42% from the Mid-Atlantic states, 25% from New England, and 4% from foreign countries. The class has slightly more women than men, and intended majors also fall evenly into the categories of humanities, social sciences, and natural sciences and math. The evenness of the academic interest of incoming students is unusual for a liberal arts college and reflects Wesleyan's across-the-board academic strength.

As for measured academic performance, most (60%) ranked in the top 10% of their high school classes with 6% as valedictorians or salutatorians. The SAT I medians are 600 verbal and 660 math.

About 60% of students attended public high schools, 36% attended private schools, and 4% parochial schools. Nearly 32% of the class are minority students—11% black, 12% Asian, 9% Hispanic. Thirty percent of the class applied under the binding early decision plan. The entire class was admitted on a need-blind basis, meaning that a student's financial situation has no bearing on admissions decisions. Wesleyan is one of a handful of schools in the country that can afford to admit whoever it wants. With 40% of students receiving scholarships and about two thirds of the student body receiving some form of aid, a real range of socioeconomic levels is represented on campus. Many students have jobs while on campus, and some even work their way through.

Tuition is not cheap, but Wesleyan guarantees to give any student who is admitted the full amount of aid he or she needs. Most Wesleyan literature emphasizes in bold type that students should never fail to apply for admission because of their financial situation. The motto is "Apply, see what happens, and then make a fair decision."

All Wesleyan aid is awarded based on financial need. An aid award is usually a package deal combining scholarship money, student loans, parent loans, and a government-supported work-study position. For the most recent academic year, the average scholarship award (the gift part of the package) equaled about $11,800, about half the annual tuition and fees.

ACADEMIC ENVIRONMENT

"I applied to Wesleyan because of a wonderful visit I had there in the fall of my senior year of high school. By this time, I had visited a bunch of schools, and I thought I knew what I was doing. 'College is college,' I had decided. 'I think I'll be happy no matter where I wind up.'

"I reported to the admissions office early in the day and did the admissions office things and had a very comfortable interview. I ate in the freshman dining hall and went to sit in on classes. Seeing those classes in action made me change my 'College is college' conclusion (My observations of these classes are especially telling because I had misread the course schedule and I wasn't even sitting in on classes I had chosen!)

"Everyone in those classrooms—the students and the professor—wanted to be there. Discussion flowed naturally. Professors didn't lecture from withered yellow pages, students didn't write letters in class, no one gave easy answers to questions, and no one talked for the sake of making a good impression. When people disagreed, no matter how excited the discussion, they still listened to each other. The passion that I saw on my first visit to Wesleyan was genuine. I saw plenty more classroom passion when I was on campus full-time, and I know Wesleyan students feel personally maligned when sixties activists criticize the youth of the nineties for being apathetic."

The academic program at Wesleyan is designed to encourage students to explore. Every student must take a minimum of 34 courses. Every student must choose and fulfill the requirements for a major concentration. No student may count more than 14 courses from one department towards graduation credit, the idea being that your academic focus shouldn't be too narrow. It's almost too simple, but these are the *only* requirements.

There is one hitch. Wesleyan has a system of almost-requirements, called Expectations for General Education. In this carefully chosen title the word *expectations* seems to imply academic breadth through guilt. Still, you never have to take a certain course at a certain time with your entire class slogging through the same reading list. Under the system of expectations, students are expected to take courses from three different departments in each of Wesleyan's academic categories: humanities and arts, social and behavorial sciences, natural sciences and math. Each student should take two introductory courses from each category during freshman and sophomore years, and an upper-level course from each category while an upperclassman. Almost all students complete their expectations, and most people change their direction during their college years. The loose structure at Wesleyan gives some framework for students to find themselves, or at least find their interests.

To give students the freedom to explore, plenty of courses are open to nonmajors, even in the sciences. For instance, a popular physics course, Nuclear War, requires more papers than lab work and includes guest appearances by professors from the departments of biology, economics, government, and sociology. The preregistration system is difficult to explain, but any student with common sense gets scheduled into his or her classes of choice.

Most students try each semester to take classes taught in different styles. There are many opportunities for close or individual attention from professors, but few students would want to take a full load of seminars in one semester. One thousand student-created tutorials take place each year, often as one-on-one projects with professors. Student-faculty relations tend to be close and comfortable.

There are some large lecture classes, usually introductory science and social science classes and a few literature survey courses. Wesleyan's largest classroom, second only to the hockey rink in seating capacity, doubles as a movie theater on weekends and seats about 250. Classes this large almost always break off into smaller sections for labs or workshops.

Few liberal arts colleges the size of Wesleyan could support departments as specialized as molecular biology and biochemistry or film. Several innovative seminar programs designed as interdisciplinary majors require students to apply for admission: the College of Letters combines literature, history, philosophy, and foreign languages; the College of Social Studies combines history, government, philosophy, and economics; the Science in Society Program is a humanities-oriented approach to the impact of science. Students can study the overlap between two or more disciplines through interdepartmental majors, such as the biology-psychology program, Afro-American studies, medieval studies or East Asian studies. The strength in the arts is impressive, as is the number of students and alums who do professional work in the arts. The range of languages offered at Wesleyan includes (besides the standard French, German, Spanish, Italian, Latin, and Greek) Chinese, Japanese, Hebrew, Russian, Arabic, Swahili, and even some Native American languages through the anthropology department. However, some of these departments, such as Italian, are miniscule. And if you really want to pursue languages of the Middle East, Wesleyan can only just get you started.

Through cooperative programs with Columbia University and the California Institute of Technology, Wesleyan students can earn both a Bachelor of Arts and Bachelor of Engineering degree in five years. Wesleyan's Educational Studies department can grant secondary-school teacher certification. Students can study on other campuses through one of Wesleyan's overseas study programs, currently in Paris, Heidelberg, Rome, Madrid, Kyoto, Sheffield, Jerusalem, China, Latin America, and the Soviet Union. The Twelve-College Exchange, a group of New England Colleges, offers exchanges within the United States and to programs abroad. Actually, for domestic exchanges, Wesleyan is the most frequently exchanged to school of the group.

Where Wesleyan is strong, it is very, very strong. Professors from the popular departments of biology, economics, English, film, government, history, and music are particularly notable and noted nationally. Members of the faculty include writer Annie Dillard (*An American Childhood* and the Pulitzer Prize winning *Pilgrim at Tinker Creek*), organic chemist Max Tischler (largely responsible for breakthroughs in penicillin production and a variety of vitamins and winner of 1987 National Medal of Science), writer Paul Horgan (*Fault of Angels and Great River: The Rio Grande in North American History*), Robert Wood (Secretary of U.S. Housing and Urban Development Department under Lyndon Johnson, former president of the University of Massachusetts, author of *Suburbia: Its People and Their Politics*), biographer Phyllis Rose (author of *Parallel Lives: Five Victorian Marriages*), Janine Basinger (film authority credited with bringing the collections of Clint Eastwood, Ingrid Bergman, Elia Kazan, and Frank Capra to Wesleyan's Cinema Archives, author of *The "It's a Wonderful Life" Book*), jazz saxaphonist Bill Barron, historian William Manchester (*Death of a President* on John F. Kennedy, *American Caesar* on General MacArthur, and three volumes of *The Last Lion: Winston Spencer Churchill*), experimental music composer Alvin Lucier ("Music on a Long Thin Wire"), Martha Crenshaw (authority on international terrorism, editor of *Terrorism, Legitimacy and Power: The Consequences of Political Violence*), and writer Elisabeth Young-Bruehl (*Hannah Arendt: For Love of the World* and *Anna Freud: A Biography*). Students have the chance to pursue their interests to quite advanced levels with well-reputed scholars in all fields.

Wesleyan's demand that professors be teacher-scholars is no mean feat. The flexibility that they have under the system of expectations is one of the pluses that keeps them happy. They are not bound to the same core courses year after year. If a professor teaches a course, it is because he or she chooses to teach that course. They choose the course size and style, be it a freshman seminar or a large lecture.

Faculty research, with the exception of some sabbatical taking, has immediate benefits for students. Professors often teach new classes based on their current research, and if their interests shift, they are free to shift the focus of their classes. One of my professors came to Wesleyan as a scholar of Victorian literature and Shakespeare, but after writing several biographies she began teaching nonfiction writing. I was quite comforted as a student to see that even she marked her manuscripts with lots of red ink in the process of writing and editing.

One of my favorite pieces of Wesleyan trivia is that per student and per square foot, Wesleyan has more lab space than any other science research institution in the country. The facilities are unsurpassed for a school this size. The possibility of students doing research on campus is a particular plus in the sciences where multi-million-dollar grants support faculty research. Student research sometimes leads to coauthoring papers with faculty members, an opportunity usually limited to graduate students at other institutions.

"In selecting my courses and fulfilling my general education expectations, I practically learned the course book by heart. I never anticipated how difficult a time I would have in making final decisions. ('It's like looking in a box of jewels,' my

adviser said to me). In high school, I had been fairly sure of my interest in English and had a big scene with my guidance counselor when I decided not to take science in my senior year. During my freshman year at Wesleyan I spent a lot of time talking about my writing courses with a friend who in turn told me about her biology and chemistry courses. (Although students do not spend 24 hours a day submerged in academia, it is fairly normal to enjoy your classes and to talk about them with your friends.) Her labs sounded more and more interesting, until finally, at the end of the year, the students were observing the effects of hormonal changes in mice. Students gave different doses of hormones to mice, weighed the nests of each mouse, and found that the mice that were chemically tricked into thinking they were the most pregnant built the biggest nests. The data was compiled into charts even I thought were beautiful. This sophisticated kind of experiment seemed infinitely more meaningful than the burning of wood chips, which I had done a lot of in high school. So I signed up for Introductory Biology the next term.

"In my stubborn way I'm sure I would not have enjoyed a required freshman science as much as I enjoyed the biology course I chose. I liked it so much I almost majored in biology. I did a lot of sorting and thought about majoring in history, then educational studies, psychology, classics, but finally I decided I wanted to be an English major after all. I ended up doing what I had intended way back in high school, but the difference is that I am an English major who can carry out a scientific experiment. And I wouldn't trade all the sorting out for anything."

SOCIAL LIFE

Anything goes. Despite Middletown's close proximity to more cosmopolitan places such as New Haven and Hartford (each a half-hour away) and to Boston, New York, and Providence (each two hours away), most students stay on campus during the weekends. Middletown, a town of 45,000 with both farmland and factories nearby, has shopping, restaurants, and not much nightlife. The campus itself is the main draw for Wesleyan students.

The Center for the Arts is busy on weekends. Usually several plays, concerts, and dance events take place, some impressive student productions and some professional. The Wesleyan Film Series digs up great and unusual old classics as well as recent big-name pics. Wesleyan attracts speakers on their lecture circuits, and athletic events draw supporters. Different housing options lead to different kinds of parties and social gatherings: Cafe Candide at the French House, Bad Poetry Coffeehouse at West College, parties in dorms dominated by freshmen, small gatherings at student houses, dancing and beer-on-the-floor at frats. Annual campus-wide parties attract fun bands like the Del Fuegos and Camper Van Beethoven. (Students still talk about when the Grateful Dead played Wesleyan in the early seventies). There is even an annual costume benefit sponsored by Students for Reproductive Choice, the "Come as Your Favorite Form of Contraception" Ball.

Social calendars are filled at Wesleyan, though it would probably not be called a party school and could not possibly be called a dating school. The campus social life does not fit neatly with a label. Although some students prefer hanging out in the Tunnels (underground passages connecting dorms and painted with the cleverest of graffiti) to hanging out in the Student Center, campus life does have a central focus. People seem comfortable with a relaxed, unstructured social system. There is very little peer pressure. Whatever an individual wants to do or not do is fine.

The social life at Wesleyan doesn't quite have the tiny college coziness typical of schools a bit smaller. However, the atmosphere does not come close to the anonymity of an urban school, where students will find themselves surrounded by complete strangers once class is over. Students make friends all over campus, through classes, sports teams, theater groups, student organizations, even in the library. Still, the most important tie that binds at Wesleyan is the freshman dorm friendship. Most students will choose to live with their friends from freshman year all the way through school. Freshman year is the only year that your social life will be partially set up for you. Sophomore year is sometimes a rude awakening when social lives are further hindered by the aftermath of the housing lottery. Although Wesleyan guarantees housing for all students, sophomores, having the fewest lottery points, are usually scattered around campus. Upperclassmen live in a more real world situation where they must take more initiative to keep up with their friends. Similarly, transfer students need to be fairly outgoing because they don't have a freshman-year base of friends to draw on.

"'You can't sit around and wait for the phone to ring,' people say of campus life. But at what school and in what life can you do that? Wesleyan is a hopping place, and students are enterprising. Every semester when I received the calendar of events, I circled in red all the events I wanted to be sure to see. I'd vow not to miss any of them. Between being busy and being forgetful, I never caught up with all the little red circles. But I was never bored. My favorite part of being at Wesleyan was that no matter what hour of the night it was, I could always find someone to talk to. Trips to 24-hour diners (the Middletown area is famous among New England diner connoisseurs), trips to the kookiest Dunkin' Donuts in the world, tree-climbing, and traying (sledding in cafeteria trays) down Foss Hill, weather permitting, are popular nighttime adventures."

EXTRACURRICULAR ACTIVITIES

The social life at Wesleyan is inextricably tied to the housing system. The choices available beyond dormitory living add a lot of color to campus life. Residents of special interest houses work together to promote the house theme on campus. These houses include: German House, La Maison Français, Malcolm X House, International House, the Bayit for the Jewish community, the Adult Continuing Education (ACE) House, Latin House, Asia House, Womanist House, Community Services House, and the Outhouse (sponsored by the Outing Club). About 15% of students are involved with the nine campus fraternity houses. These frats bear little resemblance to the ones portrayed in movies—three are coed, one is even a literary society, and all are expected to turn coed within several years. Some minority students belong to nonresidential chapters of fraternities and sororities. Upperclassmen can either live in special interest houses, fraternities, apartments, modern townhouses, or traditional New England clapboard houses or opt to stay in the dorms. Some students live off campus, but rarely more that three or four blocks away.

About 70% of students have the luxury of living in single rooms, including freshmen. Freshman dorm styles include traditional Clark Hall with its suites and quads, modern halls of singles and doubles in Butterfield and Foss, a group of reconverted houses, and the liberal atmosphere of West College. In assigning freshmen dorms, the housing office tries to match lifestyles but also to mix students as much as possible. By the end of orientation week, freshmen know their hallmates and at least recognize the other dorm residents.

The freshman cafeteria, Mocon (for Moconaughy Hall), with its central balcony, *Gone With the Wind* staircase, and round glass walls, is set up perfectly for people watching. After two semesters of Mocon meals, many faces will have become familiar. Some upperclassmen eat at Mocon as well, but usually their meal plans include eating at the student center or at dining coops sponsored by fraternities and special interest houses. Many upperclassmen have their own kitchens and organize cooperative dinners with their friends.

Outside of class the student body supports a tremendous amount of activity. They serve on every university committee, including the Board of Trustees. They also allocate funds for all student groups and enforce the Honor Code. Among the 200 organizations are groups focusing on community service, politics, the arts, ethnic and cultural interests, and athletics. Many student volunteers work in Middletown's soup kitchens, hospitals, and women's shelter. The "8-to-8" student-run listening service is available 24 hours a day. Voter registration, political campaigns, and human rights receive a lot of attention—Wesleyan is no ivory tower. The student-run '92 Theater and Captain Partridge's Theater Workshop organize drama events on stages other than the Center for the Arts Theater. Singing groups, social-racial awareness groups, publications with various political viewpoints abound. WESU-FM, the campus radio station, captures a large part of Connecticut's listening audience.

Intercollegiate athletics received a big boost a few years ago with the completion of the Freeman Athletic Center, a $19 million athletic complex complete with a natatorium, an eight-lane outdoor track, and a state-of-the-art field house. All of the schools in Wesleyan's Division III league, the NESCAC, are required to maintain practice schedules that do not conflict with athletes' academics. None of these schools does athletic recruiting or offers athletic scholarships. Wesleyan athletes do have fans, but the university does not own their bodies.

Our most successful teams recently have been cross-country, crew, men's baseball, men's soccer, and Nietzsche Factor, the untiring Ultimate Frisbee Club. Sunday afternoon intramural sports are so popular that most sports have three levels of competition. Over half the student body participates, and the faculty, administration, and physical plant employees have manned some winning teams as well.

> *"In campus activities, any student with time, energy, and talent is welcome—including freshmen. I came to Wesleyan with an interest in radio. By November of my first year, I was a licensed DJ with my own show. My high school friends at other colleges were told they could shelve records for two years when maybe a time slot would open up for them."*

GRADUATES

Rick McLellan, the director of Wesleyan's Career Planning Center, has a favorite statistic about Wesleyan: the two largest employers of Wesleyan graduates are Goldman-Sachs investment banking firm and the Peace Corps. Wesleyan students do a variety of things after graduation, just as they did while on campus, and they seem to meet with success. Acceptance rates to professional schools are about 90% and Wesleyan graduates have won more Watson Fellowships for self-designed study projects than students from any other school in the country.

About 15% of Wesleyan students go straight on to graduate school. Five years after graduation about 75% will have attended some kind of graduate school. Of a recent class, 13% are in law school or law-related fields, 12% are employed in education, 13% are in graduate school, 13% in medicine or health care, 12% in the arts. The largest group of graduates are in business (35%).

This balance of alumni professions serves Wesleyan undergraduates well. Networks of minority alums are also well established. Alumni are frequent sponsors of student internships over winter breaks and semesters off. Most recent graduates or seniors will contact alums for career advice. I was shy about doing this at first, but the people I met had such interesting jobs and were so willing to share their experience that job hunting became easier and—almost—fun.

"Initially Wesleyan was the only thing I knew I shared with the alums I contacted. But their advice was particularly appropriate. I learned from their example that, although my life's plans weren't 100% nailed down, I could certainly find an interesting, challenging job. They set me looking for jobs where I would be given different types of responsibilities and that I could shape somewhat to my interests. My impression from the advice of alums and from my own experience in the working world is that graduates of Wesleyan gravitate towards situations that require fast-on-your-feet thinking. This is partly from our predisposition and partly from Wesleyan's preparation, but surely this reflects Wesleyan itself."

SUMMARY OVERVIEW

Students at Wesleyan truly appreciate the school's unusual position as a small university. In many ways Wesleyan feels much larger than it actually is. The depth and breadth of courses and fields of study available as well as the level of sophistication of facilities go beyond what is possible at many of the small, highly competitive colleges with which it is most frequently compared. As at larger universities, most Wesleyan professors devote time to research projects and papers. However, Wesleyan is primarily a teaching institution. Students benefit from having teachers who do research and stay on the cutting edge of their fields. Because most classes are small, students have personal contact with their professors. Sometimes students have the opportunity to assist professors with research work or arrange individual tutorial classes. Often students and professors at Wesleyan become friends.

Like a larger university, Wesleyan has a well-mixed student body with students of many different backgrounds and interests. But because the student body is small, it is difficult for a student to remain completely insulated within a group of similar people. Most Wesleyan students I know agree that in spite of how much they learned in classes, they have learned as much outside of classes from contact with other students.

There are some flip-side quirks to Wesleyan's having a mixed student body and a wide range of choices in a small environment. Students are expected to take advantage of the choices and freedom they have. A student who does not want that responsibility will not do well at Wesleyan, nor will a student who expects everyone on campus to do the same things.

Just as the campus community demands a great deal of its individuals, a great deal is demanded of Wesleyan as well. Surprisingly harsh criticism and campus shake-ups occur if anyone feels that the university falls from ideal performance in any way. Certain debates become especially diverse when arguments are built around contrasting pictures of how Wesleyan should ideally function. The strength of individual's feelings about Wesleyan may be a tribute to the community, but the strong words used in debate often surprise strangers.

In the end, there isn't much room for complacency. Although complacency is easier, Wesleyan believes, that, in the long run, students learn and grow and get much more out of a challenging education. I did.

Suzy Walrath, B.A.

Williams College

THE PROGRAM

"On an art history final, I was asked to choose three pieces of modern American art for a museum: these works would represent all of modern American art. I chose some pretty standard pieces for the first two. Then for the third I took a risk and chose Claes Oldenburg's "Giant Tube of Toothpaste," a sculpture of exactly what it says. I still had not figured out whether this sculpture was good, or even if it was art, but it had done something very important: it had raised those questions and forced me to think, to reevaluate my ideas. If it did the same for my museum-goers, I reasoned, I would have done more than my job; I would have contributed immeasurably to the art world, simply by making people think. This is what Williams is all about: taking risks and making people think. The college's goal, regardless of your major, is to make you think, question, and redefine your own ideas a little more clearly. That is its job, and that is its contribution to the world."

Williams is one of the few colleges in America to require each of its students to pass a swimming test in order to graduate. In that simple requirement lies the heart of William's philosophy of education. Williams does not want to send out into the world people who are fit to live only in a library or classroom. Williams wants to foster living, breathing adults, capable of meeting the world's challenges—more important, capable of adding to their world in some significant way. One of the oldest and most prestigious small liberal arts colleges, Williams owes its success to its goal of teaching both the mind and body of every student—through rigorous and stimulating classes, a diverse and exciting faculty and student body, and the widest range of extracurricular activities imaginable. Everything at Williams works together to develop in its students a thoughtfulness, an enthusiasm, and a fullness of understanding that will help ensure a rewarding life in the real world after Williams.

599

"Two things you'll notice when you visit Williams:

• At four each afternoon everyone's heading off to a rehearsal, a game, a practice, something. Classes end, but the day has a second half to it. After dinner, the same phenomenon occurs: lecture, movies, meetings, concerts, games. Sure, you'll spend time in the library. But never because there's nothing else to do.

• The uniform at Williams seems to be Williams sweatshirts, sweats, T-shirts, etc. I have never seen another set of students so proud to wear the school's name. I myself have four different Williams sweatshirts, along with scores of T-shirts from intramurals, activities, etc. Why, if we are in Williamstown, do we need to advertise Williams? Williams students wear Williams paraphernalia because they are proud and happy to be there, and they don't care who knows it!"

All of this does not mean that you cannot specialize at Williams, nor that you will not be worked hard academically. You will spend a lot of time in the library and classroom. But Williams is not noted specifically for business or economics or science. Williams is noted for liberal arts. You will take a little of everything; you will try activities that you might never have had the time or inclination for if you were concentrating on business, and so on. You will find that learning involves much more than a book or classroom.

The Williams students and even the campus itself contribute to this more-than-academic program. The students are diverse and enthusiastic about sharing their talents: you might learn to ski from one friend, to knit from another, and to speak Russian from a third. The campus is small, so everyone is in contact with each other and everyone lives relatively close. You might be an art major living in the science quad or a bio major living right next door to the history building. No one is sequestered; no one is grouped. At the same time there is room to breathe on the 450-acre campus located in the northwesternmost corner of Massachusetts, nestled among the beautiful Berkshire Mountains and bordered by a 2000-acre forest. When your four years at Williams are over, you will have learned a lot about one or two fields and a little about many others. More important, you will have learned how to think about, question, analyze, and contribute to your world.

GETTING IN

"Admissions is a crazy process at any school. In my senior year of high school, six of us decided to go to Williams. Six from one public high school—that was unheard of. More important than the number, however was the fact that we were six totally different people—an artist, a math whiz, a military history buff, an ardent political philosopher, and two of us English types (who

had never gotten along). If they liked Williams, I was sure it would be completely wrong for me. I was wrong. Williams had a niche for each of us."

Williams is one of the most selective colleges in the country. In a recent year, more than 4600 high school seniors applied to the college. A total of 1224 were accepted; 500 of those decided to attend Williams. There is no one kind of student who gets into Williams; students come from public, private, and parochial schools, from 50 states (and D. C.) and 41 foreign countries. The common denominator seems to be that all who get in are talented. That talent might be academic, athletic, artistic—there's something to every Williams student that runs below the surface, an initiative, a spark, an interest in things that you won't see everywhere.

So you have that spark. You're interested. You're up for the challenge. What makes it easier to get in? You will have an easier time getting in, all other things being equal, if you are a minority or a foreign student, as Williams is strongly interested in creating a diverse student body. In recent years, about 25% of all four classes have been members of a minority group. International students comprise 3.1% of the class of 1996. It will also help if you are a legacy—that is, if one or both of your parents went to Williams or if you have some other familial connection to Williams. The Williams alumni organization is one of the most loyal in the country, and the college sees nothing wrong in paying them back by treating their children a little differently.

The best bet for getting in, regardless of all this, is the student who has talent and sustained interest in a few different areas, one who has faced up to a couple of different challenges—intellectual and otherwise—and one who might add something to the school. The college wants students who can teach something to the college and who will also be up to the challenge of learning from the college.

The academic standards at Williams are high. Almost half of the entering class were in the top tenth of their high school class; no one was below the top half. Sixty percent of those entering had SAT I scores of 1300 or above, with the average score on SAT II exams somewhere between 600 and 700. There are students at Williams who score well above these averages and students who score well below. There are also students who score well above these averages and do not get into Williams, as Williams is not out to be a scoring factory. Williams wants students who are fun to teach, who will give to the college and learn from it. In short, Williams wants people of character.

"I was terrified by my Yale interview. The woman seemed incredibly sophisticated, and the way she asked, 'What kinds of things have you written, Katrien?' made me feel like a fool for not having published some collection of poetry yet. I am sure my uneasiness made me sound quiet or stiff; I just could not be myself. Being my first interview, it set the tone for the rest, and I walked into my Williams interview very nervous. What a change! There sat a young alum, complete with Williams painter's hat, no less,

ready to answer my questions about Williams. If he asked tough questions, I don't remember them. I could be me; and I'm sure I sounded a lot more intelligent and interesting than I had in the Yale interview. Williams started to win me over right then. Any school with alumni who wanted to put me at ease, wanted to help me get in rather than keep me out—that was my kind of place."

The best way any college gets a sense of an applicant's character is through his/her interview. Interviews are not required in the admissions process, but there is no reason not to have one. These interviews are not frightening. The admissions committee just wants an idea of its applicants' character—are they open? friendly? bright? interesting? Interviews are conducted by alumni representatives who live all over the country, Have an interview. Meet an Eph (as Williams students call themselves, after founder Ephraim Williams) firsthand and see if he or she seems like someone with whom you'd want to go to school.

FINANCIAL AID

Williams is an expensive place to go to school, which might make a student hesitant about applying there. The entire expense for one year at Williams, including tuition, room, board, and a student activities fee, is $25,560. The admissions process at Williams is need-blind; that is, it admits students without looking at the student's financial situation. Whether students will need aid or not has no bearing on the decision to admit them. Once a student is admitted, the college determines the financial aid award.

All financial aid awards at Williams are based on need. There are no scholarships for athletics, arts, academics, and so on. If that seems unfair, remember: everyone at Williams is talented. That is why they are there. How could the college hope to distinguish one talent as being more worthy of financial aid than others? In order to determine financial need, the college looks at parents' income, assets, family size, and the number of children the family has in college. The student is expected to contribute his or her summer earnings to the cause as well. If a family is seen to need aid, the package will consist of a grant, a loan, and a campus job for the student, all of which will make up the difference between what the family can afford and what the cost is. Williams also urges students to apply for outside scholarships, state grants, and so on.

There are many other payment plans and loan options; all are described in the Williams prospectus and application. The most important thing is that everyone who is determined to need aid gets it and gets it for all four years, as long as his/her academic progress is satisfactory. Most recently, 37% of the students at the school showed a need for aid, and the awards ranged from $1000–$24,000, with the average being a $15,200 package. The median family income for those assisted was $56,800. The cost of Williams is high, but the school is dedicated to seeing that all of its students can meet it.

ACADEMIC ENVIRONMENT

All Williams students must complete 32 semester courses (four per semester) in order to receive the degree of Bachelor of Arts, and within those 32 must be three semester courses in each of the three divisions of the curriculum. Division I has fine arts courses: English, music, art, languages. Division II consists of social studies courses: history, political science, sociology. Division III includes the science and math courses. Each division looks at the world from a different perspective, so the student is required to take courses in all three. In addition, there is a new requirement that students take a one-semester course on peoples and cultures, designed for students to understand cultural pluralism in America and the world. Other than these broad requirements, the college requires a swimming test and four semesters of physical education. By the end of four years every student ought to be able to face the creative, cultural, analytical, and physical challenges of the outside world.

At Williams, students declare their majors at the end of their sophomore year. (They can change them, of course). Within each major there are other requirements, but the student has plenty of opportunity to mold his own program within the major. In all, students are left with at least 17 free choices; that is, 17 course spaces to fill with anything they might want. My class had 80 double majors at graduation, clearly showing that there is plenty of room in the schedule to fulfill the requirements of even two majors! Courses offered range from the most basic college course such as English or Psychology 101, to student-initiated courses such as Non-Violence and Social Change, or extremely specialized courses in literature, art, or science. Class size ranges from 100-person lecture courses, to Oxford-style tutorials, to one-on-one independent study or thesis work. Students can audit courses or take fifth courses for a pass/fail grade or a regular grade. There is plenty of freedom to design your own education and get as much as possible out of four years in Williamstown.

> *"Choosing my English major was easy. It was almost automatic; I was the daughter of two English teachers. But who had ever heard of American studies? What did someone do with an American studies major? I was deciding to double-major in something when I was not even sure what it was! There was something about the first couple of Am. stud. courses that made me feel like this was what I really wanted to be doing. By my senior year, my English major was primarily a complement to my American*

studies, and it was in American studies that I wrote my senior thesis. As I was writing my thesis, I knew I had made the right choice: I loved what I was writing. I couldn't stop thinking about it. That whole second half of the year was grueling: I had never worked that hard on one project. But I truly loved doing it. That is half the secret at Williams: you'd better love what you do because you do an awful lot of it!"

The search for a major to love is not as hard as you might think. The majors available to students are many and varied—there were 29 different major fields of study represented in a recent class, along with 125 double majors and 11 contract majors (fields of study that the students enveloped and pursued independently, usually combining college offerings), English, history, and political science attract the most majors, with art, economics, and psychology also popular choices. Even when 97 students are history majors, those 97 are in no way clones. There are history majors who focus on American, diplomatic, or modern history, for example. No one at Williams would think of saying that one experience is superior to the other. Every student learns to read more critically, analyze more thoughtfully, think more clearly about our world—and that is Williams' goal.

All of this would mean nothing if the professors teaching these courses weren't excellent. At Williams, the faculty has the same energy and spark as the students. Rarely will a student come away from a course without being impressed—even awed—by the professor's knowledge of his/her field and his/her range of experience in that field. Professors at Williams are not stuffed shirts, living only in the classroom, unaware of new ideas of trends in the world. They practice what they teach. They are writing books, doing research or studies, discovering things in their subject area, all the time! Graduate students teach in only one area at Williams— introductory art history. Otherwise, at Williams students get their learning straight from the masters. Students learn astronomy from a nationally known astronomer, history from a renowned political scientist, or poetry from an award-winning poet. Even with a faculty of this caliber, students are not underlings; they are partners in this learning process, often getting the opportunity to help professors with research, writing, and even publishing. It is impossible to pick one department that is particularly excellent: all of the professors' enthusiasm about their subjects is infectious, and it is topped only by their desire to share it with their students. They are available all the time: their offices are open to student visits; they love an invitation to go to lunch or dinner. They are as excited about what they are doing as the students and just as excited to be doing it at Williams.

The truly unique aspect of the Williams academic experience, besides the excellent faculty and diverse offerings, is the 4-1-4 academic calendar. Williams has a four-month first semester and four-month second semester, and in between them is a one-month term, called Winter Study. Winter Study is all of the advantages of Williams, without the academic pressure. Imagine the entire month of January and only one class to take. First-year students are required to take one of seven interdisciplinary seminars. Upperclass students can spend the month in classes such as

Chinese Calligraphy, the Chemistry of Winemaking, the Economics of Sailing, Victorian Mysteries, and Puzzle and Problem Solving, or something created by the student and approved by a faculty adviser. Students can hone a skill they already have or try something they've never thought about doing. The best part: it is pass/fail. So there the students are in Williamstown, only one course to pass for an entire month, the best skiing in the Northeast about 20 minutes away, all of their friends within walking distance. . .it is the most relaxing, enjoyable month imaginable. The students *want* to come back to Williams after Christmas break. How many schools can say that.

But back to reality. During the rest of the year, academic life is tough at Williams. Students work themselves hard. Faculty expect it, and the students expect if from themselves. At times the pressure is thick, but it doesn't have to be unpleasant. Most students seem to enjoy what they are doing; it would be impossible to keep it up otherwise.

SOCIAL LIFE

Williams' reputation has long been that of a country club—the image seems to be of preppy men and women frolicking in the Purple Valley. That image exists more in the college guides than in reality. Yes, Williams is as beautiful as any country club. Yes, students play squash, tennis, golf, swim, and ski. But this is the most intellectual country club ever created. Yes, there are an astounding number of L. L. Bean sweaters around. But that is not Williams—that is New England. It is cold in the Berkshires—and let's face it, duck boots are practical in the snow. And students wear sweats to class far more often than they do L. L. Bean outfits. Williams is neither as homogeneous nor as dull as a country club. The students are diverse, and they are casual. Put it together, and you get a number of different things going on during the weekends.

> *"Some of my best times at Williams were spent sitting in my living room, in front of a fire, playing charades with my closest friends. Not everyone's idea of a rollicking good time, I know. But luckily at Williams there were some other folks who did see it as a good time. That's the key to the Williams social life. What's your idea of a good time? A campus party? A political discussion? A movie, lecture, concert? A walk through Hopkins Forest? All of the above? There is no one brand of social life at Williams. You'll find people interested in all of the above. You create your own social life. If charades is your thing, do it! If not, you'll find something else."*

The traditional outlets for blowing off steam abound at Williams—namely, beer and parties. Alcohol plays a major part in the social lives of most Williams students, as it probably does at most colleges. If it is more obvious at Williams, it is because all of the drinking is concentrated into on-campus parties. There are only two places to drink off campus within walking distance—the drinking age in Massachusetts is 21—so the general trend is to go to the campus parties, where there is drinking, dancing, and conversation. There are usually two parties a weekend, open to the entire campus, leaving Sunday for back-to-the-books day.

Other options on the weekends or at night? There are always movies, lectures, concerts, performances, and conversation. Because of the academic demands of Williams, the social life has even worked its way into the most academic place of all—the library. The third floor is the designated social floor; it is understood that students will talk and visit more there than on other floors. So even students who are studying can fit some social life in between chapters, if they want. If a student can't find something social to do at Williams, she or he probably isn't looking very hard.

The other major rumor—besides that it is a country club—is that there is no dating at Williams. The truth of this depends on how one defines dating. Everyone I knew at Williams had a boyfriend or girlfriend at one point or another, if not for the whole four years. So there is certainly serious dating. What there isn't is casual dating, and there are a couple of logical reasons for this. The casual atmosphere, first of all. Few people go on dates. The town is small, so there aren't that many places to go on an official date. It's much easier to go to a party with a group of friends. Also, the size of the school makes everyone pretty familiar, which makes it awkward to date someone with no intention of starting a serious relationship, for you know you will see that person again, and you can be quite sure that many other people will know that you saw him/her in the first place. Casual dating is not the norm at Williams. On the other hand, it is not at all hard to date someone seriously. In fact, I am married to my Williams sweetheart, as are many other Ephs I know.

What is more important than a lack of casual dating, however, is the fact that there is a very healthy relationship between men and women at Williams. The opposite sex is demystified at Williams. Men and women do not blush or swoon in each other's presence; they are very used to each other and come to see each other as potential friends and supporters. Men and women live right next to each other. They take the same classes. They play the same sports. (Yes, there are women's rugby, hockey, lacrosse, and crew teams, as well as teams for almost every other sport men have). If there is a lack of casual dating, there is no lack of interaction between the two genders at Williams. It is a healthy, friendly, supportive interaction.

For outside social life, there are plenty of neighboring colleges—RPI, Mt. Holyoke, Amherst, and there's a bus that runs right to Boston from Williamstown. Buses also run daily to New York City, and for the more local tastes there is public transportation to the nearby town of North Adams, where there is more variety in movies, stores, and restaurants. All of the necessities and plenty of the luxuries are available in Williamstown, but when cabin fever hits, there are plenty of places students can go.

The social life at Williams grows out of the college itself, and it is just as diverse as the college. It can be intense—when Williams students party, they party pretty hard because they work hard. It can be mellow, goofy, or sophisticated. It can be mindless; it can be intellectually challenging or stimulating. There is something for everyone because the students are responsible for creating it.

EXTRACURRICULAR ACTIVITIES

Williams students work hard. They play hard. Guess what? They throw themselves into their extracurricular activities hard, too. Perhaps because of its location, perhaps because of the kind of students there, Williams offers more activities for 2000 people than seem imaginable. There are over 100 student organizations at Williams, ranging from groups with serious political goals to groups looking to have serious fun. At the beginning of each year, the Purple Key Society sponsors a fair, at which all of the activities are represented, and freshman can hear about them, meet the members, and sign up. They might try WUFO (Williams Ultimate Frisbee Organization), the James A. Garfield Republican Club, or a service organization, like Big Brothers. The activities echo the dedication and diversity of the Williams students. There are over 20 musical groups, eight different publications, at least 12 club sports, and dozens more clubs of every kind and range of seriousness.

It is hard to say what the most popular clubs at Williams are, for each has its own devoted following. The men's and women's rugby club are two of the most popular, along with Amnesty International, and the public interest group Masspirg. Some of the more vocal groups are the Black Student Union, the Feminist Alliance, and the Bisexual, Gay, and Lesbian Union. A student is not pigeonholed into belonging to one type of organization. Nothing stops a member of a singing group from playing rugby or a member of a political club from being a juggler. Williams people have many different talents, and they are not worried about choosing between them—use them all!

Athletics is a vital extracurricular activity at Williams, and nearly everyone seems to participate at some level. Among the Division I teams at Williams are squash, skiing, and rugby. The swimming team is traditionally excellent, with a number of swimmers qualifying for nationals each season. Last year, virtually every team had a winning record; they won many Little Three New England, and ECAC titles. Football, with a 7–1 record ended a 23-game winning streak. Many participants in various sports received All-America and Academic All-America honors. The most hotly contested games in every sport, however, are the Little Three games. Williams, Amherst, and Wesleyan have a rivalry that will outlast the pyramids.

> *"You know something's different at the very beginning of a Williams-Amherst basketball game. You had to get there an hour early just to get in. Fans are waiting outside for people to leave so that they can get a seat, but nobody's moving. When the Amherst*

team is announced, every Williams fan opens a newspaper, handed out before the game, and ignores the team. When Williams sinks its first basket, the gym erupts in a shower of purple and gold streamers, stopping play while the fans cheer. Some unlucky Amherst player is chosen to be the goat, and every time he touches the ball, Williams fans chant his name over and over until he gives it up. At any spare moment, two guys run on the court and spell Williams out for the crowd. No one is quiet. No one is worried about being Division III or having no one over six-three on the court. Everyone just wants to beat Amherst."

Casual athletes abound at Williams. The many squash courts are available to anyone at any time—when the first-rate Williams team is not practicing. The new Chandler Gymnasium has an Olympic-size pool and diving well, as well as rowing tanks and a weight room complete with Nautilus and free weights. Other sports facilities on campus include the Lansing Chapman Hockey Rink (converted to indoor tennis courts in the off-season), which is used for intramural hockey on Sunday nights and very informal broomball any other time, the Towne Field House, with an indoor track, which is used also for pre-season practice by the baseball, softball, and lacrosse teams, and some of the most beautiful outdoor football, baseball, soccer, and lacrosse fields you will ever see. Whatever level of play you seek, you'll find it at Williams.

Williamstown also hosts two nationally respected art museums: the Williams College Museum of Art and the Clark Art Institute, which houses one of the finest collections of impressionist paintings in the country, as well as other art. If you are a budding artist or an art lover of even if you've never thought about art for a second, these are two great places to hang out for an afternoon.

There are no fraternities, sororities, or eating clubs at Williams, so housing is not connected to the extracurricular activities in any way—except that it is the houses who organize the campus parties. But anyone can come to those parties, and everyone does. Is there better housing than at Williams? If so, I've never seen it. Freshman year, the students live together in "entries" (sections of a dorm, usually with about 30 students). At the beginning of sophomore year, each student chooses housing for the next three years. Sophomores might end up in the oldest building on campus—the oldest extant dormitory in the country—West College. Or in the most modern dormitory, with cafeteria built right in—Mission Park. Or an old fraternity house. Each place fits differences in social lives, differences in aesthetics. Regardless, nearly everyone has a single room after freshman year, sometimes as part of a suite. Some of the older rooms are huge, with fireplaces, porches, separate living and bedrooms; some are small, modular bedrooms, with a separate living room for the whole suite; some are average bedrooms (in Williams terms—they would be primo at many other schools I have seen a lot of smaller rooms at other colleges—with people sharing them!). Each house at Williams has its own style, its own character.

GRADUATES

"Three months before graduation, I got a job for the next year. Following the Career Counseling Office's advice, applying early, driving down to New Jersey in the snow for an interview—all of it had paid off! My roommate had gotten a job earlier that month. When I told friends outside of Williams about our situation, they were amazed. 'You haven't even graduated, and you already know you have a job?' they asked. They couldn't believe it. Williams makes you expect that you will have a job before you graduate. You have to step outside of Williamstown, talk to people from anywhere else, to realize that this is NOT the norm! Then you realize just how hard Williams has pushed you, how much you've come to expect of yourself, and how lucky you are."

Eighty-nine percent of a recent Williams class graduated in four years. About 67% of that class was employed right after college; 19.6% went on to graduate school; 1.4% traveled for a while; and 11.7% were undecided or job hunting.

What were those 67% who were employed doing after Williams? The overwhelming image of a Williams senior year seems to be seniors in business suits trying to join the corporate world, and indeed many of them do join it. They are probably the most visible, but they are not the only kind of graduate. If you want to be an investment banker, yes, your liberal arts degree from Williams will help you. But it can open a number of other doors, too. Right now I have friends in publishing, sales, consulting, banking, law school, med school, master's programs, Ph.D. programs, Japan, teaching, traveling, coaching, fishing in Alaska, working on election campaigns, and working at Williams. What can you do out of Williams? Anything you want.

The Office of Career Counseling's sole purpose is to find graduates jobs. They'll help you write a résumé, prepare you for interviews, and show you where to look in the first place. About 95 employers visit Williams in the spring to recruit new employees—everyone from the top notch corporate firms to nonprofit organizations. More and more employers want students who are widely educated, who know how to read, to write, and to think, rather than graduates who specialized in accounting or business. More and more employers realize that students who have met the challenges of Williams will succeed at any job.

"The first job application letter I ever wrote turned out to be to a Williams graduate. He immediately sent back a personal response, recalling some of his days at Williams, expressing interest in interviewing me. I felt that, since he knew what he had gone through at Williams, he would know how hard I had worked and would feel very confident in my abilities, simply because I was a Williams grad. I was right. He hired me and three more Williams grads for his staff."

Alumni are very helpful in finding graduates jobs. There is a definite loyalty to the school, to anyone who has lived there and studied there, that is very warm and reassuring in the outside world. That bond does not show itself only in jobs for graduates. The Williams alumni organization is one of the most loyal and active college alumni organizations in the country. With reunions every summer, alumni trips and seminars during the year, and special programs at Williams during the summer, the alums keep in touch with each other and with Williams. Alumni donated over $4 million to Williams last year, and the participation rate in the donation drive was 62%. Once you've lived at Williams, played there, worked there, it is impossible to detach yourself. No matter when you graduated or what you majored in, the Williams experience is a bond for all graduates.

SUMMARY OVERVIEW

Williams is a small liberal arts college. It does not have an immediately recognized name although that is changing. It is not an athletic powerhouse. It is in farm country in the corner of Massachusetts. There is no big city within an hour. It's cold. In spring, Billsville becomes Mudville. The work takes 100% effort, even when you have only 50% of the time you need. So why do over 4000 people apply there every year to get into a 500 person class?

The primary strength of Williams is an intimacy and energy that larger schools lack. With only 2145 total students (with graduate students in only art and development economics), undergraduate students are assured of working closely with the excellent faculty. Williams has well-known teachers: Michael McPherson, economics; Jay Pasachoff, astronomy; writers Jim Shepard, Louise Glück, and Lawrence Raab; Mark Taylor, religion—all working with undergraduate students, sometimes one-on-one, sometimes in lecture classes. Because the campus is generally open and unlocked, all students have access to the college's excellent facilities for athletics, computers, music, and science, and live a stone's throw from two nationally respected art museums. Those famous names you see in the brochure—you'll meet them, if you want to, not across a 200-person lecture, but at dinner, in the snack bar, or at a movie. Those facilities you see pictured—you can enter those anytime and use them. They aren't for graduate students or the people who manage to get keys. They're yours.

Williams's biggest strength is (modestly speaking, of course) the students it attracts. The students at Williams are interesting, terrific people. You won't like everyone, of course. But you'll be amazed at the various talents and interests you'll come across. The head of the colleges' service organization is now studying at Oxford University as a Rhodes Scholar. An expert organist also heads the first-year student orientation camping trip. The head of the College Council works with dysfunctional adolescents. And so on! Students come to Williams with something to add to the college and leave the college even more ready to add to the world by virtue of all the people they have met and challenges they have overcome along the way.

The school does have its weaknesses. Williams is small—2000 undergraduates. Williamstown makes that 2000 even smaller. There is no real city nearby. There are no nightspots and only one bar and one movie theater and so on. Some folks cannot survive for four years in that kind of atmosphere. Even if you do not think of yourself as a city person, you will probably need to get away to Boston or New York once or twice in order to gasp a breath of city life. The college also offers plenty of exchange and study-abroad programs for junior year, allowing students to broaden their horizons a little. Still, most of your time will be spent in Williamstown, with the same 2000 people, for four years.

Even with that many bright young people, Williams is not a perfect world, with no sexism, racism, division, or animosity. The lack of fraternities, the vocal outlets like the Feminist Alliance, the Black Student Union, the Bisexual, Gay, and Lesbian Union, all help to create awareness of and spark debate on these faults, but the divisions exist. This is a fault of the world rather than a fault of Williams, but students should be aware that even in Williamstown, where students leave their rooms wide open, there are still some minds tightly closed.

Williams has other faults. A comprehensive list is impossible, however, for some would call it too conservative, others too liberal. Some hate the mismatched architecture; others think it adds charm and character. Some want more focused majors; others want more freedom. No place is perfect for everyone, or even for anyone. Fortunately, none of the faults is so great as to ruin the potential of the Williams experience.

Four years at Williams are four years filled with challenge, fun, and learning. Everything at Williams is there for the students to enjoy—the mountains, the people, the activities—and they do plenty of enjoying. But somehow those mountains, those people, those activities all manage to teach something along the way, too.

Katrien Sundt, B.A.

Yale University

THE PROGRAM

"You went to Yale? You must be smart." This is the response I often get after telling people I went to Yale. The response indicates Yale's widely accepted reputation as one of the academically strongest colleges in the nation. Some outsiders often do not realize that Yale, as an Ivy League school, is much more than a collection of books and bookworms or a haven for the social and intellectual elite.

Certainly Yale's academic program receives well-deserved attention. Yale attracts professors who are experts in their respective fields, creating a very strong diverse faculty. There is a great amount of intellectual energy at Yale, generated by both students and faculty. However, the strong academic program at Yale constitutes only one aspect of many that set Yale apart from similar institutions and, therefore, should not be considered Yale's only defining characteristic.

The image of Yale as an elitist institution is much further off base. Although its history of old money and patriarchy cannot be changed, Yale has moved with the times and is now considered a very liberal and socially diverse school. Yale's wealth and the wealth of some of its strongest alumni are notable, but the "Old boy—Old Blue" Yale no longer exists, except in the minds of some of its alumni.

In order to get an accurate picture of Yale, you must start with the basics.

Yale is a liberal arts college. Students study English, history, and philosophy, to name a few, with the intention of learning to think rather than of being trained for a particular vocation. Yale does not offer majors in career-directed fields such as communications, business, or marketing.

Yale is a large college. The college has approximately 5200 undergraduates with 1279 in a recent freshman class. However, compared to state universities, Yale is cozy. Furthermore, the entire university (the college and the graduate schools) has only 11,000 students. The college dominates the university, comprising half of the total university population. The size is such that although you will not graduate knowing everything about everybody in your class, you will also have to work to gain complete anonymity.

Yale is a New England school, located in New Haven, Connecticut. In choosing a college, location is often a significant factor. New England is recognized as a liberal and intellectual corner of the country. It is known for its beautiful autumns as well as its many strong educational institutions. Almost invariably, half of the nation's top ranked colleges are in the New England area. New Haven, however, is not a typical quaint New England college, but a medium-sized, blue-collar city. It is located an hour-and-a-half (about $8 by train) from New York City, and two-and-a-half hours from Boston. Its proximity to New York is a definite bonus, but outsiders often don't realize that New Haven itself has a lot to offer. New Haven falls somewhere between a booming metropolis and a college town. Although Yale is the single largest entity in New Haven, without Yale, New Haven would continue to thrive, as a major industrial center in Connecticut. Yale's particular relationship with and location in New Haven contributes to every student's education. Yale is located in the middle of the city but still maintains a feeling of enclosure.

Yale is a campus school. Although located in the middle of New Haven, Yale stakes its claim and does not lose the feel of being a university because it is organized on city blocks. From the streets you can see the varying architectural styles, predominantly Gothic but also many others. Many of the buildings encircle courtyards that enable students to escape from the bustle of city life. From the outside, Yale is simply a collection of city blocks; from the inside, however, students feel a true campus atmosphere. Yale is not a commuter school; a good part of the Yale experience comes from outside the classroom in other campus activities. In fact, due to the strong sense of campus and the variety of activities that are linked with campus life, very few students choose to live off campus.

> *"The image of the Yale campus that will remain fixed in my mind is that of the evening of the first snow my freshman year. The snow came down quickly, starting around 9 P.M., and soon the Old Campus—the largest quad where all the freshmen live—was covered, first by fresh snow and soon after by the entire freshman class. Everyone left term papers and finals studying behind to take a break to participate in a spontaneous campus-wide snow celebration. We had snowball fights, played snow football, and generally frolicked all night long. I sensed a feeling of camaraderie, a sense of belonging, among my thousand-plus classmates, somewhat akin to the feeling four years later at graduation."*

Yale is characterized by diversity, particularly in the student body. Although the basic facts create an adequate snapshot of Yale, they cannot provide the specific qualities that make Yale a unique and special place. There is a variety in all aspects of Yale life: the courses, the students, the activities, even the libraries.

> *"The determining factor in my choice to attend Yale was the diversity of its student body. During my visit to Yale I was*

amazed at the wide variety of backgrounds and interests of the students I met. Furthermore, I found that the diversity did not serve to be divisive. It seemed to me that at some larger school people's interests determine their social groups: the jocks hang out and live with the jocks, and the artists hang out and live with the artists, etc. At Yale I found soccer players rooming and party-ing with pianists and chemists, which I can now attribute to its small (enough) size as well as its open-minded students.''

Yale offers one of the finest academic programs in the country. Although aca-demics do not constitute the whole of Yale, the quality of education provided at Yale should not be downplayed. Even for the nonintellectual, the academic opportunities are both interesting and challenging. The academic atmosphere is intellectually stim-ulating, such that even the most unwilling students develop enthusiasm for learning and studying. Furthermore, Yale has one of the most extensive sets of resources in the world, covering a wide variety of topics in extreme depth. The Yale library system contains a little bit of everything: one of the 11 remaining original Guttenberg Bibles, today's *Wall Street Journal,* even an entire collection of books written about the impact of gospel music on the civil rights movement (all of which I read for a research paper). Yale boasts the fourth largest library collection in the country.

In developing an image of Yale, it is important to remember that Yale is first and foremost an educational institution, with excellent academic facilities, including faculty and resources. Yalies never tire of complaining about how much work they have to do, and they do work hard, by and large. In addition, Yale has a lot to offer besides academics; despite how much work they have, almost all Yalies take advan-tage of the opportunities that lie beyond the classroom. A Yale education encom-passes far more than the academic excellence with which most people associate the university.

GETTING IN/FINANCIAL AID

"I remember when it hit me that my Yale classmates, seemingly ordinary, were very distinguishable from my high school class-mates. I was having ice cream at Durfee's—the on-campus Sweet Shoppe—with a new friend. He was large, laid-back and goofy, and I had therefore pegged him as a big, dumb jock. In the course of our conversation, he informed me that he intended to major in physics and was taking the highest level physics course open to freshmen. This jock was also smart! Furthermore, he wanted to organize a string quartet; he was also an accomplished cellist. He did not disappoint me, however, as far as my jock image of

him was concerned; after a successful rowing career at Yale, he went on to compete in the Olympics. I realized that as ordinary as my classmates seemed, each one by virtue of having been admitted to Yale, was most likely intelligent and interesting in some unique way."

For the most part, I believe students enter Yale with one of two preconceptions: either that Yale is full of geniuses and they will never survive or that they are the smartest person around, having been told that throughout secondary school. Both groups realize their misconceptions early in freshman year. The latter sees that every high school has a valedictorian, many of whom go to Yale, and that at Yale 1400-plus SAT I scores are not uncommon. The former come to realize that Yale accepts only people who can do the work; the acceptance letter represents the admission committee's faith in the applicant's ability to be a successful Yale student. As Yalie's are fond of saying, "The hardest part is getting in."

Despite the varying trends in college admissions, Yale always remains a popular choice and typically has about ten times more applicants than places (12,991 for a recent class of 1308). As Yale seeks to maintain a diverse student body it is difficult to pin down the type of person guaranteed admission. Grades and scores play some role in the admissions process, as the committee wants to admit students who have demonstrated the ability to do the work. With such a large number of applicants, however, the committee could probably fill each class with 4.0s and 1400s. In order to prevent this, the committee weighs all the information about each applicant and usually seeks well-roundedness. Interviews, essays, and recommendations are all taken into consideration. In deciding what type of essay to write, remember that you want it to tell the committee something about you that is not evident from other parts of the application.

In compiling a diverse class, the committee also gives attention to minorities, geographical distribution, and legacies. The Yale student body is comprised of students from all 50 states and over 80 countries. At the same time, there is a large concentration of students from the New England area. Twenty-five percent of the student body are minorities; 10% are legacies. In addition, Yale is currently working to promote and strengthen its science departments and is therefore seeking to admit prospective science majors.

Yale has a need-blind admissions policy; financial need is disregarded in the admissions process. This means that you will not be rejected because you apply for financial aid. The downside of this policy is that you may be accepted without being given all the financial assistance you need. Almost half of all Yale students are on financial aid. Although work-study is not necessarily a component of all financial aid packages, good paying on-campus jobs abound. The on-campus minimum wage is around $5 per hour, and dining hall workers can earn up to $8 per hour. Being on financial aid does not pose problems for many Yale students because for the most part, it goes unnoticed among the student body.

ACADEMIC ENVIRONMENT

Since its establishment almost 300 years ago, Yale has preserved its philosophy of being a liberal arts institution. The late Yale president turned baseball commissioner Bart Giamatti never tired of explaining the value of a liberal arts education and the importance of learning to think. Giamatti himself was a testament to the fact that the skill of thinking can be used in any field from academics to baseball.

Yale offers over 2000 courses, taught by a very strong faculty. Yale's commitment to undergraduate education is widely evident, most notably the introductory courses taught to freshmen by scholars of international renown. The administration constantly reinforces the belief that Yale is primarily an undergraduate institution. Although Yale's graduate schools are very well respected, they remain small and do not detract from the undergraduate program, unlike the situation at many of the school's well-known competitors.

> *"The faculty at Yale are truly committed to the education of their students. This became particularly evident to me my senior year. I had never taken a history course at Yale, despite the fact that it is Yale's strongest department. My experiences with the subject had led me to believe that the study of history was entirely boring, nothing more than the regurgitation of facts. By my last year at Yale, I had been persuaded to give history another chance. I decided to take a freshman introductory history course in American foreign policy. The course was taught by Gaddis Smith, who is enough of a legend at Yale that most people refer to the huge lecture course simply as Gaddis. Gaddis (the person) did not let me down, delivering engaging lectures dotted with his personal experiences with noted politicians. For me, Gaddis made history come alive, enabling me to realize the necessary link between past, present, and future. In fact, Gaddis (the course) was the only lecture course I took at Yale in which I did not miss a single lecture. Furthermore, Gaddis himself directed a few of the sections—smaller discussion groups that met once a week—so that 30 or 40 freshmen had the opportunity to interact with this legend in a seminar-type atmosphere. And, like all professors at Yale, Gaddis held open office hours once a week, during which any student could talk with the professor one-on-one."*

History, English, and economics are the most popular majors, respectively, but there are a significant number of science majors. More than 60 majors are offered, ranging from Near Eastern literature to molecular biophysics and biochemistry (MB&B). Furthermore, students may design their own majors if their proposal meets with the approval of the academic committee and there are many interdisciplinary possibilities also, such as environmental studies.

Although there are no required courses at Yale, students must meet certain distribution requirements. Each student must take two classes in each of four distribution groups—English and languages; the humanities (including history, art, music, philosophy, and other disciplines); the social sciences; and mathematics and the natural sciences (don't worry, they offer Physics for Poets and Rocks for Jocks).

> *"My decision to major in philosophy came as a surprise to my friends and my parents, even to me. I had come to Yale open-minded but unenthusiastic about writing paper upon paper. The open, loosely structured academic requirements enabled me to experiment and test a wide variety of subjects. I took my first philosophy course to satisfy my humanities requirement. The professor and subject (ethics) both seemed interesting and the work load light—a perfect requirement satisfier. Unexpectedly, I became intrigued by the thought process involved in philosophical analysis and took another philosophy course, then another. At Yale, you do not have to choose a major until the beginning of junior year; this enabled me to test a variety of subjects I never touched in high school before concentrating on one."*

Each student must also demonstrate proficiency in a foreign language. This requirement can be satisfied either by AP scores, a proficiency test, or completing the immediate level course at Yale (two years if you have no or little previous knowledge of the language). Although the normal four-year course load at most colleges is 32 credits, a Yale degree requires 36. Thus, Yalies master the art of juggling five classes simultaneously.

One unique advantage of attending Yale is the shopping period. Shopping period is the first two weeks of each semester, so named because students shop for classes. Whereas students at most other schools have to preregister for classes during the previous semester or over the summer, students at Yale may attend almost any course offered during the first two weeks of the semester. At the end of the two weeks, they pick their schedule, having had the opportunity to hear the professors and receive lists of the requirements. This enables students to choose courses they will find interesting, as well as balance tests versus papers, morning classes versus afternoon, and lectures versus seminars. With the 36 credit requirement, shopping period also enables students to balance their work loads by taking fewer but harder classes one semester and more but easier classes alternately.

The academic pressure at Yale was certainly not as intense as I had anticipated. A laid-back student in high school, I expected to be the anomaly at Yale, surrounded by overachievers, each of whom was used to being the smartest. Yes, Yalies are a motivated bunch, and, yes, they do work hard. For the most part, however, students recognize the futility of academic competition. This atmosphere is enhanced by the fact that there are no GPAs and no class rankings, making it difficult for students to compare themselves with their classmates. For the most part, students get *A*s and *B*s. It seems that, having gotten into Yale, students use their energy to explore all that Yale has to offer, not to compete academically.

SOCIAL LIFE/RESIDENCE LIFE

The residential college system is probably the single most important factor that distinguishes Yale from schools with comparable academic reputations. Your residential college becomes a vital part of your identification as a Yalie. By and large, the first question you will be asked upon meeting another Yalie is , "What college are you in?" The college system affects almost every aspect of life at Yale. The colleges have been described as "like fraternities but better." Like fraternities and sororities, they provide housing, food, and a sense of belonging. However, they are coed, are not selective or exclusive, and involve the entire student body.

The student body at Yale is divided into twelve colleges: Berkeley, Branford, Calhoun, Davenport, Ezra Stiles, Jonathan Edwards, Morse, Pierson, Saybrook, Silliman, Timothy Dwight, and Trumbull. Every student, whether living in a college or not, is affiliated with a college. All freshmen are placed in a college prior to matriculation; part of your Yale identity is determined even before you arrive. This process ensures random placement of incoming students so that each college maintains a diverse student body. Despite the random placement, some colleges still have reputations—the jock college, the artsy college, the famous people college, and so on. The reputations are mostly due to traditions and mostly unfounded.

> *"My college, Ezra Stiles, was known as the geeky college my freshman year, due to its three-year history of winning the Gimbel Cup—awarded to the college with the overall highest grades. It didn't take long for us to reverse this tradition. My junior year we won the Tang Cup—an unofficial drinking award. My senior year we successfully launched a year-long crusade to win the intramural award, the Tyng Cup, thereby earning the reputation of the jock college. Thus, reputations are not to be trusted."*

Each college is a quad, with its own courtyard. Almost all students live in suites with a number of bedrooms off a common living room, often with beautiful oak paneling and a fireplace. Types of rooms and suites vary from college to college. By junior or senior year, most students can live in singles if they want.

Although placed in a college, all freshmen except those in Silliman and Timothy Dwight live on Old Campus during their freshman year. This enables freshmen to get to know their classmates before they move into their colleges sophomore year. Old Campus is the classic freshman quad, with a huge courtyard in the middle, inspiring Frisbee games and suntanning in the fall and spring and massive snowball fights in the winter.

Aside from being a dormitory, each college has such a complete set of facilities and such a diverse schedule of activities that it is possible for a student never to leave, except to attend classes. Each college has its own dining hall, common room, TV room, 24 hour library, computer room with Macintosh word processors, laundry room, intramural teams, theater society, student-run late night snack bar, social activities committee, college council, and more. Other facilities vary among colleges but include game rooms, dark rooms, music practice rooms, squash and basketball courts, weight rooms; Calhoun even has its own sauna.

Dining halls serve as the social centers of each college. Aside from being a place to eat (food at Yale is above average on the institutional scale), dining halls are seen as the place where all students of the college congregate daily (and nightly). All students who live on campus—over 80% of the student body—are required to have a full meal plan. This ensures that you can find most of your friends in the dining hall on any given evening, You are not restricted to eating in your college and may eat at any of the other colleges and many of the graduate school dining halls. All freshman eat breakfast and lunch in Commons, an overwhelming dining hall with seating capacity of more than 1500. Commons is closed in the evenings and on weekends, giving the freshmen an opportunity to eat in their colleges and get acquainted with the upperclassmen.

The colleges also play a major role in the social life of Yale students. Although Yale is not a party school of *Animal House* proportions, there is usually a wide variety of social events each weekend. Each college has a Social Activities Committee (SAC) that throws campus-wide parties. There are usually at least one or two SAC parties each weekend. These are often the classic beer and tapes parties although each college throws one or two special parties annually. For example, Morse and Stiles team up once a year to host Casino Night, a forties-style semiformal party featuring gambling and dancing, complete with cigar girls and Monopoly money. Most colleges have one or two formal dances each year. SACs also host happy hours, trips to the beach and to Mets' games, and midweek study breaks. Due to the legal drinking age of twenty-one, all SAC parties serve alcohol only to students with a Yale-issued drinking ID.

Since the recent implementation of this alcohol policy, fraternities and private parties have become increasingly popular. For the most part, fraternities and sororities play a very small role in campus life. There are only six or seven fraternities and three sororites, with membership of around 5% of the student body. Fraternities and sororities do not affect most students' lives, except to provide another party to go to on Saturday night. Room parties, suite parties, hall parties, and off-campus parties provide most of the social life after freshman year. There are also a handful of good hangouts in New Haven where students congregate late nights and weekends.

There is never nothing to do at Yale. If you're fortunate enough—or carefree enough—to be able to skip studying for a while, there is always a wide range of activities going on. Yalies never have enough time and are typically forced to establish priorities and make decisions in order to get everything done.

EXTRACURRICULAR ACTIVITIES

The extent of extracurricular activities is so large that it would be impossible to mention all of them. Suffice it to say that if you are interested in something, there's likely to be an organization, group, or team for you. If not, you can probably start one.

Almost all Yalies are involved in some type of athletic activity. Twenty percent of the student body are varsity athletes; Yale has 32 varsity sport teams. There is also a variety of club sports, from polo to cross-country skiing. Intramurals involve the largest number of Yalies. Each college has its own set of intramural teams that compete with the other colleges for the coveted Tyng Cup, awarded each year to the college with the best overall intramural record. Although intramural teams are competitive, they are open to players of all levels and present a good opportunity for you to get to know other people in your college. There is a wide variety of intramural sports, from classics like soccer, tennis, and coed touch football to strange creations such as inner tube water polo.

There are a variety of political, cultural, special interest, and support groups. These groups have become so dominant and vocal on campus that the current campus joke is that white males are the only group that does not have some particular cultural or support group. There are a number of campus publications as well. The *Yale Daily News,* the oldest college daily newspaper, maintains its reputation for providing the most complete account of campus happenings. Because Yale is located in a metropolitan area, there are also plenty of opportunities for community service.

Yale is well known for its performing arts community. Every college has it own theater group, and the dining halls provide available stages. Plays, musicals, singing groups, and improv comedy groups abound and are usually opened to anyone willing to audition. On any one weekend, you are bound to find at least four student productions or performances happening.

> *"My roommates present a good example of the wide variety of activities available. While I was busy doing gymnastics or working at the Yale women's center, one of my roommates was rowing for the crew team, another publishing a literature and art quarterly, a third coordinating all intramurals for my college, and a fourth dancing with the leading Yale dance group. Although our schedules were such that we often didn't see each other until late at night, we all got a feeling for each person's activities and also got to meet a wide variety of people."*

It does not do justice to the extracurricular opportunities at Yale to attempt to describe them in a few paragraphs. The variety and number of organizations are overwhelming. Furthermore, in most cases you do not have to be an expert in the field in order to become involved. Athletes who have never sung before join singing groups; people who have never written for a publication report for the *Daily News*. Yalies realize that a Yale education does not consist entirely of classes, professors, and books. Everybody is involved in something, if not in many things.

GRADUATES

The diversity of the student body is reflected in the variety of paths that Yale alumni choose to follow. Most Yalies do not settle down immediately after college into steady careers; some never settle down. My Yale friends are presently scattered across the country and the globe. Having graduated, Yalies feel that assurance that whatever paths they follow and risks they take, they have their degree from Yale to back them up.

> *"I have found in my job searches that a Yale degree carries a great deal of weight. The general public believes that anyone who attended Yale must be bright and capable (even if this has not been demonstrated). In simple terms, a Yale degree opens doors."*

Although only 20% of a graduating class enters graduate school directly, a much larger percentage eventually get graduate degrees. Significant portions of each class attend medical and law schools. Due to high salaries and heavy on-campus recruiting, many students choose to work in business for a few years after college although they, too, may eventually attend graduate school. There are prominent Yalies in many fields. There have been Yale presidents, Yale Supreme Court justices, Yale Oscar winners, even Yale pro football players.

The Yale alumni network is very strong, often serving to assist recent graduates in their job searches. The alumni network is particularly useful when a Yalie moves to a new city. Each city has its own Yale Club, and its members are usually well connected in the community.

> *"Having been taught how to think at Yale, graduates are prepared to enter almost any field they choose. It was not until I left Yale that I realized how special it is. My academic education prepared me well, but what I missed most was the open-mined atmosphere that rarely exists in the real world. Having been a part of this atmosphere, two Yalies will always share a common bond, even if they graduated three decades apart. This feeling keeps the Yale network strong, providing assistance to current, future, and past Yalies."*

SUMMARY OVERVIEW

"During my senior year, I asked many of my friends what led them to choose Yale and if they had been surprised or disappointed. The responses were varied although most people agree that visiting the Yale campus helped convince them to attend. Even those who had come to Yale for a particular reason—to study music or play baseball—agreed that it is the people who make Yale special."

The open-minded atmosphere at Yale and the unique residential college system are two of the most important strengths of Yale. The former guarantees a free exchange of ideas and the development of each student's individuality. A great feeling of respect for each student's interests contributes to this atmosphere. The latter provides an opportunity for intimacy and camaraderie, without the exclusion or prejudice that is often found in the fraternity system, that would otherwise be hard to achieve at a large school.

The academic program is what has given Yale its name and reputation. Due to the variety and depth of Yale academics, few schools in the country even attempt to compete. This reputation is further backed up with excellent resources. The Yale administration asserts that a student can get the best education available at Yale, and students agree.

Very few graduates have major complaints about their time at Yale. There are two commonly voiced complaints. One is about the weather, for which the university cannot be blamed. Along this same line, New Haven is also the subject of some dissatisfaction. If your idea of college involves an isolated haven, a little college town in which the campus news is the only news, New Haven is not for you.

Second, Yalies always complain about their work. As there are so many opportunities at Yale, students must make sacrifices of their time in order to keep up with the challenging work load. They usually agree, however, that in order to get something out of their classes, they must put in a certain amount of effort. The work at Yale is demanding and challenging and therefore precludes 24-hour-a-day parties—an image of college that some students seek to create.

In one sentence, Yale is a friendly place with an intellectually stimulating atmosphere that happens to provide plenty of fun as well. Having spoken to students from many schools, I remain very happy with my decision to attend Yale. Furthermore, it is hard to find a disgruntled Yalie, at least one that wouldn't be equally disgruntled at any school. All of my Yale friends agree that they chose the right school. That seems to me to be the best recommendation of all—the satisfaction of the students at Yale and Yale graduates.

Janet Levine, B.A.

Summary Overview

The top 50 colleges share common characteristics. They all have well-defined educational missions, excellent faculties, strong and varied student bodies, and a broad range of extracurricular activities. All excel in at least one area and, in most cases, in many.

Despite these similarities, each of the top 50 has its own distinguishing characteristics. Each has distinctive strengths, academic programs, and social life. For example, Chicago's dominant theme is its intellectualism...Berkeley prides itself on its diversity. Columbia's core curriculum sets it apart...Virginia's liberal arts tradition is its hallmark.

In short, each of the top 50 provides an excellent educational experience, but each does it in its own way.

AMHERST COLLEGE

Amherst College is a small undergraduate institution noted for the quality of its faculty, students, and graduates. Dedicated to the principles of a liberal arts education, Amherst encourages the development of a questioning, critical mind and of awareness of social issues in current life and throughout history. Located in a valley near four other colleges, Amherst students enjoy the benefits of both intimate classes and a wide range of cultural activities. Amherst is a hard school to get into, but it is even harder *not* to get a great education there.

BATES COLLEGE

Bates College, in Lewiston, Maine, is a true liberal arts college. It is the school's aim to provide its students with a breadth of knowledge, not just training in one specific area, allowing its graduates to pursue an infinite number of career and lifestyle paths after graduation. Bates is small, with fewer than 1600 students, and has a faculty entirely committed to giving these students one of the finest educations available anywhere. Bates was the first college in New England, and the second in the country, to accept both men and women, and has never had fraternities or sororities—two facets that give the college its aura of egalitarianism. Bates' small size, beautiful setting, wonderful faculty, ideals of equality for all, and commitment to education, make it the ideal place for students to spend four school years.

BOSTON COLLEGE

Boston College is a Jesuit university located in Chestnut Hill, a suburb of Boston, Massachusetts. It is renowned for its liberal arts offerings as well as its social and intellectual challenges. There is an established core curriculum, dedicated to encouraging students to think for themselves. This includes an introduction to various aspects of philosophy and theology as well as European history, and social and natural sciences. The Jesuit influence is strong but it never dominates the commitment to education. There is great diversity not only in academic offerings but in extracurricular activities as well. This diversity renders Boston College an attractive option for students from all cultures and walks of life. It is very much an institution that places primary responsibility for success in academics on the individual. Because of this, maximum intellectual and spiritual growth is realized.

BOWDOIN COLLEGE

Bowdoin is an excellent, small liberal arts college that has a knack for making innovative policy changes. These changes help to stimulate debate and interest in the college's future direction. Such interest keeps Bowdoin strong. The faculty is as committed to teaching as most students are to learning. The atmosphere is academic in nature but usually not competitive or high pressure. An active and changing social scene can break up any academic blues, which do occur. Bowdoin is a close and rich community, but driving a mile in any direction leaves it far behind, and the whole Maine coast lies ready to be explored.

BROWN UNIVERSITY

Brown University is an Ivy League school located in Providence, Rhode Island. It offers a flexible liberal arts curriculum that allows students to plan their own academic programs. There is no core curriculum, and no courses are required except those necessary to complete a major. With a student-faculty ratio of ten to one, Brown offers the benefits of a small college but incorporates the research and scholarship of a large university. The academic program is complemented by a broad range of extracurricular activities in which students are expected and encouraged to participate. It is a school that is distinguished by its progressive and innovative approaches to education—a school that allows students to be full partners in the educational process.

BRYN MAWR COLLEGE

Bryn Mawr College is an all women's college located in Bryn Mawr, Pennsylvania, about ten miles west of Philadelphia, and is one of the Seven Sisters schools. The school is distinguished by its strenuous academic environment, its emphasis on responsibility to community, and its insistence on academic integrity and curiosity. The student body is extremely diverse, coming from 49 states and 47 foreign countries. The core curriculum is flexible, offering majors in numerous academic disciplines as well as interdepartmental and independent majors. As the first American college to offer studies leading to the Ph.D. for women, Bryn Mawr has a long history of preparing women for academic and professional challenges, and continues to encourage and promote excellence in women's education.

CALIFORNIA INSTITUTE OF TECHNOLOGY

Caltech provides a specialized education centered around mathematics, science, and engineering in a research-oriented environment that doesn't get covered with snow in the winter, isn't so large that you have to use public transportation to get from the dorms to campus, and won't ever require you to wear a sweater around your shoulders when you go to class. Located in Pasadena, California, Caltech provides students with the opportunity to work with and possibly even become a Nobel Prize winning world-renowned scientist. Caltech boasts a student-to-faculty ratio of three-to-one, unparalleled research resources, and an honor system that works.

CARLETON COLLEGE

Carleton College is a small undergraduate institution located in Northfield, Minnesota. Within its diverse yet close-knit community, students, faculty, and staff all strive to create an open social and intellectual environment. The school stresses a well-rounded education, requiring students to complete a basic core of liberal arts courses. Professors generally are very accessible, and they are as committed to teaching as their students are to learning. With Minneapolis and St. Paul less than an hour away, students have access to a major metropolitan area. However, they always can come home to the warmth and intimacy of a small midwestern town. Carleton College may be far removed from the main cluster of well-known eastern liberal arts schools to which it often is compared, but in its isolation it has acquired its own reputation for academic excellence and for attracting bright, talented, and enthusiastic individuals.

CARNEGIE MELLON UNIVERSITY

Carnegie Mellon is a private, highly competitive university located in Pittsburgh, Pennsylvania. The student body is comprised of nearly 7000 undergraduate and graduate students, and boasts a student-to-faculty ratio of nine to one. This is a school that prides itself on challenging students to become innovative thinkers, and pushes them to do so by not simply learning material but by going a step farther and applying it to real-life situations. At times called the Professional Choice, Carnegie Mellon is for the student who has an idea what he or she wants in life, and has the motivation to pursue it. Graduates go on to pursue careers in Fortune 500 companies, on Broadway and in Hollywood, and at prestigious graduate schools worldwide.

CLAREMONT MCKENNA COLLEGE

Hands-on-experience is a phrase that traditionally conjures up images of trade schools or ads for the U.S. military. Because of this, among America's most selective schools, only the youthful Claremont McKenna College would dare apply such a description to its name. Founded on the English Oxford model, yet daily creating its own tradition, CMC focuses its faculty, programs, and resources on preparing students to meet the demand for ethical leadership in business, government, and the professions. CMC students conduct independent research, help decide school policy, talk with distinguished guest speakers over dinner and wine, and play volleyball with their professors. Because CMC's uncommon personal attention fosters extraordinary personal achievement, hands-on-experience separates Claremont McKenna College from every other college or university in the country.

COLLEGE OF WILLIAM AND MARY

William and Mary is part of the Virginia state college system with roughly 35% of its students hailing from out-of-state. The program is a broad-based liberal arts curriculum strong in both science and nonscience departments. Students must complete a minimum core requirement of courses outside their intended major. The faculty teach all classes and are very accessible to the undergraduates. Anything you may want to get involved in, William and Mary probably has it, despite the school's relatively small size (5400 undergraduates). The college community is close-knit, bound by common honor codes, and there is very little academic competition among the students. The college has an excellent placement record among graduate and professional schools. William and Mary has a perfect mix of a strong, personalized education on a pleasant, active campus.

COLUMBIA UNIVERSITY

Older than the nation itself, Columbia College is a liberal arts college in the traditional mode, complete with a required set of core classes, an approach that is back in vogue in higher education. Its 32-acre campus on the Upper West Side of Manhattan creates an oasis for learning. An air of street-wise sophistication dominates the nation's smallest Ivy and from Museum Mile to the East Village dance clubs, students regard all of New York City as their campus.

CORNELL UNIVERSITY

On a beautiful campus in upstate New York, Cornell offers study in seven widely varying colleges for about 13,000 undergraduates. Any student can easily find an interesting area of study, and Cornell's large library system and wide range of activities provide further resources to the hungry student. Although Cornell can be a large, impersonal school, students who bring a desire and a determination to learn, to experience, and to enjoy will cherish their days at Cornell.

DARTMOUTH COLLEGE

Dartmouth College combines a strong emphasis on undergraduate education and a devoted faculty in the pristine rural environment of Hanover, New Hampshire. The school is renowned for its innovative method of language instruction and its advanced computer network. Its flexible calendar system, the D-Plan, allows many students to study abroad for one or more terms. By the end of the decade, new facilities in science and psychology, an addition to the library, and a new student center will complement curriculum changes that will require all students to engage themselves intellectually by means of a "culminating senior experience." Traditions such as the Homecoming bonfire, outdoor trips for first-year students, and the school's intangible "sense of place" help explain why most Dartmouth alumni have a life-long attachment to their school.

DAVIDSON COLLEGE

Located in Davidson, North Carolina, Davidson teaches students to think critically and to work hard, useful skills in any line of work. Davidson specializes in preparing students for professional schools, especially medical, law, and business. The work load is tremendous, making Davidson a demanding school to attend. Davidson works toward producing well-rounded graduates by emphasizing extra-curricular activities ranging from intramural sports to student government to campus committees. With a stringent Honor Code governing both classroom and campus, Davidson has an environment of trust and ethical conduct.

DUKE UNIVERSITY

Duke University was once one of the best schools in the South. But in recent years a subtle change has taken place: Duke is now one of the best schools. Period. Duke emphasizes freedom for intellectual and personal growth, both academic and social. Graduates have a high acceptance rate at graduate and professional schools and are generally employed in high-paying jobs along the East Coast. Duke's greatest strength is a good balance between serious academic pursuit and an active social life.

EMORY UNIVERSITY

Emory University is a hard-charging newcomer to the ranks of the nation's top universities. Newly inherited millions have lured top students and scholars to its suburban Atlanta campus, building Emory's reputation for liberal arts excellence almost as quickly as it constructs new buildings. Its 4500 undergraduates are a largely conservative, preprofessional group seeking a top-flight education without the anxieties and cold weather of more well-known Northern schools. The university is no social or athletic powerhouse, but Emory and Atlanta are both taking off like rocket ships, and going along for the ride promises to be extremely rewarding.

GEORGETOWN UNIVERSITY

Georgetown gives students an excellent, well-balanced liberal arts education. The faculty is uncommonly committed to the undergraduate students, and the academic program is demanding. Although it is a city school, it has a lovely campus. The varied life experience and backgrounds of the students allow them to learn from one another. The students themselves are conservative but spirited in their partying and dedicated to social work. Four years at Georgetown is exhausting and exhilarating. There is so much to do that you are always busy, never bored, and constantly stretching.

GEORGIA INSTITUTE OF TECHNOLOGY

The Georgia Institute of Technology offers students who are interested in mathematics and science an opportunity to enrich their education through a broad mix of tradition, fundamentals, and state-of-the art research. Located in Atlanta, the school has 31 majors in five areas: engineering, science, management, computing, and architecture. By focusing its energies on a primarily scientific curriculum, Georgia Tech is able to offer its students one of the best educational opportunities in the United States. The college's goal of producing top quality graduates combines a rich blend of extracurricular options and the cultural advantages of the city with first-rate teachers and researchers to produce an atmosphere that is conducive to both learning and excelling.

HARVARD UNIVERSITY

Harvard, located in Cambridge, Massachusetts, is a coeducational liberal arts institution. As a member of the Ivy League, Harvard has a traditional reputation for intellectual excellence and international influence. Harvard (along with Radcliffe, an institution that merged with Harvard) has an enrollment of nearly 6600 students and offers an A.B. in approximately 50 departments. Admission is most competitive with most applicants in the top 5% of their high school graduating classes. Yet the college is also known for the diversity of the student population. The academic and cultural resources available are among the best available anywhere, and it is for good reason that Harvard represents the best in a college education.

HARVEY MUDD COLLEGE

Harvey Mudd College in Claremont, California is a school of science and engineering with 600 students. It is academically rigorous, offers only six majors (biology, chemistry, computer science, engineering, mathematics, and physics), and accepts a wide variety of students with various interests outside of math and science. Every student is required to take about one-third of their courses in a major, one-third in a core of math, science, and engineering, and one-third in the humanities. The greatest feature of the school is its honor code, which requires integrity from each student, allowing a very open atmosphere for personal and academic growth. It also is near Foster's, the world's greatest doughnut shop.

HAVERFORD COLLEGE

Haverford is a small, liberal arts college with one of the finest reputations for academic excellence in the United States. Small classes, intelligent students and faculty members, extensive resources, and an intimacy that resembles that of a family's enables Haverford to provide its students with a unique, hard-won education. No student leaves Haverford without a firm liberal arts base, and few leave lacking a greater understanding of their fellow classmates and a lingering sense of honor imbued by the school's honor code. With a long history of dedication to both education and honor, Haverford blends traditional values with modern resources, facilities, and ideas.

JOHNS HOPKINS UNIVERSITY

Johns Hopkins is a liberal arts university founded on the European model of graduate schools: that students should learn from active researchers. That tradition continues at Hopkins, where a small student-to-faculty ratio and an emphasis on depth offer the undergraduate a graduate-level standard of scholarship. Ranked with the best Ivy League schools, Hopkins has an intensity few can match. Though more competitive than some may like, it is a training ground for achievers in all fields, science and the humanities. Though a Baltimore institution, the school has an international faculty and student body. Johns Hopkins combines the grandiosity of an international university with the intimacy of a graduate school.

MASSACHUSETTS INSTITUTE OF TECHNOLOGY

MIT is the world's premier institution for science and engineering education. You can study everything from the heavens (earth and planetary sciences) to the depths of the seas (ocean engineering). Everything is taught with a heavy technical and quantitative bent—although some of the social sciences (economics, political science) are also first-rate. The Institute's greatest strength is the synergy between a world-class faculty and a student body that shares a natural curiosity about the world and how it works. Despite the heavy pressures of demanding academic programs, nearly all undergraduates get a chance to take advantage of this relationship and get involved with the research projects of their professors. Located in Cambridge, a few minutes downstream from what is perhaps the country's most famous college, students take pride in the fact that, although MIT doesn't have the name recognition of Harvard, there's no place where people work harder to learn more.

MIDDLEBURY COLLEGE

Middlebury College is a small, eclectic liberal arts college tucked into Vermont's lovely Champlain Valley. Its strong and varied curriculum is loaded with international spice—the college operates six schools abroad, and its summer language schools are internationally famous. With a student-to-faculty ratio of 11 to one, Middlebury's classes tend to be small and intense. It's an intimate academic experience—professors most often get to know their students quite well. The academic program is augmented by a wide variety of extracurricular activities (Middlebury operates its own ski area, among other things), and students tend to be involved in many things at once. Middlebury provides the best of two worlds: students take full advantage of the college's deeply rural setting, but there's also the ever present buzz of events and ideas.

NORTHWESTERN UNIVERSITY

Northwestern manages to provide what many colleges and universities can't: a challenging academic program and the real world experiences that put that knowledge to the test. Each of the university's six undergraduate schools offers internships and field-study programs that give students the chance to see if what they've learned in the classroom will help them in the job world. Class sizes vary widely, but most professors are readily accessible. The school is located on the shores of Lake Michigan in Evanston, Illinois, birthplace of Prohibition. But a broad range of campus activities will make any student forget that bit of trivia. And besides, one of the world's best cultural and entertainment playgrounds, Chicago, is just to the south.

POMONA COLLEGE

Pomona College combines the personal advantages of a small college with the resources of a larger university, culminating in a well-endowed liberal arts institution with a tradition of excellence. The classes are small, the faces friendly, and the sun evershining. The other five colleges in the Claremont System give Pomona College the depth and resources of a much larger university. Classes and course schedules for just about every need are available, and the extensive exchange programs with institutions both domestically and abroad make Pomona an ideal place for those wanting to stretch their horizons. Pomona College lets the students create what they want, to a reasonable extent, and the option to do nothing also is available. The relative freedom allowed at the college, the abundance of educational and cultural opportunities, and the time, space, and setting given the students make the Pomona diploma a valuable one.

PRINCETON UNIVERSITY

Princeton distinguishes itself by its almost total commitment to undergraduate education. With few graduate programs to divert the attention of top professors, Princeton offers an unparalleled opportunity for undergraduates to experience close contact with a first-class university faculty. This contact is increased by Princeton's preceptorials and the required senior thesis, which is prepared under the close supervision of a professor and often becomes a student's most treasured academic experience. In addition to its top-notch academic program, Princeton offers an impressive social and extracurricular environment, which attracts a wonderfully diverse student body.

REED COLLEGE

Reed is a small liberal arts college in Portland, Oregon. It is well known for its commitment to undergraduate teaching, its disregard for divisions between disciplines, and the quality and rigor of its curriculum. The low student faculty ratio and the college's belief in the effectiveness of conference-style teaching encourage debate and interaction both inside the classroom and out. Socially, individual expression is valued highly; stifling expectations are not. And extracurricular activities exist as an opportunity to participate, not spectate. It is a community of apparent opposites, where traditional educational theories mix with a unique social atmosphere in a way that is all Reed's own.

RICE UNIVERSITY

Intense is the watchword at Rice, where nothing—not academics, not social life, not extracurriculars—takes place at half speed. Students are as quirky as the campus's Italianate architecture: they elect male homecoming queens, train almost religiously for the university's annual bike race, and are proud that the university's Marching Owl Band doesn't march. The oak covered Rice campus is only a few miles from downtown Houston. With an undergraduate enrollment of about 2700, Rice isn't as well known as its Ivy League cousins; but with its strong points— among them emphasis on undergraduate education, low tuition, good financial aid, the college system, active social life on campus, and warm Houston winters—it shouldn't be long until it is.

STANFORD UNIVERSITY

Stanford is the new kid on the Ivy League scene. Having just celebrated its Centennial, the school Leland Stanford founded on a farm south of San Francisco can boast of world-class teachers and researchers in almost every field and a top-notch athletic program to boot. But the school is also doing some soul-searching to define its academic mission as it enters its second century. It is trying to remain premiere among science and engineering schools and at the same time bring its liberal arts curriculum and faculty up to par with the very best in the world. As it is, Stanford combines excellent academics and a varied social life in one of the most beautiful locations in the country.

SWARTHMORE COLLEGE

Swarthmore College is a small liberal arts and engineering college located on a 330-acre arboreal campus in Swarthmore, Pennsylvania, an outlying suburb of Philadelphia. Famed for its academic intensity and small classes, Swarthmore gives its students a lot: personalized academic attention, the chance to trade classes for intimate seminars during the last two years of study, an endless panoply of extracurriculars—from political action committees to science fiction societies—and a close-knit social scene that revolves mostly around all-college parties. Swarthmore students take their education seriously, for the most part, and their lives passionately; the atmosphere, both in the classroom and out, is heated, critical, and stead-fastly progressive.

TUFTS UNIVERSITY

Tufts is a small liberal arts college located in Medford, Massachusetts. It is made up of the College of Liberal Arts and Sciences and the College of Engineering. Tufts also has seven professional and graduate schools. The small size of the college offers students the chance to work closely with faculty. One of Tufts's greatest assets is its student body. The school encourages students to learn from their peers as much as from their instructors. Having fewer than 5000 under-graduate students, Tufts can feel small and comfortable but still challenging and exciting at the same time. Located just outside one of the country's biggest college towns, Boston, the extended campus of the city offers more variety to things a Tufts student can experience.

UNIVERSITY OF CALIFORNIA/BERKELEY

Cal's most distinguishing characteristics are the diversity and excellence of its faculty and student body. Because it is a world-renowned academic institution, Berkeley draws students and faculty from the 50 states and numerous countries across the globe. Currently, there are 12 Nobel Prize winners on the faculty as well as numerous other prize-winning professors. Berkeley, which is known for its graduate program, has an undergraduate program that offers studies in almost every imaginable subject from Afro-American studies to zoology. Because of this diversity and excellence, acquiring a degree from Berkeley is very demanding but, once in hand, very precious to an employer.

UNIVERSITY OF CALIFORNIA/LOS ANGELES

UCLA's surest selling point is that it combines the academic thrust of an Ivy League school with the athletic spirit of a Big Ten college campus and the social excitement of a large public university. As one of the nation's top research universities, the only one established in the twentieth century, UCLA boasts Nobel laureates, Olympic champions, and world-renowned filmmakers as its faculty and alumni. Housed within one of the most influential cities in the world, UCLA offers students a metropolitan flavor unparalleled by any other institution. Its most distinguishing characteristics are the diversity of its students, academic options, and rich social environment. UCLA draws students from all 50 states as well as from across the world and allows them to develop at their own rate by exploring a number of different subjects or studying one area in-depth.

UNIVERSITY OF CHICAGO

The University of Chicago has a well-deserved reputation for academic excellence and intellectual ferment. The faculty is internationally renowned and on the cutting edge of research yet still committed to undergraduate teaching. Students at Chicago enjoy discussing ideas with faculty and among themselves. Students work hard. They graduate well prepared for graduate school or the professional world. They also party hard and enjoy an informal, intense social life in one of the most exciting and vibrant cities in the country.

UNIVERSITY OF ILLINOIS/URBANA-CHAMPAIGN

The University of Illinois is a Big Ten school located in Urbana. Although most of its students come from Illinois, the U of I attracts exceptional people from all over the globe. With a world-renowned faculty and a distinguished reputation in science, engineering, and the humanities, the U of I consistently ranks first or in the top three in many fields. What makes the school so exciting is the diversity of its 35,000 students, who study 150 different subjects and participate in more than 700 extracurricular activities. The size, reputation, high-tech facilities, and low tuition all combine to make the University of Illinois a top choice among scholars.

UNIVERSITY OF MICHIGAN/ANN ARBOR

The University of Michigan is a large, dynamic institution that offers the best in public education. Located in Ann Arbor, the school maintains a diverse student body and faculty that interact with the city around them. Michigan gives students many educational opportunities and receives high marks for its graduate and engineering programs. Founded in 1817, Michigan was one of the first public universities in the nation. The university combines a history of academic excellence with a look ahead to help students meet the demands of the present and the future.

UNIVERSITY OF NORTH CAROLINA/CHAPEL HILL

The University of North Carolina at Chapel Hill, the nation's first state university, is recognized for academic excellence and social, cultural, and intellectual diversity. Strengthened by outstanding faculty and top-notch students, the university's philosophy of liberal arts secures free thought, speech, and actions, as well as the development of an inquisitive critical mind. Located in the fast-growing Research Triangle area, students enjoy cultural events while Chapel Hill retains its village-like ambience. Competition for admission — especially among out-of-state applicants — is keen, but so is the educational opportunity.

UNIVERSITY OF NOTRE DAME

Situated on a grassy, tree-lined campus adjacent to South Bend, Indiana, the University of Notre Dame is a Catholic university where intellectual and moral development are seen as intimately related. Originally famous for football, Notre Dame continues its tradition of excellence in athletics even as its academic program has achieved a national reputation. Preprofessional studies, chemical engineering, philosophy, theology, and accounting are particular strengths, but most students come to Notre Dame for reasons beyond the strong undergraduate program, reasons that usually center on the spirit of friendly hospitality that flows from a close-knit student body.

UNIVERSITY OF PENNSYLVANIA

The University of Pennsylvania is a large school located in a residential area of Philadelphia. Known for years for its strong professional program, Penn has now established a reputation as a top undergraduate college, with programs in the arts and sciences, business, engineering, and nursing. Despite the number of undergraduates, the friendly atmosphere makes it seem like a much smaller school. Penn offers an endless variety of academic, extracurricular, and social opportunities and attracts a diverse group of talented students from all over the country.

UNIVERSITY OF TEXAS/AUSTIN

The University of Texas at Austin, built in 1883, is the flagship school of a 15—system institution. Enrollment in the state school tops 49,000, and the 16,500 business and liberal arts undergraduate students comprise a little less than half of undergraduate enrollment. Students may seek degrees in any of about a dozen schools plus several specialized graduate departments. UT is distinguished for its placement in a progressive, college-oriented city and its outstanding approach to research, which helped attract the superconducting super collider to Texas. The school's financial resources, rooted in the profits of a $3 billion permanent fund based on stocks and oil, are a key factor in its ability to encourage growth and diversification in its degree program and keep tuition extremely low.

UNIVERSITY OF VIRGINIA

The University of Virginia's undergraduate program focuses on a liberal arts background, exactly the way founder Thomas Jefferson would have wanted it. Top-notch faculty work with students to buttress the university's growing national reputation. Students balance academics with a thriving social scene and a myriad of extracurricular activities. Surrounding it all is the allure of Charlottesville and the neoclassical design of the university. The pursuit of excellence at UVa embraces an all-around quality education at a reasonable price in an unforgettable environment.

VASSAR COLLEGE

Vassar is a college that offers the strongest liberal arts education while still embracing the pioneering spirit. Vassar was the first college in the country to offer women access to education equal to that of what men were receiving at places like Harvard and Yale. It was also the first of the prestigious group of all-women colleges to develop a coeducational student body. Over 20 years have passed since Vassar made the decision to admit men, and men now comprise 44% of the campus. The curriculum is marked by its flexibility. Close student consultation with faculty members takes the place of a core curriculum. The choice of a major is virtually unlimited with Vassar's support of innovative multidisciplinary and independent programs. Vassar's idyllic 1000-acre campus is located in the heart of the Hudson River Valley, less than two hours north of New York City. Vassar's academic and physical offerings are enhanced by a diverse student body representing every state and 28 other countries.

WAKE FOREST UNIVERSITY

Wake Forest University is located in Winston-Salem, North Carolina on a beautiful, wooded campus. It is known as an excellent liberal arts school with a relatively small enrollment and a superb faculty. The university's emphasis is on teaching, and students have phenomenal access to professors. Divisional requirements within the liberal arts curriculum are numerous, and academic demands are rigorous. The school combines the friendly atmosphere of a small college with the superior facilities of a larger university. Despite its southern roots, Wake Forest is a place of increasing diversity, distinguished by the warmth of its community and the excellence of its personalized, liberal arts instruction.

WASHINGTON AND LEE UNIVERSITY

A small liberal arts university steeped in southern tradition, Washington and Lee boasts a broad, flexible liberal arts curriculum complemented by a variety of pre-professional degrees. The school's long-standing and successful honor system creates a rare and genteel environment: students schedule their own exams, take tests unproctored, and feel safe leaving their belongings unattended while on campus.

What's more, a student-to-faculty ratio of 11.5 to one guarantees close contact with the school's distinguished faculty. All extracurricular activities—of which there are many—are open to the entire student body, and students are encouraged to get involved in campus affairs. Most do. The W & L experience is unique: a first-rate liberal arts education founded on community and trust.

WELLESLEY COLLEGE

Wellesley is a small liberal arts women's college located in a beautiful Boston suburb. Its lake, trees, and Gothic buildings make it a wonderful haven for personal exploration and growth. Academically excellent, Wellesley is dedicated to diversity, drawing students and faculty from across this country and many others. Wellesley takes pride in encouraging close ties between professors and students. Wellesley women work hard both during and after their years on campus. Although it is required that a student take classes in at least three different areas, much flexibility is allowed. "She is ever changing, though ever Wellesley."

WESLEYAN UNIVERSITY

Wesleyan University offers the best of both a small liberal arts college and a major well-known university. This blend makes a surprising range of possibilities available to students. Students can mold their own educations but still get close attention from professors who are scholars in their fields. Wesleyan offers many choices and resources both in and out of class, but it is up to the student to make the most of the choices given. Students interested in that kind of arrangement find themselves very comfortable and challenged at Wesleyan.

WILLIAMS COLLEGE

Founded in 1793, Williams College is a small liberal arts college located on 450 acres in the northwesternmost corner of Massachusetts. Beyond a beautiful setting, Williams is one of the most selective colleges in the country. Williams manages to be relaxed and rigorous at the same time. The small town location invites a relaxation for four years of the real world rules of suspicion and closed-ness. The mind and the body, however, are rarely relaxed in one's four years at Williams. Students work very hard but not only in the classroom. Everyone seems to be involved in athletics, drama, music, politics, or something else other than classes—something that will exercise intellectual energy. This relaxed rigor is the essence of Williams.

YALE UNIVERSITY

Yale University is a large school, well known for academic excellence, located in New Haven, Connecticut. Its noted academic program lives up to the reputation of the Ivy League and is geared toward providing a liberal arts education. Yale has a strong faculty, top scholars in every field, most of whom are very accessible to students. In keeping with the liberal arts tradition, Yale offers a wide array of courses and majors; however, it does not offer many vocationally directed majors such as marketing or business. In addition, Yale strives to maintain a very diverse and highly capable student body. The residential college system makes Yale unique, providing each student with an identity in a smaller community within the university.

Part II

Top
College
Tips

Tips on Selecting Top Colleges

1. **Think about yourself and your interests.**

2. **Decide what you want—make a list of requirements.**

3. **Compile a list of 15–20 colleges, research, then narrow your list.**

4. **Buy college guidebooks, send for admissions brochures, and read up on the colleges on your short list.**

5. **Visit the colleges you are considering.**

6. **Talk to current students and recent graduates.**

7. **Talk to professors.**

8. **Choose schools that fit your social as well as your academic needs.**

9. **Look for schools with diverse academic strengths.**

10. **Go with your gut.**

1. THINK ABOUT YOURSELF AND YOUR INTERESTS.

When picking a school, there is no better place to start than with yourself. What do you excel in: history, mathematics, science, athletics, drama? What are you interested in: foreign countries, professional sports, writing? What kind of career do you want to pursue: law, business, journalism? How do you like to spend your time: reading, studying, watching movies, playing tennis? What are your personal goals, interests, and priorities?

Because the top schools are very different, it is important that *you* decide what kind of school and educational experience *you* want. How do you want to spend four years in the prime of your life? Which college best satisfies your needs? Where will you be happiest and best fit in? Obviously, the wishes of your parents, suggestions from friends, and advice from your guidance counselors are important. But in the end it is your choice.

2. DECIDE WHAT YOU WANT—MAKE A LIST OF REQUIREMENTS.

Okay, so you have decided to go to a top school. What next? Do you go down the most recent rankings in *U.S. News and World Report?* Do you consider only those schools within a two-hour drive from your home? Do you ask your guidance counselor at school for a list? Probably all of the above and more. What's missing is *your* list of requirements.

Do you prefer a college that is
* URBAN OR SUBURBAN?
* LIBERAL ARTS OR SCIENCE ORIENTED?
* SMALL OR LARGE?
* PUBLIC OR PRIVATE?
* HIGHLY ACADEMIC OR ACTIVE SOCIALLY?

Make a list of your requirements by asking questions such as these. Many times students apply to schools based on reputation alone or peer pressure. The schools you apply to should meet, at least minimally, your basic needs and criteria.

3. COMPILE A LIST OF 15–20 COLLEGES, RESEARCH, THEN NARROW YOUR LIST.

Too often in the beginning students pick three or four schools to apply to and that's the end of it. As a result, good schools are often overlooked or top colleges are eliminated because of the attitude "I'll never get in." At least at the outset, complete a broad list of colleges from highly selective to guaranteed admissions. Some might be reaches, but do not cross them off your list because your board scores are below their averages. All of the top colleges look for diversity and balanced classes.

Carefully consider each school on the initial list. Eliminate those that rank lower according to your acceptability criteria. Consider finances. Do not choose based solely on reputation. Research each carefully. A few hours spent deciding where to apply is small in comparison with the four years you will spend there. In the end, though, make sure you will be comfortable with all of your choices.

4. BUY COLLEGE GUIDEBOOKS, SEND FOR ADMISSION BROCHURES, AND READ UP ON THE COLLEGES ON YOUR SHORT LIST.

Information is power. The more information you have on colleges, the better your choice of schools and the greater your chance of acceptance. It is that simple. Buy two or three college guides to help you pick schools and to get different perspectives on them. Write to the school for admission applications and any other information they have available.

Then take your time and read. It is the best way to get initial information about each school, because you obviously cannot visit each campus on your preliminary list. Look at the stats; look at each college's personality; look at the cost; and think about where you best fit in. Then pick five or ten schools to visit.

5. VISIT THE COLLEGES YOU ARE CONSIDERING.

Visiting a college is like test-driving a car. You would never buy a car without a test drive, and neither should you consider a college without a visit. It is important to go when a school is in session. You should visit classes, talk to students and professors, look at housing, and see the athletic facilities. Try to picture yourself at the school. Does it feel right?

During your visit, try to get an interview. Most schools strongly recommend them. Interviews also tell you what the school is looking for. If you do well, an interview can help your chances of admission.

Finally, visit your top three choices more than once. This will give you a better indication of how well you really like the school. Sometimes first impressions are misleading, but after two or three visits you should have a good feeling.

6. TALK TO CURRENT STUDENTS AND RECENT GRADUATES.

What is it really like to go to a particular school? Just ask. Talk to friends or acquaintances who are going to or have recently graduated from that college. Current students can tell you what classes are like, what role fraternities/sororities play on campus, and so on. Their reviews tell you what is happening on campus now.

Recent graduates have perspective on the school and can provide insight into the value of their education in the real world. Some degrees hold up better than others depending on what you want to do or where you want to live.

Try to talk to a number of current students and recent alumni to get a different view of the school. Although one's college experience is unique, you should be able to get a good feel for what it is like to go to that school by talking with a number of people.

7. TALK TO PROFESSORS.

It is amazing that most students who visit a college never talk to a professor. Would you go to Washington and not see the White House? Would you go to Orlando and not go to Disney World? Would you go to New York City and not see the Statue of Liberty or the Empire State Building?

Professors are at the heart of any university. They will be the key component in your educational experience. Usually they are very accessible and more than willing to talk to prospective students. If no professors are available, that tells you something about the school. When planning to visit a school, call up the admissions office and ask whether they can arrange for you to talk with a professor or call one of the academic departments directly. Short of this, try to talk to a professor after class for five minutes.

A few words of advice. Keep it short. Ask good and relevant questions that cannot be found in the school literature. Ask yourself, is this the kind of professor I want teaching me?

8. CHOOSE SCHOOLS THAT FIT YOUR SOCIAL AS WELL AS YOUR ACADEMIC NEEDS.

Never let classes interfere with your education. Although W. C. Fields might have said something like this, there is a grain of truth to it. Education at a top college is a lot more than just attending classes. Like the army, it is an adventure. Therefore, you should consider social life as well as the academic program.

Because you will be in class only ten to 15 hours a week and probably studying an equal amount of time, the majority of your time at college will be spent in various social and extracurricular activities. Therefore, look at these activities carefully. First, what kind of students go to the school—intellects, athletes, political activists, people like you? What do they do most of the time? What are the living arrangements like? How strong are athletics? Are there clubs you would like to join?

Social life can make college the time of your life. Enjoy it.

9. LOOK FOR SCHOOLS WITH DIVERSE ACADEMIC STRENGTHS.

Think about how you pick colleges. Often people choose a school because it has the best prelaw or premed program, the best English or history department, or the foremost expert in biblical archeology. However, once at school you are exposed to new areas, often your interests change, and you pick a new major. Unless you have chosen a school with diverse academic strengths, you are in trouble.

It is not uncommon for a student to change majors two or three times during college. In fact, a major reason for going to college is to expose yourself to new ideas, people, concepts, careers,, and so on. Changing in most cases, except for the engineering disciplines, which have many requirements, is relatively easy if the school has a lot of strong departments. Therefore, look for a college that excels in a wide variety of areas. Think flexible.

10. GO WITH YOUR GUT.

In gut we trust. When all is said and done, you have to feel good about your decision. You can look at all the rankings in the world, listen to the advice of your parents, friends, and guidance counselors, and rationalize almost any decision. Still, you are the one who will be spending four years of your life there. At college, you will make lifelong friends, every year after graduation you will be asked to donate, and the first question most people will ask you is where you went to college.

It is an important decision. Be comfortable with your final choice.

Tips on Getting In

1. Work hard in high school and get good grades.

2. Challenge yourself—take the strongest, hardest academic program possible.

3. Score well on the SAT I.

4. Show why the school is your first choice and why there is a good fit between you and the school.

5. Show why and how you are unique.

6. Excel at and assume leadership positions in extracurricular activities.

7. Use only references who will guarantee a great recommendation.

8. Seek interviews and prepare for them.

9. Apply early.

10. Be yourself. Be enthusiastic. Be honest. Be sincere. And be relaxed.

1. WORK HARD IN HIGH SCHOOL AND GET GOOD GRADES.

Bottom line. Top colleges are looking for students who excel academically. Although it is not necessary to be a straight-A student, academic records can make or break college acceptance. Very few of us are brilliant enough that good grades come easy. Most of us have to work long and hard to achieve As and Bs. Therefore, work hard.

One of the most common mistakes students make in high school, according to college admissions officers at the top schools, is to slide through senior year. If this happens, either the application is rejected outright or the admissions offer is withdrawn. Senior year should be the pinnacle of your high school career. Don't blow it.

2. CHALLENGE YOURSELF—TAKE THE STRONGEST, HARDEST ACADEMIC PROGRAM POSSIBLE.

True or false: Colleges always look for and accept students with the highest grades and board scores. FALSE. Top colleges could easily fill their incoming classes with students who graduated in the top 10%. However, good grades by themselves do not guarantee admission. These grades must be achieved in hard courses, i.e., advanced placement or advanced level classes.

Most of the top colleges have admissions officers who specialize in different regions of the country. So they know the individual high schools and their academic programs. They know that Western civilization is different from AP history and so forth. They know guidance counselors at many of the top high schools. They know when someone is taking a difficult course load and when someone is padding his or her schedule with guts or gimmes. Their advice on getting into a top college is "Challenge yourself."

3. SCORE WELL ON SAT I.

Like it or not, SAT I provides the only objective means of comparison among thousands of different high schools. Although GPAs vary greatly depending on the difficulty of the academic program, the school, classroom competition and so on, SAT I is a standardized point of reference. Despite challenges that they discriminate against minorities and women, SAT I will continue to be used until something better comes along. Do not hold your breath.

Given their importance, do everything to get the highest possible score. Unless you scored in the top percentiles on the PSATs, consider coaching or tutoring for the test. Some schools offer help for free, whereas private tutors and programs are easily available. Because tutoring has been shown to improve scores and, in the worst case, you might actually learn something useful, some form of coaching is highly recommended. A good SAT I score makes you competitive, whereas a bad score might tip the scale against your acceptance.

4. SHOW WHY THE SCHOOL IS YOUR FIRST CHOICE AND WHY THERE IS A GOOD FIT BETWEEN YOU AND THE SCHOOL.

Getting into a top college is like a love affair: moderate passion produces moderate results. If you do not communicate that the school you are applying to is your first choice, then why should they accept you because thousands of other highly qualified students are dying to get in? Therefore, you must clearly communicate in each application and each interview that that school is your first choice. Because you are never guaranteed admission to any top college, your third or fourth choice may very well become your number one.

Not only is it important that the college be your first choice, but it also is critical that you demonstrate that there is a good fit between you and the school. First, look at the admissions brochures to see what the school is looking for, i.e., dedicated students, future leaders, socially concerned activists, and so on. Then show why you meet these criteria. Be honest. A common mistake is to present yourself as you think the school would like you to be rather than as who you actually are. If you honestly think you meet the school's criteria, say so. If you do not, you will be unhappy there even if you are accepted.

5. SHOW WHY AND HOW YOU ARE UNIQUE.

You are competing against a couple of thousand applicants. At least three quarters of the applicants are very highly qualified: bright, with good board scores and excellent recommendations, and former presidents of this or that organization. But only one out of five will get in. Is it luck? Is it skill? What makes the difference?

The critical factor is USP—Unique Selling Proposition. Your application must stand out. You must sell yourself. You must show why you are unique and better than the others. Although you might have been valedictorian or captain of the football team and thus unique at your high school, there are a lot of top scholars and athletic captains hoping to get into the top colleges. Therefore, the trick is to demonstrate why you should be accepted above the rest. Figure out what makes you really different and valuable to the schools to which you are applying. Did you do the best history paper in your junior year? Did you set up a tutoring program for disadvantaged youngsters? Did you overcome a handicap to achieve something? Did you gain great insight into a particular area that you would like to continue to pursue? Did your team win the regional or state championship? Think about it. This is not easy, but unique strengths will make you stand out and be accepted.

6. EXCEL AT AND ASSUME LEADERSHIP POSITIONS IN EXTRACURRICULAR ACTIVITIES.

Your parents always tell you to join the debate club, the band, the school newspaper, the pep squad, and other school activities because top colleges like well-rounded applicants. Do not believe it. The truth is that extracurricular activities are important only if you are a leader or excel in that activity. Being a jack-of-all-trades and a master of none will not help your application.

Carefully select a few activities. Then try to become president, vice president, director, or an officer in the club. Work hard at making a name for yourself and accomplishing something. This is what top colleges are looking for.

7. USE ONLY REFERENCES WHO WILL GUARANTEE A GREAT RECOMMENDATION.

By the time you apply to college in your senior year, you have little control over your grades and SAT I scores. Therefore, the primary things you can control are the application and letters of recommendation. Most students spend a fair amount of time on the application but give only passing thought to references. Letters of recommendation are given to favorite teachers, friends, of employers with a simple request to please fill it out and send it in. Good strategy? No.

First, decide who knows you best from an academic or professional viewpoint, i.e., teachers or employers. References from friends, although generally very positive, count little. Next prepare a background sheet for them outlining strengths and specific work you have done in their class or on the job. The more specific they can be, the more effective the recommendation. Third, give them a stamped, addressed envelope and tell them when the reference is due. Finally, ask them directly whether or not they will give you a firm positive recommendation. If they don't want to answer that question or their answer is negative, find someone else to recommend you.

8. SEEK INTERVIEWS AND PREPARE FOR THEM.

Given the fierce competition for the small number of places at top schools, consider anything that will help you get in. Interviews provide a great opportunity to demonstrate why you want to go to the school and what you want to do once you get there. Interviews offer a chance to personalize your application and make it come alive.

On the other hand, interviews can also be a disaster. Do your homework. Learn as much about the school as you can before talking with someone in the admissions department. Prepare your responses to the obvious questions such as why you want to go to the school. Avoid asking obvious or stupid questions such as how many books the school has in its library? Finally, above all else, be yourself.

9. APPLY EARLY.

Common sense says to apply early. Admission officers are fresher. There are more places available. There is more time to consider the application. Human nature dictates otherwise. Most people follow the adage "Never do today what can be put off until tomorrow." As a result, most high school students wait until the last minute to apply. Applications are rushed. References are given short lead times. And the chance for mistakes increases dramatically.

If you read this in September or October, start now. If it is later, start immediately. DO NOT WAIT.

10. BE YOURSELF. BE ENTHUSIASTIC. BE HONEST. BE SINCERE. AND BE RELAXED.

And this above all else: To thine own self be true. What Shakespeare said in the 1500s is as true today as it was then. The biggest mistake applicants make is trying to figure out what schools are looking for, then trying to change themselves to fit that image. Be yourself. Be honest and sincere. Most of the time, schools recognize applicants who are not being sincere and reject them. Be enthusiastic. Schools like people who show spirit and desire. Finally, be relaxed. Once you have done all you can, the schools will decide. Sit back and enjoy your senior year.

Tips on Filling out the Application

1. Look at the application from the point of view of the admissions officer.

2. Start early and get it in on time.

3. Use the application to your best advantage.

4. Make yourself shine.

5. Be creative, but avoid gimmicks.

6. Show a draft of the application to a friend, teacher, or parent.

7. Get letters of recommendation from people who really know you.

8. Proofread, proofread, proofread.

9. Type the application. Neatness counts.

10. Be honest. Be yourself.

1. LOOK AT THE APPLICATION FROM THE POINT OF VIEW OF THE ADMISSIONS OFFICER.

Congratulations. You have just been appointed admissions officer at a top college. Now comes the challenging part. You have to select an entering class. All you have to go on are the materials in the admission folder: high school transcript, SAT scores, application, letters of recommendation, and interview evaluation. Of the 1000 applications you review, you can select only one in five. However, four in five are qualified. Who do you pick?

Clearly, there are the top 5% anyone would pick: the superstars—football captains with straight-A averages, science students with major awards and discoveries, and so on. Another 5% are legacies (i.e., sons or daughters of alumni) who receive special consideration. That leaves only 10% to pick from the remaining 60%.

You look for applications, activities or qualities that stand out:

• average grades but an interest in science that reveals a particularly inquisitive mind;

• a good student with a social conscience who has worked at homeless shelters;

• an extremely well-written application that makes you laugh and think at the same time.

You look for achievement, potential, and personality.

2. START EARLY AND GET IT IN ON TIME.

College applications are like car inspections, birthday cards, and taxes. Almost everyone waits until the last minute to do anything. Mistake #1.

Most application essays require a good deal of thought and revision. It is generally necessary to send away for SAT I scores. Finally, references require sufficient time to do a good job, especially when they are bombarded by a lot of requests all at the same time.

Even when high school students start early, they figure it doesn't make any difference when the application is sent in as long as it gets there before the deadline. Mistake #2.

The earlier the application is sent in, the better the chances of admission. Simple logic: admission officers are fresher; more places are available.

Most students think that as long as the completed application is there, other materials can follow after the deadline. Mistake #3.

Generally, admissions materials are not reviewed until the application is complete. A late application puts the applicant at a severe disadvantage. Do not wait. Time is of the essence.

3. USE THE APPLICATION TO YOUR BEST ADVANTAGE.

By the time you read this, your grades are pretty well set. You have probably taken the college boards, and your references are fixed in terms of what they will or will not say. Given this, how can you influence the admissions decision when you are a high school senior?

The admissions application represents your best opportunity. Do not view the application merely as a form to fill out. Look at it as a chance to personalize what you have done and show why you should be admitted. Tell the committee what your strengths are, what makes you special, and how you can contribute to their academic and social program. Everything else you submit is hard data: grades, scores, someone else's evaluation of your talents and abilities. If you cannot make a good case for their accepting you, no one can.

4. MAKE YOURSELF SHINE.

You are in head-to-head competition with 10,000 other students. Many apply; few are chosen. Break away from the pack. Stand out in a crowd. One director of admissions from a top college put it succinctly: "Dare to be different, but do it with style."

Describe your accomplishments without boasting. There is a fine line between being justifiably proud and being obnoxiously arrogant. Muhammed Ali used to say he was the greatest, but he backed it up. For example, you were not just captain of the chess team; you were captain of the team that went to the state finals. You were not just a lead in the school play; you were destined for Broadway, according to the local paper. Think big.

5. BE CREATIVE, BUT AVOID GIMMICKS.

If you were in a B-movie melodrama like *Raiders of the Lost Ark,* you would have to be creative every ten minutes. In your college application, you have to be creative *only* once. Just be sure that what you do *is* creative and original.

If one essay question asks you to describe yourself in a word and then explain why, do not answer "succinct" and leave it at that. It has been done before, too many times. On the other hand, one top college asks applicants to fill a quarter-sized box with something that pleases them. According to the dean of admissions at that school, one of the best responses was from an electrical-engineer-to-be who rigged up a tiny light to go on when the application was opened. A music box cut out of a greeting card was not as effective because it did not say as much about the applicant's interest or talents.

Be creative!

6. SHOW A DRAFT OF THE APPLICATION TO A FRIEND, TEACHER, OR PARENT.

No one is perfect. The best writers in the world from Dickens to Hemingway to Bellow all have editors who review and suggest revisions of their work. Their writing is better for it. After you have filled out the application, let it sit for a week (assuming you have enough time). Then read it again. If you are satisfied, give it to someone you respect and ask him or her to review it and make comments. This might be a favorite teacher, friend, or a parent.

This step is critical because we all lack objectivity about ourselves. We need an independent view to tell us whether we are too modest, too arrogant, too vague, too specific; we also need an outside judgment about whether we have answered the questions completely. Once you get the comments back, think about them and make changes accordingly. If you don't agree, ask a second person to review the application. Seriously consider the comments, but in the end it is your application and you should be comfortable with it.

7. GET LETTERS OF RECOMMENDATION FROM PEOPLE WHO REALLY KNOW YOU.

Wouldn't it be great if Lee Iacocca or Senator Kennedy could write a letter of recommendation for you? It might be great, but it would not necessarily help you get into a top college, unless you worked for Chrysler and knew Iacocca on a professional basis or worked closely with Kennedy on his political staff. Otherwise, their recommendations would most likely be heavily discounted.

Colleges are interested in your ability to do well academically, get the most out of college, and graduate. Letters of recommendation should shed light on your ability and potential to do these things. The more professionally oriented and more specific the recommendation. the better colleges are able to evaluate you. Therefore, look for references who know you well and ask them to write on your behalf.

8. PROOFREAD, PROOFREAD, PROOFREAD.

To the admissions committee, your application represents you. It highlights your strengths, weaknesses, and personality. It can tip the balance either way. Careless errors, typos, and incomplete sentences tell the committee you are at best careless and at worse don't care. Either way, you lose.

Proofread your application. Have someone else proofread it. Then proofread it again. Act as if your acceptance depends on it because it does.

9. TYPE THE APPLICATION. NEATNESS COUNTS.

Imagine reading a ten-page application. It takes awhile. Imagine reading 1000 ten-page applications. It would take a long time. As a result, admissions officers look for shortcuts—they skim certain materials and read others very quickly. Now imagine that the application is not typed. It slows down the process significantly and makes the application not only more difficult to read, but, more important, more difficult to understand. As a result, more time and effort is spent literally *reading* the application than trying to *evaluate* it.

Type. Neatness counts. This sounds like advice from your elementary school teacher. Still it holds. All things being equal, neatness can sway opinions, and, in cases where differences are small, why take a chance? Be neat.

10. BE HONEST. BE YOURSELF.

One of the most common mistakes applicants make is trying to second-guess what admissions committees are looking for. Almost all directors of admissions will tell you there is no perfect candidate profile. Top colleges are looking for well-rounded classes with exceptional individuals.

If you try to be something you aren't, chances are you won't get in. Trust yourself and your abilities. Be honest. Decide what you want. Be *yourself.*

Tips on Financing College

1. Explore all options: civic groups, alumni clubs, and so on.

2. Discuss cost with your parents.

3. Consider part-time jobs.

4. Work summers.

5. Start early.

6. Call the financial aid officer at the school(s).

7. Take out government loans.

8. Work out a budget and stick to it.

9. Check out top state school systems.

10. Treat education as an investment. Don't be afraid to go into debt.

1. EXPLORE ALL OPTIONS: CIVIC GROUPS, ALUMNI CLUBS AND SO ON.

Very few of us have $25,000 readily available each year to put toward a college education. Over four years, that's $100,000. Do you have a rich aunt or uncle? If not, explore all your options.

There are many community, civic, and educational groups that offer loans and scholarships. The major difficulty is finding them. Talk with your high school guidance counselor, read all school notices (even the ones you normally ignore), and go to the school library and look for potential sources. Some scholarships are based on need, but others are based on merit. Some are highly restrictive, whereas others are surprisingly liberal.

If the past is any guide, college expenses will continue to increase faster than inflation. So actively search for financial support.

2. DISCUSS COST WITH YOUR PARENTS.

College is expensive. In most cases, parents are a major source of financial support. Loans and scholarships often are based on family income. Finally, parents can provide helpful advice. Given their critical role, it is important to discuss college cost with your parents at the beginning of your school search.

Because schools vary greatly in cost, investigate the full range of alternatives from low-cost, state schools to the most expensive Ivy League colleges. More expensive does not necessarily mean better, but most schools in the top 50—with the exception of state-supported colleges—cost more than $25,000 per year. Then discuss with your parents what financial support they are willing to provide. This will help determine how much you need to come up with and possibly influence your decision as to which college to attend.

3. CONSIDER PART-TIME JOBS.

Under the best circumstances, going to college is a full-time occupation. Learning is much more than classes; it is the entire educational experience: academics, social life, extracurricular activities, and so on. There is more to do than there are hours available to do it. Nevertheless college costs so much, it is sometimes necessary to look for part-time jobs.

First, see if there any part-time research or teaching positions in your major or an academic field that interests you. Next check out jobs that offer flexibility and/or the opportunity to study, positions such as dorm proctor, library assistant, and so on. Finally, check out on-and off-campus jobs in the cafeteria, bookstore, and so on. These are the obvious alternatives. You might also investigate off-campus jobs in careers you are thinking about. Who knows? You might even learn something.

4. WORK SUMMERS.

Summertime, when the weather is fine, is a great opportunity to make money for college. Most students recognize this and go for high-paying, high boredom jobs. Welcome to the real world.

Good summer jobs are hard to find, but they are out there. Talk with professors, go to the placement office, and use whatever contacts you have. Look into working part-time during the school year with the possibility of working full-time in the summer. Start early, work hard at getting a good job, and hope you get lucky.

5. START EARLY.

It is not easy to raise $25,000 especially when you are eighteen, unemployed, and have limited earning capacity for the foreseeable future. Start early. There are numerous sources, all of which require extensive applications, financial statements, and so on. All have different requirements, different deadlines, and different paperwork. Because you may be looking at paying back loans for a long time, look at the different options, apply to as many as possible, and continually search for new funding sources. Start with the college, check out federal loans, and make a budget.

6. CALL THE FINANCIAL AID OFFICER AT THE SCHOOL(S).

Despite what you might sometimes think, schools are as interested in getting good students as you are in attending a good school. Therefore, they are usually very helpful in trying to arrange financing for prospective students. Call the school(s) where you have been accepted but cannot afford to go, and talk with the financial aid officer. All schools will tell you that money should not keep any student from attending. On the other hand, you may have to go heavily into debt. Think about how much you are willing to borrow, who is willing to loan you money, and what financial package each school offers. Then decide.

7. TAKE OUT GOVERNMENT LOANS.

Although federal and many state governments have been cutting back in recent years, government loans still are widely available with some of the lowest interest rates on the market. The federal government offers the Stafford Student Loan Program, whereas many states have loan programs available for their residents.

These programs offer government guarantees and competitive interest rates with reasonable payback periods. Many colleges require students to apply for government loans before they become eligible for other school aid. In any case, if you or your parents pay taxes, you have contributed to these government loan programs. Therefore, you might as well take advantage of them.

8. WORK OUT A BUDGET AND STICK TO IT.

It would be great if you did not have to worry about money, if you had an inexhaustible supply, and if the $25,000 per-year cost was the proverbial drop in the bucket. However, if your income bracket is not within the top 1%, it is necessary to make a budget and stick to it.

The majority of college costs are fixed: tuition, room and board, and books (to a large extent). As a result, it is difficult to reduce most of these expenses unless you switch colleges. Assuming you do not want to do that, make up a budget before the semester begins. Estimate your total expenses, your projected income, and balance the two.

It is easy to spend money in college and difficult to make it. Careful planning and budgeting can help. The rest is up to you.

9. CHECK OUT TOP STATE SCHOOL SYSTEMS.

Expensive does not necessarily mean better. Most of the top 50 colleges are private and cost a lot to attend. On the other hand, there are a number of state colleges with excellent programs, including the University of California at Berkeley, the University of Virginia at Charlottesville, the University of North Carolina at Chapel Hill, and William and Mary. Each charges substantially less than its private counterparts. Further, there are additional reductions for in-state residents.

If finances are a major issue, check out the top public universities. Also investigate the possibility of establishing in-state residency for your second year. This can lower costs further. Finally, carefully consider your fit with a public college. Most public schools are larger and more impersonal. These schools may not be appropriate for you if you are not outgoing and assertive in seeking individual advice and attention.

10. TREAT EDUCATION AS AN INVESTMENT. DON'T BE AFRAID TO GO INTO DEBT.

It has been popular of late to view education as an investment because college grads earn substantially more than those with only high school diplomas. However, an argument can be made that in general top college grads, by virtue of credentials, contacts, and intelligence, do better than the general population of college graduates.

Clearly, it pays to go to college from a financial standpoint. However, the rewards are far greater than only money. College teaches you how to think and exposes you to new ideas. From a total perspective, financial, social, educational, and personal development, college is probably one of the best investments you could ever make.

Therefore the initial heavy outlay for college must be viewed against later rewards. It is never easy to pay back loans, but in the end a top college education certainly is worth the price.

Tips on Succeeding

1. Be yourself. Indulge your interests.

2. Stay on top of the work by learning to budget your time and studying efficiently,

3. Set priorities.

4. Take advantage of faculty.

5. Get help if necessary

6. Balance academic and social life.

7. Attend classes, take good notes, and do your homework.

8. Make grades secondary to learning. Be willing to try new things.

9. Have fun.

10. Keep things in perspective.

1. BE YOURSELF. INDULGE YOUR INTERESTS.

College is the best of times. Independence. Freedom. Limited responsibility. The opportunity to do and try new different things is unbelievable. Therefore, take advantage of the situation.

Indulge your interests. Do things you have never done before and will never be free enough to do again. Try new things. You will never have such broad exposure to so many different areas. Take risks. There is no better time to do it with so little downside. Finally, be yourself. College is the time to define who you are and who you want to be. Do not waste the opportunity.

2. STAY ON TOP OF THE WORK BY LEARNING TO BUDGET YOUR TIME AND STUDYING EFFICIENTLY.

The word *all-nighter* was probably invented shorty after the first college was established. The work load at college is heavy, and you have to manage your time effectively. The easiest solution is to stay on top of work. Do assignments each day. Do not put papers off until the end of the semester. Do not let one or two courses slide. It is always more difficult to make up work than to do it on time.

Learn to budget your time. Figure out how much work you need to do each week then spread it out over six or seven days. Learn to study efficiently. Form study groups and spread the work load. The more efficiently you study, the more time you have for everything else.

3. SET PRIORITIES.

Classes are to education what the heart is to the body: a vital part but not the only one. College is an academic, social, and personal experience. It is important to develop each of these elements of the experience. Therefore, decide what you want to do and what you want to get out of college. Then set priorities.

The academic program should be your first priority. But social and extracurricular life should be a close second. Most colleges stress learning that takes place both inside and outside the classroom. Try to combine extracurricular activities with your classroom training. Do not let a preoccupation with classes interfere with your total educational experience.

4. TAKE ADVANTAGE OF THE FACULTY.

Professors are sometimes viewed solely as classroom teachers. You attend their classes three times a week for 60 minutes and get feedback through exams and a final grade. Period. That's like going to a football game and leaving after the first quarter. Sure, it's enjoyable, but you have missed three quarters of the game. In the same vein, you missed a large part of what a faculty can offer if you interact with professors only by listening to lectures and taking exams.

Professors have a lot of wisdom and insight to offer, not only about academic subjects. Talk to them after class, meet them during office hours, and invite them to dinner with a group of students. Use them to help obtain summer and permanent jobs. Discuss academic difficulties and, if appropriate, personal problems. Use professors to expand your learning and your entire educational development. You will be glad you did.

5. GET HELP IF NECESSARY.

College can be tough. There are work load pressures, social pressures, and the ever present grades. Some problems are small and can be easily resolved, whereas others are more complex and require significant attention. One common mistake that many college students make, especially freshmen and sophomores, is that they do not seek help when they need it. This is important when problems occur either inside or outside the classroom.

Academic difficulties can be addressed by seeking support from fellow students on small issues or from professors if there are major concerns. Social or personal problems can be handled by seeking counsel from the guidance center or again, professors. Most top schools recognize the pressures students face and have set up elaborate support systems.

When difficulties arise, do not wait. Many students avoid doing anything until the problems become major. Get help early in the semester. Everyone needs help at some point or another in their college career. Smart students recognize it early and do something about it.

6. BALANCE ACADEMIC AND SOCIAL LIFE.

College is neither endless work nor a permanent spring break. Balance the academic and the social. Take your classes seriously and do the work. Then party. Most students at top schools adopt the motto "Work hard, play hard."

The most common complaint these students have is that there is never enough time to do everything they would like: take a variety of courses ranging from French literature to zoology, go out for crew, explore some arcane field in physics or history, have time just to think. Success at college means learning to set priorities and balance the academic and the social so that you can do everything.

7. ATTEND CLASSES, TAKE GOOD NOTES, AND DO YOUR HOMEWORK.

No one said it was going to be all fun. Going to college means going to classes, taking notes, and doing homework. Some students have the attitude that you can skip classes, borrow someone's notes, skim the reading, then take the final. But why bother to go to college at all? You might as well get your degree from the back of a matchbook cover.

A major part of learning occurs from the interchange between professor and students and among students themselves in the classroom. It may be possible to get good grades without attending class, but it is not possible to get a good education that way.

8. MAKE GRADES SECONDARY TO LEARNING. BE WILLING TO TRY NEW THINGS.

We are all grade conscious. That's how others evaluate us and to some extent that's how we evaluate our own worth. Grades are important, but they should be secondary to learning. If you are a music major, experiment with physics. If you are a history major, investigate poetry. College is a once-in-a-lifetime opportunity to look at many different subjects.

Don't worry about grades. Use college to broaden your horizons, inside and outside class. Do community work, join the school newspaper, do the things you have always wanted to do but never had the time or opportunity for. That is the real benefit and advantage of a top college education.

9. HAVE FUN.

College is serious business. So what? That doesn't mean you can't have fun. Never again will you be with as many other individuals with whom you will have as much in common.
  • Form a rock band.
  • Party till dawn.
  • Go to the mountains or the shore.
  • Play intramurals till it hurts.
  • Attend concerts.
  • Rock away the night.
  • See the latest Japanese film.
  • Try Brazilian food.
  • Play inner tube water polo.
  • Discuss metaphysics over espresso.
Think about what you always wanted to do. Then do it. Have fun!

10. KEEP THINGS IN PERSPECTIVE.

Keep repeating to yourself, "It's only college, it's only college, it's only college." We all sometimes take things too seriously or blow things out of proportion. College is important, but it is not the beginning and end of life.

College is important because it's a ticket to a career. It's important because we learn a lot. It is important because it is a major rite of passage.

Yet we all survive the college experience. Most of us are more knowledgeable, happier, and more satisfied with ourselves for having done so. There are good times, and there will be bad times. By keeping college in perspective, we can live through the bad, relish the good, and be more content in the long run.

Good luck and enjoy!

Part III

Top Perspectives from Admissions Insiders

An Insider's Perspective The University of Michigan

BY THEODORE L. SPENCER
DIRECTOR, OFFICE OF UNDERGRADUATE ADMISSIONS

"Today, more is expected of college grads than ever before," cartoonist Cathy Guisewite told University of Michigan graduates at last year's commencement. The U of M alumna and creator of the comic strip "Cathy" was right on target. Because of the competitive nature of college admissions, the same can also be said about high school students applying to college.

As with most highly selective universities, the competition for admission to the University of Michigan has become more difficult in recent years. For example, in 1980 a student presenting a grade point average of 3.0 and an SAT score of 1000 or an ACT score of 21 was, in most cases, admitted. Today, that student would likely be rejected. One reason it is more difficult to be admitted is that in 1980 fewer than 10,000 students applied to the University of Michigan, while this year almost 20,000 students applied. And these students have outstanding academic qualifications. Today, most U of M applicants have at least a 3.5 GPA or higher, are in the top 20% of their class, and have standardized test scores averaging between 1090 and 1200 on SAT I and 25 to 30 on the ACT. Each year we enroll between 4500 and 5000 students, so the large application pool versus the smaller number of final enrollees is the most important reason that it's difficult to be admitted.

Of the total number of students enrolling each year, about 70% are from Michigan and 30% from outside the state. It is true that it is harder to be admitted if you are from out of state because, as a state university, we believe it is important to give a slight edge to state residents. Also, each year we enroll about 11% Asian American, 8.5% African American, 5% Hispanic/Latino American, 5% Native American, and 2.5% international students. Michigan promotes the idea of a diverse student body, and therefore one of our goals in the Admissions Office is to admit students from many different backgrounds and geographic areas. Some would argue that our admissions policies favor one group over another. But, says James J. Duderstadt, president of the university, *"We are convinced that for the university to achieve excellence in its fundamental missions of teaching and scholarship, it seems clear we must reflect the growing diversity of America and the world around us among our people and our activities."*

Although admission to Michigan isn't easy, the majority of the applicants are qualified, and about 60% of in-state applicants are admitted. That is because many students elect not to apply if they do not believe they are qualified. Another reason is that we tend to admit students who are extremely well qualified first, and those students tend to have acceptance offers from many schools. Once we determine that these highly qualified applicants are going elsewhere, we begin to make offers to other students, including those on our delayed list.

So what do we look for in applicants? Most students apply to our two largest schools, the College of Literature, Science, and the Arts and the College of Engineering. Admissions requirements for both schools are very similar. Freshmen can also apply to five smaller units—the School of Natural Resources and Environment, the School of Nursing, the School of Art, the Division of Kinesiology, and the School of Music. Each school's admissions requirements differ somewhat from LS&A and Engineering. But all applicants are judged on their perceived ability to succeed, in combination with grade point average, exam scores, high school curriculum, essay, class rank, and extracurricular activities.

Michigan does not use an admissions committee to make its selections, but relies on the admissions counselor to make those decisions. Decisions on applicants are made on an individual basis. No specific class rank, grade point average, test score, or other qualification in itself will ensure admission. The counselors consider the strength of an applicant's high school background, including the degree of difficulty of courses selected, academic achievement, and special and unique accomplishments, both in and out of the classroom. In general, the admissions requirements include a B average or above beyond the ninth grade in a rigorous, college-preparatory program. Besides the basic educational requirements, including successful completion of a college-prep curriculum and standardized test scores, our admissions counselors concentrate on the courses and grades you received in the tenth and eleventh grades. Other than these general requirements, we also look for characteristics that set a student apart from other applicants. At Michigan, we seek to enroll and graduate students who are academically excellent, accomplished in extracurricular endeavors, and who reflect the socioeconomic and racial diversity of the state of Michigan and the nation.

Because we are unable to admit every student who applies, and because most of our applicants have very similar academic and extracurricular qualifications, we also use other factors to assist us in making decisions on applicants on our delay list. We review such factors as extracurricular activities, essay information, counselor recommendations, and alumni affiliation of parents, grandparents, and siblings to help us break ties. If your application is on delay status, we will review it in March or April, sometimes as late as June, to once again select the best-qualified students. There is not really much you can do in the way of influencing that decision. If we need additional test scores, we will write you and ask to have them sent or we will let you know if we need your senior grades. Each year we admit several hundred students from the delay list, and my best advice is to continue to do well in your senior year classes and, if you can, be patient.

WHAT DISTINGUISHES SUCCESSFUL CANDIDATES FROM A LARGE POOL OF HIGHLY QUALIFIED APPLICANTS?

When reviewing applications, counselors consider the quality of the high school curriculum as much as any information applicants provide. The successful candidate to the University of Michigan generally has taken at least four or more advance placement (AP) or international baccalaureate (IB) courses and/or seven or more honors courses. Given the wide disparity in high school course selection and offerings, we give more consideration to those courses clearly identified as Honors and AP/IB. Achievement of a respectable GPA in these demanding and challenging courses indicates to us that the student is highly motivated and committed, and should be well prepared for the academic rigors at the University of Michigan.

Many high school counselors indicate that all their courses are college prep, and their students should be given AP or Honors credit. Well, that puts us in a difficult position, and we try to give extra consideration to high schools that offer at least 16 AP/IB/honors courses, and who also send at least 70% of their students to college. Because we feel that honors and AP courses help prepare students to do well on standardized tests, we also give additional credit to schools whose students average at least 1000 on SAT I or 22 on the ACT or higher. So my advice to students interested in applying to Michigan is simple: take college prep courses, achieve a strong GPA, and enroll in the most advanced courses offered in your high school.

WHAT THREE PIECES OF ADVICE WOULD I GIVE TO AN APPLICANT?

At Michigan, admissions counselors spend a lot of time reviewing applications, looking for those academic qualities, extracurricular activities, and personal qualities that will help us select students who can develop and grow educationally and personally at our university. Our process includes identifying students before the senior year and, in most cases, recruiting, admitting, and encouraging them to enroll. We try very hard to identify students who are interested in enrolling at U of M by doing things like getting the names of students who achieve top GPAs and test scores, as well as Merit Scholars. In addition, we also receive names from alumni, high school visits, college fairs, mail and phone requests, and from as many other resources as we can conceive.

However, in spite of all these well-thought-out methods of identifying students, we still miss some very well qualified students who are interested in Michigan. Students should view these oversights from the University of Michigan (or from other colleges) as mistakes. If the school you didn't hear from is among your top choices, then my advice is to call or write and ask for an application or whatever information you need. They will be happy to hear from you. Along with that advice, I offer three other additional bits of inside information to students interested in applying to Michigan. They are:

- apply early,
- visit the campus
- prepare for the SAT I and ACT exams.

Let me briefly discuss why they are so important.

APPLY EARLY

Although our deadline for submitting applications is February 1, our rolling admissions policy means that we try to give students a decision within four to six weeks after they apply. Although we pay a great deal of attention to *not* filling the class before the deadline date, fewer positions may be available near the deadline, depending on the volume and quality of applications in a given year. But keep in mind that we are an office of admissions, not rejections, so we will do everything we can to give you an advantage in our rolling admissions process, including waiving the application or enrollment deposit deadline for individual special situations.

CAMPUS VISIT

One of the best ways to find out more about the college you are considering is to visit the campus. Classrooms, laboratories, studios, gymnasiums, and football and basketball arenas can provide an excellent glimpse of the interaction between teachers and students, as well as of students themselves. Interviews are not required as a part of the U of M admissions process. However, both prospective and admitted students and their parents are invited and encouraged to visit our campus and meet with an admissions representative in a small group setting during both daily and special campus programs.

Our daily prospective student campus visits are designed to whet your appetite. There are normally two sessions a day, at 10 A.M. and 2 P.M., and they include a presentation from an admissions counselor as well as a brief walking tour of campus. It is a good idea to call first to make sure we reserve a space for you. Once you are admitted, you will be invited to the campus and, in fact, be given several opportunities to visit. These day-long visits allow you to spend more time touring and meeting with faculty, students, and staff from units such as the Housing Division and the Financial Aid Office.

Now, I realize that not everyone can visit the campus, perhaps because they lack the time or the money. But here is something you should know: We currently have an arrangement with Northwest Airlines that allows students and family members planning to visit the university to receive up to a 40% discount on *full-fare tickets* and a 10% reduction for already-discounted fares.

So come see us if you can, because with our academic excellence, incredible campus life, and the resources in and around Ann Arbor, you will discover what it means to be a Michigan student. The comparison I often make is that most people would not buy a house or a car unless they inspected it in person. Since your investment in your college career includes a great deal of time and money, try to visit the campus.

PREPARE FOR THE SAT I AND/OR ACT EXAM

Regardless of which university you attend, the combination of high school grades and test scores will most likely be a major factor in determining your admission. For schools like Michigan, although we also combine the subjective data (essay, extracurricular, and personal strengths) with the objective data (test scores, curriculum, and GPA), *the objective data outweighs the subjective.* The high school record is by far the most significant predictor of academic performance at the university. Test scores come in a strong second. Because so few people have the God-given ability to take a test and score well with little or no preparation, we have found that the students who do best on these exams have:

- taken AP/IB, honors, and college prep courses in high school
- taken test improvement classes, either at school or privately
- spent time on "do it yourself" preparation

Of the three, I believe the first option will yield the best test results. However, I also recognize that taking prep courses can help some students improve their scores. I would recommend that students first consider test-prep courses offered in high school before investing a great deal of money in more costly test-prep services. In fact, many people can improve their scores by using a do-it-yourself book in combination with some help from tutors, teachers, or other students. The bottom line is that it is a good idea to do one, two, or all three. You do not have to worry about which test we accept at Michigan. We accept both the ACT and SAT I. We will use whichever test results offers an advantage to the student. One additional hint: Indicate on your application your previous and future test dates. That way, if your previous scores were low, we may postpone our decision until we receive your new scores. There is a place on our application to indicate the test dates.

CONCLUSION

Finally, what does it mean to have a degree from the University of Michigan? We are proud of the fact that our graduation rate is among the highest in the nation. The majority of students enjoy their college years at the University of Michigan. The Michigan experience offers students an exceptional academic background and social experience to begin their job careers.

Before students graduate from Michigan, they are offered many opportunities to prepare for the upcoming job search. Throughout the year, the Office of Career Planning and Placement offers workshops that focus on resume writing, cover letters, interviewing techniques, networking, and self-assessment. Placement counselors also arrange for on-campus and off-campus interviews with companies throughout the state, nation, and world. Job-posting boards are maintained outside the office, and students can sign up daily for face-to-face interviews with representatives from both large and small companies. The result has been that Michigan alumni have done extremely well in finding good jobs immediately after graduation. About half of all graduates go on to make a minimum of $40,000 a year during their early earning years after graduation. In addition, the influence of University of Michigan alumni is tremendous. Their power and leadership are widely recognized and they provide a very effective network for other graduates. Michigan can claim the largest number of degree holders, not just in the Big Ten, but in the entire nation, with more than 300,000 living alumni. In addition, Michigan has produced alumni who continue their education in graduate and professional schools. In fact, the University of Michigan has the highest law school and medical school acceptance rate, around 85%, of any undergraduate program in the United States.

Students leave Michigan having gained an excellent education, self-confidence, and the security of knowing that businesses recognize that a degree from the University of Michigan means they have successfully completed one of the best college programs in the world.

> *Theodore L. (Ted) Spencer has served as director of the Office of Undergraduate Admissions at the University of Michigan since 1993, following four years as associate director. He earned a B.S. degree in political science from Tennessee State University in 1963 and an M.A. in sociology from Pepperdine University in 1979. After graduation from Tennessee State, he entered the United States Air Force, retiring with the rank of lieutenant colonel in 1976. Ted is also a graduate of the Military War College and served for 12 years as associate director of admissions at the United States Air Force Academy in Colorado Springs.*

An Insider's Perspective Yale University

BY RICHARD H. SHAW JR.
DEAN OF UNDERGRADUATE ADMISSIONS AND FINANCIAL AID

College-bound students spend 12 years preparing for the opportunity to be scrutinized, analyzed, dissected, and exposed during the college application cycle. Perhaps at no other time in your life have you been asked to tell all. Further, you find a whole cheering section behind you willing to give you their best advice at any point you ask. Parents, teachers, school officials, coaches, friends, friends of the family, and even your long-lost uncle are all involved in giving you their best counsel. Hopefully they will do this by maintaining a neutral perspective. Sure! In reality, you have to deal with subtle and not-so-subtle direction about the best approach to getting into the college of your choice. Colleges and universities have added more overload by filling your family mailbox with information of the possibilities open to you. Color brochures of every shape and size are sent to give you an accurate summary of the merits of hundreds of colleges and universities. At some point, your college literature filing system prevents you from easy access to your room. The pictures of beautiful buildings with large white pillars and happy undergraduates make you wonder what you have been missing; they excite you about the college years ahead. The most frenetic of you have added guidebooks, computer disks and, yes, even cordial messages over the Internet. You try to stay level-headed through all of this.

I remember my own experience when applying to college! The clear advice I received both from my high school guidance counselor and the dean of admissions, was when you apply to college, do not be shy—do not hold back. Little did

I know then that I might someday be sitting in this chair reviewing and evaluating applicants to Yale. I recall that I was not very thoughtful about how I should select an institution to which to apply and, in fact, I was attracted to certain schools by the pretty pictures they sent me. If hindsight were 20/20, I would do it differently, and certainly be more reflective. Fortunately, the school I went to was my first choice for the right reasons, and hence I did not have to face the consequences of enrolling in other schools about which I knew very little.

If you are reading this book it is a good sign that you are taking a thorough approach to choosing colleges and universities to which you will apply. It is extremely important that you make a list of those attributes that are important to you, because you are talking about a place where you will spend the next four years of your life. You know best what is most important to you and should go with your instincts as well as utilize resources that help you in your search. What we are talking about here is trying to make a good match between you and the institution. This means you must be aware of the general profile characteristics of the schools you are considering and their unique and special qualities, that is, how are they the same and how are they different? Most important, how will the school contribute to your development and how might your own special accomplishments and abilities augment the college's environment? In fact, it is a marriage of sorts . . . one in which the goal is to develop a lasting and positive relationship.

I would suggest that students come to Yale because of the very clear commitment to undergraduate education, the quality of the teaching faculty and the residential college system. Students choose to enroll at Yale because the school is clearly committed to ensuring that undergraduates experience all that is humanly possible, both in the classroom and outside. Yale promotes and takes pride in scholarship, while encouraging students to test their own boundaries by getting involved in endeavors they would not have thought of when they first arrived from high school. The learning environment encourages curiosity and experimentation in an extraordinary array of academic disciplines. A Yale objective is to ensure that students develop the capacity to write well, analyze information effectively, and integrate what they have learned with the challenges of life following graduation. Yale provides a community experience, promoting friendships between students, faculty, and staff that last a lifetime. This is done in an urban setting where volunteerism is an asset and caring a strength.

So there you have it—reasons to apply! You have also assessed your position and determined that you are a realistic prospect for admissions and now commences the admissions process. The most commonly pondered question is, "What do I do to get in?" What is the admissions committee looking for? This is a legitimate concern among highly selective institutions such as Yale. We have almost 13,000 applicants, and are striving to enroll a class of about 1320. Most applicants present academic credentials suggesting that, if enrolled, they can do the work. We are honored by an applicant pool of very strong students. We have the luxury and, some would suggest, the daunting task of selecting the Yale class from among many qualified students. We take this challenge very seriously! So what is the secret?

Our goal is to bring to Yale a group of students whose backgrounds suggest that they will thrive. We want to attract young people from every walk of life and every geographic location. We are interested in strength of character and a high level of accomplishment to date. We like students with a lot of energy and intellectual curiosity, which will allow them to have an exciting experience here. We care that they were involved in their school or community and that they made a difference. We are intrigued by those who pursued an interest and excelled at it; this runs the gamut: athletes, student government, forensics, Model U.N., writing, theater, music, community service, journalism, language, science and mathematic competitions, and so on. We go well beyond what is recorded on the transcript, to look at the depth and breadth of the curriculum attempted in high school as well as what was done outside the classroom. If you had to work at a job, we want to know that. If you had special challenges or experiences, it is important for us to be aware of them. I would reemphasize that writing an application is not a time to be restrained. However, I would also suggest there is a difference between being honest and forthright about who you are in an engaging way, while balancing the reflections with some humility.

Admissions officers at Yale are seeking to know you through your earned record in the classroom, recommendations from your teachers, and the report from guidance officials. These evaluations will be supplemented by an interview we conduct in our office or the one you have conducted in your community by our alumni, and, very importantly, we will get a glimpse of you through your essays.

THE ACADEMIC RECORD

Your success in the classroom is the foundation of our review. We look at the types and rigor of the courses you take and your earned record in these courses. We evaluate the type of learning environment you are in and the systems by which your performance is assessed. In fact, the admissions officer that has primary responsibility for the review of your application has developed expertise about your school and community environment no matter where it is in the world. We review your grades and also assess your relative competitiveness in your own class by reviewing class rank (or distribution of grades within the class if rank is not available). We supplement the review of your classroom experience by looking at external indicators. This would include outcomes on the SAT I and SAT II tests, or the ACT. We go further to see if you have been given special recognition and awards by your school or by outside organizations. This might include national language, writing, mathematics or science competitions. These supplemental indicators may, in fact, suggest a relationship between your experience and the academic major you have indicated on your application. Many applicants to Yale submit tapes of their music performance, slides of their art work, unique computer programs, or samples of award-winning writing or science activities, and the like. These too are considered, if appropriate. In other words, the review is comprehensive and your own special efforts are acknowledged.

TEACHER AND SCHOOL RECOMMENDATIONS

Applicants are encouraged to take these requested recommendations seriously. The best advice would seem obvious. You should select teachers that know you well and are familiar with the caliber of your work in their courses. I would suggest that, if feasible, you ask teachers from more recent classes, although the key is to select individuals that know you best and who you believe will give an honest and constructive appraisal of you. Generally, students have less control over the school report because guidance counselors are assigned. The student should make an extra effort to make an appointment with the college counselor and discuss the application process. Further, it is wise to take part in college counseling programs beginning in your junior year. Again, the counselor's knowledge of you will only be as good as the information that can be gathered from you and other members of the school community. In schools that do not have a college counselor, we ask that a recommendation come from a third teacher. Also, if you have had an opportunity to take a college course while in high school, you want a recommendation from that faculty member.

EXTRACURRICULAR/COMMUNITY INVOLVEMENT

In the Yale application, students are asked to summarize their extracurricular involvements in school and community. The admissions committee is interested in your commitments to outside activities and these become a factor in the overall review. Involvement in school athletic programs, student government, journalism, clubs, community service, music, the arts, and so on, are of interest, particularly where we see a sustained involvement and leadership. The level of accomplishment may encourage special consideration by an intercollegiate sport at Yale or by the faculty in a particular field. Students are encouraged to indicate awards and honors in these activities, as well. As mentioned earlier, we are in part assessing how your special accomplishments might contribute to Yale, so it is important for us to know of your interest and commitment to activities outside the classroom.

THE ESSAYS

Essay questions are there to give you the opportunity to say, "This is who I am, and I want you to know me." A commonly asked question is, "What should I write about?" That is an important question and is truly one of the more mystical parts of the process. We do not want to give you the outline—we want to give you the space to tell us what you think is important for us to know in context with the rest of the application. We give you a place on the application to list your activities and accomplishments, so the essays should not be a place to regurgitate these things. It is important for you to know that we read them, as we do the whole application, several times, and your writing content, quality, and creativity, play a part in our review. However, the focus should be on you as a human being rather than you as a future Pulizer Prize winner. You should be careful to read the essay question before you respond to it. You should not assume that all schools are asking for the same response. You should assess how your honest and personal response is relevant to the college that is considering you as an applicant. Obviously, good writing makes for good reading, so you should be thoughtful and expressive.

THE INTERVIEW

The interview for Yale is voluntary. The vast majority of students applying have an opportunity to visit with alumni in their home communities. About 9% actually have appointments on the campus. These interviews give the student an opportunity to personalize the application process. The time you spend with an alumnus or admissions interviewer gives you a chance to talk about and expand upon experiences that have been important to you in your life. Questions that may be posed by individual interviewers may be different, but certainly the goal is the same. We want to evaluate how your preparation and interest might be in concert with the Yale environment. This is an opportunity to communicate who you are and supplement the information you have presented in the written application. We are hopeful that talking to an alumnus or admissions interviewer will also give you a chance to ask questions about the kind of environment we have here. The key in the interview process is to have a conversation that you find as rewarding as does the person with whom you are meeting.

Yale attracts as applicants, and ultimately admits, a wonderfully diverse student body with many and varied talents. We cannot really define the characteristics of the perfect applicant because in determining an admitted class, each student brings unique qualities and idiosyncrasies to the mix. Thus, there is no magic formula or silver bullet for successful applicants. Rather, it is a combination of proven achievement, high potential, and a good match between the applicant and the college. This is not to say that unsuccessful applicants do not have high achievement or potential. Rather, we select those from a highly qualified applicant pool who we believe are the best and who will contribute the most.

It is correct to say that we are looking for students who are well-rounded as much as we are interested in students with special strengths that will contribute to our having a diversified entering class. When students enroll in the residential colleges, we believe the individual strengths they bring will augment and enhance the general living and learning environment. We would suggest that students who are admitted show in some way a capacity to lead, express a motivation to test their own limits, exhibit an inquiring mind, engage in extracurricular life with enthusiasm, and have a sense of caring about others. We intend to attract applicants from all walks of life, religions, cultures, and backgrounds, as well as geographic locations. We admit students without regard to their ability to pay. We take special pride in ensuring that students admitted to Yale will have their full demonstrated needs met, within the boundaries of federal and institutional needs analysis. This allows every student an opportunity to take advantage of a place where the focus is truly the total nurturing of the individual undergraduate.

At Yale we suggest that present or recently graduated undergraduate students provide the best testimonies. That is why, in general, this Barron's guidebook is valuable. It gives you an opportunity to hear the voices of undergraduates about the places they have become a part of. There is no better personal resource for you than hearing those who are presently enrolled or recently graduated from the college.

EPILOGUE

Over the years, we have experienced an amazing array of gimmicks and efforts to grab our attention. Students have sent samples of candy they have made, boxes of helium-filled balloons intended to float out when opened, which expressed the applicant's love for Yale, or video tapes of personal expressions about why they are the right student to be admitted. While these extra efforts amuse and entertain the staff in our mail room, they do not make their way to the committee review.

Our focus is on those application materials that are highlighted in this essay. Be assured that your application will get a thorough reading and that your merits will be considered by the admissions committee. The committee is comprised of professional admissions officers and Yale faculty, each with equal influence on the final decision. It is a democratic process in which fairness and equity is the rule. As you well know, not all applicants can be accepted, but we believe that most students will apply to a wonderful array of colleges and universities. If you conduct your college search well and give yourself strong options and alternatives our bet is you will be quite successful. Good luck!

Richard H. Shaw Jr., the dean of Undergraduate Admissions and Financial Aid at Yale University, has held numerous positions in higher education management as well as in national professional organizations. Prior to Yale, Dean Shaw served four years as Director of Undergraduate Admissions at the University of Michigan, five years as Associate Director of Admissions and Records at the University of California at Berkeley and, earlier, as Director of Admissions Processing and Associate Director of Admissions at the University of Colorado in Boulder.

An Insider's Perspective California Institute of Technology

BY CHARLENE CONRAD LIEBAU
DIRECTOR OF ADMISSIONS

What do an opera singer, Olympic athlete, and Caltech student have in common? Passion. For the opera singer it is passion for music and performance, for the Olympic athlete it is passion for sport and the dream of breaking a record, and for the Caltech student it is passion for learning and an insatiable curiosity about the world.

Passion is emotion, intense feeling, enthusiasm. Being passionate about science means not only professing interest, and perhaps even love, for math and science subjects, but a willingness to spend lots and lots of time asking, "Why?" and then spending even more time finding the answer.

Passion requires devotion, time, and energy. Do you find that you spend half the night staring at the sky—not because you are dreaming, but because you are trying to identify the constellations? Or do you talk with friends hour after hour, discussing the ethical dilemmas posed by biotechnology? For the Caltech student, devotion means a willingness to work on a project or problem until solved, without thought to the time on the clock. It also means you don't give up—you spend the time and energy necessary to complete a project when everything that could possibly go wrong, does. Just as the musician practices the same piece of music over and over to master it, just as the athlete runs the same distance again and again to improve stamina and speed, so the scientist repeats an experiment, reworks the problem, changes the conditions, tests and retests, until the problem is solved.

Caltech seeks students who are passionate, especially about science and math. A passionate (and motivated) student is one who is willing to challenge himself or herself—willing to go beyond what is required in school, willing to enroll in the most advanced courses available, willing to pursue a topic or subject independently. A passionate student will undertake a research project in an area of special interest, even though there is no requirement to do so. A motivated student seeks opportunities. Oftentimes high schools offer only the introductory-level, basic courses in math and science—the motivated student routinely puts forth that extra effort—spends time and energy—does what others might call "extra credit." For one student it might take the form of setting up a lab in the basement and tinkering with electric circuits, for another it is spending summer at space camp, and for another it is getting up at 4:30 in the morning to fit in workout and practice time in order to be on the swim team.

Passion for science is critical, because the Caltech curriculum focuses primarily on research and instruction in the fundamental sciences of mathematics, physics, and chemistry. In fact, the core curriculum, a requirement for all students, begins in the freshman year and includes two year-long courses in mathematics and physics, a year of chemistry, and a course (each term) in the humanities or social sciences. While it is possible to graduate with a major in literature, history, social science, or an independent studies program, all students must fulfill the Institute's core curriculum in math, physics, and chemistry.

The focus at Caltech, while clearly on study in mathematics, science, and engineering, is also on learning how to learn. In the core curriculum, students learn more than answers, or even how to find the answers; they learn the "why" behind the answer. The emphasis at Caltech is on education rather than training. Learning and understanding the essentials will prepare students well for whatever develops in science and technology.

An important part of learning is creativity, which the Admissions Committee also looks for in applicants. The linkage is clear. The world of research—of discovery—requires the scientist to be willing to view problems from different perspectives, to look at the world in new ways, to try something new. How do you look at problems? Do you ask questions? Do you make connections between thoughts and ideas that others don't make? Do you use your imagination when you think? As the commercial asks, "Are you content to 'stay within the lines,' or are you willing to go outside the lines to solve problems?"

Caltech asks its applicants to be creative when it asks, "Please fill the space below with something interesting," and then provides sixty-eight square inches of blank paper. As you might suspect, the range of responses is wide and has included poetry, essays, drawings, new solutions to old problems, and even a recipe for chocolate chip cookies. Just as is true of responses to other essay questions, there are no "correct" answers, or in this case, prescribed ways to fill the space, but including this question as part of the application allows students to demonstrate their creativity. Whether it be through writing, music, art, or approach to problem solving, Caltech applicants should convey a spark of creativity, a willingness to meet challenges in new ways.

Caltech also asks its applicants to demonstrate an active interest in math and science. Participation in science fairs, math contests, research projects, and the like help convey this interest. Faculty members who read and evaluate applications are impressed by students who "tinker," students who enjoy taking things apart and, after awhile, putting them back together!

What distinguishes the successful candidates from the many who are qualified? Clearly, ability and preparation in math and science are important and serve as the base line for successful applicants to Caltech. High school preparation should include four years of mathematics with calculus highly recommended, a minimum of three years of English (four years are recommended), and one year each of chemistry, physics, and U.S. history/government.

The best-prepared students are those who do very well in these courses and who also enrich their courses of study with additional college preparatory work. Additional science, history, social science, and humanities courses expand the student's program and are good preparation for juggling the full college load.

Beyond ability, preparation, demonstrated interest, motivation, and creativity, there are two additional qualities students should develop if they are serious about studying science: perseverance and a willingness to work with others.

While research—discovery—can be exhilarating, it is also very hard work. Students should be willing not only to challenge themselves and to ask why, but to persevere and not give up, to persist even when the work becomes routine and tedious. In summarizing her four years as an undergraduate, a recent alumna and now university professor, commented, "My four-year experience at Caltech revolutionized the way I thought about science, society, scientific endeavors, and myself. We weren't pampered or sheltered from the realities of big-time science, which may include long hours, odd behavior, and hard work."

The second important quality is the willingness and ability to work with others. Quite often math and science courses in high school encourage individual effort and competition between students. At Caltech, course work is collaborative. Students work together in study groups, lab groups, and as members of teams to solve problems. As a current Caltech senior remarked, "Thank goodness we can collaborate on many of the homework sets. If you had to do all your homework alone, you'd never graduate! It sometimes takes three or four students to solve a problem. That's one of the things that contributes to the widespread atmosphere of cooperation here. Everyone is willing to help and be helped. You don't just learn about science or engineering here. You learn the importance of working alongside others and the excitement of sharing ideas." Science at Caltech is a cooperative effort, just as it is in research labs and in industry across the nation. For example, a good test of your willingness to work with and help others is whether or not you tutor others in subjects that come easily to you.

Lest you think Caltech is all work and no play, smile on. At Caltech a sense of humor is also a way of life; wit and cleverness characterize the campus. Pranks enjoy an important place in Caltech history and lore; some have become legendary. Among the more famous examples of Caltech pranks is the incident during a Rose Bowl game when the scoreboard lit up Caltech v. MIT instead of the names of the battling Pac-10/Big Ten teams. Then there was the celebration of the Hollywood Centennial when, during the dark of night, the famous hillside HOLLYWOOD sign was altered to read CALTECH, and the time a Model T was dismantled, moved, and reassembled in a student's room. The Admissions Committee is looking for well-balanced students who not only take their science seriously, but also their fun. Examples of life before college help your chances of getting into Caltech.

There is one aspect of Caltech life for which students don't specifically prepare—but need to be aware of—for it guides the conduct of all campus life: the honor code. Stated quite simply, the honor code is expressed in few words:

> *No member of the Caltech community shall take unfair advantage of any other member of the Caltech community.*

Students, faculty, and staff alike adhere to the code and, as a result, trust, respect, and honesty are hallmarks of Caltech campus life. On a daily basis, the code translates to take-home midterm and final exams that are not proctored, and students being issued keys to campus buildings.

If asked to give advice to future Caltech applicants, my suggestions would include the following:

• Challenge yourself—in your course work and by seeking opportunities that further expose and develop your interests.

• Add credibility to your interests by participating in an activity that demonstrates you truly understand what you are talking about. Noting your interest in engineering carries weight when you can point to the rocket you just built in your garage and launched, much to the consternation of your parents and neighbors, but to the delight of your friends. (In fact, one applicant blew up the family garage in his attempt, which we surely don't recommend!)

• Develop a range of interests that take you beyond a single focus. When you broaden your horizons, you open yourself to a variety of challenges. You will learn lessons that can carry you through the challenges of studying math and science. That is, you will learn to work with others whose interests and perspectives may differ from yours. You also learn, through experience, how to react to setbacks. Research is beset by setbacks—how you react can determine whether or not you will persist or give up. Having experienced a setback in a high school class, on a team or other activity, may well provide the impetus you need to keep trying. Persistence in the face of apparent failure or adversity is necessary to successfully pursue science and engineering.

Graduation from Caltech carries with it great pride and a sense of accomplishment. In the words of one alumnus:

> *"I came here expecting a challenge . . . and one of the things I told myself—why I wouldn't have wanted to go anywhere else, even after going through all you have to go through at Caltech— is you know you've done the best you can do. You know you've challenged yourself to the utmost. If you go to another school, maybe you wouldn't know what you could have done."*

The realization that you have met a challenge, and met it successfully, generates confidence in knowing what you *can* do.

For students who are truly passionate about math, science, and the world of technology, who are creative, have a sense of humor, and who welcome a challenge, Caltech may very well be the right match. As one sophomore asks, "Ever been awakened at 3:14 A.M. by twenty people yelling 'pi-time'? Ever wondered if Domino's will deliver a pizza ordered through the mail? Ever talked to people for so long that you didn't realize the sun had risen an hour ago? Ever tried to make a pickle glow? If you never have but would like to, or even have some great ideas of your own, then Caltech is the place to be."

> *Charlene Conrad Liebau is Director of Admissions at Caltech. She received her undergraduate degree from the University of California, Berkeley, and her master's degree from Stanford University. In addition to her interests and activities in higher education, she has an active interest in the governance of independent schools, serving as a trustee and consultant. Charlene has also been active in the community, serving as a director on the boards of philanthropic, cultural, and service organizations.*

Appendix

Comparison Charts
on the
Top 50 Colleges*

In nearly all cases, the colleges provided the information in this Appendix. Estimated figures are given for SAT I scores when the school chooses not to release specific scores.

COMPARING THE COLLEGES

School	Number of Applications	Entering Students	M/F Ratio	SAT I Verbal	SAT I Math	SAT I Comb	Academic Strength
Amherst College	4,823	418	47/53	628	675	1303	Liberal Arts
Bates College	3,754	458	51/49	600	650	1250	Liberal Arts and Sciences
Boston College	15,522	2,250	48/52	565*	645*	1210*	Liberal Arts/ Sciences/Pre-professional
Bowdoin College	3,662	431	50/50	610	665	1275	Liberal Arts
Brown University	13,222	1,423	54/46	620	680	1300	Liberal Arts
Bryn Mawr College	1,583	329	0/100	650*	630*	1280*	Liberal Arts
California Institute of Technology	2,012	231	77/23	639*	757*	1396*	Science and Engineering
Carleton College	2,782	528	51/49	625*	660*	1285	Liberal Arts
Carnegie Mellon University	8,647	1,150	67/33	570	660	1230	Electrical and Computer Engineering/ Fine Arts
Claremont McKenna College	2,066	232	53/47	610	670	1280	Economics/ Government/ International Relations
College of William and Mary	8,169	1,256	44/56	590	640	1230	Liberal Arts/ Sciences
Columbia University	7,856	870	51/49	620	670	1290	Liberal Arts
Cornell University	20,076	3,103	53/47	595*	685*	1280*	Wide Range
Dartmouth College	9,521	1,057	53/47	650	710	1360	Liberal Arts
Davidson College	2,724	451	53/47	600	660	1260	Liberal Arts
Duke University	14,324	1,730	54/46	655*	710*	1365*	Humanities/ Sciences

* estimate   **mean

Three Most Popular Majors	Class Size	Expenses	Academic Pressure	Social Environment
English, History, Political Science	22–25	$25,060	Strong	Small College Town
English, Biology, Psychology	15	$25,180	Moderately Intense, Self-generated	Something for Everyone
English, Political Science, Psychology	18–21	$24,048	Moderately Intense	Friendly, High Involvement in Campus Community
Economics, Government, History	15–20	$25,240	Self-determined	Small Town/Small College
History, International Relations, Political Science	15	$24,454	Moderately Intense	Friendly/Low Key
English, Biology, Psychology	15–20	$24,915	Intense	As You Like It
Engineering, Physics, Electrical Engineering	12	$23,327	Intense	Suburban, Friendly, Intellectual
English, Biology, History	19–24	$19,620	Intense	Close-knit and Supportive
Electrical and Computer Engineering, Drama	30	$22,760	Intense	Nestled Between Neighborhood and City
Economics, Government, International Relations	19	$24,500	Moderately Intense	Close-knit Community
Government, Business, English	28	$ 8,854 $17,776	Self-determined	Small Town/Friendly
English, History, Political Science	15–20	$25,774	Self-determined	Small Diversified Community/Big City
Biological Science, Economics, Government	Varies	Varies by School and Residency	Self-determined	Active/College Town
Government, History, Biology	5–50	$27,165	Intense	Small College Town
History, English, Psychology	10–20	$22,534	Intense	Small Town
Biology, Economics, History	17–40	$24,974	Moderate	Open/Friendly

School	Number of Applications	Entering Students	M/F Ratio	SAT/ Verbal	SAT/ Math	SAT/ Comb	Academic Strength
Emory University	9,653	1,190	50/50	585	660	1245	Liberal Arts/ Science/ Business/ Nursing
Georgetown University	12,659	1,449	49/51	600*	650*	1250*	Liberal Arts
Georgia Institute of Technology	7,875	1,798	73/27	560	673	1233	Engineering
Harvard University	15,261	1,619	55/45	N/A	N/A	1340*	Liberal Arts
Harvey Mudd College	1,388	170	66/34	660	740	1400	Engineering/ Sciences
Haverford College	2,466	952	51/49	620	670	1290	Natural/ Physical Science
Johns Hopkins University	7,794	952	62/38	600	700	1300	Sciences/ Humanities/ Engineering
Massachusetts Institute of Technology	7,136	1,097	61/39	635*	745*	1380*	Sciences/ Engineering
Middlebury College	3,871	493	50/50	605*	645*	1250*	Languages/ International Relations
Northwestern University	13,515	1,867	50/50	590	670	1260	Science/ History/ Performing Arts/ Engineering
Pomona College	3,293	379	51/49	630*	690*	1320*	Liberal Arts
Princeton University	14,363	1,161	56/44	650	700	1350	Liberal Arts
Reed College	1,966	327	52/48	603	632	1235	Liberal Arts
Rice University	7,779	620	57/43	655*	715*	1370*	Liberal Arts/ Engineering
Stanford University	14,609	1,589	50/50	640	702	1342	Entire Range
Swarthmore College	3,349	328	51/49	650	700	1350**	Liberal Arts

* estimate   ** mean

Three Most Popular Majors	Class Size	Expenses	Academic Pressure	Social Environment
Social Sciences, Psychology, Business Management	22–38	$25,350	Moderately Intense	Wealth of Opportunity
Government, English, International Politics	27–34	$25,595	Noncompetitive	Close-knit/Cosmopolitan
Electrical, Mechanical, Civil Engineering	32	$ 8,112 $12,702	Intense	Friendly, Southern City
Social Science, Biology, English	25	$22,080	Extremely Competitive	Major College Town
Engineering, Physics, Math	10–15	$20,800	Intense	Big Family
Biology, History, English	19	$25,250	Intense	Warm and Friendly
Biology, International Studies, Biological Medicine, English	35	$25,540	Intense	Big City
Electrical Engineering, Computer/Science Mechanical Engineering	20–30	$22,230	Intense	Best-attended Parties in Largest College Town
English, Psychology, History	20–30	$25,750	Intense	Rural Eclectic/Diverse
Economics, Political Science, Engineering, History	24	$21,924	Moderately Intense	Lively
Social Sciences, Biology, English	14	$25,120	Self-determined	Open/Low-key
History, Politics, English	N/A	$25,810	Intense	Active/Eating Clubs
Biology, English, History	15–20	$25,600	Intense	Relaxed/Off-beat
Engineering, English, Biology	18	$16,495	Intense	Quirky and Friendly
Economics, Biology, Engineering	Varies	$25,465	Very Rigorous	Suburban and Cosmopolitan
Political Science, English, Economics	12–20	$22,160	Intense	Close-knit

School	Number of Applications	Entering Students	M/F Ratio	SAT/ Verbal	SAT/ Math	SAT/ Comb	Academic Strength
Tufts University	7,880	1,170	47/53	586	654	1240	Liberal Arts/ Engineering
University of California/Berkeley	19,873	3,206	53/47	570*	680*	1250*	Sciences/ Engineering
University of California/ Los Angeles	23,406	4,130	50/50	515	613	1128	Engineering/ Liberal Arts
University of Chicago	6,262	924	53/47	620	670	1290*	Common Core Studies, Research
University of Illinois/ Urbana-Champaign	15,616	5,734	57/43	520	619	1139	Engineering/ Liberal Arts
University of Michigan/ Ann Arbor	19,393	5,068	53/47	540	650	1190	Classics/ Economics/ Engineering
University of North Carolina/Chapel Hill	15,041	3,331	41/59	527	594	1121	Liberal Arts
University of Notre Dame	9,300	1,878	58/42	580	670	1250	Engineering/ Liberal Arts
University of Pennsylvania	13,739	2,346	51/49	598	678	1276	Liberal Arts/ Business/In- terdisciplinary
University of Texas/Austin	14,320	5,545	52/48	527	608	1135	Architecture/ Business
University of Virginia	14,921	2,764	47/53	573	644	1217	English/History
Vassar College	3,760	612	38/62	610	625	1235	Liberal Arts
Wake Forest University	5,923	948	50/50	575	625	1200	Liberal Arts
Washington and Lee University	3,620	443	60/40	618*	662*	1280*	Commerce/ Mass Media
Wellesley College	3,385	570	0/100	620	660	1280	Liberal Arts
Wesleyan University	5,482	727	46/54	600	660	1260	Liberal Arts/ Sciences
Williams College	4,673	500	51/49	660	690	1350	Liberal Arts
Yale University	12,991	1,308	53/47	670	720	1390	Liberal Arts/ Sciences

* estimate   **mean

Three Most Popular Majors	Class Size	Expenses	Academic Pressure	Social Environment
English, International Relations, Biology	25	$26,172	Moderate	Friendly/Outgoing
Electrical Engineering, Computer Science, English	Varies	$ 8,728 $16,427	Intensely Competitive	Large City Excitement
Biology, Psychology, Economics	Varies	$11,974 $19,673	Intensely Competitive	Supportive
Biology, English, Economics	10–25	$25,616	Work Hard/ Play Hard	Residential Community
Psychology, Biology, Electrical Engineering	Varies	$ 9,864 $14,664	Intense	Friendly/Happening
Psychology, Engineering, Biology	28	$11,650 $25,350	Moderately Intense	Varied/Open
History, English, Psychology	Varies	$ 5,330 $12,372	Self-determined	Happening
Government, Premed, Accounting	20–35	$21,240	Work Hard/ Play Hard	Warm and Friendly
Finance, History, English	10–19	$26,126	Moderate	Lively
Liberal Arts, Business, Psychology	48	$ 6,885 $11,175	Moderately Intense	Extremely Social and Diverse
English, Government, Psychology	44–58	$ 4,480 $13,052	Very Rigorous	Excellent
English, Political Science, Psychology	7–20	$25,170*	Intense	Cosmopolitan
Biology, Business, History	25–27	$18,115	Moderately Intense	Friendly and Close-knit
English, History, Economics	15	$18,700	Very Rigorous	Excellent
Psychology, English, Economics	18–21	$24,700	Intense	Close-knit Community
English, History, Biology	17	$25,390	Self-generated	Comfortable and Friendly
History, English, Political Science	10–40	$25,560	Intense	Small College Town
Life Sciences, English, Political Science	Varies	$26,350	Moderately Intense	Friendly, Busy

REPUTATION CHART

School	Reputation
Amherst College	First-rate Liberal Arts School
Bates College	Great Regional Rep—Spreading
Boston College	Jesuit Ivy
Bowdoin College	Innovative/Well-regarded Liberal Arts
Brown University	Top-notch Liberal Arts
Bryn Mawr College	Best Women's College
California Institute of Technology	Leading Edge Science Tech
Carleton College	A Rennaissance School
Carnegie Mellon University	The Professional Choice
Claremont McKenna College	On the Verge of Greatness
College of William and Mary	Strong Liberal Arts—Well Balanced
Columbia University	Top-notch Liberal Arts
Cornell University	Diversified Academic Excellence
Dartmouth College	Top-rated Liberal Arts
Davidson College	Demanding Liberal Arts Curriculum
Duke University	Thorough Coursework/Versatility of Graduates
Emory University	On the Brink of Greatness
Georgetown University	Traditional/Value Oriented
Georgia Institute of Technology	Hell of an Engineer
Harvard University	Internationally Premier College
Harvey Mudd College	Best Specialty Engineering College
Haverford College	Liberal Arts Center
Johns Hopkins University	Academic Think Tank
Massachusetts Institute of Technology	Premier Science and Engineering Institution
Middlebury College	Liberal Arts Personified
Northwestern University	Midwest Ivy

School	Reputation
Pomona College	Best Liberal Arts West of Mississippi
Princeton University	Quintessential Ivy League
Reed College	Best Liberal Arts School
Rice University	Top-notch Science and Engineering
Stanford University	Ivy League/Best
Swarthmore College	Best Liberal College
Tufts University	Strong All Around
University of California/Berkeley	International Intellectual Center
University of California/Los Angeles	World-class University
University of Chicago	High-powered Academics
University of Illinois/Urbana-Champaign	MIT of the Midwest
University of Michigan/Ann Arbor	Best All Around
University of North Carolina/Chapel Hill	Public Ivy
University of Notre Dame	Top-notch Undergraduate Program
University of Pennsylvania	Strong Multifaceted University
University of Texas/Austin	University of the First Class
University of Virginia	Great Academics
Vassar College	Innovative and Independent
Wake Forest University	Liberal Arts Bastion
Washington and Lee University	Best Kept Secret in the South
Wellesley College	Intellectual Haven
Wesleyan University	Top-notch Liberal Arts
Williams College	Top-notch Liberal Arts
Yale University	Finest Liberal Arts—Creative

Notes on Contributors

TOM FISCHGRUND
(Editor)

Tom received a B.A. from Tufts, a Ph.D. from MIT, and an M.B.A. from Harvard. He has taught public administration and done government research. He has written three books, *The Insider's Guide to the Top Ten Business Schools, Match Wits with the Harvard MBA's,* and *Fischgrund's Insider's Guide to the Top 25 Colleges.* He currently is a marketing executive with Coca-Cola.

JUDITH ABRAMS

Judith graduated from the University of Michigan/Ann Arbor with a bachelor's degree in English in 1989. While at Michigan, she wrote for *The Michigan Daily.* After graduating, she worked as a freelance writer for *The Ann Arbor Observer* and *Michigan Today,* U of M's alumni magazine. Currently she is working as a reporter for *The Lake City Reporter,* a North Florida newspaper that is part of *The New York Times* Regional Newspaper Group.

NICK ANDERSON

Nick graduated from Stanford University with an A.B. in English in June 1988. At Stanford, he was a reporter and executive news editor for the *Stanford Daily,* an independent newspaper, the largest on campus. Since graduating, he has worked as the city reporter for the *Palo Alto Weekly,* writing news, features, columns, and book reviews.

LAURENCE ARNOLD

Laurence graduated from Cornell's College of Arts and Sciences in 1988. A history major, he spent three years as a reporter and one year as associate editor on the *Cornell Daily Sun.* After graduation, he was a reporter for the *Daily Register* in Shrewsbury, New Jersey. He now works for the *Courier-News* in Bridgewater, New Jersey.

ANDREW BARRON

Andrew graduated from Davidson College in 1987. While at Davidson, he was editor of the student newspaper, the *Davidsonian.* He currently works as a newspaper reporter for the *Herald* in Rock Hill, South Carolina.

ADAM BELL

Adam graduated in 1988 from the University of Virginia with a degree in history. He served as news editor of the daily paper there. Adam was a summer intern with the *Charlotte Observer* in 1987 and is currently working as a staff writer for the *Bucks County Courier Times,* a daily paper near his suburban Philadelphia home.

ADAM BIEGEL

Adam graduated summa cum laude from Emory in 1993 after majoring in political science and English and editing the student newspaper. After graduation, he worked on a U.S. senator's staff in Washington D.C., and as a newspaper reporter in Little Rock, Arkansas. A Bethesda, Maryland native, he is currently attending the University of Chicago Law School.

BECKY BIEGELSEN

Becky is a 1989 graduate of Carleton College, where she majored in classical studies. While on campus, she was very active in athletics, theater, and music. She recently completed a musical theater training program at The American Musical and Dramatic Academy in New York City, and currently is working as a producer and promotions assistant at classical radio station, WNCN.

PAMELA BOL

Pamela is a 1987 graduate of Brown University. She concentrated in English and graduated with honors in creative writing. In addition to her studies, she rowed on Brown's crew team for four years. Presently, she is working toward her master's in English creative writing at New York University. She also works part-time for a book scout.

MARSHALL BOSWELL

Marshall received his B.A. with honors in English from Washington and Lee University in 1988. He received his M.A. in English from Washington University in St. Louis and is now teaching English at the University of Miami. His fiction has appeared in *Shenandoah* and *Playboy,* and he currently is finishing his first novel.

MARLENE CASILLAS

Marlene received her baccalaureate degree in English from the University of California/Los Angeles in 1989. While at UCLA, she worked as a staff writer for the *Daily Bruin* and as a volunteer in pediatrics at the UCLA Medical Center. Upon graduation, Marlene went to work as a journalist in the Sacramento area.

IRIS CHANG

Iris is a 1989 graduate of the University of Illinois/Urbana-Champaign, where she majored in journalism and minored in math and computer science. Throughout college she freelanced for a number of different publications, including *The New York Times,* the *Associated Press,* and the *Chicago Tribune.* She currently is completing a master's degree at Johns Hopkins graduate school.

GARRETT CHOI

Garrett graduated from the California Institute of Technology in 1989 with a B.S. degree in Engineering and Applied Science with an emphasis in Mechanical Engineering Design. Following graduation, he was drafted into the Undergraduate Admissions Support group. He has been employed with the Rocketdyne Division of Rockwell International Corporation as a systems integration engineer on the *Space Station Freedom* program since 1989.

JOAN CLIFFORD

Joan graduated from the University of North Carolina at Chapel Hill in 1988 with a degree in English and creative writing. Afterwards, she wrote features for the *Fayetteville Observer* in North Carolina and currently is a life-style writer for the *Daily Progress* in Charlottesville, Virginia.

SARAH E. DAVIS

Sarah is a 1988 graduate of Bryn Mawr College, where she received her A.B. degree *magna cum laude* with honors in English. She worked for a year as a writer and editor for a typesetting house in Philadelphia. She currently is a free-lance writer.

JONATHAN DOUGLAS

Jonathan is a 1992 Phi Beta Kappa graduate of Dartmouth, where he received his A.B. degree with high honors in music. While at Dartmouth, he wrote for several alumni and student publications, played in the marching band, sang with the Glee Club, and was a fan of the game. After graduation, he spent a year working for *Duke Magazine* before enrolling in graduate school in music.

SCOTT ELLIOTT

Scott graduated from the University of California/Berkeley in 1988. While there, he was president of the Senior Class Council and now serves as chairman of the Class of 1988 Endowment Fund. Scott majored in economics and plans to attend law school. He currently works for a law firm in the litigation department.

KELLY THOMAS FORLINI

Kelly is a 1988 graduate of the Georgia Institute of Technology's College of Management. While at Tech, she was active in both the student newspaper and the Office of Undergraduate Recruiting. She and her husband, a 1986 Georgia Tech graduate, currently are residing in Alexander City, Alabama, where they are both employed by the Russell Corporation.

LOREN FOX

Loren received his B.A. in writing seminars from Johns Hopkins University in 1988. While at Hopkins, he began writing for several newspapers and magazines. He currently works as a reporter and editor for a newspaper in the New York area.

DWIGHT GARNER

Dwight is a 1989 graduate of Middlebury College, where he received a B.A. degree with highest honors in American literature. He has worked as a freelance writer for *The Village Voice, The Boston Phoenix,* and *The New York Times.* He currently is an editor with *The Vermont Times.*

VARUN GAURI

Varun graduated from the University of Chicago in 1988 with a degree in Fundamentals: Issues and Texts, an interdisciplinary program in the humanities. His focus was heroism and morality. He currently lives in New York City and works for the Hastings Center, a research institute that examines problems in biomedical and professional ethics.

JONATHAN GAW

Jonathan graduated from Pomona College in 1989 with a concentration in government and public policy analysis. While at Pomona, he was editor of *The Student Life,* the college newspaper. Currently he is a staff writer with *The Los Angeles Times.*

NATALIE CAPONE GILLESPIE

Natalie graduated from Carnegie Mellon University in 1989 with highest honors, receiving a B.A. in professional writing and visual communications. While at Carnegie Mellon, she was editor-in-chief of the yearbook and a resident assistant.

After graduation, she married a fellow Carnegie Mellon graduate, and currently is an internal communications writer for Westinghouse in Pittsburgh.

LISA GRAY

Lisa graduated from Rice University in 1988 with a double major in English and sociology. While at Rice, she was editor-in-chief of the student newspaper, the *Rice Thresher.* She is now working as a technical editor and freelance writer in Houston.

DAVID GRUMHAUS, JR.

David is a 1988 graduate of Princeton University where he received an A.B. degree in history. At Princeton, he was president of the University Press Club and a member of the Cap & Gown Club. He currently is working as an analyst with an investment bank in New York City.

ZOE HEINEMAN

Zoe graduated from Georgetown University's School of Foreign Service in 1987. While at Georgetown, she was involved with the radio station, the Lecture Fund, the Russian Club, Cabaret, and the Grace Notes (an *a cappella* group). She currently coordinates seminars and conferences at the Kennan Institute for Advanced Russian Studies, a branch of the Smithsonian Institution in Washington, D.C.

LANE HENSLEY

Lane graduated from Duke University with a major in religion in 1987. He is a member of Sigma Chi fraternity and is a former senior editor of Duke's student newspaper, the *Chronicle.* Lane worked in Duke University's Publication Services for one year and now works in Washington, D.C., for the Bureau of National Affairs, Inc.

STEFANIE HIRSH

Stefanie received her B.A. with a double major in English and Italian from Middlebury College in March 1993. While at Middlebury she was an editor and reporter for both *The Campus,* the college newspaper, and *Artemis,* the gender issues magazine, as well as news announcer for WRMC-FM. She also worked as student assistant in the Public Affairs Office where she wrote articles for the alumni magazine and press releases. She is currently pursuing a career in journalism.

MARK HUDIS

Mark received his B.A. with a major in English from Haverford College in 1990. While at Haverford, he wrote a humor column for the school newspaper, acted in several theatrical productions, and sang with the Haverford Humtones, the school's oldest, finest, and best looking *a cappella* singing group. Currently freelancing both feature and news articles for local newspapers, he spends his days as a copy editor for a Connecticut-based news wire service.

ROSILAND JORDAN

Rosiland is a 1988 graduate of Harvard-Radcliffe Colleges in Cambridge, Massachusetts, with an A.B. (*cum laude*) in romance languages and literatures (French civilization). During her four years, Rosiland was secretary of her dorm council, played rugby (wing), was a stage manager for the Harvard Gilbert and Sullivan Players and also wrote for the *Harvard Independent.* She is attending the Columbia Graduate School of Journalism.

KENNETH G. LAU

Kenneth graduated *magna cum laude* from Claremont McKenna College in 1988 with a double major in political science and literature. While at CMC, Ken served as one of the first Dunbar student fellows for the Gould Center for Humanistic Studies and as director of the *Playbill* film series; and spent a semester studying abroad at Oxford University. Currently attending UCLA Law School, Ken also participates in a Child Abuse and Neglect Research fellowship by working as a volunteer law clerk for the Los Angeles Department of Children Services County Counsel.

CINDI LEIVE

Cindi graduated with high honors from Swarthmore College in 1988. While on campus, Cindi, an English major and religion minor, worked as a writing associate and as managing editor of the student newspaper, *The Phoenix*. She currently works as a staff writer at *Glamour Magazine*.

JANET LEVINE

Janet is a 1988 Yale University graduate with a B.A. in philosophy. At Yale, she was a member of the varsity gymnastics team, a volunteer tutor in the New Haven public schools, and a member of Yale's Women's Center. She currently is working on Capitol Hill in Washington as a research assistant for the House Committee on Ways and Means. She plans to attend law school.

J. REESE MADDEN

Reese graduated from Bates College in 1993 with a B.A. degree in Political Science. A member of Phi Beta Kappa, he played on the Bates Tennis Team, was a Geology teaching assistant, and sat on the Honors Study committee. Reese currently works at The Tennis Center at Steamboat, in Steamboat Springs, Colorado.

FLYNN McROBERTS

Flynn received his B.S. in journalism in 1989 from Northwestern University's Medill School of Journalism. While at NU, he worked at the campus newspaper, *Daily Northwestern,* as a columnist, news editor, and editorial cartoonist. He now is working at *The Chicago Tribune* as a reporter.

LINDA BETH MILCH

Linda graduated with highest honors from the University of Texas at Austin in 1989 with a bachelor's degree in journalism. She worked for two years at the campus newspaper, *The Daily Texan,* and spent a semester as a foreign exchange student in Monterrey, Mexico. She currently is working as the assistant city editor of *The Odessa American* in Texas.

ALISON MILLS

Alison is a 1990 graduate of Boston College, where she received a B.A. with honors in English. While an undergraduate, she was active in the university's Fulton Debating Society where she enjoyed success as a competitive public speaker. She currently is in the process of applying to graduate programs in journalism.

JOHN A. OSWALD

John graduated from Columbia College in 1988 with a B.A. in political science. While at Columbia, he was a reporter for the *Columbia Daily Spectator* and its managing editor in 1987. He served as campus stringer to the *New York Times* and to *New York Newsday.* Upon graduation, he interned for the *Los Angeles Times* and presently is a reporter for the *Jersey Journal* in Hudson County, New Jersey.

BRENDON REAY

Brendon received his B.A. in classics from Reed College in 1987. While at Reed, he played on and coached the school's club basketball team and worked as an intern in the admissions office. He worked as a copywriter in high-tech advertising and public relations for three years, and now attends graduate school in classics.

AMY RESNICK

Amy graduated from Tufts University in 1988. She received a bachelor of arts degree with honors in international relations and history. She worked for a year as a town reporter for the *Wayland/Weston Town Crier* in Massachusetts and is now an associate editor for *Facts On File*.

JANA RICH

Jana received an A. B. from Vassar College in 1988. While at Vassar, Jana majored in psychology with a correlate sequence in women's studies. She also was a member of committees on admission and curricular policies. Jana currently works in public relations in New York City.

KYLE G. ROESLER

Kyle is a 1989 graduate of Harvey Mudd College. He is a writer by nature, and has written a three-act play, "Preoccupied in Suburbia," and is working on his first screenplay, "Man with a Mission," and his first novel, *Helen of Torrance*. He currently is aiming high for the air force in Colorado Springs, Colorado.

KATE SARDOU

Kate graduated with a B.A. from Berkeley in 1993. She majored in economics and minored in demography. While at Berkeley, she was president of the local Panhellenic chapter (representing all sororities on campus). She is currently consulting.

LAURA SHAW

Laura graduated from the University of Pennsylvania in 1988 with a major in American civilization and a minor in English. While at Penn, she served as a reporter and editorial page editor for the *Daily Pennsylvanian,* the student newspaper. She also wrote a student column for the alumni magazine. She is currently a student at Columbia Law School.

JAY SMITH

Jay graduated from Wake Forest University in 1990 with a B.A. in history. He then enrolled in a master's degree program at Yale University in international relations. Currently, he is on leave from Yale to work with *Foreign Policy* magazine at the Carnegie Endowment for International Peace in Washington, D.C.

LINDA SOMMERS

Linda graduated Phi Beta Kappa from Wellesley College in 1989. She played varsity field hockey and lacrosse all four years, and was captain of both teams her junior and senior years. She also was active in dorm government. She currently is using her philosophy and Spanish double major to travel abroad and contemplate graduate school.

JOHN STAUD

John graduated from the University of Notre Dame in 1987 with a B.S. degree in chemical engineering and a B.A. degree in English. A recipient of a Mellon Fellowship in the Humanities, John currently is pursuing a Ph.D. in English at the University of Michigan.

HAROLD A. STERN

Harold finally received his B.S. and Master of Science degree from the Massachusetts Institute of Technology in May, 1989, after having been a student for nearly six years. He majored in computer science and received the joint degree as part of his work at General Electric as a co-op student. Outside the classroom, he was editor-in-chief of the *Tech*, MIT's student newspaper.

KATRIEN SUNDT

Katrien is a 1987 graduate of Williams College, where she double-majored in English and American studies. She taught English at the Delbarton School in New Jersey for two years, and then in August 1989 she was married to a 1986 Williams graduate. She has since moved to Pennsylvania, where she attends graduate school.

MICHAEL TOWNSEND

Michael graduated with honors in English from Bowdoin College in 1990. At Bowdoin, he was editor-in-chief of the *Bowdoin Orient*, the student newspaper. Following graduation, he worked for two years in Bowdoin's office of College Relations as a Sports Information and News Intern. He is currently a free-lance writer of fiction and nonfiction.

SUZY WALRATH

Suzy received her B.A. with a major in English from Wesleyan in 1987. While at Wesleyan, she worked as a resident adviser in a freshman dorm, a WESU-FM DJ, and a senior interviewer in the admissions office. She is currently working in the communications department of the U.S. Committee for UNICEF.

MARK WANNER

Mark received an A.B. in biology and a minor in English from Bowdoin College in 1986. He was the Sports Information Fellow at Bowdoin for the year after graduation. He then studied microbiology at the University of Virginia for one year. He currently is working for a small publishing house.

KEVIN WILLIAMS

Kevin graduated with honors from Amherst College in 1988. An English major and creative writer, Kevin is a fellow in the Teaching Program at Columbia Teachers College in New York, preparing for a career teaching high school.

GREG ZENGO

Greg is a 1988 graduate of the College of William and Mary, where he received a B.S. degree with high honors in chemistry and linguistics. He currently is pursuing an M.D. at Emory Medical School and is active in the William and Mary alumni network in the Atlanta area.

TOP 50 SCHOOLS BY REGION

New England

Amherst College	MA
Bates College	ME
Boston College	MA
Bowdoin College	ME
Brown University	RI
Dartmouth College	NH
Harvard University	MA
Massachusetts Institute of Technology	MA
Middlebury College	VT
Tufts University	MA
Wellesley College	MA
Wesleyan University	CT
Williams College	MA
Yale University	CT

Middle Atlantic

Bryn Mawr College	PA
Carnegie Mellon University	PA
Columbia University	NY
Cornell University	NY
Georgetown University	DC
Haverford College	PA
Johns Hopkins University	MD
Princeton University	NJ
Swarthmore College	PA
University of Pennsylvania	PA
Vassar College	NY

South

College of William and Mary	VA
Davidson College	NC
Duke University	NC
Emory University	GA
Georgia Institute of Technology	GA
Rice University	TX
University of North Carolina/ Chapel Hill	NC
University of Texas/Austin	TX
University of Virginia	VA
Wake Forest University	NC
Washington and Lee University	VA

Midwest

Carleton College	MN
Northwestern University	IL
University of Chicago	IL
University of Illinois/ Urbana-Champaign	IL
University of Michigan/ Ann Arbor	MI
University of Notre Dame	IN

West

California Institute of Technology	CA
Claremont McKenna College	CA
Harvey Mudd College	CA
Pomona College	CA
Reed College	OR
Stanford University	CA
University of California/ Berkeley	CA
University of California/ Los Angeles	CA

BARRON'S NEW STUDENT'S CONCISE ENCYCLOPEDIA
A Complete Reference Guide For School & Home, 2nd Edition

Compiled by the editors at Barron's

Here's the all-in-one reference guide that *gives you the important facts about virtually every topic imaginable* — in a compact, easy-to-use format that's packed with beautiful illustrations. Every major academic area is covered, from Literature, Art, History and the Social Sciences to Business, Mathematics, Computer Science and General Science. Plus, study and test-taking techniques help you boost your grades. And, you'll find expert tips on money management, diet and exercise, first aid — and other practical pointers on daily living. Diagrams, charts, tables and maps help make all the facts easy to understand! 1,300 pages, hardcover with dust jacket, $29.95, Canada $38.95 (6329-5)

WRITING A SUCCESSFUL COLLEGE APPLICATION ESSAY, 2nd Edition

By George Ehrenhaft

This step-by-step guide can mean the difference between getting into the college of your choice — and getting a rejection letter! It teaches you how to select an appropriate topic for a college application essay, and then how to develop ideas effectively in paragraphs that have *impact.* You'll easily learn how to edit, revise, and polish your essay until it's "letter perfect." Actual student essays are included with helpful critiques. 128 pages, paperback, $9.95, Canada $12.95 (1415-4)

BARRON'S PROFILES OF AMERICAN COLLEGES, with Supplementary Computer Disks, 20th Edition

By Barron's College Division

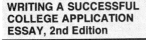

This new edition of America's number-one college guide reports on more than 1,500 accredited four-year colleges. Many Canadian and Mexican schools are also profiled. A separate section on easy-to-locate tinted pages presents Barron's comprehensive *Index of College Majors,* which helps you find colleges offering courses that most nearly match your interests and aptitudes. A brand new feature with this edition is a pair of $3\frac{1}{2}"$ computer disks—one for Windows and the other for Mac. They'll help you use your computer to fill out college application forms, compile your own academic profile, and write personalized college application letters. 1,800 pages, paperback, $23.95, Canada $31.00 (1752-8)

AFTER THE SATs

By Anna Paige

Written by a student for students, this practical guide to college offers first-hand advice on topics such as arrival preparations, living arrangements, establishing relationships with teachers and friends, selecting courses, extracurricular activities, and more. Humorous cartoon illustrations. Paperback, 224 pp., $9.95, Canada $12.95 (4477-0)

All prices are in U.S. and Canadian dollars and subject to change without notice. Order from your bookstore—or directly from Barron's by adding 10% for postage (minimum charge $3.75, Canada $4.00) New York State residents add sales tax.

ISBN PREFIX: 0-8120

BARRON'S

Barron's Educational Series, Inc.
250 Wireless Blvd.
Hauppauge, N.Y. 11788
Call toll-free: 1-800-645-3476
EXT. 204, 214, or 215

In Canada:
Georgetown Book Warehouse
34 Armstrong Ave.
Georgetown, Ontario L7G 4R9
Call toll-free: 1-800-247-7160

(#1) R 3/96